INTERNATIONAL BUSINESS AND TECHNOLOGICAL INNOVATION

INTERNATIONAL BUSINESS AND TECHNOLOGICAL INNOVATION

DANIEL D. ROMAN
Department of Management Science
George Washington University, Washington, DC

and

JOSEPH F. PUETT, JR.
Department of Business Administration
Alfred University, Alfred, New York
and
Information Systems
Worthington Group, McGraw-Edison Co.
Wellsville, New York

North-Holland
New York · Amsterdam · Oxford

Elsevier Science Publishing Co., Inc.
52 Vanderbilt Avenue, New York, New York 10017

Sole distributors outside the United States and Canada:

Elsevier Science Publishers B.V.
P.O. Box 211, 1000 AE Amsterdam, The Netherlands

Library of Congress Cataloging in Publication Data

Roman, Daniel D.
International business and technological innovation.

Bibliography: p.
Includes index.
1. Technological innovations. 2. International economic relations. I. Puett, Joseph F., Jr. II. Title.
HC79.T4R63 338′.06 82-5150
ISBN 0-444-00715-6 AACR2

Manufactured in the United States of America

To Roz and Arlene

Contents

Preface

International trade is facilitated by the exchange of goods and services. Goods may be in the form of convertible raw materials or as finished products. The harvesting or extraction of raw materials, services provided, or the finished products, transferred from one economic entity to another, reflect the technological need and ability of the parties to the transaction.

Technology is a critical component in international trade. Technology can vary from crude labor-intensive activity, leading to an end-product, to highly complex methodologies, requiring considerable capital inputs. Complex technologies often evolve from scientific discovery. Science is knowledge oriented and technology is application directed. In essence, technology is the "state of the art" in a socioeconomic environment. The technology of a society represents the composite usable knowledge that the society applies and directs toward the attainment of cultural and economic objectives. Technology, in some form, exists in every cultural organization. Technology is, additionally, a product of invention and innovation.

Invention, innovation, and technology play a big part in international competitive strategies of developed nations, and in efforts by emerging nations to improve their standard of living.

The level of sophistication in international business has increasingly intensified during the 20th century and, more explicitly, since World War II. At the conclusion of World War II, the United States was the dominant economic power in the world. The U.S. position of economic preeminence in the near post World War II period was in considerable part due to broad technological leadership. Since the 1960s, the U.S. position of leadership has eroded across several technologies. Nations have rebuilt their productive and economic systems based on aggressive technological development. Such nations (Japan and West Germany as two primary examples) have emerged as significant forces in international trade.

The ability to develop new technologies or improve existing ones is not limited to geographic or national areas. Technological development frequently requires extensive resources, both material and human, and involves economic, political, and social factors beyond a single national jurisdiction. As a result, technological development often cannot be localized and, as a consequence, has broad international implications.

This book attempts to go beyond the traditional foundations of international business. It appears that technological ability and leadership are becoming increasingly critical factors in international competitiveness. Therefore, the focus of this book is on the technological implications in international business.

The book is divided into six sections. Section I provides an overview of innovation and technology, as well as potential economic impacts in international business. Section II examines international science and technology policies, as well as some relevant international trade policies. Section III looks at the various aspects relevant to technological development, such as technology forecasting, technology assessment, environmental impact, technology transfer, and appropriate technology. The fourth section deals with technological innovation and international purchasing of technology. Section V represents a view of the many factors management must consider in an international technologically dynamic operational environment. The concluding section—VI—is a brief examination of some present and some possible impacts of technology and internationalism.

Any project of this magnitude involves the help of many individuals and the resources of several organizations. The authors wish to acknowledge the following organizations and people for assistance, suggestions, and moral support:

The International Institute for Applied Systems Analysis, Laxenberg, Austria;

Professors Phil Grube and Cliff Fawcett and Mario Kamenetzky of The World Bank;

Gail Aguilia who diligently interpreted our hieroglyphics; and

The U.S. Department of Commerce for their assistance and guidance.

Daniel D. Roman
Joseph F. Puett, Jr.

SECTION I:

Macro Considerations

CHAPTER ONE

Introduction

The International Business Environment

International business decisions have become increasingly difficult as a result not only of the complexity of the international business environment but also of the compounding factors of national goals and objectives in the nation where the business is to be conducted. There are increasing competitive pressures from the industrialized nations of the world who have attained technological parity with the United States, particularly the Europeans and Japanese. These nations are intent on competing with the Americans in global markets; rising feelings of nationalism and anticolonialism (direct or de facto through technological dependence) are causing businessmen to reconsider many of their strategies and tactics in reaching world markets. The increasing costs of reaching these global markets, the scarcity of raw materials, rising wages, spiraling inflation, tariff barriers, currency revaluations, international politics, and other factors in international business are causes enough to require business to be very selective in choosing strategy and accompanying tactics for the most efficient method of conducting international efforts.

Technological Impact

Technology is a critical component in international trade. Technology is the "state of the art" in a socioeconomic environment. The technology of a society represents the composite usable knowledge that the society applies and directs toward the attainment of cultural and economic objectives. In essence, technology is how things are accomplished. Different societies will use different methods, varying in degree of methodological sophistication to reach goals.

Technology, in some form, exists in every cultural organization. In many instances, relative technological efficiency or unique technological skills become the basis for international trade. Technology is a product of invention and innovation.

Invention, innovation, and technology play a big part in international competitive strategies of developed nations and in efforts by emerging nations to increase their standard of living. Quality-of-life standards are primarily related to Science, Innovation, and Technology, and are the direct result of organized research and development.

Developing Nations

Developing nations seek greater self-reliance and greater autonomy in the management of their affairs. They also desire to achieve self-sustaining growth and want to achieve the ability to develop and/or evaluate existing technologies and alternatives, as well as the economic, social, and cultural implications of using certain technologies. They are concerned with the ability to choose, transfer, adapt, develop, and apply technology in view of local assessments and priorities. It must also be recognized that there is a considerable range of technological capability in developing countries. Some of the developing countries have little current capacity for internationally competitive technological innovation, whereas other developing nations, such as Argentina, Brazil, and Mexico have expanding technological capabilities.

Technology and Developing Nations

The efforts of the developing countries to achieve self-sustaining growth have often been hindered by the lack of an indigenous scientific and technical base. Without such a base, their economies cannot be integrated or competitive in the international system. Development and transfer of science and technology have emerged as major goals in developing countries; they are increasingly determined to evolve their own capabilities in these areas and to gain greater access to the business know-how of the industrialized world.[1]

However, developing nations often tend to view technology transfer suspiciously. The importation of technology is frequently seen as placing a nation in a position of technological servitude or, worse yet, in a position of dependence on a second-rate or noncompetitive technology. Rather than a deterent to technological development, technology transfer can be the means for compressing the time needed and resources required to reach international technological parity. Japan is a noteworthy example of a nation importing and, subsequently, building on existing technological bases. Apparently, the Soviet Union and China are retreating from earlier positions of technological isolationalism and are adapting the Japanese strategy to accelerate technological development. To successfully effect this strategy, nations must selectively choose which technologies to import and, subsequently, develop. In addition, intense nationalistic pride must be suborted to ultimate national welfare. Total technological self-sufficiency for developing nations is not feasible or possible. The establishment of priorities for technological development should coincide with intensity of national need and availability of human and natural resources.

Technology and Developed Nations

The industrialized nations likewise have recognized that they cannot rely on a policy of self-sufficiency regarding technological competence. They must, at times, rely upon others to provide the knowledge of specific technologies, products, and processes. Consortiums of nations to develop high technology products are becoming an instrument of competition. Licensing and teaming of large industrial firms to develop and produce expensive complex systems are becoming commonplace. Coproduction or technological consortiums by a group of suppliers from several nations of a highly complex system, such as a commercial airliner, typifies the business arrangements that have evolved. These types of arrangements have become feasible due to scarce resources, increasing costs of research and development, high risk, and perhaps most important, political pressures.

The national policies, natural and financial resources, and national political, social, educational, and economic environment of various nations with a need for technology-based products dictate the conditions for business to follow in world markets. Technology, i.e., the application of science, has largely contributed to the emergence of highly developed societies. Innovation, the adoption of that technology to specific needs, provides the mechanism for change. The importance of science and technology in natural and international development efforts to achieve self-sustaining growth has long been recognized. In recent years, it has taken on a new perspective with the increasing interdependence of nations and the scarcity of basic commodities, such as energy. The problem is universal. It applies to the economic welfare of developed, developing, and underdeveloped nations.

To participate in these world markets, it becomes crystal clear that the modern day businessman must know not only the market factors in international business but also the technological implications of doing business in a global market. These implications transcend the traditional factors of culture, language, and institutional differences, to include a myriad of barriers and facilitators in reaching these global markets.

It is necessary to create an awareness of the integral coupling of international business, i.e., business activities that cross national borders, including management processes and transmission of various types of resources and services with the technological implications of doing business in a global market. These latter implications vitally affect the survival and growth of business in these areas.

International Transactions

Transactions among political entities, business organizations, political divisions, and among organizations operating out of different political jurisdictions, have rapidly increased since World War II. International business transactions involve the exchange of goods, services, and raw materials. International transactions have been stimulated by several factors. From all indications, international business transactions will increase in the foreseeable future, spurred by more materialism in the developed nations, the emergence of new markets in developing countries, the need for more effective utilization of the world's natural and human resources, and changing life patterns reflecting technological innovation.

The Growing Technological Disparity

Living standards have generally improved in the developed nations of the world. As people have become more affluent, the demand for more, better, and a greater variety of goods and services have increased. Countries that had much of their productive capacity destroyed during World War II, especially Germany and Japan, have rebuilt. The results have been dramatic as new industries and technologies have emerged. Unfortunately, the extent of technological innovation has actually widened between the developed and developing nations. According to United Nations' figures, six countries—United States, Great Britain, France, Japan, Russia, and West Germany—account for approximately 85% of all spending and 70% of all human resources for research and development. It is conjectured that somewhere near 72% of the world's population resides in developing countries and less than 3% of research and development expenditure are spent by these nations which have less than 13% of the world's scientists and engineers.[2]

Reflecting the statistics in the preceding paragraph has been the emergence of the transnational business organization which is invariably based in developed nations. Transnational* business operations are not new, but the growth and scope of such operations have come into sharper focus since World War II. To give some dimension to the importance of the transnational firm, it has been estimated that business companies operating internationally account for approximately 25% of the world's productive effort.[3]

There frequently has been some discernible technological progress in the developing nations, but progress has not always been consistent, predictable, or satisfactory. The developing nations have often made advances in health

*There are definitional differences in terminology among international, multinational, and transnational firms. In the text, international, multinational, and transnational terms are used interchangeably when in fact a distinction can be made. According to Dr. Eric Ferguson of the Dutch government in a personal interview, an international firm does 20% or less of its business outside its home country; a multinational firm does at least 50% of its business within its country of national base; a transnational country does not have a national home base and it does no more than 20% of its business in any one country. Another definition is that a multinational has offices in two or more foreign nations. A transnational merely does business across international boundaries and, accordingly, the terms are not interchangeable by definition.

delivery systems and improved agricultural methods. Some developing nations have established the roots of a technologically innovative productive system. Others have laid a potential foundation for future technological innovation as a consequence of wealth generated by indigenous natural resources.

Negative and Positive Aspects

There have also been negative aspects which cannot be ignored. We seem to live in a world of perpetual political crisis. Terrorism and international hooliganism are forces which must be contended with. Politically inspired international tensions have become the norm. Shortages of vital materials have also become a way of life, exacerbated by population pressures and waste. A major percentage of the world's population still does not enjoy reasonable living standards or a desirable quality of life.

Despite negative aspects, the world situation is far from hopeless. There are signs of desirable progress. A new social consciousness appears to be evolving for people and their environment. Political governments can provide a receptive atmosphere for social progress. Where such environments exist, private enterprise has often been an important implementing vehicle.

Localized business activities have, in many instances, expanded nationally and internationally in response to market demand. International market response has frequently reflected distinct technological capabilities. Technological innovation can be applied to the effective utilization of raw material sources, the development of highly specialized and skilled services, and quality goods at affordable prices. No individual, operating unit, or nation has a monopoly on brain power. Knowledge exchange, e.g., technology transfer, is manifested in the exchange of services, goods, and methods to utilize natural resources.

Economic activity fostered by technological development is encouraged by the firm doing business nationally and internationally where incentive is provided by profit. Another aspect is that natural resources may not always be sourced at the point(s) of need. Effective utilization of these natural resources may require relocation, extraction or harvesting, assembly, processing or transformation, and movement of these goods to markets. The multinational firm often is instrumental in providing know-how, capital, management, and distribution channels, leading to ultimate "use" utility. The multinational firm is also a prime factor in the international disbursement of technology; some form of technology can be the currency in international exchange.

Technological Innovation—An Overview

Technology and Economic Growth

The economically aggressive nations in the world usually have a strong research and development capability and a history of technological innovation. Economically stagnant societies often are technologically stagnant societies. A progressive and productive technology is essential for economic well-being.[4]

Manufacturing companies in the United States are spending billions of dollars each year for research and development of new products and improvement of existing products to extend the marketing life of those products. Foreign competitors are also expending vast sums in an unending race for technological leadership and international market dominance. The effective utilization of such resources mirrors the successes or failures in the marketplace.

In the United States, some technologically dynamic industries derive most of their current business from products that did not exist 20 years ago.[5] One study indicated that somewhere between 46 and 100% of short-term corporate growth could be derived from new product development.[6] It is now commonplace for large technologically dynamic companies to derive 50% or more of current sales from products developed and introduced in the past ten years.[7] Comparable findings were reported in a study conducted by the Joint Economic Committee of Congress.[8]

Advancing technological frontiers by research and development activity gives no assurance that new products will always be successful. On the contrary, most new products are unsuccessful; it has been estimated that 60 to 90% fail.[9]

Resource allocation which is channelled to new product research and development represents quite a problem where the failure probability is so high. Private industry is constantly confronted with product obsolescence as new developments threatened to limit the market life of existing goods. Also, shifts in consumption patterns can materially affect the existing product structure. Combined with the very high cost of product development, and the need of innovation for survival, these factors create a real managerial dilemma when the question arises of diverting resources to technological innovation. The development of technologically innovative processes is also very important. Process innovation facilitates the exploitation of a technology. Obsolete processes and facilities can compromise the competitive position.

Increasing Reluctance to Invest in Technological Innovation

Because of the high risk and uncertainty—as well as considerable cost—there is a growing reluctance in the United States to invest heavily in long-term technological innovation. The deterioration of technological innovation in the United States has already materially affected our position in international trade and competition.

Statistics can be misleading! The statistics indicate increasing expenditures for research and development in the United States, but the figures do not show the true picture. Distortion is due to inflationary factors and the nature of the effort purchased by these research and development funds. We are generally pursuing a policy of incremental technological development which is, in the short run, relatively safe. There are very important problems associated with long-term knowledge generation directed to significant technological innovation. The unfavorable risk environment is reflected by a shortage of available venture capital. Since the 1960s and more pronounced in the 1970s, companies have increasingly been dominated by financially oriented management. In a financially oriented operational environment, the pressures usually are for quick and predictable returns. An operational philosophy directed to achieving quick and predictable returns is not compatible with the risk and uncertainty associated with technological innovation.

Technological progress and economic well-being, as mentioned, are closely related. The rate and extent of technological innovation in the United States has slowed. There is increasing concern that in many industries in the United States technological innovation has become evolutionary rather than revolutionary. Our major economic competitors have been willing to be patient on long-term investments and subsequently have increasing reaped the rewards of technological innovations. The United States has been, as a consequence, losing leadership along a broad horizon of technologies to nations where the operational environment has been more supportive of major technological innovation.

"A hostile climate for new ideas and products is threatening the technological superiority of the U.S."[10] Reflecting the increasingly conservative attitude on technological innovation is the movement of the RCA Corporation, which has been at the forefront of electronic technology, into the takeover of CIT Financial Corporation. It would appear that RCA has chosen financial involvement over technology. In the RCA financially dominated situation, high technology gambles that lead to new industries and future profits have apparently been delayed or shelved.[11] RCA, like many other traditionally high-technology companies in the United States, is buying an increasing amount of its technology from foreign sources. The operational philosophy of short-term payoff discourages long-term research and subsequent development.[12]

Another factor affecting the U.S. position on technological innovation is how and where the bulk of research and development funds are spent. Since World War II, in the neighborhood of 40 to 55% of government research and development expenditures have been for defense-related technology. No attempt is made to make value judgments since persuasive arguments can be advanced pro and con for these expenditures. What is significant though is the fact that West Germany and Japan have been virtually prohibited from spending vast sums on space and defense research and have subsequently diverted their research and development expenditures to the commercial fields.[13] We are now buying products from these two countries which we once sold to them; this compounds our trade deficit.

A more conducive setting could be inspired if the U.S. government would establish policies and provide support to encourage technological development. A government can stimulate or retard technology. Government can be involved in three possible ways:

1. In totalitarianist political states, where the degree of effort and direction is orchestrated by the government. While some high-level technological innovation has emerged from such environments, as in the Soviet Union, it can be generalized that technological innovation, especially commercial innovation, is not usually noteworthy or consistent in such jurisdictions. This is evidenced by Soviet purchase of many technologies in automotive, electronics, information, and agricultural areas.
2. In situations where industry has primary responsibility for technological innovation, the government's role is normally passive in providing stimulation for innovation. Primary government involvement is regulatory. This is, basically, the current situation in the United States.* Some regulation and control are undoubtedly necessary, but regulation can become stifling if politically motivated and sensitive to many diverse pressure groups. Restrictions, rather than incentives, can be disastrous where foreign competition is not hobbled by onerous regulations.
3. The third possibility is where the government takes an active role in promoting technological innovation. This is not to infer a form of socialism but instead cooperative effort. The American economic success has been founded as an incentive system and any cooperative effort should be directed to the continued stimulation of incentive in the private sector. In this situation, partnerships are formed among government, industry, and universities to encourage technological innovation. The government could act as a directional force and sponsor, but the immediate control and incentive rests with industry, utilizing government and educational resources. If the economic successes of Japan and West Germany are indicators, it would appear that this policy has excellent prospects for encouraging technological innovation.

Figure 1-1 indicates a probability that a highly bureaucratic political environment can lead to comparatively low-technological innovation whereas an environment with a minimum of political bureaucracy will tend to foster high-technological innovation. The assumption is that an excessively bureaucratic system stifles incentive.

Another Look at Technology

A comprehensive understanding of technology is impeded by limited perspective. There are many facets and interrelationships that impinge on the technological progress. The greater the complexity, the greater the interactions and the more difficult the solution. It can be a costly mistake to attempt to treat "a" technological component to the exclusion of other factors which might have a significant bearing on the ultimate success of the undertaking. Technological development should be approached as a package concept. To illustrate: According to Poats, of the approximately 350,000 known plant species, a

*There have been some indications of a shift in U.S. government policy during the early phases of the Reagan administration.

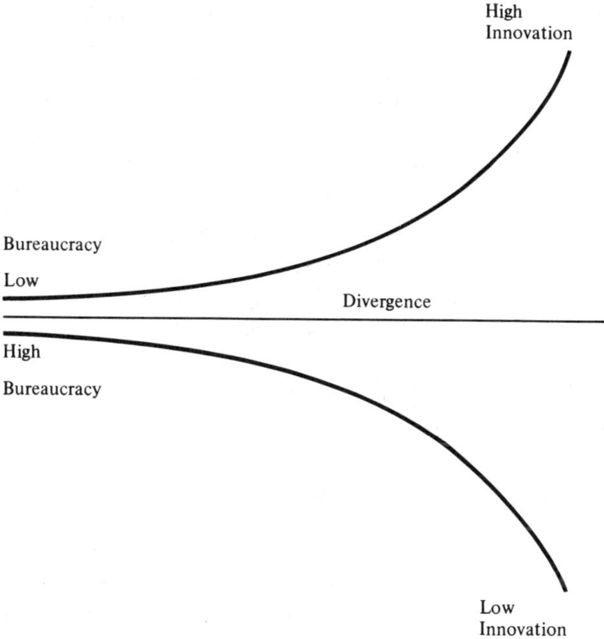

Figure 1-1. Bureaucracy and innovation.

dozen represent the source of 90% of the world's food supply. Crops such as rice, sorghum, corn, sugar cane, beans, peanuts, bananas, wheat, coconut, barley, potatoes, soybeans, and cassava contribute the bulk of the world's food. The number of food species has actually declined over the centuries as there has been increased concentration on the more productive species. There has been research and development to improve those species which are the most productive relative to resource requirements and yield potential.

> Improved strains have been developed and more efficient methods for growing these species have also resulted. The results have not always been unmitigated blessings, but have at times created serious unforeseen corollary problems. There have often been difficulties in educating people to change to new crop varieties and new farming methods. Where there has been successful transitions and introduction of new strains, the resulting crop has, on occasion, proved a surplus embarrassment because there were no provisions for the development of roads or distribution systems to bring the crops to market.[14]

Worse yet, the people were too poor to buy the products which were available.

In most developing nations, distribution systems are either very inadequate or are nonexistent. Problems frequently surface as a result of undeliverable food surpluses because increased productive efficiency has eliminated the need for farm labor, and in many developing nations the heaviest population concentrations are in the rural farm areas. This compounds unemployment. Fewer gainfully employed people have cut down the economic base for effective demand. At times, unanticipated difficulties have occurred in providing irrigation requirements. On occasion, new agricultural technologies have led to capital requirements in societies where there are severe capital restrictions. Or, where there has been a successful transition, a new affluence has developed for some and there is a greater disparity of income for others. This aggravates the already poor living standards for those who have not benefitted from the technology and leads to social and political frictions.[15]

Introducing a technology is critical. A given technology can be a blessing in one society or a disaster in another. The benefits and shortcomings resulting from a given technology should be anticipated and evaluated before adoption. This introduces the idea of technological modification to suit the host environment.

A Systems Approach to Understanding Technology

In a world community that reflects interdependent as well as dependent characteristics, no individual, group, organization, or political entity can truly operate in an independent vacuum. Each unit is, in fact, a cog, subunit, or component of a larger operational unit which becomes a part of a global system.

The Macro Components of Technology

An encouraging note is the growing worldwide interest in technology, its management, and the constantly increasing thrust of academic research. The areas of research and the attendant literature resulting therefrom have expanded dramatically starting in the 1970s.

Potential contribution is considerable for research that is in process and is anticipated relative to understanding the many hues of technology. What has been missing is a holistic view of the technological process. Identifying all the relevant components and putting them into a meaningful context is no simple task.

It is almost inconceivable that a decision having any important technological impact can be isolated and confined to a narrow political, geographic, or economic jurisdiction. The technological factors must be considered in the light of direct and indirect national and international implications. Nationalism is an inescapable element that has to be recognized and accommodated for in any attempt to alter existing technology. Nations have pride, and nationalism fosters identity. No nation wants to think of itself as second-class and, subsequently, a recipient of second-class technology. Nationalistic attitudes are too frequently impediments to the most beneficial use of technology. Not all nations are equal in human and material resources. A spectrum exists from extremely resource-poor nations to extremely resource-rich nations. Technology—the applicability, adoption, modification, and utilization—should be considered in the light of the nation's social, political, economic, and cultural position. Nations must consider their resources, their needs, and their immediate, short-, and long-range goals in harvesting technology for the national welfare. Priorities and programs must be determined and will vary nation to nation.

The determination of priorities and programs should evolve through systematic exploration of alternatives. Of paramount importance is a consideration of national goals, in concert with national resources. Aspirations must be compatible with resources—existing and potential. National assets include human resources, natural resources, locational resources, and climatic resources. Exploitation of these resources should parallel national developmental requirements. In exploiting the economic resources, nations must plan. A national science and technology policy can provide planning guidance. Science policy and subsequent planning can, and should, be influenced by forecasting technological developments which probabilistically will occur. A nation should determine the advantages and disadvantages of inhouse development or outside purchase of nationally relevant technology. Competitive factors, available resources, most effective utilization of available resources, and national priorities should be most relevant considerations in developing a technology. In line with forecasting technological development is the corollary requirement to anticipate the potential environmental impact of that technological development. Overestimates of technological benefits, or miscalculation of the negative effects, can lead to serious problems. Another component in the decision to pursue or not pursue a given technology, or to establish a desired technological level, are the prospects for marketing that technology. Marketing technology would involve internal and external possibilities. What is the range of the technology? What is the appropriate technology for a particular country? To what extent can the technology be transferred in its developed form? What are the legal restraints in international market exploitation? What forms, devices, or methods can be used in transferring and marketing the technology?

The Micro Components of Technology

Research is the forerunner of technology. The extent and direction of research is often a product of direct government involvement or government subsidy. Depending on national political ideology, government participation in research can range from absolute and direct involvement and control to a guiding force manifested by government resource diversion. The relative role of government, industry, educational, and nonprofit institutions will vary according to political philosophy, national objectives, and economic factors, including degree of risk.

The end product of science and technology will also reflect interactions between government, industry, educational, and nonprofit institutions. At the micro or operating level, resources are invariably limited. To maximize potential results and minimize resources used, planning and control procedures must be established, project selection methods must be determined, and there must be an estimate of organizational resource requirements. It is also important that micro operations reflect macro operations. Many procedures indicated under the macro factors must be repeated with an application thrust at the micro level.

The Interdisciplinary Aspects

The interdisciplinary aspects are the tools and are critical to relating and bonding the macro and micro components into a viable system. The inclusion of several academic disciplines such as behavioral science, systems theory, law, management, finance, marketing, operations research, economics, political science, information technology, and international business are representative but not all-inclusive disciplines which must be understood and integrated if a realistic picture is to be developed.[16]

Organization

This book is organized to provide a logical progression and understanding of international business subject to technological impacts. Section I provides a foundation and includes an introductory chapter indicating an overview of the subject and Chapters Two and Three look at the economics of international business and technological innovation.

Section II looks at international science and technology policies and trade policies reflecting technological innovation. The third section deals with macro and micro considerations in anticipating technological development and opportunities. Local and international impacts of technology are discussed, including assessment as to relevance and environmental impacts. This section also explores the range of benefits and incurred obligations induced by technology transfer, including the various transfer processes and examination of appropriate technology consistent with a nation's needs, resources, and capabilities. Related material in this section examines alternatives of purchasing technological innovation in the international market, the advantages and disadvantages of acquisition practices, and a view of procedures and complexities involved in bringing technological products across political jurisdictions. The fourth section involves the diffusion of technology including the procurement and marketing of technological innovation.

The fifth section is micro/macro-oriented and is concerned with the multitude of decisional factors involved in developing a technological infrastructure. The section also covers traditional and new forms of international cooperative arrangements, the environmental settings that have nurtured these arrangements, and issues such as protection of international proprietary rights and national security considerations. The sixth section is an epilog looking at some present and possible future impacts of technology and internationalism.

Endnotes Chapter One

1. "GIST", Bureau of Public Affairs, Department of State, January 1978, page 1.
2. "UN Technology Meeting Lacked Clear Direction," *Science*, September 21, 1979, Vol. 205, page 1236.
3. *An Introduction to Policy Analysis in Science and Technology*, a Report, No. 46, UNESCO, Paris, France, 1979, page 54.
4. Edwin Mansfield, "Contribution of R&D to Economic Growth in the United States," *Science*, 4 February 1972, Vol. 175, No. 4021, page 477. Also, Nathan Rosenberg, "Thinking about Technology Policy for the Coming Decade," *U.S. Economic Growth from 1976 to 1986; Prospects, Problems and Patterns*, studies prepared for the use of the Joint Economic Committee, Congress of the United States, Vol. 9, *Technological Change*, January 3, 1977, page 1, and "The Impact of Regulation on Industrial Innovation," *National Research Journal*, National Academy of Sciences, Washington, DC, 1979, pages 8–9.
5. *Investing in Scientific Progress, 1961–1970 Report*, NSF, 61–27, Washington, DC: National Science Foundation, 1961, page 7.
6. *Management of New Products*, 4th edition, New York: Booz, Allen, and Hamilton, Inc., 1964, page 6.
7. *Ibid.*, page 2.
8. "Report of the Joint Economic Committee, U.S. Congress," 88th Congress, 2nd session, 1964, page 65. (See also Dexter M. Keezer, "R&D—Its Impact on the Economy," *Challenge*, December 1963, page 7.)
9. J.E. Stafford and J.A. McNeal, "Organizing for Product Planning," *Advanced Management Journal*, January 1964, page 28.
10. "Vanishing Innovation," *Business Week*, July 3, 1978, page 46.
11. "RCA Chooses Financing Over Technology," *Business Week*, September 3, 1979, page 88.
12. *Ibid.*
13. "Vanishing Innovation," *op. cit.*, page 47.
14. Rutherford M. Poats, *Technology for Developing Nations*, Washington, DC: The Brookings Institute, 1972, page 28.
15. *Ibid.*, pages 20–21.
16. Daniel D. Roman, *Science, Technology and Innovation: A Systems Approach*, Columbus, Ohio: Grid Publishing Company, 1980, pages 13–16.

CHAPTER TWO

International Economics

The Global Market

Technology as a Basis for Trade

For decades economists were prone to believe that there was a difference between the goods that were traded *between* countries and the goods traded *within* a country. Eventually, their studies led them to a different perspective. International trade is a natural extension of national commerce which takes place between people and regions. Since the beginning of recorded time, people have exchanged goods and services—long before the advent of money. These goods and services represented those items for which a particular individual or group had a demonstrated proficiency to produce or offer. They obviously were competing in the marketplace, albeit a limited one. These transactions are termed "bartering."

It was only natural for people to band together for the purposes of commerce. As the ancients perceived a particular technology they quickly recognized the inherent economic potential—witness the arrowhead, the metal knife, and gun powder. These are but a few of the early examples of technology offered for trade between groups of people within regions. As man has become more sophisticated, the regions became states within nations, and the spirit of enterprise continued to be pervasive. If the item or service was in demand in another region, it was naturally traded there. This fostered a problem—the form of payment. Once a mutual basis for exchange was overcome the stage was set for international trade, and thus the reality of a global market.

This chapter will explore the realities of the factors of production, comparative advantage, absolute advantage, and provide an insight into the production possibilities of nations. World currencies will be examined and a framework will be established for studying international trade. Chapter Three will cover the contribution of technology to international economics, trade, and commerce.

The Factors of Production

Controlling the Factors of Production

In any society, country or nation there exists a limited amount of the factors of production. These factors are capital (C), labor (A), and land (D).* For our purposes we will restate the factor "land" and title it "natural resources" or N, as this is more germane to the discussion.

It should also be apparent that while "capital" (C) is normally perceived to be capital equipment, amounts of funds and perhaps amounts of credit, it also pertains to technology. A nation that has accrued sufficient amounts of capital can make outright purchases of technology. This is happening today in the Middle East where Saudi Arabia, Iran, and the United Arab Emirates are purchasing a wide spectrum of Western technology. It should be noted, in addition, that technology will tend to flow in response to availability of and in exchange for natural resources.

The endowment of these factors will vary from country to country and, indeed, from time period to time period. Some countries fortunately have been blessed with great amounts of natural resources but are sparsely populated (for example, the Soviet Union and Canada). On the other hand, some nations have large numbers of people but relatively few natural resources; Japan and India are prime examples.

Of particular importance from the international perspective, however, is *how* and by *what amounts* a certain nation *produces*; given a fixed amount of these factors of production. Thus, it is appropriate to state that national output, Y will depend upon the amounts of these three factors employed at a particular point in time. We, therefore, are enabled to say that:

$$Y = \sum C + \sum A + \sum N \tag{1}$$

It is therefore apparent that to some extent a nation is able to adjust the nature of its economic output by controlling and manipulating the variety and amounts of the factors of production. For nations whose outputs are planned in detail, such as the members of COMECON,[1] the equation is more easily kept in balance. In the capitalistic and socialistic societies, the task is not as simple. The United States and members of the European Common Market,[2] to a more limited extent, make their adjustments through the application of tax rates, investment tax incentives, indirect governmental involvement, and wage and price policies. Extant import and export policies and tariffs are also cogent factors. For the most part, however, the total of national output of the

*The French Economist J.B. Say added a fourth factor—the entrepreneur who assumes the risk and management associated with the other three factors of production.

so-called Free-World nations is determined by the collective opinions and perceptions of hundreds of thousands of individual entrepreneurs. These people, in point of fact, are guiding the destinies of their nations through their search for a profit.

Some Economic Theories Affecting International Trade

Theorists have identified four significant reasons for international trade. These are condensed into these categories:

1. Differences in the actual costs of the actual factors of production.
2. Actual or perceived differences in technologies.
3. Decreasing costs of production normally resulting from increased output.
4. Differences in taste between areas.[3]

Absolute and Comparative Advantage

A concept underlying the pure theory of international trade was developed by the classical economist, David Ricardo *circa* 1810. He theorized that nations engaged in trade because of "the special ability of a country to provide one product or service relatively more cheaply than other products or services."[4] This theory explains why a country capable of providing a relatively broad range of goods and services at a cost lower than any other country (having an absolute advantage) should nevertheless concentrate on selling those products or services for which its cost advantage is greatest. Thus, a country should selectively optimize its production and leave the production of some goods to other countries. Succinctly then, each country should specialize in those products or services which may be produced more efficiently as compared to other countries. The principle of comparative advantage is applicable to business organizations as well as nations. Ricardo noted,

> Two men can both make shoes and hats, and one is superior to the other in both employments, but in making hats he can only excel his competition by one-fifth or 20% and in making shoes he can excel him by one-third or 33%;—will it not be for the interest of both that the superior man should employ himself exclusively in making shoes, and the inferior man in making hats?[5]

Ricardo's classic example of the law of comparative advantage is explained by focusing upon the production of wine and textiles in Portugal and in England. Production of the two products in each of the two countries is as follows:

	Production	
Product	**In Portugal**	**In England**
Wine	80 hr/unit	120 hr/unit
Textiles	90 hr/unit	100 hr/unit

The above example reflects the labor theory of value—that is, production is expressed in terms of the units of labor required to produce one unit of product. Note that Portugal has an absolute advantage in the production of both wine and textiles, since less units of labor are required to produce both wine and textiles in Portugal as compared to England. However, in terms of comparative advantage, Portugal has a comparative advantage in the production of wine while England has a comparative advantage in the production of textiles (one bottle of wine could be exchanged for only eight-ninths of a unit of textiles in Portugal, while the same bottle could be exchanged for one and one-fifth units of textiles in England).[6] For trade to commence and continue there must be a two-way street so that goods and payment may be exchanged. Both parties must have the opportunity for commerce. Invariably there is some mutually agreed upon common exchange unit. If one country only buys and the other only sells it follows that since resources are limited, the common exchange unit will eventually be exhausted. If this happens trade will either cease or another acceptable unit will have to be agreed upon. Ricardo's theory, in essence, was directed at the continuation of trade by both buying and selling and the effective use of scarce resources.

Labor Theory

Classical economists had the belief that if the product of an industry could be sold for more than the value of the labor it contained, additional labor would transfer into that industry (from other occupations) to earn abnormal wages. This transfer would continue until the price of the product was brought down to the value of its labor content. The converse was also believed true. If a commodity sold for less than its worth of labor, labor would move away into other occupations until the gap closed. After a period of time labor would have spread itself among several regions of a country thus equalizing wages. The regions then would produce and sell to each other what each region can make the cheapest.

It was believed that while the above explained movement of the factor "labor" within a country, this same theory was not valid to analyze factor mobility from an international perspective. It was presumed that the factors of production were relatively "immobile" internationally. If wages were higher in the United States than in Spain, they would stay higher because migration (immigration) cannot take place on a scale sufficient to eliminate discrepancies. This analysis was eventually rejected as the tendency for the return to labor to be equal throughout a country was seen to be incorrect. Labor is not homogeneous. If there was an increase in the demand for horseshoes, the wages of blacksmiths rose above those of brewers. It was recognized that there was not a great class of labor with a single wage, but rather, a series of noncompeting groups among which the tendency to equalize wages was weak or nonexistent.

Opportunity Costs

A void developed following the rejection of the classical labor theory of value since it was recognized that labor was not homogeneous and that goods were not produced by labor alone. What then was the explanation for the movement of goods across international boundaries? Gottfried Haberler, during the 1930s, made available his theory of "opportunity costs," and helped remove the veil of indecision.[7] This theory is best expressed using "production possibility curves."[8] As may be seen from Figure 2-1 the price of a given output, in the long run, can be measured in terms of how much of some other output a country has to give up in order to obtain additional units of the first good. Figure 2-1 represents a situation of constant returns to scale where a proportionate increase in inputs increases outputs by the same proportion. Note that the factors of production (or their absence) actually constrain and at the same time define the perimeter of possible output. This case is one of relatively poor productivity.[9] One unit of change in steel output causes an equal reaction in the agricultural sector.

Figure 2-2, on the other hand, is an example of increasing returns whereby a proportionate increase in inputs increases output more than proportionately.

In each case the magnitude of the production possibilities are severely limited by the gross amounts of natural resources, capital, and labor available at that precise moment in time. From Figure 2-2, it may be readily deduced that a relatively small shift in the factors causing a reduction in wheat output from W_1 to W_2 will directly increase the output of cloth from C_1 to C_2. This is a proportionately greater output.

The slope of the production-possibilities curve [the marginal rate of transformation (MRT)] measures the number of units of one commodity or service that

Figure 2-1. Production possibilities with constant returns.

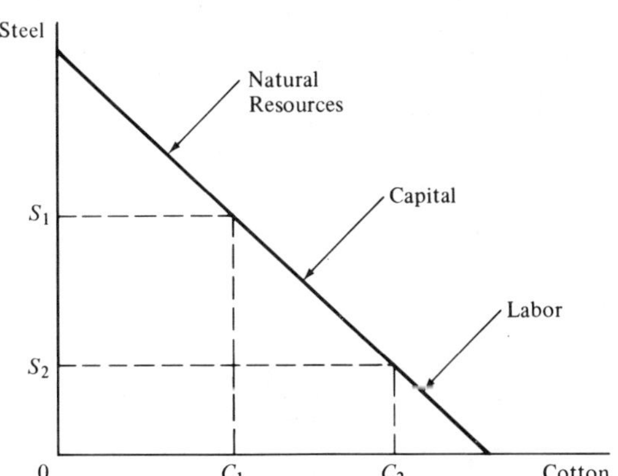

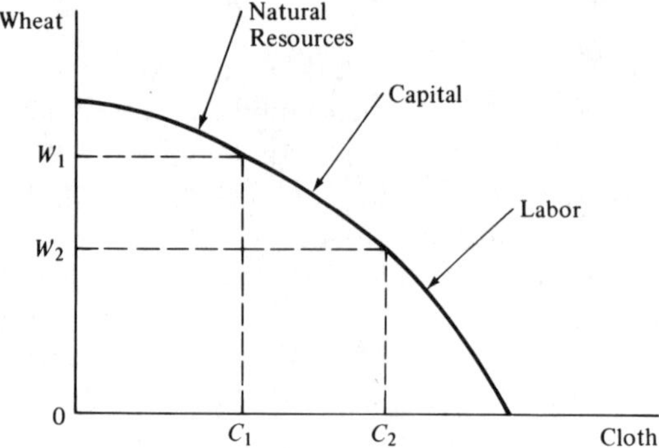

Figure 2-2. Production possibilities with increasing returns.

must be given up to obtain one additional unit of the other commodity or service. Thus, as may be deduced from Figure 2-2, the quantity of wheat indicated by distance W_1 to W_2 must be given up to obtain added units of cloth due to the shift in output from C_1 to C_2. The marginal rate of transformation is based upon technology, i.e., (a) relative factor endowments, (b) proportionate factor intensities, and (c) returns to scale. It is these differences in factor efficiencies which create the basis for trade between countries—that is, the relative abilities of different countries to produce different products at different levels of efficiency.

Introduction of the demand side of the equation (supply = demand) enables us to perceive an equilibrium position—the point at which the marginal rate of substitution (MRS) of consumers [measured by the slope of a consumer's indifference curve (IC)] is tangent to the production possibilities curve. The equilibrium is achieved at point T_E in Figure 2-3. This figure represents a one-country, two-commodity model. It is at point T_E that the country would produce to satisfy the relative national demand for both wine and cloth—

Figure 2-3. One-country, two-commodity equilibrium model.

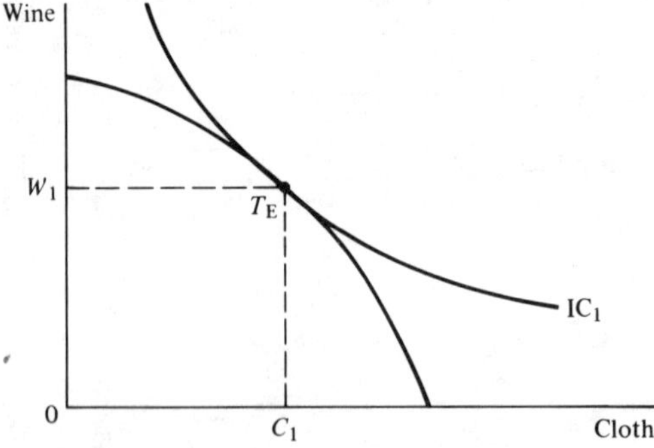

amounts W_1 for wine outputs and C_1 for cloth outputs. Remember that the magnitude of the production possibilities frontier, $W-C$, is delineated by the amounts of $C-A-N$ available at that point in time. Thus, outputs of commodities and services are a combination of the factors of production and the demand for those products by consumers at a specific point in time. Over a period of time the factors may increase or decrease.

Based upon the relative efficiencies of two countries (such as Portugal and Great Britain) in the production of two commodities (such as wine and cloth), it is clear that both countries will likely benefit from trade of the commodity in which it has a comparative *advantage* in exchange for the commodity in which it has a comparative *disadvantage*. Accordingly, a necessary condition for equilibrium in a two-country, two-commodity world is

$$\text{MRS}_\text{P} = \text{MRT}_\text{P} = \text{MRS}_\text{GB} = \text{MRT}_\text{GB} \tag{2}$$

where

$$\begin{aligned} \text{MRT} &= \text{marginal rate of transformation} \\ \text{MRS} &= \text{marginal rate of substitution} \\ \text{P} &= \text{Portugal} \\ \text{GB} &= \text{Great Britain} \end{aligned}$$

However, another condition is also necessary in order to reach equilibrium, and that is

$$\text{EX}_\text{P} = \text{IM}_\text{GB} \tag{3}$$

$$\text{IM}_\text{P} = \text{EX}_\text{GB} \tag{4}$$

where

$$\begin{aligned} \text{EX} &= \text{exports} \\ \text{IM} &= \text{imports} \end{aligned}$$

The above are the two necessary and sufficient conditions for achieving equilibrium in a two-country, two-commodity world. Figure 2-4 depicts such a situation.

Figure 2-4. Two-country, two-commodity equilibrium model.

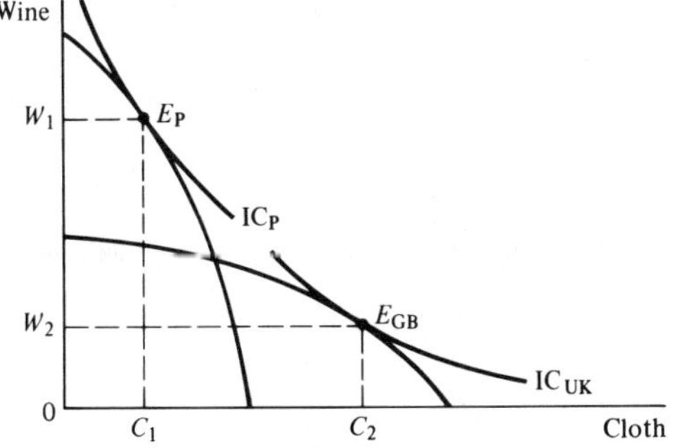

Here the situation $W_1 - E_P - C_1$ represents a point of equilibrium whereby Portugal is producing a great deal of wine—probably more than can be consumed nationally. On the other hand, Great Britain is producing at $W_2 - E_{GB} - C_2$ where they are likely overproducing cloth. Portugal very likely requires cloth and Great Britain wine—thus, the stage is set for international trading.

Monetary Exchange

For the most part it is not convenient to conduct the world's trade on a barter basis. Money or "monetary credits" have a definite advantage as a "unit of exchange."[10]

To illustrate the importance and convenience of money from the standpoint of international trade consider two different currencies and countries than in our previous example: francs of France and marks of Germany. Table 2-1 relates the units of output of the two countries in terms of two commodities, cloth and wine.[11] The table is relating units of output per unit of labor input—labor output efficiencies. Now assume that wage rates for the average workers are 300 francs in France and 100 marks in Germany. Table 2-2 compares the per-unit price of cloth and wine in terms of domestic currency units. Prices in Table 2-2 are a function of the relative efficiency of output from Table 2-1 and wages as paid. Therefore, in France, cloth costs 10 francs $(300 \div 30 = 10)$ and in Germany it costs 5 marks $(100 \div 20 = 5)$. In this illustration, France has an absolute nonmonetary cost advantage for producing both goods. If trade is to take place, however, France must allow and perhaps even encourage some measure of production in Germany.

Currencies, just like any other commodity, have prices. The international phrase is "currency exchange rate." This is the price of one currency in terms of another. There are a number of factors which establish these exchange rates—among these are the relationship of one nation with another, the political strength of a nation, and the economic strength of a nation. We will discuss the theory of exchange rates in more detail later.

If the exchange rate is 3 marks = 1 franc, France would like to import both cloth and wine. It would be paying 5 marks instead of 30 for cloth and 10 marks instead of 45 for wine. (See Table 2-3.)

Another way of looking at this situation is to consider the cost of goods if a person in France were to convert their entire paycheck into marks. They would

Table 2-1. Units of Output[a]

	Cloth	Wine
France	30	20
Germany	20	10

[a]Per worker–day of input.

Table 2-2. Price in Domestic Currency[a]

	Cloth	Wine
France (franc)	10	15
Germany (mark)	5	10

[a]Per units of output.

negotiate through a monetary exchange and obtain 900 marks for their 300 francs. They then would purchase cloth for 5 marks and wine for 10 marks from Germany. On the other hand, the Germans would have little desire to purchase either cloth or wine from France. Consider the exchange. For the paycheck of 100 marks, a German would obtain 33.33 francs ($100/3 = 33.33$). Cloth would cost 10 francs and wine 15 francs. The cloth would have consumed one-third of the francs and the wine almost one-half.

At this exchange rate, very little bilateral trade will occur. An adjustment is required in the exchange rates or the prices of both countries must come into a better balance in order to open the "two-way street" of international exchange.

Price Changes

In the preceding example, prices would have been more in line (that is, more equal) if the wages of workers in France were lowered and those in Germany were raised. Sound easy? In theory, at least, it is.

Trade is facilitated where the opportunity exists to buy "cheap" in one environment and sell "high" in another environment. The differential is profit and is the incentive to enter into transactions. Merchants in France, perceiving the opportunity for profit, convert francs to marks or procure and ship some other common exchange unit to purchase both goods. Let us focus on just one good—cloth—as we continue this scenario. At the outset, relative prices, demand, and supply for both countries are depicted in Figure 2-5. Note that cloth is relatively more expensive in France than in Germany. The tendency then is for French merchants to seek German cloth. The French merchants will accept payment in francs or any precious substance having value in virtually

Table 2-3. Germany's Monetary Cost Advantages[a]

	Prices in marks	
	Cloth	Wine
France	30	45
Germany	5	10

[a]Exchange rate: 3 marks = 1 franc.

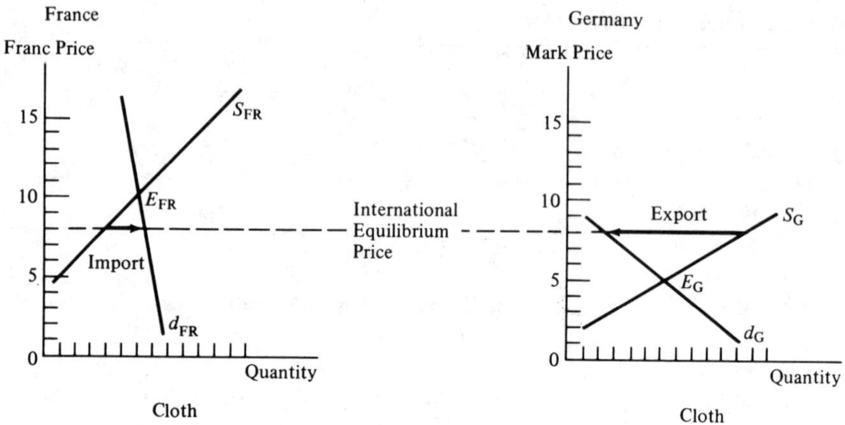

Figure 2-5. International equilibrium.

all markets (such as gold). The German merchants will accept marks or a precious substance. The Germans would be reluctant to accept francs, however. The reasoning here is that after a time it would be difficult to spend the francs. Goods are far too expensive in France. So, of what use are the francs to the people and merchants of Germany? There is nothing in France that would induce them to spend there, given the level of prices.

The French continue to put pressure on their merchants for more and more German cloth. This will occur for as long as the quality is perceived to be equal and the price is below that of commercially produced French cloth.

As added quantities of cloth are demanded and produced, the relative wage rates of German workers will rise in response. French wages, albeit at a slower rate, will tend to decline because Germany is "more competitive."

If the situation continues, the wages of the two nations will tend to equalize at the point (the international equilibrium price) as indicated in Figure 2-5. In reality, however, this situation will have been likely exacerbated by the introduction of tariffs, quotas, or other exchange restrictions (to be discussed in detail in later chapters). These "barriers to trade" will have served to raise the price of the German cloth to levels of that produced in France. Other factors which affect this natural "leveling process" are recessions and rapid inflation.

Exchange Rate Changes

Adjustments in the rates of exchange between two nations are possible as the relative "worth" of the individual economies change over time. This change in the value of an economy is normally a gradual process given political stability.

Consider that France obtained a large stockpile of gold, perhaps as a result of the discovery of North Sea oil deposits. Gold, as has been mentioned, is an acceptable "medium of exchange" in all nations. Gold could be used to directly purchase goods from Germany or could be converted into marks and then used to purchase the goods.

After a period of "free trade" (the absence of trade barriers) the stockpile of gold in France would have diminished somewhat. As more and more cloth is purchased, additional quantities of gold flows into the coffers of Germany. As may be observed from Figure 2-6, there is a net flow of gold from France to Germany. As Germany accumulates gold, the overall value of the German economy, from the international perspective, tends to rise. Thus, after a period of time, as Germany's economy is "worth" more and France's less, the relative exchange rates will tend to come more in line—more toward a one-for-one par. Therefore, just in the sense that a person may become increasingly wealthy, so can a nation also accumulate wealth (and power).

It is important to note that the "leveling" process may occur with a nation importing more than it exports in a "gross" sense. The nation's economy tends to become "soft"; its people are existing on credit and living off the good graces of their trading partners.

Other factors that affect the relative exchange rates are much more subtle. These include high national unemployment rates, low productivity, goods of poor quality, severe decline in national resources, and many other equally insidious causes.

The matter of rates of exchange and prices of goods is a delicate one. To fully appreciate the fragile nature of the international marketplace, one has only to ask oneself why a particular good costs as it does on the domestic market. Tie to this analysis the attitudes of different people, the objectives of different governments, and the realities of natural disasters, and one can see why there is a natural fluctuation in exchange rate between nations.

International Balance of Payments

Economic Transactions

International trade presupposes a foreign exchange rate between domestic and foreign currencies. It is this exchange rate that forms the "mechanism" for

Figure 2-6. International trade.

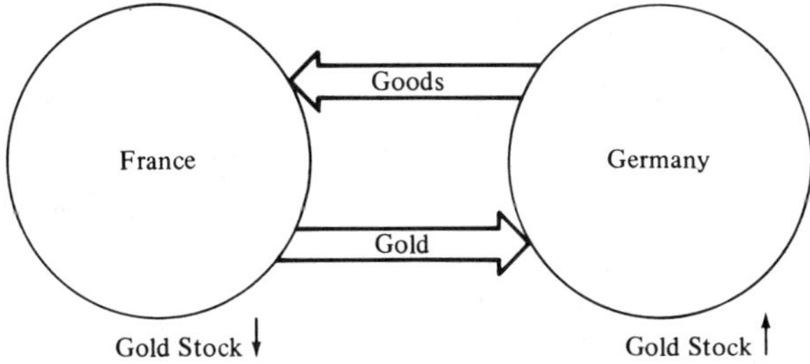

trade. Without this common economic basis nations would be reluctant to trade with one another.

In view of the fact that (a) exports do not always equal imports, and (b) we do not live in a simple two-country, two-commodity world, it is necessary to review the concept of the balance of payments. The balance of payments is a systematic record of all the economic transactions between one country and the rest of the world in a given period, usually one year.[12] Therefore, just as we as individuals must balance our checkbooks, so must nations balance theirs as well. They maintain records that result in calculations of national deficits and surpluses.

Conveniently, accounting for the balance of payments is accomplished by the familiar double-entry bookkeeping system. Each transaction between the resident and a nonresident leads to two entries in the balance of payments. Usually one of these entries is a credit and the other a debit. For example, the accounting entries to record an American export of merchandise valued at $2000 to Mexico would be that shown in Table 2-4. If, on the other hand, an American buyer purchases merchandise valued at $2500 from a Mexican producer, the accounting entries would be that shown in Table 2-5.

Simplistically, each transaction leads to one debit and one credit entry; thereby keeping a balance in the balance of payments. The accounting balance of payments, i.e., the sum of all credits minus the sum of all debits can never be anything but zero. However, this is not the point of international balance deficits and surpluses; it is necessary to examine the above transactions in more detail for the answer.

Consider, for example, the $2000 merchandise export from the United States. There is a conceptual difference between the two accounting entries. A Mexican buyer wished to purchase the American goods. The motive was autonomously based on an active preference for the American product. The "export" entry is therefore independent of any other entry in the U.S. balance of payments. The other entry, "payments received," passively followed as a *result* of the transaction. Consider a purchase of a stereo tape deck. You buy the tape deck because you wish to have it—not because you wish to make payment for it. Making payment for the tape deck is a passive consequence of your active desire for the product.

Therefore, one of the two entries to each international transaction is active, while the other is passive. If the active entry is a credit, then the passive entry must be a debit, and vice versa.

Table 2-4. U.S. Balance of Payments

Debits	Credits
Payments received $2000	$2000 Merchandise exports

Table 2-5. U.S. Balance of Payments

Debits	Credits
Merchandise imports $2500	$2500 Payments made

The distinction between active and passive entries leads directly to a concept of imbalance in the balance of payments. In Table 2-6 both the export and import transactions are reflected in four entries. The active entries are placed into the "active account," and the passive entries are placed into the "passive settlements account."

It follows, therefore, that a county has a balance of payments deficit if active debits exceed active credits or if passive credits exceed passive debits. A country has a balance of payments surplus when active credits exceed active debits or if active debits exceed passive credits. A simple way of analyzing the impact of a given flow on the balance of payments is to determine the direction of the flow of cash involved. If the net flow is inward, the effect is positive (surplus); if the net flow is outward, negative (deficit). Thus, an active entry is a credit when payment is received for it; it is a debit when payment must be made.

Some examples will help illustrate these principles. Country A may sell services to foreigners in the form of transportation, tourism, and insurance. Such service exports are active credits because payment is *received*. Country A may decide to give foreign aid in the form of a grant to another nation. Although this is a unilateral transfer, one active and one passive entry must be made. Foreign aid gifts carry an active debit entry along with a corresponding passive credit entry of "payments made." In the case of lending and borrowing, the active entry "lending" is a debit, while the active entry "borrowing" is a credit, each offset by a credit "payments made" or a debit to "payments received."

Table 2-6. U.S. Balance of Payments

Debits		Credits	
	Active account		
Merchandise imports	$2500	$2000	Merchandise exports
Net active (deficit)	500		
	Passive settlements account		
Payments received	$2000	$2500	Payments made
Net passive		500	(Deficit)
Accounting balance	$4500	$4500	

Technology Transfers

There are some transactions that do not constitute a balance of payment issue. Technology or skills may be exported on the basis of a long-term contract or as a capital contribution to a foreign enterprise. The capitalization of that technology or skill is not recorded in the balance of payments.

Accounting Gaps

Realistically, the actual international balance of payments accounting for a given nation is not so easy. In order for the double-entry method to be applied, both entries of each transaction must be known to the recorder. While this is the case with most transactions, there are others whereby only one entry, usually the passive one, becomes known. Such borderline transactions may be due to gaps in the recording network or to illegal transactions. In order to keep the accounting balance intact, some balancing entry (an active debit) must be made. In the U.S. balance of payments this entry is called "errors and omissions." In short, if the active and passive accounts do not balance, the passive settlements account is accepted as correct and the active account is adjusted by means of the residual active errors and omissions entry.

The U.S. Position

An examination of the international accounts of the United States should serve to put this topic into proper perspective. The balance of payments for the United States consists of the following accounting entities:

1. *Current account*. This consists only of goods and services, and therefore represents exports and imports, including interest and dividends.
2. *Capital account*. This consists of both long-term and short-term investments.
3. *Unilateral transactions*. This is that which makes up a net surplus or deficit and which results in compensatory movements. If receipts (credits) of a country are less than its payments (debits), a deficit results. On the other hand, if credits are greater than debts, a surplus results.[13]

The so-called "liquidity balance" measures changes in the U.S. external liquidity position in relation to all foreigners; while the "official reserve transaction balance" (or "official settlements balance") measures changes in the U.S. external liquidity in relation to foreign official institutions only. The major purpose of keeping these records is to inform governmental authorities of the international position of the country, to aid them in reaching decisions on monetary and fiscal policy on the one hand and trade and payments questions on the other. While the example of accounts above relates to the United States, it is apparent that all nations maintain similar accounts.

It is essential to differentiate the concept of the balance of trade from that of the balance of payments. The balance of trade consists of *part* of current account only—that is, the merchandise balance—the difference between the *value of the goods that a nation exports and the value of the goods it imports*. If exports are greater than imports, a "favorable" balance of trade is said to exist; if imports are greater than exports, an "unfavorable" balance of trade is said to exist. However, these terms remain as part of an earlier era of economic thought, and do not indicate goodness or badness of themselves; thus, a favorable balance of trade could be as undesirable to a country with a surplus balance of payments as would be an unfavorable balance of trade to a country with a deficit in its balance of payments. It is instructive to note that the United States had experienced a favorable balance of trade each year since the 1890s until 1971. During that time several deficits in the balance of payments were experienced.

While this discussion is theoretical, it is well to use the United States as an example of how a nation can move from a state of *favorable* balances of payment to one of *unfavorable* balances.

Figure 2-7 represents the posture of the United States since 1945.[14] Note that while the stock of gold is decreasing, the liquid liabilities are steadily increasing. The country is suffering from rising inflation and lower productivity. The wealth of income per capita is declining. There are a number of factors that have been identified as the root-cause. Samuelson has identified the following as the causes for the U.S. chronic payments deficit:

1. Too much inflation at home.
2. Overgenerosity in aid and military programs.
3. Lack of trust in the dollar.
4. Discrimination abroad against American goods.
5. The rapid growth of productivity abroad.
6. High investment abroad by American firms.
7. Quadrupled price of OPEC oil.[15]

Figure 2-7. Trends in U.S. gold stock and liquid liabilities.

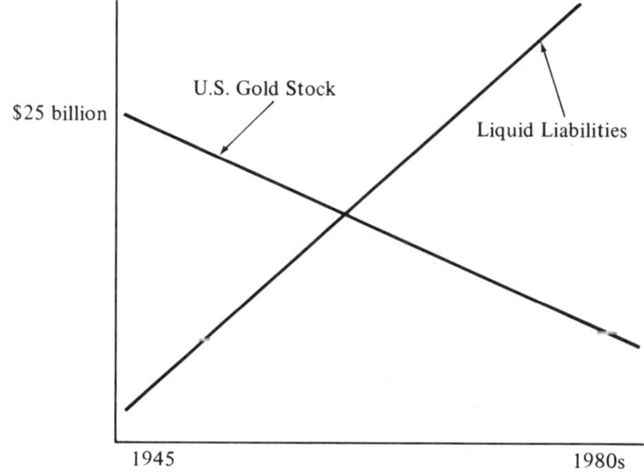

These factors no doubt have been the forces driving down the relative worth of the U.S. dollar and backing the United States into an "economic box" in the late 1970s. These same factors lurk around the corner for a number of other nations—West Germany, Japan, and perhaps the Middle-Eastern oil rich nations. The difficulty being that as a nation comes under international pressure, the process of recovery is difficult.

Monetary Systems

Background

Monetary systems obstensively serve the dual purposes of a medium of exchange and a store of value. Monetary systems existed as far back as ancient civilizations. However, these ancient systems frequently were inadequate and as a consequence in order to facilitate trade, barter was often practiced. The variety and nature of goods was comparatively limited so the barter process was not too difficult.

The world has become much more complex due to the amount of choices, the technological sophistication of goods, and the geographic spread of operations. Barter may still occasionally be feasible, but as a generalization it is no longer an effective method to transfer goods and services. To simplify international exchange it is important to seek some common exchange denominator. Monetary systems serve this purpose.

Prior to World War I, the external values of currencies were mainly determined by their worth as expressed in gold or silver. Furthermore, this worth was realizable only if there was no restriction placed on the convertibility of the national currency into either of the two metals. Traditionally, a currency was considered to be fully convertible if notes and coinage could be freely exchanged for gold at a nation's central banking facility (e.g., the U.S. Federal Reserve Bank). Convertibility into gold ceased to be practicable after World War I.

Under a bimetallic system (standard), it was normal for nations to establish gold and silver ratios. This ratio was intended to limit speculative buying of gold and silver and movements from one metal to the other. At the outset, the set ratios may have reflected the current availability balance between silver and gold, but the mining and refining activities soon caused imbalances.

By the beginning of the 20th century, countries like Great Britain and the United States had implemented the "Full" of "Specie Gold Standard." Countries with no access to mined gold and the less developed nations adopted the Gold Exchange Standard. Nations on the Gold Exchange Standard maintained their foreign reserves in the currencies of countries following the "Full Gold Standard."

After the First World War, most nations found it necessary to abandon the Full Gold Standard; there was not enough gold to go around. Most countries then adopted the Gold Exchange Standard or a modified version. Some countries relied largely on gold but others preferred to keep the bulk of their reserves in countries which settled official claims in gold. The term *hard currency* which before 1939 would have referred to a currency backed by large gold holdings now describes one with large foreign currency reserves.

The Gold Bullion Standard was introduced by Great Britain in 1925. This Standard was blamed for the General Strike of 1926 and a national economic stagnation and was abandoned in 1931. In 1933, the United States devalued the dollar by raising the price of gold from $20.67 to $35 an ounce. These two incidences plus currency problems in Germany caused a scramble by other countries to protect their currency and trade in relation to all the other nations—termed by many, a "beggar thy neighbor" approach. Competitive depreciations to promote exports and curb imports, inconvertible currencies, exchange controls, currency blocks of nations, and bilateral trade agreements became common.

By 1935, the international monetary crisis, coupled with the gripping global depression, had splintered the international monetary systems into five groups:

The Dollar Area. United States and most Central and South American nations.

The Sterling Area. British Commonwealth and Scandinavian countries.

The Gold Bloc. Western European countries.

The Exchange Control Area. Central and Southeastern Europe, dominated by Germany.

The Yen Area. Japan and Japan's possessions.[16]

Argentina, Brazil and Chile depreciated their currencies against the U.S. dollar, but adopted exchange controls that rendered their currencies inconvertible. Canada depreciated its dollar by 10% against the American dollar, but remained convertible. The currencies of the Sterling Area, the Yen Area, the Dollar Area, and those of the principal Western European nations (excluding Germany and Italy) remained fully convertible from one to another up to the outbreak of World War II.[17]

The Second World War brought an end to any monetary stabilization that may have been achieved in the late 1930s. The strain on the world's resources was much too great for the previous systems to be reestablished, and a realignment of economic relations between nations was thought to be necessary. The clearest aspect of this readjustment was the emergence of the United States as the undisputed leader of the Western world. U.S. shipments of armaments and essential common goods during the war had been the backbone of the Allied war effort. Therefore, at the urging of the United States, the major Allied leaders met at Bretton Woods, New Hampshire, in 1944 to establish a postwar international monetary system.

Perhaps realizing the need for a stable structure to facilitate restoration of an industrial world largely devastated by the war, or perhaps cognizant of the new structure of power among the nations resulting from the war, or perhaps dissatisfied with the previous times of instability and problems with gold-base systems, they forged ahead on a newly conceived fixed rate monetary systems. The agreement was signed in 1944 and took effect in 1945. It created among other entities, an International Monetary Fund (IMF), with the following objectives:

Promote international monetary cooperation.

Expand and balance growth in international trade.

Promote exchange rate stability.

Maintain monetary arrangements.[18]

The fixed rate system had these features: Each member nation defined a par value for its own currency in terms of gold or the U.S. dollar; the United States defined the value of the dollar in terms of gold only; each nation agreed to regulate the market exchange rate for its currency within a band of plus or minus 1% of its par value; and, nations could change the par value of their currencies after consultation with the IMF. The change was termed a *devaluation* if the new value was lower, a *revaluation* if higher.

Each nation upon joining the IMF was assessed a quota to be paid, one-fourth in gold and three-fourths in its own currency.[19] This pool of gold and national currencies became available to nations when needed for short-term balance of payments problems and adjustments. The IMF also provided temporary assistance to member nations experiencing monetary difficulties.

More specifically, the IMF will sell a particular foreign currency to a country which needs that currency for its operations in the foreign exchange market (to be discussed in the next section). The buying country pays with its own currency. In fact, these purchases are more properly viewed as foreign currency loans, as they are to be repaid to the IMF within five years. These are limits to IMF borrowing. Any nation may automatically borrow up to 25% of its quota. This automatic drawing right is called a nation's *gold tranche*. Borrowing in excess of the gold tranche is possible, but not automatic. Such additional borrowing falls into a nation's *credit tranche*. In order to make credit tranche loans, the IMF will have to be persuaded that the borrowing country is taking appropriate measures to adjust its balance of payments deficits, such as anti-inflationary monetary and fiscal policy. This persuasion becomes more difficult as the credit tranche percentage increases.

The Bretton Woods system was a gold-dollar system with flexibility. The dollar was the central currency—it alone was defined in terms of gold, and all other currencies were defined in dual terms: dollars and gold. Over time, gold and the U.S. dollar became the most popular reserve assets, and eventually dollars, which were more plentiful and were interest earning, prevailed over gold as a reserve asset. The United States with its worldwide foreign aid spending, aid to reconstruction, and its troops on foreign soil ensured that dollars were plentiful.

Monetary Devaluation

For a time, the Bretton Woods monetary system worked well. It was designed to give the nations of the world a stable monetary system with flexibility through occasional devaluations and revaluations of par values to handle any imbalances without too much disturbance of the overall stability. However, some situations related to the operations of the flexible adjustment process began to signal future problems:

1. The adjustment process depended upon the voluntary action of the nation involved in response to economic pressures.
2. Over time the dollar became overvalued.
3. Nations with a surplus payments balance were reluctant to revalue their currency because curtailed exports would mean losses of jobs and business.[20]

An eventual monetary crisis began to evolve. It concerned the major nondollar world currencies and gold in the late 1960s and the dollar in the 1970s. The pound sterling underwent a crisis and was devalued in 1967. In 1968, gold was the cause of a crisis of a different nature. Members of the London gold pool (the United States, United Kingdom, Belgium, Italy, the Netherlands, West Germany, and Switzerland) who had agreed in 1961 to control the price of gold in the London free market gave up in March 1968. They had used a great deal of their national gold stocks in a futile attempt to keep the price of gold stable. The French franc was devalued in 1969, followed that same year by the West Germany mark which was revalued (illustrating West Germany's growing industrial progress).

This deteriorating situation prompted the IMF to create in 1969 a special form of paper money. *Special Drawing Rights* (SDRs) are issued to member nations in order to give them additional reserve assets with the IMF. They are sometimes called "paper gold" and can only be used within the IMF system. They are equivalent to lines of credit for nations in times of payment problems.

By August 1971, it became clear that the United States faced its first modern currency crisis. In the late 1960s the U.S. involvement in the Vietnam conflict had a strong impact on the American balance of payments and trade. Domestically, Vietnam spending put strains on the American economy and contributed toward the increasing rate of inflation, weakening confidence in the soundness of the dollar. Also, the enormous cost of aid to Vietnam, and other foreign military aid programs accelerated the outflow of dollars and increased the severity of the balance of payments and trade deficits.

In August 1971, the United States placed a 10% surcharge on imports, imposed a 90-day freeze on wages and prices, and suspended the gold convertibility of the American dollar. In effect, the U.S. action terminated the Bretton Woods Agreement. The international monetary markets remained closed for a week. World currencies were afloat against the dollar as financial experts struggled for a negotiated settlement.

The Group of Ten and the Smithsonian Agreement

Over a period of four months, difficult and sensitive monetary negotiations were conducted by the finance ministers from the Group of Ten.[21] They met in London in September 1971, and in Rome at the end of November. Much of the negotiations focused on modifying the American and European positions that the other side make all the concessions. Finally, the major issues were settled in December when the United States agreed to accept a devaluation of the dollar and a general realignment of all other currencies. The arrangements became known as the "Smithsonian Agreement."

The Smithsonian Agreement called for a 9% devaluation of the dollar and other currencies were revalued (increases of 16% for the yen and 13% for the West German mark). Additionally the official price of gold was raised from \$35 to \$38 per ounce. Member nations agreed to maintain currencies within a band of plus or minus 2.25% around the new central values, and the dollar remained unconvertible into gold.

Although the Smithsonian Agreement was greeted with enthusiasm initially, the old problems did not evaporate. The Smithsonian realignment did not fulfil its promise, and after incurring further deficits in 1972, the United States was forced in February 1973 to devalue once more. The price of gold was increased by another 10% and the dollar was allowed to float against all currencies—fixed rate systems had come to an end after 29 years.

Monetary Upheavals

Monetary upheavals since 1973 have been numerous but an overall solution has yet to be found. To list all conferences, places, names, descriptions of new schemes, plans, systems—sliding pegs, crawling pegs, flexible rates, etc.—would fill a volume and contribute little to the discussion. Combinations of floating and loose snake agreements may in the long-term provide the answer to the age-old question of whether or not to have fixed exchange rates. Until a nation has its economy operating efficiently with a moderate level of inflation there is little point to joining a fixed or flexible exchange rate system; it is better to continue a currency float, or even to devalue from time to time.[22]

The Foreign Exchange Market

Just as any commodity has a price, so does a currency. In order to facilitate international trade and, just as importantly, to produce a profit, individuals and institutions have established foreign exchange markets. These are markets in the typical sense of the word, where currencies are bought and sold for a price.[23]

The price is relative to the availability of the currency and its perceived value in the eyes of the buyer. Just as common stocks are traded in commercial stock brokerage houses so are currencies traded on exchange markets. The currencies of a number of major countries are traded within and among financial centers. The major markets are located in New York, London, Paris, and Zurich. Many traders participate at each of the centers, and the centers are in constant contact with one another.

It is common practice for major banks to deal in foreign exchange for their customer's convenience. These activities include the purchase of proceeds of exporters and supplying the currencies needed by importers. They also deal in foreign exchange at two levels. First, since it is impractical for a bank to hold large inventories of many currencies, they go into the market to even out their position when supply and demand among its customers for a given currency fail to balance. Second, they maintain contact with banks in other countries. Foreign currency is bought and sold between them through cable transfers, which is nothing more than a transfer of credit. A cable transfer causes a deposit lodged in a foreign bank to change accounts.

It should be kept in mind that some inducement initiates these transactions and motivates the people involved. This inducement is normally a commission. Even currencies with official fixed prices are normally allowed to fluctuate within relatively small limits, and thus exchange rates are continuously moving.

It is this movement and the hint of profit which attracts *arbitrage*.

Arbitrage is a general term for buying something where it is cheap and then selling it where it is dear. Foreign exchange arbitrage occurs where traders are adept at recognizing inequities in the market and capitalizing on the differences. For example, if the price of Belgian francs in New York fell below that price in London by a degree (greater than the transactions cost) it would pay to buy francs in New York and sell them in London. This obviously would continue until the price leveled. Arbitrage also keeps exchange rates fairly constant among the many traded currencies. To illustrate the lure of arbitrage, consider that you had $1000 to use in "playing" the money markets. In this case, we will disregard the transactions cost. With the $1000 you buy Belgian francs in New York, sell the francs in Paris for Swiss francs, then sell the Swiss francs for dollars in Zurich. If, after all this activity, you have more than $1000, the exchange rates were not consistent. It should be obvious that if you made a profit you would continue the "round" until the rates were driven into a level posture.

Also operating in the foreign exchange market are speculators. These speculators are willing to take "open positions," thereby committing themselves to a future scale. They are betting on the rise and fall of exchange rates.

Charles P. Kindleberger has noted that when the foreign exchange market gets out of equilibrium it can be restored in one of a number of different ways; these include the following:

1. National authorities buying up excess supply or supplying excess demand over a period and waiting for the dust to settle. This is called "financing the deficit or surplus in the balance of payments." Within limits, disequilibriums can be financed. Over time, however, the country would run out of reserves and credit.

2. Shifting the demands for foreign goods and the supply of goods for export by altering domestic national income.
3. Rationing the supply of foreign exchange (foreign exchange control).
4. Allowing changes in the exchange rate.[24]

International Multiplier Effect

Closed Economy Multiplier

Spending within the various domestic economic segments usually results in magnified effects throughout the economy in proportion to the marginal propensity to consume. In the same vein, an autonomous shift in domestic investment or in exports will cause a change in national income in the same direction. Decreases in these expenditures will lower national income; increases will raise it. The resulting change in national income will be a *multiple* of the autonomous change in investment or exports.

In an economic sense, it is necessary to assume that exports take place out of current production, rather than from past production (disinvestment of inventories or transfers of existing assets). This means then that exports increase income. Additionally, exports are assumed to be a constant at every level of national income. It is presumed that the nation is exporting commodities which it either does not consume at all or for which its demand is inelastic. This assumption is appropriate for a primary producing nation such as Chile—exporting copper and using very little—it is not appropriate for the United States producing and exporting consumer goods. In America, as well as in all developed economies, exports and consumption and exports and investment are both *competitive* rather than independent. An increase in income under this circumstance will lower exports, and exports may be taken as a falling function of income. The realities of the developed economies are ignored in this explanation of the closed economy in order to gain an appreciation of the effects of the multiplier; to do otherwise would unduly exacerbate the discussion.

The foreign trade multiplier may be understood through an analogy with the domestic multiplier. It is necessary to represent the simplest kind of system in which there are savings and investment schedules, but ignoring governmental expenditures, taxes, transfers, and the like. Savings are a rising function of national income with a negative vertical intercept (dissavings occurs at zero national income), as in Figure 2-8a. Investment is a constant at every level of national income as may be seen in Figure 2-8b. Combining these two schedules, Figure 2-9, by superimposing the investment on the savings schedule gives us the equilibrium level of national income (Y), where

$$\text{Income Produced} = \text{Income Received} = \text{Income Spent} \qquad (5)$$

Income produced is the sum of consumption goods and services ($C+I$); income received equals consumption plus savings ($C+S$). Investment goods

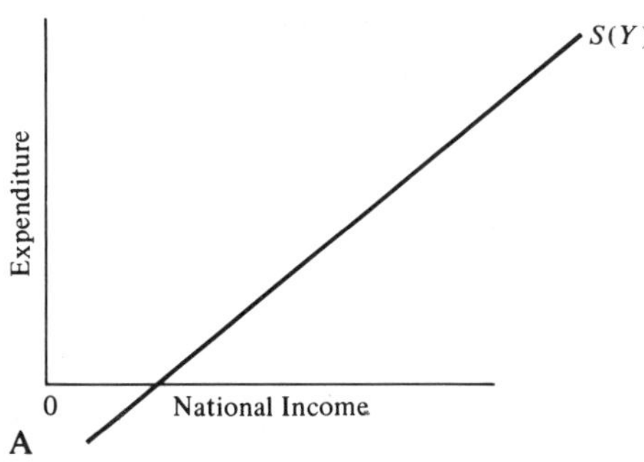

Figure 2-8a. Savings schedule.

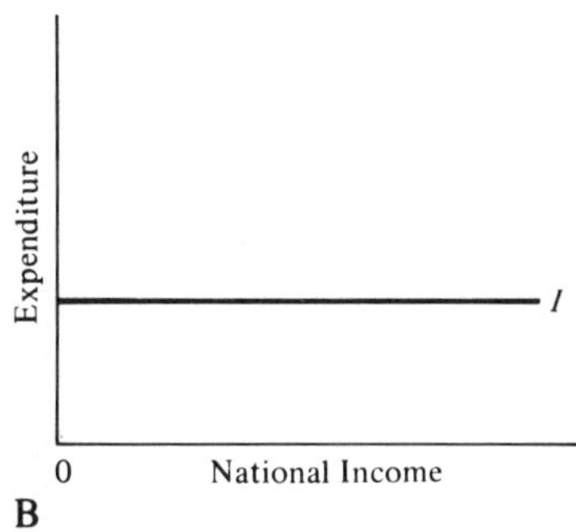

Figure 2-8b. Investment schedule.

are defined to include any goods originally intended for consumption and not sold. Therefore, the value of consumption goods produced equals the value of consumption goods consumed or

$$\begin{aligned} C+I &= C+S \\ C &= C \end{aligned} \tag{6}$$

Therefore

$$I=S \tag{7}$$

The equilibrium level of national income is that level where the savings and investment schedules intersect.

Now suppose that there is an autonomous change in the investment schedule, from I to I' in Figure 2-9; national income is increased. The amount of this increase is determined by the combined effects of the increase in investment and the domestic multiplier. Thus, we wish to determine the change in national income (ΔY) caused by the change in investment (ΔI). The determination is either geometric (from the characteristics of the triangle $\Delta Y - \Delta I$ in Figure 2-9) or by algebra. Algebretically, ΔY is ΔI times the reciprocal of the

Figure 2-9. Multiplier in closed economy.

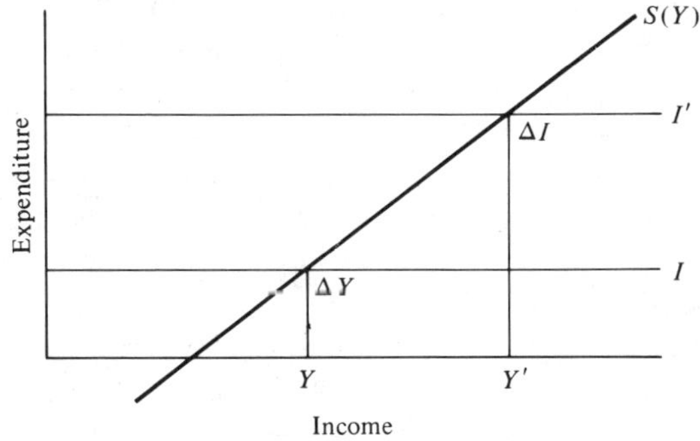

slope of $S(Y)$. The slope of $S(Y)$ is $\Delta S/\Delta Y$, and its reciprocal is $1/\Delta S/\Delta Y$ and is the multiplier. Therefore, in order to obtain ΔY, it is necessary to multiply the multiplier ($1/\Delta S/\Delta Y$ or $1/\text{MPS}$, where MPS is the marginal propensity to save), times ΔI.

We know that I equals S at equilibrium levels of national income. Therefore, in equilibrium,

$$\Delta I = \Delta S \tag{8}$$

Dividing both sides by ΔY,

$$\frac{\Delta Y}{\Delta I} = \frac{\Delta Y}{\Delta S} \quad \text{or} \quad \frac{1}{\Delta S/\Delta Y} \quad \text{or} \quad \frac{1}{\text{MPS}} \tag{9}$$

This, then, is the multiplier in a closed economy where the change in income equals the change in investment times the multiplier:

$$\Delta Y = \frac{\Delta I}{\text{MPS}} \tag{10}$$

Foreign Trade Multiplier

Determination of the foreign trade multiplier necessitates an analysis of the impacts of exports and imports on levels of national income. To determine the effects of foreign trade, continue to assume no government spending and also that goods produced (Y) plus imports (M) are equal to goods bought ($C+I$) plus goods exported (X). If there are *no* savings and *no* investments, all income is spent on consumption, and Y must equal C.
Therefore,

$$Y + M = C + I + X$$

and

$$I = 0, \quad Y = C$$

therefore,

$$X = M \tag{11}$$

Exports are equal to imports at equilibrium levels of income. The relationship between imports and national income may be expressed as the average propensity to import. The average propensity to import is the dollar value of imports as a percentage of total national income, or the proportion of national income spent on imports. The average propensity to import, at various national income levels is the import schedule or the propensity to import (Figure 2-10a). The average propensity to import at various levels of national income is denoted by $M(Y)$ in the figure. The marginal propensity to import is the change in imports associated with a given change in income. The marginal propensity to import is the slope of $M(Y)$.

Figure 2-10b notes that earlier assumption that exports will be constant at every level of output. Given the schedules of imports and exports, one can determine the level of national income. This is seen by combining Figures 2-10a and 2-10b into Figure 2-11.

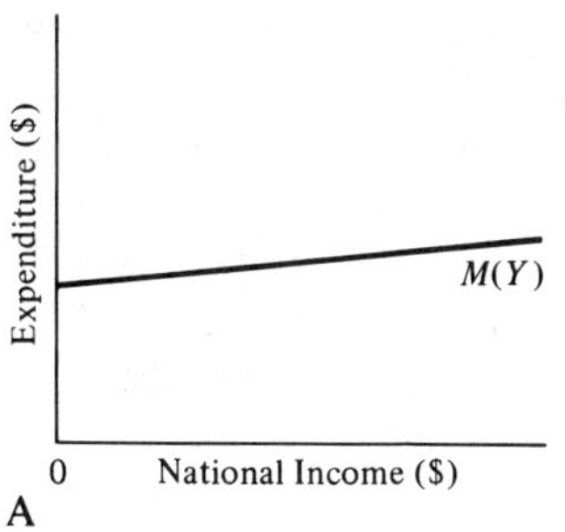

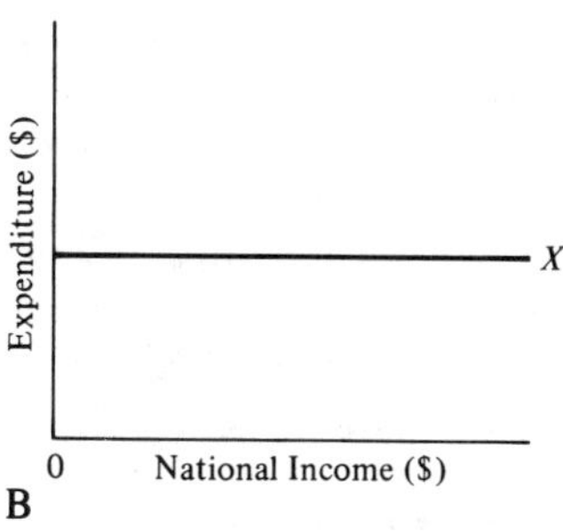

Figure 2-10a. Propensity to import.

Figure 2-10b. Constant exports.

It is now possible to derive the foreign trade multiplier for this simple economy. If for some reason exports shifted from X to X', the change in income from Y to Y', is the change in exports multiplied by the reciprocal of the slope of the impact schedule (the reciprocal of the marginal propensity to import). Therefore,

$$X = M$$

at equilibrium

$$\Delta X = \Delta M.$$

Dividing both sides of the equation into Y, we get

$$\frac{\Delta Y}{\Delta X} = \frac{\Delta Y}{\Delta M} \quad \text{or} \quad \frac{1}{\Delta M/\Delta Y} \quad \text{or} \quad \frac{1}{\text{MPM}} \tag{12}$$

Clearly, any increase in exports in an open economy without domestic savings as investment will raise the equilibrium level of national income to the point where the increment of new exports is matched by an equal increase in imports. Income will continue to grow because of the increases in consumption until the cumulative increase in imports tends to become an offset.

A shift in the import schedule will also affect national income. Assume that exports remain unchanged. Figure 2-12a shows the effects on national income

Figure 2-11. Foreign trade multiplier.

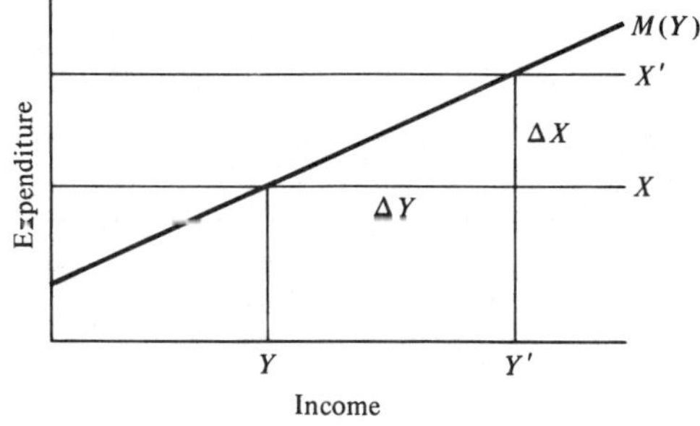

brought about by a reduction in imports. Such a shift may occur because of a change in tastes or an internal shift in income distribution or tariffs or foreign inflation or a host of other reasons. Thus, such a shift causes an increase in the national income levels (Y').

In Figure 2-12b, an upward shift in imports has occurred. Note how such a move has actually caused a reduction in the levels of national income (Y'). Such shifts may occur because of changes in tastes, lower foreign prices for commodities, or domestic shortages (U.S. oil shortages in the 1970s and 1980s).

Impact upon Commerce

The impact of the foreign trade multiplier has been felt in the global economy. For example, during the Great Depression of the 1930s countries repeatedly used policies to switch domestic expenditure away from imports and toward home goods, in order to raise the utilization of domestic resources. These policies reduced income and employment abroad. One nation's reduced imports were another's reduced exports. Such policies were the so-called "beggar-thy-neighbor policies" mentioned earlier. The effects of such policies did not usually accomplish the desired results. Nation A's diversion of expenditure from imports would lower nation B's income, and thus reduce B's imports

Figure 2-12a. Balance of payments effects of increase in investments.

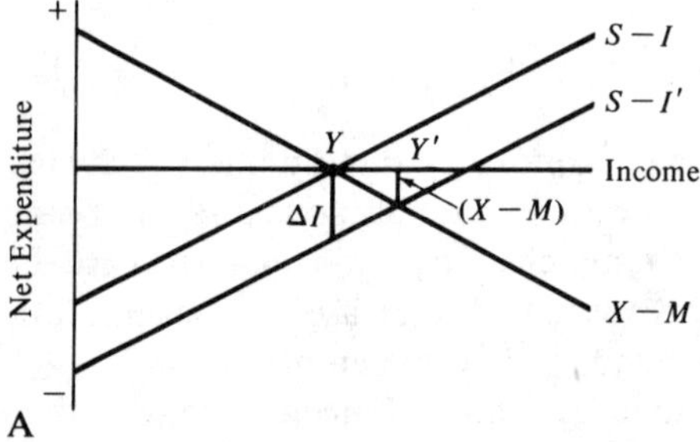

Figure 2-12b. Balance of payments effects of decrease in investments.

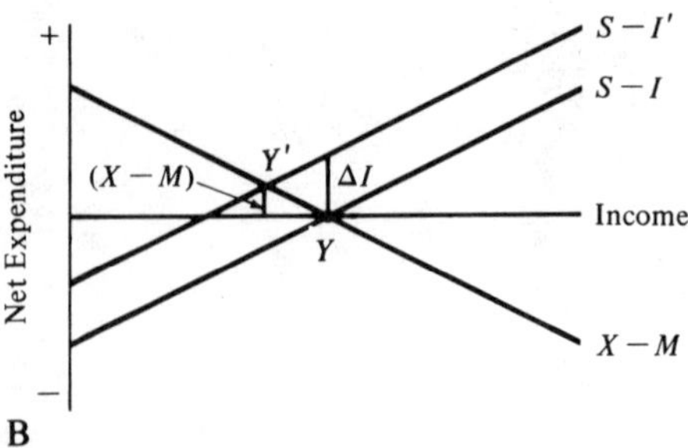

from A. The net effect of the policies could be calculated only by subtracting from the multiplier-induced increase in nation A's income the induced decrease that would ensure from the fall in nation A's exports to B. Most likely, nation B would not be idle and would retaliate against A's action by cutting imports and thus, both nations would be net losers.

Figure 2-13 shows the effects upon a nation's balance of payments of a shift in only one of the four schedules, domestic investment. Recall that $X+I=S+M$; then $X-M=S-I$. This says that a nation's balance of payments on current account equals the difference between savings and domestic investment. Therefore an increase in domestic investment will displace the $S-I$ schedule downward to $S-I'$ [because the negative term $(-I)$ is increased]. This raises national income from Y to Y', but opens up a balance of trade deficit (the line D in Figure 2-13). The deficit D is less than the amount of investment increase ΔI because increased savings (multiplier minus 1/MPS) partially offsets the shift caused by additional investment.

Further analysis of the multiplier's effect upon balance of payments may be observed by increasing or decreasing imports—which would move the $X-M$ schedule up or down, respectively—a change in the import schedule down or up, which would have the same relative effects on the $X-M$ curve; or a change in the propensity to save. Increases in exports, decreases in imports, decreases in investment, and increases in savings all help the balance of payments. Movements in the opposite direction hurt it.[25]

Some economists feel that occasionally a foreign trade accelerator may be prevalent. It is similar to the domestic accelerator. An increase in investment may take place in the export industries. An increase in American expenditures

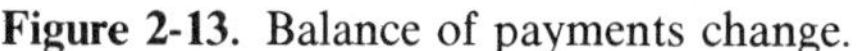

Figure 2-13. Balance of payments change.

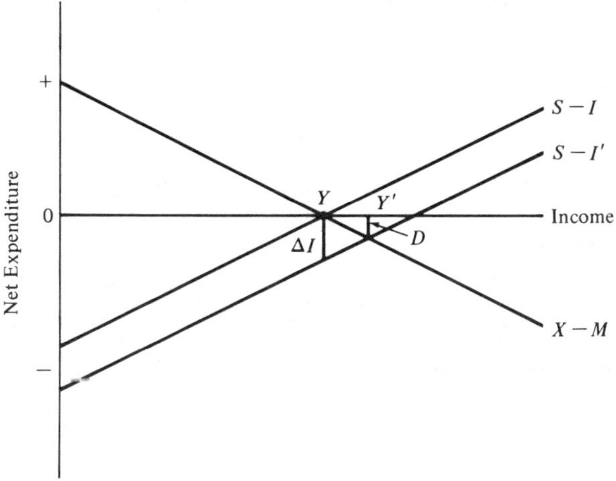

for oil in Saudi Arabia may lead to further Saudi oil exploration ventures. Or the general propensity created by the expanded-exports may lead to new investments in industries producing for home consumption—the case with modern Saudi Arabia.

Clearly, when one studies international business and global commerce, an appreciation of the effects of the international multiplier is necessary. There is indeed a correlation between international trade, and the effects of one nation's policies reverberate throughout the world's economy.

Summary

This chapter dealt with a number of important issues of international economics. While it is impossible to mention all international economic theories, it was necessary to develop a framework for a subsequent appreciation of the contribution of technology to world economic development and of the reasons for international trade.

Surfaced were the dual concepts of absolute and comparative advantage. Regardless of the relative production power of a given nation, if trade is to take place, each potential trading partner must seek to produce some good for which they have a comparative advantage.

Bartering on an international scale is simply not feasible, therefore monetary systems were developed. Difficulties are implicit when nations attempt to establish a value relationship between various currencies. Several international monetary crises have been the outcome.

Finally, just as there is a multiplier effect in domestic trade, so is there an international multiplier effect. Changes in investments, savings, imports and exports have a profound effect upon the balance of payments posture of a given nation. Therefore, if the world is to remain at peace and attempt to better the standard of living of all people, it is necessary to realize that no nation is alone—what each does in the way of domestic policies affects the livelihood of all other nations and their citizens.

Endnotes Chapter Two

1. COMECON is the acronym for the Council for Mutual Economic Assistance, which consists of the Soviet Union and its six Eastern European partners—Czechoslavakia, Romania, Poland, East Germany, Hungary, and Bulgaria.
2. European Economic Community (EEC) is more usually known as the European Common Market. Originally established by Belgium, France, Italy, Luxembourg, the Netherlands, and West Germany. Subsequently, Great Britain, Ireland, and Denmark have joined the EEC. Since 1976 the group is known as the European Community (EC). Both terms will be used in this text. It is expected that Spain and Portugal will join.
3. R.D. Hayes, C.M. Korth, M. Roudiani, *International Business: An Introduction to the World of the Multinational Firm*, Englewood Cliffs, NJ: Prentice-Hall, Inc., 1972, p. 50.

4. *The McGraw-Hill Dictionary of Modern Economics*, New York: McGraw-Hill Book Company, 1965, p. 100.
5. David Ricardo, *Principles of Political Economy*, Everyman's Edition, p. 9., as reported in P.T. Ellsworth and J.C. Leith, *The International Economy*, New York: Macmillan Publishing Co., 1975, pp. 46–49.
6. For a more detailed analysis of the laws of absolute advantage and comparative advantage see P.T. Ellsworth and J.C. Leith *op. cit.*, pp. 46–58.
7. See G. Haberler, *The Theory of International Trade*, London: William Hodge & Co., Ltd., 1936, Chapters 9–11; and G. Haberler, *The Theory of International Trade*, London: Macmillan & Co., Ltd., 1937. Also see G. Haberler, "Real Costs and Opportunity Costs" in *International Social Science Bulletin*, Spring 1951.
8. Production possibility curves (also known as transformation curves) relate one input (or one package of inputs) to two outputs; they relate the quantity of the input to several outputs: or

$$X = f(r_1, r_2)$$

$$y(x_1, r_1, r_2) = 0$$

   Thus, in Figures 2-1 and 2-2 the quantities of two outputs are shown along the axes. The curve is normally drawn concave to the origin reflecting diminishing returns.
9. Productivity is a measurement of the value of goods and services produced by a company or nation, divided by the hours or work required to produce them. Both measurements are in dollars or other currency.
10. Lester V. Chandler, *The Economies of Money and Banking*, 5th edition, New York: Harper & Row, 1969, Chapters I, II.
11. For a comprehensive synopsis of the relative complexity of monetary exchange see Hayes, Korth, Randin, *International Business*, *op. cit.*, pp. 60–64.
12. The International Monetary Fund (IMF) defines a country's balance of payments (B/P) as "a systematic record of the economic transactions during a given period between its residents and the residents of the rest of the world." IMF, *Balance of Payments Concepts and Definitions*, Washington, DC: Pamphlet Series No. 10, 1968, p. 4.
13. Many fine references are available for a more detailed analysis of the national balance of payments. Included are Paul A. Samuelson's *Economics*, 10th edition, New York: McGraw-Hill Book Company, 1976; Charles P. Kindleberger's *International Economics*, 5th edition, Homewood, IL: Richard D. Irwin, Inc., 1973; and P.T. Ellsworth and J.C. Leith's *The International Economy*, *op. cit.*
14. United States Department of Commerce statistics furnished author in January 1980.
15. Samuelson, *op. cit.*, pp. 715–717.
16. League of Nations, *International Currency Experience*, Geneva: League of Nations, 1944, p. 198.
17. F.R. Root, *International Trade and Investment*, 4th edition, Cincinnati: South-Western Publishing Co., 1978, pp. 346–347.
18. T.G. Evans, *The Currency Carousel*, Princeton, NJ: Dow Jones Books, 1977, p. 4.
19. The size of each country's quota was set according to its international trade volume, stock of reserves, and other measures of relative economic importance.
20. Evans, *op. cit.*, pp. 6–7.
21. Formed in 1962, the Group of Ten consisted of Belgium, Canada, France, West Germany, Italy, Japan, the Netherlands, Sweden, United Kingdom, and the United States.
22. R.G.F. Coninx, *Foreign Exchange Today*, New York: John Wiley & Sons, 1978, pp. 31–35.

23. An excellent reference dealing with foreign exchange is Richard E. Caves' and Ronald W. Jones' *World Trade and Payments: An Introduction*, Boston: Little, Brown and Company, 1973.
24. Kindleberger *op. cit.*, p. 322.
25. For a more comprehensive discussion of the multiplier and its effects see Kindleberger, *op. cit.*, Chapter 20; Root, *op. cit.*, Chapter 13; and, Caves and Jones, *op. cit.*, Chapter 17.

CHAPTER THREE

Economics and Technology—Research and Development

Science and Technology

Relationship

Science and technology are generally considered as two sides of a coin—science, the obverse, being the search for and acquisition of knowledge; and technology, the reverse, being the application of knowledge to the needs and desires of mankind. Scientific research may or may not explicitly precede technological innovation. During the Industrial Revolution, inventions such as the steam engine, telegraph, cotton gin, and electrical distribution systems were made before a hard scientific base for such an innovation had been established. As Albert Teich has noted,

> While today we are inclined to identify the two (science and technological innovation) quite closely they have not always been seen this way. In fact, a number of analyses show that, until recent times, science and technology progressed more or less independently of each other. Today's close identity between the two is a result of the explicit recognition on the part of society that scientific research, which in its purest sense is the pursuit of knowledge for its own sake, provides the basis for technological advance.[1]

It is technology that affects the lives of man. Technology provides the tools—the power, the methods and processes, and the machines—used by today's industrial enterprises to produce the multitude of goods and services available in the global markets. Technology produces the employment and the wealth and creates the demand for the outputs of industry.

Edwin Mansfield has said,

> Without question technological change is one of the most important determinants of the shape and evolution of the American economy. Technological change has

improved working conditions, permitted the reduction of working hours, provided an increased flow of products, old and new, and added many new dimensions to one way of life.[2]

Technology and Progress

Thus, with technological innovation, mankind has pulled itself from the mud of the nut and berry gatherer's era, through the Stone, Bronze, and Iron Ages, the Industrial Revolution, and into what has been called the Second Industrial Revolution. However, not all of the world's people have made the transition. In the underdeveloped nations of Africa, Asia, and South and Central America many people still exist in pre-Industrial Revolution conditions and, pathetically, some even in Stone Age surroundings.

To paraphrase John Donne, no nation is a scientific or technological island, entire of itself. Technology provides the key to opening the "door of plenty" to even the poorest developing nation. Proper technology utilization represents great promise for improving economic standards in developing nations. Improved economic standards should afford the means for a better life. A better life would include increased lifespan, relative freedom from sickness and disease, improved productivity and social contribution, and the means to acquire and enjoy material goods and services. Technology may be made available by the process of international trade and commerce.

International Economics—Science and Technology

World Commerce

The world, at least in terms of commerce, is becoming increasingly smaller. There are a number of factors contributing to this trend; among these are

Improved communications.

Tolerance of national goals.

Threat of global destruction.

Improved technology.

As the world shrinks, the necessity for international trade becomes more apparent. From a national perspective, it is becoming increasingly common for nations to consider the realities of comparative advantage, foreign exchange, price changes, and even factor mobility. Just as the United States developed markets after World War II for the future through the Marshall Plan, so do other developed nations assist in the growth of the developing nations. Technology is often that common bond, that element which facilitates international trade.

A Reference

Up to this point, we have only alluded to the relationship between economics and science and technology. We may define economics as "the science that treats of wealth, its nature, production distribution, and consumption and accompanying relationships."[3] Science is "systematized knowledge obtained by study, observation, and experiment."[4] Technology is "the science of the industrial arts."[5] There is a natural relationship between economics, science, and technology. Human wants and needs are virtually insatiable, but the resources required to satisfy these wants and needs are limited. Seldom are there sufficient resources to satisfy all peoples; therefore citizens, governments, and commercial enterprises spend vast sums of money in developing, producing, distributing, and consuming commodities in the present and future.

The Importance of Science and Technology

Investment in scientific knowledge and in its application to productive uses has become an important characteristic of developed nations. Benefits from the development and utilization of knowledge are many and varied. They are evident in improved health for millions of people as well as in greater understanding of outer space. They include new products that enhance the quality of life and new techniques that expand the productivity of the world's human and physical resources. While an accurate evaluation of those benefits that directly improve economic performance is difficult (to say nothing of the less tangible benefits), it is widely agreed that science and technology (S&T) plays a significant role in controlling the economies of the world. S&T has led to new products and industries, and contributes in important ways to solving today's complex economic and social problems.

The entire character of civilization has been gradually modified by the development of science over the centuries; it is the great on-rushing tide of technological change of the past two or three decades which has demanded that consideration of scientific and technological policies be lifted into the very highest councils of government.

Figure 3-1 graphically displays the natural relationship among political decisions, economic decisions, and decisions affecting science and technology. There is a natural overlap among and between these vital areas of national and international concern. The model illustrates the importance of interface between these factors within any nation—whether developed or developing. It is essential that this synthesis result in both national and international policies which require mature, careful consideration of all inputs, whether endogeneous or exogeneous in origin.

Technological Change and International Implications

Edwin Mansfield has maintained that "technological change is one of the most important determinants of the shape and evolution of the American economy."[6] Mansfield identifies aspects of change such as improved working conditions, new and old products, and the contributions in such areas as automated production facilities, and the medical sciences. However, he also points to the negative aspects of technological innovation—military mass destruction weapon systems, air and water pollution, and the effects of change upon

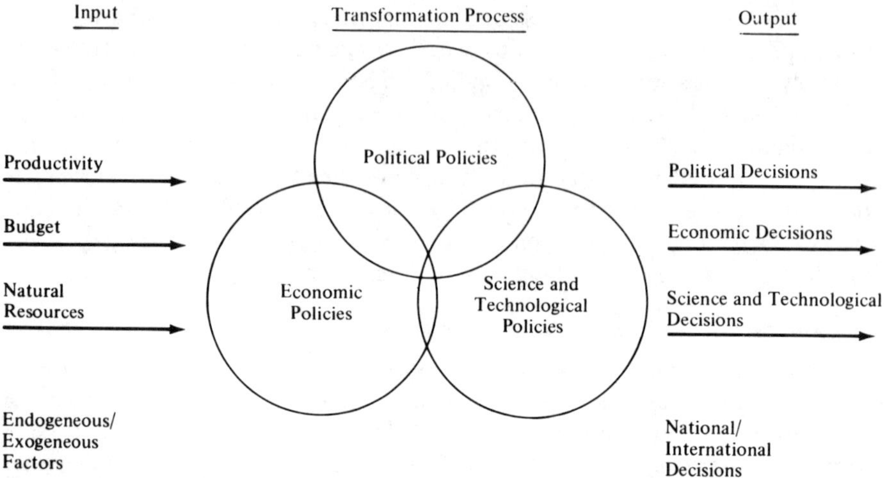

Figure 3-1. Economic/political/science and technology synthesis.

agriculture.[7] Thus, while change may have benefits, there are many unwelcomed by-products.

Given the state of technological change at any point in history, it was not surprising that individuals and organizations turned to international commerce. The lure of expected profit motivates the introduction of new products and services into both domestic and international markets. Figure 3-2 is based upon Ricardo's economic theories as previously discussed. The perimeter OABC is the output for two nations which *have not* engaged in international trade (from A–B is the output of the home country; B–C represents foreign country output). The curve O–A–D–C is the output of both nations engaging in international commerce. The shaded area represents the opportunities for expanded profits.[8] Science and technology are natural partners of economics, as through the application of new technology international commerce is facilitated and enhanced.

Before a company seeks to expand its commercial activities into another nation's economic sphere, several germane questions must be answered. These include the following:

1. What factors of production are present?
2. What are the costs of operations?
3. What will be the political reception?
4. What technology is appropriate for that culture?
5. In what form will renumeration be offered?
6. Where will the product be produced?
7. What barriers to trade are present?
8. What are the tax liabilities (both in the new market and at home)?

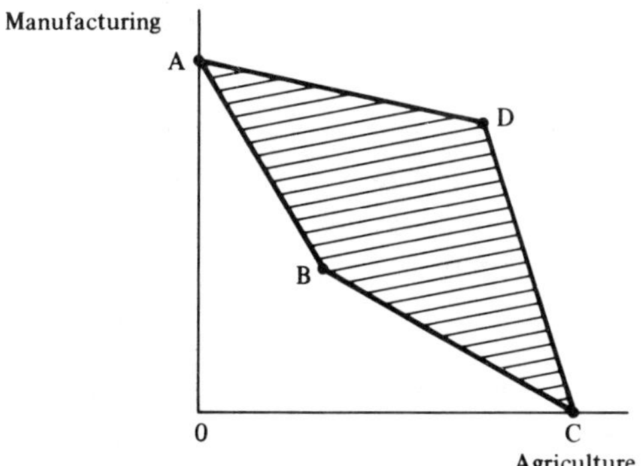

Figure 3-2. World transformation schedule.

9. From where will the work force be drawn?
10. Do we know enough about them to be trading in their marketplace?

Before a nation seeks or accepts technological change there are also questions to be considered. These are the following:

1. What is the purpose of the technology?
2. Does it allow for positive results?
3. What national benefits will accrue?
4. What will be the short-run and long-range benefits of the technology?
5. What is "fair" payment for the technology?
6. What are the likely effects of the technology?

The situation is complex, and often exacerbated by a lack of information. The advent of international commerce does bring with it change. Some change occurs immediately, while in other instances it develops over time.

Technology and Business

Economic Development

Technology may be viewed as a prime mover in the course of economic development. It has been credited with raising the relative productivity levels of the world. Because technology permits the more efficient use of productive resources, it has been described as "the vital growth component in each of the four traditional economic input factors: land, labor, capital and education."[9] It is the actual technological application of the factors of land, labor, capital, and education, rather than their mere presence, which determines a nation's potential for economic growth.[10] The transnational enterprise, through its propensity for technology transfer, can play a vital role in improving a nation's resource productivity and thus substantially contribute to its economic development.

The impact of technology extends far beyond its impact on productivity—it affects the base economic structure of a given economy. The introduction of new methods of production usually produces changes in the kinds and amounts of inputs used by each industry. Each new industrial technology requires different kinds and amounts of energy, raw materials, parts, and components as compared to the technologies replaced. As a consequence, technology often is a factor in the determination of world trade patterns.[11]

Transnational Enterprises and Technology

There is a natural and mutual interdependence between the transnational firm and technological innovation. Traditionally, transnational firms are found in industries that devote a relatively high proportion of their resources to research and development (R&D). The bulk of the world's R&D is in fact performed by these firms.

Transnational enterprises are a formidable element in the world economy. They profoundly impact upon, and often dominate, the evolution of scientific and technological achievements in the countries in which they operate as a result of direct investment activities, nonequity technological, managerial, and marketing contractual relations, and the acquisition of machinery, spare parts, plants, and services. In all of these areas, a nation's technological evolution must reckon directly with the crucial role played by the transnational corporation.[12]

Transnational firms have existed for centuries. Trading in and transferring technology has been an inherent part of their activities. Controlling some phase of technology frequently results in a competitive advantage. The technology asset usually is created as a result of investing in a highly risky process. Commercial application of that technology involves an even larger risk. The value of the technology is determined not by the cost of generating it, but by the utility it achieves in the marketplace. That value is difficult to determine, because it is a derivative of the commercial success achieved by the products made possible by the technology. Thus, technology's value is a function of the commercial opportunity it makes possible modified by the alternative technologies available to the prospective purchaser. Seldom is there an actual market for technology *per se*; value must be determined by negotiation. The whole system of goals, measurements, and rewards in business is predicated on determining exchange values, and then determining whether or not mutual benefit can be derived from the exchange. Cost does not determine value, but it certainly influences whether production will take place.

R&D Market Considerations

Research and development are prelude to technological development. R&D is an investment which is necessary for new products. New products are important for growth and survival in technologically dynamic industries. Investment costs for product development are generally high, and risk is compounded by market uncertainties. Unless there are strong profit motivations there will be reluctance, in view of cost and risk, to invest in technological development.

Much of the R&D effort does not come to a commercial application. Past studies have indicated that the greatest cause of failure in commercializing new technology is inadequate coupling with the market. Consequently, proposals by developing nations that R&D be divorced from business considerations and simply treated as an activity in its own right does not appeal to business organizations faced with the realities of making a profit.

Specific technologies should be tailored to each local situation. The actual modes of procurement will differ for each technology as will the manner in which they are applied and the types of control exercised over them by the receiving nation.

Business, Technology, and Developing Countries

No developing country can make adequate use of technology unless it has an appropriate scientific and technical infrastructure in the public, private, educational, and corporate sectors. A very critical problem facing developing nations is the selection of technology for industrial development. The selection of industrial sectors to be developed in a host nation depends on the relative factor endowments of the country, the markets to be served, the priority given to human needs, the pressures for military development, the ties to regional associations, the openness of the international markets, and other related considerations. To adopt technologies appropriate to the industrial sectors selected for development by the nations requires considerable knowledge about sources of alternative technologies. Most developing country governments recognize that even after they have identified the technologies required, they must negotiate for the transfer if the country is not in a position to develop the technology. Unfortunately, all too often, officials of developing nations are not adequately prepared for these negotiations. Longer-lasting and more beneficial contracts result when all parties to the agreement have access to relevant information and the skills to use it effectively. It is obvious that when one party to a negotiation has leverage resulting from skill, economic, and technological advantages a one-sided agreement will likely result. The other side will feel "gouged and taken," especially later when results point to the resulting benefits favoring the transnational enterprise.

Parenthetically, however, transnational firms have often failed in adequately communicating their position. To go into new markets, especially in developing countries, entails a high risk position. There must be adequate inducement and mutuality. Developing countries frequently are unrealistic in their perception of a technological transaction. They see only the advantages accruing to the transnational firm.

The companies should recognize that information is the basis for good decision making and that better contractual relations arise when both parties have access to adequate and relevant information and know how to use it. There can be significant joint benefits where there is technological development. The transnational firm gains markets, profits, and often access to natural resources. The developing country builds an economic base resulting from human and natural resource utilization, market development, and technological know-how.

Some Additional Motives for International Investment

Several inducements for international investment by transnational companies have been mentioned in previous sections of this chapter. There are many other motivations which may or may not be directly anchored to technological considerations. Following are some of the more common reasons:

Need to circumvent tariffs in order to protect export markets.

Realization of efficiency and effectiveness by producing in market vs exporting to it.

Possibility of realizing lower production costs by producing components abroad.

Fear that competitors may capture potential, lucrative market.

Fear that competitors may threaten domestic position by securing cheaper sources of supply.

Need to diversify product lines to avoid fluctuations in earnings.

Desire to assist licensees in need of expansion capital.

Desire to avoid home nation rules and regulations, e.g., U.S. antitrust laws.[13]

In a more general and usual sense, however, the basic reasons impelling corporations to invest abroad is the desire for profit and the fear that their present or prospective market position will be lost to foreign or domestic competitors. As with domestic investment, foreign investment must be weighed in terms of alternative investment opportunities. A usual objective is a return on capital within a reasonable time period and with a reasonable differential for the risks involved in foreign operations.

Technology Multipliers

For most economists, the "Keynesian multiplier" effect—created by multiple expenditures of incremental investments in a society—is a primary means of stimulating economic growth. In direct investment situations, there is a discernable lead–lag time frame for economic impact. In technological investment, there can be considerable variation from investment time to return time as well as the extent of the multiplier effect.

When a firm invests in some "hard" capital good (i.e., a new plant) or in a "soft" investment (such as marketable securities), there are definite dimensions as to the foreseeable growth. This is not the case when those same investment dollars are turned to technological innovation. In successful technological innovation, the money literally breeds more money through original product generation and through subsequent improvements and changes to the original product. Further, there are both direct and indirect benefits from the effect. Those direct effects accrue for the originator, expressed in terms of returns on investment and increases in productivity; indirect returns will be generated for customers who make cost savings and by forcing suppliers to provide more sophisticated components or equipment at higher quality or lower cost. Additionally, families of related products may evolve as a consequence of the original technological development.

No doubt, some will argue that the Keynesian multiplier effect and the technology multiplier effect are totally different. Not so![14]

Reflection will enable a rational person to recognize that the technology effect is one of focus and direction of investment. Because of the inherent risk, an investment in technology requires more deliberation and more propensity for risk than a mere investment in plant, property, and equipment. The crux, then, is that *returns on investment* from technological choices will likely be exponential, while those from "hard" investments will usually follow linear patterns.

Many of the transnational firms have exhibited the characteristics of "risk takers" because they have shown a continuing willingness to invest in technological change. These investments are apparently returning huge rates as they tend to be among the world's largest corporations—IBM, Philips, Hoechst, Unilever. The technology multiplier effect has enabled them to grow, expand, and penetrate more markets.

Technological Development

Use

The development of a technology capability base is by itself sterile. The technology must be utilized and technology utilization requires adaptation, promotion, and sales. If a technological breakthrough occurs which cannot use existing production or marketing resources, the firm is faced with a dilemma of ignoring or discarding the new technology, of selling the technology to organizations which can adopt and utilize it, of arranging for a technology transfer by licensing agreement, or, if the technology has high growth and profit potential, modifying the organization so that distribution and production can accommodate a new market.

A U.S. Government report has noted that "Japanese firms have become highly versatile and commercially effective in operating up and down the product cycle—evolving manufacturing know-how from the less sophisticated products and components to the more complex and profitable items."[15] The authors of the report further state that this extension of research to business accounted for the Japanese technological advances from small black-and-white TV sets to the more complex color apparatus in ten years.

Advancing Technology

For the past two decades there has been growing acceptance of technological innovation as one of the primary determinates of corporate competitive strength. This has led to pressures for increasingly heavier expenditures for R&D programs by individual firms and nations.

Professor Bela Gold has identified five kinds of primary benefits offered by investments in technological development:

1. Realizing competitive advantages through new and often better products and processes.
2. Obtaining know-how and knowledge which can be subsequently sold.
3. Maintaining competitive position.
4. Portraying images of innovative and progressive management.
5. Minimizing disadvantages of input factors.[16]

Research for Foreign Markets

There are several recognizable strategies of research and development that lead to products for overseas use. Traditionally, the great majority of U.S.-based transnational's R&D effort has been for domestic markets. New products have subsequently been moved into overseas markets virtually unchanged. Another related strategy is to adopt a product or manufacturing process to locally supplied (and often somewhat different) raw materials, or a more labor intensive manufacturing process, or a local market with unique consumption characteristics. This latter effort often necessitates additional development work, usually accomplished in the overseas laboratories.

A third approach is to recognize and employ spin-offs of technological products. Product changes, modifications, or developing related products would depend on the market. The market demand could vary significantly between developed and developing nations.

An additional alternative, albeit a seldom used one (a notable exception being Japan), is where R&D is undertaken primarily for new products for specific overseas markets. However, there are indications that this strategy will become increasingly important in the future.

There are natural advantages and disadvantages associated with each strategy. In the first instance, the risk associated with the R&D effort is greatly reduced, but there are some disadvantages in trying to make simple extensions of the product into a vastly different market. The second approach could be more costly but may be less risky and more palatable to many nations. This strategy entails local involvement in production, use of local raw materials, and market adoption. The third possibility is a natural strategy for profit-minded, risk-averting firms. It involves an extension of product technologies coupled with a degree of consumer "pull."

There are a number of influences that should enhance greater future reliance upon the fourth strategy—R&D specifically for certain nations. Among these influences are the following:

1. Greater insistence by foreign nations that transnationals use locally purchased raw materials and labor.
2. Rapid increases in indigenous technically qualified personnel.
3. Growing recognition of the power of the consumer.
4. Fear of competition from nations such as Japan which does "tailor" goods to specific markets.

Clearly, the successful transnational firm will be encountering and accommodating more discriminating consumers in the foreseeable future. This reality will force the more enlightened and enterprising firms into a careful, deliberate form of product development strategy.

When comparing the strategies, certain characteristics appear important:

Relative costs of development.

Relative likelihood of commercial success.

Relative magnitudes of resulting market rewards.

Relative disruptions in organizational arrangements capital allocations, materials requirements, labor relations, and marketing patterns.[17]

Product Influence

When choosing among the alternatives, it is necessary to recognize the influence of the technological and market characteristics of the particular industries under consideration. And, in addition, careful attention should be given to the resource constraints, managerial preferences, and guiding objectives of the individual firms making the decisions. For example, in consumer goods industries management might circumvent radical technological improvements toward seeking evolutionary improvements. In industries subject to rapid technological advances it may be advantageous to make heavy commitments to developing major innovations.

Technological improvement efforts may be expected to vary among firms within industries. In part, this may be due to substantial differences in the volume of resources available. Firms with limited resources are less likely to reach beyond modest, low-risk, short-term projects than those with more ample endowments. The experiential biases of management also effects the emphases of R&D programs, with technologically oriented executives being more likely than those with finance or marketing orientations to support ambitious technological ventures.

Management of Technological Risk

The existence of uncertainty with respect to future economic, ecological, social, political, and/or technological conditions results in business organizations being susceptable to varying degrees of risk. Transnational organizations as a consequence of the operational, technological, and geographical scope of their activities are generally more vulnerable to risk than are domestic companies. Management must evaluate risk exposures of the company and minimize or avoid risks where possible. At times, in high-technology industries, risk is an inherent characteristic which must be carefully managed.

Risk is defined as the likely variability of future returns from a given asset/project. The purchase of technology helps to reduce the amount of this risk.

Technological risk is said to exist for a corporation if

A new technology could emerge which would displace or seriously threaten the market currently enjoyed or anticipated for one or several of the company's products.'

Unanticipated impacts of a product upon one or more of the environments results in a significant adverse reaction by society to the product.

A noncompetitive technology induces changes in societal values which alter the market for an existing or planned product.[18]

Risk evaluation is concerned with the segmentation of several factors. As indicated, technology can have a significant impact on the firm's product lines. National or international economic conditions will affect product demand, markets, competition, and the requirement for financial resources.

Potential ecological changes, where negative consequences are possible, represent another serious risk resulting from technology. New products or processes can affect the environment. The ecological risks can be local and/or international; the risks can also involve morality or severe legal liabilities resulting from consumer or governmental actions. If technology creates social or legal problems the firm loses both in terms of public relations and out-of-pocket costs.

The social environment is the most difficult to evaluate. It certainly includes the demographic attributes such as population size and age distribution. Perhaps more importantly, however, is the fact that the social reflects the values subscribed to by that society. The cultural values of a society are important, but intellectual, religious, and ethical values must also be considered. All of these diverse elements together constitute the social environment.

Relating R&D to Corporate Goals

In the international commercial market system, the seller takes the initiative in researching and developing products. R&D generally is predicated on marketing evaluations which assess potential need and scope of demand. Prospective need has to be interrelated with the technical feasibility of developing the product, developmental costs, the various market vulnerabilities, and the prospect for profits. Additionally, the firm must have the resources to embark on technological development.

The firm committed to a R&D effort has distinct problems regarding resource allocation. Managers must balance all resources in terms of existing and planned needs. In making allocation decisions, they must consider whether the commitment covers a constant use or a special use and its susceptibility to obsolescence. Alternative uses of resources must also be considered. Objectives must be well-conceived and properly communicated; otherwise resources required by the project can be dissipated by indecision. Since product R&D may cover a considerable period, there are additional economic and technological risks which can occur due to unforseen intervening events. Objectives must be frequently reviewed and evaluated, especially where there is a long-term commitment to technological development.

A technique that may prove useful in ensuring that R&D objectives adhere to the overall transnational firm's corporate goals and objectives is the "objectives tree."

The *objectives tree* is a special form of relevance tree, showing a simple graphical representation of the relationship between a basic function and its subfunctions. It is a simple graphical and analytical method for quantitatively and qualitatively rating subobjectives, just as a functional diagram is a hierarchy of functions.[19]

For any given organizational entity, the highest-order objective appears at the top of the tree. This basic objective is a qualitative statement of the motivating force for the existence of the organization. It is usually a general, qualitative, brief statement under which the total organization operates.

The second level of the tree consists of strategies. These are the generalized approaches to be used in accomplishing the objective. These may form the objectives of subordinate organizational groupings.

The third and further levels of the objectives tree are programs and tasks within programs. These are explicit statements of the specific jobs to be accomplished, along with inherent timing considerations. A program may fit under several strategies, but it must fit under at least one.

Successive levels of the tree indicate alternative or parallel means of achieving the objective. These ways should include all those strategies or programs that can be used within the constraints on or by the organization.

Constraints on methods used to accomplish the objectives, or general principles reflecting how the organization is to operate, are called policies. Policies are not direct parts of trees, but rather provide ground rules for programs and strategies.

The objectives tree can serve to put each R&D program into perspective relative to other program elements, relative to the basic objectives of the corporation, or relative to other business or marketing approaches to the same objective. A well-conceived objectives tree can display, on a single chart, in a simple, straightforward fashion, the hierarchy of tasks, programs, strategies, and objectives into which any research and development element fits.

Some Economic Indicators of Technological Success

A definite problem for a commercial organization is an assessment of the relative success of their R&D effort. There is no single comprehensive measure which will unfailingly provide satisfactory answers. It will be up to the individual firm to identify and use those appropriate measures which suit their own organizational needs. However, there are some approaches which when combined should provide at least some indicators as to trends:

Percentage of earnings invested in R&D.

Number of scientists and research engineers as a percent of total white-collar work force.

R&D expenditures as a percent of gross profit.

R&D expenditures as a percent of net profit.

New product profits as a percentage of total profits.[20]

In any event, an attempt should be made by management to periodically audit the R&D effort to provide feedback as to actual versus expected results. Attempts to compile international comparative summaries of R&D activities and resources reveal a number of severe problems. Among these are the following:

1. National definitions differ.
2. Different survey methods are used.
3. Data in many nations are not collected regularly.
4. As data collection systems mature, comparability problems with earlier periods arise due to changes, corrections, and modified organizations. (Time series are often limited.)
5. Financial measures must be used with caution because of exchange rate problems, differences in economic systems, and standards of living.
6. Unreliable data.
7. Omission of important R&D performers.
8. Inaccurate grossing-up, extrapolation, estimation, etc.
9. Price inflation varies between nations.

Some Contemporary Economic Issues

Technology and Economics

Technology has economic repercussions. In many respects technology is an intangible. The cost of technological development at times may be determinable and at other times difficult to ascertain. The benefits of technology are usually both direct and indirect and almost invariably difficult to accurately measure. Many times evaluation of technological development is subjective. The social and economic gains may be readily apparent and the cost relatively inconsequential. There have also been instances where actual versus planned technical accomplishment has been disappointing and the obvious costs have appeared excessive.

The problem essentially is to define input–output relationships; unfortunately, this is no simple matter. If input–output relationships are difficult to establish for a single R&D project or program, and much more so for groups or organizations, an accurate national or international picture is nigh-on unattainable. It can, based on economic research, be assumed that technology is a factor in economic growth. The difficulty, as indicated, is to determine whether technological accomplishment is commensurate with its cost. Any value determination of technological contribution to economic activity is, at best, largely based on conjecture since inputs are often inaccurate, and generally acceptable methods for measuring technological output have not been developed.

There are several contemporary economic issues related to technology. Among the more important are worldwide egalitarianism, utilization of natural resources, and declining productivity. The aforementioned are considered relevant to the theme of this book and will be discussed.

Worldwide Egalitarianism

Most of the valuable, useful, and transferable technology in the world today belongs to the industrialized or developed nations—whether free market (United States, West Germany, Japan, etc.) or controlled economy countries (Soviet Union, Eastern Europe, China, and Cuba). The holders of the technology are being challenged by a new world force—the "Group of 77" or the "Third World."

Parenthetically, the name "Group of 77" stems from meetings held in Peru in the late 1960s by a bloc of 77 developing nations, all members of the United Nations. Even though they now number in excess of 120, they still retain the euphemism, Group of 77. At the moment, they constitute the largest single bloc of votes in the United Nations General Assembly.

The members of the Group of 77 expouse a radical rhetoric of a new international economic order. They are demanding and militant. They are allowing political discipline within the bloc to supersede their natural national requirements. The developing countries believe that they should receive a larger share of the world's wealth at the expense of the developed nations.

Their claim is that the developed nations have selfishly consumed more than their "fair share" of these resources. Further, the accusation is that many of the resources were garnered originally from the developing nations. The complaint has been on two levels: first, that all too often the developed nations were richly endowed with natural resources which were withheld from the poorer countries; or, second, that when resources were discovered in the developing countries they were exploited by the richer nations. Whether true or not there are indications that the Third World is being heard.

Under the auspices of the United Nations, the issue of the worldwide distribution of technological capabilities and natural resources, particularly into developing countries is regularly addressed. Several U.N. conferences on "Science and Technology for Development" have been conducted. Additionally, the United States has launched a new foundation for International Technological Cooperation with a sizable endowment of $50 million.[21] The concern about the dwindling natural resources is not new. In 1970 Erwin L. Peterson said, "Islands of plenty cannot permanently endure in a sea of want."[22] In 1969 U. Thant, the then Secretary General of the United Nations, warned members that "they had perhaps ten years left in which to subordinate their ancient quarrels and launch a global partnership to curb the arms race, to improve the human environment, to diffuse the population explosion and to supply the required momentum to development efforts." If such a global partnership was not formed, he feared that these problems would have reached such proportion that they would be beyond solution.[23]

The Third World bloc has adopted the tenets of Fabian socialism. The first of these beliefs is that of government ownership of most of the major means of production. The second is the need for redistribution of existing wealth rather than creation of new and additional wealth. The third is relief of and deserved reparation to the poor for their prior suffering and exploitation. The fourth belief is that these goals should be accomplished through parliamentary processes and not revolutionary violence. Thus, they are using their voting power in the United Nations to achieve their aims.

The key mechanism rejected by the Group of 77 is the allocation of resources, profits, and economic benefits through the operation of market forces. They perceive that the transnational corporations are the key market force mechanism in the world today.

The Third World nations are increasingly resisting development of their own natural resources by the transnational enterprises. They have taken the stand that all current technology, the resources of the deep sea beds, and the food products of the developed world should be shared free and as of the right of all mankind.

The situation in the industrialized nations is quite different. Almost all of the valuable, useful, transferable technology in the world today is owned by private companies. Those firms are managed by persons charged with obtaining profitable results from investments, to include the transfer of technology. If transferring technology to developing nations provides a negative return, managers are unwilling to enter that environment.

The developing nations take the attitude that this technology has already been paid for and therefore should be made available for all mankind.

The transnationals maintain that successful technology is a commodity just like oil, coffee, wheat, and tin. As a commodity it has a value which can be measured in terms of price. There is, therefore, a conflict between the methods of the transnational enterprises in generating technology and plowing back the profit of sales into more research to develop the technology of tomorrow and the ideals of the developing nations that this technology can be made free for all.

Utilization of Natural Resources

Lester R. Brown, the President of the World Watch Institute has observed that, "Unprecedented scarcities and price hikes have given rise to 'resource diplomacy'; they have profoundly altered the global political structure and accorded new power to raw-materials producers." He went on to say that the rise in oil prices in the late 1970s had caused a reactive shift in the global power structure that had reverberations not only worldwide, but extending into the production of agricultural goods as well. His theme is that "ecological stresses can quickly become economic stress," and therefore world leaders must have cognizance of both the diminishing returns of economics as well as the negative returns of overextending and exploiting nature.[24]

For years economists have maintained that the realities of diminishing returns could be forestalled through the application of technology.[25] Indeed, this law of economics and nature appears to have been proven by modern man—witness the eco/techno-growth patterns of the United States, West Germany, and Japan. If the world's annual economic growth pattern of 4%, which started in the 1950s, were to continue for a century, the results would be a fiftyfold expansion of the world's economies.[26]

In 1973 the Club of Rome published its "Project on the Predicament of Mankind" under the title *The Limits To Growth*.[27] Based upon earlier dynamic modeling work at the Massachusetts Institute of Technology a group of researchers led by Dennis Meadows and J. Forrester constructed a world model which was used to project a wide range of factors (e.g., food per capita, population, pollution, natural resources) into the next century under a variety of conditions. The report in short order aroused controversy and opposition from groups on both sides of the environmental–economic fence. Whatever the validity of these arguments, there seems no escaping the general conclusion that based upon present policies and with existing technologies there will be severe shortages of many raw materials before the end of the century.

The Club of Rome results led to the conclusions (among others) that the "Spaceship Earth" should take immediate action to seek concurrently a posture of "Zero Population Growth" and "Zero Economic Growth."

The underlying thesis was that if the world's population could be held constant then the dwindling resources would stretch and last for a longer period. The object is to hold the aggregate growth of the world's population at a constant level. Obviously, then, help from the international sector would be required in those nations that have an annual population explosion—India and China. The industrialized nations would be required to curb their relentless quest for ever-increasing returns on investment and would have to be satisfied with a constant return.

There are conceptual flaws in these arguments of the Club of Rome and probably factual inaccuracies. They have chosen to ignore the effects of increasing scarcity upon prices (prices would tend to climb dramatically). Higher prices would also encourage substitution of similar goods and thus help relieve the pressures of shortages, plus stretch usage. They also failed to take into account the possibilities of new technological advances that would further stretch resource availability.

At the invitation of the International Institute for Environment and Development (IIED), 25 distinguished scientists, technologists, business executives, development economists, bankers, and others met in Ocho Rios, Jamaica in 1979. They discussed the common interest of rich and poor countries in mobilizing science and technology for development. The members agreed that present world economic and technical systems were neither meeting the basic needs nor adequately serving the interests of either rich or poor nations. They also concluded that appropriate technological choices and systems could result only from well-conceived and socially relevant development objectives at the national and international levels. They focused on (1) issues related to mobilizing technology for national needs, (2) the question of technology flows and multinational enterprises in the context of new international order, and (3) the use of technology for management of global problems.[28]

Thus, it becomes apparent that the intellects of the planet are looking to technological innovation to fill the gap between dwindling resources and human needs.

The trend toward regional economic communities may well provide the framework within which smaller nations may receive the benefits of broad scientific and technological effort that individually they could not afford. For some areas of the world such as the Middle East, Southeast Asia, Africa, and Latin America, it is the only feasible approach to viable scientific contribution. There are obvious political obstacles to overcome, but through desire and patience this is an attainable goal. It may well be the obligation of developed nations to provide direct assistance in this movement. If the developed nations are not capable of direct assistance, then they should at the very least maintain a "hands-off" attitude so as not to be a deterrent.

Declining Productivity

Concern about the productivity is universal among the highly developed nations of the world. Productivity in the United States (measured as the value of goods and services divided by the hours of work required to produce them) increased approximately 2% per year on the average during the last decade. This within itself is meaningless until compared against the noteworthy growth rate of 3.2% per year from 1946 to 1966.[29] While we can develop a productivity valuation for virtually any output, we are specifically addressing the productivity of labor. This is called "total factor" productivity. Cognizance of the importance of productivity has worldwide application as labor is one of the key factors in producing goods. The data at Figure 3-3 are worth attention as it indicates relative patterns in the rates of productivity, taking into effect both gains and decreases in annual output. Notice the relative ranking of the various regions of the world.

C. Jackson Grayson Jr., chairman of the American Productivity Center has identified several key aspects as relates to productivity:

1. Few people understand the nature of productivity.
2. Information about productivity is not readily available.
3. Organizations need to audit their level of productivity.
4. Organizations need to develop productivity programs.
5. Measure is weak at all levels.
6. Both labor and management gain from productivity improvement.
7. General knowledge of how to improve productivity is lacking.[30]

Figure 3-4 illustrates the interrelationship of these key areas. These problems are not unique to a particular nation but are universal.

The importance of productivity is that it is normally accepted as the source of adequate standards of living.[31] The economic "shame" of decreasing productivity is that a nation is "wasting" the energies of its most important

Figure 3-3. Productivity growth 1970–1979. (*Source*: U.S. Department of Labor, Bureau of Labor Statistics.)

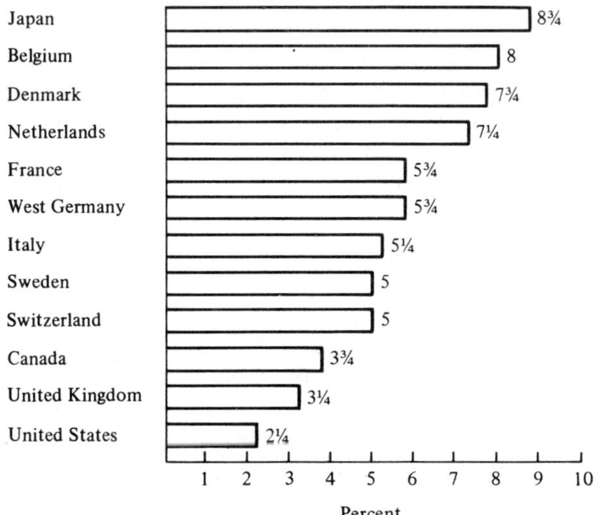

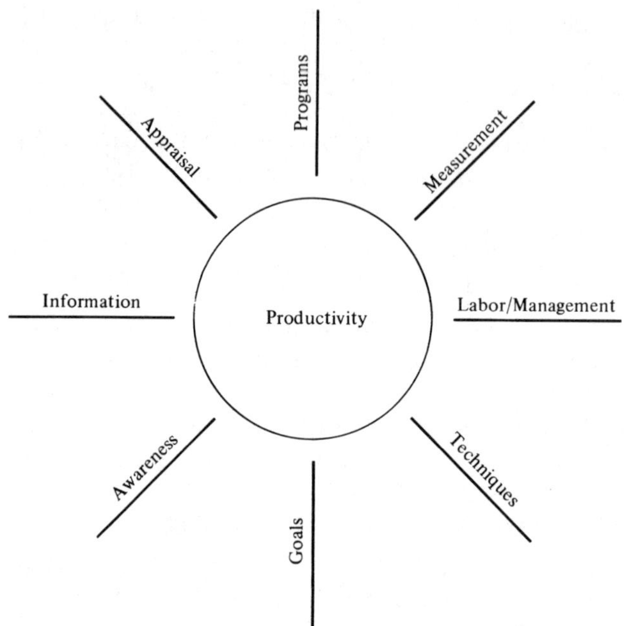

Figure 3-4. Factors affecting productivity.

asset—human resources. In many nations, the human potential is either ignored, underutilized, or not understood. The ultimate economic position of any society reflects its human quality of population which is critical.[32]

Presently there are large numbers of unemployed workers—idle resources—throughout the world. The U.S. Congressional Clearinghouse of the Future has characterized the underdeveloped nations as having "large groups of unemployed, underemployed and unskilled workers, little in terms of capital assets, and a limited technological infrastructure."[33]

Few would dispute the general concern with worldwide unemployment. There is no doubt that this is a socioeconomic ill for which a solution will be long in coming. Equally as troublesome, however, and more germane is the problem identified above—underemployed and unskilled workers.

These are the direct factors that affect the relative annual productivity rate. It is with these factors that managers must deal in order to continue their quest for efficiency and profit. Productivity is particularly troublesome to transnational corporations. Within their countries of origin labor is normally an expensive commodity and the development of labor-saving technologies is the rational course followed by these large companies. While in the developing nation labor is more abundant but less skilled, the transnational corporation is not automatically receptive to the use of less capital-intensive technologies.

It is difficult and expensive to radically change or alter manufacturing processes and techniques. The easier path is to use the existing processes and simply accept less output as the price (lower productivity).

There can be little doubt but what transnational corporations have contributed to the modernization and growth of markets within the developing nations. Increasing, however, criticism is leveled at these companies for imposing technologies which are at odds with the economic and developmental environment of the developing country.[34]

Seemingly the technologies introduced by the transnational corporations are on the whole capital-intensive and therefore act only incidently to expand employment or indigenous innovation. For the most part, this involvement serves to frustrate the developing country. The workers are seldom encouraged to achieve the higher skill levels necessary for technological independence and thus unrest and lowered output results. This emotional condition has led to serious consideration of the aspects of "appropriate technology" which will be discussed in detail in Chapter Eight.

Cognizance of appropriate technology does not within itself serve to relieve the problems of declining productivity. Since declines in productivity are likely caused by many factors, the healing process should be multifaceted. Such a process should include the functions of

Productivity assessment.

Productivity rationalization.

Productivity feedback.

These three programs assist in up-grading productivity. There is a difference between up-grading productivity and simply seeking an "increase in productivity." It is believed that an up-grade will produce the long-lasting results which have more meaning in the international arena.

The productivity assessment (Phase I) essentially is a managerial audit of the organization. The assessment is intended to discover such factors as

Operational status.

Operational potential.

Personnel status and morale.

Personnel potential.

R&D capabilities.

Product potential.

These actions may be grouped into three primary categories: process, human, and product factors. Figure 3-5 isolates each category with its separate universe of subordinate factors, any of which can have an impact upon productivity.

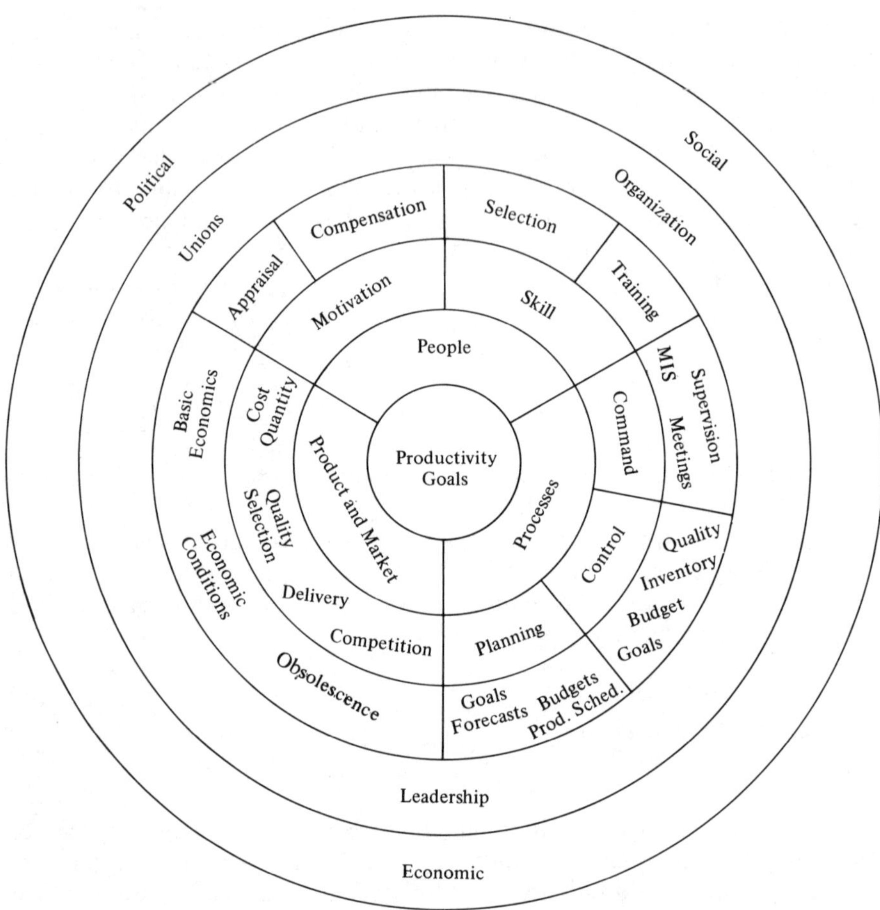

Figure 3-5. Productivity factors.

The output of the productivity assessment will be an immense amount of data which reflects the relative productivity of the various parts of the organization. Productivity rationalization (Phase II) depends upon managers (regardless of organizational level or national identity) focusing upon the interrelationship of the various critical factors (Figure 3-5), and developing specific programs to correct deficiencies. The data from Phase I are carefully organized and subjected to rigorous analysis. This analysis will result in the establishment of a list of productivity up-grade projects and their relative priority, cost, and completion deadline. Specific responsibility for each project is assigned to a manager and the projects become part of the standard management planning and control system.[35]

The final phase (Phase III) of the process of up-grading productivity is that of productivity feedback. Paralleling and following the first two phases there must be an attempt to establish productivity goals and objectives so that performance can be evaluated and assessed. Feedback should be consistent so that there is an up-to-date awareness of the relative impact upon the up-grading effort of such factors as capital investment, management practices and improvements, and labor performance.

The model illustrated at Figure 3-6 is a representation of the three phases of the productivity up-grade program. The model is equally applicable to international and national productivity problem areas.

If the long-term benefits offered by productivity up-grading techniques are to be realized, productivity improvement must become one of the performance areas for which managers at all levels are held responsible. For each manager there should be a clearly specified productivity improvement goal. The data gathered during the productivity assessment will provide a sound base for establishing these goals. Failure to integrate productivity as a routine part of each manager's job will result in a steady erosion of the productivity gains and the organization will backslide into former bad habits.

Technology's role in this program should not be overlooked. During Phases II and III managers should seek new technology and thus ensure the reality of diminishing returns is therefore postponed.

Conclusions

Technological change has certainly contributed to the economic growth of the entire world. The major change agent has been the transnational corporation. While there are many factions which would seek the demise or curtailment of the transnational enterprise, rational thinking indicates that the transnational firm is a permanent fixture and perhaps also a necessary feature.

The relationship between economics, technology, research, and development is natural. They share and contribute to the betterment of the quality of life of all mankind.

Figure 3-6. A model for up-grading productivity.

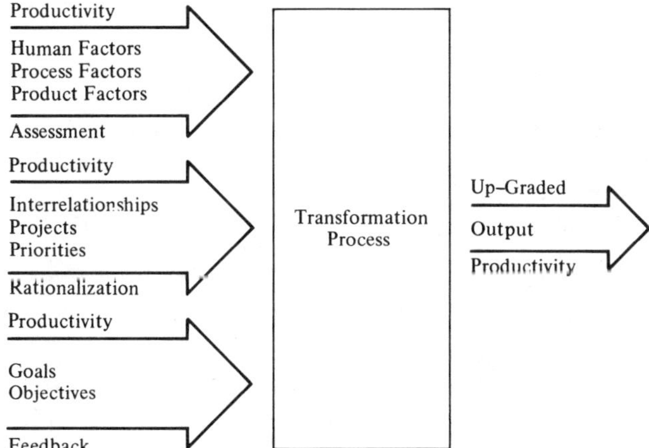

Endnotes Chapter Three

1. Albert H. Teich, ed., *Technology and Man's Future*, New York: St. Martins Press, 1972, p. XII.
2. Edwin Mansfield, *The Economics of Technological Changes*, New York: W.W. Norton & Co., Inc., 1968, p. 3.
3. *Websters' New School and Office Dictionary*, Greenwich, CT: A Fawcett Crest Book, 1974, p. 236.
4. *Ibid.*, pp. 641–642.
5. *Ibid.*, p. 745.
6. Edwin Mansfield, *Technological Change*, New York: W.W. Norton & Co., 1971. p. 1.
7. *Ibid.*, pp. 1–2.
8. For a more complete definition and discussion of Ricardian philosophy see R.E. Caves and R.W. Jones, *World Trade and Payments*, Boston: Little, Brown & Co., 1973, pp. 134–136.
9. J.B. Quinn, "Scientific and Technical Strategy at the National and Major Enterprise Level," *The Role of Science and Technology in Economic Development*, Paris: UNESCO, 1970, Chapter 4.
10. J.B. Quinn, "Technology Transfer by Multinational Companies," *Harvard Business Review*, Vol. 47, November–December, 1969, pp. 147–161.
11. T.N. Gladwin, "Technology and Material Culture," *The Cultural Environments of International Business*, Cincinnati: South-Western Publishing Co., 1978, p. 194.
12. C.V. Vaitsos, "Government Policies for Bargaining with Transnational Enterprises in the Acquisition of Technology," *Mobilizing Technology for World Development*, ed. J. Ramesh, New York: Praeger Publishers, 1979, p. 98.
13. "Policy Aspects of Foreign Investment by U.S. Multinational Corporations," *The Multinational Corporation*, U.S. Department of Commerce, March 1972, Vol. I, pp. 14–15.
14. J.B. Quinn spoke of the technological multiplier in "Technology Transfer by Multinational Companies," *Harvard Business Review*, Vol. 47, November–December 1969, pp. 147–161. His thrust made the effect mutually exclusive of the Keynesian effect. This is not the case. The focus of the investment is the key. We stress this aspect.
15. "Sources of Competitiveness in the Japanese Color Television and Video Recorder Industry," Prepared for the U.S. Department of Labor by Developing World Industry and Technology, Inc., October 16, 1978, pp. 18–19.
16. Bela Gold, "Alternative Strategies for Advancing a Company's Technology," *Research Management*, Vol. XVIII, No. 4, July 1975, p. 24.
17. *Ibid.*, p. 25.
18. F.T. Ayers, "The Management of Technological Risk," *Research Management*, Vol. XX, No. 6, November 1977, pp. 24–25.
19. R.E. Gee, "A Method for Relating Research to Corporate Goals," *Research Management*, Vol. XVIII, No. 6, November 1975, pp. 11–16.
20. "What Do We Really Know About Managing R&D?" *Research Management*, Vol. XXI, No. 6, November 1978, pp. 6–11.
21. Charles Horner, "Redistributing Technology," *Commentary*, January 1979, pp. 52–54.
22. Ervin L. Peterson, "The Use of Technology in National Development," *Proceedings of Conference on International Exchange of Technology*, Research Triangle Institute, Raleigh, North Carolina, October 29–30, 1970, p. 37.
23. Quoted in *The Limits to Growth*, a report for the Club of Rome on the predicament of mankind, Potomic Associates, April 1973, p. 17.
24. Lester R. Brown, "Global Economic Ills: The Worst May Be Yet to Come," *The Futurist*, June 1978, p. 157.

25. The Law of Diminishing Returns states that "an increase in some inputs relative to other fixed inputs will, in a given state of technology, cause total output to increase; but after a point the extra output from new inputs of the same amount will tend to decrease. See Paul A. Samuelson, *Economics*, 10th ed., New York: McGraw-Hill Book Co., 1976, Chapter 2.
26. Brown, *op. cit.*, pp. 157–158.
27. *Limits to Growth*, *op. cit.*
28. *Mobilizing Technology for World Development*, Report of Jamaica Symposium, New York: Praeger, 1979, pp. 26–27.
29. Donald Christiansen, "Productivity: Its Ups and Downs" *IEEE Spectrum*, October 1978, p. 31.
30. C. Jackson Grayson Jr., "Productivity: A Call for Action," *National Journal*, March 1978, pp. 492–493.
31. Edwin Mansfield, "Contribution of R&D to Economic Growth in the United States," *Science*, February 4, 1972, p. 477.
32. Daniel D. Roman, *Science, Technology and Innovation: A Systems Approach*, Columbus, OH: Grid Publishing Co., 1980, p. 44.
33. "Appropriate Technology: A Review," Congressional Clearinghouse on the Future, March 1977, p. 4.
34. *Ibid.*, pp. 6–7.
35. Much of the material as relates to the productivity up-grade program was adopted from Joseph F. Puett, Jr., and Wilford G. Miles, Jr., "Productivity Upgrade Program," *1980 Productivity Conference Proceedings*, St. John Fisher University, Rochester, NY, April 1980.

SECTION II:

Technology, Policy, and Trade

CHAPTER FOUR

International Science and Technology Policy

Establishing a Conceptual Framework

Defining Science Policy

Science is the forerunner of innovation and technology. The extent to which a nation is willing to commit its resources to the development of a national scientific capability is contingent on many factors, which will be discussed in subsequent sections of this chapter. National science policies have evolved as viable concepts since World War II, when there was recognition that science is an extremely important national resource.

A policy is a guide; it reflects the philosophy of an operational unit, be it an individual, a transnational corporation, or a political entity. As relevant to the theme of this book, science policy for the transnational corporation would be commitment to the range of effort and degree of support for organizational scientific and technological development and promotion. Such an activity would be influenced by the external operational environment as well as internal policy. The operational environment, national and international, could be conducive or detrimental to technological development.

National science policy is manifested by stated goals or objectives and commitment of resources. Implementation in the public sector is accomplished by legislation, resource allocation, and supportative programs and projects. National science and technology policy can be explicit and formal. A nation's science policy can also be inferred by the type of programs it supports, its attitude toward the scientific community, and the degree of governmental control exerted. To elaborate, control and involvement would reflect policy and political ideology. The roles of government and private enterprise in technological development would vary considerably between a market and a planned economy.

"Science policy" is an important concept. There is considerable latitude in interpreting science policy, so perhaps by way of amplification, further explanation is in order. The tasks of "formulating science policy," and "using science for policy," are closely intertwined. Yet, the two must be distinguished. Walsh has defined the two terms as they are commonly used:

> "Policy for science" at the federal level means decisions which affect the funding of, and organization for, research and development and the training of scientific and technical manpower in universities, government agencies, and industry. "Science for policy" denotes the scientific and technical components of government policies which also involve economic, social, and political considerations."[1]

Both meanings appear throughout the chapter.

Science Policy Objectives

Nelson indicates that in formulating science policy three distinguishable areas must be accommodated. First, science policy must be directed to the support of science, if a healthy scientific infrastructure is to exist. Second, high-level governmental decision making often must incorporate objective inputs covering scientific and technical knowledge. Third, science policy can be instrumental in channeling research and development to the achievement of national objectives.[2]

Actually, the establishment of science policy depends on the special circumstances of each country. Science policy decisions are reached after analysis of developmental strategy, economic structure, available human resources, and consideration of the national cultural organization.

An example of a science policy objective would entail the support of a scientific community. Such support would consider human resource requirements. In addition, programs to train and utilize scientists and technologists would have to be formulated.

Other objectives could be supported through resource allocations, consistent with the end product(s) the government hopes to achieve. The commitment of resources should attempt to maximize the efficient achievement of objectives. Highly trained human resources, invariably a scarce commodity, should be allocated in accordance with the most urgent national priorities. The education system should be designed for compatibility with national needs and should contribute to the development of national scientific and technological goals. In a controlled economy, this is more easily achieved than in a democracy.

Further objectives of science policy could be to encourage interface between the various societal segments. Relations should be facilitated between educational institutions, the labor market, and the production system. Another strong objective of science policy would be integrational in coordinating the components of the production system, and providing for a flow of knowledge from basic through applied science and, ultimately, to technological innovation.

Science policy should also encourage scientific and technological growth. Scientific and technological growth would depend on the quantity and quality of the scientific establishment. The quantity and quality of the scientific establishment would be encouraged or discouraged by how effective human resources are utilized. Utilization probably would be contingent on the level of scientific activity. The level would reflect both magnitude of effort and the degree of technological sophistication.

National science policy objectives should include determination of the government's role in direct or indirect support of science and technology. A government's role in a market economy would be manifested in such areas as direct financing, indirect financial supports or loan guarantees, subsidization, or selective tax policies. In addition, the government could provide strong motivational support by providing a marketplace for the products of science and technology. Government science policy could also be a deterrent in some technological areas by the withholding of critical resources. In planned economies, determination of technological direction would be absolute. Support and control would be direct and politically motivated.

Science policy objectives, as indicated, are numerous. Regardless of the sphere of activity, in order to accomplish science policy objectives successfully, provision must be made for the integration of scientific and technological research plans among the government, the productive system, the cultural environment, and the scientific community.[3] See Figure 4-1.

Some Factors and Issues Affecting Science Policy

There has been a perceptible change since the 1970s in international attitudes regarding science, technology, and innovation. Where science was once widely acclaimed as the ultimate salvation of humanity, attitudes have now surfaced where the benefits from science, technology, and innovation are viewed within

Figure 4-1. Government, productive systems, social/cultural factors, scientific community interactions.

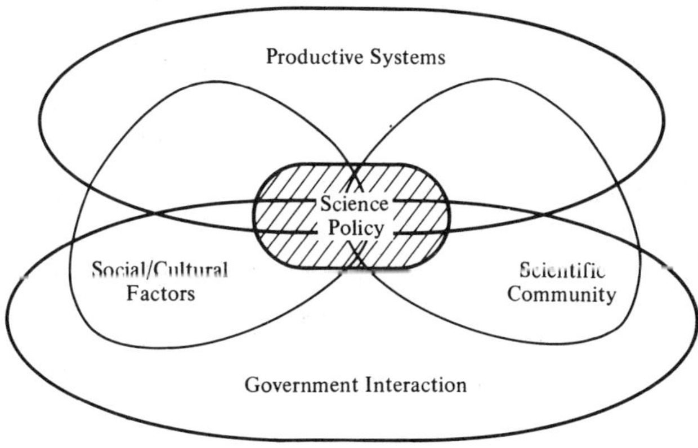

a wide spectrum ranging from wild optimism to mild skepticism to overt antagonism.

Criticism of science has developed based on interactions between science and society. Areas which were once considered politically neutral, such as atomic energy plants, massive highway networks, or weapon systems, are now subject to considerable attacks by vested interest groups. With increasing international sensitivity to the products of science, technology, and innovation, there appears to be a shift in emphasis, especially in the developed nations, to socially directed technology.[4] This is not as straightforward as it appears since resources are still necessary for socially directed technology. Nagging questions persist as to how resources should be allocated and what segments of society will benefit, or adversely be affected, from such allocations. It is an impossibility to serve all elements of society equally, much less please all societal factions involved. Invariably, resource allocation decisions are applauded by some and damned by others. While some social problems may be solved or alleviated, the probability exists, based on past experiences, that new problems will often surface as a consequence of the technological actions.[5]

One certainty emerges from any examination of science policy and that is the criticality of political support. Political support involves implementation and funding decisions. Political support invariably is influenced by public attitudes. The range of factors and issues which impinge on public attitudes is impressively huge. Without elaboration, science policy determinations can evolve from such considerations as the amount of resources to allocate to defense versus nondefense technology; determination of national needs, including social needs, with attendant priorities; methods and distributions of resource allocations; national, regional, or highly localized technological activities; national or international technological directions; determination of areas of technological concentrations, including decisions based on a broad approach or narrow intense technological specialization; and the degree of science policy decisional latitude resulting from the established political system, such as a market economy or a planned economy. Another very important factor in science policy is sensitivity to the constant shift in public attitudes, and possible impacts on technological priorities to technological programs underway.

Decisional factors, as indicated, are very complex. Complexity intensifies where technological frontiers are explored and resource requirements accelerate. In planned economies, the decision process is centralized. Decisional processes are more difficult in political societies where private enterprise exists. How much technological development should remain under the auspices of the government? What support should the government provide private interests? Often, technological development is so extensive that it cannot be localized, and private enterprise cannot afford to independently undertake development. In such cases, the technology may ultimately emerge as an international product. Again, where the technology is socially directed in a market economy, how much direct involvement and control should the government have? In the United States, the government generally has been a contractor and underwriter for social technological development. This is not a simple problem since there are constant pressures and conflicts relative to the role of government and private enterprise in socially directed technological development.

Foundations for Science, Technology, and Innovative Policy

Technological Capability

Many factors can be influential in affecting national science policy. One very pertinent consideration is a realistic evaluation of a nation's technological capability. Existing or desired capability should be viewed in terms of current, foreseeable, and long-term needs. A technological inventory could indicate capability ranges from high competence to total dependence. The cost, complexity, and availability of resources of many technologies preclude the probability that any one nation will be totally self-sufficient in all technologies needed for national well-being. The implication is that there is increasing international technological interdependence. Since a considerable part of the world's productive effort is attributable to the transnational firm, it follows that such organizations provide a valuable service in supplementing national technological capabilities. Transnationals often are the vehicles to facilitate the import or export of needed technology.

Elaborating on the preceding paragraph, it is improbable that any nation will be totally self-sufficient, or totally dependent, in all technologies. The extent of dependence, or independence, varies according to the factors indicated in the previous section. Also, national technological priorities can shift because of internal needs or external threats.

It is important to recognize nationally the developmental areas that are amenable for technological excellence. In such areas, a nation could be technologically independent and, perhaps, even export the products of that technology in exchange for technologies where there is some degree of dependence. Where there is international technological leadership, a country or company can derive extraordinary economic benefits. In the past, the United States has enjoyed technological leadership in commercial aviation and computers. Japan has become a technological leader in robotized machine tools, some phases of electronics, and in 1980 emerged as the world's largest producer of automobiles. The aforementioned are only a few examples of technological leadership in the United States and Japan. These successes have been accomplished by private enterprise in concert with a supportive government. Japan, with very limited natural resources, has to be acutely conscious of which technologies to promote in order to minimize, or neutralize, international dependence on technologies that are not economically or technically feasible for internal development. Exporting the products of technologies, where there is technological leadership in the cases cited, is achieved through firms operating in international markets. The revenues resulting from international transactions enable the purchase of other needed technologies and are important in the international balance of payments.

A nation may not have total self-sufficiency or exclusive leadership in a technology. The ultimate technological product could be a composite of international inputs. A nation, in such instances, would probably have a working capability in the technology, but there would be some international dependence, as evidenced by information exchange and product improvement. The end technological product would, as indicated, be a composite developed from international sources. The automobile is a good example of a technological development which incorporates components that have been spawned in many nations.

A nation may need a technology, but be dependent on external sources. External dependence can result because the natural resources for technological development do not exist within the country. Dependence can also be the consequence of weighing alternatives where resources do exist, but national priorities indicate a diversion of such resources to more intense needs. In addition, technological development may not be feasible, even if need and resources exist, because other nations have established a formidable technological lead; attempts to catch-up would not be cost effective. In these instances, it may be more advisable for a nation to develop a managerial and use capability and import the technology. Importing the technology could be facilitated where there are transnational firms already operating within the country or where inducements can be offered to transnationals to establish an operational base.

Perhaps the least desirable position would be where there is a need, no technological capability exists, and managerial know-how and use abilities are also inadequate. In these situations, the recipient nation has completed an almost total dependence on outside sources. This is frequently the case where developing nations import a technology. If there is little or no need for such a technology, a nation would not be compromised. There are also possibilities, more specifically in developing nations, where natural resources exist, but the country of origin does not have the technological capability to harvest or convert these resources into technologically useful products. The lack of ability often can be attributable to human resource and capital limitations. Outside sources, often transnational firms, are solicited to help develop indigenous resources. Asian rubber, Central American banana plantations, and Arab oil are just a few examples.

To emphasize what was started earlier, perhaps the most important consideration in developing a policy directed toward establishing technical capability would be the ultimate need and existing or potential capability of the initiating nation. Other factors which might be considered are market relevance, the availability of venture capital, and the existence of unique political, social, religious, or cultural problems.

Some Indices of Technological Capability

National technological planning and subsequent policy formulation could be more realistic if founded on actual and potential resources. Deciding to establish a technological capability does not, per se, guarantee accomplishment. Some standard or index of technological capability is necessary to determine if aspirations are attainable. Establishing universal standards to determine national technological capability is virtually impossible to quantify. However, there are some factors that could be used to serve as general guidelines to evaluate technical capabilities. The importance of these factors would vary, depending on the type and scope of the technological undertaking:

1. The existing inventory of trained scientists and engineers—
   a. fields of technical specialization
   b. caliber and currency of education
   c. applicability of human resource skills to present and future needs
   d. people in pursuit of formal technical education
   e. retraining, e.g., updating provisions or systems for existing professionals
   f. educational relevance to projected needs
2. Skilled technicians—
   a. availability—numbers and types
   b. formal and informal training facilities
   c. standards and quality
3. The current technological structure—
   a. types of industries
   b. level of technological sophistication
   c. local and transnational firms' actual and potential contribution to national technological goals
   d. satellite industries
4. Capital investment—
   a. modern or obsolete plant and equipment
   b. expansion or contraction of production units
   c. availability of capital
   d. prospects for capital expansion
5. The technological environment—
   a. extent of government support
   b. educational attainment of population
   c. technologists as a percent of work force
   d. utilization and productivity of professionals
   e. R&D expenditures—growth or decline—as a percent of gross national product
   f. areas of technological leadership
   g. current and anticipated scientific accomplishments
   h. internationally recognized scientific leaders
   i. political stability

The above list certainly is not inclusive. It is only a partial approach toward the evaluation of a nation's potential for technological activities. Methodologies can be developed which are more explicitly directed.

Science and Technology Policy in the United States

The Commitment of the Federal Government

Many countries, particularly in planned economies, have discernible technological policies. These policies are manifested by well-defined programs or five-year plans, geared to the accomplishments of specific technological objectives. In the United States, the government has no formal long-range technological plan. Some inference of a science policy might be deduced as a consequence of federal government support of energy programs, space exploration, national health care, defense expenditures, etc. However, even though there has been support of such programs, they have been subject to the vicissitudes of politics, public attitudes, and erratic funding patterns.

A justification for federal commitment to science and technology can be found in the Preamble, or in Article 1, Section 8, of the United States' Constitution: "To provide for the common defense and general welfare of the United States." Prior to World War II, there was comparatively little organized national R&D effort. Immediately preceding the War, during the War, and since the War there has been great growth of government support of technological development for the "common defense." Since the late 1950s, government expenditures for R&D for the "general welfare" have increased significantly.

Science and the Government

Government support of science has usually been need-directed. Such government agencies as the Bureau of Standards (established 1901), the Food and Drug Administration (established 1906), the Public Health Service (established 1789), and the Agricultural Department (established 1883) came into existence to solve problems in explicit areas. Since there was a need, research was required in order to service the need and the government became involved in scientific activity.

During World War I, and much more so during World War II, science was recognized as being essential for the national defense. A considerable percent of national scientific effort since World War II has been supported through the Department of Defense. The Department of Defense has maintained a formidable research establishment. The immediate goals of defense-supported scientific effort have been weapons systems development. Often, knowledge derived from defense-related R&D has had broader technological applications. Of great importance has been the general awakening to the power of science in solving complex problems.

Science, technology, and innovation in the private sector of a market economy are primarily profit motivated. National and international firms have to evaluate market potential, technical feasibility, and prospects for profit. Much science, technology, and innovation is required in the public sector where the immediate and direct prospects for profit are not present, where high technological and financial risks exist, and where the magnitude of resources is so extensive as to discourage short-run private involvement. In the public sector, need, rather than profit, is the prime motivation.

In a planned economic society, decisional processes as to support of scientific and technological activity would evolve around intensity of need, political expediency, resource priorities, and availability. In a market economy, there is competition between the private and public sector for resources. The federal government can, and has, provided directional force by selective scientific and technological support. Where private investment would not be forthcoming in national needs, technological development and government support is a prime motivator.

In a controlled economy, absolute government involvement is part of the system. In the United States, the issue centers around the extent of government involvement. There is constant pressure within the government to expand internal scientific capabilities, but the implementation of such a policy, where the government would be in direct competition with the private sector, would not be compatible with the U.S. political system. As a consequence, the government's role in supporting science, technology, and innovation has been primarily to select projects, allocate resources to them, coordinate them, and manage them. Only in comparatively isolated instances has the government maintained in-house capability in competition with private enterprise to perform the technical aspects of an R&D program.

Redundancy of Government Support

Government support of science and technology is often splintered. The lack of cohesive support of many programs is due to decentralization as dictated by mission orientation. As a result, the government may be involved in programs where there are related scientific and technological objectives, but the programs are administered through different branches of the government. Often, activity has been duplicated because of agency and departmental competitive inclinations.

Duplication per se is not necessarily wasteful. At times, parallel investigations in basic research or technological ventures can prove beneficial. Under conditions of urgent national need, or when the state of the art is advancing rapidly, some duplication is defensible when different groups, using different techniques, are seeking a solution. Several distinct approaches sometimes improve the probability of uncovering additional knowledge. There is no categorical answer; the intensity and range of effort are dictated by urgency, cost, and available resources.

If one considers "little science," as opposed to "big science," the cost of redundancy is sharply contrasted. In "little science," conducted by one or a small group of investigators, parallel work is usually not expensive and may be, as mentioned, productive of new knowledge. In "big science," usually performed by large organizations, there normally are high investment requirements. The duplication of effort, or acceptance of a research program with cognizance of the latest developments, can lead to large expenditures for little or no new knowledge. Consequently, the government (as a major sponsor of R&D activity) must decide where redundancy could prove advantageous. In "little science," the dominant question is the degree and type of redundancy to foster to obtain the best performance. In "big science," a decision to make a large national commitment in personnel and facilities requires the maximum amount of information available prior to the decision.

Coordination of activities and programs within the federal government has been sporadically attempted since the 1930s, with questionable success. The U.S. government is such a huge organization, composed of so many interacting groups, with differing attributes, interests, and missions that it is improbable that all these agencies could agree on a single unified direction.

Proprietary Rights on Government-Supported R&D

Much of the knowledge gleaned from mission-oriented government-sponsored R&D can be applied to products useful in the private sector. The National Aeronautics and Space Administration (NASA), in particular, has publicized the availability of such information which can, and often has been, applied to commercial endeavors.[6] However, extensive use of valuable information has not occurred because of the issue of proprietary rights.

When the government has been the customer and has supplied resources to private organizations, the general policy has been for the government to retain proprietary rights to the product, even though products with commercial potential sometimes result from federally sponsored R&D. In some instances, private enterprise has been able to use knowledge derived from government work to develop commercial products, as was the case with the Boeing 707, which evolved from the KC-135 Air Force tanker. In other instances, the organization conducting the original R&D has not had sufficient commercial opportunity, or access to R&D results, to develop marketable products.

The U.S. government is reputed to have proprietary rights to many commercially feasible products. Various agencies of the government have been willing to license private contractors to develop commercial products from R&D initially directed toward government application. Industry has been reluctant to invest resources in commercial development where the government apparently has a policy of not readily relinquishing its ownership rights. Owing to its proprietorship, the government can exercise control over commercial development and can terminate any arrangement at any time. Further difficulties are added by the political implications of giving private firms production rights to items initially researched and partially developed with public funds.

Recommendations for a Productive U.S. Science, Technology, and Innovation Policy

Starting with the 1960s and accelerating during the 1970s, there has been an erosion of U.S. leadership in several technologies. Many industries have conservatively retrenched, reflecting a risk avoidance philosophy. The uncertainties associated with R&D coupled with high costs for such effort, inflation, and the price of capital and human resources have all contributed to the declining competitive position of the United States. Critical U.S. industries such as steel, automobiles, textiles, and machine tools are a few examples of industries that have been vulnerable to foreign competition. Industries such as commercial aviation, communication, electronics, and computers where we have traditionally enjoyed technological leadership now show signs of erosion and vulnerability to foreign competition. There are several actions the federal government can take to revitalize declining industries and encourage new ventures. In the following paragraphs a few suggestions are advanced.

Industry–Government Joint Programs

The most effective competition has taken place in industries where foreign governments have provided an operational environment conducive to technological development. Japan and West Germany in particular have, on a selective basis, encouraged technological development by tax incentives, the availability of cheap capital, and various other government subsidies, including import restrictions and tariff protection. In the United States there has been an adversary relationship between government and business. In nations which have developed international technological processes there have been joint industry–government programs directed to achieving technological objectives. There has been a cooperative spirit rather than an adversary relationship.

Investment and Depreciation Allowances

U.S. industry has been hobbled by unrealistic accounting practices relative to investment and depreciation allowances. Depreciation allowances have been geared to original cost rather than replacement. During the high-inflation period of the 1970s and early 1980s depreciation reserves have been inadequate to replace worn out and obsolete facilities and equipment. This has affected U.S. productivity and been a major factor in opening the door to foreign competition. President Reagan, in his economic speech to Congress and the nation on February 18, 1981, recognized the problem and indicated the need for corrective action. Additionally, as a matter of policy, the government should take action which would encourage capital investment. Such investment would lead to more jobs and increased productivity. Investment could be facilitated by tax incentives and making the cost of investment capital attractive.

Tax Relief for R&D

R&D are part of the innovation and technology cycle. In the short run the benefits from such activity are often intangible. When economic conditions are tight, there is a tendency for organizations to cut back on R&D spending. It is during such periods of economic contraction that R&D is needed the most to develop new products and jobs to stimulate the economy. Admittedly, monitoring industrial R&D and the attendant accounting practices is difficult. Nevertheless, it is strongly recommended that incentives for R&D be provided via tax relief. Unfortunately, in the United States it appears that an operational philosophy has evolved which emphasizes the short run. This reflects the financial orientation and domination of many businesses. A tax policy encouraging long-range technological development is badly needed.

Government Proprietorship

Much useful and transferable knowledge has been generated under government sponsorship. At times there has been inducement to enter into contractual relationships with the government because the product(s) and knowledge developed under such agreement could be modified and transferred to the more lucrative commercial market. This, however, has not always happened. Many original contractors do not have the operational capabilities or incentive to convert the products. The original sponsorship invariably is justified on the basis of government need. It would seem that the fulfillment of the obligation to the government by the original contractor will satisfy a quid pro quo requirement. As mentioned earlier in this chapter, the government has retained proprietary rights and subsequent control of such information. Private interests are understandably reluctant to invest in additional developmental activity where proprietary rights are reserved by the government. The loss of such technologies is wasteful—even tragic. Two possibilities are suggested. First, since the government has paid for and hopefully received value, control, unless national security is affected, is then relinquished by the government. The contractual agreement can be considered satisfied. The knowledge should be passed on to the public domain for subsequent use. Second, if the first alternative proves to be politically repugnant the government could still relinquish direct control and proprietorship. Knowledge derived under government sponsorship could be released for subsequent control and commercial development by private interests but under royalty arrangements. Royalty payments could be an additional source of revenue to the government or could provide seed money for further technological exploration.

Cabinet Status

It is not recommended that scientific activity be centralized within the federal government. It is recognized that the various branches of government have specific missions to accomplish and are perhaps in the best position to evaluate their individual programs. While the impact of science and technology on the nation's welfare is generally appreciated, there has been inconsistency in soliciting scientific advice at the executive level of government. Various scientific advisors to presidents have ranged from influential to inept. Each president, starting with Franklin Roosevelt, has his own rapport or the lack thereof with the scientific community. The major advantages of elevating science and technology to a cabinet position would be visibility, recognition of importance, a strong focal point, and subsequent incentive to establish selected formal science and technology policy and a coordination point to determine jurisdiction, consolidate effort, and eliminate costly and unproductive duplication.

In the preceding paragraphs several recommendations relative to U.S. science and technology policy were suggested. It is an important and oftentimes controversial area and universal agreement on an action-directed program is improbable. No doubt objections could be raised to some of the recommendations. Other recommendations could be proposed where the proponents of such recommendations would advance or reprioritize programs directed to improving the U.S. science and technology posture. It was not intended to develop an absolute or all-inclusive list of recommendations. What was intended was to target in on some areas that are considered critical for national technological development and to suggest possible avenues for improved performance.

Overview — U.S. Science and Technology Policy

U.S. government scientific organization and management have executive and legislative components, but management of R&D has, for the most part, been delegated to the operational segments of the various governmental organizations. The different administrative agencies have been responsible for selecting, directing, and managing R&D.

Postulating a U.S. national science and technology policy is possible by putting many pieces together. There has been government commitment to upgrading national health, supporting national security, preserving the natural environment, improving the quality of education, and increasing educational opportunities to citizens, the conservation and proper utilization of the nation's natural and human resources, improvement of housing, transportation, and communication systems, the elimination of pollution and any unnecessary, unhealthful, or inefficient drugs and food additives, and promoting the peaceful use and exploration of outer space.[7]

Despite the programs enumerated in this preceding paragraph there is no formal U.S. policy. The dynamic nature of technology, the political implications, and the great diffusion of R&D activity within the government have not been conducive to the establishment of an explicit set of policies. As yet, no one segment of government has been charged with the responsibility for monitoring scientific activity.

Science Policy in Developed Nations—A Few Select Cases

Range of Alternatives

It should be readily apparent that given the choice in a restriction-free environment nations would select a science policy conducive to total technological self-sufficiency. The human and material resource requirements to support a policy of national technological independence are so staggering as to discourage all but the most powerful nations from even entertaining the prospects of such a policy. In actual practice, no nation has achieved total technological self-sufficiency.

In the preceding section, the science and technological environment in the United States was discussed. It has become apparent that the United States with all its bountiful resources, has been unable to maintain a world position of technological self-sufficiency. Critical natural resources create situations of dependence. Complex technological developments take place unevenly and nations lead, or lag, in certain technologies. Lead/lag situations affect national science policy decisions. In the lead situation, should increasing levels of resources be directed to these areas to maintain, or even widen, the international technological gap? In the lag situation, the criticality of the technology might be influential in directing resources to a "catch-up" policy; or, there might be the realization that there is slight probability of ultimate technological parity, resources could be channeled to potentially more productive areas, and the most expedient way to acquire the technology would be by international purchase.

Developed nations usually do have some range of alternatives which can be considered, such as technological allocation of resources to priorities and the subsequent support for such decisions. Because of resource restrictions, developing nations are confined to a much more restrictive science and technology policy decision process.

In examining aspects of science policy in developed countries, an additional caveat is in order. It might be worthwhile to look at science policy within the framework of market economies and planned economies. In the preceding section, science and technology policy in the United States was discussed. Many of the issues involved in science policy in the United States are applicable in some degree to other market economies. However, brief discussion will be directed to science policy in the market economies of France, West Germany and Japan. Some representative examples of countries with a science policy in planned economies are the Soviet Union, the German Democratic Republic, and Hungary.

France

After World War II, under the leadership of Charles de Gaulle, France launched an ambitious science policy program aimed at achieving a high level of technological excellence and international technological independence. In the post-World War II period, France, perhaps along with the United States and the Soviet Union, had the broadest technological aspirations of any of the developed nations of the world.

The French science policy, according to Gilpin, related to de Gaulle's overall political strategy.[8] The political strategy objectives were to restore France's national self-confidence after war failures, to forestall the danger of economic penetration from other countries, particularly the United States, and the perceived need for French and German cooperation in establishing an independent and economically healthy Western Europe.

The de Gaulle-inspired program met with significant, but limited, success. There were significant technological achievements, especially in the development of military weapons systems and atomic energy. However, it did become apparent that as a nation France did not have the resources to compete worldwide in all technological areas. Developed nations have generally come to the realization that total technological excellence is not a viable policy and have, as a consequence generally retreated to a defensible position of concentration to develop spheres of technological eminence where they have international competitive advantages. France appears to have also moved in this direction.

Federal Republic of Germany (West Germany)

West Germany has had a rapid and dramatic recovery from the ravages suffered during World War II. Much of the nation's productive capacity was destroyed. What remained was a quality population; U.S. assistance, an energetic, educated and aggressive population, and political stability have all contributed to miraculous post-World War II economic growth. It could be said that West Germany lost the war and won the peace.

Immediately after World War II it became apparent that government policy would be to facilitate scientific inquiry and technological application. This scientific operational environment was extremely attractive, especially to scientists in East Germany. The potential for a serious brain drain from East to West Germany was eliminated by restrictive immigration practices instituted in East Germany.

As an aftermath of World War II there has been a minimum of scientific and technological effort in West Germany for defense or military applications. The government has channeled effort into building a formidable science and technological base in selected commercial fields. The government has fostered development in high-technology industries through a variety of subsidies. Interface among government, industry, and educational institutions has been promoted in order to develop leadership in the selected technologies.

West German science and technology policy is further reflected by the numerous government sponsored institutes which maintain close liaison with industry. An open system of scientific communication has existed. German scientists have been free and encouraged to travel and interface with scientists from other countries. The government has provided an environment for scientific enlightenment. This environment has in turn paid off in many technologies such as chemicals, automobiles, machine tools, and electronics.

Japan

Japan represents a case study which is unique because of Japan's great post-World War II economic success and the Japanese technological foundation which has many characteristics dissimilar to other developed nations.

The Japanese R&D effort can be considered highly productive, considering that approximately only 1.5% of Gross National Product is spent on R&D. The comparatively low percent of GNP may be misleading in that these expenditures are almost exclusively concentrated on consumer products, with very insignificant sums being allocated to military R&D. It is estimated that about two-thirds of R&D in Japan is performed within the private sector.[9]

The major factors contributing to Japan's rapid industrial expansion, according to Inose, have been technological innovation, government policy, and a motivated labor force.[10] There have been several discernible strategies which have supported the government's policy. For instance, there has been heavy emphasis on productivity improvement, including economies of scale; there has been government support to develop an export trade policy; there has been a strategy of quickly following up inventions made elsewhere, and then adding significant improvements to improve international marketability; there has been strong government financial support; the education system has been designed to practically eradicate illiteracy, with the subsequent benefits of a highly educated and cheap work force; heavy investment has been encouraged in selected industries, such as communications, transportation, electric power, iron and steel; and, there has been attention to rigid quality control standards, resulting in quality products.

Japan has primarily concentrated its technological and innovational resources at the developmental end of the science and technology spectrum. There is relatively little basic research capability when compared to such nations as the United States, the Soviet Union, West Germany, or England. Japan has had practically no "brain drain" because of distinct language and cultural differences from other developed countries. By the same token, the monoracial composition of the population discourages the inflow of talent from outside the country.[11] Japan, as has been previously mentioned, has had heavy reliance on imported technology transfer. The result of building upon bought technology has been an outward cash flow, reflecting high royalty payments. The royalty payments have more than been compensated by the returns from the products generated as a consequence of the licensing arrangements. Japan has also started to improve its basic research capabilities, as has significantly improved its invention position as attested to by the increasing number of international patents applied for and received.

Japanese science policy has been consistent with its economic objectives. Japan has very few natural resources. To survive economically, a vigorous export system must exist; the Japanese science policy has fostered such a system. Economic growth and affluence has not, however, been attained without some negative aspects. Heavy industrialization, concentrated in a small geographic space, has created all sorts of environment problems which, if continued unabated, will impact on the quality of life. As a consequence, it is likely that Japan will have to funnel more resources in the future for internal social investment and innovation. Such activity can affect Japan's competitive position in world markets.

The Soviet Union

The importance of science in the Soviet Union is reflected in the continued expansion of scientific activity and the allocation of human and material resources.[12] If all engineers and support people are included, it is estimated that about 4% of the total work force is engaged in some aspect of science. Science is used to facilitate economic, social, productive, and cultural achievements. There also is growing interest in the use of science for the socially beneficial projects.

Science policy is manifested in planning for resource allocations, education consistent with national scientific objectives, maximizing the returns from scientific investment, and providing a physically and mentally stimulating environment conducive to scientific accomplishment.[13] To reach the goals of a productive and technologically excellent scientific capability, scientific technological advance is planned and reviewed at each developmental phase for its perspectives and societal consequences. The Soviet approach to science policy emphasizes central planning and review as the means of promising the most effective avenue to scientific accomplishment. The development and implementation of a unified national policy for science is obviously considered to be a function of the state.

Theoretically, Soviet science policy is molded by national need at the time. Policy regarding science is elastic in response to the situation. In a socialistic state, science supposedly is societally motivated. Gvishiani says the important issues in science policy in socialist countries involve coordination of scientific activities with economic reforms, motivating scientists and applying their findings to practice, improving national capability to manage and organize science, recognizing the increasing complexity of an expanding scientific system, and a logical distribution of scientific centers consistent with national needs.[14]

Science policy planning and decisions, as indicated, are highly centralized. Science planning at the national level entails financial appropriations, planning for the development of science, anticipating scientific capital expenditures, coordination of scientific activity with national development plans, coordinating work between the different scientific establishments, studying the effectiveness of scientific research organizations, and integrating the results of scientific activity into the production system. This is an interesting contrast to the inferred science policy in the United States. In the United States, science is pretty well decentralized on the theory that different organizations have different missions and, therefore, are in the best position to determine their own directions. The Soviet system of centralization combines current and long-range planning. Central planning is considered essential to channel scientific activity into problem areas deemed consonant with national needs, to minimize unproductive duplication of effort, and to encourage the development of highly specialized scientific centers.

Much of a centralized science policy can be attributed to the notion that there is a need to manage science. The management of science includes integrational activities between scientific disciplines, a directed approach to problem solving, the organization of resources to maximize results, to ensure a flow of relevant information, and a pooling of resources between Soviet bloc countries. Interestingly, it is recognized that a highly centralized scientific infrastructure also has some negative consequences. Too much centralization can lead to scientific rigidity. Unification can be a powerful contracreative influence by discouraging difference of opinion and challenge to existing knowledge. Some parallelism and competition among scientists cannot only be healthy, but also productive.[15] In a planned society failures have political repercussions; in a market dominated society planning failures have economic consequences and in some situations political overtones.

The German Democratic Republic (East Germany)

Science policy in the German Democratic Republic did not come into focus until the 1950s, when the country entered a phase of socialist industrialization. The goals of the first Five Year Plan (1951–1955) were to alleviate problems resulting from war damage, a divided country, concern for the existing scientific–technological base of production, the organization and capacities for R&D, and the educational system.[16]

When the first Five-Year Plan was launched, it was perceived that the GDR generally and technologically lagged behind industry in capitalistic countries. The technological lag could be traced to such factors as a brain drain to West German companies and the Soviet Union, the curtailment of scientific/technological information from market economy countries, and restrictive Western country trade policies. Even though technological deficiencies were recognized, simple correction by establishing science policy guidelines was not possible. In East Germany there was relatively little experience in planning for science and technology; it was deemed that more urgent national priorities existed, and there were reservations in the scientific community against central planning for science and technology.

Despite difficulties, resources for science and technology were made available in the first Five-Year Plan. Funds were allocated and technical educational institutions were created. Start up was painful and slow since there was internal competition for resources, especially trained engineers and scientists who were needed both in industry and in the newly formed educational institutions. The difficulties encountered emphasized the need for the planning of science and technology. Initially, planning was highly centralized, but concentration of planning was considered detrimental to innovation and, as a consequence, there was a departure from this policy. The result has been some decentralization by mission, with attendant R&D capabilities tied into a level of expected accomplishment. The new system allowed for more operational interpretive latitude, even though coordinated effort of science and technology continued to exist.[17] In the mid-1960s, a program, the Inter-Governmental Parity Committee on Economic and Scientific-Technological Cooperation, was entered into between the GDR and the USSR. This was consistent with the need to exchange technological information within the Soviet sphere of influence.

After evolutionary processes, it appears that there now is a commitment to centralized planning for science and technology. "Even inventions are being planned today, though the actual time and concrete way of solving the problem cannot be forecast exactly. The practicality of central technological planning has also been sufficiently proved though its forms did not meet all the requirements already in the beginning."[18]

Science policy objectives are to integrate science and technology into the overall management and planning processes. It is felt that innovation can be planned for and managed, starting with investment in R&D, the graduation of such effort into production and, subsequently, to marketing and utilization. There are long-range goals for stable economic growth, consistent with social welfare. Specific areas for technological development are identified as energy, natural resource development and utilization, improvement in the effective use of resources, production increases including export capability in such fields as heavy engineering and instruments, and the further development of new machinery and equipment for material processing and heavy industrial production. Consistent with the aforementioned objectives is the desire to improve basic research capability, which is considered the forerunner of technological development.

*Hungary**

Science policy in Hungary follows the patterns of a planned approach to science and technology which exist in the Soviet Union and in the German Democratic Republic. There are, however, a few notable differences in techno-

*The material in this section is based on interviews with Janos Vecsenyi, Bureau for Systems Analysis of the State Office for Technical Development, July 9, 1980, and Zolton Roman, Director, Research Institute of Industrial Economies, the Hungarian Academy of Sciences, July 10, 1980, Budapest.

logical development, perhaps due to the relatively small size of Hungary and its dearth of natural resources.

Hungary's operation in science and technology follows a five-year plan which is part of longer-term technological planning. The country does not have a minister of science, but it does have a special government committee to establish science policy. The committee consists of representatives from different branches of the government. Due to the diverse composition of the committee, coordination becomes an important activity.

Except for a very small enterprise, the economic activity is state owned and controlled. What appears to be a departure from the USSR and GDR systems is the degree of decentralization of R&D. For the most part, what R&D financing is available is also decentralized and is mission oriented. The added operational elasticity would seem to place Hungary somewhere between a planned and a market economy, especially since the bulk of technological effort is on micro scientific projects directed to internal improvements. It was estimated that only about five percent of scientific activity was in larger-scope projects in which there was strong central planning.

The micro technological concentrations seem to be based on national priorities, in an attempt to bring the country up to technological parity with more scientifically advanced nations. The priorities for technological development are energy, environment control, conservation, and effective use of natural resources, the development of electronic capabilities, specifically in information fields, and the encouragement of the biochemistry discipline.

Major Hungarian problems in creating a technologically advanced system are human and natural resource limitations. The Hungarian educational system is considered to be good. It was estimated that about one-third of the national industrial employment was in engineering and related fields. A difficulty has been proper utilization of these people. Human resources have not been maximally motivated and, as a result, productivity approximates 50% of similar activity in Western Europe. People are often overqualified for their assigned jobs; the system may be too rigid for professional work preferences; and, as mentioned, motivation appears to be weak due to job assignments and an inadequate recognition and material reward system.

The country has severe natural resource limitations. It is essentially an agrarian economy. Technological development has concentrated primarily on the home market since it is not thought the country has the technology to be competitive in world markets. There is limited export of agricultural products, aluminum, iron, steel, pharmaceuticals, textiles, coal, and ore. The products that are exported are not technologically sophisticated, and often these export products are similar qualitywise to products from developing nations. Most exports, about 55–60%, are sent to socialist countries, and the balance are sent to market economies. Exports at times compromise local consumption but are considered necessary to get currencies used to import needed technologies. An interesting aside, when one of the authors was in Hungary he sought to buy

Herndon China which is a national product. Except for a few hotel gift shops where the prices were higher than in the United States, this commodity was not locally available. It is exported in exchange for hard foreign currency needed to offset financial obligations incurred from imports.

A significant deterrent to technological development, and the establishment of an ambitious science policy, is the availability of funds for development purposes. Only agricultural products appear to be a foreseeable exportable surplus. The country is dependent on the import of much of its raw materials and technology. Payment for these necessary imports represents a constant drain of foreign exchange and does not permit the accumulation of surplus funds to invest in internal technological development.

Science Policy in Developing Nations

Some Characteristics of Developing Nations

In the preceding section, science policy was discussed as a process in developed nations. A further distinction was made in recognizing some characteristics of countries in which there is primarily a capitalistic or market dominated political system and countries where there are socialistic planned economies. There is another identifiable sphere in the world which is constituted of the Third World bloc of developing nations. In applying the term "developing" to these nations, qualification is necessary. Some of the developing countries do have primitive economies, such as Yeman, Chad, Thailand, and Bolivia, which have, as yet, not adjusted to the 20th century. Other so-called developing countries, such as Argentina, Brazil, and Mexico, have made significant economic and technological progress and are able, in some technologies, to compete favorably with the developed nations.

Third World countries constitute the bulk of the world's population, but do not have even a moderate proportion of the world's wealth. It is estimated that these nations have somewhere between 70 and 80% of the world's population and only perform 4% of the world's R&D. Economic development in these countries could lead to a tremendous effective demand for goods and services. Unfortunately, however, there are significant constraints in developing nations which tend to retard economic development. Some, most, or all of the following characteristics exist in economically deprived nations: overpopulation, nutritional problems, inadequate health care, poor and insufficient educational facilities, weak or nonexistent scientific infrastructure, political instability, an elitist society, and insignificantly strong middle class to act as a political anchor, shortage of capital for investment purposes, a labor- (as distinct from a capital-) intensive production system, a high proportion of the population unemployed or underemployed, often shortages of critical natural resources, primarily agrarian economies and ineffectual use of the land, low productivity, dependence on more affluent nations for much of its technology, balance-of-payment problems, high inflation, scarcity of goods, low per capita income, climatic extremes, a strong religious and/or cultural infrastructure, and, compared to developed nations, a poor quality of life.

As indicated, not all the aforementioned characteristics exist in all developing countries. In some developing countries, many of the problems do exist; still, in other developing countries, many of the nationally debilitating characteristics do not or have not existed. Many countries in the throes of developmental progress have initiated reforms that have obliterated these problems or improved these situations.

Science Policy Considerations

Even though there are some commonality of problems in developing nations, it would be unwise to treat science policy in sweeping generalizations as universally applicable to all such nations. Allowances must be made for social, political, cultural, geographical, and economic differences. There are, however, some factors which touch, to some degree, on technological development in most developing nations.

Science policy in developing countries should enable the country to use its natural and human resources to its best advantage, to improve its trading position, specifically in areas where there are markets which afford the opportunity for reciprocity, improve government management of internal activities, promote better communication, improve national defense for political survival, and improve the quality of life.[19] Unfortunately, it appears that insufficient effort in R&D is directed to improving the quality of life of people in developing nations since most international R&D effort is not goal oriented for the needs of the poor.[20]

In formulating a science policy which has a reasonable chance for some degree of fruition, developing nations must be cognizant of the factors that tend to impede technological development. Some of these factors have been identified and will not be elaborated upon. A few are deemed important enough to warrant additional discussion.

Developing nations should create policies that encourage capital accumulation. Savings are the most obvious route; but, if there is political and subsequent currency instability, there is a natural reluctance to put money in banks where it can productively be reemployed. Where there is lack of confidence in the local system, there is a "capital bleed" to nonproductive investments, such as precious metals, gems, or art objects. Or, there might be a flight of capital for investment in other more politically stable countries.

With a few notable exceptions, such as the oil-producing nations, most developing nations are capital poor. The economic systems in such nations do not produce surpluses that the government can channel into technological investment. If governments in developing countries attempt to build up surpluses by revised tax structures, they may find an unreceptive environment and additionally aggravate an already critical capital shortage by further discouraging investment. Many of these governments have nationalized key industries.

Rather than provide surplus capital, these industries, which are either subsidized or inefficient or both, act as a further drain on capital accumulation.[21]

Oftentimes, technological development is restricted by the quantity and quality of available natural and human resources. Natural resources are indeed critical assets in the economic development of a nation; natural resources per se do not guarantee that a nation will be innovative and technologically aggressive. Many developing nations do not have extensive, unexploited natural resources. The real ultimate wealth of a nation, however, is its human resources. A well-educated, well-motivated, healthy population can circumvent many limitations that initially may appear insurmountable due to inadequate natural resources. No better example to support this contention can be advanced than to cite the Japanese, Koreans, and Scandinavians. Science policy in developing nations should put strong emphasis on human development.

Human development can be fostered by intelligently planning the educational system to train people in needed skills where there are immediate and rewarding employment opportunities. Transition from technological reliance to technological independence can be bridged by judiciously using nonnationals as teachers and as advisors.

Developing nations, in line with human resource utilization, should establish policies that will facilitate the development of itinerate management skills. Invariably, developing nations suffer from a shortage of qualified, educated, and experienced local managers. Dependence on foreign managers can lead to cultural and communication problems. Communication problems are indicated, as distinct from language problems. Foreigners may be adept at the language, but as a result of a different cultural orientation, may not be able to communicate effectively.

Science policy concerned with human resource development should also consider skill transitions at nonprofessional levels. Developing nations invariably are predominantly agrarian and have a low inventory of human skills readily transferable to advanced technological processes. Without policies to cope with transition, production problems will probably be aggravated.

Market and distribution systems are also an integral part of technological development. It may not be feasible to attempt to compete in established markets; it may be far more practical to develop local industries and markets. Science policy would then entail considerations of how much support, what kind of support, and how much protection from foreign competition is necessary or desirable.

Developing countries often have little leverage in world trade. Trade restrictions frequently are imposed by developed nations to protect their work force against "cheap" labor. Even in the export of raw materials, developing nations frequently suffer from relative price differentials between exports and imports.[22]

Science policy in developing countries should be realistic. Attainable goals, as distinct from idealistic goals, should be established. Priorities consistent with technological goals and economic growth objectives should be created to divert resources into productive channels. Additionally, systems must be developed which are compatible with the nation's culture and resources, and which also will, in the long run, enable the country to attain an internationally competitive technology.

Basalla has indicated seven tasks which are prerequisite to making a transition from a scientifically dependent society to a position of technological capability:

1. Scientific negativism based on religious and philosophical beliefs must be eliminated and replaced by positive attitudes toward science.
2. The scientist must enjoy social approval of his or her efforts.
3. A workable relationship between science and government must be established where the scientist receives financial support and encouragement and government maintains a neutral stance in scientific matters.
4. Science should be integrated in the educational system at all levels.
5. Science should be promoted through the formation of national organizations.
6. National and international scientific communication should be encouraged.
7. There should be the maintenance of a technological base to serve as a foundation for the growth of science.[23]

Science Policy and Innovation

Political Ideologies

In the preceding sections, science policy was discussed within the context of market directed political systems, planned economies, and developing nations. Invariably, the different political systems have technological objectives and national priorities which are brought into focus through science policy. Many times, despite differences in political ideologies, the national technological objectives are strikingly similar; in essence, the end goals are approximately the same, but the methods to achieve these goals vary among governments.

Technological goals in several instances are quite specific. Less specific but certainly implied in examining science policy in political systems is that innovational processes are critical to the achievement of technological objectives. It has become apparent after research into science policy that all political systems at least outwardly are striving for an innovative society. Some systems have obviously been more successful than others in stimulating an innovative climate. What negative factors affect national innovation? What positive national environmental conditions encourage innovation?

Negative Factors Affecting National Innovation

Societal pressures are often compelling forces for short-run projects in political systems. These pressures are reinforced by the desire of incumbants to maintain their office. Innovation and technological development often are long-term, high-risk processes. In many political divisions, the population rank and file do not comprehend the long-term benefits to be derived from investing in the scientific establishment. Often there is poor communication between the public and the scientific sector. All too frequently people only see the costs of scientific effort, the immediate benefits, if there are any, and sometimes the negative fallouts. There is normally a failure to appreciate the long-term benefits and multiplier effects of a successful scientific program. Many times esteemed products, vital services, and general societal benefits emanate from some obscure scientific work which is only vaguely traceable. If there is an indifferent or hostile national attitude to resource support, if there is no recognition and acclaim for scientific effort, and if there are pressures for short-run plastic results, it follows that innovation will not thrive in such an environment.

Innovation requires a proper economic, political, and cultural climate. Government policies can go a long way toward the encouragement or discouragement of innovation.[24] To be more explicit, excessive government controls as well as government indifference can affect innovation. Lack of national direction as exemplified by no discernible goals or priorities can act as a discouragement. High costs and considerable risk can be negative factors if the government is unwilling to underwrite all or part of the effort. Capital availability including the cost of money, opportunity costs, and profit prospects all impinge on the innovational decision process. Protection of innovations by patent policy or trade practices can provide inducement. The failure to recognize the importance of basic research as well as mission-directed research can also impact ultimately on innovation. There is a need for predictability of government support and the government's willingness to invest in long-term projects. The failure of government to adequately support university scientific effort and coordinate such activity with industry can lead to negative synergism. A program aimed at the general populace to educate them to the benefits and contributions of science, technology, and innovation is advisable. The tendency of governments to be sporadic in their treatment of science can lead to unpredictability, subsequent confusion, and destruction of morale and motivation in the scientific community.

One variable affecting innovation is the individual. Environmental factors may be negative, or at best neutral, but even without positive inducements some individuals are motivated to creativity. In a more receptive environment, these people would probably be more productive than in a restrictive situation. Fortunately, the human spirit being what it is, some innovation will happen in spite of economic, cultural, or political barriers.

Some Positive Factors That Could Induce Innovation

Many of the negative factors affecting national innovation can be reversed to provide positive incentives. Rather than belabor the obvious, this section will examine some additional factors that could provide positive inducements for innovation.

Claiborne reports that the Israeli government is earmarking more state capital for high-innovational projects which are directed to develop export products.[25] To give tangible support to this program, the Israeli government is transferring scientists from academic projects to the private sector. There are some interesting implications in the aforementioned. Too often, ties between academic and industrial organizations are tenuous at best. The academics frequently fail to translate their work into tangible and understandable concepts. The industry counterparts are also victims of their environment. The degree of their technical sophistication will vary, according to the technical objectives of their organization. An effective system to encourage knowledge exchange and utilization, with positive objectives and government support, can create an innovative climate. In the case cited, government support in Israel extends to grants of up to 80% of the cost of new product development, the availability of government loans for working capital, and liberal tax incentives to encourage industrial and private investment.

A very important factor in Israel's push for an innovative national environment is its investment in people and education. The country has a large reservoir of highly trained scientists, many who have immigrated from other countries. The government has attempted to provide an intellectually stimulating environment in the industrial sector to encourage innovation. New enterprises are being fostered and are rapidly forming as a result of direct government financial support.[26]

Despite the restrictions of climate, geography, natural resources, and quantity of population, Israel has had accelerated industrial growth; much of the industrial growth has taken place as a consequence of innovation. The methods used in Israel to encourage innovation could well lead to productive research in this area.

Japan has been a large importer of technology. Japanese product and process innovation has converted imported technology into internationally marketable products. The Japanese economic success can, in large part, be attributed to favorable government/industry relations. It appears this partnership between government and industry is expanding to encourage the development of selected high-technology industries.

The emerging science policy goals are designed to have less future reliance on innovational conversion of imported technologies, and more effort in locally developing basic innovational technologies which can be exported. Many of the technologies that have been developed in Japan have been exported to developing countries. To illustrate, steel mills in Taiwan, shipbuilding factories in South Korea, and desalinization plants in the Middle East have resulted from Japanese exported technologies.[27] The exported technologies have primarily required large numbers of industrial workers. The Japanese are now working on capabilities to computerize many heretofore manual operations, by use of sophisticated electronics and industrial robots.

The Israeli and Japanese cases have been used to illustrate the innovational force that can occur as a consequence of government working in concert with industry. An overall receptive national innovational climate can exist and several suggestions are possible to increase innovational motivation.

There must be incentives. Incentives can vary among organizations, political systems, and individuals. In private industry the primary incentive is profit.

The opportunity to start up and direct an innovative enterprise. Available venture capital. The encouragement of entrepreneurship. The chance for personal material gains resulting from successful innovation.

A mobile society. The opportunity to move from one technical environment to another.

Information exchange. Easy access to information sources, within and outside the immediate political jurisdiction. The exposure to new ideas. Cross-pollinization with people from other disciplines, other industries, and other countries.

A patent protection environment.

A long-term government commitment to an intellectual society. Minimum or no concern that shifts in political ideology will obviate the work or lead to some form of retribution based on political considerations.

A positive environment for creativity. Allowance of interpretive latitude. Avoidance of established dogma which prevents the exploration of new avenues to knowledge.

A recognition and reward system for more entrepreneurial innovations.

Closer interface between industry and universities, including practitioners, faculty, and students.

The recognition that innovation can be managed. The avoidance of overmanagement, as distinct from good management.

Understanding the value of people investment. Provide basic educational and continuing education opportunities.

Science Policy and Internationalism

Thoughts on National Science and Technology Policy

It must be remembered that science and technology are means to an end, not ends in themselves. The development of a high-level scientific capability is a futile exercise if there is no application or technological utilization. Nations with limited resources cannot afford the luxury of a misdirected and unproductive scientific organization. The scientific establishment must be supportive of national technological objectives.

One important decision area is the relative balance of effort between science and technology. There really can be no simple or categorical answer as to where resources can be most effectively utilized. This would vary from situation to situation, nation by nation, and from one technology to another. Research provides a learning foundation on which long-term benefits can accrue. On the other hand, needs may be apparent and immediate and successful development effort can be more contributive, surer, and productive in the short run. Or, it may be outright cheaper and more expedient to import certain technologies, rather than invest scarce resources in their development.

A relatively common problem found in developing nations is underutilization of basic research capabilities. In many instances, bright young people are sent to foreign countries for their formal education. The learning derived may reflect education which is responsive to the host country's needs and casually or totally unrelated to the needs of the visiting scholar's country. Often, students return to their home countries and are disillusioned to find little or no employment of their newly acquired skills. For nations with limited human and material resources, this is reckless extravagance and poor planning.

The political environment is also crucial to science and technology policy. Political ideologies range from commitment to free enterprise to total state control. In such possible environments, R&D can be performed independently of government support and with minimal government control. R&D can also take place within a partnership structure where the government provides the funds and industry performs the work with some governmental control. In the extreme situation, the government has total involvement in scientific and technological direction and development.

Another consideration in viewing science policy is the uncertainty and unpredictability of public attitudes, which have a telling impact on the political environment. A shift in public opinion can be politically influential in supporting or not supporting technological projects. A good example is the initial commitment and subsequent withdrawal of support to the U.S. supersonic transport program. There has also been a change in public attitude from intense environmental concern to an emphasis on energy. These shifts in attitudes make it politically expedient to divert funds to areas where there is strong and immediate public support. In such an operational milieu, poor projects may be sponsored and promising projects may be discarded as not being politically feasible.

Another possibility for consideration in establishing science policy is an extension of effort beyond national boundaries. Many nations having geographical proximity have common problems and limited resources. A pooling of scarce resources, in concerted effort, could be more productive and less risky than individual undertakings. A good example of this approach is the Central American Common Market. There is the problem of nationalism which is a frequent deterrent to cooperative efforts in many parts of the world.

A nation must also carefully consider where, when, and what type of technology should be introduced. Employing technological forecasting and assessment might prove useful in the decision process of whether to embark on technological development. A variation of economic opportunity cost can be used to explore possible alternative technological investments. Such investments should consider a multiplier effect with regard to the greatest probable return consonant with national welfare.

A carefully considered and intelligently managed science and technology policy could be contributive to increased political and economic independence, the establishment of a structure for future national income generation, the development of technologies that are sensitive to national needs, the opportunity to educate, develop, and utilize people, and the fact that knowledge feeds on knowledge.

International Aspects

Science and technology have not only been instrumental in changing social structures within nations, but have also been forces having dramatic impact on the internationalism. Science and technology have affected international relations as a consequence of weapons systems development, with their attendant potential for massive destruction, the increasing international technological interdependence, the technological requirements for natural resources, increasing population pressures, and the development of technologies that have worldwide application.[28]

Technology crosses national boundaries in addressing such problems as disease eradication, pollution, arms control, use of common natural resources such as oceans and the sky, energy shortages, international crime, etc. In the not too distant past, science and technology were considered almost exclusively national resources. It has become more and more apparent that in the present and future science and technology must be used to solve critical problems that cross national boundaries.

Selective international scientific cooperation can lead to positive synergistic results. The need for common problem solutions may be the ultimate force for international cooperation and world peace. Perhaps an early manifestation of this is the growing number of international cooperative arrangements and technological consortiums. Cost is a considerable factor in technological development. The availability of resources and the cost of developing technology can certainly perpetuate the differences among nations, unless cooperative strategies are evolved and implemented.

Firms operating internationally can be effective implementing agents. Profit motivation can circumvent political reluctance. Also, the transnational firm may be able to facilitate technological development and utilization internationally and avoid roadblocks created by strong nationalistic tendencies.

Science and Technology Policy Within a Systems Context

Many elements germane to science and technology policy have been identified and discussed. Figure 4-2 is an attempt to place these elements in some perspective.

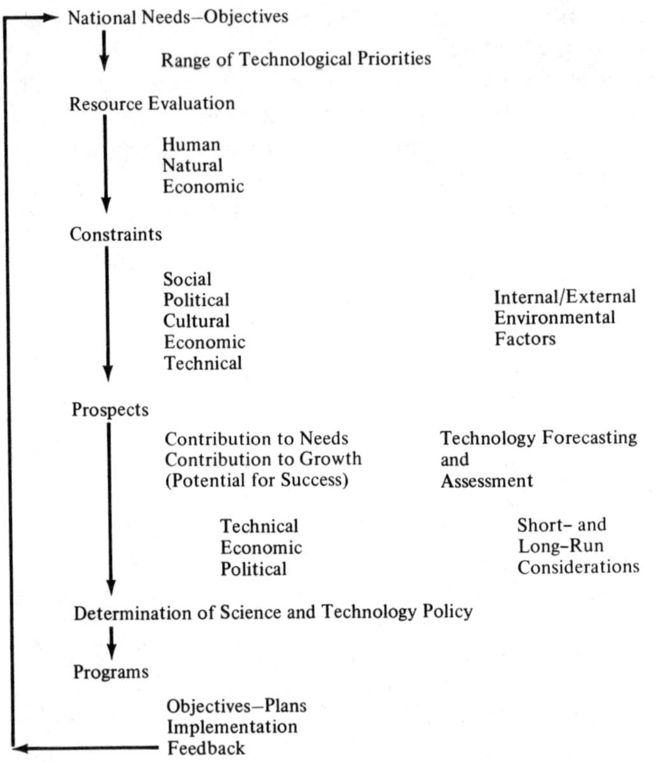

Figure 4-2. A systems approach to science and technology policy determination.

Endnotes Chapter Four

1. John Walsh, "Science Policy: Detent, LDC's New Dimensions," *Science*, December 28, 1973, p. 1326.
2. R.R. Nelson, "Closer Integration of Science Policy and Economic Policy," in *Technological Innovation: Government/Industry Cooperation*, edited by A. Gerstenfeld with the assistance of R. Briainard, New York: John Wiley & Sons, 1979, p. 198.
3. "Excerpts from the Final Report of CACTAL," Pilot Project on Transfer of Technology, Regional Scientific and Technological Development Program, Department of Scientific Affairs, Washington, DC, SG/P. 1 PPTT/6, September 1973, pp. 6–8.
4. E. Layton, "Conditions of Technological Development," in *Science, Technology and Society*, edited by Ina Spiegel-Rosing and Derek de Solla Price, London and Beverly Hills: Sage Publications, 1977, p. 216.
5. *Ibid.*, p. 217 and D. Nelkin, "Technology and Public Policy," pp. 393–441.
6. See *Spinoff 1980—An Annual Report*, National Aeronautics and Space Administration, Washington, DC: U.S. Govt. Printing Office.
7. Science and Technology Policy—Conference Report (to accompany H.R. 10230), 94th Congress, 2nd session, House of Representatives, Report No. 94-1046, April 26, 1976, pp. 1–3.

8. Robert G. Gilpin, Jr., "Science, Technology, and French Independence," in *Science Policies of Industrial Nations*, edited by T. Dixon Long and Christopher Wright, New York: Praeger Publishers, 1975, p. 115.
9. T. Dixon Long, "The Dynamics of Japanese Science Policy," pp. 133–168. *Ibid.*
10. Hiroshi Inose, "Government Policy and Innovation in Japan," in *Technological Innovation: Government/Industry Cooperation*, edited by Arthur Gerstenfeld, New York: John Wiley & Sons, 1979, pp. 140–158.
11. *Ibid.*, pp. 141–158.
12. Jermen Gvishiani, "Soviet Science Policy," in *Science and Technology Policies*, edited by G. Strasser and E.M. Simons, Cambridge, MA: Ballinger Publishing Co., 1973, p. 174.
13. *Ibid.*
14. *Ibid.* p. 176.
15. *Ibid.*, pp. 178–181.
16. Heinz-Dieter Haustein, "Planning of Technology in Industry," unpublished paper, International Institute for Applied Systems Analysis, Laxenburg, Austria, undated, p. 3.
17. *Ibid.*, pp. 4–7.
18. *Ibid.*, p. 10.
19. Ziauddin Sardar and David G. Rosser-Owen, "Science Policy and Developing Countries," in Spiegel-Rosing and Price, op. cit. pp. 538–539.
20. *Mobilizing Technology for World Development*, published for the International Institute for Environment and Development and the Overseas Development Council, New York: Praeger, 1979, p. 29.
21. Sardar and Rosser-Owen, *op. cit.*, pp. 542–543.
22. *Ibid.*, p. 545.
23. G. Basalla, "The Spread of Western Science," *Science*, 156, May 5, 1967, pp. 612–621.
24. Bradley Graham, "Somethings Happened to Yankee Ingenuity," *The Washington Post*, September 3, 1978, G1, and Howard K. Nason, "The Environment for Industrial Innovation in the United States," Gerstenfeld, *op. cit.*, pp. 76–77.
25. William Claiborne, "Israel Pushing to Export 'Ingenuity'," *Los Angeles Times*, December 31, 1979, Part II, p. 11.
26. *Ibid.*
27. "Japanese Seek to Export High-Technology," *Herald Tribune*, June 24, 1980, p. 13.
28. Eugune B. Skolnikoff, "Science, Technology and the International System," Spiegel-Rosing and Price, *op. cit.*, p. 507.

CHAPTER FIVE

International Trade Policies

Trade Policy and National Growth

Trade Policy and Change

National trade policies are susceptible to change. Trade policies can be formulated to encourage the influx of capital and subsequent development of new industries. Policy can also reflect political isolationism, as was the situation in China until the 1970s. Selective protection of key industries or the exclusion of competition until infant industries can be established can also be objectives of trade policy. Additionally, trade policies can be reflected by the relative markets for new technologies offered, and the likely degree of competition posed by the nation or group and/or its commercial enterprise.

In essence, trade policy is affected by the national and international political environment, by economic factors, by societal considerations, and by technology. Each of the aforementioned is subject to volatile change which can impact on a nation's trade policy.

Stages of National Growth

Many theorists are of the opinion that international trade is a determinant in a nation's economic growth. In order to appreciate the level of growth that can be achieved it is necessary to understand the "process" of commercial growth.

W.W. Rostow identifies five stages of growth that have characterized all societies:

Traditional society.

Preconditions for takeoff.

Takeoff.

Drive to maturity.

Age of mass consumption.[1]

The "traditional society" (Stage I) is one in which very little change occurs. There is a ceiling on per capita productivity and income because of the absence of modern science and technology. Examples include the early civilizations of the Middle East, Medieval Europe, and the dynasties of ancient China.

The "preconditions for takeoff" (Stage II) is a term allocated to the transitional stage when societies develop the conditions necessary for the third stage. While in this stage, a society likely shows some characteristics of both the traditional and the new. The key feature of these societies is their political development. Nations at this stage are normally building a centralized national state. There are both ancient and modern examples—France and the United States during their revolutions and most of the members of the Third World today.

The "takeoff" stage (Stage III) is where the traditional resistances of a society are weakened and are finally overtaken as the society enters upon a process of cumulative growth. Technology, organization, and modern attitudes are the dominant features of the society. As agriculture becomes commercialized and more productive, the workers begin to leave the land to satisfy the expanding need for industrial labor. This stage normally lasts one or two decades. The forces at play during this stage transform the political, social, and economic structure of the society so that steady, sustainable growth is enabled. Notable technologies include textiles and steel. Since World War II, Mexico, Brazil, Egypt, Israel, and Taiwan have experienced this stage.

In the "drive to maturity" stage (Stage IV), the economy moves beyond the industries that originally provided the momentum for takeoff. The society usually has the capacity and technology to produce virtually anything required. Industrial processes became progressively more sophisticated. Notable technologies include electronics and chemicals. The nation assumes a different role in world trade: More and more goods are produced at home, altogether new impact requirements arise, and modern technology creates new export products. Historically, approximately 60 years are required for a nation to move from stage II through IV. Few, if any, of the developing nations have yet made this transition.

In the "age of mass consumption" (Stage V), a society develops affluent living standards and places a definite emphasis on the production of durable consumer goods and individualized services. The notable technology at this stage is the automobile. The United States entered this stage during World War I; Western Europe and Japan made the transition in the late 1950s.

There is little argument that this model is a constrained glimpse of technological/political/economic development. A definite limitation is the impression that each stage logically follows its predecessor. It is important to recognize that a given society may stagnate prior to takeoff due to some internal condition, such as a population explosion, which prevents improvements in standards of living. The majority of the developing nations are still building the preconditions for takeoff. The most important factors for most are technology and its paralleling capital formation. The key to developing these factors is that nation's trade policies.

Technology and Trade Patterns

Technological Influence

There are a number of "continuous disturbances" and "dynamic imbalances" taking place in the world economy. It has been postulated that the influence of economic change on the patterns of trade may be caused by various technological factors. It is appropriate to examine these factors in terms of an "international product life cycle"[2] (see Figure 5-1).

In this instance a new product is developed, or similarily, a new process is discovered, which assists in manufacturing the new product. The firm initially introduces the item within the bounds of the domestic market. Product research and development probably occurred within a developed nation, because of the availability of capable scientific talent and a stable political environment, which encourages innovation.

After a period of local use and product acceptance, the firm will tend to look for wider markets—perhaps in foreign lands, especially in the developed nations. Normally developing nations are not a market where a technology is first introduced. Time, cost, culture, and often technology modifications are factors to be contended with before developing nations become economically viable markets for new technology.

International Competition

International business is highly competitive. New and marketable technology affords a business or nation a competitive advantage. Many nations have entered into trade agreements which protect inventions and innovation from

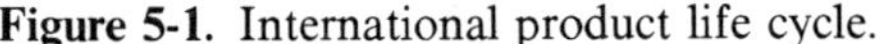

Figure 5-1. International product life cycle.

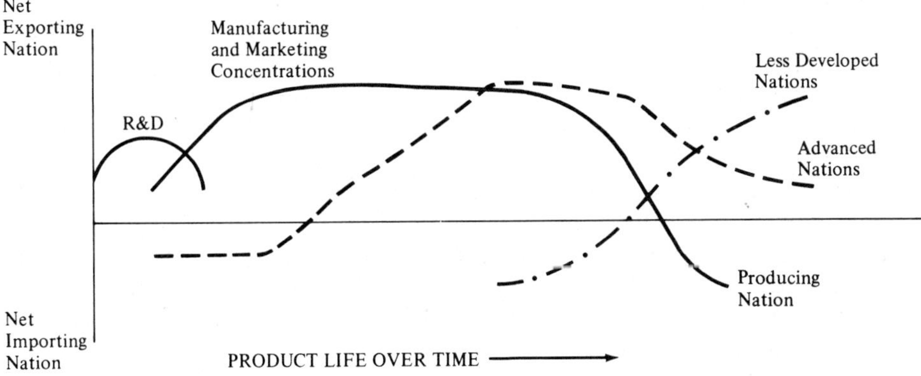

infringement. Unless an invention or innovation is completely protected by patents, it likely will be imitated or copied by others. The first competition appears in the domestic market, then in the overseas markets. International competition may come from rival domestic companies or from foreign companies. In either case, the firm is in constant jeopardy of losing its market position gained by the introduction of technological innovation.

Much international trade competition results from technological innovations developed in the United States, West Germany, Japan, Great Britain, and France. Technological innovations on a lesser scale have also been introduced from other developed countries such as Italy, Sweden, Canada, and Israel. With the general exception of Japan, the nations mentioned invariably process a technology from applied research through various developmental stages to commercialization. The Japanese have some applied research capabilities. They have, however, been aggressive competitors by building on proven and successful technological innovations developed in other nations. Growing awareness of fierce Japanese technological competition has been manifested in several countries by discussions or actual trade restrictions. A prime illustration is a possible quota imposed on the number of Japanese automobiles that can be exported to the United States.

Need

Innovation frequently is the result of need recognition. The cost of need fulfillment can be assessed in terms of economic and social benefits. Often technological innovation is process rather than product directed. Process innovation has not been given the attention it deserves. Process innovation enables efficient production which in turn enhances a competitive position. Most of the literature on technological innovation is directed to product innovation.

Developing nations usually have a large pool of comparatively cheap, unskilled, underemployed labor. Developed countries, as part of the international competitive process, tend to substitute capital for labor. The production goals are mass produced, cheap, standard products. Labor in developed nations is generally comparatively expensive, skilled, and in relative short supply. As a consequence, business based in developed nations seeks either labor-saving technological innovations or production sites, usually in developing nations, where there is an abundant source of cheap labor.

In the past, even though American labor was obstensively expensive compared to foreign labor, in terms of real cost, American labor was actually competitive. This was true because of capital investment, modern technology, and the high productivity per labor unit. There has been an erosion of this position due to several reasons, such as the obsolescence of U.S. capital equipment in many industries, lagging technological development, and decreasing productivity. There is now intensified foreign competition where there has been productive investment in new technological processes, capital equipment, which has often resulted in lower costs and higher productivity per labor unit.

There is a need for a resurgence of American technological development. The deteriorization of U.S. leadership in several industries has compromised the U.S. international trade position. Trade protection of technologically outdated industries is not the answer. What are the range of international trade policies and how can such policies be employed to encourage technological development in order to be internationally competitive? The following sections of this chapter will examine some of the pertinent issues.

The Case for Free Trade

Rationale

Before examining the various trade policies of individual or blocs of nations it is well to examine some of the underlying reasons why trade between nations is beneficial.

Without international trade the productive and subsequent consumption patterns of a nation would be limited. The opportunity to freely sell and buy commodities in a world market opens up the possibilities of consumption choice of goods and services.

An argument can be advanced that uninhibited trade can provide a directional force for the effective use of resources. For instance, if world prices are high for some technologies, effort and resources will be directed to markets where there are profit inducements. Such resources would be channeled away from less productive or profitable avenues. A nation may have natural advantages in exporting some technologies. In a free world market a nation could concentrate its productive efforts where it has natural advantages and buy goods that it cannot economically produce or where it cannot effectively compete. Or, based on the law of comparative advantage, scarce resources can be directed to the production of goods and the development of technologies where there is a comparative advantage to be gained by the employment of available resources.[3] In a free world market based on comparative advantage, needed goods could be acquired from foreign sources even though these goods could be produced cheaper domestically.

Following the rationale of the Ricardian theory, the movement of resources in response to different world prices is the source of additional (productive) gains from trade. The Ricardian model also assumes a difference in a given technology from one country to another.[4]

Market Systems

The fundamental motivation for trade in a market system is the expectation of profit resulting from the exchange. In this respect, trade occurs for the same reasons among nations as it does between groups of people or regions within a particular country.

In the not too distant past theorists were likely to explain international trade in terms of natural factor endowments. This explanation is becoming less accepted today. Economists have noted that trade in industrial goods can occur even in the absence of factor endowments. Apparently, many of the important comparative advantages of industrial nations are artificial and arise from product differentiation, technology gaps, and economies of scale.[5] Classical theory has not explained why firms choose to make direct investments rather than trade. International business in the 1970s was characterized by increasing instances of direct investments; this is a serious shortcoming of theory. Modern analysts have therefore been inclined to feel that

> It is becoming increasingly evident that this traditional approach is entirely inadequate for the 1970s. The theory does not explain real-world trade flows very well, and in concentrating on nation-to-nation flows the theory deals with phenomena that are becoming less significant. In looking at trade from the country's point of view, we have lost sight of the fact that, except in certain special cases, countries do not trade with each other, companies do.... Many of these business firms' critical decisions involve decisions on reinvestment of earnings or raising funds in foreign countries, neither of which results in any flow across borders. The decision to export, usually seen as something quite separate from capital flows, is coming to be looked upon as inextricably linked with the decision to invest; to decide to export is a decision *not* to invest in plant, and vice-versa. Contrary to classical theory, such decisions are based more often on demand and competitive considerations than on seeking lower cost production sites.[6]

Direct Investment

Another distinct reason for the establishment of the various trade policies is the propensity of transnational firms to engage in direct foreign investment. In this situation a firm invests abroad when it can earn a higher rate of return overseas after considering the risks and costs of operating in a different political and legal environment. To be successful, the firm must have some advantage over its competitors that it can transfer from one country to another. Additionally, the advantage should be of a nature that is not readily achievable by the local firms.

Direct investment usually occurs because of "some imperfections in markets for goods or factors, including among the latter technology, or some interference in competition by government or by firms, which separates markets."[7]

Gains from Trade

There are positive gains to be obtained from international trade, both for a nation and for the transnational firm. For a nation, it is obvious that international trade increases the variety of goods available for consumption. Often it is either impossible or not economically feasible to produce certain goods within a country even though the demand for such goods may be great. Importation may result in availability at a lower cost which, in turn, presents the possibility of more widespread consumption.

It is normally accepted that the increased variety of goods available through trade enhances the standard of living within a country. It provides new consumption experiences plus the possibility of buying products that more closely meet the requirements of varying lifestyles. International trade opens the world market to producers of these goods, thereby allowing more efficient and profitable production than would be possible with only local sales.

Sometimes natural resources, or derived products, cannot be developed with a given nation—no matter how technologically advanced that country may be. Scarce resources and commodities such as iron, tin, and copper must be extracted where they are found. Since they likely form the basis for industrial production, the only recourse may be international trade. The United Kingdom and Japan are examples of nations which depend on such trade to keep their production facilities in operation.

The quantity of goods available for consumption will likely increase through international trade. A given country, by concentrating production on the items having the greatest comparative advantage, can trade a portion of this output for goods that have comparative disadvantage. The importation of goods that are produced more efficiently abroad results in a greater variety and usually better quantity of goods on the home market than if the resources were applied to the production of goods when the country does not have a comparative advantage.

Another realistic explanation for world trade is that because of the widening of the markets it is possible to expand plant size. This, in turn, leads to more capital formation and normally higher levels of employment.[8] Also, it is possible that when such expansion results in scale economies, the likely benefits of lower costs will be available to either domestic or foreign customers, or both.

A final, but equally important issue, is the recognition of the "two-way street" of trade. It should be emphasized that the importation of goods, services, and capital are necessary to provide foreigners with the means of payment for domestically produced exports.

Benefits for the Transnational Firm

The transnational firm has a direct and obvious interest in international trade—profits. Producers not only expect a profit on the commodities sold abroad but they likewise see foreign markets as a basis for expanding production beyond the limits set by the domestic market. Exports enable many industries to

Keep their labor and capital fully employed.

Rapidly expand production.

Realize lower operating costs.

Distribute sales more widely.

The international production and marketing efforts are geared toward expanding markets for the firm's products. However, early penetration of the foreign market may have as its goal the preempting of the market from potential local competition or from firms from other nations offering similar products.

By nature of its operations, survival of the transnational enterprise is based on the importance of international trade to the transnational enterprise. The data in Table 5-1 illustrate the contribution to total profits made possible by international trade by some American companies. Comparisons of transnational firms formed in other nations provide similar results.

While many manufacturing industries in the United States historically have not been highly dependent on foreign markets, the significance of these foreign markets is growing. Consider, for example, the company which has only 15% of its output in foreign trade; the loss of that 15% may dramatically affect profits which could drop by more than 15% because of the impact on efficiency and overhead allocation.

A worldwide dispersal of production and marketing capacity provides opportunity for increased profits and encourages operational flexibility. An integrated logistics system can capitalize on the advantages of production and marketing in specific localities.

Barriers to Free Trade

Restrictive Practices

In general, two types of policy measures are used to control the movements of goods across national borders. One is the tariff, which is a duty levied on imported and exported goods. Tariffs can take a variety of forms, ranging from specific duties to physical characteristics of traded goods.

Table 5-1. U.S. Transnationals in World Trade

Company	Percentage of Net Earnings	Percentage of Sales	Percentage of Assets
International Systems & Controls	112.0	63.1	63.1
Black & Decker	63.0	55.1	38.6
F.W. Woolworth	58.9	34.7	37.6
J.W. Thompson	58.7	43.8	33.8
I B M	55.5	50.0	35.8
Coca-Cola	55.0	44.0	37.0
NCR	49.9	49.0	46.8
Scholl	49.3	47.5	48.0
Johnson &Johnson	47.7	30.8	33.0
Standard Oil of California	47.6	59.1	43.3
American Standard	43.7	45.8	39.7
Gillette	43.0	51.2	60.6

Source: 1978 Annual Reports of these companies.

The other basic commercial policy measure is the quota, which restricts, on a quantitative basis, the amount of goods permitted to be traded internationally. Quotas can range up to a complete embargo on the trade of certain types of products, can be administered on a geographical basis where preference is given to certain countries' goods, and can be administered so that companies within an industry affected by a quota may apply for a specified percentage of the trade that is permitted during a given period.

Tariffs and Economic Theory

A *tariff* is a tax on foreign trade. It usually makes foreign commodities more expensive. Tariffs alter the allocation of resources, change both domestic and world prices, and redistribute income among countries and among the various productive factors within a country.[9] It is a schedule of duties or taxes levied on products as they cross national boundaries. The terms "tariff" and "duty" are often used interchangeably, although the latter refers to the money amount of tax collected by reason of a tariff.[10]

Tariffs may be applied on products as they are exported, when imported, or when in transit through a third country. Transit duties have virtually disappeared in recent years, although they were among the earliest forms of taxation. Import duties are used by virtually every nation; whereas, export duties would shift comparative advantages against the exporting nation and are therefore seldom used.

Tariff duties can be levied in one of three forms or in combinations. An *ad valorem duty* is stated as a percentage of the value of the product (e.g., 12% of the value). A *specific duty* is expressed as a fixed amount per some quantitative unit (e.g., $2.00 per barrel). The *compound duty* combines features of ad valorem and specific duties (e.g., 10% of value plus 50 cents per piece).[11]

Protectionists Arguments

There is a constant dialog between economists, trade unionists, and politicians as to the worthiness of tariffs. Protariff theorists, over time, have surfaced several justifications for tariffs. The nine most salient effects which deserve mention are (1) the protective effect, (2) the consumption effect, (3) the revenue effect, (4) the redistribution effect, (5) the terms-of-trade effect, (6) the competitive effect, (7) the income effect (8) the balance-of-trade effect, and (9) the infant industry effect.[12]

A tariff is prohibitive when the protective effect is sufficient to expand domestic production to the point where it will satisfy domestic demand without imports. If foreign competition is kept out by tariffs, domestic industry can become relatively sluggish with subsequent poor productivity. However, it is natural for domestic industry to attempt to persuade government to raise barriers and thus be covered by protective anticompetitive measures. Evolving industries often argue that they would gain a comparative advantage if they could get started. The argument is that confronted with foreign competition such infant industries may not be able to survive initial financial and developmental problems. Tariffs would give, theoretically, some preliminary relief, and taking a long-run view this does have economic merit.[13] Where an industry has developed under a protective tariff umbrella removal of the tariff or other protective measures would likely cause injury to the industry.

The consumption effect where there is a protected industry is almost always adverse. It serves to raise prices so that the consumer pays more for each item he consumes to purchase because the industry has been permitted to develop under noncompetitive conditions. The redistribution effect represents a higher price and higher profits for domestic producers. Marginal producers can exist on such a protective environment. In all probability where the purchase and import of technology is restricted, the local industry will be technologically weak and noncompetitive in markets where it is not protected.

Governments have historically used foreign trade as a basis for raising revenues. Developing countries are likely to be dependent on a portion of government revenues coming from tariff duties. It does follow through that if the tariffs are extremely restrictive and protective, imports will be excluded and no revenues will be derived. Countries have to determine which industries to protect and establish selective tariffs which can in some instances lead to exclusion and in other situations to revenue.[14]

Tariff Systems

As a rule most countries have two major lists in applying their tariffs: (1) a list of goods subject to custom duties, and (2) a list of goods permitted to enter the country free of duty. Classification in the dutiable list may be made according to (1) alphabetical arrangement, (2) magnitude of the duty, or (3) the attributes of the goods. The Brussels Tariff Nomenclature (BTN) which classifies products according to their physical substance has been adopted by some 100 countries that account for two-thirds of total world trade. Among the industrial countries, only the United States and Canada continue to use their own tariff classifications.[15]

Tariff schedules may have one, two, or three different duties for each dutiable article. A nation is said to have a "single column," a "double column," or a "triple column" tariff system, according to the number of different duties appearing on its schedules for each product. Duties established by national law are termed "autonomous," and those resulting from treaty arrangements with other nations are called "conventional."

Tariff Mitigation

To resolve the conflict between import protection and export promotion, tariff systems commonly mitigate the effects of duties through drawbacks, bonded warehouses, and free zones. A *drawback* is a refund of duties and internal taxes to an exporter who exports a product that was previously imported into the country. The United States currently refunds 99% of the original tariff duties as a drawback.

Dutiable imports may be brought into a customs territory and left in *bonded warehouses* free of duty. Imported goods may be stored, repacked, manipulated, or further processed in these areas according to the laws of the particular country under strict governmental supervision. The goods may be later reexported free of duty or withdrawn for domestic consumption upon payment of customs duties.

Isolated, enclosed areas with no resident populations offering extensive facilities for handling, storing, mixing, and manufacturing imported and domestic goods without customs intervention are termed *free zones*. These areas enlarge the benefits of a bonded warehouse by eliminating customs supervision and offering suitable manufacturing facilities. Free zones are also called free ports; however, true free ports are whole cities, or sections of a city, isolated for trade purposes.[16]

A related consideration is the "customs area," which is a geographical area within which goods may move freely without being subjected to customs duties. It generally, but not necessarily, coincides with national boundaries. At times a customs area includes more than one country and is therefore known as a "customs union." The significance of both of these arrangements is that goods move within the area without payment of tariffs or duties. The European Common Market is a customs union.

Supplementing tariffs as barriers to trade are a number of quantitative restrictions. Quantitative measures, like tariffs, are tools of national economic policy designed to regulate the international trade of a nation. They, however, are much more direct in that they impose absolute, definitive limits upon specific items, thus inhibiting market responses and foreign trade. Economists often believe tariffs to be less noxious than these measures.[17]

Import quotas are the most usual form of quantitative restriction. There are three distinct types of quotas in use: (1) unilateral quotas, (2) negotiated bilateral or multilateral quotas, and (3) tariff quotas. The *unilateral quota* is a fixed quota that is adopted without prior discussions or negotiation with another country. Imposed solely by the importing nation, it frequently creates friction, antagonism, and retaliation, which undermines its success.

Under a system of negotiated *bilateral or multilateral quotas*, the importing nation negotiates with various supplying nations before declaring the allotment of the quota by defined shares. These quotas tend to minimize pressure by domestic importers upon their own government and tend to increase cooperation by foreign exporters.

Tariff quotas provide for the importation of a specified quantity of a product which is permitted to be imported at a given rate of duty—or perhaps duty-free. This restriction, then, combines features of both quotas and tariffs.[18]

Export quotas may also be subjected to quantitative restrictions by government action. Quantitative export controls are designed to accomplish the following:

To prevent strategic goods from reaching unfriendly powers.

To assure all or the greater part of certain products in short supply for the home market.

To permit the control of surpluses on a national or international basis to achieve production and price stability.[19]

The objectives are more positively achieved by quotas than by tariffs. Like import quotas, export quotas may be unilateral when established without prior agreement or multilateral when imposed because of agreements.[20]

Other Nontariff Measures

Nontariff trade barriers are becoming increasingly prominent even though nations are working under the auspices of the General Agreement on Tariffs and Trade (GATT).

GATT is a relatively informal organization, having no permanent secretariat. Meetings are held every few years. Perhaps the best known of the GATT activities was the mid-1960 "Kennedy Round," which was the sixth GATT tariff conference. GATT attempts to lower barriers to trade and where there are barriers to encourage the application of such barriers on a nondiscriminatory basis. It also serves as an arbitrator when violations of trade agreements are alleged.

GATT calls upon member countries to levy indirect taxes on goods in the country of destination vis à vis country of production. This is the "destination principle."[21] One of the primary targets of GATT has been the practice of "dumping." Antidumping regulations are aimed at preventing the selling of products in one national market at lower prices than those received in other national markets (to include the seller's own domestic market). There are essentially three identified categories of dumping—sporadic, predatory, and persistent. *Sporadic dumping* occurs when producers dispose of unexpected surpluses abroad at lower prices than at home.

Predatory dumping occurs when producers use low prices to weaken or drive out competitors in a foreign market. After competition is eliminated, the victorious producer is able to charge high monopoly prices. Japan has been accused of using this tactic in the United States with their color televisions and automobiles.

Persistent dumping refers to the continued foreign sales of products at lower prices than at home. Such dumping may reflect the existence of a foreign demand more price-elastic than domestic demand. Japan apparently has used this tactic in attempting to sell steel at prices lower than U.S. competitors. Persistent dumping may also arise when producers price exports so as to cover only variable costs while covering fixed costs on the domestic market. In essence, the home market is exploited by paying higher prices and subsidizing exports which are lower priced than locally available.[22]

Customs Cooperation Council (CCN) was formed to promote cooperation among members on matters dealing with customs duties. The CCN strives to obtain a uniform interpretation and application of customs conventions adopted by member governments. It also plays a role of conciliator in the settlement of disputes arising out of the interpretation and application of such conventions.[23]

The Coordinating Committee (COCOM) is formed by 15 countries which use their national license requirements to control exports to Eastern Europe and Far Eastern Communist countries. The controlled items have been declared strategic and have been compiled into an embargo list. Items of high technology are usually included on this list. Requests for exceptions may be presented to COCOM for evaluation on a case-by-case basis. Member nations are Belgium, Canada, Denmark, France, West Germany, Greece, Italy, Japan, Luxembourg, the Netherlands, Norway, Portugal, Turkey, the United Kingdom, and the United States.[24]

Subsidies are sometimes paid by governments to domestic producers or exporters to stimulate expansion. Subsidies may be extended in the form of outright cash disbursements, tax exemptions, preferential exchange rates, governmental contracts with special privileges, or some similar favorable treatment. Since these subsidies result in a cost advantage, they are an indirect form of protection.

Goods thus protected by subsidies tend to nullify the protective aspects of import duties. To reinstate the intended level of protection, importing countries often impose a special surtax (or countervailing duty) in addition to the usual tariff duty. This effectively restores the original value structure.

Taxes in addition to the customs duties also are directed at imported goods. These are normally in the form of excise taxes and processing taxes, and are aimed at compensating for similar taxation of domestic goods.

Excise taxes are collectable upon the entry of the goods through customs. Processing taxes are payable upon the first domestic processing in the case of raw materials and semifinished goods. Road taxes are sometimes used to discriminate against imports. Border tax adjustments are indirectly applied to imports. This tactic has been used by the European Common Market against American goods.[25]

Procurement policies of national and local governments allow for discriminatory treatment of foreign products. The "Buy American" regulations of the United States give domestic producers up to a 50% price advantage over foreign suppliers on Department of Defense contracts and up to 12% on other government procurements. This sort of discrimination is matched in other nations, either by overt legislation or administrative practice.

Technical and health policies refer to a variety of measures with respect to safety, health, marking, labeling, packaging, specifications, and standards. Although imposed for health and safety reasons, these barriers may tend to discriminate by imposing greater hardships on importers than on domestic producers. In Canada, for example, canned goods may be imported only in containers approved by the government.[26]

The location, size, and structure of a market itself may deter international goods from entering a given marketplace. Just as large companies in a domestic market tend to ignore unimportant hamlets and villages, so companies involved in international commerce are likely to overlook small markets when vastly broader potential of larger ones remains untapped. Furthermore, a country may be excluded from international trading because size or remote location make it uneconomical or unprofitable as a market. In the final analysis, natural market barriers are probably the most important deterrents to international trade. If markets appear to offer promise of great profits, most of the governmental, exchange, and psychological barriers can be surmounted by entreprenural businessmen.[27]

There are numerous other nontariff barriers to trade—far too many to mention in this brief space. However, as a last issue, the "boycott" has become much too prevalent to omit. A government boycott is an absolute restriction against the purchase and inportation of certain goods from other countries. A public boycott can be either formal or informal and may be government sponsored or sponsored by a given industry. It's not unusual for the citizens of a country to boycott goods of other countries at the urging of their government or civic groups.

A particularly insidious type of boycott has developed recently; the economic boycott used to achieve political ends. In 1978 goods of some countries were subject to boycott because of the nations' attitudes toward black rights. Arab countries boycott Israel and Israel in return boycotts them over the Palestine question. Cuba is boycotted by Brazil and South Korea because it supports revolutionary activities there. South Africa trades openly with many of the countries boycotting it and covertly with others.

Open markets are needed if world resources are to be developed and utilized in the most beneficial manner. It is true that there are extreme circumstances when market protection may be needed and may be beneficial to national defense or the encouragement of infant industries in developing nations. The temptation, however, is always toward excessive market protection or, more correctly, excessive producer protection, because the customer seldom is the beneficiary.

Assessment of World Trade Policy

Overview

The actual issue of free trade versus protection has been debated over several centuries. The pure theory of international trade demonstrates that for the world as a whole, free trade leads to a higher level of output and income than no trade. Free trade also enables each nation to obtain a higher level of production and consumption than can be obtained in isolation. Under perfect competition, free trade achieves a worldwide allocation of resources that meets the requirements of Pareto optimality: It is virtually impossible to make any nation better off (through reallocation) without making some other nation worse off.[28] Therefore, most contemporary economists are reluctant to unequivocally support the free trade arguments. In pure economic terms, the Pareto optimality theory says that free trade equalizes the marginal rate of substitution in production and the marginal rate of substitution in consumption for each product and for each nation. Simple logic implies that (1) real-world markets tend to depart frequently from conditions of pure competition, and (2) that there is not necessarily any parallel between higher income and higher welfare at *both* national and international levels.

To state that the "allocative efficiency of free trade may not be optimal" is a poor argument for protection. It is more an argument of competitive markets through policies such as the U.S. antitrust laws. It appears that protection is an ineffectual policy tool to correct the defects and weaknesses of imperfect competition as compared to the more direct tools. There is little assurance that the trade restrictions actually imposed by a government will add to economic efficiency. From a pragmatic point of view, it appears that increases in restrictions will lower economic efficiency.

Economic Welfare

The second issue of the Pareto optimality hypothesis is that of economic welfare. Even with optimality in the allocation of national and world resources, it would not unconditionally follow that free trade would also optimize national and world welfare. The primary reason is that competitive markets determine not only the prices of goods but also factor incomes (prices). By the process of adjusting relative prices, free trade is also altering income distribution among individuals and groups within and among nations.[29]

It follows, therefore, that protection is normally an inappropriate policy with which to attempt higher levels of welfare for a group or nation. This has been demonstrated in the United States when the government attempted to redistribute income through some agricultural programs. The effect was to promote agricultural self-sufficiency. It probably would have been more desireable to directly subsidize farm incomes from general tax coffers and leave the markets free to allocate agricultural production both nationally and internationally.[30]

For the most part the welfare of a nation is reduced by import protection. However, viewed more closely, it becomes readily apparent that through trade barriers, specific factors of production associated with a protected industry gain in increased welfare. In lobbying for trade protection, industry producers and labor unions are, in effect, attempting to improve their own well-being. Their gain will be at the expense of another industry or group.

It is apparent that those groups favoring protection would gain little public support if they argued in terms of their own private gain. They, therefore, couch their arguments in terms of some form of national interest or blessing. They are usually able to rally many followers behind a national banner.

For the most part, arguments against free trade attempt to show that

Advantages are outweighed by disadvantages.

National economies are exposed to outside economic forces.

Price systems and pure competition, as underlying assumptions, are lacking in the real world.[31]

The apparent reason for the success of the protectionists in shaping national and international trade policies lies in their ability to convince policy makers that their private interests coincide with the national interest.

Trade Policies of Developed Nations

Trend Toward Free Trade

Free trade, as has been discussed in preceding sections of this chapter, will always be, to some extent, threatened by various governmental and market protective barriers. There have been counterpressures exerted as a consequence of dwindling natural resources, increasing technological interdependence, intensified specialization, and a trend toward cultural and market compatibilities in developed nations.

Since World War II there has been a trend in many industrialized nations to work toward cooperative arrangements for freer trade.[32] A prime example to support the aforementioned is the European Common Market.

The United States

After World War II the prevalent U.S. attitude was one of conciliation. As a result, several international measures were undertaken to liberalize trade and payments between nations. Primarily because of American leadership, plans were initiated for the creation of a multinational system of world trade. The culmination of the planning was manifested in the conceptualization of the International Monetary Fund (IMF), the International Bank for Reconstruction and Development (The World Bank), and the International Trade Organization (IRD).[33]

The IMF and the World Bank became realities and materially assisted in the postwar recovery of Allied and Axis nations. Parenthetically, they are both in full operation today.[34]

The third body, the International Trade Organization, was never accepted by the world's leading trading nations. Its function had been envisioned as the liberalization of trade. Pending the anticipated ratification of the organization's charter, a provisional agreement, the General Agreement on Tariffs and Trade (GATT—previously mentioned), was created in 1948. Therefore, ITD has never existed and as a result the "provisional" nature of GATT has been infused with rather permanent life.[35] The primary activities of GATT have been (1) tariff bargaining, (2) quantitative restrictions, and (3) settlement of free trade disputes.

During the years immediately after World War II, and into the early 1960s, U.S. foreign trade policy essentially consisted of adhering to the spirit and philosophy of making the objectives of GATT workable. During this period the United States tended to widen and reinforce the "technology gap" created during World War II.

In 1962, the United States passed the Trade Expansion Act in direct response to the progressive establishment of a customs union by the European Economic Community (now called the European Community). The provisions of this Act granted the President broad authority to reduce or eliminate U.S. import duties in return for similar concessions from the EEC and third countries. The key importance of EEC markets to the United States and the threat that these markets would become limited by protectionist policies convinced John F. Kennedy's administration that the United States must make a strong effort to bargain down common market trade barriers and prevent, or mitigate, the trade diversion that menaced the export interests of countries outside the EEC. By this point, U.S. balance of payments were in a continuing deficit posture and this factor lent urgency to this decision.

Therefore, in May 1963, the ministers of the GATT, at the urging of the United States, met in Geneva in what is called the "Kennedy Round." The primary issues addressed were tariff disparities between the United States and the EEC, various agricultural issues, and for the first time nontariff trade barriers.

Only a few months after the Kennedy Round (1967), several bills were introduced in the U.S. Congress calling for quota protection on imports of textiles, shoes, watches, steel, dairy products, and many other products. By 1970, protectionists were pressing Congress to introduce scores of issues aimed at providing some varying amount of protection to their particular area of interest. They had been increasingly encouraged by a sympathetic Congress and various campaign-pledges of Presidents Johnson and Nixon.

These moves by the protectionists came to fruition with the Trade Act of 1974. The Act contains a mixture of both liberal and restrictive provisions. The Act provided the President with certain negotiating authorities necessary for participation in the GATT Tokyo Round. Additionally, the Act contained measures intended to pressure other countries to be more generous in their concessions to the United States during the Tokyo Round; it introduced the notion of reciprocal nondiscriminatory treatment, made it easier for a domestic industry to be "protected" against imports, and granted the President more authority to retaliate against "unfair trade practices."[36]

The Tokyo Round (the seventh round of talks since 1947) officially opened in Tokyo in September 1973, but very little was accomplished until the passage of the Trade Act of 1974 (signed into law in January 1975). To encourage participation by non-GATT nations, a Trade Negotiating Committee (TNC) was established to investigate tariffs, agricultural cooperation, nontariff barriers, safeguards, tropical products, and industrial sectors (such as metals, electronics, etc.). The Tokyo Round has been noted as making a start toward dealing with the almost limitless expense of nontariff trade barriers by adopting six new rules or "codes." The participating nations agreed to set up codes and agreements strengthening the authority of the Geneva-based GATT to deal in trade violations.[37] Agreement was reached to cut world tariffs an average of 33% on some 5,700 items over an eight-year period. The significance of the Tokyo Round was that the principal trading nations were negotiating to liberalize trade at a time of economic turbulence and turmoil.

An important element of post-World War II American trade policy has been the state of East–West tensions. Shortly after the end of the war, the United States began to view its trade relations with the Soviet Union and other communist nations as a political question to be handled separately from commercial policies toward noncommunist nations.

In 1949, the Export Control Act was passed, placing strategic controls on American exports to communist countries. Approximately 1,300 product categories (and their associated technology) were identified and categorized. Export of these items was prohibited without prior approval from the U.S. Department of Commerce in the form of validated licenses. The Act, however, has subsequently haunted U.S. businessmen. In the 1960s most of the items and associated technology became available to communist buyers from other developed nations. Often allied nations have acted as brokers or intermediaries in the transfer of U.S. products and technology to communist bloc countries.

In 1969, the Export Administration Act enabled the Department of Commerce to remove some 2,000 individual items from the export control list, thus bringing the United States into closer agreement with the export control lists of Western European countries and Japan.[38] Additionally, the Department could approve for export any listed item that was freely available from other Western nations.

Throughout the early 1970s more U.S. export controls were liberalized as part of a general softening in trade relations between the United States and the communist countries. However, as the 1974 Trade Act made the granting of "most favored nation treatment" to communist nations contingent on their removal of emigration restrictions, trade relations once more deteriorated.

The decade of the 1980s will likely see a changing of the American attitude toward world trade. International trade has become increasingly important for the United States. During the 1970s, exports grew from 4.3% of the gross national product in 1970 to 8% in 1980.[39] Exports now account for 20% of domestic goods production, one out of every seven American manufacturing jobs and $1 out of every $3 earned by American corporations.

Thus, while the United States will be seeking more markets for its agricultural, high-technology, and service industries, it likely will be establishing greater barriers against automobile, steel, and apparel imports. Domestic policy issues will be viewed in international terms. "Successful management of the U.S. economy will require successful management of the global economy," according to U.S. government officials.[40]

Western European Community

Rather than assessing each of the Western European nations individually, it is more reasonable to discuss trade policy as it relates to Western European countries belonging to the European Common Market.

The United States played a dominant role in initiating European unity with the Brittan-Woods Conference and the Marshall Plan. The Marshall Plan led to the development of the Organization for European Economic Cooperation (OEEC) which administered the $12.5 billion channeled by the United States for European recovery.

In 1951, the European coal and steel community was created, which was the most direct forerunner of the Common Market. In 1957, the Treaty of Rome was drafted and subsequently ratified by France, West Germany, Italy, Belgium, the Netherlands, and Luxembourg, thus creating the European Economic Community (Common Market). In 1970, Great Britain, Ireland and Denmark joined the community, with Turkey and Greece being granted associate membership in 1978. Greece was admitted as a full-fledged member in January 1981. Spain and Portugal early in the 1980s were negotiating for membership.

The founders of the EEC intended it to be a truly common market; so much so that economic policy was supplemented by concurrent political policy. As a point in fact, the change in name of the group to European Community in 1976 illustrates the power, political intentions, and dynamics of this customs union.

The main feature of the EC is the creation of a customs union for both industrial and agricultural goods, involving the abolition of all restrictions on trade among member countries and the creation of a common external tariff. A second objective is a full economic union with free movement of persons, services, and capital, and progressive harmonization of social, fiscal, and monetary policies. The probable ultimate objective is a political union of all member nations.

Although trade in industrial products within the EC is no longer obstructed by tariffs and quotas, it is not yet as free as trade within a single country. Many nontariff trade barriers still trouble intraunion trade traffic, such as differences in customs classifications, varying taxation systems, border restrictions, and state monopolies. In the 1960s the EEC introduced a common agricultural policy that eliminated restrictions on mutual trade and established single minimum selling prices (intervention prices) and base prices (target prices) throughout the community. In the 1970s the common agricultural policy has been troubled by food surpluses, fluctuating exchange rates, and a deterioration of farm income. High agricultural support prices encouraged overproduction in butter, sugar, wine, beef, grains, and other products. It appears that the common agricultural policy has encouraged inefficient farm production and has strained relations with other nations, as the EC has not only cut down on farm imports through variable levies and occasional embargoes, but also subsidized the export of food surpluses.

Community workers and their dependents can move freely among the member countries responding to employment opportunities. They receive the same rights and social security benefits as do nationals, all the while retaining any accrued rights and benefits earned in any other member nation. Statutes have been introduced before the EC Council which would eliminate legal obstacles that currently discourage cross-national mergers, branches, and subsidiaries.

The EC has moved in the direction of the United States, by accepting antitrust provisions. The EC attempts to distinguish between "good" and "harmful" cartels and monopolies. In general, business agreements and concentrations that help improve the production or distribution of goods or promote technical and economic progress are legal in the community provided that they do not eliminate competition in a "substantial" part of the market.

The EC has taken positive steps to reduce tax frontiers among member states, by requiring all to use a value-added system. The value-added tax (VAT) is added at each stage by the seller. Therefore, border tax adjustments reflect accurately the turnover taxes accrued at that point by the product.

The static effects of the European Community as a customs union involves both free trade among its member nations (liberalization) and, at the same time, restrictions on imports from nonmember or third countries (protection). The liberalization tends to eliminate internal tariffs and other barriers, thus stimulating new trade among members without displacing third-country imports. However, the protection aspect occurs in that member nations now purchase from each other what they formerly purchased from third countries.

Because of its economic size and dynamism, the external policies of the EC have a pervasive influence on the composition, direction, and volume of international trade and investment. The basic policy of the EC toward third nations is expressed by the common external tariff and the variable import levies on agricultural products. The discrimination implicit in the common tariff and variable levies is a cause of concern to all third countries. This concern was readily apparent during the bargaining sessions of the Kennedy and Tokyo Rounds.

Ironically, the United States has consistently supported the European Community in its efforts to develop economic and political unity in Western Europe. Although the EC remains the primary American export market, the United States has been aggravated by the trade diversion efforts of the common agricultural program and the EC's preferential agreements to Mediterranean nations.[41]

The decade of the 1980s has dawned with a gloomy outlook for the European Community. Economic growth in 1980 in the nine EC nations, which account for some 80% of Europe's industrial capacity, averaged 1.3%.[42] The commission is painting a bleak picture for the early years of the decade of the 1980s. Economic growth slowed further to 0.6% for 1981, and unemployment reached a level of 7% (nearly eight million people). The applications of Spain and Portugal for EC membership may well be delayed for several years due to economic conditions. France, in particular, has opposed the entry of Spain and Portugal. Thus, the 1980s are likely to lead to increased protectionism as the trade policies of the European Community are tightened in favor of member nations. Indeed, some members are considering protecting and subsidizing ailing industries to save jobs.

European Free Trade Association (EFTA)

The European Free Trade Association was a grouping of nations who in 1960, for a variety of reasons, chose not to join the European Community but desired economic integration. The original group consisted of Austria, Denmark, Norway, Portugal, Sweden, Switzerland, and the United Kingdom. The member nations agreed to remove internal tariffs on nonagricultural products in several steps and achieved this goal ahead of schedule by 1966. EFTA was later to accept Finland and Iceland.

The group did not have the political desires of the European Community. As a free trade area, there was no provision for a common external tariff. Consequently, rules as to origin and location of production were adopted to ensure that only goods that originated in the area benefited from the tariff reductions.

When Great Britain joined the Common Market, EFTA essentially ended as a significant trade grouping. However, those nations which have not joined the EC do enjoy a free trade area treatment from the community.

Council of Mutual Economic Cooperation (COMECON)

Formed in 1949, The Council of Mutual Economic Cooperation coordinates trade and other forms of economic relations among the centrally planned economies of Eastern Europe. COMECON consists of Bulgaria, Czechoslovakia, East Germany, Hungary, Poland, Romania, and the U.S.S.R. The Council has promoted some international product specialization. However, the centrally planned countries secure more of their needs from domestic production than do most capitalist nations. A large share of the availabilities for export or needs for import is determined after decisions have been made on the composition and volume of domestic output. Consequently, foreign trade has often been a means of providing for unplanned shortages or disposing of unplanned surpluses.

Trade decisions are normally made by the various state trading organizations which have full responsibility for buying and selling a particular product. The state trading companies are separate from those state enterprises which produce or consume the product. Because of this system of control, and the implicit absence of any necessary link between the cost and price of a product, it has been difficult to apply the trading rules of the market-oriented GATT to bilateral agreements between COMECON nations and nonmembers.

In sharp contrast to their political influence and military power, the COMECON nations have made but modest contributions to world trade. Their emphasis on self-sufficiency, bilateral trade balancing, and preference for intrabloc trading have all contributed to reducing trade volume with the noncommunist world. Foreign import restrictions, especially anticommunist discrimination, lack of marketing know-how, and poor product quality have placed involuntary constraints on their ability to export to the West. Without exports, importation from the West has been impeded by lack of foreign exchange.

The key to any increased East–West trading lies in the hands of the Soviets. The United States uses its political influence to affect Western trade with COMECON. The existing political climate often is a determinal factor in trade between the United States, Western European countries, and the communist bloc countries.

The U.S.S.R. commenced a new five-year plan in 1981, the 11th of the Bolshevik era. It is possible that the Soviets will be able to improve somewhat on poor agricultural and industrial performance in 1979 and 1980. However, most Westerners tend to believe that the Soviet Union will be facing some bleak times until 1985.

Japan

Japan has historically been a "closed system." The Japanese distribution system for goods, for example, stems from the early 17th century, when cottage industries and a burgeoning urban population spawned a merchant class. Although postwar Japan has become one of the world's leading industrial nations, the nation has essentially remained closed or semiclosed to foreigners.

Traditionally, there are close ties between Japanese peoples, families, and companies. These ties have resulted in formal and informal barriers that have effectively discouraged imports into Japan.

In recent years, as Japan has increased its output into foreign markets, other nations have become increasingly concerned about the protectionist attitude of the Japanese government. The United States and other nations have pressured the Japanese to reduce their restrictions of the entry of foreign goods and investments. The United States in particular has mentioned the possibility of retaliation through increased restrictions on Japanese business access to American markets. A hostile U.S. Congress could well impose import restrictions on Japanese automobiles or other products, and it is conceivable that the

EC would follow suit. Such a trade war is possible in the 1980s but unlikely. The Japanese government has indicated a willingness to open its doors to foreign goods and investments. It is also likely that world pressures will reduce the extent to which the government provides subsidies to national industries.

Trade Policies of Developing Nations

Protectionist Attitudes

Usually the export problems of the developing countries are commonly aggravated by their own trade and general economic policies. The dominant goal of government policy makers appears to be economic development. Economic development is usually construed to mean industrialization rather than self-sustaining economic growth. The policy tools chosen by many developing countries to advance their economic development have been economic controls, trade protection, and inflation. The adoption of such policies means essentially rejecting free markets, international specialization, and monetary stability. The disregard for the concept of comparative advantage and the neglect of internal and external balance have created serious problems which prevent or impede the attainment of their development goals.[43]

A Compromised Position

Developing countries complain that they are unable to follow the examples of earlier industrial leaders, such as West Germany, France, Japan, because the external conditions they face are different. They contend that the terms of trade run against them, and that the fault lies in conditions in the developed nations. The lack of progress of trade in the developing nations in so distressing to them that they claim to suffer from neoimperialism or neocolonialism. The point begs some analysis.

For trade under unequal bargaining conditions to be regarded as exploitation or not depends upon one's perception of alternatives. If the alternative to international trade is concerted push toward improving the productive structure of the developing nation and to limit its dependence upon imports, then trade is exploitative; and, waiting until development is complete is unexploitative. However, if the alternatives lie between trade and no trade and no development, with the developing nations producing raw materials and agricultural goods, then no trade is exploitative and trade is unexploitative. This situation is similar to one where a rich man employs a poor person to work for minimum wages—in a sense it is exploitative; but not to hire in the first place, with an alternative of unemployment is also exploitative.[44]

To illustrate the use of trade policies to further national goals consider that in some parts of the world, tariffs have been used to attract foreign investors. At times the potential size of a market does not warrant the construction of a plant. Governments committed to development are prepared to offer incentives to attract investments by transnational firms, including tax concessions, subsidized factories, and a guaranteed domestic market by introducing tariffs or quotas. Later, these same enterprises may be offered incentives to export their products.

Trade Policy and the Transnational Firm

Trade policies of developing nations should also be examined from the perspective of their view of the transnational firm. Conflict between the transnational enterprise and the host government may derive from four sources: from the fact that it is a *private* enterprise and thus may clash with social and national goods; that it is *large* and hence possesses market and bargaining power which may be used against the interest of the host country; that it is foreign, and hence may be serving the national interests of a foreign nation; and that it is usually "*Western*" and thus may transfer inappropriate know-how, technology or management practices, or products designed with characteristics not needed in less-developed countries.[45]

It naturally is not possible to analyze all developing nations. As a consequence, only one nation, The People's Republic of China, will be examined, as well as several of the trade cartels.

The People's Republic of China (PRC)

Trade between China and the rest of the developed world generally ceased in 1950. However, in 1971 trade opportunities for the West were once again opened. In the intervening years most trade was with other communist nations.

Traditionally the Chinese have viewed exports as a means of payment for necessary imports and the PRC has striven for a balance between exports and imports. During the early 1950s, however, the PRC developed an unfavorable balance of trade as it exported minerals, agricultural products, and consumer goods for Russian raw materials and machinery.

Since 1972, the United States and the PRC have been engaged in trade. China tends to be restrictive in the same sense as is any communist nation. Imports must be cleared and approved by the appropriate Foreign Trade Corporation—an agency of the Ministry of Foreign Trade. Additionally, the bureaucracy of the PRC is causing increasing Western concern. Cultural, language, and idealogical differences frequently are impediments to trade.

Despite the inherent difficulties indicated in the previous paragraph there are bright prospects for increased trade between China, the United States, Japan, and Western European countries. There has been a discernible shift in policy in China away from economic and technological isolationism. China has tradable raw materials. The United States, Japan, and Western European countries have high-technology products which are desirable to China. Based on the type of international trade in the early 1980s it is possible to surmise that China, as Japan did in the past, sees the import of high technology as a reasonably quick and efficient method to afford the transition to a technologically advanced society.

Cartels

A cartel is a grouping or association of commodity producers which attempt to control the market for that commodity through the use of pressures such as price-fixing, allocation of markets, restriction of supplies, or other such monopolistic practices. Cartels have been formed at one time or another in the industries of mining, metals, chemicals, ceramics, electronics, textiles, insurance, and traffic.[46]

Perhaps the most visible of the cartels is the Organization of Petroleum Exporting Countries (OPEC). Formed in 1960 to exert more control over the international oil companies operating in the producing countries, it began to stretch its muscles in 1973–1974 with the infamous oil embargo.[47] The objectives of the organization are to raise the taxes and royalties earned by member nations and to gain more control over production and exploration.[48]

Since OPEC produces approximately 85% of the world trade in oil, they have been in a position to control supply and prices in the short run. The crisis of 1973 was a devastating combination of politics and economics when OPEC embargoed oil exports to the United States and the Netherlands, cut-back worldwide production, and quadrupled oil prices, forcing the world's economies into an unprecedented energy crisis. The OPEC price hikes have continued into the 1980s and have constrained economic growth in dependent oil importing nations. It has caused a decline in real disposable income and has induced cuts in real consumption and investment. Also, exorbitant prices have been a direct cause of inflation and have reduced the energy intensity and productivity of industry. For the three years 1974 to 1976, the OPEC-induced loss in production has amounted to $550 billion.[49]

OPEC's power has been applauded by a number of Third World nations as a major step to rectify the perceived imbalance of power and wealth between the "have and have-not" nations. The success of OPEC naturally has stimulated interests of other raw material producers, and associations have been proposed or formed for coffee, iron ore, bauxite, and copper, but have not achieved the success of the oil cartel.

Regional Trading Agreements

In recent years there has been a tendency for numerous developing countries to form trading groups. The major groups, date of establishment, and member countries are

1. Latin American Free Trade Association (LAFTA), 1960: Argentina, Brazil, Chile, Mexico, Paraguay, Peru, Uruguay, Colombia, Ecuador, Venezuela, and Bolivia
2. Central American Common Market (CACM), 1960: Costa Rica, El Salvador, Guatemala, Honduras, and Nicaragua.
3. Central African Customs and Economic Union (UDEAC), 1964: Cameroon, Central Africa Republic, Zaire, and Gabon.

4. Arab Common Market (ACM), 1964: Egypt, Iraq, Jordan, and the Syrian Arab Republic.
5. Regional Cooperation for Development (RCD), 1964: Iran, Pakistan, and Turkey.
6. East African Community (EAC), 1967: Kenya, Uganda, and the United Republic of Tanzania.
7. Caribbean Free Trade Association (CARIFTA), 1968: Barbados, Guyana, Jamaica, Trinidad and Tobago, Antigua, Dominica, Grenada, Montserrat, St. Kitts-Nevis-Anguilla, St. Lucia, and St. Vincent.
8. East Caribbean Common Market (a subgroup of CARIFTA), 1968: Antigua, Dominica, Grenada, Montserrat, St. Kitts-Nevis-Anguilla, St. Lucia, and St. Vincent.
9. Andean Group, formed in 1969 as a subgroup of LAFTA: Bolivia, Chile, Colombia, Ecuador, Peru, and Venezuela.
10. West African Economic Community (CEAC), 1972: Benim, Ivory Coast, Mali, Mauritania, Niger, Senegal, and Upper Volta.[50]

It is apparent that these nations hope that an enlarged market and greater internal competition will yield benefits from economies of scale in production and the more efficient use of resources. Also, it is their hope that these benefits will exceed any costs resulting from trade diversion, and that the net gains will be distributed equitably among members.[51]

The United Nations Conference on Trade and Development (UNCTAD)

While the United Nations naturally was established to serve the needs of all nations, most of its recent activities, as relates to international trade, have been directed to achieving an international redistribution of income. In 1964, The United Nations Conference on Trade and Development was convened and attended by representatives of 119 nations.

UNCTAD was an outgrowth of the desires of the developing nations for accelerated growth and económic modernization. The previous free trade ideology which assumed a static economic structure did not fit the needs and aspirations of the developing countries.

The developing nations adopted protectionist policies to encourage infant industries. They were convinced that they must diversify into manufacturing from agriculture and raw material extraction, because of expanding world demand for finished goods.

In each of the UNCTAD conferences, the developing countries have made major demands on the developed nations. They have demanded, for example, unilateral tariff reductions on imports of manufactured goods from the developing nations. They have also pressured the International Monetary Fund into making credits available to countries that suffer a fall in export earnings because of a decline in export prices.

Under prevailing economic arrangements, the developing countries feel that they have not participated equitably in world prosperity during periods of economic expansion and have supported a disproportionate share of the burdens of recessions. Consequently, they are now demanding an "integrated" program of commodity agreements, including a common fund for buffer stock financing, and a series of proposals for facilitating the transfer of technology to the developing nations.[52]

Summary

There is little doubt that international trade involves a great deal of mutuality. However, it is a natural inclination for nations and people to develop a protectionist attitude as jobs, economic security, and national well-being are threatened. Over the years, therefore, most nations have resorted to tariffs or nontariff trade barriers to protect their industries and profits.

Developing and developed nations tend to be at odds as to the proper trade policy measures to employ. Developed nations usually are less protectionist in their overall approach to world trade. Developing nations feel exposed and think that the developed nations have exploited them and thus tend to adopt protectionist policies.

Numerous trading arrangements, groups, and cartels have been formed over the years. These all tend to have similar objectives—protection of their members at the expense of nonmembers.

For the transnational enterprise the globe consists of "three worlds" each with its own objectives and strategies. The industrialized world frequently favors free trade and specialization and is not overly concerned about changing the basic structure of the world economy. The developing nations tend not to favor free trade and would use trade arrangements to achieve structural economic changes in their own and all other economies. The centrally planned world would like to expand greatly its trading relations with the other two "worlds" but with a minimum of change in internal economic structure.

Endnotes Chapter Five

1. W.W. Rostow, *The Stages of Economic Growth: A Non-Communist Manifesto*, Cambridge, MA: Cambridge University Press, 1960.
2. L.T. Wells, Jr. (ed.) *The Product Life Cycle and International Trade*, Boston: Graduate School of Business Administration, Harvard University, 1972. Our explanation is somewhat similar to his. However, we stress the importance of research, development, and the interface with marketing. In addition, see R.E. Caves and R.W. Jones, *World Trade and Payments: An Introduction*, Boston: Little, Brown & Co., 1973, pp. 218–225.
3. David Ricardo, *The Principles of Political Economy and Taxation*, New York: Penguin, 1971, Chapter 7.
4. Richard E. Vaces and Ronald W. Jones, *World Trade and Payments: An Introduction*, Boston: Little, Brown & Company, 1973, Chapter 7.
5. Franklin R. Root, *International Trade and Investment*, 4th edition, Cincinnati: South-Western Publishing Co., 1978, p. 90.

6. David S.R. Leighton, "The Internationalization of American Business—The Third Industrial Revolution," *Journal of Marketing*, July 1970, pp. 5–6.
7. Charles P. Kindleberger, *American Business Abroad: Six Lectures on Direct Investment*, New Haven and London: Yale University Press, 1969, p. 13.
8. A sharp exception to this statement is possible based upon the development of microelectronics and robotry. See Colin Norman, "The New Industrial Revolution," *The Futurist*, February 1981, pp. 30–42.
9. Caves and Jones, *op. cit.*, p. 229.
10. R.D. Hayes, C.M. Korth, and M. Roudiani, *International Business: An Introduction to the World of the Multinational Firm*, Englewood Cliffs, NJ: Prentice-Hall, Inc., 1972, p. 66.
11. *Ibid.*, p. 66.
12. A.M. Freeman, *International Trade: An Introduction to Method and Theory*, New York: Harper & Row, 1971, pp. 135–136.
13. See M. Chacholiades, *International Trade Theory and Policy*, New York: McGraw-Hill Book Co., 1978, pp. 525–539, for a complete discussion of the effects of this argument.
14. Freeman, *op. cit.*, pp. 107–120; and, P.G. Samuelson, *Economics*, 10th edition, New York: McGraw-Hill Book Co., 1976, pp. 692–703.
15. P.H. Combs, *Handbook of International Purchasing*, Boston: Cahners Books, 1971, pp. 85–86.
16. See *Exporting to the United States*, United States Customs Service, Department of Treasury, September 1977.
17. Caves and Jones, *op. cit.*, p. 286.
18. Root, *op. cit.*, pp. 134–135.
19. The United States has an active export control program. The objectives are specified in the *Overview of the Export Administration Program*, Bureau of Trade Regulation, U.S. Department of Commerce, October 1979. In addition to satisfying U.S. internal requirements, America cooperates in an international security export control system, maintaining controls over exports to communist nations. The administration of the overall U.S. export control system is based upon licensing requirements. Licenses (approval) are required for every good to be exported. The U.S. Department of Commerce cooperates willingly in communicating this program; contact the nearest U.S. Department of Commerce, Industry and Trade Administration, Bureau of Trade Regulation, Office of Export Administration, Washington, DC 20230.
20. Root, *op. cit.*, pp. 135–136.
21. A.V. Phatak, *Managing Multinational Corporations*, New York: Praeger Publishers, 1974, p. 96.
22. Root, *op. cit.*, pp. 139–140.
23. Phatak, *op. cit.*, p. 51.
24. *Overview of the Export Administration Program*, *op. cit.*, p. 8.
25. Root, *op. cit.*, pp. 140–141.
26. *Ibid.*, p. 142.
27. International bodies that help foster international trade and reduce the effects of barriers are numerous. In addition to GATT, CCN, and COCOM, there is the Organization for Economic Cooperation and Development (OECD), United Nations Regional Economic Commissions, Inter-American Economic and Social Council (IA-ECOSOC), Economic Commission for Asia and the Far East (ECAFE), and other organizations concerned with specific commodity problems, such as the International Coffee Organization and the International Coffee Advisory Committee. Objectives and policies of many of these organizations will be discussed elsewhere in this text. Specific information concerning their activities may be obtained from either the United Nations, New York City, or from The United States Council of the International Chamber of Commerce, 103 Park Avenue, New York, NY 10017.

28. Root, *op. cit.*, p. 146.
29. *Ibid.*
30. *Ibid.*, p. 47.
31. *Ibid.*, p. 149.
32. P.R. Cateora and J.M. Hess, *International Marketing* 4th edition, Homewood, IL: Richard D. Irwin, 1979, p. 69.
33. In 1944 representatives of the Allied Nations met at Brittan Woods, New Hampshire in order to plan and control the international financial and trading relations of the post-World War II world. The planning was broken into three major areas: monetary problems, financing problems, and trade problems.
34. See R.D. Hayes, C.M. Korth, and M. Roudiani, *International Business: An Introduction to the World of the Multinational Firm*, Englewood Cliffs, NJ: Prentice-Hall, 1972, Chapters 4 and 5, where the objectives, accomplishments, and shortfalls of these agencies are outlined.
35. For a comprehensive discussion as to the aims and direction of GATT see Root, *op. cit.*, Chapter 7.
36. Public Law 93-618.
37. Clyde H. Farnsworth, "Toughening Attitudes on World Trade," *The New York Times*, February 8, 1981, section 12, p. 11. For more information on the Tokyo Round contact the Office of the United States Trade Representative, Washington, DC. See also Peter Nulty, "Why the 'Tokyo Round' was a U.S. Victory," *Fortune*, 99 (10), May 21, 1979; and "Tokyo Round Concessions Can Significantly Improve World Tariff Structure," *Business America*, 2 (13), June 18, 1979.
38. The Coordinating Committee (COCOM) consisting of the NATO nations and Japan was formed to multilaterally determine export controls to Eastern European Communist nations. The COCOM list has been substantially smaller than the U.S. list.
39. Source is U.S. Department of Commerce statistics.
40. Farnsworth, *op. cit.*, p. 11.
41. Root, *op. cit.*, p. 218.
42. Statistics made available by the Executive Commission; European Community, Brussels, Belgium.
43. Root, *op. cit.*, p. 426.
44. C.P. Kindleberger, International Economics, 5th edition, Homewood: IL: Richard D. Irwin, 1973, pp. 84–85.
45. P. Streeten, "Costs and Benefits of Multinational Enterprises in Less-Developed Countries," in *The Multinational Enterprise*, ed., J.H. Dunning, New York: Praeger Publishers, 1971, p. 251.
46. R. Kahler and R.L. Kramer, *International Marketing*, 4th edition, Cincinnati: South-Western Publishing Co., 1977, p. 390.
47. "The Birth of OPEC, and How It Grew," *Business Week*, January 13, 1975, pp. 78–79.
48. "OPEC: The Economics of the Oil Cartel," *Business Week*, January 13, 1975, p. 77.
49. "How OPEC's High Prices Strangle World Growth," *Business Week*, December 20, 1976, p. 45.
50. Adopted from R.E. Baldwin and D.A. Key, "International Trade and International Relations," in *World Politics and International Economics*, ed., C.R. Bergstem and L.B. Krause, Washington, DC: The Brookings Institute, 1975, pp. 107–108.
51. S.H. Roback, K. Simmonds, and J. Zwick, *International Business and Multinational Enterprises*, Homewood, IL: Richard D. Irwin, 1977, pp. 137–138.
52. *Ibid.*, p. 131.

SECTION III:

Technology—Micro and Macro Factors

CHAPTER SIX

Technological Forecasting, Technology Assessment, and Environmental Impact

The Dynamic Technological Environment

Awareness of Change

There are very few societies in the world that have not been or are not now in the process of being affected by change. Introducing change in societies where there are centuries of cultural heritage is extremely difficult. Technology can impinge on tradition and subsequently alter the societal structure. Subservient populations, dominated by political or religious institutions, have in the past usually resisted changes where the existing social order could be disturbed. Often in such cases the societies' ability to grow or perhaps even survive has been jeopardized.

Cultural, technological, and political isolationism can prove to be economically disastrous. The paradox is that economic crises can lead to political change which, in turn, could affect established cultural patterns. There has been a growing awareness of the dynamics of technological change. The impact of technology has for some nations led to minor cultural modifications and in other nations there has been a significant alteration of traditional cultural practices.

China is a prime example of a nation which has taken drastic actions to affect social–economic transitions considered necessary for political survival. Many other countries (e.g., India, Mexico, Venezuela) have instituted programs to cope with the changing world technological environment. In these examples the cultural impact has not been as pronounced as in China.

Organizations are also vulnerable to technological change. Past success can lead to present complacency. Organizational vested interests are "sacred cows" and they invariably tend to protect the status quo. Failure to recognize and respond to change and technological innovation can affect the organization's position in the competitive marketplace.

To develop a technology that has market impact takes time. To be oblivious of such technologies in process is a cardinal management sin. A defensive response also takes time, during which established markets previously considered safe can erode. Often leaders of industry act defensively instead of actively pushing technological frontiers to maintain their position. It is no longer possible to coast on technological and market leadership. In industries where the technology is dynamic or subject to competitive technologies, failure to take a productive aggressive approach will often result in the loss of position in a very short time. Years of market dominance can disintegrate in a short time where the competition technologically catches up and even passes the firm. Classical examples are the American automotive, steel, and machine tool industries.

Business organizations as well as nations must be alert to technological developments and evaluate potential technological change. Such change can materially affect organizational goals and the scope of technical and geographic operations.

Obsolescence

One important distinction between developed and developing nations is technology. Developed nations operate in an environment of dynamic technological change. In these societies the knowledge and skill levels of the population are generally well above their counterparts in developing nations, there is a capital-intense rather than a labor-intense productive system, and the productive system tends to be technologically sophisticated.

A dynamic technological environment entails change which could precipitate human and capital obsolescence. Technological change is often considered necessary and beneficial. There are also often negative results from technological change and there are proponents who advocate a simpler technological approach.[1] A categorical pro or con attitude toward technological change is unrealistic. Since the mid-20th century there has been an acceleration of technological development. It is reasonably safe to assume that technological change is an irreversible process. On such an assumption it becomes increasingly important to anticipate and manage technological change. Knowledge, as reflected in scientific accomplishment and technological application, can obsolete and subsequently affect existing skills and industries. New occupations not yet identifiable will emerge and new processes and products will lead to the birth of new industries.

There has been significant impact of technological developments such as atomic energy, jet aircraft, computers, and transistors to give only a few examples. In the foreseeable future technological developments are highly probable in genetics, geriatics, increasing use of the earth's resources through the use of satellite remote-sensing devices, mechanical devices to replace human organs, lasers, mari-culture, the development of new synthetic materials, the economic desalinization of sea water, the creation of new energy sources, weather and environmental controls, and communication systems, to cite just a few possibilities. The aforementioned, plus other technological breakthroughs which loom on the horizon, make it important to plan for the integration of these developments.

Planning to Cope with Technological Change

In some environments, managers must be alert and plan to compensate for change; in other situations, a prime managerial function is to instigate technological change. In either case, the manager must be aware of technological impact and be sensitive to the need for more precise planning for the future.

Planning and subsequent successful implementation are critical for long-term growth and perpetuation. The need for successful planning is more pronounced when the organization operates in an internationally dynamic and competitive technological environment. Effective planning can take place after identification of informational requirements, the location and use of valid and relevant informational sources, correct interpretation of the data, and reasonably accurate prognostication. The accomplishment of the aforementioned is quite difficult in view of the amount, dispersement, and availability of information. Awareness of potential technological development is critical. The concept of technological forecasting has been a response to this need; it is future oriented. Technological assessment and environmental impact are closely aligned with technological development and will be discussed in subsequent sections of this chapter.

Technological Forecasting

The Objective of Technological Forecasting

A distinction should be made between general forecasting activity and technological forecasting. General forecasting can be short, intermediate, or long range. It is primarily directed to anticipation of the level of economic activity within an established time frame. The sales forecast is basic for operational planning. Based on the sales forecast, planning is instigated on product schedules, material acquisition, human resource requirements, facilities and equipment needs, cash flow, capital expenditures, and profit expectations. Technology forecasting is more explicit than general forecasting.

Technology forecasting is not concerned with immediate economic activity; it is directed at the assessment of technological development.[2] In essence, a technological forecast endeavors to identify the nature or extent of the technical change and within a reasonable time period. Technology forecasting involves technology transfer. The transfer of technology can take place at vertical or horizontal levels.

Vertical transfer of technology represents the progressive phases in the development of a technology. The phases entail discovery, creativity, substantiation, development, and engineering. The engineering phase leads to a functional technological system that could involve a hardware product, a process, or a intellectual concept. According to Jantsch, the extension of the vertical transfer by substantial subsequent technology transfer represents technological innovation.[3]

Forecasting technological change is important in determining national and business strategies. What technical developments are possible? Feasible? What new fields are evolving? What resources are or will be required? What risk factors are involved? The concept of technological forecasting is valid but the methodologies and accuracy of such forecasts often suffer in reliability. The discussion in the following section covers some of the mechanics and problems.

Exploratory and Normative Forecasting

Technology forecasting can employ exploratory or normative methods. The exploratory method is a passive approach. In this method the forecast starts from the existing base of knowledge and proceeds to the future on the assumption of logical technological progress; it is an analysis and reporting of anticipations. There are problems with such an approach based on available information, the ability of the forecaster, and the interpretation of the data. Often critical information is not available because of security or proprietary rights. Also, significant technological developments can take place in other fields which will subsequently affect the field of technology being forecast. At the time the forecast is made possible transfer processes are not known or if known the means for successful transfer may not be obvious. Despite inherent limitations, exploratory forecasting has distinct attractions.

It would seem that most industrial firms could effectively use exploratory forecasting. Reasonable identification of emerging technology and analysis of technological implications could provide clues for the firm as to competition, possible expansion of existing product lines, related product lines—which the firm should ease into—and new product areas where a foothold could provide a competitive edge. In short, a look into the future would enable better planning, more effective use of resources, and considerable avoidance of human and capital obsolescence.

Normative forecasting represents an offensive, action-directed approach to technological development. Normative forecasting is goal oriented in that future technical objectives are identified and programs formulated to accomplish those objectives at a time which is considered reasonable and attainable. In exploratory forecasting there is extrapolation from the present to the future based on expectations. In normative forecasting a future date is established and the extrapolation is from the future to the present. Technological gaps are identified which might act as constraints to the attainment of the technological objectives. Using this method to focus on the problems to be surmounted and solved, resources can be segregated and allocated.

Since resources are limited, normative forecasting could be used in deciding priorities. Decisions could be made in conjunction with cost effectiveness studies to determine whether the mission requirements are as critical as presented, are possible within the stipulated time, and if the ultimate accomplishment of the mission is worth the resource expenditure. Perhaps the best example of how normative forecasting was employed is the U.S. Apollo Space project.

Normative forecasting has been used by the U.S. government in military and space programs. Private firms could use normative forecasting to push technological leadership. Before undertaking an aggressive technical approach, the firm would have to examine national and international markets, evaluate market potential against developmental costs including risk and technical feasibility, decide on what future avenues it should travel, and then make the decision as to whether the project should be undertaken.

Jantsch contends that, presently, the most difficult technological forecasting problem is establishing the correct time frame in normative forecasting. In exploratory forecasting difficulty exists in conceiving an end effect in the future due to the time covered, but it is relatively simple to prognosticate compared to the normative forecast difficulties. In the normative method, the forecast is predicated on objectives, requirements, and sociological factors; the problem is the assumption that present requirements or anticipations are representative of the future.[4]

Technological Forecasting Techniques

Forecasting the future is at best a tenuous proposition. Invariably, intervening factors take place which could not be anticipated at the time of the forecast. The further the forecast delves into the future, the greater the probability will be that unforeseen developments will occur, which in turn could affect the validity of the forecast. Forecasters constantly search for procedures or techniques that will more accurately open the door to future events. The state of the art is such that there is no one technique or approach that is universally adapted, acknowledged, or reliable. Invariably, there is some degree of methodological innovation in forecasting. Techniques used in forecasting technological development cover a spectrum ranging from relatively simple naive intuitive approaches to extremely complex procedures.[5] Most of the techniques are academic, with limited practical adoption. Classification of the techniques can be refined to intuitive, extrapolative and correlative, logical sequence or network-type techniques, and future scenarios.

Intuitive forecasting is probably the most common approach to technological prediction. This is a simple, direct, and inexpensive technique. It can be done by individuals who seem to have a faculty for anticipating future technological developments (the so-called genius approach), or by consensus. This represents an "educated guess" approach. It can vary from a very naive approach, sort of a "off the top of the head" prognostication, to a much more intense look based on an extensive sampling and consensus of authoritative opinion. Delphi, the best known technique under this classification, was developed by Olaf Helmer of the Rand Corporation. Inquiries using the Delphi technique can ask authoritative opinion for a time assessment as to expectation when a particular development is probable. The Delphi inquiry can also seek a quantity assessment including an expected time frame and/or a probability of achieving technical goals within a stipulated time frame.

A plethora of methods exist which are essentially variations of PERT. *Relevance trees*, *graphic models*, *planning–programming–budgeting systems* (PPBS), *mission networks*, *decision trees*, and *systems analysis* all use network construction and/or extrapolation and correlative methods to derive technical forecasts.

If numbers are any criteria, it would seem that after some variation of Delphi, the network technique is the most popular avenue to technological forecasting. Networks help in identifying and establishing a logical pattern from an existing point to an anticipated goal. An intuitive technique, regardless of individual technological perception, might ignore or minimize a significant obstacle to technological attainment. On the other hand, the network system is vulnerable in that all critical events might not be recognized, parallel technology might be ignored or unknown, information may be inaccurate, fragmentary, or misinterpreted (leading to wrong conclusions) and, finally, optimism or pessimism might permeate the forecast.

Scenarios on the future are another approach to technology forecasting. Herman Kahn has been one of the foremost proponents of this approach. In a sense, scenarios are narrative extensions of decision trees. The scenario is developed on the assumption that an event or events will occur and a descriptive attempt is made at logical extrapolation of what might follow from the event or events. Many possible scenarios can evolve from a single technological development. For instance, optimistic, pessimistic, and probablistic (according to the interpretation of the scenario writer) scenarios can reflect a spectrum of possibilities suggested by a single event or a series of related events.

Many techniques have been developed to forecast technological development. Some of these techniques appear to be quite scientific but of questionable reliability, and cost factors have limited these approaches in their application. Most technological forecasts have relied on nonquantifiable and subjective factors before conclusions have been reached. In studying this field no discernible differences, relative to accuracy, have been found between complex sophisticated techniques and relatively simple naive techniques. This might explain the popularity of the Delphi technique or its derivatives.

International Business and Technological Forecasting

As an organized concept, technological forecasting is relatively new. However, as an intuitive process employed by management it has been used in varying degrees for a considerable period of time. Transnational firms from the United

States, Great Britain, Japan, West Germany, France, and several other countries have long been aware of the implications of technology and the subsequent impact on business competitiveness and profitability. Much of the economic dominance of Japanese firms in some technologies can be attributed to the ability to anticipate markets and technological developments.

To be useful, technological forecasting does not have to be precise. If an innovation can be identified, and if the innovation can be translated into constructive action within a reasonable and discernible time frame, it can substantially contribute to the decision-making process.

Often, long-term commitments are undertaken on the basis of short-term technology. In many cases, inability to anticipate technology leads to built-in obsolescence. Attendant to obsolescence are high modification costs to update facilities and operations, difficulty in selling change to entrenched interests, and failure to exploit market potential.

An illustration of potential benefit from technological forecasting would be in product development. The technological forecasters have not yet developed the precise refinement of being able to localize specific innovations within a technological continuum. However, most technologies follow an S-shaped curve and evaluation of existing and anticipated status of the technology can be meaningful in the decision to undergo or forego investment in product development. The technical scope, cost, and time to develop a new product may be attractive or unattractive after technological forecasting information is assembled.

Generally, technological forecasting can assist management in several ways. It can represent an organized approach to a selective search for information. It can provoke thought by expanding horizons. It can help provide perspective and facilitate interdisciplinary communication. It can encourage operational sensitivity. It can assist management in determining the magnitude of anticipated change and provide a basis for estimating costs and requirements for people, facilities, and equipment. It can aid in giving direction to product development and market penetration. It can assist in recognizing national and international competition and other possible restraints, such as natural resources or technological limitations. It can, depending on the nature of the operation, encompass worldwide activities, or it can be used to focus on a relatively small geographic area. It can be used to help determine sociological and economic trends.[6]

James Bright has probably been the most active disciple in promoting technological forecasting to American industry. When the concept was first developed in the United States, primarily for government activities, the interest level was reasonably intense, but it waned in the 1970s. Surprisingly, there has generally been a much more enthusiastic reception to technological forecasting in Europe than in the United States.[7] While the level of U.S. interest may be stabilizing or even declining there appears to be increasing European interest, especially in the Western European countries.

Technological forecasting in proper context should seriously be considered as an addition to the management process. As Jantsch so aptly stated,

> Technological forecasting is not yet a science but an art, and is characterized today by attitudes, not tools; human judgment is enhanced, not substituted by it. The development of auxiliary techniques, gradually attaining higher degrees of sophistication (and complexity) since 1960, is oriented towards ultimate integration with evolving information technology.[8]

Technology Assessment

The Need for Technology Assessment

Science and technology have been used to solve many societal problems. Often improvement of the quality of life can be attributed to technological development. Technology, despite beneficial impacts, has not always been an unmitigated blessing. There have been miscalculations of costs and benefits and instances where unforeseen negative factors have surfaced as a consequence of technology. The results of technological change frequently have far-reaching impacts. Major technological developments have international ramifications and are difficult or impossible to confine within geographic boundaries. There is increasing pressure for better use of dwindling world resources. There are competitive technological alternatives for the use of world resources; there is, especially in the United States, increasing pressure for better and more reliable products. All these factors have been instrumental in the voluntary or compulsory review of the potential side effects of technological development.

Technology should be approached as a holistic concept. Technology is not the exclusive province of any societal segment. Because of the potential for negative effects it is becoming increasingly apparent that technology must be planned. In order to plan technology, there must be some level of expectations from technology. This is where technology forecasting is applicable. Technical feasibility, by itself, is not sufficient. It must also be known if a technical innovation is economically justifiable and socially and politically acceptable. When the societal consequences are evaluated and considered it then becomes technology assessment.

Technology Assessment Objectives

Technology assessment goes beyond self-interest evaluation of such factors as technical feasibility and profitability. Too much and too many are involved to have innovation decisions dictated by relatively short-run and partially representative considerations.[9] Technology assessment should be an adjunct activity to technological forecasting to help provide guidance for better utilization of technology.

In defining technology assessment, David Kiefer says,

> Technology assessment is an attempt—still halting and uncertain—to establish an early warning system to control, direct, and, if necessary, restrain technological development so as to maximize the public good while minimizing the public risks.

> It is, no less, a new approach to allocating scientific resources, setting technological priorities, and seeking more benign alternatives to the technology already at hand.[10]

Technology assessment should go beyond the immediate direct impact of a technical innovation. Joseph F. Coates suggested that a technology assessment should involve policy studies designed to systematically explore broad societal impacts resulting from technological introduction, expansion, or modification.[11]

A broad range of complex questions must be investigated in a technological assessment. For instance, What is the present state of the art in the technology? Where, directionally, does it appear to be going? What are the prospects for technological application? What forces might affect potential application? What possible consequences can be anticipated of the application? What are the cost and benefit considerations? What societal interest groups are apt to be affected by the technology, and what actions by these vested groups can be anticipated to support their position?[12]

By way of further elaboration, Coates says,

> The goal of technology assessment is to examine the risks, the benefits and the consequences implied by a technology and to put into the hands of a decision-maker, better information about the possible consequences of alternative actions.[13]

It would appear that the primary objective of technology assessment is to anticipate possible consequences of technological change. Anticipations can be developed into scenarios that identify possible good or bad consequences, potential trade-offs, and suggested courses of action to minimize or eliminate the negative aspects of potentially desirable technologies.

A Few Methodological Suggestions

Methodology or technique for a technology assessment, as in a technology forecast, requires procedural innovation. The scope of the technology would be an influential determinate of the methodology employed. Jones suggests seven major steps in making a technological assessment:

1. Define the assessment task.
2. Describe relevant technologies.
3. Develop state-of-society assumptions.
4. Identify impact areas.
5. Make preliminary impact analysis.
6. Identify possible action options.
7. Complete impact analysis.[14]

Within the framework outlined by Jones, a more detailed structure could be built to support a technological assessment. Or, as mentioned, other approaches considered more responsive to the immediate problem could be employed.

Joseph Coates also acknowledges the inherent difficulties associated with developing a universally applicable procedure or method for technology assessment. He maintains that there are three fundamental conditions that dictate the technology assessment approach: the subject, the budget, and the primary user. He also identifies ten modules of a technology assessment:

1. Definition of the problem, the technology, issue or project to be assessed.
2. Definition of alternative systems to be examined.
3. The unfolding of impacts.
4. Evaluation of the significance of impacts.
5. The decision apparatus.
6. Defining options and alternatives.
7. Parties at interest with regard to a particular technology.
8. The importance of recognizing and analyzing the impacts of variation on the technology under consideration.
9. The prominant place of exogenous factors in any technology assessment.
10. Examining all the above to come to some set of conclusions.[15]

Another possible alternative to assessing a technology would be to employ an advocate or vested interest approach. In the formative stages of a technology, impetus usually comes from sources such as science, industry, military, or the other branches of government. The sponsor(s) are inclined to view potential technological development as it most directly affects their immediate activities and interests. The ultimate technological results could have reverberations that materially affect other interest groups. Undesirable downstream consequences can be avoided or minimized by communication and research.

It is suggested that each segment of society which might be affected by the technology be represented in exploring possible technological implications. Each group would approach the problem in the light of its own self-interest. For instance, the technologists would, among other things, look at the state of the art, technical feasibility, the time frame for technical accomplishment (hopefully in conjunction with alternatives and competing technologies), potential application, and obsolescence. Additionally, the technologists would explore the availability of technical resources and possible government interest, as a prelude to requesting government support in the early R&D phases. If industry and not the government is the immediate partner with the technologist, the support decision might be made after consideration of such factors as organizational objectives, profits, costs, existing products, growth potential, international aspects, competition, and potential government regulation and/or support.

The significant point is that decisions to push technology can, and often are, made unilaterally where the prime motivation is provided by either the government, industry, or the technologists; or the decision can be bilateral, with two of the aforementioned three interest groups in partnership; or all three groups may be parties to a trilateral agreement. It has become increasingly apparent that the technologists, government, and industry do not have the right nor sole domain in determining the direction of technology. Labor and the general public, among others, must be represented and economic factors must be evaluated in order to provide a more realistic impact analysis. It is possible that other special interest groups would also have to be represented so that technological perspective can be accomplished. It is also probable that a technological development of any magnitude would have international consequences. As an example, a technology which can affect the environment must be evaluated for international implications.[16]

A matrix approach can also be used in a technology assessment. The matrix could be useful in national technological assessment or by the firm as a means to evaluate technological alternatives. Assuming the case of the transnational, an overall assessment can be made of past, present, and anticipated markets. Products, processes, and resources can be assessed. Technology forecasting could be beneficial in determining the evolutional potential of existing products and new areas where there is promise for technological development.

A systematic approach could provide the most practical path and greatest potential for success in the determination of which operational areas to emphasize, the establishment of priorities, and the selection of special goals. Unless realistic priorities are formulated with a reasonable chance for fulfillment, limited resources could easily be dissipated with few accomplishments. The matrix approach suggested could provide management with perspective and help focus decisions on desirable and allowable priorities. Once priorities are determined sequential activities within these priorities can be set in motion to accomplish the technological and operational objectives.

Environmental Impact

Technology Assessment and Environmental Impact

The Office of Technology Assessment (OTA) was originally established by congressional authorization to provide information to Congress on the potential affects of technology. As a result of consumer and legal pressures, technological assessments, in a much more limited way than those performed under government auspices, have frequently been employed in the private sector. Food, drug, and cosmetic products in particular, are usually subject to exhaustive testing and evaluation before being put on the market. It should be pointed out that there generally are no universal international product standards. A product which the U.S. Food and Drug Administration might reject could surface in other countries where product test standards are less stringent.

The original high expectations for technology assessments performed by or administered by the OTA have not been realized. However, the concept and use within the U.S. government has broadened considerably. A parallel technology evaluation procedure, Environmental Impact, is now a common practice in the various governmental agencies that deal with some phase of technology. An organization soliciting government support on a project involving technology must generally include with the request (proposal) a comprehensive statement as to the affect such a project might have on the environment.

Evolutionary Development

There have been adverse impacts on the natural and man-made environment caused by heavy population concentrations; the ineffective disposal of wastes; pollution in air, soil, and water caused by toxic materials; poor use of natural terrain including intensive agriculture, forest destruction, and soil erosion; and other uneconomic use of natural resources.[17] The increasing encrouchment on the natural environment can substantively affect the quality of life. Environmental changes could also lead to undesirable hazards to public safety, health, or welfare as well as having negative impacts on other life forms.

Until the 1960s there was little or no significant government control. Government action prior to the 1960s was primarily addressed to rectifying the results of environmental disasters rather than taking a preventative approach. Emphasis and intensification of the problem was brought about by the emergence of analytical methods that were able to detect foreign substances in human tissues which in turn could affect health and life expectancy.[18]

During the 1970s the people in several nations became increasingly concerned. What had started as basically a conservation movement expanded in recognition that threats to all life forms were developing. These first groups, while vocal, and usually socially affluent, had relatively little impact on governments and legislation. The movement had not come into sharp focus until the 1960s when increasing pressures were brought against the U.S. government for political intervention. Pressure with political force resulted from environmentalists merging into a cohesive block. Cohesiveness often took the form of public appeal, financial support for environmental programs, and exercise of the voting franchise at the polls to support environmentally sympathetic candidates.

The problems that precipitated concern and subsequent legislation are not confined to any one political jurisdiction.

International Aspects

Each political division has some areas of comparability with other political jurisdictions. The extent and degree can, and probably will, vary depending on a variety of factors. Many environmental problems that might initially be local ecological problems tend to spread beyond established political boundaries and subsequently become international in scope. For instance, deforestation in parts of Africa has lead to soil erosion and unproductive deserts which are extending beyond national boundaries with deadly cancerous certainty. The Rhine River which flows through France and Germany before reaching the Netherlands picks up pollution enroute to the Atlantic Ocean and must ecologically be reckoned with by the time the river flow reaches the Netherlands. Countries bordering on the Mediterranean Sea must be concerned with the deterioration of that body of water as a food source and a recreational outlet.

Spurred by the problems cited and more active public involvement, many countries have passed pollution control legislation. The legislation has not been easily born because there has generally been contrapolitical pressures brought to bear by industrial interests. Industrial concerns have centered around the position that pollution controls increase production costs. Firms operating in internationally competitive markets are loath to generate any costs which could compromise their competitive position. However, noteworthy legislation has been passed: The United States has the NEPA (National Environmental Protection Act), passed in 1969; the Environmental Protection Act (EPA) was passed in 1969 in Sweden; in Great Britain the Control of Pollution Act was passed in 1974. Japan and Canada, while not having any specific national legislation appear to be in the process of centralizing and coordinating environmental matters.[19]

From the preceding paragraph it can be seen that there is increasing international awareness and action on environmental problems. Besides direct legislative control, environmental anxieties have been expressed in many other forms such as bilateral and multilateral treaties, tariff policies, and regional collaborative agreements based on commonality of problems, interests, and natural resources.

The National Environmental Policy Act

The National Environmental Policy Act (NEPA) requires that in planning a project, consideration must be given to any possible effects the project might have on the environment as well as the technical objectives of the project. The NEPA requires a comprehensive look at decisions that could affect the public interest. In essence, project management decision processes have to include technical, economic, social, cultural, and environmental factors. Before NEPA decisions were primarily based on economic and technical aspects.[20]

In complying with NEPA, three significant areas must be addressed:

The *environmental inventory* is a comprehensive description of the existing physical environment of the area where any action is proposed. The environmental inventory serves as an evaluation basis to determine possible impact(s) of the project.

The *environmental assessment* is the second stage during which possible outcomes are investigated which might affect the environmental inventory. In accomplishing this objective an attempt would be made to forecast any environmental change, the extent of the anticipated change, and the significance of the change.

The *environmental impact statement* is a summary of the two previous phases.[21]

According to Canter, there are five components in an environmental impact statement: basics, the environmental setting, evolution of impacts, determination of the approach, and an impact statement following established guidelines.[22]

The environmental impact statement should contain both the primary and the secondary positive and negative aspects of a proposed course of action. This would entail an evaluation of possible direct and indirect consequences of the action. This process closely parallels technology assessment procedure. By attempting to uncover possible negative aspects, action can be directed, as a result of anticipation, toward eliminating or neutralizing negative features. The aforementioned assumes that the potential benefits outweigh the potential liabilities and added beneficial weights can develop by anticipating and eradicating possible contrabalancing ill affects. This phase involves consideration of possible alternatives.

An environmental impact statement should also weigh short- and long-run factors such as productivity and the societal contribution therefrom versus the uses of the environment and the ultimate environmental effects that might be anticipated. The underlying consideration in this approach is concern for future generations as well as present needs.

A final aspect would be a look at any possible irreversible and irretrievable commitment of resources based on project authorization. This is an anticipatory attempt to evaluate the impact of permanent changes which could take place and how the natural environment might permanently be altered.

The Procedural Approach

In an environmental impact statement the procedural approach is extremely important in identifying relevant areas which might be affected. Hundreds of environmental impact statements have been filed with the U.S. government. Guidance as to preparation procedures and identification of possible impact areas can be obtained by looking at environmental impact statements that have been filed and are available from the U.S. government. Examination of environmental impact statements that have led to project authorizations would be useful in identifying critical areas for concern and to avoid gaps which could delay project approval or result in project rejection as a consequence of an unacceptable environmental impact statement. The nature of the proposed project would also provide assistance in developing the structure of the environmental impact statement. Canter, by way of illustrating possible areas, says the environment can be divided into such categories as physical and chemical characteristics, biological, cultural, and ecological relationships. It is possible that the socioeconomic environment would also have to be accommodated.[23]

Pollution Control

Pollution can be controlled in any of several different stages:

a. At the source.
b. Where discharged into the environment by neutralizing treatment.

c. In the environment by adding dispersants.
d. By protective gear to reduce human exposure.
e. Through immunization.
f. By treatment of affected groups.[24]

Of the above possibilities preventative measures, rather than corrective procedures, are more desirable; most effort, as a result, is primarily in the preventative phases. Pollution control, as exercised by the government, can be direct or indirect. Direct controls could involve operating procedures to minimize pollution risk. The government could, and in practice does, establish nonhazardous acceptable levels of pollution. A good example of this is the automobile pollution standards.

Indirect controls might involve positive economic incentives offered by governments to encourage private investment in pollution abatement devices. These incentives could be offered as direct investment grants, tax relief, or low-cost loans, or perhaps by affording industrial protection from foreign competition. The government can also police industry and impose fines or other types of penalties for noncompliance with pollution standards.

Public Participation

Earlier in this chapter it was stated that projects are initiated and championed as a result of some vested interest or interests. The usual process involves two or more parties with some mutuality of anticipated benefit resulting from the successful completion of the project. Normally one individual or group would perform and the other would finance or support in the expectation of utilization of the end product. In technologically complex projects several groups can have varying degrees of involvement. Each participant in a project usually has a gain motivation. The real or perceived gains of the participants would not necessarily be the same. However, the point is that the participants do have some vested interest and do hope, as a consequence of participation, to derive some benefit. Gains or benefits for participants could result in direct or indirect loss to nonparticipants.

In the preceding section on technology assessment a vested interest model was proposed, the reason being that any project of any technological magnitude that has possible consequences affecting others beyond the immediate project participants should be objectively scrutinized to look at potential undesirable aspects. The rationale for this suggestion is based on past practices where technological impacts on the general public have often been treated lightly and subverted to the interests of strongly vested groups. Canter supports the position that there be public participation in the environmental impact process. He indicates six general objectives for public participation: (1) education, information dissemination, and coordination; (2) selection of problems, need, and value determinations; (3) development of ideas and problem solving; (4) impressions and feedback on suggestions; (5) examination, analysis, and evaluation of alternatives; (6) consensus based on conflict resolution.[25]

Canter further divides the public into four segments such as people who are directly affected by the project, the ecologists concerned with environmental preservation, the public who would derive direct benefits from the proposal, and the public who put environmental preservation secondary to the maintenance of their standard of living.[26] Public representation, based on intensity of interest, can range from a few public groups to a very diverse public representation. Realistically, most of the public is apathetic, resigned, and nonresponsive unless there is a direct and serious threat to their specific vested interests.

Inducement and Environmental Concern

Motivation and inducement for environmental concern are extremely important. Positive inducements rather than negative primitive actions would seem to be the better route to follow. Policing and enforcement actions are expensive and have limited success. A supportative voluntary constituency could be far more effective in maintaining a healthy environment. No doubt with a little ingenuity several attractive inducements could be possible. In the following paragraphs just a few ideas are suggested.

Compliance with government-imposed environmental impact regulations adds to the cost of doing business. In most cases the technology already exists to cope with pollution problems, but there is resistance since business is reluctant to incur nonproductive costs which can compromise the organization's competitive position. Industry constantly rails about governmental regulation. Public exploitation and disregard for social responsibility usually leads to negative public response and subsequent restrictive legislation. Restrictive legislation can be forestalled by intelligent forward-looking policy and action. Many industries have associations. Industrial association charters can be expanded to establish environmental impact standards. Self-enforcement of standards would have many advantages, such as comparability of costs which would not compromise an organization's market position, less government interference and regulation, not to mention the additional costs incurred due to compliance, and a favorable public relations image.[27]

Good public relations in view of current attitudes is extremely important. This can be a major inducement. Any costs associated with a program of environmental responsibility could be compensated for by public good will and possible increased sales volume. It would seem that an advertising campaign incorporating specifics about an organization's environmental protection program and technological responsibility would be effective. Favorable or unfavorable corporate publicity often has a lasting public affect which can be translated into consumer marketplace decisions.

Many nations enjoying economic prosperity can trace such affluence to enlighted government industry relations. Japan, Germany, France, Austria are just a few examples of the aforementioned. There is a feeling of partnership and neutrality anchored in the knowledge that a politically healthy and economically prosperous nation serves the general interest; this is achieved by cooperative effort rather than skepticism and mistrust. Unfortunately, while this lesson has been learned by some of the United States' most persistent competitors, it has or yet not generally been learned and practiced in the United States.

The government can be a strong ally rather than an operational hindrance. Addressing the discussion to environmental and technological impacts, the government can protect industry through a variety of internationally used devices. In exchange for adhering to safe and responsible environmental and technological practices, industries can be rewarded by means of tariff protections, tax relief, which is a form of subsidy, for instigating environmental controls, low-cost loans, and, considering that the government is by far the largest purchaser of goods and services, by giving preferential buying treatment to organizations which demonstrate environmental responsibility.

The preceding paragraphs merely make a few suggestions. Many other inducements can be used effectively to motivate organizations into environmentally and technologically responsive practices.

Environmental Impact and Technology Assessment

On the surface it appears that technology assessment and environmental impact are practically identical concepts. There is unquestionably a very close philosophical bond between the two concepts. If a distinction is possible, it appears that technology assessment is approached primarily as an evaluation of the consequences of developmental technological action. Environmental impact is used in such instances as well as in more technologically mundane types of projects.

Actually, it is very possible that significant differences between technology assessment and environmental impact actually have become obscured and, in fact, both with minor or hair-splitting differences are really the same thing in slightly modified packages. To support the aforementioned, there have been technology assessment projects as cloud seeding over some western states and proposed airport construction projects in the Florida Everglades and in Long Island Sound. The cited projects, and many others of a similar nature, performed under the auspices of the Office of Technology Assessment (OTA) could easily have come under the National Environmental Policy Act. Many projects evaluated under procedural requirements dictated by the NEPA could just as easily have been the subject of a technological assessment. It may be that the only real difference between the two concepts is jurisdiction; what has happened, not unusual in Washington, is that the same street is identified under two different names. This position can be reinforced by similarities in methodologies which have been designed for comparable informational objectives.

Whether there are extensive or trivial differences in technology assessment or environmental impact, the objectives of each approach are essentially the same. Both seek to minimize potential dangers from technology as a result of ill-conceived or poorly planned projects. From all indications this is not a present fad; in view of global ecological problems it is quite safe to assume that there will be increasing activity to evaluate any significant technological projects to assess potential environmental impacts.

Managerial Implications

Managers operating in national and international environments should be cognizant of technological impacts. The state of the technology frequently provides a competitive edge for moving into international markets. The decision process to develop international markets has to factor in potential negative aspects consequenced by technological side effects, social pressures, and awareness of national legislation or international restrictions which could affect the sphere of operations.

The manager is responsible for organizational survival and survival is associated with profitability, planning, the developing technology, innovation, achieving objectives, proper utilization of resources, organizational image, product introduction, and legal responsibilities. In an increasingly competitive international marketplace it is obviously important for the manager to be aware of technological developments and the possible impacts of such developments.

In this chapter an attempt has been made to focus on the relevant aspects of technological developments. Technological developments frequently affect the multinational organization. Technology forecasting and assessment undoubtedly have taken place in multinational organizations. Such activities have generally been relatively unsophisticated and informal. It might well be, considering technological acceleration, complexity, and international impacts, that forecasting and assessing such developments be put in sharper organizational focus and become formalized functional activities.

Endnotes Chapter Six

1. See E.F. Schumacher, *Small is Beautiful*, Harper and Row, 1975.
2. See E. Jantsch, *Technological Forecasting in Perspective*, Paris: Organization for Economic Cooperation and Development, 1967, p. 15. Also see M. Cetron, "Prescription for the Military R&D Manager: Learn the Three Rx's" unpublished paper presented to The NATO Defense Research Group Seminar on Technological Forecasting and its Application to Defense Research, Teddington, Middlesex, England: November 12, 1955, p. 2.
3. Jantsch, *op. cit.*
4. *Ibid*, pp. 29–32.
5. Extensive treatment of technological forecasting techniques can be found in M.J. Cetron, *Technological Forecasting*, New York: Gordon and Breach, 1969; Jantsch, *op. cit.*; and J.R. Bright (ed.), *Technological Forecasting for Industry and Government*, Englewood Cliffs, NJ: Prentice-Hall, 1968.
6. D. Roman, *Science, Technology and Innovation: A Systems Approach*, Columbus, OH: Grid Publishing, 1980, pp. 122–123.

7. A representative example is H. Jones and B. Twiss, *Forecasting Technology for Planning Decisions*, London: The MacMillan Press, 1978.

8. Jantsch, *op. cit.*, p. 17.

9. David M. Kiefer, "Technology Assessment," *Chemical Engineering News*, Vol. 48, October 5, 1970, p. 44.

10. *Ibid.*

11. Joseph F. Coates, "Technology Assessment—What It Means to You, Your Profession, Your Corporation, Your World," unpublished paper presented to the Chemical Marketing and Economic Division, American Chemical Society Annual Meeting, New Orleans, March 21, 1977, p. 1.

12. Martin V. Jones, "A Technology Assessment Methodology—Project Summary," MTR-6009, prepared in cooperation with and for the Office of Science and Technology, Executive Office of the President, Washington, DC: The Mitre Corporation, June 1971, p. 3.

13. Coates, *op. cit.*, p. 1.

14. Jones, *op. cit.*, p. 7.

15. Coates, *op. cit.*, pp. 7–9.

16. Roman, *op. cit.*, pp. 129–130.

17. Joseph L. Rodgers, Jr. *Environmental Impact Assessment, Growth, Managements and the Comprehensive Plan*, Cambridge, MA: Ballinger Publishing Co., 1976, pp. 1–2.

18. D. Eva and H. Rothman, "Control of the Environmental Impact of Technology," in *Directing Technology: Policies for Promotion and Control*, edited by R. Johnston and P. Gummett, London: Croom Helm, 1979, pp. 156–157.

19. *Ibid.*, p. 162.

20. L. Canter, *Environmental Assessment*, New York: McGraw-Hill, 1977, p. 1.

21. *Ibid.*, pp. 1–3.

22. *Ibid.*, p. xiii.

23. *Ibid.*, p. 46.

24. "Environmental Engineering: A Guide to Industrial Pollution Control," *Chemical Engineering*, April 27, 1970.

25. Canter, *op cit.*, p. 222.

26. *Ibid.*, p. 223.

27. There might be situations where the costs of voluntary compliance might not be significantly higher or perhaps even less than the costs of involuntary compliance plus the costs incurred in reporting and adhering to government regulations.

CHAPTER SEVEN

Technology Transfer

Definition, Purpose, and Utilization

A Frame of Reference

Technological change results from the generation of ideas, the creation of knowledge, and the employment of ideas and knowledge to develop new products, processes, or additional information. Knowledge and information are sterile until they are used. The use of knowledge and information involves a transfer from the knowledge originator or the information source to its application.

The 20th century, more particularly the latter half of this century, has been characterized by the tremendous development of new knowledge and the tremendous expansion of information which have fostered rapid technological change. No individual sect, business organization, or nation has a monopoly on knowledge and information. Knowledge and information to a greater or lesser extent are created in all societies. With so much knowledge and information being produced there are problems in locating, disseminating and utilizing the knowledge and information. Often knowledge and information emanating from one environment directed toward a specific application can be applied to similar situations in other environments with or without some modification, or can be used in nondirect but related applications. This is technology transfer.

Technological change is precipitated by a cycle of invention, innovation, and diffusion. The invention phase involves the idea and knowledge development; innovation is conversion of knowledge to a useful process or product; diffusion is the end application. For reference purposes the terms technology transfer and diffusion are used synonymously.

Explicitly, technology transfer can be defined as

> The process of collection, documentation and successful dissemination of scientific and technical information to a receiver through a number of mechanisms, both formal and informal, passive and active.
>
> The transfer process begins when it has been established that a technological advance has significant relevancy in a directed or different application and that a necessary adaptation can be made. The process occurs naturally between participants who understand what has to be done to permit effective utilization.[1]

Purpose

Technology transfer is certainly not a new phenomenon. Archaeologists have uncovered primitive tools of ancient societies. These tools reflected the then existing technology. The actual tools or the methods for their production represented knowledge or technique that was passed from one generation to the next. This was a transfer of technology. The technology of these early periods was very crude by modern standards and technological change was extremely slow. It has only been since the 1970s that technology transfer has extensively been formally recognized with resultant international attention and research. Early technology transfer was primarily motived by the need to survive. Since the 1970s there has been increasing international realization that the effective transfer and utilization of technology impinges not only on survival but on economic well-being and the quality of life as well.

Awareness of the importance of technology transfer can be associated with the realization of impacts related to technological acceleration. Technology has become increasingly complex. There is a constantly growing information base. The development of sophisticated technology frequently involves high costs and risks. There are pressures for more effective use of diminishing resources. More effective use of diminishing resources can be accomplished by building upon knowledge and information that already exist rather than unproductive duplication of effort to produce noncumulative results.

Technology and technology transfer are nationally as well as internationally important. Transfer and utilization processes within a nation affect industrial development and competitiveness. Transfer can facilitate progress by identifying, filtering, modifying, and employing information generated in one operational environment to another operational environment with resultant time and resource savings.

The effective use of technology can have many beneficial returns. Since it is improbable that any one nation would have the capacity to develop all the technology required within a socioecopolitical system, it follows that there must be some dependence on technology developed within other political jurisdictions. Transferring technology from one socioecopolitical environment is not always an easy process. However, the potential benefits from technology transfer, problems notwithstanding, are considerable. For instance, technology transfer can be a device to strengthen the local production system; it can provide information and subsequent training; it can serve as a stimulant for further research and development; it can facilitate a more competitive position in the international marketplace; it can strengthen local capabilities; it can serve as a vehicle to integrate knowledge; it can assist in closing the technological gap between developed and developing nations; and it can very conceivably lead to a better quality of life. The aforementioned are by no means all inclusive, but they do serve to give some indication of motivational factors.

Utilization

Technology utilization follows the transfer of information. The information can be derived as a consequence of government or private industry directed activity. The knowledge produced can be converted into products, processes, or services in either or both the public and private sectors. It is also possible that there is a horizontal or secondary application of the technology. The technology initially developed for a specific mission may be subsequently modified and used in other situations. Utilization actually extends beyond transfer because it is the application of technology to the creation of a marketable end-product or service.[2]

The complexities involved in the transfer and utilization of technology are highlighted in a report prepared by the Committee on Technology Transfer and Utilization of the National Academy of Engineering. As indicated in the report, many possibilities exist for utilization:

Organizing and assembling the results of R&D.

Information dissemination.

Need identification and applicable technology evaluation. This phase identifies possible users and technological adoption requirements.

With user assistance, the correlation of need and existing technology.

Cost benefit analyses.

Market evaluation to ascertain ultimate utilization.

Technology assessment—potential technological impacts.

Funding indigenous organizations with the capability for transferring the technology into practical utilizations.

Evaluation of resource requirements and resource availability.

Coordinating suppliers and users relative to use and supply characteristics.

Performing additional engineering which may be required to adapt technology to local needs.

Business planning, e.g., production and operational costs, financing, market planning, provision for product service, and product pricing.[3]

Vertical and Horizontal Transfers of Technology

Vertical Technology Transfer

Vertical technology transfer represents a flow from basic, or laboratory research, through developmental stages, and ultimately to production and technology.[4] The vertical transfer of technology can represent a flow from invention to innovation to diffusion. Inasmuch as each phase in the operational flow has distinctive characteristics there must be accommodation for people and organizational variances and coordination to facilitate transfer from phase to phase.

Since vertical technology transfer entails technological progression from science to a completed product, there seems to be a trend toward organizing R&D by vertical integration. Stated another way, all research that is germane to the transfer, such as fundamental, applied, or developmental, is consolidated in a "mission-oriented" organization.[5]

Horizontal Technology Transfer

Horizontal transfer of technology represents a wide range of possibilities. Horizontal transfer is essentially the transfer of established knowledge or processes from one operational environment to another.[6] There can be horizontal integration of research through organizational methods which group scientific disciplines or technologies. In such instances, the orientation would have a *discipline-* rather than a *mission*-directed approach. It is an oversimplification to infer that technology is transferred exclusively by horizontal or vertical processes. In practice, technology can be effectively transferred both horizontally and vertically incorporating techniques to bridge the gaps between discipline- and mission-oriented R&D.

Government working in concert with industry can significantly encourage horizontal technology transfer. To illustrate the aforementioned, the government can

Make available low-interest-rate innovation capital to industry in technologies that support national developmental objectives.

Provide tax incentives.

Place high priorities on training people for employment in these technologies.

Afford preferential treatment to foreign specialists in this industry.[7]

Transnational corporations are also an extremely effective vehicle for horizontal technology transfers. It has been estimated that in 1970 transnational corporations were responsible for about one quarter of the world's production.[8]

Transnational companies are deeply involved with horizontal technology transfer especially in developing countries. By the nature of their operations they offer a range of alternatives for technology transfers. In accepting a transfer of technology a receiving nation must consider its technological options, the adaption of the technology to local needs, the potential of the technology to provide the opportunity to develop independent production capabilities, and the ability of local organizations to manage the technology.[9]

Linking Vertical and Horizontal Technology Transfers

Linkage of vertical and horizontal technology transfers depends on the extent that the technology(ies) have to be adapted. In the transfer process, the modification may be slight which simplifies the situation. Where radical alterations are necessary, the transfer of the technology is obviously much more complicated, and linkages are, accordingly, more difficult and challenging. In situations where linking problems are apparent, careful considerations should be given to the transfer of such technologies in terms of needs, priorities, and costs. Decisions would be required as to whether the technology should internally be developed, whether the outright purchase of the technology is possible, or whether some intermediate position should be taken between complete independence and complete dependence.

The Diffusion of Technology

Need Stimulation

A significant motivator for technology transfer is need. The identification of need stimulated by effective demand provides impetus for bringing people and information together. In the diffusion process, need induced linkages are formed between the innovator, the producers, and the user. Such linkages are important for transferring technology. However, the linkages are subject to variation due to the nature of the technology, the type of functions, and the timing of the transfer.[10]

Technology may also be viewed as an essential production input. As a needed ingredient in production, technology is, in essence, a commodity that can be bought or sold in various forms: Technology can be represented in the form of intermediary or capital goods; it can be manifested in the form of specialized human resources; it can also be in the form of technology or commercial information, which is either easily accessible or proprietary and subject to constraints.[11]

Some Considerations Prelude to Transferring Technology

A technology that is operable and successful in one environment could prove to be a disaster in another operational milieu. The decision to transfer or not transfer a technology could revolve around the consideration of several factors:

Market and technical feasibility studies.

The range of technologies considered and the choice of technology.

Industrial processes.

Engineering factors.

Facilities requirements and availability.

The existing human resource inventory and training requirements.

Management.

Marketing intelligence.

Process and product design improvements.[12]

Delineation of the scope of the problem is also important in directing activity for transfer and use of technology. Information requirements must be identified and relevant information subsequently collected, organized, and interpreted. Information should be coordinated with and adapted to need. Evaluation must be accomplished relative to existing technology and actual need applicability or the extent of technological modification required. Cost–benefit analyses can provide some insight as to the value of the technology or possible alternative actions. Market research can be influential as to the technology potential, looking at such factors as intensity and extent of need, competition, resource requirements, and resource availability. The determination of performance standards desired by consumers and attainable by producers with necessary product engineering is still another of several possible considerations.[13]

Transfer Levels

There are many environments where technology transfer takes place. Each environment has its own idiosyncrasies affecting technology transfer. To give some idea of the magnitude involved, technology transfer can take place

within the organization,

within a group,

within an industry,

between industries,

government to government,

industry to government,

within a discipline,

between disciplines.

In addition, it is possible that technology transfer could involve communication between several different diffusion levels. Communication is difficult in a complex homogeneous environment but in a complex heterogeneous environment the communication problems are compounded.

The amount, diversity, and dissemination of information can create all sorts of problems in the transfer of technology. Some of the reasons information gaps develop are the amount of information being generated, the increasing size of organizations, geographic dispersion, language barriers, semantic difficulties within a common language, and organizational decentralization and diversity of operations.

With the aforementioned problems in mind, it is understandable that reading, screening, interpreting, and transferring information to the right people at the right time can present a monumental task. Also, information sources may not be universally applicable or may not be known by the people or organizations looking for some transfer of technology. Failure to exploit the proper information source at the right time can thwart the process of technology transfer.[14]

Methods for Transferring Technology

The transfer of technology may be calculated as in the case of a licensing arrangement where one company gains access to the technology developed by another company. The transfer of technology may also be more subtle and indirect as in situations where knowledge derived in one environment can be modified and adapted to a different use in another environment. There are many sources of information that can be converted into technology. Some of the more relevant vehicles for technology transfer will be discussed in this section. Each of the methods is worthy of extensive treatment; the subject could easily be expanded into a separate volume. The purpose of the following discussion is to provide breadth and awareness rather than intensive depth.

Most governments have involvement with some aspects of research and development. In some countries there is a ministry of science, which serves as an information focal point. In the United States most government agencies are mission directed, and as a consequence information is more dispersed. However, the U.S. Printing Office does have information which has been generated under the auspices of the different agencies and to some extent does operate as a governmental clearing house. More in-depth specialized information is still better obtained from the individual agencies. A good example is the National Aeronautics and Space Administration (NASA), which has extensive information available to the public.[15]

The U.S. government is probably the most prolific generator and source for information in the world. Much of the information resulting from government-sponsored studies is not used because of the general lack of awareness of the extent, scope, and availability of such information. In the past attempts have been made to broaden the use of available data through the use of information dissemination centers and data banks. Despite such attempts, diffusion has generally been very poor considering the amount of existing information and the costs connected with information development.

Another serious difficulty as to the government's role in technology transfer is knowledge which has been developed and supported by public funds. The knowledge is often freely available; it cannot be given freely as an exclusive property right to a commercially directed activity. There are use restrictions since the knowledge was created by means of public funding. When there are restraints of this nature, organizations in the private sector are unwilling to make resource commitments on products, processes, or services when they do not have exclusive control. There is an exception when such knowledge is developed under government contract for government requirements, but the knowledge derived therefrom can be legally transferred by the generating organization to commercial products over which it does have direct control. In many instances the potential commercial fallout provides additional incentive for government contracting.[16]

People are one of the most important methods for transferring technology. Professional people operating in high-technology environments usually have good-to-excellent intra- and interorganizational mobility. Professional people are normally conscious of an obligation to keep current in their field. As a consequence, they may periodically become involved in further formal education, short specialized seminars, professional meetings,[17] directed research, and part-time teaching. Transnational firms can move people temporarily or permanently with relative ease. Exposure to different operations or similar operations in different settings can prove stimulating and lead to suggestions and subsequent technology transfer.

People may be the information transferring vehicle within geographically confined operations, between operations that are geographically dispersed, or from outside sources to internal operations. Unfortunately, information flows from outside and from within the organization can be impeded by real or artificial barriers. Intense narrow functional orientation, the tendency to compartmentalize within an organization on the basis of professional specialization, diverse organization activities, and imagined proprietary information rights are impediments to internal transfer of technology.

Still, people interactions are one of the most effective means for transferring technology. The potential barriers indicated in the preceding paragraph can be circumvented by encouraging more people to communicate and by specifically recognizing people within the organization who are good information transmitters. Exposure of these people to informational sources is an important part of the technology transfer process.

The literature, including books, specialized newsletters, technical and professional journals, and trade magazines are other useful informational sources. With so much literature being created it is an impossibility to locate, let alone read, all the applicable material being turned out. Abstracts are often misleading. Frequently by the time the information is published it is old because of the time elapsed from idea inception to publication. Or, the research findings may be technologically significant so there is an understandable reluctance to publish such information, which is considered proprietary, until the originating source has been able to exploit the information. Also, better sources might exist giving access to the information before it is published.

Time is a very important asset. Surveying the literature must be on a selective basis. Most high-technology organizations maintain technical libraries. The relevance, currency, and access to these libraries are important. Too often, unless there is direct research applicability, reading during the course of a normal day's activity is not encouraged. But, as mentioned, the literature can provide valuable clues for the productive transfer of technology. In some instances there can be a direct application of the information. On other occasions information can be taken out of direct context and fruitfully transferred and employed in areas not directly related. The ability to bridge the gap from one technology to another is an instance of horizontal technology transfer.

Consulting services represent another avenue to technology transfer. Since World War II, the United States has been a formidable exporter of professional services. International consulting has been an important activity. The extent and total impact of such activity as a transfer method or as a factor in international trade and balance of payments is poorly understood. There has been comparatively little research in this area, and subsequently the literature is sparse. No doubt a great deal of internal consulting takes place among the various divisions of the transnational business firms. This can be a relatively quick and easy way to transfer technology.

International consulting has been used in transferring technology in technical fields and in management. International consulting services have been provided in several ways. Information can be transferred as indicated, among the different national and international divisions of the transnational business firm by internal consultation. Private business firms, such as Bechtel, may provide specialized international consulting services. Government organizations like the Peace Corps and AID can sponsor programs for international service. A considerable amount of consulting has been provided ree to developing countries through international nonprofit organizations. The extent of such activity varies, but essentially most of them provide some form of consulting and technical assistance to developing nations. A few of the more active of these organizations are the United Nations, the Organization of American States (OAS), the World Bank Group, and the Organization for Economic Cooperation and Development (OECD).

Much international consulting is done by individuals who are independent entities. One of the authors has, on several occasions, had consulting assignments which transcended national boundaries. In the course of these assignments, he has encountered other independent consultants with different national affiliations. Because of the nature of such activity, it is practically impossible to determine the volume of effort or the impact on the transfer of technology.

There is considerable international dependence on consulting services to provide knowledge and facilitate the transfer of technology. International consulting has become extremely competitive; it is no longer the province dominated by the United States. Japan, West Germany, Great Britain, Italy, Israel, and France are a few countries who are active competitors in international consulting. With the emergence of international competition in consulting, there have also been some shifts in international attitudes relative to such services. Americans, or other nations for that matter, are not always warmly welcomed, even if their knowledge and services are needed. Invariably the purchaser of such services does not want a lasting relationship. They usually hope to use the knowledge purchased to provide a transition for their own technological independence. Another development is the consulting opportunities in Soviet bloc countries. This represents a sharp change in Soviet policy. Soviets have come to the realization that buying and employing relevant technology is, in the long run, quicker and cheaper than trying to develop their own technology when such technology already exists and often is available in the world marketplace.[18]

Many international cooperative arrangements have evolved which facilitate the transfer of technology. An example is licensing. Licensing is an arrangement whereby one party, usually having some proprietary control (e.g., through the use of a patent, copyright, trademark, or know-how) of a product or process, gives a second party the "right of use" contingent on performance requirements and payments. Coproduction is another technology transfer device. Coproduction takes place when two firms from different nations enter into an agreement to produce an end product. In this situation one firm usually provides most of the technology and some of the product components. The other firm also produces some components and assembles the end product in the country of ultimate use. A technological consortium is another cooperative venture which generally involves technology transfer. Technological consortiums are ventures between two or more nations and/or between two or more companies where extensive resources are required to accomplish a technological objective. The consortium can involve partnerships among nations, firms, or nations and private enterprise. A joint venture is another business form that facilitates technology transfer. A joint venture has some similarity to a technological consortium but usually does not require the magnitude of resources, have the same degree of high risk, or involve the level of technology regarded in a consortium. The motivation for a joint venture might be where there are resource limitations or political restrictions, such as a requirement for local partners. These cooperative forms will be more fully discussed in Chapter Fourteen, International Cooperative Arrangements.

The transnational firm is one of the best agents for change and channels for technology transfer. The transnational enterprise, by nature of its size, the scope of its operations, and the geographic dispersement of its activities, is uniquely adapted to transferring technology. Some of the ways the transnational firm can transfer technology are by products, services, training, direct investment, the buying and selling of products or services, and R&D. The transnational organization, with geographically and operationally extensive activities, can transfer knowledge easily with a minimum of political and proprietary difficulty.

The most obvious but perhaps the least discussed vehicles for technology transfer are educational institutions. Education assumes an imparting of knowledge and such a process involves the transfer of information. Technology transfer takes place not only as part of the formal educational system but also as a consequence of special informal nondegree educational and training programs.

The education unit, formal or informal, degree or nondegree, is the ultimate method for information diffusion. The diffusion or transfer process comes through the dissemination of knowledge which may not be new but is generally new to the attendees. In some cases where there has been original research at the education center the information conveyed represents new knowledge frontiers. There are many instances in which useful and productive technology is created outside the confines of the educational institution. This information is ultimately received, processed, and filtered through educational channels. Technology transfer also happens as a casual occurrence as distinct from a designed process as a result of the informal interface and exchange of information among the participants in educational programs.

The formally established educational institutions may at times be slow to respond to new technological developments. At times there may be inclinations to follow at a discrete distance when new knowledge is evolving. At other times the educational institution may be the precipitating influence for the generation of knowledge. Whether the educational operational environment might be technologically aggressive, passive, or even defensive, it is safe to say that information will eventually permeate educational institutions for subsequent analysis, evaluation, processing, and dissemination.[19]

Technology Transfer and Internationalism

Technology as Leverage in International Exchange

Technology, more specifically the products and services spawned from a marketable technology, is fundamental to international exchange. Where national technological development has taken place in product and service areas, and where demand or need is not localized, there can be international competitive and subsequent economic advantages. For the most part, international trade is enhanced by the need for raw materials, products, and services. Some nations have extensive raw materials, but lack the technology to convert these natural resources into commercially desirable products. This frequently is the situation with developing nations.

Some nations, such as Japan, have practically no natural resources and are dependent on other nations to supply required raw materials. Japan's economic affluence mirrors that nation's ability to import and convert raw materials effectively, to import selected technologies intelligently, to innovate from the base of the imported technologies, and to transfer the converted innovated technologies into international markets.

Some nations are only partially dependent on imported raw materials or transferred technologies. These nations may have some of the natural resources required in a technologically progressive society; they may also have varying degrees of competence in many technologies. Surplus raw materials and technologically advanced products can be marketed internationally and the returns therefore used to purchase needed raw materials and technologies.

What has become increasingly apparent is that a nation with advanced technology does have important leverage in international affairs. Edward E. David has said,

> Technology has become the preferred currency of foreign affairs. It is the bedrock of detente with the Soviet Union, improved relationships with China and our ability to dilute centuries old issues in the Middle East. Nations eye a technological, not a geographical, "heartland." Tomorrow's security will come not from mutual fear of MIRV's and ICBM's but from mutual dependence of each country on the other's technological resources, natural resources and markets.[20]

Technology Transfer — Developed to Developed Nations

It is easy to have a preliminary misconception of technology transfer. A significant portion of the literature on this subject is directed to technology transfer from developed to developing nations. A plausible explanation is that the bulk of the literature on this subject originates in the international nonprofit organizations and their mission is invariably tied to developing nations.

There are untapped market prospects in developing nations. The actual effective demand in developing nations, however, is weak because of low per capita income and the inequitable dispersion of national wealth. The effective demand in the developed nations has been increasing and this in turn has provided stimulation for technological development. Most technology transfer actually takes place between developed nations, more specifically, between transnational firms operating in and among developed nations.

A transnational organization may operate globally or may concentrate activities in a few select countries. The operational end products can be identical from nation to nation or they can have moderate-to-extensive modification to accommodate local markets. The transnational firm can have international product identification or it can control diverse activities where there is more identification with the industrialized production in different countries than with the parent organizations. Most consumers do not comprehend the extent of technology which has been transferred and incorporated into products used internationally.

The transfer of technology can be direct, and product identification from one nation to another is obvious. The transfer process can be, and often is indirect, gradual, and less obvious. Product identification from one nation to another may be, in such cases, obscured. Modification in some instances can be so extensive that the original technology is almost unrecognizable.

Direct transfers, such as a McDonald's to Paris or Vienna, a Colonel Sanders Kentucky Fried Chicken in Tokyo, or a Toshiba to Los Angeles are apparent. However, technological diffusion can be very subtle, often there is not general awareness by the host or recipient organization or nation of the transferred technology. For one example, while in Paris, one of the authors was told that Alka Seltzer was a French product. In the United States much more technology is imported than most Americans realize. The imported technologies may be modified or gradually incorporated into products that are considered essentially American. Few Americans, without reflection, appreciate technology not originally American which has been transferred to the automobile. To illustrate, the American automobile may incorporate such transferred technological components as radial tires, rack and pinion steering, disc brakes, fuel injection, and bucket seats. These components have become an important and integral part of the automobile.

The technology transfer between developed nations seems to be stimulated by give and take. The give and take relates to a community of products common to these nations. True, there are variations based on cultural preferences, such as manual vs automatic automobile transmissions or a preference for nonairconditioned cars in Europe as against such a preference in the United States. Despite the preponderance of literature on technology transfer from developed to developing nations, as previously indicated, the bulk of technology transfer takes place between developed nations such as the United States, Canada, and the Western European nations.

Technology Transfer to Developing Nations

It is easier to transfer technology from a developed to a developed country than from a developed to a developing country. In developed countries related products or processes might exist, adaptable production facilities are available, a core of technical expertise can be employed, and a discernible market is present or can be developed based on an affluent society.

Developing nations hunger for the same form of technology that is used in more technologically advanced nations. Any variation or modification is viewed suspiciously and regarded as exploitative. To use an analogy, it is like desiring beautiful party clothes, which first do not fit, and second are not functional, considering that the recipient is working in the fields and not going to a party. Considering the psychological aspects it should be apparent that transferring technology from a developed to a developing country must be done on a highly selective basis. The conditions or motivations for the transfer can be significantly different from the transferor to the transferee. Many times host nations have accepted or courted technology transfer for economic development when such development would not, at the time, be possible without foreign assistance. Technology that may initially be welcomed may eventually become a source of friction.

The developing nation in promoting the import of technology must consider long-range as well as short-range implications of technology transfer. There should be a development strategy. It is important that the host country carefully consider the type and extent of its natural and human resources. The receiving country must develop analytical methods including some accommodation for cost–benefit analysis to evaluate alternative technologies, the transition problems associated with technological adaption to indigenous conditions, and the prospects for participation in the creation of new technology.[21]

As part of the analytical process in determining the feasibility of technology transfer, the developing nation has an extensive range of factors which must be considered: What are the national priorities? Can the imported technology foster the training of people? Will the new technology encourage the development and growth of local educational institutions? How will the imported technology affect the quality of life? How effectively are the resources being used? Can educational and productive forces be coordinated for a positive synergistic effect? How does the technology transferred fit into the existing production system? Can the technology transferred be used to reinforce the present system and provide impetus for growth and expansion of that system?[22] Or, will the transferred technology cause disruption and compound national problems? Specifically, the technology transferred from a developed nation could be capital intensive, whereas the developing nation has a large unemployed or underemployed human resource base. If the imported technology is not new but only a variation or an improvement of an existing technology the net result can be displacement of human resources, which in turn compounds the employment problem.

Careful consideration of the aforementioned factors can provide invaluable insight as to whether to accept or reject the transfer of a technology. The conclusions from the analysis might indicate that the technology is not appropriate because it uses scarce resources inefficiently and does not employ plentiful resources. The output or product may not be compatible with local markets or needs. The transferred technology, rather than providing a bridge for additional internal technological development, may actually perpetrate technology dependence. Another consideration is unequal bargaining power between the parties to the transfer, with the advantage usually being on the side of the seller. The price for the technology can be too high after careful consideration of available resources and alternative opportunities. Buying an expensive technology can add to the economic problems of a developing nation by affecting its balance of payments.[23]

The transnational firm can have a catalytic role in a nation's economy. Generally the establishment of a national operation involves the transfer of management, special skills, and capital. The new enterprise provides local employment and the training usually necessary for indigenous labor to become productive. Such an operation can help the host nation in building an economic foundation. There can be a multiplier effect if the industry or industries imported spawn other industries. Local enterprise can learn by means of direct and indirect technology transfers. Local entrepreneurs can competitively be forces to emulate some of the transnational's activities or can hire employees trained by the transnational to bring new insights and acquired skills into local business. The transnationals also encourage technology transfer by building needed facilities. They provide added stimulation for education by importing new knowledge into the area, often as part of R&D activities, and by training users to provide direct and auxiliary services.

Like any other activity or operation there is not unequivocal acceptance or absolute agreement of benefits of the transnational enterprise. Many developed and developing nations view the transnational as a threat or a problem rather than an asset. Labor unions feel that the transnational may establish production operations in foreign countries because the price of that labor is cheaper.[24] This, in effect, leads to local unemployment. There has been criticism that the transnationals are not good guests and are not sensitive to local needs and problems. At times the technology transferred is considered too sophisticated for local use; at other times the technology is considered not sophisticated enough and is really second-class and exploitative technology. There have often been additional criticisms that transnationals, to protect their vested interests, become politically involved and support unpopular political factions.

The Sale and Control of Transferred Technology

Mutuality — Beneficial Exchange

There are usually two parties to the transfer of technology. If the transfer is to be successful, both parties must perceive and achieve benefits. How the technology will be transferred depends on several factors.

If the technology is very recent and technologically complex the probability is that it will be transferred as a package. The supplier would have high control of the technology. The supplier might have additional leverage as a consequence of managerial and technical skills which do not exist in the receiving nation. The resources available to the supplier in the receiving country and the investment and risk can also affect negotiations and the form of the transfer. In some cases there is strong product identity with a trademark or brand name, and even though the technology is not sophisticated the recipient nation may make concessions to acquire access to the product. The local industry capability may be such that there has to be reliance on the supplier to produce the goods for local consumption. The practice as to capital–technology–management packages and packaged technology transfers are subject to wide variations according to the nature of the technology, the owner of the technology, the country of origin, and the receiving country.[25]

"Highly packaged" transfers tend to provide the supplier with monopolistic advantages. The "packaged" transfers generally represent some form of licensing for process technology and probably also include direct equity investment by the supplier of the technology.

Reasons for Packaging a Technology Transfer

There are three significant reasons for "packaging" technology transfers. First, when there has been "packaging" and the supplier has equity participation the chances are that the supplier will exercise considerable control over production operations. Second, the receiving enterprise may have little or no expertise in the technology and may actually solicit a "packaged" transfer to facilitate production and minimize risk. Third, the recipient may want access to a brand name or a trademark owned by the supplier. To receive the identified product the recipient may be willing to make concessions to the seller by which the seller maintains substantial technical and managerial control over the operation.[26]

National Policy Considerations in Transferring Technology

Need to Establish a National Technology Transfer Policy

During the 1970s economic and political issues involving the transfer of technology came into focus. Questions pertaining to the free movement of technology from one political division to another were precipitated by such situations as the Control Data Corporation's desired sale of computer equipment to the Soviet Union. The United States in the 1970s allegedly had a significant lead in computer technology over the Soviet Union; issues raised relative to Control Data's right to sell the equipment revolved around the potential military application of this equipment which was obstensively to be used for peaceful monitoring of weather conditions. In addition, the equipment was far advanced over any known existing Soviet equipment; it was assumed that Soviet possession of this equipment would enable them to quickly bridge the existing technological gap in this field. The sale and export of this computer was subsequently held up as a consequence of U.S. government intervention. Control of transferred technology may be more illusory than real where there are transnational operations. A prohibition of a direct transfer between two countries can be circumvented by a transfer from one country to another, which may be politically permitted, and then having the second country, acting as a broker, complete the transfer to the third country.

Developing nations have strongly advocated the transfer of technology as a means of achieving technological parity with the more technologically advanced nations. There has been increasing reluctance on the part of developed nations to transfer technology as a relatively free good or as a "give-away." First, developed nations are unwilling to subsidize the R&D that invariably precedes technological development and, second, the free or relatively free transfer of a technology raises the spectre of creating a potential competitor.

Starting in the late 1970s, it became apparent that national policies on technology transfer, which had heretofore been nonexistent, were evolving.[27] The formulation of technology transfer policies is of concern to both developed and developing countries. It has been suggested that in the United States a technology transfer policy would have to recognize issues involved between the Western industrialized nations and Japan and between Western countries and communist bloc countries.[28] The transfer of technology between North and South countries raises additional issues and considerations.

Reactions from Developing Nations

As previously discussed, developing nations view technology transfer processes with skepticism, and often have, in fact, a hostile attitude. Hostility emanates from a widespread belief in developing countries that transferred technology from developed nations is almost invariably exploitative. Reflecting such negative attitudes are the growing number of laws and regulatory agencies in developing countries to control the flow and payments for transferred technology. Illustrative of the aforementioned, the Andean Pact countries of Bolivia, Colombia, Ecuador, Peru, and Venezuela have set up regulations of foreign capital where there have been technology transfer payments. Control includes registration and subsequent government approval where there have been royalty or related payments for the use of technology. Extending such controls, these countries have also prohibited royalty payments from subsidiaries to parent companies and are no longer permitting packaged sales of technology.

Further restrictions have been imposed, which require that each technological import be separately justified as to cost and the availability of competing technology. Brazil, Argentina, and Mexico have screening processes on imported technologies and restrictive payment schedules for royalties.[29]

Controls on Transferring Technology

Growing concern relative to uninhibited transfer of technology is being manifested in nationally developed control procedures. Controls reflecting evolving national policies are being formulated where restrictions on the free movement in and out of technology are perceived to have possible detrimental national consequences. In order to determine the feasibility of transferring technology in and out of a nation, some institutional mechanisms should exist.[30]

Most nations have procedures, or rules, governing international transactions. The degree of control can vary according to national political philosophy, the nature of the technology as when national security would be compromised, the appropriateness of the technology, the extent of technological dependence incurred, or balance of payments problems. Excessive institutional controls can discourage the transfer of technology; lax controls, on the other hand, which fail to recognize significant implications involved in exporting or importing technology, can lead to technological dependence or a failure to exploit indigenous natural and human resources.

The establishment of institutional controls must be in concert with national policies dealing with science and technology.[31] Institutional controls to provide guidance and perspective must be formulated with the entire science–technology spectrum in mind as distinct from a more narrow approach directed specifically to immediate technology transfer. Institutional control variations affecting the transfer of technology are extensive. Indicative of some control considerations are the following:[32]

Industrial Investments. The granting of investment licenses may take into evaluation such factors as the end product, its impact on the local economy, capital sources, local partnerships and investment, and balance of payment implications.

Project Analysis. A look at project compatibility and the local technological environment. Is the project technologically feasible within the environment? What impacts—favorable and unfavorable—might be expected as a consequence of the project? Such impacts could include extension of educational capabilities encouragement of peripheral industries, or the utilization of natural resources, ecological problems, and displacing people in the labor market to cite a few possibilities.

The Financial Aspects. This could include import and export of capital, currency restrictions, the availability of capital either internally or else externally by means of favorable loan arrangements with such international institutions as the World Bank, or perhaps there might be direct and total dependence of imported foreign capital. The long-range implications of such dependence must be evaluated.

Import Controls. Control of technological imports may result due to the need to foster the establishment of new industries, to protect existing industry from foreign competition, or to limit technological imports to transfer products or services which are deemed compatible with local needs and priorities. This control area might also consider pricing strategies designed to "dump" products in order to eliminate or compromise local production.

Control of Exporting Technology. The transfer of technology may not be compatible with national interests. Such transfers might involve selling high technology which could be converted from peaceful to military applications. Such transfers could also act as a form of technological subsidization to recipient nations since the donor or transferring nation would have underwritten developmental costs. The transfer of an advanced technology could affect a nation's competitive and economic position.[33]

The establishment of national control procedures through institutional arrangements relative to technology transfer should not proceed oblivious of innovational impacts. Technology transferred and properly utilized can be a compelling force for technological expansion and innovation; witness the Japanese experience. Institutionalism, or bureaucratic approaches, normally mitigate against innovation. The development of a national paranoia against technology import can easily lead to a national philosophy dictated by short-term activities which really perpetrate status quoism; this is often viewed as a relatively safe decisional position. What is required is the courage to take an intelligent long-term position and carefully examine innovational possibilities, consequenced by technological transfer processes, and selectively imposing controls which are compatible with long-term technological objectives.

Technology Transfer Policy Between Developing Nations

Developing nations can also benefit substantially from transfer of technology from other developing nations, especially where there is geographic proximity. Apparently, the pooling of resources and technological consortiums between developing nations has not been a common phenomenon. There should be strong incentives and national policy to encourage such transfer. Developing nations with geographic proximity invariably have common problems and a community of interests. These nations frequently have difficulty in solving problems by technological approaches because of limited natural and human resources. Combining resources can lead to the solution of common problems when individual effort might be ineffective. Added compulsion for mutual effort could occur where the technological problem(s) cannot be geographically restricted to one political domain.

Policy formulation should consider technological objectives. Technological objectives can range from immediacy to long-range technological development. It is also possible that the developing nation may derive no immediate direct benefits from the technology, but the long-term indirect benefits gained can be substantial in capital and knowledge formation which can be used for other developmental projects. Several technologies may be developed simultaneously. Then technologies should be evaluated in a systems context for compatibility with overall technological objectives.

Some Further Thoughts on a Technology Transfer Policy

The determination of technical policy is of great importance in overall national development. Technological policy would provide guidance in ascertaining the applicability and desirability of a transferred technology. Some overriding considerations in technology transfer policies are the strengthening of innovative technological capacity problem solving directed to regional needs, recognition of population constraints, and the transfer of a technology which can afford opportunity in attaining direct national goals or prove vital in developing international technological competitiveness.[34] Often political entities cannot facilitate effective technological development and transfer. The transnational firm with extensive resources, can, if properly employed, be a valuable vehicle in improving a nation's technological capabilities.

Problems and Advantages of Technology Transfer

Problems

The transfer of technology from one socioecopolitical environment to another should be preceded by careful analysis and planning. The introduction of a new or significantly modified technology often must anticipate and provide for a transitional period.

A recipient nation, motivated by a strong sense of nationalism may erect political and economic barriers to the transfer of a technology. Such barriers are manifested by import quotas, high tariffs, or outright exclusion due to a real or imagined threat of economic dominance leading to political vulnerability. Developed nations may place restrictions on imported technology to avoid technological dependence or unfavorable trade balances, or in response to local interests desiring protection. Developing nations, often capital poor, may need and want the technology but may place operational restrictions which discourage potential donors in the light of capital requirements, marketing and production start-up problems, and high risk. Additionally, potential donors could be dissuaded by the political instability of the recipient nation. The usual expenses and difficulties associated with transferring technology will be deterrents if there are no long-range expectations.

There are problems often encountered in the technology export country. Obstacles may develop where production is planned in a recipient country because of the fear of exporting capital and employment. The technology can involve national security considerations which could lead to legal sanctions against the firm by the parent country.

The quantity and quality of a nation's labor force can be a factor in transferring technology. Most developing nations are labor intensive and most developed nations are capital intensive in their production systems. The technology transferred from one economic system to another could cause serious disruptions to the work force. Transferring technology such as the production of a product to a developing country must take into account the amount of labor, the skill levels, and local factors affecting the working conditions. Often, firms seeking new production outlets are initially encouraged by large reservoirs of available and cheap labor. Too often there is disenchantment after the commencement of operations when it becomes apparent that the skill level is marginal or nonexistent, training is required with its attendant time and cost, there is low productivity, and there are quality control problems.

If local labor conditions are viewed realistically and planned for, the firm can derive a production benefit and ultimately a marketing benefit as a consequence of increased employment and spending power. The firm moving into a developing country should infuse a technology that creates rather than eliminates jobs. This is very relevant since most production-directed technologies are usually aimed at increasing production efficiencies to be internationally competitive; consequently, there is a shifting, changing, and eliminating of jobs. In a sense, the social consequence of technology is a very important consideration, and technological development should be planned with serious accommodation for utilization of human resources.

There are also serious attitudinal problems associated with the transfer of technology. Developing nations want freely transferred technology to narrow the technological gap between the developed and developing nations. The attitude of developing nations is generally that there is a moral right and justification for the free transfer of technology.

The developed nations seem to be increasingly skeptical about transferring technology without some retention of control and residual economic benefits. Of specific concerns are the huge expenditures to develop technology and the risk involved without retaining proprietary rights. It is generally felt among U.S. industries that the acquisition of technology by LDCs could provide them with an advantage in international markets.[35] An editorial in *U.S. News and World Report* decried the giving away of U.S. know-how. There is a feeling that transferred U.S. technology has materially helped foreign nations, allies and potential enemies as well, in closing the technological gap in military as well as economic power.[36]

There is a natural reluctance to "give" something of value away. Knowledge and information are often considered proprietary by individuals, organizations, and nations. Sometimes undue restrictions are placed on information, either because of the desire for competitive advantages or because of security requirements.

Samuel N. Bar-Zakay suggests that a donor of technology may be reluctant to delegate authority to a recipient for the following reasons:

1. The donor may not want to lose control of proprietary information.
2. The donor may want to stay in the picture to protect the investment.
3. The donor may want to create continuing dependence.
4. The recipient may not be able to assume control.[37]

It is also possible that a donor may be reluctant to transfer technology because there is insufficient prospect for return on investment. Or there is the fear, as previously mentioned, of ultimate competition. Jack Baranson further identifies barriers as problems of quality control, economics of size, and adaption difficulties to local conditions—for example, technical capability in the form of skilled technicians and applicable facilities.[38]

In some instances, cultural influences are so strong that an extensive transition is required before the recipient can operationally adopt the technology. In a complicated technology, innumerable factors must be considered before the technology can successfully be transferred. Cultural attitudes, such as the way of doing business, can impede transfer. In addition, a complicated technology usually involves interface with satellite industries. Where these satellite industries do not exist and where there are import restrictions, the transfer of technology may present almost unsurmountable obstacles.

There are several other possible impediments to technology transfer. Language can present formidable obstacles to understanding or proper interpretation of the information. Knowing what information is really relevant and knowing where to look for that information are other barriers. Much time and useless effort are expended in a fruitless information search or in performing unneeded work to gather knowledge which already exists and is available. It has been said, "If every scientist and engineer working in R&D would cut ten minutes a week from the time spent finding and evaluating data, it could save $100 million annually in R&D expenditures."[39] There is the possibility that the information is old, and newer and better data exist. With the time lag between information generation and dissemination it is important to tie into the most current information sources possible. Another problem on transfer is an understanding between the parties as to what is wanted and needed. There may be good faith on the part of both sides, but miscommunication can lead to misunderstanding and frustration. One of the authors was involved in such a project in the Dominican Republic where the scope of the activity was delineated by the sponsoring organization. The sponsor's interpretation of the issues involved was substantially different from the perceptions of the transferees. The result was an ineffectual transfer of technology caused by a communication breakdown.

There are many other elements in technology transfer. Few technologies are static. Importing a technology suggests the need and means to maintain that technology as a viable force. It must be recognized that technology can rapidly become obsolete and relatively worthless, unless there is commitment to keep building and incorporating changes as well as adopting the technology to local conditions.

Advantages

The previous section discussed many problems associated with the transfer of technology. Despite the problems, the potential advantages resulting from a successful transfer of technology can provide motivation to solve or minimize the applicable problems. There can be important economic and political benefits which accrue as a consequence of technology transfer. National needs can be satisfied quicker and cheaper with more effective use of scarce human and natural resources. Instead of the costs and the technical risks related to technological development, resources can be used to buy and build upon proven technologies. Resources can also be diverted to the development of new technologies which promise long-term benefits.

Selective technology transfer can help create new jobs, upgrade the labor force, and expand purchasing power. Increased productivity results in a greater range of economic choice and fosters economic progress. Technology transfer can provide the impetus to build new facilities or upgrade existing facilities. Production improvements should follow. Technology transfer can encourage expanded production by opening up new opportunities.

Expanded and improved production capability should improve a firm's or a nation's competitive position and decrease dependence on outside technological sources. Technology transfer can, as in the case of Japan, afford the opportunity for technological acceleration and the subsequent attainment of technological parity.

The transfer of appropriate technology can lead to political and sociological benefits. The technology should be utilized for community needs and interests. It should use human and natural resources for sociologically beneficial purposes. If there are improved economic standards leading to a better life with relative freedom from sickness, hunger, and material needs along with an expanded life expectancy, the economic attainments are consistent with sociological benefits. To accomplish economic objectives and social well-being there must be the right political climate.

Technology transfer can be instrumental in economic progress and sociological development. In such a milieu, political freedom and stability should thrive.

Endnotes Chapter Seven

1. "Technology Transfer and Utilization: Recommendations for Redirecting the Emphasis and Correcting the Imbalance," a report prepared by the Committee on Technology Transfer and Utilization of the National Academy of Engineering for the National Science Foundation, National Academy of Engineering, Washington, DC, 1974, pp. 4–5.
2. *Ibid.*, p. 5.
3. *Ibid.*, pp. 6–8. Also, *Excerpts from the Final Report of CACTAL Related to Transfer of Technology*, Brasilia, D.F., Brazil, May 12–19, 1972, Pilot Project on Transfer of Technology, Regional Scientific and Technological Development Program, Department of Scientific Affairs, Washington, DC, pp. 16–17.
4. *An Introduction to Policy Analysis in Science and Technology* #46, UNESCO, Paris, 1979, p. 49.
5. *Ibid.*, p. 54.
6. *Ibid.*, p. 49.
7. *Ibid.*, p. 54.
8. "Major issues arising from the transfer of technology to developing countries," UNCTAD document TD/B/AC, 11/10, Rev. 1, International Group on Transfer of Technology, 3rd session, 1974.
9. *An Introduction to Policy Analysis in Science and Technology*, *op. cit.*, p. 51.
10. "Federal Laboratories and Technology Transfer: Institutions, Linkages, and Processes," *National Science Foundation*, NSF-RA-R-74-018, Washington, DC, March 1974, pp. 39–40.
11. *Guidelines for the Study of the Transfer of Technology to Developing Countries*, United Nations, TD/B/AC, 11/9, New York, 1972, p. 5.
12. *Ibid.*
13. *Technology Transfer and Utilization*, *op. cit.*, pp. 7–8.
14. D. Roman, *Science, Technology and Innovation: A Systems Approach*, Columbus, OH: Grid Publishing Co., 1980, p. 181.
15. See *Spinoff 1980: An Annual Report*, National Aeronautics and Space Administration, Washington, DC, April 1980.
16. Roman, *op. cit.*, p. 184.

17. For a comprehensive discussion on professional meetings see E.B. Peters and D.D. Roman, "The Transfer of Scientific and Technical Information to Developing Nations," International Associations, 1973, no. 11.
18. Roman, *op. cit.*, p. 191.
19. *Ibid.*, pp. 198–199.
20. Edward E. David, Jr., "Moon Technology—Five Years Later," *The Wall Street Journal*, August 2, 1974.
21. *Guidelines for the Study of the Transfer of Technology to Developing Countries*, United Nations, TD/B/AC, 11/9, New York, 1972, p. 6.
22. *Excerpts from the Final Report of CACTAL, op. cit.*
23. *Guidelines for the Study of the Transfer of Technology to Developing Countries*, *op. cit.*, pp. 6–7.
24. William W. Winpisinger, "The Case Against Exporting U.S. Technology," *Research Management*, Vol. XXI, No. 2, March 1978, pp. 19–21. The author maintains that a unrestricted policy of technology transfer will, in the long run, negatively affect business and labor.
25. *Guidelines for the Study of the Transfer of Technology to Developing Countries*, *op. cit.*, pp. 15–16.
26. *Ibid.*, pp. 9–10.
27. *Technology Transfer and the Developing Countries*, Report of the Task Force on Technology Transfer, Chamber of Commerce of the United States, April 1977, p. i.
28. *Ibid.*
29. *Ibid.*, pp. 12–13.
30. *Guidelines for the Study of the Transfer of Technology to Developing Countries*, *op. cit.*, p. 48.
31. *Ibid.*
32. *Ibid.*, pp. 49–50.
33. A good discussion on this issue is contained in "Know-How for Sale: Concern Grows Over Rising U.S. Exports of Skilled Technology to Overseas Firms," *The Wall Street Journal*, September 5, 1979, p. 44.
34. *Excerpts from the Final Report of CACTAL related to Transfer of Technology*, *op. cit.*, pp. 17–18.
35. "Issue of Technology Transfer is Snag for 1979 U.N. Meeting," *Science*, October 7, 1977, p. 37.
36. Marvin Stone, "Giving Away Our Know-How", *U.S. News and World Report*, March 13, 1978, p. 96.
37. Samuel N. Bar-Zakey, "Technology Transfer Model," unpublished paper, The Rand Corporation, Santa Monica, CA, November 1970.
38. Jack Baranson, *Industrial Technologies for Developing Economies*, New York: Praeger, 1969.
39. Fred U. Wetzler, "Data Banks for R&D," *Research and Development*, June 1977, p. 54.

CHAPTER EIGHT

Appropriate Technology

A Foundation

Semantic Confusions

It is often possible to have minor variations in the interpretation of a single concept. Gradations of shading, which essentially express the same idea, frequently lead to confusion rather than enlightenment. Appropriate technology is the most widely used identification of the concept to be discussed in subsequent sections of this chapter. It is also considered important that in order to avoid semantic confusion identification and discussions of some variations to the basic theme are necessary.

Sardar and Rosser-Owen[1] identify several possible nomenclatures expressing, if not the same, at least closely parallel concepts such as soft technology, humane technology, new alchemy, peoples' technology, radial hardware, and biotechnics. To this list can be added more widely used descriptions such as *alternative technology*, *relevant technology*, *efficient technology*, and *adaptive technology*, as well as the most common terms, *intermediate* and *appropriate technology*.

Alternative technology[2] is not a concise philosophy. Alternative technology is considered technology with the following characteristics: labor intensity, small scale, localized, participatory, simple, and easily manageable. Alternative technologies are geared to satisfying local consumption requirements with a small surplus. Also, alternative technologies use unskilled indigenous labor in the production of a simple end product. Capital requirements are minimal and the equipment used is not capable of mass production. In fact, the means for production are frequently equipment abandoned as obsolete by more technically advanced societies. The essential strategy of alternative technology is to employ the unemployed and underemployed in rural areas of developing countries. A conflict arises when immediate needs are satisfied by technologically simple methods which in the long run tend to thwart efforts for modernization.

Robinson[3] adds a distinction in *efficient technology*. In explaining efficient technology he feels that an efficient appropriate technology involves the production of a good at a competitive price. A competitive price entails consideration of scarcities, opportunity costs, exchange rates, balance of payments, and the availability of capital. Robinson uses inputs and substitutions from the four factors of production: labor, land, capital, and entrepreneurship as determinants of ultimate efficiency of a technology.

Additional refinement is suggested by Veldhuis[4] in discerning between *appropriate* and *relevant technology*. Veldhuis maintains that a relevant technology is consistent with societal and political goals. Decisions relative to relevant technology are the responsibility of government. Such decisions entail the amount of investment and in what technologies the investment should be made.

Still another variation on the basic theme is that of *adaptive technology*. Schacht[5] feels that technologies must be adapted to the specific needs and situations of each individual country. An adaptive technology, by this definition, appears to become an appropriate technology. Adaption also implies modification; contra to the level of expectations of developing countries, an adaptive technology might not be a current or a competitive technology. However, an adaptive technology does imply elasticity or a transformation ability to change and adapt to evolving environmental pressures.

Intermediate Technology

Appropriate technology has evolved from intermediate technology; intermediate technology is associated with the late British Economist, E.F. Schumacher[6] who developed the concept during the 1960s. Fruition of Schumacher's ideas is found in his book, *Small is Beautiful — Economics as if People Mattered*, which has had a profound global impact. As the ideas expressed by Schumacher have taken hold, there has been a transition from intermediate to appropriate technology. The terms *intermediate* and *appropriate technology* frequently are used synonymously when there are, in fact, significant differences.

According to a World Bank report, there is a definite distinction between intermediate and appropriate technology.[7] Intermediate technology is applicable to transitional technology. A technology can be primitive, with the connotation of inherent inefficiencies, or it can be a capital-intensive, advanced technology, utilizing specialized resources. Intermediate technology represents some middle ground between technological extremes. It is important to note that an intermediate technology may not be an appropriate technology.

Another element in discerning between intermediate and appropriate technology regards unfavorable interpretation relative to intermediate technology. Many developing countries view intermediate technology as second-best or second-hand technology.[8] Schumacher recognized this interpretation of intermediate technology and felt objections stemming from this interpretation were really psychological. There was, and perhaps is, a feeling among developing nations that intermediate technology means withholding the best and foisting off inferior and outdated technology.[9]

Appropriate Technology

In evaluating an environment to attempt to determine the appropriateness of a technology, a broad range of factors must be considered. A technology which might be appropriate at a given time or place might not be appropriate at a different time or at a different place.

It is important to recognize that appropriate technology is not a second-rate technology. By definition the technology is appropriate to the environment in which it is employed. As a consequence, while it may not be the best technology in all possible environments, it is the best technology for a given environment at a given time. Jequier says an appropriate technology is best for the need consistent with the culture, such as a good reliable inexpensive resource limitation, the water pump or a roof for a slum dwelling. Considering inherent resource limitations, the water pump or the roof may reflect real ingenuity and innovation to meet needs using simple processes and available materials.[10]

There is almost complete association between appropriate technology and developing countries. This is too narrow an interpretation. Developed countries must also consider the limitations imposed by available resources and the competition for these resources as factors to be evaluated relative to the feasibility, sophistication level, and appropriateness of a technology.

There does seem to appear to be general agreement as to which component elements are essential in determining the appropriateness of a technology. Synthesis, by way of definition, would be that an appropriate technology would contribute to the improved social and economic conditions of a society by developing technological capabilities environmentally suitable in consonance with need, resources, labor, and capital.

In reaching possible agreement as to what constitutes an appropriate technology, consideration must be given to such elements as social and environmental goals, evaluation of technological impact, compatibility of the technology with needs in relation to social and economic conditions, the availability of capital, the type, quantity, and quality of indigenous labor, the cost of the technology and its subsequent dispersion, the scale or size of the technology and the existence and accessibility of natural resources.

Appropriate technology incorporates soft or social technology, as well as hard or engineering technology. Appropriate technology, to be effective, must accommodate custom and tradition.[11] There must also be recognition that in a given society the level of appropriate technology may, in the short run, be lower than that technology in other societies because of differing environmental requirements.[12]

An excellent and perceptive overview of appropriate technology is provided by Kamenetzky.[13] He expresses concern as to the focus of attention on ownership of the means of production between the state and private enterprise, to the exclusion of human factors. Regardless of ownership or control, according to Kamenetzky, the really critical human considerations, which he calls psychosocial factors, are how the production and distribution of goods and services are organized. In identifying very important additional components in determination of the appropriateness of a technology, he urges people participation in decision processes that affect their daily lives, some equity in income distribution, and the incorporation of psychological satisfactions, as well as economic benefits, into the process.

Kamenetzky aptly summarized appropriate technology as being sensitive to human needs, and in concert with such needs, optimizes the use of indigenous resources, protects the environment, minimizes the frustrations and unpleasant aspects of work, provides for increased worker and consumer participation in decision processes, encourages equitable income distribution, and reduces physical risks to workers.

In summation, appropriate technology will vary from situation to situation. To solve the problem of what constitutes appropriate technology, many elements must be integrated to reach some reasonably equitable solution. Not only are the elements as such important, but the degree or combination of these elements is also compelling in establishing an appropriate technology.

Planning Appropriate Technology

Environmental Constraints

An appropriate technology in one environmental setting could be an inappropriate technology when transferred to another social–political location. Technology environmental constraints would vary according to political systems, natural resources, cultural idiosyncrasies, demographics, and the sophistication level of national technological development. Social need would also be a critical factor in establishing national priorities and appropriate technology.

To generalize, an appropriate technology in a developed country might be a technology that contributes to political stability by affording consumer satisfaction and to economic well-being by supplying goods, services, and jobs. The appropriateness of the technology could be questionable even in another developed country unless technological modification takes place to accommodate environmental variations. The same technology could be inappropriate in a developing country because of additional environmental factors. Another paramount consideration is that even though a technology may be immediately appropriate in one environment, such technology could have negative impacts beyond the intended sphere of operations. Specifically, a technology that appears to be appropriate in one environment may be inappropriate because of ecological disturbances, the uneconomical use of scarce resources, or questionable international morality.

Ecological disturbances can result by destroying the balance of nature. Overpopulation or maldistribution of population is often a strong contributor to ecological problems. Population control measures in nations where such controls are most urgently needed have generally been nonexistent or inept.[14] Parallel to overpopulation are such problems as malnutrition, unemployment, and misuse of available land. Land abuse takes place due to overgrazing and deforestation, which subsequently leads to erosion. A pertinent example is the Sahara desert. It is estimated that each year the Sahara desert geographically erodes over an area twice as large as Cyprus.[15]

The uneconomical use of scarce resources affects the appropriateness of a technology. Wasteful habits have become a worldwide syndrome.[16] Conservation and appropriate technology are closely related. There is often extravagent use of energy. Intelligent use and moderate restraint could be globally beneficial. Waste is also evident by pollution. The discarding of materials before their economic life is over (or which can be regarded for reuse) is wasteful and contributes to pollution.

International morality can also impinge on the appropriateness of a technology. Plants raised in such countries as Turkey, Mexico, and Bolivia may contribute to those nations' income. When those plants are converted into drugs for illicit international trade the consequences of the technology go beyond geographic boundaries and acceptable international morality.

Developing countries have environmental conditions that frequently do not exist or differ in significant degree in developed countries. Some of these environmental factors which are often common to developing countries are high unemployment or underemployment of human resources, a predominantly unskilled labor force, a low literacy rate, a disproportionate percent of the population being poor, a practically insignificant strong middle class, inadequate educational facilities, insufficient health systems, malnutrition, and a primitive marketing mechanism.

Most developing nations are deficient in some critical national resources or have debilitating climates. There are, however, very apparent exceptions where economic resources exist and are exploited (for example, oil), or where resources exist but technological exploitation has not taken place (for example, South America). In some of the wealthier developing nations, the average per capita wealth is high, but of course this is illusory since there is maldistribution of the wealth and little of the wealth trickles down to the average person.

Nutritional resources also vary from critical deficiencies to no major problems among developing countries. In some countries, there is agricultural capability, but the population has outstripped the productive capability. In other countries, there are climatic or topographical problems creating inherent restrictions on food production. And, in other developing countries, food is no real problem, but inefficient marketing systems act as distributional restraints.

Each nation must evaluate environmental conditions relative to its existence. Each nation must determine what technologies are necessary, have promise, and are appropriate. The technology, the developmental level of the technology, and the degree of appropriateness will vary from environment to environment. National and local planning are essential as a prelude to the promotion of appropriate technology.

The Political Setting

It is possible to recognize the concept of appropriate technology politically and establish policy accordingly. At this writing there are no formal national policies on appropriate technology but a few African countries such as Nigeria, Tanzania, Ethiopia, Chana, and Kenya have created appropriate technology organizations.[17]

A political setting is generally critical to national technological development and could specifically be an instrumental factor on developing technology(ies) that are nationally appropriate. In developing countries there frequently is political instability and the political environment retards more often than abets appropriate technology. Whether the country is developed or developing, a politically stable regime with an operationally conducive environment can encourage private enterprise and subsequent investment. Government policies can be influencially directive in promoting technology. There can be calculated balancing of import and export controls; there can be liberalizing of licensing restrictions on importing and exporting raw materials; there can be provisions for tax incentives for investment, as well as for investment protection; there can be government subsidies to encourage high-risk projects; the government can provide incentive as a potential market for technologically developed products; there can be currency stabilization; there can be the promotion of product exports to encourage industry and capital formation; and there can be reasonable government controls on wage standards and other regulatory areas. The government can materially promote technology in some instances by underwriting, or direct financing of, socially desirable projects.

Appropriate technology can also be a product of political will and technological opportunity. Nelkin maintains that technological opportunity is contingent on the availability of the appropriate technology along with the receptivity of the political environment to embrace technological change.[18] Need and technological capability must coexist. To support this position Nelkin cites the case of the need for better automotive safety, where the technology existed and where the issue was politically viable to the U.S. Congress. There may also be situations where there is political receptivity, such as the desire for a cure for cancer, but the technology is not available. Or, the technology may exist, as in the disposal of solid wastes, but political pressures are weak. Another possibility is where neither the political nor technological pressures are strong enough to lead to solutions. Examples cited by Nelkin are mass production of artificial organs or general availability of low-cost housing.[19]

Degree of Appropriateness

To some degree all technologies are susceptible to environmental forces. The potentially negative impacts, based on environment, may discourage technological development. If negative factors can be neutralized, eliminated, or are minimal considering the potential for positive gains, technological development can proceed. To sponsor appropriate technology, it would be well to view such technology as to its degree of relevance or dimensions of appropriateness. The World Bank distinguishes four dimensions of appropriateness:

1. *Appropriateness of Goal.* Does the technology support the goals of development policy?
2. *Appropriateness of Product.* Is the final product or service delivered useful, acceptable and affordable to the intended users?
3. *Appropriateness of Process.* Does the production process make economic use of inputs?
4. *Cultural and Environmental Appropriateness.* Are the production processes, the products delivered, and the institutional arrangements compatible with the local environment and cultural setting?[20]

The above criteria suggested by the World Bank are useful as a starting point. Often there are many additional factors which are relevant and which must be evaluated before the degree of the appropriateness of a technology can be approximated.

Micro and Macro Aspects in Planning for Appropriate Technology

Both micro and macro elements enter into planning for appropriate technology. Promoting appropriate technology is primarily a macro approach. However, in a market economy some appropriate technology can evolve from micro effort. This would, in effect, be a bottom-up approach. Normally appropriate technology development would be a top-down macro approach. The extent of micro/macro planning latitude appropriate technological development would be susceptible to political influences, i.e., a market or a planned economy.

Commitment to appropriate technology involves planning and political support. Implementation of appropriate technology could be the exclusive domain of either the state or the private sector, or it could be a direct partnership or modified joint undertaking between government and private interests. This would vary according to the type of technology and national political ideology.

Long-range objectives must be identified to focus planning. Short and intermediate planning goals should be consistent with long-range objectives. Too often, such fundamentals are ignored due to short-run political pressures.

Politicians depend on public support for election and continuity; they are prone to look to the immediate future, the short-run payoff, rather than consider long-range consequences that might involve short-range sacrifice. As a consequence of the political environment, there generally is government by crisis rather than planning, rational development, and activity.

At times it is difficult to disassociate micro and macro factors. There often is a cause-and-effect relationship between such critical national and world problems as overpopulation, natural resource shortages, human skill development, inventory and utilization, maldistribution of wealth, terrorism, and pollution to indicate just a few problems. The intensity of some of the problems indicated would vary from society to society. Solving such problems using the concept of appropriate technology would require determination of national priorities and political commitment and planning based on anticipated benefits and liabilities.

Trade-offs undoubtedly would have to be made. Cost-effective analysis would have to take many factors into account. Is the technology highly localized? Is it regional? Does it have national implications? Is there export potential? What capital is needed and is capital available? Can capital formation be encouraged? How does this affect the population? Can jobs be created? Can new skills be developed? Can productivity and consumption be improved? To what extent are increased productivity and consumption desirable? What segment of society will benefit? Where is the most pressing need? Will this technology eliminate or relieve this need? Will satellite activities be encouraged? Will the technology contribute to balancing population distribution? Does the technology affect traditional cultural patterns? How? What possible impacts will result? Are there any health or moral considerations? Is there qualified management available to direct such technological activity?

It is also very possible that a technology may be needed but the resources required for technological development either do not exist or are so expensive in absolute or relative costs that technological development is impossible or unfeasible. As has been indicated, planning for appropriate technology is a complex process. The decision to support or not support development should be made after examining micro and macro factors and as a holistic process.

Appropriate Technology and Environmental Compatibility

The Operational Environment

There are stories such as building highways that lead nowhere or large modern airports where the traffic will not support such an endeavor. An appropriate technology should accomplish planned technical objectives and should also be compatible with the operational environment. It would be foolish to design a super four-lane highway using capital-intense equipment in a nation where ox carts are the normal transportation vehicles, where labor is plentiful and capital is scarce, and where there would be limited or no use of the capital equipment on similar or subsequent projects. What are appropriate methods of highway construction in one environment may be totally inappropriate in another environment.

The technology, to be appropriate, should be compatible with the production and market environment. To elaborate, N.V. Phillips, the Dutch transnational company, has a special unit that designs systems for Third World adaption. It is not unusual for Third World nations to desire production facilities that are not consistent with their environmental requirements or resources. Frequently these nations want high-production, technologically sophisticated, and expensive plants, but local markets are small and will not support such output. Additionally, because of capital limitations, which are almost inevitable, equipment must be simple, inexpensive, and maintainable. Also, management procedures should be adaptive and not complicated.[21]

An appropriate technology would entail need, a receptive environment, and available resources. All three of the aforementioned components have to be present before the system is designed. Existing technologies may require modification or repackaging to do the job. Departure from traditional methods may be indicated. Materials which are locally abundant may be employed where such materials would not normally be used, or might prove inadequate or too expensive in other environments. For example, in northwestern Florida, many secondary roadbeds are made from compacted oyster shells.

Products may have to be redesigned for local acceptance and use. These same products, as modified, would not be appropriate in other environments. A few further examples would be as follows: simple agricultural irrigation systems using hand pumps rather than electric equipment in areas where labor is plentiful and electricity or generators are not available or are economically beyond the means of the users; simple housing to provide adequate shelter and sanitation facilities which are affordable to poor people; inexpensive transport systems to facilitate communication and exchange, products which can be produced labor intensively.

Nontechnical Appropriateness

Haustein, Maier, and Robinson contend that there are other factors of importance besides technical appropriateness.[22] Appropriate technology usually involves social adaptation; change must be compatible with present and predicted national requirements. Also, the development of technological potential must be in response to demand. Demands and national goals must be coordinated.

It is very important to realize that all technologies do not proceed in their development at an equal pace. In any country it is probable that different technological levels will exist. An example of this is illustrated in Table 8-1.

In all countries it is very possible that less advanced technological systems exemplified by "A" to "C" may coexist. However, in developed countries "A" and "B" technologies will contribute relatively little production volume; there

Table 8-1. Levels of Technology

Level	Content	Example
A. Technology	Manual drive, task execution, control and logical functions	1. Drop spindle 2. Spinning wheel 3. Improved spinning wheel
B. Technology	Substitution of mechanical for human energy (power tools)	Spinning wheels with external drive power
C. Technology	Substitution of mechanical for human energy and task execution	1. Self–actor 2. Ring machine 3. Open-end spinning
D. Technology	Complete substitution of mechanical–technical for human operation, including control and logical functions	1. First-generation automated equipment 2. Second-generation automated equipment

Source: Data from Haustein et al., "Appropriate Technology."

will be different levels of technology which operate as segments of an integrated national system. Haustein et al. are of the opinion that the concept of intermediate technology is fundamentally concerned with advancing semi-mechanized technologies, class "B," but concentration of effort in this range of technological development will not be conducive to improving the standard of living in developing countries.[23] Further, it is not feasible to jump from the technological level "B" to a high-technological level, "D." Generally developing countries are unable to make such a transition because of investment inadequacies and labor skill shortages. Developing countries are faced with the necessity of designing a technological system that recognizes resource restraints and the developmental levels of the different technologies that can be used most effectively within the political system. If such objectives were achieved this would be an appropriate technology. In achieving appropriate technology there must be an holistic technological approach rather than the development of a technology as a single or isolated factor. Haustein et al. stress that while the prevailing view is to segregate individual technologies or technologies of a specific technological level, this is an unrealistic and impractical approach.[24] Appropriate technology, whether in a developed or in a developing country, must be considered in concert with other technologies and with an awareness that some total optimum return point can be approximated by using an efficient mixture of types and levels of technologies.

Table 8-2 is an attempt to indicate the impacts of possible technological levels relative to meeting the technological needs in developing countries:

1. An attempt should be made in governmental technology to achieve the proper mixture among technologies "a," "b," "c," and "d."

Table 8-2. Impact of Different Technology Levels[a] on the National Economy of Developing Countries

	Levels of Technology								
Criteria	**a1**	**a2**	**a3**	**b1**	**c1**	**c2**	**c3**	**d1**	**d2**
Effects on growth of production	0	1	2	2	2	3	3	3	3
Better satisfaction of basic income needs	0	0	1	1	2	3	3	4	4
Employment effect on capital growth savings	3	3	3	3	3	2	1	0	0
Effect on labor skills	0	0	0	1	2	2	3	4	4
Impact on national division of labor	0	0	0	1	3	3	4	4	4
Use of national resources	4	4	4	3	3	3	2	1	1
Integration in national market	4	4	4	4	3	3	2	2	2
Accommodation on national condition	4	4	4	4	2	2	1	0	0
Linkage to international developments	0	0	0	0	1	2	3	4	4
Sum of benefits	15	16	18	19	21	23	22	22	22
Expenditure Criteria									
R&D intensity	0	0	1	1	2	2	3	4	4
Demand to the infrastructure	0	0	0	1	2	2	3	4	4
Optimum production scale	0	0	0	0	1	2	3	4	4
Import share	0	0	0	1	3	3	4	4	4
Sum of expenditure criteria	0	0	1	3	8	9	13	16	16

Source: Data from Haustein et al., "Appropriate Technology".

[a]Evaluation: 0 = without importance; 1 = little importance; 2 = medium importance; 3 = high importance; 4 = very high importance.

2. A dominating role is allocated to technologies "b1," "c1," and "c2." This results from the benefits and criteria expenditure.
3. It appears necessary that in order to improve technological capability in a developing country transitions are required to go from technology "a" and "b" to "c3" and "d1" and to develop technology from level "c" to "d."[25]

Marketing considerations and available credit are other factors that must be provided for in designing an appropriate technology. Market institutions have to be organized and credit has to be made available for small manufacturers, farmers, and homeowners. Preliminary success resulting from properly designed technologies can lead to more advanced technology.[26]

The design of the technology may also have strategy implications. The strategy to increase the productivity of a small landowner in a developing country may incorporate such elements as land and tenancy reforms, credit availability, dependable water supply, improved seeds and agricultural methods for better and more voluminous crops, and available public services such as roads, power, health, drainage, irrigation, storage facilities, and transport systems.[27]

Designing a system to achieve appropriate technology objectives is far more complicated than it appears at first glance. The design of such a system immediately requires sensitivity to the operational environment with appropriate modification. To accomplish the immediate objectives of the appropriate technology, the system should strategically be designed to envelope extrinsic factors that can have a determinate bearing on the technology. In designing an appropriate system, there must be cognizance of size implications. As Schumacher asked, What is an appropriate scale? He felt that scale is a very crucial factor.[28] Added considerations relative to size would be how much growth is possible or desirable. Another extremely important aspect of designing a system for appropriate technology would be the implications beyond the immediate technology. What related activities might be affected—positively or negatively? What peripheral or new activities might be encouraged to support the technology, or what activities would emerge as a consequence of derived demand? There could be important multiplier affects and such a possibility should be given strong weight in designing an appropriate technology.

Technologies Which Can Be Inappropriate

Environmental Incompatibility

The prospect of developing a technology might be abandoned because after evaluation the technology is deemed to be inappropriate. An inappropriate technology has been defined as a technology which is not properly compatible to the local environment or is not technologically suited to that environment.[29]

The tendency is to think in terms of a technology being too advanced for a given environment but the possibility also exists that the technology will not be advanced enough to warrant resource expenditures relative to prospects for contributive gain. Environmental compatibility is, of course, fundamental. Even though there is a distinct requirement for a technology it can subsequently prove to be inappropriate because of design and engineering inadequacies. Many technologies have to be designed or redesigned and developed to accommodate the specific operational environment. A technology that is operationally efficient in one environment may not be operationally successful in a different environment.

There are discernible susceptibilities to inappropriate technologies. Factors contributing to adaption of inappropriate technology would be strongly directive government policies, the overpricing of labor, and the underevaluation of capital and foreign exchange. There could be internal discriminations against small farmers or producers as a consequence of inadequate credit or financial help, controls of raw material exports and imports, the lack of technological information and support, and managerial assistance. There are also the vested interest groups who may benefit from imported technology that is appropriate to their narrow interests, but which is very inappropriate to the total nation.[30]

Inappropriate Imported Technology

Before importing a technology, analysis of short- and long-range benefits and liabilities is important. There may be compelling short-run reasons to import a technology such as the technology exists and is known; there is operational experience, the technology can be procured in packaged and guaranteed form, and there can be quick application with external technical assistance.

In the long-run, such imported technologies may actually be inappropriate for a variety of causes. The various cost components, such as local prices, real costs of capital, labor, and foreign exchange, may be excessive or incompatible with local capital availability. Another cause for incompatibility may stem from size. A large-scale technology may not be properly utilized in the host country, making it inefficient costwise. This could lead to another difficulty in local pricing. The technology may not be appropriate to the market and may not be competitive with comparable products available in the international market. Still another very relevant consideration is associated with the continued dependence on the imported technology to the exclusion of developing local technology. The last argument is certainly not invariably true. Japan has been a frequent importer of technology but, rather than becoming dependent on imported technology, has used such technology as a base for the development and exploration of advanced versions of the imported technologies.

What might initially appear to be an appropriate technology can easily become an inappropriate technology if adequate allowance is not made for environmental factors. Frequently, there are institutional changes that must be accommodated, as well as necessary engineering modifications. Educational processes may be dictated in gaining public receptivity and government support.[31] Additionally, an imported technology may work very well in an environment where there is a capital-intensive structure and labor-saving devices represent an economic expediency. A good example is the development of mechanical agricultural harvesters because of labor problems and costs. The introduction of such a technology in a labor-intensive society could be a disaster by compounding unemployment.[32]

Appropriate Technology and Innovation

Negativism

Puristically and idealistically, the concept of appropriate technology appears to hold promise for societal and global improvement. Actually, there is much skepticism or overt negativism in some quarters as to the usefulness and validity of appropriate technology as a guiding principle and working doctrine.

In developed societies, it is possible to argue that no central body, probably politically motivated, has the omnipotence to determine the appropriateness of a technology. In a relatively free market directed society, technology should be determined by demand and supply forces in the marketplace.

There are very definite barriers to the acceptance and utilization of appropriate technology within developing countries. Many critics in LDCs view appropriate technology as "technological imperialism." They feel appropriate technology affords Western nations a vehicle to control poor countries for exploitation purposes; under this concept, Western countries would have continued access to vital resources needed to perpetuate the Western lifestyles.[33]

Many developing nations are not interested in appropriate or intermediate technology, which they consider as second-class technology. These proponents of technological parity desire to model their technologies along the lines of the advanced and capital-intensive technologies which are reflective of the industrialized nations.[34]

There really is no either/or position. Unqualified categorical commitment to either primitive or advanced phases of technology is not logical. Different technologies and different developmental phases of those technologies may vary nation-to-nation and in degree of appropriateness. Uncritical acceptance of advanced technology in a generally technologically depressed environment may create strains on the socioeconomic system. The technologies that are capital intensive may be very inappropriate and the barriers formidable in societies characterized by an unskilled labor force, high levels of unemployment, poverty, and the lack of an effective market mechanism.[35]

There are other barriers to appropriate technology; barriers to any technology exist to some degree in developed and developing societies. The appropriateness of a technology in any society must, among other things, be sensitive to size and size constraints, capital availability, political stability and receptivity, vested interest pressures, management availability, currency parity, wage laws, taxes, and the human inventory.

Underlying this discussion is the assumption that what is good and relevant in one society may not be commensurately good or relevant in another society. Appropriate technology is closely related to technology transfer and to innovation. Appropriate technology must be determined before technology transfer processes can be intelligently employed. Such transfers can result in productive innovation.

The Challenge

Innovation is not a simple process. The complications of an innovation process are invariably compounded by environmental constraints. To develop a technology requires innovation; the complexity of the technology will no doubt prove an innovative stimulant. Technological development can be approached in one of two ways: puristically, where the technology evolves with primary emphasis on the technology and secondary considerations adoption to possible operational environments; and applied, as in the case of appropriate technology where development is in direct response to "an" operational environment. In the second example the innovational challenge is quite acute.

There are, to be sure, innovational restraints in developed nations. These restraints are parallel to innovational restraints in developing countries with a few very significant differences. In all societies there are some degrees of restraint emanating from political, social, cultural, and economic systems. For instance, innovational motivational pressures and directions could be quite different in planned and market economy political systems. The one compelling difference affecting innovation between developed and developing countries is the innovational climate. Without attempting any value judgments, developed countries have invariably technologically progressed. Technological progression has been a by-product of innovation. Innovation and attendant change have been recognized and accepted within environmental limits in developed countries. On the other hand, environmental pressures resulting from political, social, cultural, and economic factors are almost always more pronounced in developing countries.

Developing countries are frequently characterized by societies which are technologically static when compared to developed nations. Again, without attempting to argue the good or bad aspects, developed nations have been subject to significant cultural changes. There has often been an erosion of traditional institutions. New values and new systems are evolving and dynamic technological change takes place in a generally but not universally responsive society. In a change-directed environment innovation represents a premium activity.

The developing nations are restricted in innovational processes. A static or slowly evolving society invariably is not receptive to change and innovation. Change and innovation must affect established patterns of behavior and entrenched institutions. Experimentation is further restricted by resource limitations. Considering the natural resource limitations of most developing nations, real innovation is required to use what resources do exist effectively to improve the quality of life. Developing nations also almost always suffer qualitative shortages of human resources. The Japanese experience has indicated that properly channeled innovation can circumvent natural resource limitations if there is a quality population.

A conclusion might be that developing nations are reluctant to affect cultural changes and at the same time they desire innovational technologies which if successfully transplanted must lead to the erosion of established cultural systems. A realistic approach is indicated. Appropriate technology is a desired goal. The appropriate technologies in developing societies present an awesome innovational challenge. Innovating an appropriate technology involves using the physical resources available, recognition of the limited range of human skills, provision for technological opportunity for the extension of human skills, and the need for a technology that will not immediately be disruptive of established institutions.

Endnotes Chapter Eight

1. Sardar, Z., and D.G. Rosser-Owen, "Science Policy and Developing Nations," in *Science, Technology and Society*, edited by Ina Spiegel-Rosing and Derek de Solla Price, London: Sage Publications, 1977, pp. 564–567.
2. *Ibid.*
3. Robinson, Austin, "The Availability of Appropriate Technologies," in *Appropriate Technologies for Third World Development*, edited by Austin Robinson, London: MacMillan Press, 1979, pp. 26–27.
4. Veldhuis, K.H., "Transfer and Adaption of Technology: Unilever as a Case Study," in *ibid*, p. 219.
5. Schacht, Wendy H., "International Technology Transfer to the Developing Nations and the Role of Appropriate Technology: A Background Paper," *Studies in Taxation, Public Finance and Related Subjects*, Science Policy Research Division, Congressional Research Service, Library of Congress, August 22, 1977, p. 461.
6. Schumacher, E.F. *Small is Beautiful — Economics as if People Mattered*, New York: Harper and Row Publishers, 1975.
7. *Appropriate Technology in World Bank Activities*, Document of the World Bank, Washington, DC, July 19, 1976, Appendix 1.
8. Proposal for a Program in Appropriate Technology (revised edition), 95th Congress, 1st Session, February 7, 1977, p. 11.
9. Schumacher, *op. cit.*, p. 181.
10. Jequier, N. "Appropriate Technology: Some Criteria," appearing in *Towards Global Action for Appropriate Technology*, edited by A.S. Bhalla, New York: Pergamon Press, 1979, p. 3.
11. Proposal for a Program in Appropriate Technology, *op. cit.*, p. 107.
12. *Appropriate Technology in World Bank Activities, op. cit.*, p. i.
13. Kamenetzky, M., 1978. "Psycho-Social Stability and the Appropriateness of Technology," unpublished research paper.
14. Richmond, Frederick U. "The Future of Egypt," *The Futurist*, December 1977, p. 367.
15. Eckholm, Eric, and Lester R. Brown, "The Deserts Are Coming," *The Futurist*, December 1977, pp. 361–369.
16. Purcell, Arthur H., "The World's Trashiest People," *The Futurist*, February 1981, pp. 51–59. Also see Schacht, W., W. Renfro, and K. Bea. "Appropriate Technology: A Review," Washington, DC, prepared for the Congressional Clearing House on the Future, the Library of Congress, Congressional Research Service, March 21, 1977, p. CRS-14.
17. Proposal for a Program in Appropriate Technology, *op. cit.*, p. 14.
18. Nelkin, D., "Technology and Public Policy," in Rosing and Price (eds.), *op. cit.* pp. 393–442.
19. *Ibid.*, p. 400.
20. *Appropriate Technology for World Bank Activities*, *op. cit.* p. 5.
21. Otten, A.L., "Pilot Plant Tests and Trains, Aiding Third World Industry," *The Wall Street Journal*, February 27, 1981, p. 25.
22. Haustein, H.D., Maier, H., and J. Robinson, "Appropriate Technology," unpublished working paper, International Institute for Applied Systems Analysis, Laxenburg, October 1979, WP-79-95, p. 4.
23. *Ibid.*, p. 7.
24. *Ibid.*
25. *Ibid.*, p. 8.

26. *Appropriate Technology in World Bank Activities*, *op. cit.*, p. IV-V.
27. *Ibid.*, p. 4, Appendix 2.
28. Schumacher, *op. cit.*, p. 66.
29. *Appropriate Technology in World Bank Activities*, *op. cit.*, Appendix 1.
30. *Ibid.*, p. ii.
31. *Ibid.*, pp. 2–3.
32. Proposal for a Program in Appropriate Technology, *op. cit.*, p. 86.
33. *Ibid.*, p. 13.
34. Schacht et al., *op. cit.*, CRS-5.
35. *Ibid.*

SECTION IV:

Diffusing Technology

CHAPTER NINE

International Procurement of Technology (I)

Introduction

New Products

In 1972, Fujitsu Ltd., a leading Japanese computer manufacturer, bought 22% of Amdahl, a small American computer firm. The purchase agreement included an opportunity for Fujitsu to increase its holdings to 39%. Amdahl is a competitor of IBM Inc. in the "large computer mainframe" sector. This acquisition has allowed Fujitsu to acquire sufficient technology to enhance Japan's capacity to manufacture similar computers and, in addition, to satisfy domestic demand, thereby threatening U.S. export markets throughout Asia.[1] This example represents a common marketing problem—consumer demand but no product available. The answer: Purchase the technology if necessary!

As mentioned in earlier chapters new products are essential to company growth as well as for an expansion of national economic frontiers. New product development is an integral part of business—as necessary as finance, marketing, and production. The actual contribution of new products to a company's growth varies from company to company and from industry to industry. The contribution rate will naturally be higher in "technologically dynamic" industries in which growth and survival are usually contingent on the successful introduction of new products.[2] A new product can be something new to the marketplace or something the consumer has never bought before. Also, a new product to the manufacturer can mean a change in the form, content, production process, package, or method of distribution of an existing product.[3] A Booz, Allen, and Hamilton study concluded that growth industries have been heavily oriented toward new product development. For the most part, those industries expending the most resources to develop new products experienced the greatest growth.[4]

New products do not just happen. They are the result of one or more of the specific actions as seen in Figure 9-1, and may be either discrete or deliberate combination of these factors. Each industrial enterprise normally has two sources of supply—within the company itself, or outside sources. It is natural that a firm doing business internationally would attempt, as a first choice, product genesis from within existing corporate boundaries. Internal development can include intrafirm research (basic research and/or applied research), intrafirm product development, or intrafirm product improvement.

In the event that total internal product development is not possible or feasible and if a discernible and desirable market does exist, an attempt to meet that demand may require some level of utilization of outside sources to supplement internal capabilities. While all of the options illustrated in Figure 9-1 are viable, this chapter will focus upon the purchase of technology, either outright or by licensing agreements. Table 9-1 indicates the advantages and disadvantages of an in-house R&D effort, outright technology purchase, and licensing (in-flow) technology.

Make or Buy Decision Factors

There are significant advantages in maintaining internal R&D capability, such as the creation of proprietary knowledge, the opportunity to train specialists in new technologies, product control, and attracting professionally accomplished people to the organization. On the other hand, purchasing technology requires

Figure 9-1. New product genesis.

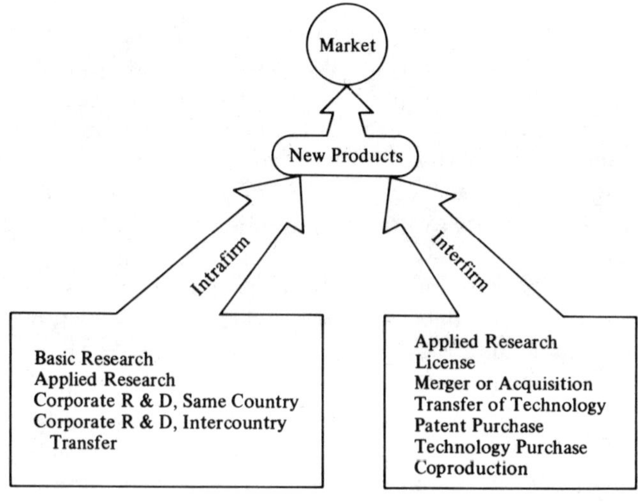

Table 9-1. Acquiring New Product Know-How

	In-House R&D	Purchasing Technology	Licensing (In-Flow)
Advantages	1. Obtain proprietary knowledge 2. Train specialists prior to production 3. Future revenues 4. Proprietory control 5. Attract professionals to organization	1. Little R&D 2. Low technical risk 3. Low financial risk 4. Full production enabled 5. Buy proven or successful technology	1. Obtain knowledge and know-how 2. Can calculate risk 3. Low R&D costs 4. Train specialists prior to production 5. Moderate period prior to full production 6. Low financial needs 7. Buy proven or successful technology
Disadvantages	1. High risk 2. High cost 3. Development time	1. Minimal proprietory knowledge 2. Training possible only after production commences 3. High purchase cost 4. Low competitive technological advantage 5. Limited control 6. Limited technological capability	1. Extensive search required 2. License fees required 3. Moderately high costs 4. Limited control 5. Technological dependence

little or no R&D, has little associated risk and cost, and enables rapid market penetration, because only proven technology is purchased.

There are several ways in which technology can be bought, ranging from an outright purchase of a design or patent, several intermediate arrangements requiring technical collaboration and/or equity participation, to direct investment in a wholly owned subsidiary. Licensing (in-flow) usually necessitates further R&D, provides time for some training of specialists, but is virtually risk-free and allows fast entry into markets.[5]

Technology acquisition can also be influenced by the sophistication and secrecy of the technology, the proprietary control and corporate policy of the seller, the absorptive capacity of the buyer, and the urgency and evaluation of opportunity costs.[6] Further, buying the know-how externally involves many other considerations, such as the following:

Locating sources of technology.

Contracting for technology.

Governmental regulations and restrictions.

Cost and financial analysis.

Quality.

Legal and security matters.

Additionally, when the technology purchase crosses political jurisdictions, difficulties in effecting a transfer are often compounded by currency conversions and cultural differences in how business is transacted.

Sources, Problems, Identification, Evaluation, Selection

Problems in International Technology Acquisition

International purchasing, as indicated in the preceding paragraph, is far more complicated than local acquisition. Endemic factors are the following:

Greater distances and lead times.

Communication differences.

Problems of interpretation or understanding.

Governmental regulations.

Currency conversion.

Trade regulations (tariffs and quotas).

Weights and measures.

Insurance, shipping, customs, legal requirements.

Inspection provisions (quality standards).

National differences as to customers, financial methods, and business practices.

National security.

Balance of trade problems.

Identifying the Source

The first step in crossing national boundaries is to purchase technology after need has been determined and after a *buy* rather than a *make* decision has been reached is the location of the source. Appendix A is a comprehensive listing of sources. The search usually begins by researching the following:

Professional publications (domestic and international).

Trade publications (domestic and international).

Foreign trade intermediaries and services.

International banks.

Trade fairs.

Miscellaneous sources.

The knowledge requirements are such as to probably transcend the capabilities of any single person, especially where a complex technology is involved; as a consequence, a project team is usually formed. The project manager's primary function is to coordinate the various necessary activities such as source location, technical capability analysis, managerial ability, financial responsibility, and legal implications. Included in the legal sector are such considerations as negotiations, standards, contracting, methods of payments, and accommodation for political factors. When all the necessary skills are identified, it becomes readily apparent that several different organizational functions will be involved in the acquisition process.

Foreign Trade Intermediaries and Services

It is possible that a firm has a large degree of technological internal capability, and the infrequency or the nature of its requirements to seek international technological assistance is not economically feasible to form a specialized project team. The firm may do most of its business with satisfactory domestic sources which has precluded it from developing internal foreign acquisition capability. Another possibility is that the firm does not have the internal resources or technical skills and sophistication to organize foreign technical acquisition teams. Where one, more, or all of the aforementioned conditions exist, the firm may find it easier to rely on specialized organizations or individuals who serve as international intermediaries to facilitate technology transfers.

"Foreign trade intermediaries and services" are collectively the variety of organizations and firms conducting "middleman" operations involved in importing or exporting. The following categories are designated in the trade according to major service provided. It should be apparent that any particular firm may perform one or more of the services. Import/export intermediaries are as follows:

Trade firms (export management companies).

Import/export merchants and wholesalers.

Import/export commission houses.

Agents and representatives.

State-controlled companies and agents.

Customs brokers.

Technology brokers.[7]

Each of these internuncios will be discussed in some detail. The extent of their involvement in a specific technology purchase transaction will depend upon such factors as the nature of the product, the nations involved, the legal elements of the contract, the nature of payment, and how the product is to be marketed internationally.

Trade firms or export management companies (EMC) deal in the import and export of technology, products, and equipment of every sort. They generally provide all functions associated with importing and exporting. They often provide all-around full services such as docks, transportation and shipping facilities, and financial services. They generally afford the advantages and convenience of worldwide operations and in-depth know-how. They offer lower internal operating costs and relatively shortened lead times. Costs are usually quoted on a commission basis. Use of these firms must be weighed against the expense of dealing with a foreign firm directly, the shortened lead time between identification and procurement, and lack of knowledge of the proposed supplier.

Import/export merchants and wholesalers are individuals and firms that already own or specifically purchase technology for the purpose of resale. They sell abroad through their own outlets. As they assume all the risks and perform all the intermediate steps, their fees are generally higher than those of EMCs.

Import/export commission houses act for exporters abroad, selling within a given nation on a commission basis. They, therefore, act as either a selling agent or buying agent. Such houses generally do not have the technology or merchandise billed to themselves although they handle many of the customs and shipping details. It is not unusual for a single firm to conduct both the import and export function.

Agents and representatives are resident in the buyer's country and represent particular foreign sellers. They may be either firms or individuals and normally do not assume financial responsibility, since their commission is paid by the seller. The risk of loss usually remains with the seller. Their primary interest is that of the seller and they act as a distributor. They usually are responsible for entry/exit details and necessary coordination with appropriate governmental agencies. They normally are under contract for a definite period of time (renewable by mutual consent). The contract defines territory, terms of sale, method of compensation, and other more specific details. They may operate on either an exclusive or nonexclusive basis. A possible disadvantage is that the seller has given up control over the marketing and sale, which may have future consequences.

State-controlled companies and agents are found in those nations having state trading monopolies—where business is conducted by a few government-sanctioned and controlled trading entities. The agents are either quasigovernmental firms, official governmental employees, or foreign governmental agencies empowered to conduct the importation and/or exportation of technology and goods. The fees and contracts will depend upon the types of contracts, nature of the technology, and extent of services rendered. Such agents do, however, enable expediting the transaction through governmental channels and the avoidance of "red tape."

Customs brokers act as agents of importers or exporters to handle the complex and exacting process of clearing the technology and perhaps prototypes in or out of the countries involved. These firms (although individuals occasionally so function) conduct freight-forwarding services in addition to their customs activities.

Technology brokers are "finders" and sellers of technology on the international stage. They help to provide a *match* of technology and productive capacity. Their function is to bring together buyers and sellers of technology of different nations. They are the "middlemen" of technology transfer. Their basic role is to bring the source and the user together with an inherent savings in time and money.

The objectives and activities of the technology broker are as follows:

1. To determine the specific opportunities for technology transfer in terms of specific requirements—to be guided by "market pull" rather than "technology push."
2. To identify appropriate sources of technical breakthroughs, scientific information, and other technological developments that will meet identified needs.
3. To build bridges between sources and users.
4. To follow through initial contacts with other services, skills, and inputs to accommodate commercialization.[8]

The brokers work for fees, paid by the originator of the search procedure. A variation of this activity will be discussed in more detail in a later chapter.

International Banks

International banks are willing to provide assistance in the worldwide search for technology. Often, large corporations will consult with the international banking department of their corporate bank for trade inquiry in a particular foreign country as well as credit investigation. The correspondent bank of the company's bank will often accomplish the inquiry or credit investigation if the company's bank does not have offices in that particular country. There are numerous banks and other financial institutions that involve themselves in international operations, providing assistance in locating the technology sources and financing the purchase. Table 9-2 provides an overview of potential sources for financing international purchases.

Overseas subsidiaries of U.S. or European banks are usually in the forefront in their willingness to service investors. Local banks often provide excellent service, may have invaluable contacts not accessible to foreign banks, and often may be the only bank available. Private individuals, as contacted by banking agencies, can also be extremely attractive as sources of financing in terms of cost, freedom of restrictions, government controls and/or bank traditions (which often severely encumber bank activities).

Other Sources

Other sources of information and services are available. The majority of those listed are more prepared to assist only American firms. Similar agencies, offices, and sources are affiliated with each of the major developed nations. The U.S. sources to be discussed are as follows:

National governmental agencies.

Trade missions.

Seminar missions.

Catalog shows.

Table 9-2. Foreign Technology Financing

	Form of Assistance[a]		Parent Company	Currency
	Loan	Equity	Guarantees	Source
First country				
Parent	X	X	N	O
Financial agencies	X	X	X	O
Gov't agencies	X	N	X	D, O
International agencies	X	X	X	D, O
Second country				
Commercial banks				
Local	X	X	X	D, O
First country office	X	X	X	D
Private individual	X	X	X	D
Government	X	X	X	D
Third Country				
Intracompany	X	X	N	O
Commercial bank	X	X	X	O
Open Market				
Eurodollar	X	N	X	O
Security market	X	X	X	O

[a] X = available; N = not available; O = other; D = domestic.

Trade centers.

Telephone books.

Chambers of commerce.

National governmental agencies such as the U.S. Department of Commerce are committed to aiding U.S. businesses searching for foreign opportunities. The Department of Commerce maintains up-to-date listings, termed "export contact lists," of foreign buyers, distributors, and agents for various products in many countries. The information is stored on a master computer file designated as the "Foreign Traders Index" (FTI). The file contains information on more than 140,000 importing firms, agents, representatives, distributors, manufacturers, service organizations, retailers, and potential end-users of products in 143 countries. Newly identified firms are added to the file; information is available in three forms: (1) Export Mailing List Service (EMLS), (2) FTI Data Tape Service (DTS), and (3) trade lists. The EMLSs are specially targeted retrievals for individual requestors wishing to obtain lists of foreign firms in selected countries by commodity classification. Information includes name and address of firm, name and title of the chief executive officer, type of organization, year established, relative size, number of employees and sales personnel, and product or service by Standard Industrial Classification (SIC) number. The DTS offers information on all firms included in the FTI for all or selected countries on magnetic tape. Users can retrieve various segments of the data in unlimited combinations through their own computer facilities. Trade lists are available in two forms: (1) lists of controlled trading companies in countries where state-owned or controlled organizations conduct foreign trade, or (2) lists of business firms in selected developed countries contained in the automated Foreign Trader Index. These lists give names and addresses of foreign companies dealing in specific products in more than 100 countries. They also identify importers and dealers, giving names and addresses, the size of each firm, classified by the products they handle and services they offer, and the acceptable language of correspondence.

World Traders Data Reports produced by the U.S. Foreign Service provide commercial information on individual overseas firms whose names may have been located from the Trade lists. These reports are much more detailed. They describe the size of the firm, year established, product line, sales territories, and names of principal owners and officers. They list the type of organization, method of operation, capital, sales volume, general reputation in trade and financial circles, name of firm's trading connections, and an evaluation of the foreign firm's suitability as a trade contact for U.S. firms.

The Agent/Distributor Service (ADS) of the Department of Commerce can assist in locating interested and qualified agents or distributors in foreign countries. Upon request, U.S. Foreign Service personnel will make direct inquiries with appropriate overseas representatives to determine their interest in a proposal. The names and addresses of up to six foreign firms are furnished to the requestor for direct negotiation. This service is best utilized when market indicators point to an existing or potential demand and when tariff barriers or other import restrictions are favorable.

The Trade Opportunities Program (TOP) established by the Department of Commerce also furnishes U.S. business with detailed opportunities with overseas buyers—private and government, as well as notices of foreign companies offering to represent U.S. firms overseas. Americans indicate the specific product categories, type of opportunities, and countries for which they wish to receive leads. The information is coded into a computer. As leads are reported from foreign sources, they are computer matched with U.S. requirements. Individual trade opportunity notices are automatically sent to subscribers of the service. These trade leads are generated by more than 200 American Embassies and Consulates overseas that cable information to the TOPs in Washington, DC. The program has two levels of participation: (1) individual notices against a specific request, and (2) general notification published weekly in the *TOP Bulletin* revealing all the trade leads of all types, direct sales, representation, and foreign government tenders, developed in the period.

Reports on commodities, industries, and economic conditions may be prepared by U.S. Foreign Service officers. Additionally, in-depth foreign market surveys are frequently prepared by private research organizations on contract basis as part of the Department's "Foreign Market Report Program." These reports are available to individuals.

The Foreign Buyer Program is designed to increase the purchase of American products and services by foreign business visitors to the United States Facilitative services include identifying U.S. suppliers, services, and technology. The service also includes setting up itineraries, business appointments, plant visits, seminars, and other arrangements suited to the visitors' business needs.[9]

The Import–Export Bank of the United States (Eximbank) is a financially self-sustaining, independent U.S. government agency whose primary purpose is to facilitate the export of U.S. goods and services. Eximbank works closely with the Overseas Private Investment Corporation (OPIC) to put together appropriate export and investment financial packages. Eximbank maintains a Small Business Advisory Services and, additionally, offers a comprehensive briefing program. Their policy calls for them to assist in the location of foreign technology for U.S. subscribers.

OPIC is also an independent, financially self-sustaining agency of the U.S. government which offers businesses appropriate guidance, counseling, and financial support in determining how and where to invest in developing countries. Insurance protection and financial services are also available. OPIC is the agency through which the federal government encourages and assists foreign investment. Its two principal operating departments are the Insurance and Finance Departments. Through their worldwide operations, OPIC has developed leads for U.S. firms seeking technology.[10]

Trade missions provide another means of identifying specific technologies. They usually consist of eight to ten companies from a specific industry promoting the sale of products or services. Members usually pay their own expenses and a share of the overseas operating costs. They will conduct business, make contacts, and sell products while on tour.

Seminar missions are similar to trade missions. The members present authoritative state-of-the arts presentations to key foreign government, industry, and technical leaders in carefully planned, well-publicized seminars—often cosponsored by local trade associations. Following the seminars, time is allocated for individual business appointments.

Catalog shows entail a promotion technique featuring special displays of product catalogs, sales brochures, and other graphic sales aids at foreign consolates, embassies, or in conjunction with trade fairs.

Trade centers are usually semipermanent installations complete with exhibition halls, visitor lounges, telephones, exhibition booths, a permanent staff, and other facilities required for a successful exhibition. The staff can usually arrange business contacts as necessary and appropriate.

Telephone books from the major foreign cities can also often provide a source of information. They usually offer only scanty leads, which can be more fully developed in combination with some of the aforementioned sources.

Chambers of commerce are to be found in the major cities of the world. They are often an invaluable source of information and assistance. They usually will have city directories, general directories, or other specialized references, as well as trade journals covering industries of importance in the region. In many large communities, chambers of commerce publish classified buyers' guides, manufacturers' guides, or lists of international traders in their localities. They are well-informed on business in the area, and are in a position to advise and make recommendations.

Evaluating and Selecting Sources

A foreign supplier's failure to perform, especially if it is a specialized sole source procurement can lead to a crisis situation. The buyer must have a high level of confidence that the supplier will perform per agreement so proper supplier evaluation is critical before making any significant procurement commitment. Foreign, *vis à vis* domestic procurement can be aggravated by gaps in communications, legal and financial matters, quality and measurement standards, determinations of real costs, and length of lead times.[11]

Language can be a stringent barrier to successful foreign purchasing. Often industrial purchasing entails highly technical specifications so communication and mutual understanding are of vital importance. Mutual fluency in a language is essential to minimize misunderstanding but even this fluency will not alleviate all problems. Cultural, religious, environmental, and other socioeconomic factors are all potential reasons for different interpretations of words and phrases.

Purchase laws are different in each country. Necessarily, buyers and sellers should exercise more precision and care than normal when negotiating international contracts. Each is working from a different legal framework. Financing and foreign purchase is complicated by the various currencies involved and the constant change in values relative to each other.[12]

Quality presents special challenges for negotiators. All too often there is a tendency, particularly in the public sector of developing countries, to substitute quantity for quality.[13] Quality often is relative and is a multifaceted combination of cost, measurements, standards, workmanship, materials, and level of technology. Nations on metric systems of measurement have to be prepared to convert American engineering data from inches to millimeters, feet to centimeters, and yards to meters. On the other hand, Americans buying overseas find that they will have to specify quality characteristics that were implicit in domestic agreements. These intricacies tend to be worked-out over time but can spell trouble for new trading partners. Realistically, physical separation of trading partners complicates even the most simple problem and can cause time delays in the acquisition process.[14]

There may be greater real costs in buying overseas than is initially apparent. Costs of the technology search, legal arrangements, tariff and custom duties often are not perceived until after the contract has been negotiated. They are insidious factors because they are not present in domestic situations. Even when there has been international procurement experience it is difficult to cost all items fully until after the acquisition has been completed.

These ingredients combine to make purchasing international technology a tedious and exacting process. Such factors as need, available technology, cost advantages, and control of the technology must override inconvenience and complexity. Selecting a source with whom one can work and trust, and who is dependable, is especially critical in the international arena.

Source Evaluation

Eligibility of the candidate suppliers should be determined by the buyer before any time-consuming and costly negotiations take place. The analysis should seek to assess internal operational elements such as related experience, management, reliability, financial responsibility, quality reputation, and external elements such as governmental regulatory constraints, technology competition, national security, balance of payments restrictions, and public attitudes. A potential seller may be disqualified due to national rules, policies, and regulations such as

> "Buy America Act," "Soviet Controlled Areas," "U.S. Products—Military Assistance Program," "Duty Free Entry—Canadian Supplies," "Patent Rights," "Rights in Technical Data," "Military Security Requirements," "Preference for Certain Domestic Commodities," and "Ocean Transport of Government-Owned Supplies."[15]

The objective is to identify those factors which may indicate potential problems and weed them out as soon as possible.

Techniques of Evaluation

Techniques of evaluation to determine supplier capability vary with the complexity and relative cost of the purchase. The evaluation process must be conducted on two levels: (1) evaluating the worthiness of the technology and (2) assessing the capabilities of the supplier. Appraisal techniques may include the following:

Technology/Source Screen.

Technology/Source Evaluation Sheet.

Technology/Source Value Index.

Of the above techniques, the Technology/Source Screen is the most simplistic. Facts pertinent to the technology and the supplier are collected and listed for each alternative. Alternatives are then evaluated which best fit organizational needs in terms of quality, cost, reliability, ease of transfer, ease of assimilation, and any other factors that are germane to the procurement.

The Technology/Source Evaluation Sheet procedure is an often-used technique.[16] A number of important considerations are enumerated—for example, cost of technology, ease of transfer, governmental regulation, effect on present products, technical opportunity, materials availability, and competition; the candidate technology is then evaluated from "1" to "5" for each of these factors. "1" is "very poor" or a low rating, and "5" is "excellent" or especially favorable. The process may be refined by applying numerical weights to each factor which might reflect organizational goals, policies, and strategies. Table 9-3 is an illustration of such an evaluation. In this instance, a similar sheet would be developed for every alternative under consideration. Total scores would be compared. Additionally, there may well be company-imposed minimum scores, which further assists in the decision process. The scores in the example could vary between "0" and "5." The example represents an item with an above average rating.

The Technology/Sources Value Index is a more sophisticated, mathematical analysis of the cost and revenue variables. The resulting index would provide

Table 9-3. Technology/Source Evaluation Sheet

A **Characteristic**	B **Weight**	C **Rating**	D **Factor Score** **(B × C)**
Cost	.30	5	1.50
Transfer ease	.20	4	.80
Governmental regulation	.05	4	.20
Effects on products	.05	3	.15
Technical opportunity	.10	4	.40
Materials availability	.10	3	.30
Competition	.20	3	.60
	1.00		3.95

the basis for comparison between competing technologies and a ranking among them. The formula is

$$\text{TSVI} = \frac{\text{ST} \times \text{TE} \times \text{D} \times \text{S} \times \text{GR} \times \text{P/L}}{\text{TC}}$$

where

TSVI = Technology/Source Value Index

ST = Technical success (scale 1 to 5)

TE = Transfer ease (scale 1 to 5)

D = Forecasted demand (annual demand)

S = Seller dependability (scale 1 to 5)

GR = Governmental regulations (scale 1 to 5)

P = Expected profit (per unit)

L = Life of product (in years)

TC = Total cost (all identifiable costs)

The variable as selected would be a reflection of corporate policies, and aspirations.

Other more rigorous evaluation techniques such as breakeven analysis, linear programming, rate-of-return, opportunity cost evaluation, and cost–benefit analysis calculations could also be used. However, they are more appropriate for selecting the actual technology *vis à vis* the seller of technology.

Contracting for Technology

Direct vs Indirect Purchasing

After selecting the supplier, consideration should be given to "direct" versus "indirect" transactions.

Direct purchasing refers to the direct contractual relationship with a foreign firm as distinct from placing an order for foreign technology with an intermediary. Direct purchasing requires the involvement of the buyer in all aspects of international transaction and can reduce costs significantly by eliminating the "middleman." Certain outside agencies may, however, be required for such specialized services as foreign clearances (export brokers), entrance clearances (customs brokers) or freight forwarders for handling prototypes.[17] Direct purchasing may be feasible if there is sufficient volume, frequent purchases, and no specialized skills or procedures involved outside the existing organizational skill inventory.

Indirect purchasing refers to the purchase of imported technology from import merchants, commission houses, import wholesalers, or trading firms. It is essentially a domestic transaction whereby an order is placed with an importer who assumes all responsibilities, risks, and the handling of all details and making delivery as specified by the buyer. The degree of difficulty encountered usually depends on the nature of the product. The more complex and technologically advanced the item, the more involved the time consuming the transactions. The ability of the buyer and other company personnel to handle complex transactions can influence decision for either "direct" or "indirect" involvement.

Negotiation

Negotiation of the actual contract is technically similar to those techniques used domestically. The difficulties encountered usually lie in the following areas:

Language and mode of communication.

Systems of currency, weights and measures.

Sociotechnocultural characteristics.

Management style and "rules of the game."[18]

Effective foreign supplier contact and proper negotiations are vital to avoid misunderstandings that could result in contract problems. Negotiation and subsequent contract terms agreeable to both parties are extremely important because the resolution of legal problems in international transactions is invariably costly, time consuming, and difficult where there are different political jurisdictions.

The larger foreign firms are likely to be familiar with American business practices, and can be expected to behave much as U.S. firms. There are, however, predictable national personality differences. For instance, the Japanese are notorious for being indirect; causing many Americans to complain of receiving a "snow job." They are constantly wined and dined by their Japanese hosts, taking long periods before and between business sessions. Negotiations, therefore, are obscure and indirect, and American impatience must be curbed as it is not appreciated.

Relations with the members of COMECON (the communist bloc countries) pose very special considerations. Here the buyer/seller is dealing with a governmental agency rather than a private firm. This presents unusual problems of bureaucratic "red-tape" and requires particular care and deliberation.

As each culture has its own code of ethics, what is acceptable in one culture may be taboo in another. Business ethics among the technologically advanced nations are usually similar, but there are still minor differences. The buyer/seller of technology would be well advised to receive an in-depth, comprehensive briefing as to ethics and mores of the host nation prior to commencing negotiations. As an example, it is not unusual for negotiators to exchange gifts in many countries; this is particularly true in Japan and most Middle-Eastern countries. The buyer/seller should have a gift for each host which is to be presented at the time of departure. To ignore this custom would be an insult.[19]

The actual negotiation process may range from being a "simple walk through" of the details, or it may be a lengthy, taxing, complex process. Regardless, the buyer should ensure that certain elements are discussed; these include the following:

Purchase terms.

Title transfer.

Degree of technical support.

Means of payment.

Time-length of the agreement.

Specifications.

Nature of prototypes.

Responsibilities of seller and buyer.

Schedule of transfer.

Error redress.

Punitive measures.

It must be recognized that successful buyers have a sophisticated approach to negotiation. They realize that they can only negotiate those points which the supplier is willing to concede. Some of the principles that have been applied to successful negotiations are the following:

Put yourself in the seller's shoes.

Let the seller do most of the talking.

Give the seller room to "save face."

Satisfy the seller's needs.

Speak with the proper person.

Sell the seller.

Discuss and settle one point at a time.

Do not rush the process.

Be honest and impersonal.[20]

There is no way that a buyer can force a seller to do what he wants—or vice versa. Preliminary informal contact is often an ideal way to achieve a meeting of the minds so that each party can appreciate the other's goals and often eases the formal negotiation process.

The object of negotiation is agreement. Most authorities feel that the issues should be discussed in the order of their probable ease of solution. With this approach an atmosphere of cooperation can develop that may facilitate solving the more difficult issues. Traditionally those issues germane to the seller are presented first, followed by those issues of interest to the buyer. An air of agreement must prevail, for once the party adopts the position of "take it or leave it," negotiations can break down! This atmosphere is particularly difficult to maintain, but is even more important in the international arena because of the likelihood for misunderstanding. It is often preferable to reach no agreement than to reach an unsatisfactory agreement. The successful negotiator habitually enters negotiating sessions with higher goals than the adversary and generally achieves them.[21]

Purchase Contracts

Essential elements of contracts are basically the same throughout the world. To be valid and enforceable, a contract must contain four basic elements: (1) agreement ("meeting of the minds") resulting from an offer and an acceptance, (2) competent parties, (3) considerations or obligation, and (4) a lawful purpose.

The Uniform Commercial Code of the United States says that "conduct by both parties which recognize the existence of a contract is sufficient to establish a contract or sale although the writings of the parties do not otherwise establish a contract." Especially important in technology contracts are the conditions that may be attached to the transfer. Often these conditions restrict the freedom of the purchaser to buy and sell commodities related to the technology thus transferred, and may sometimes stipulate how the benefits of future technological advances by the buyer are to be exploited, how the contracts are to be terminated and where disputes are to be arbitrated.[22]

A valid contract must be only consummated by persons who have full contractual credentials. This is often a problem when dealing with agents of foreign governments. The agent may not have full contractual authority and hence be incapable of signatory authority. It is well to ascertain the extent of the trading agent's official capacity early in the negotiating process.

In addition to a meeting of minds, a valid contract must also contain the element of obligation. Most purchase contacts are bilateral; that is, both parties agree to do something they would not otherwise be required to do. The important point is the mutuality of obligation.[23] The importance of bargaining can hardly be overstressed. The acceptable price to the seller may lie between the marginal cost of transferring the technology and the price that would drive the buyer to other sources of technology. The price to the buyer will lie between zero and the net (after allowance for profit) discounted stream of benefits that is expected from the new technology, or the net cost of finding alternative sources of technology.[24]

A contract whose purpose is illegal is automatically illegal and void. A contract whose primary purpose is legal, but with one or more illegal ancillary terms may be either void or valid, depending upon the severity of the illegality and the extent to which the term(s) may be separated from the contract.

A controversial aspect of international purchasing termed "offset" is becoming an increasingly prevalent special clause of international purchase contracts.

In essence, an offset arrangement is that in which the seller agrees to spend a certain percentage of the sales price in the buyer's country. The buyer's objective is to "offset" a portion of the hard costs in payments other than currency—perhaps through coproduction (to be addressed in a later chapter), or perhaps in commodities. Almost all offsets share these common elements:

The overture for offset usually originates with the buying country or company.

The offset agreement is formalized in a separate contract after an "agreement in principle" has been reached in the main sales contract.

The objective of the offset arrangement is leverage for the buying country.[25]

Both buyers and sellers should have cognizance of offsets as they may well be proposed in the negotiating process.

Technology Purchases

Purchases of technology will generally fall into the following categories:

Raw materials.

Low-technology goods.

High-technology goods.

Services.

Raw materials technology purchases will normally be relatively less complicated than the purchase of high-technology items. The purchase of raw materials can vary from material in its raw state to material that has been converted and can be directly employed in production processes. Conversions processes might range from simple processing to technologically sophisticated conversions. Grading or quality standards are factors that must be accommodated in contractual arrangements. It is possible that where highly technical conversions have been made and there are unique characteristics of the raw material there might be contractual provisions which require the seller to provide on-site assistance and followup.

Low-technology goods usually present the least amount of problems. Here, the purchase of technology is forthright and there are relatively few areas for misunderstanding. The technology is also generally well-known to the purchaser. In such acquisitions, special contract considerations might include discussions of modifications and future improvements.

High-technology goods are the most difficult for which to contract. There are many variables, and often new technological frontiers are involved for the buyer or seller or both. There may be a failure to include in the contract items such as technical specifications, quality standards, materials and material technology, machinery specifications, and future developments and changes. The manufacture and production of high-technology goods normally require close coordination including on-site assistance and technical advice.

Service contracts are relatively easy to negotiate. These contracts will normally specify the level of competence, frequency, and duration of assistance desired. These matters should be included in the body of the main technological purchase package.

As indicated, there are many pitfalls in the contracting process. It is important that the buyer be cognizant of the following items, regardless of the nature of the purchased technology:

Contract terms.

Patent restrictions.

Engineering specifications.

Delivery dates.

Governmental restrictions.

Cost.

Endnotes Chapter Nine

1. "Technology Transfer from Foreign Direct Investment in the United States," Report of Seminar Series, National Academy of Engineering, National Academy of Sciences, Washington, DC, 1976.
2. Daniel D. Roman, *Science, Technology, and Innovation: A Systems Approach*, Columbus, OH: Grid Publishing, 1980, pp. 387–388.
3. *Ibid.*, p. 288.
4. *Management of New Products*, 4th ed., New York: Booz, Allen and Hamilton, 1964, p. 2.
5. William Marcy, "Acquiring and Selling Technology—Licensing Do's and Don'ts," *Research Management*, May 1979, pp. 18–19.
6. Sanjaya Lall and Paul Streeten, *Foreign Investment, Transnationals and Developing Countries*, Boulder, CO: Westview Press, 1977, pp. 66–68.
7. This listing was modified from those included in "An Operational Approach to International Purchasing," by C.L. Scott and Eddie S.W. Hang, TRW Inc., 1975. This publication is a comprehensive guide to U.S. firms desiring to purchase internationally. The services as listed conform to existing U.S. Department of Commerce definitions and service categories. Another excellent guide is "A Basic Guide to Exporting," a U.S. Department of Commerce publication.
8. The U.S. Department of Commerce has a number of publications available which explain these programs in more detail and list fees. These pamphlets include *Export Contact List Services*, November 1979; *The Agent/Distributor Service*, August 1978; *Export Information Services*, September 1979; *Trade Opportunities Program*, March 1979.
9. *Export Information Services*, U.S. Department of Commerce, September 1979.
10. *The Small Business Market in the World*, U.S. Department of Commerce, 1979, pp. 24–25.
11. Dean S. Ammer, *Materials Management and Purchasing*, 4th ed., Homewood, IL: Richard D. Irwin, 1980, pp. 380–382.
12. *Ibid.*, pp. 381–382.
13. Jorge A. Sabato, "Quantity versus Quality in Scientific Research: The Special Case of Developing Countries," *Impact of Science on Society*, Vol. XX, No. 3, 1970, p. 187.

14. Ammer, *op. cit.*, p. 382.
15. Scott and Hong, *op. cit.*, p. 1.11.5.
16. R.B. Chase and N.J. Aquilano, *Production and Operations Management: A Life Cycle Approach*, Homewood, IL: Richard D. Irwin, 1977, p. 27.
17. Scott and Hong, *op. cit.*, p. 1.11.9.
18. *Ibid.*, p. 1.11.5.
19. Ammer, *op. cit.*, pp. 387–388.
20. *Ibid.*, pp. 411–413.
21. Lamar Lee, Jr., and Donald W. Dobler, *Purchasing and Materials Management: Text and Cases*, 3rd ed., New York: McGraw-Hill, 1977, pp. 158–169.
22. Lall and Streeton, *op. cit.*, pp. 67.
23. Lee and Dobler, *op. cit.*, pp. 493–495.
24. Lall and Streeton, *op. cit.*, pp. 67–68.
25. John Whitmarsh "Offset: The International Negotiating Game," *Purchasing World*, May 1978, pp. 48–52.

CHAPTER TEN

International Procurement of Technology (II)

Cost Components

Price Analysis

Foreign procurements many times are justified regardless of relative costs because of the need and the availability of technology. Normally, however, unless other overriding factors exist, foreign procurements should be justified in terms of economic advantage determined by cost analysis. Importing involves many more obvious and less obvious expenses than does domestic purchases. These extraneous costs should be added to the sales price to estimate the final cost of the order.

Whether in periods of inflation, or price stability, or recession, obtaining technology at the "right price" can mean the difference between a firm's success or failure. The right price means that the price is fair and reasonable to both the buyer and seller. There is no set of pricing principles that precisely calculates what constitutes a fair and reasonable price. In order to determine the right price for a particular purchase, there are a number of variables and relationships that must be evaluated.[1] Those elements of total cost to be examined include the following:

1. Intermediary's fees.
2. International processing, transportation, and wharfage fees.
3. Insurance costs.
4. Tariff duties and taxes.
5. Communication and travel expenses.
6. Currency exchange costs.
7. Packaging and marking fees.
8. Price of technology.

Intermediary Fees

Intermediary fees will vary depending upon the service rendered and the complexity of the transaction. These fees may be expressed as a percent of the total transaction, as a specific cost, or as a combination of both. These fees should be delineated in a contract prior to consummating the final deal. Fees will tend to be higher in those instances when the intermediary assumes title and, thus, bears risk.

International Processing, Transportation, and Wharfage Fees

International processing, transportation, and wharfage costs are factors in virtually every procurement. Many of the technical terms used in international marketing are quite different from those prevailing in domestic operations, and the lack of uniformity causes confusion and misunderstanding. International marketing prices are quoted as net or as list prices when purchasing in quantity. A net price indicates that the specific quoted price is not subject to trade or quantity discounts. A list price is a general price published in a catalog, price list, or advertisement, or otherwise given out by the exporter.[2]

International marketing price quotations and terms can indicate the following: (1) transportation and related changes and cost items included in the price, (2) the respective duties of seller and buyer, and (3) their respective liability in case of loss or damage.[3] The nature of the product, its classification for shipping charges, method of handling, method of shipment, and distance determine transportation costs which must be factored into the final costs.

There are a number of terms commonly used in international commerce to describe responsibility and price. These terms of trade are as follows:

Ex (point of origin) price.

F.O.B. (free on board) price.

F.A.S. (free alongside) price.

C.I.F. (cost, insurance, and freight) price.

Ex dock (named port of importation) price.

Miscellaneous quotes.[4]

Ex (point of origin) *price* is the price quotation under which the exporter's liability for loss or damage, duties, and costs included in the price are at a minimum. This term is also quoted as *ex factory*, *ex mill*, *ex mine*, *ex plantation*, and *ex warehouse*. An example might be "Price quoted is $10,000, ex warehouse, Le Havre, France." In this instance, the seller's responsibilities end at the Le Havre, France, warehouse.

F.O.B. (free on board) *prices* represent a wide range of quotas. Included are the following:

1. F.O.B. (named inland carrier at named inland point of departure).
2. F.O.B. (named inland carrier at named inland port of departure, freight prepaid or allowed).

3. F.O.B. (named inland carrier at named point of exportation).
4. F.O.B. vessel (named port of shipment).
5. F.O.B. (named inland point in country of importation).[5]

F.O.B. defines the place and time at which title passes from seller to buyer as the merchandise is officially loaded "free on board" by some common carrier. Regardless of the arrangement, the buyer ultimately pays the transportation bill, and also bears any extra costs resulting from carrier selection. An example is "Price quoted is 1200 DM, F.O.B. barge, Frankfurt, West Germany, for export." Here, the seller loads the items for export, with proper documentation.

F.A.S. (free alongside) *prices* also do not extend delivery beyond the port of export. This quotation includes delivery of goods free alongside, but not on board, the vessel at the port of export. The seller is expected to place the goods alongside the vessel or on the dock on the date designated, pay any heavy lift charges, provide clean docks or ship's receipt, and be responsible for such delivery. "Price quoted is 2300 FF, F.A.S. vessel, Le Havre" is a typical example.

C.I.F. (cost, insurance, and freight) *price* is a situation whereby delivery and costs are carried beyond the port of exportation. The seller is required to provide and pay for transportation to the port of discharge, including inland transportation to the port of export, port handling charges, and ocean freight to the foreign port of destination. The seller must also provide, upon buyer request and at his expense, certificates of origin, consular invoices, and other necessary and required documents. An example of this trade term is "Price quoted is 45000 yen, C.I.F. Tokyo." This quote includes practically all costs from point of origin to Toyko, Japan. The buyer is responsible for war risk insurance and fees for foreign government documents.

Ex dock (named port of importation) *prices* include the cost of goods and all additional costs necessary to place the goods on the dock at the named port of importation with any duties paid. Here, the seller pays war risk insurance, certificates of origin, consular invoices, costs of landing, wharfage, taxes, and customs duties, and is liable for loss and damage. The buyer merely takes delivery. "Price quoted is $2800, ex dock Rotterdam" is an example of this term.

Miscellaneous quotes also exist which are hybrids of the aforementioned terms of trade. Notable among these are C.I.F. & C. (cost, insurance, freight and commission), C.I.F.C. & I. (cost, insurance, freight, commission, and interest), and C.I.F. landed (cost, insurance, freight, landed).[6]

Insurance Costs

Insurance costs are normally specified in the terms of trade as outlined above. Several exposures are coverable by insurance. The majority of international transactions recognize the requirement for war risk insurance, marine insurance, fire insurance, all risk insurance, and rail or land carrier insurance. Exporters usually take out open insurance policies which set forth risks for which there is insurance. Every shipment that is made by the exporter under this open policy is certified to the insurance company, with complete descriptions, value, and other appropriate details. This open policy protects the exporter on all shipments, provided the insurance company is notified of details.

Marine insurance differs from many other forms of insurance in that the insured has a choice of a vast variety of risks against which insurance can be affected. These risks, in broad categories, are as follows:

1. Free of damage insurance.
2. Fire and sea perils.
3. Fire and sea perils with average.
4. All risk insurance.[7]

Tariff Duties and Taxes

Tariff duties and taxes may be substantial expense items and justifiably deserve investigation prior to finalizing the procurement. When a tariff is ad valorem, the duty imposed on a particular import good depends on how it is classified in the tariff schedule and how it is valued by the customs authorities. Complicated and obscure tariff nomenclatures coupled with ambiguous rules of classification give customs authorities latitude for arbitrary classifications. The resulting uncertainty (and the higher duties in many instances) can become a strong deterrent to trade.

The United States Customs Service will generally quote fees for a prospective imported item if the following information is furnished:

1. A complete description of the goods. Samples, sketches, diagrams or other illustrative materials may be submitted when the imported item cannot adequately be described in writing.
2. The method of manufacture or fabrication.
3. Specifications and analyses.
4. Quantities and costs of the component materials with percentages, if possible.
5. Whatever information you have as to the (a) commercial destination of goods within the United States and (b) chief use of the goods in the United States.[8]

The majority of the developed nations will render similar advanced quotes if furnished with these same items of information.

Goods may be entered into a country by the consignee named in the bill of lading under which they were shipped, or by the holder of such bill of lading duly endorsed by the consignee. When the goods are consigned "to order," they may be entered by the holder of the bill of lading, duly endorsed by the consignor. In most instances, entry is made by a person or firm certified by the carrier bringing the goods to the port of entry to be the owner of the goods for customs purposes. The document issued by the carrier in such cases is known as a "Carrier's Certificate," and substantially shows the information noted in items 1 to 5 above plus gross weight, foreign port of landing and sailing date, and the identification of the carrier, voyage/flight number, and arrival date. When goods are not imported by a common carrier, possession of the goods at the time of arrival is normally sufficient evidence of the right to make entry in most countries.

In addition to the basic customs duties, certain excise and processing taxes may be assessed. Consular fees and documentary fees are also a real expense.

The consular fees are charged for the issuance of a consular invoice; which is an invoice certified by the consulate of the destination country.

Documentary fees are normally charges for the processing of the various import, export, and financial documents.

Certificates of origin are often required. These are documents provided by the exporting company, and are usually verified by authorities in the exporter's country. The document certifies the origin of materials and/or labor used in the manufacture of the purchased item.

Communications and Travel Expenses

Communications and travel expenses add to the total price of the item to be purchased. These costs are appropriately included in domestic purchases; the sheer distances involved in international transactions make these more salient considerations.

Communications include any media used by buyers such as telex, letters, and telephone. Travel expenses are the direct expenses of buyer representatives involved in the transaction. Travel expenses may be minimal when some type of intermediary is employed. On the other hand, where there are direct negotiations between the buyer and seller, travel expenses can become formidable especially if a new or complicated technology is involved requiring extensive coordination between the parties to the transaction.

Currency Exchange Costs

Currency exchange costs are an item which must also be factored into the final cost of the item. These are the gains and losses resulting from the exchange of the currencies of the buyer and seller. In addition to changes in par value between the currencies, which often may be volatile, there are exchange fees associated with the specific conversion of one currency into another.

Packaging and Marking Fees

Packaging and marking fees while normally slight are nevertheless one more item to add to the growing total price. The packaging expenses will, of course, be in direct relation to the bulk of the item, its degree of fragility, and the mode of transport to be used. Marking will consist of destination identification, attachment of necessary import/export documents and identification of the shipper.

Price of Technology

Price of technology refers to the quoted price of the item. Care must be taken that none of the direct expenses outlined above have been intentionally or inadvertently included in this quoted price. The actual reproduction costs of the item purchased could be substantially lower than the price quoted and subsequently paid. The price paid, where the product purchased entails sophisticated technology, probably includes R&D costs, monopolistic or oligopolistic pricing where sources are limited or controlled by patent or other protective devices. Also, if the technology is new or developed for a specific customer price determination may be difficult inasmuch as there may not be any basis for comparative analysis. A reasonable or fair price may be agreed to on subjective determination of "use value."

Table 10-1 represents a compilation of the various charges and responsibilities. The traders in international commerce must be knowledgeable of all legal and customary requirements and remain alert to pitfalls. The contract must be specific on all items involved in the purchase and actual transfer of the item.

Financial Analysis

Need to Evaluate Alternatives

It is possible to consolidate the numerous costs associated with procurement and with a fair degree of accuracy, estimate or compute the landed cost of any transaction. The methods available for final analysis are numerous, but some are especially noteworthy; these are specific pricing, value rationalization, and cost–benefit analysis. Regardless of the method, the objective is a basic cost comparison among alternatives, whether domestic or international, in an attempt to optimize the new product development budget.

Specific Pricing

Specific pricing entails the gathering of the details of the transactions, listing them sequentially, in a common currency, totaling the component costs and comparing the results. Care must be taken that all pertinent data are obtained for all viable alternatives. Candidly, the prudent transaction is one in which foreign technological opportunities are compared against domestic possibilities. This allows for more definitive decision making.

To illustrate this technique, presume that a U.S. firm, after a national and then worldwide search, has identified a West German technology that will apparently meet its needs. An intermediary is employed. U.S. officials fly to Frankfurt where negotiations commence as to cost, duration of license, prototypes, and technical assistance. The U.S. businesspersons do not speak German, but this, fortunately is no hindrance as the Germans speak fluent English. A preliminary agreement is finally hammered-out and is then brought to the attention of the hierarchy of both firms for approval. The contract is agreed upon and the transfer of product and technology begins. The agreement stipulates that the cost is F.O.B. Frankfurt, July 3, 198X. The intermediary is to make arrangements for transportation and documents from Germany to the United States. Each cost is to be specified and listed for individual payment. The U.S. company is to have a customs broker handle importing the prototypes, tools and dyes, and necessary paperwork. The U.S. purchasing agent eventually runs a postprocurement audit on the transaction. The results at 1.90 Deutsche Marks to one U.S. dollar are as follows:

	DM	U.S. $
Cost of technology	105,450	55,500
Transportation (prototypes and dyes)	3505	1845
Insurance (all)	190	100
Tariff duties		200
Communication and travel		3300
Intermediary (5% of cost)	5273	2775
Packaging and marking	550	290
Currency exchange (1%)	1150	605
		$64,615

Specific pricing allows for each item of expense to be identified and analyzed. Expenses over and above the actual cost of technology added approximately 15% to the total cost of the package. Granted, some added costs would have been involved in the case of a domestic procurement.

Value Rationalization

Value rationalization, while more involved and tedious, does allow more input from the decision makers. The technique combines the procedures of value engineering and value analysis. Value engineering is defined by the United States Department of Defense as

> an intensive appraisal of all the elements of the design, manufacture, or construction, procurement, inspection, installation, and maintenance of an item and its components, in order to achieve the necessary performance, maintainability and reliability of the item at minimum cost.[9]

The purpose of value engineering is to make certain that every element of cost contributes proportionally to the function of the item.

Value analysis is used in the analysis of the purchased item attempting to identify a lower-cost substitute or "better buy."[10]

Value rationalization combines the objectives of both these approaches with an attempt to analyze a technology, identify costs at each stage, and seek lower costing alternatives. The procedure calls for an analyst to develop a checklist of pertinent questions:

Does the item have any design features that are not necessary?

How much does it weigh?

Table 10-1. Foreign Trade Terms[a]

Services \ Terms of Trade	Ex Point of Origin	F.O.B. Named Inland Carrier Named Inland Point of Departure	F.O.B. Named Inland Carrier Named Inland Point Freight Prepaid to Named Point of Exportation	F.O.B. Named Inland Carrier Named Inland Point Freight Allowed to Point of Exportation	F.O.B. Named Inland Carrier Named Point of Exportation
Warehouse storage	S	S	S	S	S
Warehouse labor charges	S	S	S	S	S
Export packing[b]	S	S	S	S	S
Loading at origin	B	B	S	S	S
Inland freight	B	B	B	B[c]	S
Transportation at port	B	B	B	B	B
Port storage	B	B	B	B	B
Forwarder's fee	B	B	B	B	B
Consular fee[b]	B	B	B	B	B
Ocean carrier loading	B	B	B	B	B
Ocean freight	B	B	B	B	B
Marine insurance[b]	B	B	B	B	B
Foreign port charges	B	B	B	B	B
Foreign taxes and customs	B	B	B	B	B

Source: After George W. Tomlinson, *Pointers on Export Letters of Credit*, Philadelphia, PA: The First National Bank, 1953.

[a]b = Buyer; S = Seller.
[b]Export packing, war risk insurance, and consular fees depend upon sales contract.
[c]Shipped collect and deducted from invoice amount.
[d]Buyer pays subsequent charges prior to delivery on dock.
[e]May be seller's responsibility in some contracts.
[f]Buyer pays charge, while seller is responsible for arrangements.
[g]Seller responsible for inland freight.

F.O.B. Vessel Named Port of Shipment	F.O.B. Named Inland Point in Country of Importation	F.A.S. Named Port of Shipment	C. & F. Named Point of Destination	C.I.F. Named Point of Destination
S	S	S	S	S
S	S	S	S	S
S	S	S	S	S
S	S	S	S	S
S	S	S	S	S
S	S	S[d]	S	S
S	S	S[d]	S	S
B[e]	S	B	S	S
B	S	B	S[f]	S[f]
S	S	B	S	S
B	S	B	S	S
B	S	B	B	S
B	S	B	B	B
B	S[g]	B	B	B

What are alternative technologies and their costs?

What are alternative transportation systems?

Can weight be reduced?

Can domestic technologies be identified?

Can alternatives be identified for each of the elements of total cost?[11]

In using this and similar checklists, the analyst evaluates the item under consideration seeking maximum economy and reduction in the cost of the technology through the following means:

Establishing methods to analyze and measure basic value inherent in design, materials, and method of transfer.

Collaborating with engineers, procurement, and transportation specialists to seek low-cost alternatives.

The analyst would then prepare an evaluation sheet whereby the element costs of each of the alternatives would be compared.

Table 10-2 illustrates a worksheet used in value rationalization. Data would be collected and alternatives sought for each of the listed elements of cost. The objective is to enable the analyst to "engineer" the lowest-cost most effective solution.

Cost–Benefit Analysis

Cost–benefit analysis is a tool which can be used to distinguish whether a particular foreign technology, given all pertinent costs, is a worthwhile strategy. The techniques are similar to those used in capital budgeting. Since success in any business is usually measured in terms of profits, this procedure attempts to measure an estimated benefit or return from a particular item of technology consistent with costs. To illustrate, consider the following examples of relative simple cost–benefit ratios:

$$\text{Index} = \frac{\text{Estimated Product Value} \times \text{Estimated Chance of Success}}{\text{Estimated Total Cost of Technology}}$$

or, using an estimate of commercial success (CS) and technical success (TS), expressed as a percent, and the cost of procurement and marketing:

$$\text{Index} = \frac{\%\text{T.S.} \times \%\ \text{C.S.} \times \text{Annual Sales}}{\text{Technology Cost} + \text{Marketing Costs}}$$

A slightly more sophisticated approach is to use present value of benefits and costs since future funds are of less value to an organization than equivalent present values, using some appropriate rate of compound interest. The simplest form of the type of cost–benefit analysis consists of calculating for each possible project, the ratio of the present value of expected future benefits to the present value of expected future project costs. The aim of such selection

Table 10-2. Value Rationalization Worksheet

	Sunk Cost	Current Fiscal Year (FY)	FY + 1	FY + 2	Factor Weight	Total Value
Foreign Alternative						
A. Technology cost						
1. Preferred (as is)						
2. Redesigns						
3. New materials						
B. Transportation cost						
1. Barge–ship–train						
2. Train–ship–train						
3. Air–ship–air						
C. Insurance						
1. All risks						
2. Destruction only						
D. Intermediary						
1. Export broker–customs broker						
2. Export broker						
E. Tariffs and taxes						
1. No alternatives						
F. Currency exchange						
1. No alternatives						
G. Communications and travel						
1. Full negotiation team (five people)						
2. Partial team (three people)						
Domestic Alternative (Similar comparison of alternatives for each cost element)						

system is to maximize the present discounted value of benefits obtained from the spending of a product development budget. The solution to this technique is to rank the proposals in decreasing order of cost–benefit ratio.

As a group, the cost–benefit ratios have a lot to offer. It is an easily understood technique and adds a less subjective aspect (more quantitative approach) to alternative costing. It appeals to the nonresearch-oriented, financially oriented manager.[12]

Payment and Financing

In general, there are four methods of payment for foreign technology:

Advance payment (cash in advance).

Bills of exchange (drafts).

Payment after receipt and inspection of item (open account).

Payment upon receipt of documents evidencing shipment (letter of credit).

From the standpoint of the buyer, "cash in advance" would be the least desirable method of payment while an "open account" arrangement would be the most advantageous. The "letter of credit," however, is a form of financing that protects both the buyer and seller in virtually any foreign transaction.

Cash is both a method of remittance and a term of payment, but it is rarely used as a method of payment in international procurements. Cash may be called for with the order, or against certificates of manufacture as work on a complex item progresses, or at a time of shipment, or at the time and place of export. Cash methods of payment, at best, are unattractive to a buyer. In the case of cash upon shipment, the buyer assumes the entire burden of financing the shipment; he has experienced an out-flow of funds for a considerable time before receiving the item; incurring a loss in the rise of working capital as well as a loss in interest. The buyer is also completely dependent upon the honesty, solvency, and promptness of the international seller.

Cash may be demanded when the buyer is unknown or of doubtful commercial standing, when internal conditions in a country force exporters to guarantee payments, or, when the exporter needs cash in order to complete the transaction.

A departure from the strict terms of cash with orders occurs in the requirement of partial cash in advance. The amount of prepayment is generally sufficient to reimburse the exporter for packing, freight, and all other transportation charges to and from the foreign destination, as well as insurance and all other expenses that the exporter would lose in case the shipment were refused by the importer and returned.[13] In addition, some prepayment would probably be demanded by the seller in the purchase of high-technology products. This would be desirable from the seller's position in that in the event that the order were cancelled there would probably be a very limited market for a customized or specialized product.

Bills of exchange, or drafts, are the most common method of payment in international commerce. Bills of exchange provide a documentary evidence of obligation; and the financial burden is borne by neither the exporter nor the importer.

Drafts are drawn by the seller, calling for the buyer either to pay or to accept for payment a designated sum of money at a determinable future time. Acceptance consists of an acknowledgment to this effect written across the face of the draft and signed by the drawee (buyer), thus obligating him to provide payment of the amount stipulated within the period of time designated.[14]

A draft drawn without collateral documents attached is known as a clean draft; while one with certain stipulated documents of shipment, insurance, or origin is known as a documentary draft. In international commerce, the documentary draft is the more common.

There are three parties to every draft transaction:

The Drawer. The person who executes the draft (the exporter).

The Drawee. The person on whom the draft is drawn and who is required to meet the terms of the document (importer).

The Payee. The party to receive payment (exporter or exporter's bank).[15]

The time at which payment of a draft is to be made is known as tenor or issuance. With respect to their tenor, bills of exchange are of three kinds: sight drafts, arrival drafts, or date drafts.[16]

The sight draft calls upon the drawee to accept and pay the draft upon "sight" or presentation. In some countries it is customary for a bank to hold a draft to await the arrival of the goods for which the draft is drawn before presenting it to the drawee.

An arrival draft, which calls for payment upon the arrival of the merchandise, would tend to avoid the difficulties arising from the delivery of a sight draft before the receipt of the goods. These are not used all that often, as sight drafts are normally executed with instructions to the bank to defer presentations until the goods arrive.

A date drafts calls for payment on a specified date or specified number of days after the date. The maturity is definite but rigid and inflexible.

Figure 10-1 illustrates a trade bill transaction. The example involves a sight draft (payment in 30 days), with the transaction in U.S. dollars.

1. The American exporter ships to a French buyer, with billing in name of exporter.
2. Exporter delivers the draft and shipping documents to the American bank, which sends draft and shipping documents to the French bank.
3. The French bank notifies the importer that the documents have arrived and presents the draft to the importer for acceptance, payment in 30 days.
4. Upon accepting the bill of exchange, the shipping documents are surrendered to the importer, who may now claim the shipment.
5. The accepted bill of exchange is returned to the American bank.
6. The exporter discounts the draft and receives advance payment.
7. The American bank, in turn, disposes of the bill in the acceptance market (there are brokers, buying and selling trade and bank acceptances arising in international commerce).
8. Upon receiving funds, the American bank is now in a liquid position again, having discounted the draft.
9. When the 30-day maturity approaches, the bill is sent to the French bank by some financial institution that had purchased it from the American bank.
10. The French bank receives payment from the French importer in francs and the conversion of francs to dollars in made by the French bank.
11. The funds are transmitted to the present holder of the trade acceptance.

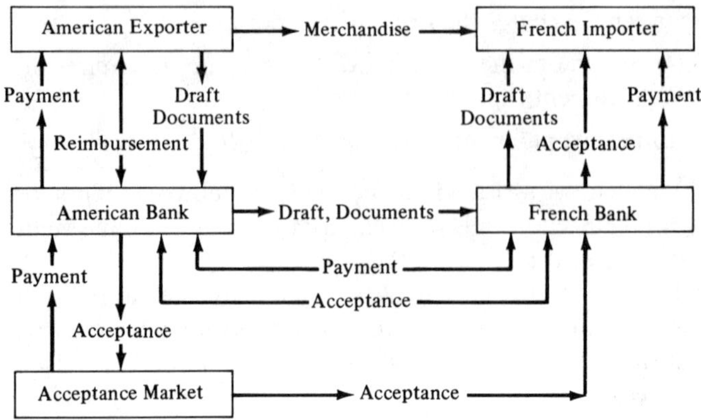

Figure 10-1. Trade bill transaction: 30-day payment.

12. The American exporter settles with the American bank to complete the transaction.

Open accounts are the opposite extreme from cash in making payments for international transaction. In an open account system, goods are shipped to a consignee without documents calling for payment. The commercial invoice of the exporter indicates the liability. Payment for goods is usually stipulated as a certain number of days after date of shipment, or occasionally it may be left to the discretion of the buyer.

Sales on open account can be safely made only to customers of the highest credit standing and then only when political and economic conditions are stable and favorable. Distance is also a definite factor in determining open account payment.

Letter of credit methods of payments use drafts drawn upon a bank and not upon an importer, thus becoming bank acceptances rather than trade acceptances. The commercial letter of credit is a financial instrument issued by a bank at the request of a buyer whereby the bank undertakes to accept and/or pay drafts drawn upon the bank by the seller of the merchandise. The seller is governed by the requirements as set forth in the letter.

The three essential parties to a commercial letter of credit are the following:

1. *The Opener, Account, or Importer*. The buyer who opens the credit.
2. *Issuer*. Bank that issues letter of credit.
3. *Beneficiary or Accrediter*. Seller in whose favor the credit is opened.[17]

The types of letters of credit vary to fit conditions. The principle types of commercial letters of credit are revocable or irrevocable, confirmed or unconfirmed. The privilege of revocability refers to the right of the issuing bank to revoke the transaction to honor drafts drawn on it. They may be cancelled or modified at any time and without notice to the beneficiary. When, however, the credit has been transmitted to a correspondent, changes are enabled only upon written notification by the correspondent, prior to payment. In actual practice, letters are considered as being irrevocable.

A letter of credit is confirmed when a correspondent bank in the exporter's nation allows the exporter to draw a bill of exchange against it without recourse. The bank will not confirm the letter of credit unless it is also irrevocable. With an irrevocable, unconfirmed letter of credit, the exporter is still exposed to the risk of nonpayment by the issuing bank. In this process the exporter avoids risk as long as the exporter meets the stipulations regarding goods, shipment, payment terms, accompanying documents, and similar provisions.[18]

Figure 10-2 illustrates the letter of credit mechanism and Figure 10-3 defines the governing relationships between the parties to the letter of credit transaction.

The usual documents required are the bill of exchange; commercial, customs, and consular invoices; bill of lading (or air waybill); insurance policy or certificate; and packing lists.

Figure 10-2. Letter of credit mechanism: Flow of goods and documents.

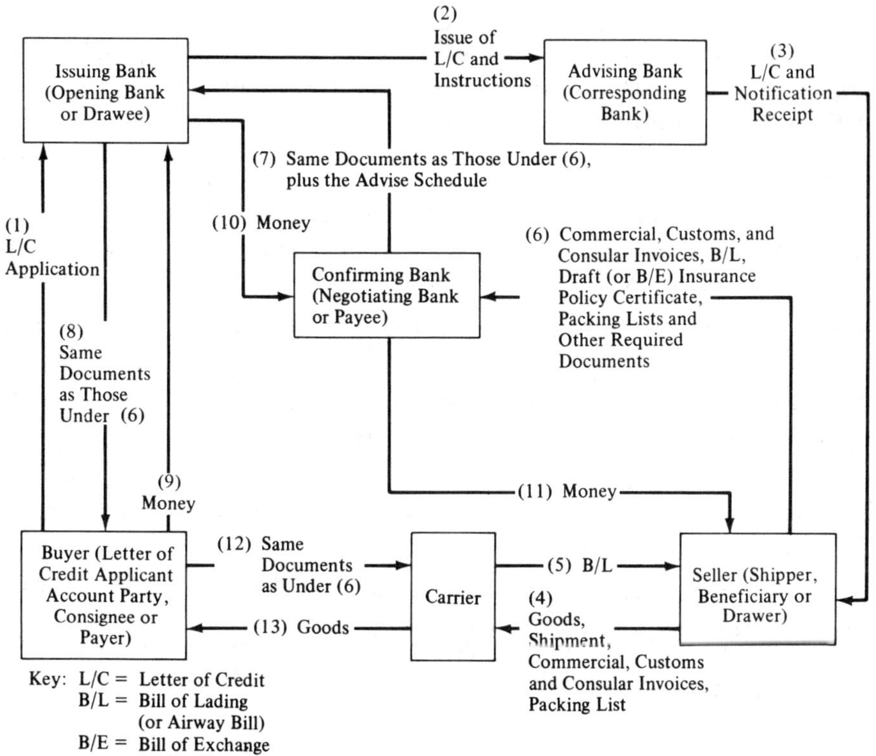

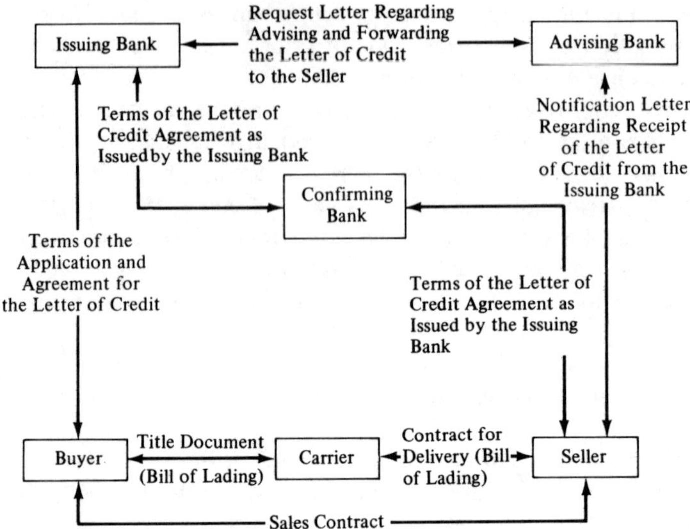

Figure 10-3. Relationship among the parties to the letter of credit.

Most international banks can advise and handle all details of the letter of credit. Buyers should be familiar with the letter of credit mechanisms in Figures 10-2 and 10-3, as to their content and their relationship to the terms and conditions of their particular transaction.

Currency

Payment must be made in the particular currency of the country agreed to during negotiation and specified in the order. In general, there are four ways in which the risks of foreign exchange fluctuations may be allocated:

Buyer assumes all of the risk and agrees to pay a fixed amount in the currency of the seller's country.

Seller assumes all of the risk and agrees to accept payment in the currency of the country of the buyer or at a fixed exchange rate.

The risk is shared by the buyer and the seller.

The risk is transferred to an international bank by hedging via the foreign exchange contract.[19]

Once the parties have agreed upon the responsibility for risk, care must be taken to reduce risk by the assuming party. This may be accomplished by forecasting the foreign exchange rate fluctuations, identifying potential strategies, or hiring a specialist.

In forecasting fluctuations, one must look to long- and short-term psychological, technical, and market bias factors. The strategies available include matching maturity of payment to other transactions, shift financing (accepting exposure by borrowing weakening currency and repaying when that currency is weakest), or hedging the risk by purchasing a foreign exchange contract through banks or other financial institutions. At times, firms will turn to specialists to assist in the currency exchange process. These people may well recommend translation of funds in a third nation's currency and subsequently back into the seller's currency.[20]

In some nations, the buyer must report to that government transactions that require the transport of funds above a certain level to another nation to nation. In the United States the level is $5000.

Other Procurement Considerations

There are a number of general items that may be a factor in a particular procurement. These include legal and nonperformance claims, arbitration clauses, various security matters, governmental policies, and postprocurement followup.

Legal Considerations

When engaging in international commerce, the transnational firm will encounter many pitfalls on the way to a successful procurement. These snags are varied and often reflect moods of the times as opposed to a historical evolution of laws. Before discussing remedies to nonperformance of contracts, it is well to generalize about legal aspects of international marketing.

In the international arena, the law of the exporting or importing country may govern, depending upon the prevailing provisions of the law. The parties may agree on the law that is to govern. Commercial usage is important in helping to decide controversies.

The legal systems of the free world are divided between common law and code law. The United States (and, in general, the United Kingdom) follow common law (precedents), while the rest of the free world follows code law (inscribed codes). There is, however, a tendency in common law jurisdictions to codify certain elements of commercial law. Trademarks, designs, and commercial names may be used to illustrate the difference. Under common law, the first user has legal ownership; under code law, the first to legally register becomes the owner. International conventions have been attempting to reconcile some of these differences.

Patent laws of the various countries differ more widely than do those relating to other industrial property. These laws are under constant change. International agreements are standardizing this area.

Merchants in code law countries are required to register in a commercial court, revealing certain information pertaining to their commercial standing (e.g., nature of business, amount of subscribed capital, etc.). There are many more partnership arrangements in code law countries, while corporations are more prevalent in the common law jurisdictions.

Sales laws tend to vary in terms of conditions of sales (i.e., time-payment), and law of agency from one nation to the next. A power of attorney is universal and is essential to transacting foreign business. Bankruptcy and insolvency are more rigidly legislated in code countries. Taxation in the international marketplace often results in double taxation due to the multiplicity of laws.[21]

The legal systems of the world are so varied and complex that it is beyond the scope of this text to explore the laws of each country individually. There are, however, legal problems common to most international purchase transactions which must be given special attention. The following list includes those elements most prone to legal difficulty:

1. Rules of competition pertaining to collusion, discrimination against certain buyers, promotional methods, variable pricing, and exclusive territory rights.
2. Cancellation of distributor or wholesaler agreements.
3. Product quality laws and controls.
4. Packaging laws.
5. Warranty and after-sales exposure.
6. Price controls, limitations on markup or markdowns.
7. Patents, trademarks, and copyright laws and practices.[22]

One of the problems aggravating legal settlements is determining what legal system will have jurisdiction when commercial disputes arise. A frequent error is to assume that disputes between citizens of different nations are adjudicated under some supranational system of laws. Unfortunately, there is no judicial body to deal with legal commercial problems arising between citizens of different countries. It is often erroneously implied that there exists a body of international law to which all foreign trade activities are subject. The confusion probably stems from the existence of international courts, such as the World Court at The Hague and the International Court of Justice, the principal legal organ of the United Nations. These courts are operative in international disputes between sovereign nations but not between private citizens. Unless a commercial dispute involves a national issue between states, it will not be heard by these international courts.

When international commercial disputes arise the problems must be settled under the laws of one of the countries concerned. The paramount question in a dispute is "Whose law governs?" Jurisdiction over private, international legal disputes is generally determined in one of three ways: (1) on the basis of jurisdictional clauses included in the contract, (2) on the basis of where the contract was entered, or (3) on the basis of where the provisions were to be performed.

When it becomes apparent that a dispute cannot be settled on a private basis, more determined action must be taken. Many transnational organizations prefer a settlement through arbitration than a suit. Lawsuits in public courts are to be avoided for a number of reasons, ranging from costs, time delays, and harm to public images, to fear of unfair treatment and difficulty of collecting awarded damages. It has been suggested that the settlement of every dispute should follow three steps: first, try to "placate" the injured party; if this does not work, "arbitrate"; and finally, "litigate." The final step is to be taken only when all other steps fail.[23]

Commercial Arbitration

As commercial arbitration is generally voluntary, it is dependent upon the voluntary inclusion of an arbitration clause in contracts or, in the absence of such a clause, upon voluntary submission of the dispute after it occurs. Arbitration is a quasijudicial process where an impartial third party, acting as an arbitrator, evaluates the situation and comes to a determination leading to a settlement of the dispute. The arbitrator's decision is binding on both parties and barring fraud or conspiracy, will be upheld in a court of law. Arbitration is making headway largely because of the shortcomings of litigation in trade matters. Many trade disputes are not matters of law but of fact, and in many instances such questions of law as do arise in interpreting a business contract are of secondary importance. The tendency of commercial arbitration is in the direction of tribunals consisting of unbiased arbitrators who are experts in their fields, or at least are businessmen who are familiar with the sorts of facts and practices that arise in the course of a trade dispute.

The more extensive use of commercial arbitration is also due, in part, to higher business standards and better business ethics. Its use has undoubtedly been furthered by the enactment of improved arbitration statutes worldwide and by the organized efforts of commercial organizations. Many of these commercial organizations have conducted campaigns of education, published carefully devised arbitration rules, set up permanent arbitration machinery, and taken active measures to place their facilities at the disposal of exporters and importers and domestic businessmen. There are today what might be described as four basic systems of commercial arbitration: (1) the British system, (2) the International Chamber of Commerce system, (3) the Soviet Union system, and (4) the Western Hemisphere system.[24] While each varies in scope and procedure the objective is common: resolving commercial disputes.

Commercial arbitration has distinct advantages over direct legal action. The arbitration process is faster and cheaper. It also encourages a continuing relationship between the parties where a honest difference in a particular transaction exists. Legal actions can result in strained feelings and preclude future business transactions between the litigants.

Security Matters

Another group of troublesome items in international commerce is the industrial property rights. Exporters, investors, licensors, and others involved in international business have a vital stake in protecting their patents, copyrights, and trademarks. In most countries these rights can be protected, but it is still necessary to acquire protection for each country individually throughout most of the world.

There is as yet no overall international patent and trademark system. With relatively unimportant exceptions, no country has recognized internally the patents or trademarks issued by others. There is, however, general agreement among nations on a basic rights of patent and trademark owners.

It is important that the industrial property rights receive careful legal attention in the contract. In most instances, the purchase of technology is, in effect, a purchase of the industrial property right. The transaction should be reviewed by competent legal people to ascertain that the buyer is indeed receiving expected rights.

Governmental Policy Concerns

A complex matter which often becomes an irritant in international technology purchases is governmental policies. These policies are multifaceted and involve the attitudes of the governments of both buyer and seller to the technology being transferred.

The sale or purchase of technology is especially troublesome as it may run contrary to the national economic policies of one or all the countries involved. These sales usually involve the transfer of funds, types of production, and the transfer of jobs from one country to the other. The question often boils down to one of the firm's perceived allegiance to national policies. For example, a French subsidiary of an American computer manufacturer, in deference to American allegiance, did not solicit computer sales from Eastern Europe despite pressures from the French government. The international logic of the multicountry company comes to coexist with that of nationalism. An international manager feels himself no less a German, Englishman, or American when he tries to remove existing tariffs and controls in order to expedite international trade.

If, through a series of acquisitions, mergers, and exchanges of stock, what was once a 90% American-owned company becomes 30% American, 20% British, 20% German, 20% French, and 10% Italian—What is it then? Is it American, British, German, French, or Italian? Such companies have developed. Governments are experiencing difficulty in dealing with them. The national policies are often not adequate to cope with this situation. Therefore, the prudent transnational will attempt to "calm governmental waters" prior to entering into negotiations for technology as either the buyer or the seller.

Postprocurement Followup — The Audit

A final consideration should be the conduct of a postprocurement audit. The purpose is to assess the value of the completed product acquisition process. This process may be very formal or simply a matter of an "after action report." In any event the audit will assist personnel in future technology procurements.

The formal approach would entail gathering all factor costs and matching them to the sales and benefits of the product in production. This will take place after the technology has been purchased, production strategies developed, production scheduling systems conceptualized, quality control issues resolved, and the items have been manufactured, distributed, and sold.

The audit helps to establish whether it was "worth the effort." This procedure will also assist in justifying (if appropriate) future foreign purchases of technology on a quantitative basis of merit.

Outside Technology Sources

Size as a Factor in Technology Procurement

A study of 500 innovations selected from a field of 130 indicated that larger firms (5000 and more employees) tended to demonstrate lower reliance on external sources of technology. Smaller firms (less than 1000 employees), despite being more oriented toward outside sources of technology, experience more difficulty in properly identifying and evaluating technology and integrating technology to meet their specific requirements.

The innovations were introduced into the marketplace during the years 1953–1973, and originated from the countries of Canada, United Kingdom, France, West Germany, Japan, and the United States. The 500 innovations were considered by an international panel of experts as most important in terms of technological, socioeconomic, and political importance. The objective of the study was to determine and compare, on the basis of the data, the underlying trends and characteristics which are indicative of the relative innovativeness of the different countries.[25] Thus, while the larger firms are not as inclined to look outside their own resources for technology, they do avail themselves of that possibility; and, small firms frequently go to an outside source, despite subsequent difficulties.

Sherman Gee found that a paradox exists because firms more disposed to utilizing external sources of technology are the smaller ones who depend primarily on their own innovativeness to remain competitive.[26] Studies by Collier, Kamien, and Schwartz have indicated that the smaller firms and independent inventors produce a disproportionately larger share of innovations than the larger firms which are more concerned with maintaining a favorable return on investment.[27] It is the smaller firms, ironically, that are at a disadvantage in their capability to exploit technology sources effectively because of their more limited technical capabilities and capital resources. Very probably their smaller technical and capital base could be the principal factor underlying their higher utilization of outside technology. Large firms possess more extensive technical and financial means for capturing the full benefits of outside technology. However, the larger firms tend to be less reliant on outside sources than the smaller ones. Also, the larger firms are not as prone to accept high-technical risks.

Medium-sized firms (1001–5000 people) on the surface would appear as the most likely to benefit from internal research and development. Their internal resources are greater than the smaller firms, but products and pressures are less demanding than the larger firms. However, Gee found that innovations from firms of this size tended to take the longest to come to fruition, ostensibly because of their low dependence on external sources of technology. Heavy reliance on internal sources constitutes a significant handicap in their case inasmuch as their internal resources are more limited compared to the larger companies and their relatively lower external orientation would cause them to overlook many outside technological opportunities.[28]

A strategy for improving the technological innovation rate for different-sized firms thus becomes more clearly crystallized. Basically, an overall increased sensitivity to and utilization of outside technology must be developed paralleling the internal development of resources and capabilities. A heavier dose of external orientation is especially needed in the case of the medium to large companies in order that outside technologies may better compliment their in-house strengths.

Summary

At least six sources of stimuli for technological innovation can be identified:

1. Consumer needs.
2. New products of suppliers.
3. Inventions (internal and external).
4. Corporate acquisitions.
5. Production technology.
6. Internal R&D.

Studies, both in the United States and Great Britain, have analyzed the sources of technically innovative ideas which spawned successful products. A significant 60–80% originate from sources other than science-based internal R&D. Acquisition of external technology is often critical in the innovative process.

The information in Chapters Nine and Ten has not been directed toward a particular method or means of technological conveyance, but rather toward outlining and defining many relevant factors and procedures. Some will be clearly more pertinent to a particular acquisition/procurement than others.

The international commerce arena is frought with opportunities for mistakes, miscalculations, and disappointment. *Caveat emptor* must certainly be uppermost in the minds of the purchasing executives involved in a foreign purchase contract. With cognizance of proper caution, adherence to the following considerations should result in a successful technology purchase:

1. Identify a need and evaluate the technological requirements that must be met to satisfy that need.
2. Match available technology with the specific need or ultimate use.
3. Execute a continuing series of relevant benefit–cost analyses.
4. Define the market potential and other pertinent parameters that will determine potential utilization.
5. Examine possible consequences that may result from fulfilling the needs along with their internal and external impact.
6. Locate potential suppliers who are able and available to translate the technical information into practical reality.
7. Determine the resources and other requirements necessary to produce the product, service, or process.
8. Associate sources and uses to ensure proper and adequate standards, characteristics, performance, and constraints of product, service, or process.
9. Perform adoptive engineering, as required, to develop product, service, or process or to acquire missing elements.
10. Establish a detailed plan to determine acquisitions, production and operational costs.
11. Acquire necessary financing.
12. Create a marketing plan for the product, service, or process.
13. Initiate procurement in accordance with the procedures as outlined in Chapters Nine and Ten.

Interfirm and international trade in scientific and technological knowledge has long been part of the industrial scene and shows no signs of abating. There are advantages and disadvantages in purchasing technology. The purchase of technology obviously speeds the product to the marketplace. The total cost may be in some circumstances considerably lower than if discovered and developed within the firm. Only successful technologies are purchased. Expensive R&D with its attendant high risk is eliminated.

A disadvantage of depending entirely on the purchase of other people's technology, especially in competitive process industries, is that there is a high probability that the purchasing firm will never be first to market the product and may have continuing technical and financial deficiencies which can affect profits. A further disadvantage is that the firm which has no technology to sell may find it difficult to buy, since in some industrial firms cross-licensing and technology exchange agreements are a significant way of doing business.

Endnotes Chapter Ten

1. Lamar Lee, Jr. and D.W. Dobler, *Purchasing and Materials Management: Text and Cases,* 3rd ed., New York: McGraw-Hill, 1977, p. 91.
2. R.L. Kramer, *International Marketing,* 3rd ed., Dallas: South-Western Publishing Co., 1970 pp.145–147.
3. *Ibid.* p. 133.
4. Dean S. Ammer, *Materials Management and Purchasing,* 4th ed., Homewood, IL: Richard D. Irwin, 1980, pp. 133–135.
5. *International Rules for the Interpretation of Trade Terms*, 1936.
6. See Kramer, *op. cit.*, pp. 135–145 for an excellent examination of these various terms of trade.
7. *Ibid.*, pp. 170–175.
8. Exporting to the United States, United States Customs Service, Department of Treasury, September 1977, p. 9.
9. Armed Services Procurement Regulation, Section 3-406.3.
10. R.B. Chase and N.J. Aquilano, *Production and Operations Management: A Life Cycle Approach,* Homewood, IL: Richard D. Irwin, 1977, p. 613.
11. Modified from *Basic Steps in Value Analysis*, National Association of Purchasing Management, New York, pp. 4–18.
12. A. Paolini and M.A. Glaser, "Project Selection Methods that Pick Winners," *Research Management*, May 1977, pp. 26–27.
13. P.R. Cateora and J.M. Hess, *International Marketing*, Homewood, IL: Richard D. Irwin, 1979, pp. 627–628.
14. P.H. Combs, *Handbook of International Purchasing*, Boston: Cahners Books, 1971, p. 46.
15. F.R. Root, *International Trade and Investment*, Cincinnati: South-Western Publishing Co., 1978, 4th ed., pp. 224–226.
16. Kramer, *op. cit.*, p. 267.
17. *Ibid.*, p. 280.
18. Root, *op. cit.*, pp. 226–227.
19. For an explanation of hedging techniques and tactics see L.C. Nehrt, *International Finance for Multinational Business,* Scranton, Pa: Intext Educational Publishers, 1972, Chapter 7.
20. C.L. Scott and E.S.W. Hong, "An Operational Approach to International Purchasing," TRW, Inc., 1975, pp. 1.11.10-1.11-12.
21. See Kramer, *op. cit.*, Chapter 11 for an excellent discussion of the legal aspects of international commerce. *Foreign Business Practices,* U.S. Department of Commerce, November 1974, is also a definite source of information on these issues.
22. "151 Checklists—Decision Making in International Operations," *Business International*, 1974, p. 84.
23. Cateora and Hess, *op. cit.*, pp. 190–191.
24. See Kramer, *op. cit.*, pp. 218–220, and Cateora and Hess, *op. cit.*, pp. 191–207 for a full discussion of arbitration systems, and their individualities. See also *Foreign Business Practices, op. cit.*, p. 15, for an especially enlightening article on U.N. enforcement of arbitral awards.
25. S. Feinman and W. Fuentevilla, "Indicators of International Trends in Technological Innovation," Final Report, Gellman Research Associates, Inc., Jenkintown, PA.
26. S. Gee, "Factors Affecting the Innovation Time-Period," *Research Management*, Vol. 21, January 1978, pp. 37–42 reported very comprehensively on the results of the Feinman and Fuentevilla report. His analysis is excellent and in-depth.

27. D.M. Collier, "Research-Based Venture Companies: The Link Between Market and Technology, *Research Management*, Vol. 17, May 1974, pp. 16–20; and M.I. Kamien and N.L. Schwartz, "Market Structure and Innovation: A Survey," Report No. NSF/RDA/73/6/3/, Northwestern University, Evanston, IL 60201.
28. Gee, *op. cit.*, p. 42.

CHAPTER ELEVEN

Technological Innovation

Technology and Change

The Innovation Process

The innovation process culminates with the introduction of new products, processes, or services to the market. According to Heinz-Dieter Haustein,

> Innovation potential is the ability of effectively introducing new technical devices and organizational solutions into the production process and, subsequently, the market.[1]

Larson says, "By definition, innovation means change—discarding the old way and adopting a new one."[2] Much of the impetus for technological innovation results from R&D. But, as Twiss observes, technological innovation transcends the activities of a single department responsible for R&D. Technological innovation is a total organizational involvement leading to the profitable application of the technology.[3]

Technological innovation involves highly complex decisions, including what technology to develop, evaluation of the state of the art, evolutionary or revolutionary changes, market appraisal, potential risk, product control, the national and international political and economic environment, competition, and the immediate operational environment, specifically, organizational processes that might abet or retard the innovation process.

With so many interacting considerations, there is a need to understand what advantages exist in technological innovation, how it takes place, and what external and internal environmental and operational factors serve as stimulants, or barriers, to technological innovation.

The Cycle

The innovation process is only one phase of a cycle. The complete cycle is invention, innovation, and diffusion. Invention is distinct from innovation and is the first stage in the cycle. Invention involves the demonstration of a new technical idea by designing, developing, and testing a working example of either a process, a product, or a device. Invention is a separate and distinct area from innovation, but it must be remembered that invention is frequently the prelude to innovation, which is primarily a conversion process leading to application. A much simpler distinction between invention and innovation revolves around the verbs "to conceive" and "to use." Invention entails a conception of an idea, whereas innovation is use, wherein the idea or invention is translated into the economy.[4]

The diffusion of technology is a technology transfer process. Diffusion can occur in any of several ways: directly by people, by the literature, by attending conferences and exchanging information, by the outright purchase of goods or services, and through licensing, franchising, coproduction, technological consortiums, or direct investment.

Innovation and Technological Competition

A Disintegrating U.S. Position

At the end of World War II the United States was the undisputed world technology leader. There were significant technological developments resulting from scientific investment during the war which provided the impetus for new products and industries. New industries and products revolved around technological processes innovated in electronics, medicine, computers, nuclear fission, propulsion systems, etc.[5]

Unfortunately, even though the United States still enjoys leadership in some technologies, there has been a failure to sustain eminence in many important areas. Lagging innovation and technological growth have subsequently affected the U.S. international competitive position. It can be inferred that the United States has been largely living on technological capital developed during World War II and there is evidence that this capital is dissipating.

Many industrial countries have taken a technologically aggressive approach to catch up or even pass others by accepting the attendant risk and investing in innovation. The result has been new or better products, more efficient production processes and modernized production facilities.

There is increasing international competition as a result of a technological leveling of the process. Nations that formerly imported technology are now exporting products evolving from invention and innovation. It has been reported that in the 1950s the United States introduced into world markets approximately 80% of the major technical inventions, whereas in the late 1970s the U.S. share had dropped to less than 55%.[6]

Problems

The recent experience of the United States might serve to illustrate some of the problems related to innovation. In the 1970s, despite the acceleration of invention, there were alarming indications that the technological innovation process had slowed down in the United States. The dollar expenditures for R&D had increased, but in absolute terms of real dollars adjusted for inflation, there had not been much exciting growth.[7] Industry became cautious and generally appeared to have drifted to an evolutionary, as distinct from a revolutionary, technological innovation strategy. Management often became cautious and risk-resistant.[8] A trend of short incremental, but safe, steps seems to have developed.

A risk-resistant conservative approach to sponsoring innovation might be attributed to the high failure rate generally associated with the introduction of new technology. The estimated failure rate of new products has ranged from 60% to 90%. However, a study reported in 1980 maintained in a five year period preceding the release of the study there was a failure rate of only one in three for major new products introduced in that time frame. Significantly, the study survey covered 148 medium- and large-sized companies and involved important new products, as distinct from products that had undergone some modification.[9]

In some industries survival is contingent on innovation. Technological development has been especially rapid in communications, microelectronics, computers, and scientific instruments to indicate a few dynamic industries which have had a tradition of innovation. Other industries, such as steel, chemicals, paper, packaged goods, and automobiles, seem at least during the 1970s to have technologically retrenched as far as important innovations are concerned.[10]

Another deterrent to technological innovation has been the availability and cost of capital. Starting in the late 1970s there was increasing emphasis on the need for technological investment. High interest rates, questionable profit prospects, and limited capital all have been negative investment factors. Despite high interest rates and uncertain economic conditions, the 1980s appear to be the start of a new era of optimism for investment in high-technology activities. An article in the *Wall Street Journal* reported the comparative easy availability of venture capital for emerging high-technology firms.[11] Access to venture capital can be a major stimulant to technological innovation.

The Science, Technology, Innovation Spectrum

The Technology Model

A better perspective of the relationship among science, technology, and innovation can be provided by Figure 11-1.

The effort spectrum ranges from pure research to technology. The model is

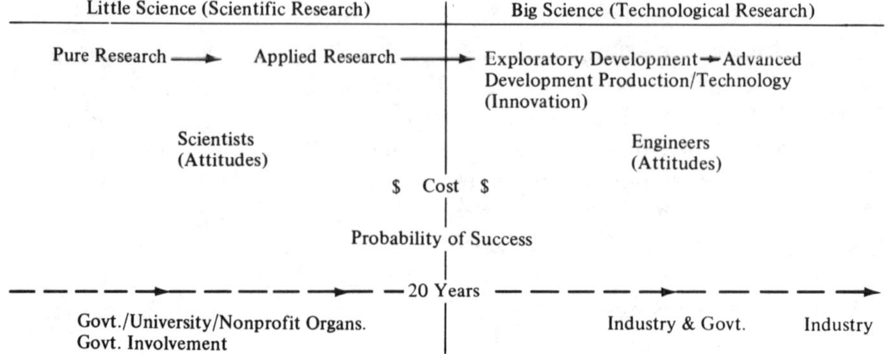

Figure 11-1. The technology model.

one dimensional for simplicity and does not attempt to accommodate technology transfer, nor does it provide for all intermediate phases which are possible, from pure research to technology. In a complicated technology, it has been estimated that the lead time between a scientific discovery and its technological application is about 20 years.[12]

Little Science (Scientific Research)

In the pure and applied research phases, scientific effort is conducted, for the most part, by small teams of scientists. These early phases are generally characterized by a high failure rate, long research times, relatively low costs; work often is performed in universities or nonprofit organizations and, predominately, by scientists. There are, of course, exceptions, such as some research on solid-state physics, high-energy particles, molecular biology, or nuclear fusion. These early phases are primarily knowledge generating or invention oriented. Since the probability of immediate success, in terms of commercial innovation, is comparatively small and the lead time to marketing is long, industrial firms are usually reluctant to invest heavily in this phase of knowledge creation. However, this is a vital phase in developing scientific capability and priming the pump for future discovery. This area is primarily the province of university, government, and nonprofit operations, and government support in these phases is critical if a viable national scientific base is to be established.

Some additional thoughts: The initial phases in the creation of knowledge are usually the domain of scientists. Managing scientific research is far more difficult than managing technological research inasmuch as these are much more intangible. Innovation invariably involves something of a tangible or use nature. Also, scientists' organizational attitudes differ, on the average, from engineers' organizational attitudes; the scientist in these phases is interested in discovery, professional growth, and peer acclaim. He or she tends to associate mainly with the profession, and organizational affiliation is only a secondary factor—a vehicle which affords the scientist the opportunity to pursue his or her professional objectives, which frequently are not immediately compatible with innovation.

Big Science (Technological Research)

The second part of Figure 11-1 depicts Big Science. The closer R&D moves toward technological fruition, the greater the cost. Technological research generally is expensive. Depending on the anticipated end-product of the research, it can be performed by the government, by industry, or by government and industry in some concert. Also, relating to the type of developmental work with expectant innovation, as an end-product, performance may be by small or large organizations. In short, the industry/government marriage and the organizational size of the partners would depend on the nature of the technology.

In the advanced phases of technology, engineers rather than scientists are more often involved or responsible for accomplishing technological objectives. The engineers generally see a more tangible product which has organizational association. As a consequence, engineers tend to be organizationally, as well as professionally, directed. Their operational environment definitely reflects innovation possibilities.

Engineers see their career, professional growth, and material benefits being derived from the organization. The organization invariably has product or service identification, and organizational affiliation is commitment to professional scope and direction. In essence, the engineer tends to be more organization oriented, whereas the tendency of the scientist is to be more function, or activity, directed.

Possible Objectives of Missions

There are many purposes of science and technology, among them are the following:

1. Discovering and furthering knowledge.
2. Developing new products.
3. Improving existing products.
4. Finding new uses for existing products.
5. Improving production processes.
6. Finding potential uses for by-products or waste products generated by present production.
7. Analyzing and studying competitors' products
8. Providing technical service to functional departments in the organization.

The R&D operation can perform one, several, or all these services. It can operate as a subsidiary and support group in a product-centered enterprise. Or it can fulfill a fundamental function as it does in the defense industry, where R&D may or may not be directed toward the production of hardware in volume. It can be organized primarily for technical service either as part of an organization or as a separate organization. Also, it can pursue a purely exploratory purpose, with the objectives of discovering and expanding knowledge rather than applying it. In the United States, government and military R&D organizations can also be distinguished, although comparatively little R&D is actually conducted in these. They are mainly responsible for contracting government and military work to industry, determining requirements and specifications, and managing the work through control, coordination, and evaluation.

Considering the objectives and organization of science and technological research, is research a separate industry? Part of an industry? An adjunct operation? A means of transition?

One very important additional idea is suggested. It is highly probable that large and complex organizations doing R&D will have performance requirements in more than one of the service areas indicated. Such organizations may actually, to varying degress, be involved in all eight of the service sectors indicated. Identifying and accomplishing the fundamental mission of the R&D organization is paramount. Resources can easily be dissipated in supplying nonrelated or casually related mission services. There is also a wide spectrum of professional services which can be performed. The various service areas usually require different skills and professional interests. Failure by management to comprehend mission and service requirements will lead to poor organization, ineffective use of human resources, and disgruntled professional employees.

What is strongly suggested by the above discussion is that R&D can be instrumental in accomplishing a variety of missions which are supportative of innovational objectives. Failure to comprehend the several possibilities indicated can result in ineffectual organization as a consequence of ineffectually utilizing personnel. Management must recognize the range of activities that are possible, delineate operational goals, and allocate resources, especially human resources, that are compatible with the operational objectives.

Types of Innovation

Range

Innovation is an inclusive term covering a wide range of operational and environmental connotations. Innovation is possible in the context of social, economic, product, process, procedural, and managerial situations. In some instances, there is a very fine line of demarcation in the above, especially in making a distinction between managerial and economic innovations. There is also a marked tendency to think of innovation primarily as product-directed innovation.

Social Innovation

Social innovation and government involvement are practically inexorable. Solutions to many public sector problems require innovation. Some of the more obvious public problems in need of innovative solutions are urban renewal, environmental pollution, crime and terrorism prevention, water purity and shortage, public transportation, disease eradication and health maintenance, the elimination of poverty, highway safety, and public education.

The solving of social problems usually entails interaction and cooperation between public and private sectors. At times, private innovations in the industrial sector have created conditions which necessitate social innovation in the public domain. There are instances when the advancement of private innovations is dependent upon the environment of social innovations. Examples to illustrate the aforementioned are the pollution problems created by the automotive and chemical industries. Industrial innovations may be contingent on the availability of natural and human resources; to provide these resources social innovations are required.

Government should provide encouragement for the employment of private resources in social innovation. The government incentives for innovative solutions can be stimulated by (1) defining social problems, and establishing social priorities, (2) providing opportunity and incentive for profit in the development of solutions, (3) engaging in intensified planning for innovative solutions, (4) legislating regulatory measures and other controls to compel or encourage industry to act consonant with public welfare, and (5) taking initiative in social innovation when inadequate incentives do not exist for such effort for the use of private resources.[13]

Economic Innovation

There is a growing body of literature on innovation. Various aspects of innovation have been investigated by Solow, Roberts, Gold, Griliches, Shapiro, Twiss, Kendrick, Utterback, Terleckyj, Mansfield, Arrow, and von Hipple, to name just a few. At times, the literature is contradictory or confusing. It appears, though, that there is a strong consensus that technological innovation is important, but the social and economic effects of R&D specifically, and innovation generally, are not known well enough to present quantitative indicators of these effects with confidence. Many of the studies that have been conducted differ as to method, range, and conceptualization; this adds to the difficulty of formulating a composite picture. However, some of the conclusions that might be inferred from these studies are as follows:

1. There is a positive, high, and significant contribution of R&D to economic growth and productivity.
2. The investment in R&D and innovation yields a return as high or often greater than the return from other investments.
3. There are benefits to the industries which purchase new and/or improved

products from innovating companies. Often, the benefits to the recipients of innovative technology equal or exceed the direct benefits to the innovating companies.
4. There may be underinvestment in R&D and innovation relative to the future potential benefits to the firm and to society.
5. Existing measures of economic performance, such as Gross National Product or productivity indices, are only partially reflective of the contribution that R&D and innovation make to the economy and society.[14]

Twiss maintains that technological innovation is vital for survival. In an analysis of business failures there were significant instances where innovators failed to translate technological creativity into profitable operations. The real challenge is not only to innovate, but to innovate for profitability. Twiss says technological innovation is critical in the survival and growth of most industrial operations and should not be left to chance.[15]

Product Innovation

Most managers operate in a short-term environment. The pressures are for quick results and risk avoidance. Innovation is fraught with risk. Failing to innovate can also represent a high-risk situation. It is not difficult to enumerate situations where competitive forces have led to the spawning of new products and entirely new industries which have neutralized or eliminated existing products and industries. The U.S. economy has thrived and grown on innovation, and departure from this operational philosophy can lead to technological vulnerability.

As technology has accelerated, there have become stronger competitive pressures to innovate. Competition born from innovation has led to products which perform old functions better and products which make new functions possible: Three examples that can be cited are xerography, synthetic wash and wear fabrics, and instant photography.[16] Innovations that drastically affect existing industries and which frequently lead to new industries very often do not emanate from established companies in established industries. Synthetic fibers were developed by the chemical industry rather than the textile industry. High-speed ground transportation development has extended from the automobile and railroad industries to the aerospace and electrical manufacturing industries. Instant photography was developed outside the conventional photographic industry. Xeroxing was not a product innovated by the office equipment industry.[17] The aforementioned illustrations can be supplemented with numerous other examples. The message should be obvious that competitive pressures lead to innovation and a no-risk reluctance to innovate operational policy can sooner or later prove disastrous.

Process Innovation

Process improvement affords considerable latitude for innovation. Products may be needed, which is technology demand-pull. The successful introduction of these new products may be directly related to product producibility.

Producibility, especially with new products, may be contingent on process innovations. Also, in a period of cost escalation, the threat exists that price increases could take the product outside its normal consumption range. Process innovations can reduce production costs, increase profits, improve the organization's competitive position, and enable the firm to penetrate markets that were previously not economically feasible. Process innovation may be in large or small organizations, but normally one would tend to think of process innovation as a large-enterprise activity where economies of scale would provide innovational incentives.

Procedural Innovations

There is a tendency for individuals and organizations to become bogged down in routine procedures. Operations change and operational climates may also change, albeit at times unperceptibly. Often, routines or procedures are not reviewed or recast innovatively to reflect shifts in operations. Procedural innovation, in mechanical processes or thinking processes, can be instrumental in more effectively utilizing the organization's resources. This, unfortunately, is often a neglected area, but it offers fertile innovational possibilities.

Managerial Strategy and Innovation

Management is a big variable in the innovation process. Management would be the instigating or moving force in the innovational possibilities previously suggested in this section. Organizations usually reflect management's strategy and operational policies.

Firms can be technologically aggressive, defensive, or passive. Operational philosophy can mirror the general environment, the nature of the industry, the particular company, the degree of competition, and most certainly, management attitudes.[18] Operational strategy reflects policy and affects planning. Ansoff establishes three classifications to describe how firms approach strategy:[19]

1. *Reactors*: A passive approach because firms in this classification do nothing to anticipate problems. Problems are solved as they occur.

2. *Planners*: Companies in this category anticipate and plan for problems.

3. *Entrepreneurs*: Companies which fall into this classification are technologically aggressive. They anticipate not only problems but also opportunities.

Market-oriented strategy is very important in planning for innovation. Market planning strategies must be developed systematically to anticipate and maximize opportunity for long-range growth and profit targets. Corbin identifies four main forces which create pressures for marketing strategies: greater size and complexity of business operations, increased competition, rapid change factors that affect the technological and marketing environments, and intensified pressures for new products and markets.[20]

Strategy, as suggested by Twiss, can involve consideration of several factors. What possible growth is possible from current products? Is it possible to expand the market by extending the product line? What prospects exist for penetration of new markets? What can be done to improve the competitive position by reducing production costs? Can profits be increased and operational control enhanced by vertical integration, even though there is no volume increase in the end-product sold? To what extent is growth feasible by acquisition or merger?[21]

Developing and implementing an innovation strategy is not a simple process. In the process, operational strategies can be dominant. Operational strategies can be motivated by a strong technological orientation, where decisions can tend to be one-dimensional technical decisions. Technical people can become obsessed with technical novelty and forget that to be an economic success customers must be able to respond to and use the product. Or, operational considerations involving producibility and cost may become so overriding as to discourage potential innovation with its implied deviation from the safe incremental approach.

There are times when market innovation strategy cannot be divorced from operational innovation strategy. J. Fred Bucy, president of Texas Instruments, presents a telling argument for the marriage of both innovation and operational strategies. Exclusive of some critical defense technology, most U.S. technology is generally freely available. The availability of American technology comes about through foreign purchases and subsequent imitation of U.S. products. It also transpires through information exchanges at technical meetings and dissemination of research data published in technical journals. The free and easy access to American technology throughout the world is unusual, especially in view of the costs required to generate such technology. What is not freely available is the operational know-how to produce better products at competitive prices. According to Bucy, the U.S. still maintains a competitive edge in some fields because of innovation in operations which reflects design and manufacturing technological advantages.[22]

Environmental Impacts on Innovation

The Climate for Innovation

Differences in operational climates can facilitate or retard innovation. Impacts on innovation may reflect the political environment, industry characteristics, and the method of operational organization. Figure 11-2 indicates some of the environmental impacts on innovation.

The Political Environment

A government can be a compelling force in providing a receptive or negative climate for innovation. The political environment can abet or retard innovation both within the public and private sectors. Cultural influences are usually

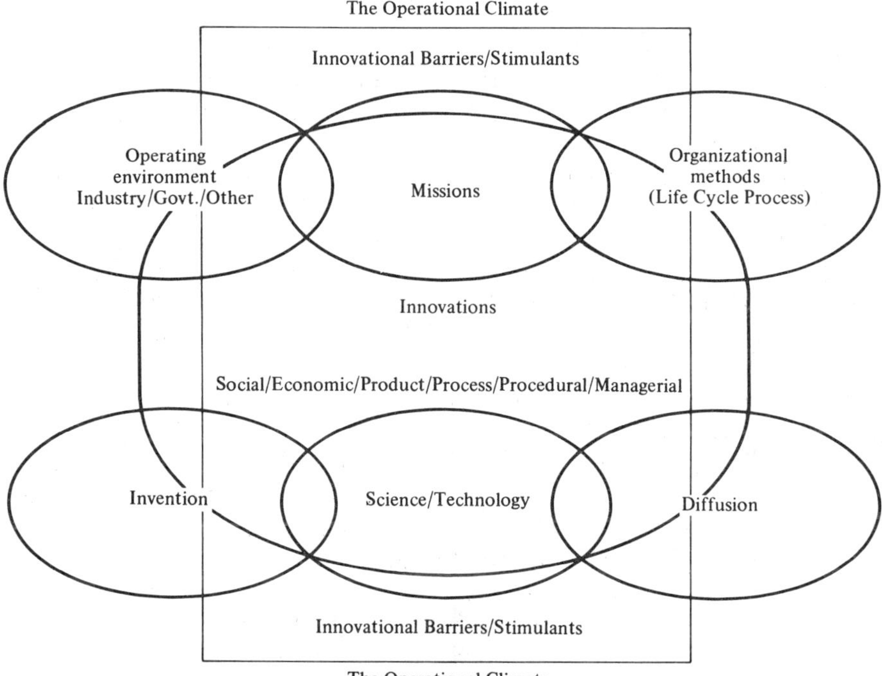

Figure 11-2. Environmental impacts on innovation.

mirrored in political systems. Political systems cover a range from totalitarian to democratic and from an implied obligation of morality and public responsibility to an elitistic controlled system with questionable public accountability.

The benchmark frequently used for measuring an organization's performance is profit. However, many organizations, especially governmental organizations, do not function under a profit-directed motivation. What criteria can be applied to determine the effectiveness and efficiency of an organization? Chester I. Barnard has said that for an organization to continue to exist, either effectiveness or efficiency is necessary; and the longer the life, the more necessary are both.[23] Effectiveness in an organization is essentially its ability to achieve its objectives; its efficiency is the degree to which it actually achieves them. An action is effective if it accomplishes its specific aim. It is efficient whether it is effective or not and if the process does not create offsetting dissatisfactions.[24] The effectiveness of a cooperative effort concerns the accomplishment of an objective within the system, and is determined by the system's requirements.

Efficiency is related to the satisfaction of individual motives. The efficiency of a cooperative system is the result of the efficiencies of individuals who furnish constituent efforts, and thus can be considered to derive from the capacity of the system to maintain itself by the satisfaction it affords the individuals involved. Efficiency can be promoted by motivating individuals or by changing the individuals within an organization so that the productive results obtained can be distributed to them. Productive results, Barnard says, may be material, social, or both. An individual may obtain satisfaction from material benefits in some cases and from social benefits in others. Most people require both, though in varying levels and proportions.[25]

In government operations, material incentive would appear to be secondary to social incentives. The assumption is that material returns provide an acceptable standard of living. A more intense material environment would be the industrial setting where some correlation might be shown between material rewards and incentive to innovate. Even though material incentives would not appear to be a paramount motivational factor in government, there obviously are motivational factors which do exist and which should be investigated relative to innovation within government organizations.

Government can also provide incentives or erect barriers to industrial innovation. Government support can be direct or indirect. Government support can be manifested by subsidies such as tax incentives or protection from international competition, by being a market, or by underwriting risk associated with R&D. A good example of the latter is the development of the machine tool industries in West Germany, the Soviet Union, and Japan.[26] In France, there has been extensive effort to create markets by the development of procurement programs and trade accords. The French and West Germans have invested large sums of money to minimize risk and spur the development of key technologies. Several countries, including Japan, the United Kingdom, France and West Germany have created a favorable climate for the formation of specialized institutions whose operational objectives are to provide capital support for invention by individuals and small enterprises.

The political climate in the United States has not been consistent. The government has encouraged innovation in technologies such as aircraft, military systems, medical research, electronics, space, and computers, as a few examples. On the other hand, government regulations have been blamed for discouraging innovation in other technologies.[27]

Industry Characteristics

Industrial operational environments are infinite. Organizational patterns can be studied in a variety of ways, such as by industry, by regulated types of industries, by nonregulated types of industries, by technologically innovative industries, by technologically static industries, by old industries, by new industries, by innovative firms within an industry and noninnovative firms within the same industry, and by organizational size as an innovatively influential factor. Also, industry organizational variances, based on national or cultural characteristics, should be looked at as having an impact on innovation.

Innovation may be a by-product of a particular industry. Consumer product industries are likely to be technologically conservative. Innovations in this type of environment are not normally geared to truly new products and new markets. Innovations in such an operational milieu tend toward an evolutionary approach—the modified variation of the old theme. The more significant innovations in such a setting would probably be in production, processes, and marketing.

In an industry where technological change is rapid, constant innovation is necessary for growth and survival. If competitive pressures are intense, a strategy of heavy commitment to research, development, and innovation may be dictated. An industry subject to drastic technological change would tend innovationally toward products which are more revolutionary than evolutionary.

The volatility of the market could affect the resources devoted to innovation. In many markets the product life cycle has become alarmingly compacted. As an example, it has been estimated that in the frozen food and dry-grocery business the introduction of new products has increased at a tremendous rate and, concurrently, the average product "life expectancies" have declined from 36 months to 12 months.[28] If new products are constantly being introduced, if there is a high product mortality rate, strategy might be directed toward keeping the pipeline full of new products. Total commitment to one or a few products is not strategically feasible. Other considerations for a strategy of steady product innovations are the unpredictability of product successes and product life expectancies. A broader-based product line, buttressed by managed introduction of new products, could provide an operational hedge. Fast pay-off strategies mean less expenditures for basic research projects, which are generally long-term and are uncertain as to accomplishment and application.

Innovation strategies should be sensitive to organizational resources. Resource allocation depends on company goals and the amount and kind of resources available. The resource mix could be distributed in several ways, but should be coordinated with, and consistent with, company strategy.

Most of the aforementioned situations were primarily addressed to aggressive or offensive innovation strategy. Defensive innovation strategies do exist and should not be ignored.

Some companies enjoy greater returns from investment in R&D than other companies. This may happen because the product of the R&D may be better, or it is possible that those more successful companies are more adept at innovating from the knowledge gleaned from R&D. There are situations leading to reluctance to invest in R&D because it is easy for competitors to build on the effort. The strategy may be imitation rather than innovation. There can be significant advantages in imitation. Only successful products are copied. Major developmental costs are not incurred. Risk is minimized. If such a strategy is adapted, arrangements can be made with innovating companies to license the technology.

A compromise position is another possibility. The company may be unwilling to depend on other companies for licenses, may want to keep at the forefront of technology, and yet may also be reluctant to incur the developmental costs in the light of risk and product life uncertainties. A middle position can be affected by being the licensor, instead of the licensee. The innovation can be licensed to other companies subject to stipulated controls. In this type of situation, part of the developmental costs can be recouped from licensing fees and there still can be some control of the innovation. It is also possible to make legal arrangements to share in incremental innovations introduced by licensees. Another possible strategy that would be offensive, rather than defensive, would be for the innovating firm to take the initiative in pushing incremental innovation.

Licensing under the proper circumstances, can be very effective defensive innovation strategy. The Japanese, in particular, have enjoyed great success using this approach.

Some other defensive innovation strategies can also be considered. Legal harassment can be taken. Such obstruction can be formidable, even if it is eventually doomed. Legally retarding an innovation may give the defensive firm the time and opportunity to take countervailing measures and technologically catch up.

Another defensive tactic could be to shift product lines so the innovation does not have full impact. The product line can be broadened, or compacted, to avoid direct confrontation. With a competitive innovation, the defensive firm can also attempt to develop a market position, or market segmentation, which cannot easily be reached by the innovation.

A study by Cooper and Schendel indicated that it is possible to improve existing products substantially, even though the innovation introduced does offer an option which is directly competitive.[29] A good example to illustrate the aforementioned is the improvement of razors and razor blades, long after the introduction of the electric shaver.

One other defensive strategy merits strong consideration. If you can't beat them, join them. It could conceivably be much the simplest strategy to acquire an innovating company, which competitively is a threat, rather than engage in other defensive strategies, or attempt to fight them head-on in the marketplace.

Organization

Organization is the grouping of people and functions to accomplish specified objectives. It is based on a division of labor and a delineation of activities for administrative purposes. Human resources are organized to show functional interrelationships indicating responsibility and authority, and to establish communication. An organization may be a company, a division of government, or a military unit. It may also be a subgroup within a larger unit. Organizations, people, and functions are not constant; they must be continuously regrouped and redefined to cope with dynamic operational conditions.

Studies on organization and innovation have been conducted to look at the innovation process within organizations, including where ideas or innovations start, how innovations are processed through the organizational hierarchies, and character profiles of individuals who have been identified as organizational innovators.[30]

Organizations grow and develop personalities. Speaking anthropomorphically, it can be said that organizations evolve through infancy, adolescence, maturity, and, possibly senility. In each evolutionary phase there are tendencies toward life cycle organizational characteristics. See Figure 11-3. In some phases of the organizational life cycle the operational environment would appear to be more conducive to innovation than in other phases.

Each of the first three phases of the organizational life cycle have desirable characteristics. Management should assess the organizational operational phase and make the necessary transitional adjustments to stimulate innovation. Ideally, the organization should have the enthusiasm, the free information flow, and the extreme flexibility of infancy. The organization should have the focus of objectives, the goal of long-run perpetuation, and the confidence of accomplishment associated with adolescence. And, finally, the desirable characteristics of maturity of experience, reputation, growth, reasonable stability and market position should be sought.

Size

Economists such as Schumpter,[31] Samuelson,[32] and Galbraith[33] have maintained that by the nature of their size, extensive resources, and range of activities large organizations have a significant advantage in conducting R&D leading to innovation. Subsequent research indicates that a considerable amount of innovation takes place in technical organizations employing fewer than 5000 employees.[34] Actually innovation takes place both in large and small organizations. There are both advantages and disadvantages based on organizational size.

Large organizations, especially those operating internationally, have extensive markets. Where only a local market exists the cost and attendant risks associated with R&D may not make investment in innovation attractive. A break-even point may be reached in a domestic market with spiraling profits accruing from foreign markets. Large organizations also have extensive resources. Capital for investment in innovation is critical. With diversified operations risk can be spread to where one technological failure is not an organizational disaster. Large organizations have other important resources at their disposal which are essential for successful innovation. They have a reservoir of technical people operating from different international locations. This gives them access to skills and knowledge not available to a localized

CHARACTERISTICS	INFANCY	ADOLESCENCE	MATURITY	SENILITY	UTOPIA
Objective	Survival	Growth	Perpetuation	Survival	Growth
Personal mobility	Very rapid all levels	Rapid shake-out process, fill in organizational gaps	Frequent at lower levels, slow turnover at middle and top levels–promotion from within	Individual stagnation, age disequilibrium, static structure, entrenched hierarchy	Upward mobility, avoidance of individual obsolescence–promotion by merit–infiltration of new ideas
Formal organization	Sketchy (objective directed)	Evolving (objective directed)	Established formal structure–job descriptions (functionally directed)	Rigid (extreme functional direction)	Evolving and flexible to accommodate change–objective-directed
Functional responsibilities	Vague	Evolving	Specific–some interpretive latitude	Rigid–little interpretive latitude	Evolving and flexible to accommodate change
Proprietary interests (sacred cows)	Nonexistent	Emerging	Some definite proprietary operational areas areas	Strong territorial claims	None–organizational welfare and attendant human concern paramount
Communications	Excellent short lines	Very good	Good-to-fair definite structure based on protocol	Red tape–communication often treated as proprietary	Excellent–interface encouraged
Reaction to problems	Very fast	Fast	Responsiveness varies from slow to fast	Slow	Fast
Informal organization	Strong–objective directed	Strong–groups begin to form	Existent but not as pronounced as in previous phases	Strong–"old boy" system	Geared to accomplishment
Internal competition	Slight	Moderate	High	Extreme	Slight
Growth	Extremely rapid	Rapid	Predictable	Static	Predictable, manageable, competitive
Innovation	High	High	Moderate	Static	High
Market position	Tenuous	Being established	Entrenched	Deteriorating	Influential

Figure 11-3. Life cycle organizational characteristics.

operation. Also, a broad operational base facilitates the transfer of technology and simplifies any product modification processes necessary to accomodate selected international markets.

Large organizations also have some inherent disadvantages relative to active innovation. Complacency can result from market domination.[35] Innovation will not enhance the market position of a firm which already has a significant share of the market. Indeed, a new product could be competitive with an existing product that has proved profitable. Large organizations tend to be conservative and adapt an evolutionary product, as distinct from a revolutionary product approach, unless extreme competition forces a change in operational philosophy. Additionally, large organizations are complex with so many operating strategies that it may take a long time for an innovative idea to work its way through the system to ultimate approval and implementation. This can be discouraging and dampen the enthusiasm of people seeking to introduce new innovations.

Of course, there are advantages and disadvantages in small organizations relative to pursuing innovational objectives. There have been successful innovations such as xerography, DDT, insulin, rockets, streptomyan, penicillin, titanism, some synthetic fibers, the zipper, automatic automobile transmissions, the jet aircraft engine, the self-winding wristwatch, the helicopter, power steering, kodachrome, airconditioning, polaroid camera, the ball-point pen, and cellophane[36] which have been important contributions of independent inventors and small organizations in the 20th century. The innovations from small organizations are, as indicated, significant. Small technical organizations are generally extremely responsive to innovative ideas. Few vested interests or sacred cows have had time to develop. Communication is rapid. Enthusiasm tends to be contagious. Red tape is nonexistent or minimal. And, most important, the innovation champion frequently is either top management or else has wide decisional latitude.

Small organizations also encounter operational environmental difficulties. They usually have limited managerial, financial, and technical resources. They often are geared to a single technology or product which leads to a make-or-break situation. Another serious disadvantage is limited access to the market.

It should be apparent that there are advantages and disadvantages associated with size in stimulating innovation. Both large and small organizations contribute. Gee says that, as a generalization, innovation from smaller organizations is apt to involve a single technology source whereas big organizations are in a position to utilize multiple sources. It follows that large organizations are normally able to undertake projects of greater size and technological magnitude than projects initiated in smaller companies.[37] It is also a reasonable assumption that several important inventions have surfaced as innovations sponsored by big companies which were started in smaller organizations. The little firm, as mentioned, is frequently hampered by lack of managerial know-how, financial restrictions, and, perhaps most critical, market access, even though initial impetus was provided by market considerations. In such instances, progress is possible only so far as completion of the cycle is contingent on big companies taking over and bringing the innovation to fruition.

Market Incentives

Demand-Pull Innovation

Most successful innovation is need or market stimulated. This is "demand-pull" innovation. It is estimated that 60 to 80% of important innovations have been a response to a customer request or need.[38] There are times when a need can be perceived by an innovator which is not apparent to the consumer until the product is introduced. To support the aforementioned statement, there are many products on the market that are now considered almost necessities which were introduced along with consumer education to their need.

Awareness of a need can be communicated by a customer through a vendor's representative. In many industries, suppliers' representatives have technical qualifications and can provide advice to customers. Sometimes a customer's needs are not unique and there are broader prospects suggested by the immediate need. In such instances, alert suppliers' representatives can convey need prospects to their organization and this can provide stimulation for innovation. Another possibility is where need is based on a derived demand which is anticipated by an innovating supplier. A good example are the various software products tied in to computers.

Technology-Push Innovation

Technology-push innovation is generally initiated from the supply side. The seller in such situations innovates and then seeks a market application. The motivation for technological development is based on market potential and subsequent technology procurement pull. The risk for the technological developer is less in the demand-pull situation than in the technology-push situation. In demand-pull there is a response to the market whereas in technology-push the development is an anticipation of a market rather than to a committed response. However, the prospective returns are also much greater in the technology-push situation if the potential market analysis is correct. A technologically innovative strategy can be instrumental in establishing market identification and leadership positions which other firms may subsequently find difficult or impossible to overcome.

Users as Innovators

There are times when, due to urgent need, or lack of communication between user and supplier, the user is forced to innovate to solve operational problems.[39] The innovation probably will be incidental to the main product produced. It can affect methods, tools, equipment, or material required in the production process. Often, while these in-house innovations are crude, they are nevertheless improvements over previous technology. These innovations are generally outside the main sphere of operational activities and, here too, sharp field representatives can pick up these ideas and convey them to their organization for refinement and commercialization. The need, in such cases has been established; preliminary development, testing, and use has occurred. The more specialized producer can add refinements and has market access as an inducement for product development.

Barriers and Stimulants to Technological Innovation

Barriers

There are many formidable barriers to innovation. Considering the magnitude of the problems associated with innovation it follows that there must be some very compelling forces to encourage firms to embark on innovative activities.

Innovation implies change and change involves uncertainty. There are internal disruptions that could have an impact on part or the total organization and affect some, most, or all of the functional areas. Invariably, when change takes place in an organization, vested interests are affected. The gain or loss, real or perceived, as a consequence of change, is bound to vary in degree of organizational acceptance from all-out support to passiveness to outright resistance. The change can affect production processes, pursuing a new technology, the introduction of new products or product variations, or different operational methods.

External factors affecting innovation involve risk predicated on market environmental forces, most of which are uncontrollable. The affects of innovation and subsequent change are largely unknowns. The unknowns, internal or external, create psychological barriers which must be circumvented. The farther into the future, the greater the uncertainty. When the environment is technologically evolutionary, innovation is likely to be incremental and the change is transitional. Where the environmental pressures are for dynamic technological change, innovation can be radical and the change is revolutionary.

Organizations that have enjoyed past commercial success have a tendency to become complacent unless there are constant external pressures to innovate. Complacency goes hand-in-hand with a no-risk position. Innovation entails risk and most managements take short-run avoidance positions. Professional managers favor short incremental and predictable results.

Innovation entails market uncertainties. Market uncertainty results from consumer acceptance, market fragmentation, and competitive forces which can neutralize an innovation.[40] Related to market acceptance is the developmental cost of the innovation. Engineers and scientists are invariably optimistic. There is a tendency to underestimate developmental costs and overstate the anticipated technical accomplishment. The degree of optimism varies with the magnitude of the technical problem and the individual making the prognostications. Management must factor each situation, since there is no general rule of thumb. Perhaps it is because of the extent of technical uncertainties, where major innovations are involved, and the difficulties in coming to a realistic appraisal of the full scope of the technical problems, that have acted as a conditioner for management to sponsor short, incremental, but manageable steps.

Cost escalation can materially affect profit potential. A market analysis can be predicated on potential product demand, the range of geographic demand, developmental costs, and pricing prospects. Higher than anticipated developmental costs would affect return on investment projections and could make a prospective innovation economically unfeasible. Attendant problems would be marketable features that might have to be sacrificed to meet cost objectives and developmental time. Another problem is that the longer into the future the greater the probability that there will be some unforeseen intervening factors which could affect the marketability of the innovation.

If the innovation is revolutionary there is the chance that the product will not perform as predicted. Product failure can have an impact on the firm's reputation. In addition, with a strong consumer environment all sorts of legal obligations can evolve stemming from product liability actions.

The political environment can also serve as an innovation barrier. Legal restrictions and regulations can dampen innovation enthusiasm. A politically unstable government can discourage venture capital especially in high-risk areas. Also, government fiscal policy can be instrumental in encouraging or discouraging innovation. A good example is the extremely high tax rate in England which, in concert with high developmental costs and the high risks of innovation, acts as a negative incentive. The evolving tax structure in the United States can be taking the U.S. down the same risk-avoidance path that exists in England.

Stimulants

The theme throughout this chapter has centered on the desirability of innovation. Innovation is the product of need either through "demand-pull" or "technology-push" projects. Need is normally market stimulated but not always. Need may be socially motivated where there are limited prospects for direct profit. Usually where there is intense social need technical accomplishment is a primary consideration. Need motivated by profit prospects is primarily directed by market considerations. Innovations that are market directed fail more often due to market miscalculations than failure to achieve technical objectives. Technicians often become obsessed with the mechanical aspects of an innovation and either ignore or pay insufficient attention to the commercialization prospects.

In market directed innovation, studies have shown the primary impetus was provided by need which was dictated by market potential.[41] Need must be reinforced by the prospect of success. Mansfield and Wagner identify three probabilities that are critical for successful innovation: the probability of technical accomplishment, the probability of commercialization based on technical completion, and the probability of economic success on the assumption of commercialization.[42]

Survival can be a vital stimulant for innovation. Growth, market maintenance, and profit in some dynamic industries are contingent on process and product innovations. The electronics and computer industries are examples where rapid change and technological progress are triggered by a constant stream of competitive new products. Firms that have not innovated and have not been at the forepoint of the technology in these fields have not survived.

Innovation is not a natural process; it is forced. To bring invention to successful innovation, dedication and effort are required. Commitment is essential. First, organizational commitment is required. Without organizational interest, resources, and sponsorship, innovation is highly improbable. Top management must also be dedicated. In smaller companies, top management probably will be intimately involved with the project. Commitment requires not only organizational sponsorship, but also an innovation champion who has organizational clout and sufficient support of other people to bring the idea to fruition.

As indicated, organizational sponsorship is vital for innovation. Top management's attitudes will be reflected in the organization's willingness or unwillingness to push innovative projects. In small companies with a narrow operational base, top management will, in all probability, be involved. Most small companies came into being on the basis of an idea generated by the top people. With rapid acceleration of technology, ideas that provided initial impetus for formation may or may not continue to be feasible. Management must be responsive and flexible and shift resources to meet opportunities. In small firms, management may become wedded to the initial idea, or ideas, and not respond to new opportunities for innovation.

The availability or nonavailability of resources can be a determinate factor in stimulating or retarding innovation. Resources can be available, but interpretation of environment factors can be pessimistic. In such instances, the prospects for innovation may not appear good, even if resources are available.

A situation may exist where resources are scarce, or practically nonexistent, but environmental factors appear very favorable. In such an optimistic setting, the firm may decide to innovate and put itself into a leverage position.

Another possibility may exist in which there are surplus resources which can be diverted to innovative projects that might not normally be attempted. The incentive to use such resources could relate to updating human skills by pursuing new technologies, modernizing facilities, anticipating the phasing-out of current income-generating activities, or entering new fields.

The government can be a motivating force for innovation. Stimulation for innovation, especially social innovation, can be provided when the government underwrites the risk associated with development and subsequently becomes a buyer of the technology. Often knowledge gained through government contracts can be modified and transferred to innovations that can be introduced in the private sector. Government directed effort is, in some respects, a laboratory which can serve as a basis for evaluating further innovational prospects. The government can also provide direct stimulation for innovation in technologies by tax incentives, investment credits, subsidies, etc. Another seldom considered governmental innovational stimulant is regulation. Normally regulation is regarded as a negative innovational factor but Gillette says that in some instances regulatory approaches can be a positive innovational influence. He feels that the service-oriented regulation of telecommunications is one example which has led to technological innovation. In addition, government procurement policies and product specifications can provide incentive for innovative design and product development.[43]

Internationalism

Government Involvement

Technological innovation and the fallouts therefrom have been recognized as being critical for national welfare. Recognition of the need for technological innovation is apparent in countries politically subscribing to a market economy. During an assignment at the International Institute for Applied Systems Analysis in Laxenburg, Austria, one of the authors had extensive dealings with representatives from countries where there are planned economies. Considerable research and effort in such economies are being channeled to improving productivity and stimulating innovation. Regardless of political idealogy, a sought-for national end-product is innovation.

Innovation can be stimulated more readily in some environments than others. Governments can provide incentives to augment existing environmental conditions. Various and extensive incentives can be offered to establish R&D facilities.[44] National policies can be formulated to shorten the cycle time from invention to innovation to diffusion. Shortened cycle times can lead to advantages in international trade and competitiveness.[45] Government funding can be influential in directing innovation to priority areas. Governments can enter into joint or multiple agreements for technological collaboration.[46] Collaborative efforts may be indicated where a pooling of resources would be mutually beneficial where there are high risks involved in pushing the state of the art, and the innovations resulting from such projects would have global impacts.

Economic Development — Exports and Imports

Innovation affects national and industrial economic development. The products resulting from innovation can be very profitable. Profits derived from innovation can help in international trade balances. It has been reported that

Israel in 1967 exported locally developed products amounting to $2.5 million. At that time most Israeli exports were agricultural or noninnovational products. A government policy supporting technological innovation has been a major factor in raising industrial exports in 1979 to $783 million. There has been a transformation from a insignificant percent of technological exports to more than 30% of overall industrial exports in a period of little more than ten years.[47] Mexico is another example of a country seeking to minimize dependence on imported technology. The Mexican government is encouraging technological innovation in a wide range of agricultural and industrial applications.[48]

Israel and Mexico are just two examples. Industrialized nations have long appreciated the need for technological innovation as a means to achieve national economic development. Some developing nations such as Brazil and Argentina are making progress in fostering innovation and economic development; other developing nations have been less successful in marshalling their resources for innovation and economic development.

Companies, especially those operating in international markets, are also affected. If there are no innovational products to market, it follows that a nation's technological position will be compromised. In planned systems there are apt to be political as well as economic repercussions. In market systems there will be negative economic impacts if firms operating nationally or internationally cannot compete in the marketplace. It was reported in *Business Week* that Philips, the huge Dutch electronics firm, is encountering severe competitive pressure from Japanese industrial organizations.[49] If technological innovation is not forthcoming from domestic industrial organizations it follows that there will be increased dependence on foreign firms.

Nations can be both exporters and importers of innovation. Usually developed nations tend to have a favorable export balance of innovation, whereas developing nations often have an import balance of innovation. Importing innovation can lead to technological dependence, or, as in the case of Japan, importing innovation can be a short-cut to technological development and subsequent exportable innovation.

The exporting of technology, as previously mentioned, can have a pervasive effect on international trade and a nation's international balance of payments. The international account includes payment for such things as technical know-how, including the sale of consulting services, licensing, patent royalties, and coproduction arrangements.

Most of the international movement in transferring technology and innovation involves technologically advanced countries. For instance, the bulk of U.S. technology export has gone to Western European countries and most U.S. technology import has come from Western Europe and Canada.[50]

The export or import of innovation can have significant, if not immediately obvious, impact on the technological balance of payments. A new product or industry can be developed where no direct substitutes or competition immediately exist, such as Xerox or the computer. There can also be "displacement" innovations, such as synthetic fibers invading the natural fiber market.[51]

Untapped Markets — Developing Nations

A great market potential exists in the developing nations which have the bulk of the world's population. The United States, Canada, Europe (including the U.S.S.R.), Australia, New Zealand, Israel, South Africa, and Japan are considered the world's developed nations.[52]

The rest of the nations in the world are considered to be developing nations. The implications are staggering in the light of the population concentrated in the land area involved, and the relatively low percent of the world's total consumption found in the developing nations of the world. With their anemic per capita income, the consumption of goods and services by about 70% of the world population in the developing countries could be estimated at from 10 to 15% of the value of all goods and services consumed globally. The conclusion is that the developing nations represent a tremendous market which should be accommodated.

Developing nations usually are deficient in most advanced technologies. Need assessment and evaluation of available resources can assist in the determination of technological priorities. Concentrated effort toward selected technological excellence can lead to an environment conditioned for innovation. It is important to realize that the development of a technological capability base may, by itself, be sterile. Technological utilization requires adaption, production, marketing, promotion, and sales. To exploit the potential in developing nations, firms frequently are forced into modificational innovations in production methods and marketing procedures.

Overview

Some Relevant Questions

The subject of innovation is broad. As indicated in this chapter extensive research has taken place and is in process in order to better understand the phenomena. Investigating and subsequently understanding the implications of innovation is critically important. Following are some questions, the answers to which might serve as potential research projects. No attempt has been made to prioritize or structure the following questions.

1. It would appear that innovations processes are low in developing countries. What factors can stimulate innovation in such environments? Where has there been successful innovations? Are there any organizational patterns in such instances that can provide guidance for intensifying innovations in developing nations?
2. What types of innovations have taken place in developing countries? It is theorized that a small innovation (small by industrial country standards) in

such a society will have a proportionally larger impact than a more technologically advanced innovation in a high-technology society.

3. Can innovation be stimulated? How? Is the phase in the organizational life cycle relevant to innovation?
4. Do certain organizational environments tend to spawn innovations in specific areas? For instance,

Innovation	Environment
social	government
process	large organizations
productivity and procedural	large organizations
product	small organizations

5. Do organizations reach saturation points or diminishing innovational returns? What factors contribute to such situations?
6. Why does innovation happen or not happen? What external or internal forces seem crucial to encouraging or discouraging innovation?
7. Are some organizational forms more conducive to stimulating innovation than other organizational forms? What advantages and disadvantages are there in traditional organizational forms relative to stimulating innovation?
8. Can innovatively productive organizational forms be identified and classified by type of operational setting and type of innovation?
9. At what phase of the pure-research-through-production cycle is innovation most likely to occur? Is innovation desirable in all phases of the cycle and, if so, to what extent are organizational processes a factor to be considered?
10. To what extent do political or cultural factors affect innovation? A study might be conducted of similar industries in different social/political environments.
11. How does management affect the innovation process? Studies of high-innovation environments to determine the motivational role of management would be fruitful.
12. Are there any discernible characteristics of innovators, such as age, education, experience levels, organizational position, functional orientation, etc? Are people with some functional backgrounds more apt to innovate than people with other functional backgrounds? In what types of innovations? Is the innovation a product of the individual's functional orientation?
13. Would it be feasible to establish an "innovation" function and assign people to that function? Their sole mission will be to innovate—within their functional area of expertise—or using their functional know-how, to work in concert with other functional experts. Functional tenure in the "Innovation Department" would be subject to periodic review.
14. What are the sources of innovations within organizations? Can these be understood within the context of type of innovation, the operational environment, or functional affiliation?

15. How does technology transfer and the diffusion process, within the organization, affect innovation?
16. To what extent do reward or recognition systems within organizations serve as innovational stimulants. Is there any correlation between reward systems and intensity of innovation? If so, which reward systems appear to be most successful?
17. Are interdisciplinary interactions within organizations effective in encouraging innovation? How? What methods can be employed to encourage intraorganizational communication?
18. How can interorganizational processes be used to stimulate innovation?
19. What type of outside exposures are most fruitful in instigating thought processes leading to internal innovations?
20. Are there any discernible patterns of organization in government where there has been a high incidence of innovation? Are there variable patterns based on political ideology?
21. In looking at industrial organizational patterns and innovation, it is suggested that such studies should be structured to consider: types of industry, regulated and nonregulated industries, competitive and monopolistic industries, technologically aggressive industries and technologically static industries, old industries and new industries, large industries and small industries, and industrial variations, based on geographic location and/or cultural difference.
22. Are certain types of organizations more adept at original innovations? Are there distinct organizational characteristics where innovations emanate from initiation vis-à-vis the Japanese system of sharp improvement over established processes?
23. What affect does the constant phasing-in and phasing-out of projects, a common practice in R&D organizations, have on innovation? Is there any correlation between project life expectancy, i.e., long- or short-duration projects and innovation?
24. Is it possible to study project or work units and organizational factors associated with work where there has been innovation? If so, this might give some clues as to what types of activities encourage innovation solutions and how organizational factors act as reinforcement for innovation.
25. How does internal functional competition affect innovation?
26. Is there any correlation between organizational stability turnover or attrition rates, and intensity of innovation? Is innovation more apt to take place in organizations where there is constant people movement in and out of the organization, or where there is stability? Can attrition norms be developed to provide a climate where innovation might be stimulated?
27. How do the formal and informal organizations affect innovation?
28. From research, would it be possible to evolve a new organizational form that would be conducive to innovation?

29. How do organizational decision processes affect innovation—degree of decisional latitude as encouraging or discouraging innovation? Hierarchical or colleague authority?
30. What is the effect of physical proximity-functions or disciplines on innovation?
31. Does organizational position or rank have any bearing as to individual's proclivity to innovate? If so how?
32. Is intraorganizational mobility a factor in innovation?
33. How does seniority or organizational tenure affect individuals who might or might not innovate?
34. Does the nature of the industry—ease of exit or entry—have any bearing or tendency to innovate? Also, what types of innovations take place?

Endnotes Chapter Eleven

1. H.D. Haustein, "Human Resources, Certainty and Innovation: The Conflict Between Homo Faber and Homo Ludius," invited paper for the Sixth World Congress of the International Economic Association (IEA), Mexico City, August, 4–9, 1980, prepared under auspices of International Institute for Applied Systems Analysis, Laxenburg, Austria. November 1979, WP-79-112, p. 20.
2. Charles F. Larson, "Management for the 80's—A Challenge to Change," *The International Journal of Research Management*, Vol. XXIII, No. 5, September 1980, p. 7.
3. Brian Twiss, *Managing Technological Innovation*, Longmans Group Limited, London, 1974, p. 2.
4. *Technological Innovation: Its Environment and Management*, Washington, DC: U.S. Department of Commerce, 1967, p. 2.
5. Gilbert Kivenson, "Gain in Productivity Through the Tapping of Shelved Technology," *Industrial Research and Development*, January 1981, p. 141.
6. *Ibid.*
7. "The Silent Crisis in R&D," *Business Week*, March 8, 1976, pp. 90–92.
8. See "The Breakdown of U.S. Innovation," *Business Week*, February 16, 1976, pp. 56–68.
9. "New Product Success Rate—One out of Three," *The International Journal of Research Management*, Vol. XXIII, No. 2, March 1980, p. 3.
10. "The Breakdown of U.S. Innovation," *op. cit.* p. 57.
11. "Venture Capitalists Rush in to Back Emerging High-Technology Firms," *The Wall Street Journal*, March 18, 1981, p. 31.
12. John Verhoogen, "Federal Support of Basic Research," in Basic Research and National Goals, Report to the Committee on Science and Astronautics, U.S. House of Representatives by the National Academy of Sciences, 89th Congress, 1st Session, March 1965, p. 270.
13. *Technological Innovation*: *Its Environment and Management*, *op. cit.*, pp. 11–12.
14. *Science Indicators—1976*, National Science Board, Washington, DC: National Science Foundation, 1977, pp. 125–126.
15. Twiss, *op. cit.*, pp. 2–3.
16. *Technological Innovation*: *Its Environment and Management*, *op. cit.*, p. 7.
17. *Ibid.*

18. For a good discussion on managerial attitudes see William G. Sharwell, "A Prescription for Innovation," *The International Journal of Research Management*, Vol. XXIV, No. 1, January 1981, p. 6.
19. H. Igor Ansolf, *Corporate Strategy*, New York: McGraw-Hill, 1965, p. 104.
20. Arnold Corbin, "The Team Approach to Strategic Market Planning," *Changing Marketing Strategies in a New Economy*, Indianapolis: Bobbs-Merrill Educational Publishing, 1977, pp. 65–66.
21. Twiss, *op. cit.*, p. 28.
22. J. Fred Bucy, "Marketing in a Goal-Oriented Organization," *Changing Marketing Strategies in a New Economy, op. cit.*, p. 130.
23. Chester I. Barnard, *The Functions of the Executive*, Cambridge, MA: Harvard University Press, 1938, p. 82.
24. *Ibid*. p. 20.
25. *Ibid*. pp. 56–57.
26. Clifford W. Fawcett and Dan Roman, "Industry Overview for the Purchase of Machine Tools," *Journal of Purchasing and Materials Management*, Vol. 12, No. 3, Fall 1976.
27. See Dean Gillette, "How Regulations Encourage and Discourage Innovation," *The International Journal of Research Management*, Vol. XX, No. 2, March 1977, p. 18.
28. "New Products: The Push is on Marketing," *Business Week,* March 4, 1972, p. 72.
29. Arnold C. Cooper and Dan Schendel, "Strategic Responses to Technological Threats," *Business Horizons*, February 1976.
30. To cite a few representative studies: Louis K. Bragaw, Jr., "Some Characteristics of Successful Technological Innovations and Their Patterns," doctoral dissertation, The School of Government and Business Administration, The George Washington University, September 1970; J.M. Utterback, "The Process of Technical Innovation in Instrument Forms," doctoral dissertation, Massachusetts Institute of Technology, January 1969. A few others who have contributed in this area are A. Shapiro, E. Roberts, and J. Goldhar.
31. Joseph Schumpter, *Capitalism, Socialism, and Democracy*, New York: Harper & Row, 1942.
32. Paul Samuelson, *Economics*, 8th edition, New York: McGraw-Hill, 1970.
33. John K. Galbraith, *American Capitalism*, Boston: Houghton Mifflin Co., 1952; and *New Industrial State*, Boston: Houghton Mifflin Co., 1967.
34. See Louis K. Bragaw, Jr., *Some Characteristics of Successful Technological Innovations and Their Patterns*, doctoral dissertation, The School of Government and Business Administration, The George Washington University, September 1970; J. Jewkes, D. Sawers and R. Stitterman, *The Sources of Invention*, 2nd edition, Macmillan, 1969; A.C. Cooper, "Small Companies Can Pioneer New Products" *Harvard Business Review*, September/October 1966; James Bright, *Research, Development, and Technological Innovation*, Homewood, IL: Richard D. Irwin, 1964; Donald A. Schor, *Technology and Change*, New York: Delacorte Press, 1967; Sumner Meyers and Donald G. Marquis, *Successful Industrial Innovations*, Washington, DC: The National Science Foundation, 1969.
35. Joel B. Rosenberg, "Research and Market Share: A Reappraisal of the Schumpeter Hypothesis," *Journal of Industrial Economics*, Vol. XXV, No. 2, December 1976, p. 104.
36. *Technological Innovation: Its Environment and Management, op. cit.* p. 18.
37. Sherman Gee, "Factors Affecting the Innovation Time-Period," *The International Journal of Research Management*, Vol. XXI, No. 4, January 1978, p. 40.
38. Jordan D. Lewis, "National Science and Technology Policy—Its Impact on Technological Change," *The International Journal of Research Management,* Vol. XX, No. 1, January 1977, p. 14.

39. Pioneering studies of users as innovators has been done by Eric A. von Hippel, "Has a Customer Already Developed Your Next Product?" *Sloan Management Review*, Winter 1977, pp. 63–74, and "Users as Innovators," *Technology Review*, January 1978, pp. 31–39.

40. Frank Press, "Towards New National Policies to Increase Industrial Innovation," *The International Journal of Research Management*, Vol. XXI, No. 4, July 1978, p. 11.

41. E. Mansfield and S. Wagner, "Organizational and Strategic Factors Associated with Probabilities of Success in Industrial R&D," *Journal of Business*, Vol. 48, No. 2, April 1975, p. 175; S.M. Utterback, "The Process of Technical Innovation in Instrument Forms, Doctoral Dissertation, Massachusetts Institute of Technology, January 1969; and L. Bragnaw, *op. cit.*

42. E. Mansfield and S. Wagner, *op. cit.*

43. Gillette, *op. cit.*, p. 21.

44. Robert N. Mattson, "R&D Tax Policy," *The International Journal of Research Management*, Vol. XXI, No. 1, January 1978, p. 24.

45. Gee, *op. cit.*, p. 41.

46. "U.S. and Japan Agree on Joint Research Efforts," *The International Journal of Research Management*, Vol. XXIII, No. 4, July 1980, p. 3.

47. "Research Trends," *Industrial Research and Development*, March 1981, p. 39.

48. *R&D Mexico*, National Council of Science and Technology Conacyt, February 1981.

49. "Philips—An Electronics Giant Rearms to Fight Japan," *Business Week*, March 30, 1981, pp. 86–97.

50. *Science Indicators — 1976 National Science Board*, Washington, DC: National Science Foundation, 1977, p. 3.

51. *Technological Innovation: Its Environment and Management, op. cit.*, p. 5.

52. *UNESCO, Statistical Yearbook (1971)* p. 28.

SECTION V:

Managerial Considerations

CHAPTER TWELVE

Decision Factors in Development of Technological Infrastructure

The Transnational Firm

International Impact

As mentioned in previous chapters, the transnational firm's activities span the boundaries of several countries, influencing and touching the lives of many people and nations. These organizations are a response to economic imperatives, personal ambition, and human creativity. They are agents of vibrant change. Considerations of scale and efficiency, the search for raw materials and markets, and quantum leaps in information and communications technology are among the more obvious factors that underlie the emergence of the transnational firm.

In this chapter some decision factors are discussed which are considered relevant for management of the transnational enterprise in the development of a broad technological infrastructure base. Emphasis is placed on discussing basic determinants for the foundation that sustains the transnational firm and supports its expansion, diversification, and technological advancement. These determinants are stratified as *exogeneous* (external) or *endogenous* (internal) *factors*. They constitute those considerations necessary for successful technological generation, growth, expatiation, transfer, and improvement.

Exogenous Factors

Plurality of Exogenous Factors

The plurality and diversity of exogenous factors make it necessary for any national or continental suborganizations of a transnational company to possess the power to solve problems and issues that are peculiar to its domicile.[1]

Studies in this country and abroad show that management must continuously interact with people inside and outside the organization, and that its members—the executives—must constantly be ready to interject themselves propitiously when something threatens to disrupt the equilibrium of the organization.

Specific factors that are worthy of study are the political/legal structures of the nations involved, the economics of direct foreign investment, the cultural and educational realities of international commerce, and the industrial and public relations requiring national consideration. There are obviously many other factors that have an impact on the transnational firm; these, however, are the more salient and eminent.

Political / Legal Considerations

The primary distinction between international and domestic business firms lies in their environmental frameworks and in the organizational and behavioral responses that flow from these frameworks. As a company transcends a national setting, its environmental framework changes in countless respects. There arise new ground rules as defined by law, custom, and culture; new values; new contradictions, interactions, and balances among external forces; and new opportunities as well as uncertainties. The more extensive the company's international scope, the greater the environmental diversities surrounding it. To make rational choices among alternatives available to it in different countries, a company must be able to identify, understand, and anticipate both the negative and the positive forces of the international environment.

In domestic business where there is reasonable political stability the external factors are relatively identifiable and somewhat predictable for most firms. Changes are normally gradual and generally do not lead to any sudden or revolutionary differentiation among opportunities and constraints among diverse industries or types of enterprise. When an enterprise expands its operations and institutions beyond the domestic sphere, the environmental settings are subject to many possible variations. The constraining or the liberating factors of the environment become variables, both in space and in time. The constraints—social attitudes, public policies, price regulations, etc.—are no longer homogeneous constraints but heterogeneous variables which increase complexity as the firm expands its operational scope.

Laws and public policies governing corporate behavior and defining the limits of entrepreneurial freedom and action differ in numerous respects. There are no two countries whose laws, policies, and politics are identical. An action that is perfectly legitimate in one nation may constitute a criminal or civil offense in another; or again, an action regarded in the best interest of one community of economy may be construed as antisocial in another. A transnational corporation operating in different political jurisdictions has no single constitutional structure, no one system of federal laws, and no other common juridicial framework. The laws and public policies encountered in political jurisdictions are often based on different premises, vary in countless respects, and frequently are incongruous and irreconcilable in specific provisions. For example, the incorporation law in one country may be loose; in another the requirements may be methodical and strict. In Spain, a specified percentage of stock must be held by local nationals—this increases the facade of "dummy stockholders." In other countries, like Ethiopia, the permission to enter business may be obtained only after repeated visits and long negotiating sessions with officials. Unusual strategies are often necessary in order to initiate and sustain operations. Because of the political situation, a major industrial firm shared ownership of its Bogota subsidiary with a Colombian family. One member of the family belonged to one political party and another member to the other party. The presidency of the subsidiary alternated between the two, depending on which party was in power; business prosperity and continuity depended greatly on good governmental relations.

The political environments of different countries often vary in such a degree that uncertain operational latitude and continuity add to the normal risks of doing business. Governments change frequently, especially in developing nations, and invariably along with a change in the administration there is a change in the political climate. In an international setting, which is often politically volatile, there is an understandable natural reluctance for transnational firms to enter such environments and make extensive investment in nonportable operations. The result has been, as reported in *The Wall Street Journal*, a new functional activity within such firms for political analysis as an important part of the investment decision process.[2]

Investment

Investments in foreign environments confront corporate management with a variety of risks and uncertainties that differs materially from those involved in domestic investment decisions. For direct foreign investment the attitudes of the people and of the government officials in that country have to be carefully considered. This analysis should include a thorough study of the country's laws and the degree of vigor and method of enforcement. In some nations such as Burma, there are official statutes which favor direct foreign investment—liberal tax exemptions, guarantees against expropriation, and immunity to certain exchange controls. The government, however, generally disregards the laws and rarely enforces them. The laws are more of an indication of governmental power than as rights of business enterprises.

A stable political and economic environment offering an atmosphere conducive to a reasonably predictable operational base is an important consideration for the transnational firm seeking new investments and markets. Some entrepreneurial ventures can thrive in times of war, crisis, and political upheaval. They capitalize on uncertainty and disruption. Most businesses, however, prefer a relatively stable environment. Violent changes in government and national policies inject too many uncertainties into business decisions.

Unstable currencies or severe foreign exchange fluctuations promote justified feelings of instability and uneasiness. Additionally, disturbances such as labor strikes or undependable utilities and communications seriously hamper a firm's ability to operate efficiently.[3]

Nationalism

The transnational firm faces a unique and provocative challenge: Can a firm managed by members of particular national groups act in a way that encompasses broader multidimensional, multinational issues? Conflicts between the viewpoint of the firm in regards to a particular country and its outlook toward operations in the world as a whole can easily arise. An understanding of nationalism and national viewpoints may be imperative to successful operation of a firm whose operations extend across national and cultural boundaries.

It is apparent that "nationalism" is an elusive concept. It has been described as "a fusion of patriotism with a consciousness of nationality..." or "the individual's identification of himself with the 'we group' to which he gives supreme loyalty."[4] The "we group" to which an individual gives this loyalty may be as small as a clan or as large as an entire group of nations. The heads of political entities promote this allegiance and feeling of oneness among the members of the society in order to foster unity and cohesiveness in ventures requiring cooperation, such as industrialization and national defense. However, the interests of the transnational firm may be impaired by a type of thinking that divides the world into "us" and "them." The successful international manager is quick to recognize the potential for conflict between an action that is "optimal" for operations in a specific nation and an action that is best for the entire firm.

Traditionally, a business firm's primary objective is held to be maximization of relatively short-term profit. The economic objectives of nations may be longer term and can be formulated in terms of macroeconomic goals: growth of output, reduction of unemployment, curbing of inflation, and usually political continuity for the incumbants. In a closed domestic economy it is possible for the microeconomic objectives of the firm and the macroeconomic objectives of a nation to conflict. A company may maximize profit and be contributing to rising inflation. However, and this is important, the firm is in the final analysis bound to that economy and the extent of the conflict is limited by local politics. Within this scenario, the government can take actions to curb and control the actions of the firm.

The subsidiary of a transnational firm, however, leads a dual existence. On the one hand, it is a corporate citizen of the host country and also a unit or component in a broader system. The transnational enterprise's objective is to maximize returns to the system as a whole. It is entirely possible that maximization of overall returns will require that an individual subsidiary perform at levels not necessarily compatible with the best interests of its political host. Profits in a given country may be reduced through various managerial manipulative practices. Therefore, while the subsidiary is a resident in the host country, it is not entirely a part of it. The possibilities for conflict are exacerbated by the very multinationality of the subsidiary. It is not under the same degree of national control as its domestic competitors. The transnational firm has a greater potential for conflict with national objectives than its domestic competitors and is substantially less subject to control by the host government. The transnational firm, therefore, represents a direct threat to sovereignty—in terms of law making, control, and enforcement—that no independent nations can ignore.[5]

While the host government has less control over foreign subsidiaries than it does over domestic firms, it still has several substantial weapons which can be brought to bear. It is the sovereign, law-making and law-enforcing entity within the nation. If necessary it could expropriate assets. Long before that point is reached, however, many alternatives are available. It can place controls over remissions of profits or institute requirements for substantial local ownership and participation. There normally is a relatively congenial tradeoff. An important consideration is that the host government must be careful not to exercise undue control to preclude frightening away existing and potential investors. On the other hand, the transnational weighs maximization of worldwide corporate returns against good corporate citizenship in a given country at the risk of overall suboptimization. The transnational is usually careful not to force a government's hand, mindful of its alien status.

A transnational firm must have a good perception of the political risks involved in multination operations. Political systems are both complex and dynamic. Political change can be difficult to anticipate and political change can affect achievement of the goals of an enterprise. The firm must be concerned with home, host, and third-country relationships and with their mutual and often complex interactions.

When building the cornerstone for an organization there are numerous nationalistic factors to be considered. The list becomes longer for the transnational organization. The following tabulation is probably not complete for all situations, but it does illustrate some areas involving decisions that are influenced by nationalism:

Location of business.

Structure of business.

Market.

Product laws and codes.

Financial considerations.

Monetary considerations.

Taxes.

Industrial proprietary rights.

Investment risks.

Personnel considerations.

Transportation considerations.

Technology.

These 12 factors deserve managerial attention, as they tend to exacerbate the nature and legality of business transactions.

International and National Laws

International law is a different entity from the laws of individual nations. This is due to the absence of an international legislative body that can generate "international statutes" and a suitable body to enforce international laws, if enacted. All that presently exists is a collection of agreements, treaties, and conventions between two or more nations. Violations and deviations are usually difficult to settle and involve great expense and long legal entanglements. A good example is the territorial dispute between Argentina and Chile.

However, as more and more companies and nations are involved in international commerce, so is there a growing basis for international law. Regional economic groupings, such as the European Economic Community, are creating laws that pertain to the operations of the transnational firm. Technology is also aiding in the creation of a body for international laws. Increasingly, nations are facing common problems that require common solutions and find that technology assists in the solution. The world is definitely shrinking in terms of business relationships—aided by technological innovation.

Usually laws reflect the cultures that gave birth to them. The laws of a society are one dimension of its culture. They are the rules established by authority, society, or custom. Collectively, these rules of behavior govern the affairs of people within a society. The laws of a nation are a manifestation of its attitudes and cultural norms, and generally reflect its religious traditions. Table 12-1 is a summary of the world's legal systems. Note that over 30 nations have indigenous, nonwritten law as part of their overall legal system.

Cultural Aspects

There is little doubt as to the contribution made by technology to the change in the worldwide standard of living. There is correlation between technology and the culture of a nation. Technology is not autonomous; it can be shaped by a culture according to prevailing values and social structures, as well as natural resources and economic factors. Once introduced, technology alters society by opening new possibilities for human and business action. Therefore, technology can also be instrumental in shaping sociocultural systems as well as reflecting prevailing systems.

In formulating the strategy of introducing and marketing a technology a

Table 12-1. World Legal Systems (As of 1975)

Systems	Numbers of Countries
Common Law Systems	
Pure common law countries	7
Mixed common law countries	19
Total countries with common law elements	26
Civil Law Systems	
Pure civil law countries	32
Mixed civil law countries	39
Total countries with civil law elements	71
Moslim Law Systems	
Pure Moslin law countries	2
Mixed Moslim law countries	28
Total countries with Moslim law elements	30
Communist Law Countries	12
Indigenous Law Systems (tribal, nonliterate law)	
Pure indigenous law countries	0
Mixed indigenous law countries	30
Total countries with indigenous law element	30

prudent international manager studies the realities of the following:

Technology and value systems.

Technology and social systems.

Technology and religious systems.

Technology and educational systems.[6]

Values serve as standards for judging concrete ideas, rules, and goals; they guide choices and actual behavior. The current values of a society should play a major role in the determination of which technologies are developed and applied. A society's values provides social direction to the process of technological development. Recent worldwide efforts in the field of pollution control can be viewed as a response to the shift in values in many societies toward better "quality of life."

The *social organization* of a culture may either foster or inhibit technological development. It tends to operate as a source of authority, responsibility, and aspiration, thus, influencing the course of technological advance and the creation of material culture. Aspects of social organization in the industrial spheres, such as division of labor, specialization, and systemization will likely influence the technological process and thus the outputs as well. Alterations in the social organization are most often due to technological advances, either directly or more often indirectly.

The social processes of a given country should be studied and analyzed in great depth before the commitment of venture capital. There will likely be special considerations that demand the attention of corporate planners. Failure to adhere to local practices may well doom the success of a venture from the outset. The caste system of India is an example of where the business strategist must ensure that only the "proper" representatives are contacted, and thus only the "proper" level of worker will be employed.

Religious institutions in a culture propagate norms, customs, prohibitions, and standards of conduct that serve to influence the nature, development, and application of technology. Very often religious values are biased against technological change and the likely effects of this change after the culture. Mahatma Gandhi once said, "The machine should not be allowed to cripple the limbs of man," and was concerned that, "by working with machines we have become machines ourselves, having lost all sense of art and handwork."[7]

Political systems tend to be those interrelated factors of social structures and power/authority roles that serve to coordinate and administer the society, to maintain social order, and to provide the means for changes in legal and administrative systems. The political system provides the direction for development of technology and guides the application and use of technological advances for the benefit of the society.

There are both direct and indirect effects of the political system upon technology. Directly, technologies are recognized by political leaders as being related to decision making, communications, and information-flow, and thus influence the rationalization of the decision process. For example, leaders of many nations are concerned with training, communication systems, maintenance, spare parts, and technical advisors, before allowing the extension of computers and computer systems within their country.

Indirectly, the political system places great influence upon the technological process. Often technology is recognized as spelling problems for the society. Matters such as pollution, urban decay, resource depletion, and economic and professional obsolescence are recognized as technological "fallout." Leaders are thus reluctant to open their doors to technological change unless they accrue offsetting benefits that tend to outweigh the disadvantages. The "Third Nation" movement within the United Nations often addresses this theme.

Educational systems of a society tend to transmit knowledge from one generation to another by either formal or informal methods. Educational systems affect the technological systems by both the extent and type of technologically relevant knowledge and capacities (i.e., human resources) which make up a nation's population.

Educational advantages in many countries are reserved only for the rich, affluent levels. Educational objectives may, in such situations, be aesthetic rather than practical or functional. For a company expecting to rely upon an indigenous labor force this can create problems. In such cultures there could be highly educated people available but they may not possess the required technical skills. A company may be seeking electrical engineers and only be able to hire lawyers. As the company seeks to fill intervening positions (between top management and the labor force) they encounter serious problems. Very likely the society has not provided for the education and subsequent training of technicians who are capable plumbers, electricians, foremen, middle managers, or semiskilled machine operators. A few may exist, but far too few to satisfy the needs of the company. At the lower level, however, there will be a virtual glut of human resources. There will be many illiterate or semiliterate persons, totally unskilled in any activity needed for an industrial operation. Unfortunately, such people often cannot be effectively integrated into more sophisticated activities, especially moderate- or high-skill capital-intensive operations.

The native's view of the firm, reflecting cultural bias, must be a consideration of the corporate planners when developing the initial strategy. At present there is a discernible movement in Europe to avoid the purchase of American goods whenever possible. This is a factor to be weighed in the overall context of whether to and how to operate a business. It is conceivable that deliberate steps might be taken to conceal the country of origin of the technology.

Fears of domination of Europe's economy by U.S.-based firms are especially strong and turn mostly on technological matters, real and fancied. A persuasive agreement to this effect was presented in *Le Defi Americain*.[8] The author, J.J. Servan-Schreiber, predicated that within a life time "the world's third great industrial power, just after the United States and Russia, will not be Europe, but American industry in Europe." His reasons were the dynamism of American management and the resonant use of technology. American management in Servan-Schreiber's mind could readily adapt to changes, be organizationally flexible, and to utilize the creative power of teamwork—all direct threats to the life-expectancy of European commercial enterprises.

Geography

The geography of a nation plays an important role in the technological development of that nation as well as the establishment of its science policy. Geographical factors important to the transnational firm are size, terrain, climate, location, and supply of natural resources. It is interesting to examine the technological development of some of the world's great nations with respect to whether they were helped or hindered by geographical factors.

The United States has certainly benefited from its favorable geographical situation. The climate is generally moderate and there has been a bountiful supply of many natural resources up until recent years when it has been necessary to import a great deal of oil. Geographical factors have helped to make America the technological leader of the world.

Japan is a small island nation with few natural resources of its own. However, they have made great progress in spite of this handicap. They import critical materials such as the oil, iron ore, manganese, lead, copper, and bauxite used in their domestic production. In order to pay for all of these raw materials, Japan has a strong export program of consumer products to other nations. They have taken advantage of their skilled labor to build radios, televisions, cameras, watches, automobiles, and many other products for the export market. By keeping exports ahead of imports, Japan has been able to feed their industrial programs and maintain a good technological growth.[9]

The Soviet Union, although a great industrial nation, has been hindered in one respect by geography. The Siberia region of the USSR has vast natural resources of minerals, coal, oil, and gas. However, these resources are trapped between hundreds of feet of permafrost and the Soviets have not developed the technology to retrieve them. They are taking steps to import Western technology to mine these resources.[10] They are also taking internal actions to exploit the region. *The Washington Post* reported on a "Science Township" which was established in the mid-1950s on the Ob River to map the vast natural resources of Siberia. The "Township" is a concentration of scientists and engineers devoted specifically to speeding up and making more efficient the tapping of the region's resources.[11] *The Washington Post* also highlighted the new Baikal-Amur-Mainline Railway under construction through central Siberia. The railroad, scheduled for completion in 1983, will open the vast mineral and fuel riches of this remote region to world markets. The construction of the railroad is a tremendous technological challenge because of the extreme cold and the mountains, valleys, and swamps which must be traversed. Also, there is the permafrost which requires special insulation against heat from passing trains that could melt the frost and sink the track. Special alloy steels are needed in the track to keep it from snapping in the extreme cold. Imported technology is being used extensively in this project. Japanese-made drills are being used for tunnelling; German-made trucks and American-made earth moving and hydraulic equipment are being used to freight the rubble out of the tunnels.[12]

Tropical Africa has had considerable difficulties with its technological development, and part of the reason is its geography. It has enormous size and generally low population density. It has generally high temperatures, but great extremes of rainfall in different areas. The tse-tse fly, which prevents livestock rearing over much of the area, has hindered permanent settlement. There is a prevalence of disease, especially insect borne. There is some progress being made in upgrading the technological base of Africa, but the geographical and climatic factors noted above are definitely a hindrance.[13]

Natural resources are those basic materials provided by nature, having an economic usefulness or value. It should be noted that the presence of these in most places where people live is not accidental. Man's evolution from "forager" to "grower" led to settlement in areas where those resources necessary to support agriculture were plentiful. Man has long sought to discover, develop, extract, and use natural resources, wherever they may be found. Man has long proved to be ingenious in circumventing the vagaries of nature by developing and using technology to increase water reserves, refertilize depleted soils, and breed plants and animals that resist diseases and climatic extremes. Technological advances have allowed people to grow crops in deserts (California and Israel) and to enable animals to thrive in isolation (the Kobi beef cattle of Japan).

Natural resources provide both an incentive as well as a basis for development. The economic lure of natural resources may prove to be the motivational incentive which allows the transnational enterprise to assist in developing a viable economy in a lesser-developed nation.

Topography and climate are also factors that can play important parts in commercial operations. Environmental balances have delayed and complicated the development of Alaska's land and vast natural resources. The long periods of winter coupled with its isolated position have inhibited development of population centers. Railroads and highways are costly to build and maintain, thus reducing their number. The world has yet to significantly tap any resources of the Arctic or Atlantic regions. Whereas land may be plentiful, the cost of labor and environmental realities inhibit commercial expansion.

Utilities are those services which are necessary for industry to drive machinery, support workers, and make life more comfortable. While not a geographical factor in a pure sense, utilities are normally a function of geography. Even the most basic utilities such as water works and electric companies are either absent or rudimentary in many nations today. Transnational firms would incur abnormally high costs if these support systems have to be developed and installed in underdeveloped countries. This factor deserves careful attention, where both costs and benefits of the planned expansion are carefully weighed.

Economic Considerations

Much of the foregoing analysis can easily be interpreted primarily in technological terms, that is in the context of technological efficiency. In other words, management's international integration problem may be interpreted as essentially one of minimizing the physical inputs used to achieve any given physical output within and among internationally separated producing units. This represents technical, not economic, efficiency. The point to bear in mind is that while there are usually several technologically efficient ways of producing a specified output, at any particular time there is only a single economically efficient method—the one which achieves a given output at minimum cost. This condition may be called "ideal integration" and a transnational firm may be said to be ideally integrated when all of its scattered international output is produced at minimum cost. If the firm operates in an internationally competitive market, its ultimate survival and success will be dependent upon its ability to achieve economic efficiency by effectively integrating its international operations.[14]

The equimarginal principle of international economics states that capital and other resources should be so allocated between and within national sectors of the world economy that the returns from, or the net productivity of, the last or marginal unit of resources employed in each of the different activities shall be as nearly equal as possible.[15] This is the ideal or most efficient situation for international integration.

Application of this principle would militate that the economic decision process of the transnational firm, considering its far-flung operations, vary from nation to nation (market to market). The decisions will differ in terms of such considerations as degree of investment, ownership control, accommodation to host governments, attitudes and considerations of minority owners, relative efficiency of constituent plants and servicing units, trade barriers, and time horizons.

Technology has a major impact on world trade and the balance of payments problems of individual countries. Therefore, it is important to examine these relationships in detail. Edward David, Jr. notes that since World War II, technology has been a major positive factor in the United States' world position in trade. Technological products such as aircraft, computers, chemicals, pharmaceuticals, and agricultural products have been the backbone of American exports.[16] Edwin Mansfield indicates that American exports tend to be research-intensive goods. He notes, for example, that there is a high correlation, industry by industry, between the ratio of R&D expenditures to sales and the U.S. share of exports by all OCED countries. Based on Mansfield's research it would appear that in the United States export performance is closely related to R&D performance.[17] Industries where R&D investment is low and where technological development is relatively static are susceptible to economic stagnation and foreign competition.

There is some evidence that the U.S. position in many technological products is slipping. Michael Boretsky, a Commerce Department economist, analyzed the growing U.S. trade deficits in terms of four categories of imports and exports: technology-intensive products; nontechnology-intensive products; minerals, raw materials, and unprocessed fuels; and agricultural products. He found that the technology-intensive trade surplus was shrinking. He identified the lag in high-technology products, including electronics, chemicals, automobiles, and the like, by comparison with West Germany, Japan and other industrialized nations as a principal factor in the U.S. deteriorating balance of trade.[18]

Chemical & Engineering News reported on a related aspect of the growing problems of exploiting international markets for high-technology products. The report stated that many foreign companies are operating in economic and political climates that favor their success, whereas almost the reverse is true in the United States. Also, there seems to be a lack on the part of the U.S. government of any long-term trade policy for high-technology products.[19]

In a similar vein, Guyford Stever, a former Director of the National Science Foundation, was quoted as saying, "When you look abroad at some industries competing for world markets, they work hand-in-hand with governments. Very often we do nothing to help our own companies. We are not well equipped to carry on this battle." Stever further stated that, "There is a wide conclusion in Washington and the country at large that if the U.S. is to maintain the ability to grow, more and more intervention will be necessary in the private sector."[20]

In discussing possible reasons for the indicated U.S. slippage, David notes the declining proportion of GNP devoted to R&D (from over 3% in the mid-1960s to 2.2% in late 1970s). However, he believes that the real reason for the change is that the nation seems to be losing its interest in excellence and dedication. He believes that we are now satisfied with bland, stodgy, marginal competence. Technological innovation is probably the first to suffer under this deterioration.[21]

One important aspect of technology transfer is the rate of economic growth of the country receiving the technology. Mansfield reports on several studies that have attempted to identify the relationship between technological change arising from all sources and economic growth. One study by Robert Solow indicates that for the period 1909 to 1949, 90% of the U.S. increase in output per capita was attributable to technological change. Edward Denison's study in the 1960s indicated that "advance of knowledge" was responsible for about 40% of the increase in national income per person during 1929 through 1957. Studies have also been made of the contributions of technological change to economic growth in Europe. These studies indicated that approximately 35% of the increase in national income in Northwest Europe was attributable to new technology and transfer of technology from abroad.[22]

The increased impetus for R&D described earlier has forced the world's industrial nations to give much closer attention to their scientific and technological capabilities. The result in many countries has been a number of actions designed to improve both the training of scientists and engineers and the organization of science and technology, and to increase the efficient allocation of resources for R&D.[23]

The importance of R&D to the maintenance of a nation's economic position in the world requires that research approaches be very carefully considered. First of all, considerable funds are required to develop even the most fundamental scientific capabilities and certain areas of technology require enormous investments. Second, there is a long lead time between the conception of a new technology and the production stage; therefore, good decisions are vital to prevent much wasted time. Third, there is a rapidly growing concern about the impact of technology on the physical environment and human welfare; therefore, it is important to carefully assess and control the consequences of technological advance.[24]

State of the Art and Competition

Advances in the state-of-the-art can have a strong impact on plans for developing a technological infrastructure. A failure to anticipate the rate and direction of technological change can place an entire program of expansion and its accompanying technological effort in jeopardy.

Unforeseen technological developments can make present programs, existing facilities, and personnel obsolete. The life cycle of new products from R&D may be shorter and the product changes more pronounced than is the case with upgrades to established consumer goods. This means that technology which is market-directed can be shifted more readily and easily into other markets. Projects on hardware undergoing development can be technically sound but technologically outdated. Capital expenditures are extremely risky when a probability of extended or full economical utilization of expensive equipment is slight. The development of new materials and processes can also have a significant influence on planning. Diversification to hedge against technological miscalculation is a distinct requirement. However, indiscriminate diversification can be equally destructive and disruptive.

Competition also affects planning. It is unusual for a new product, especially a consumer product, to be so drastically different that it promptly and completely outmodes current products. In the normal course of international business events there are usually some advance clues as to the general intentions of competitors but not necessarily the form or nature of the innovation or product. Where there is proprietary R&D it is usually not possible to immediately make a direct comparative analysis of the competitor's product, and thus a company may be caught off-guard.

International competition can also revolve around operational capability, based upon technological anticipation and planning. A major technological breakthrough often cannot be anticipated, and technological leadership can radically affect the competitive position of organizations or even nations. However, it is essential for survival that organizations try to anticipate and plan for future requirements. Frequently, the organization will find the best defense to be an active offense. It can, through innovation, keep the competition reacting to their moves. A passive, waiting game can be a questionable strategy, and may well compromise a firm's very existence. Technological initiative not only gives the organization a short-run advantage, it also establishes an image which can be exploited in the future.

It follows, then, that decision making in the transnational company is emphatically a multidimensional one. The possibilities or combinations where there is a dynamic technology are staggering. Too often managers seek only the most obvious variables and factor them into the decision formula and fail to achieve imaginative decisions. In addition to the various tangible and intangible points identified in this section, there are numerous others which could affect the process. Factors which could impact upon the infrastructure decision include family ties, class structure, living/working conditions, state welfare conditions, state ownership and planning, and the various military and national defense policies.

Endogenous Factors

Strategy Possibilities

The complexity of exogeneous factors sorely complicates the determination of technological infrastructure decision factors, the matter of determining the "inside" factors is also very complex. The strategy for operating in each of the overseas markets is different and so is the necessity for variation of corporate structure and approach also different for each of the countries. In this section a number of pertinent, endogeneous factors will be analyzed. For example, the conduct of R&D in the international sphere requires certain special considerations. There are constraints and problems as well as advantages and flexibilities which are not present in R&D confined to national boundaries.

Objectives delineate the organization's mission, and planning which is aimed at achieving objectives must therefore be compatible with that mission. A dilemma often encountered by subordinate entities involves the desirability of developing a plan for technological exploration which is not consistent with current operational objectives of the parent organization. The complexities and demands of the international marketplace add to this frustration. Local operations and direction can easily be subverted to indigenous pressures.

Facilities and Equipment

A manager assessing the possibility of marketing goods and services in a newly created market is naturally concerned with the "wherewithal" with which to produce the product and to interface with the consumer. The creation of production and sales facilities and equipment represent sizeable investments. Problems in servicing a local market are further multiplied by the factors of distance, construction costs and difficulties, and time when dealing with international markets.

The major industrialized nations of the world usually have the most sophisticated and advanced facilities and equipment for conducting R&D and for producing high-technology products. The cost of such facilities and equipment has come to represent major capital expenditures on both the part of industry and governments.

The United States leads the world in R&D equipment and production facilities in areas such as aircraft and computers. Other industrialized nations have led in certain areas, such as the U.S.S.R. in steel making. In 1969–1973 the Soviets lost their leading position temporarily to Japan, who had constructed larger blast furnaces. The U.S.S.R. with its 5000 c.u.m. furnace completed at the end of 1974, again has the largest output in the world.[25]

The Soviet Union also holds a strong world position in machine tools and electric power transmission. However, in the science-based industries, including chemicals, control instruments and computers, the Soviets lag considerably behind the Western world.[26]

In studying the scientific climate in China, it is interesting to note that the Chinese lack much of the sophisticated equipment and research facilities which would be required to put their theoretical knowledge to work. During the 1970s the Chinese reported an increasing number of scientific instruments developed entirely in China, including high-resolution electron microscopes, oscillographs, multichannel analyzers, and new vertical turbine molecular pumps intended for use in high-energy physics research. All of these are claimed to be "up to world standards."[27]

Technology transfer between nations can be effected by a number of means, including technical licensing arrangements, and through work with affiliated companies. Increasingly, there is a tendency to transfer technology by means of manufacturing equipment, processing technology, and even complete "turn-key" or plant sales. *Business Week* reported in 1976 that the Japanese, long the exporters of steel, autos, and consumer electronics, are now heavily involved in exporting industrial plants and machinery. Japanese forges, auto presses, and chemical plants are flowing into the Soviet bloc, China, the Mid-East, and the Third World at such a rate that capital goods will soon account for 20% of the island country's exports. Five years earlier the figure was only 5%. The Japanese are catching up with and in some instances have surpassed the United States, West Germany, and Britain in plant technology.[28]

Another phase of plant technology is also being extensively exported by the Japanese—that of chemical processing. There are several reasons why Japan has developed the ability to export chemical technologies. First, the Japanese chemical industry has developed several unique processes in the 30 years since World War II. Second, it has absorbed, digested, and improved the imported processes during the period of high growth of the 1950s and 1960s. Third, the chemical companies in Japan have obtained experience in the export of technologies and have surplus personnel available for this work.[29]

Plant technology is even being exported in increasing quantities to the Peoples Republic of China. As of the early 1980s Japan was the major exporter to China. During the few years preceding 1976, the Chinese had been embarked on a series of complete plant purchases totaling some 2.1 billion dollars. These contracts, primarily with German, French, and Japanese firms, have been mainly for the supply of chemical fertilizer plants, power stations, steel plants, and petrochemical plants. It was further expected that metalworking and finishing equipment would find a growing market in the Peoples Republic of China as that nation implements a policy of industrial expansion.[30]

It has been reported that Israel is a fertile market for some of the United States' most advanced equipment and instrumentation. The Israelis are seeking reliable, sophisticated equipment in areas such as chemical processing, electronics, process control instrumentation, power-generating equipment, and metalworking and metalfinishing equipment.[31]

Even the Soviet Union has managed to sell some high-technology equipment in the Western world; however, their successes appear to be due less to the equipment's technological advantage than to its low price. For example, in England, Soviet-made injection-molding machines could be purchased in 1976 at prices 40% lower than for roughly comparable British made machines.[32]

The transfer of technology by either sales of facilities, equipment, processing methods or by licensing product manufacturing to other countries often bogs down because of incompatibility of the market, facilities, and equipment. An example of this is when high-volume–low-unit-cost equipment is purchased which was designed for mass production and mass markets. This leads to capital-intensive manufacture and assumes the existence of a sophisticated marketing network. The compatibility of such processes, equipment, and facilities with one national environment may not be compatible with another. Often a successful transfer requires extensive modification for receptivity to local conditions. An important consideration besides the market is local labor factors such as the quality and quantity of the labor force. Local conditions might dictate a shift from a capital-intensive production to a labor-intensive approach. In some instances it might not be feasible to establish production capabilities. Therefore, the decisions to make versus buy will be based on quite different tradeoffs.[33]

Another example of incompatibility in technology transfer is cited by Abelson and Tinker. They raise the question as to what current U.S. technology would be useful to the Third World for the long-term. Much of the United States' industrial and distribution system was designed to use readily available low-cost energy such as oil and natural gas. Some of this technology is now obsolete and possibly within a decade facilities designed to use cheap fuels may be destroyed. Most of the world needs new technologies based on the indigenous energy and human resources of the respective countries.[34]

Also, there are environmental factors to be considered. Some of the present equipment and facilities for production may not meet the more stringent pollution control requirements that are envisioned by some countries. Modifications and even complete replacements may be necessary to meet the new needs.[35]

Care is necessary to identify the problems of transferring plant technology to such remote parts of the world as tropical Africa. For example, cement plants, recently introduced there, have run into serious problems. These are generally plants with continuous rotary kilns built mainly by European contractors using imported equipment. There are many difficulties in operating and maintaining such machinery and instruments far from the source of supply. Experienced instrument and electrical maintenance engineers are often not available. Refractory linings for the rotary kilns and high chrome alloy castings for preheater grate plates are examples of essential spares which must be imported.[36]

The African countries have foundries, both ferrous and nonferrous, which make a wide range of castings. However, there is an acute shortage of trained African metallurgists, foundry and laboratory technicians, inspectors and test staff, as well as electrical and mechanical engineers to repair and maintain foundry equipment, motors, heating furnaces, and cupolas. In short, the plants are severely handicapped in their operation because of labor problems and as a result of their remote location.[37]

In general, it can be said that all plant technologies transferred to underdeveloped countries must consider the differences in design and operational criteria. The technologies needed in these developing countries do not put emphasis on automation, high performance, quiet operation, or sophisticated design. Instead, the following criteria should be stressed: low initial cost of machinery or equipment; simple operation or control; minimum maintenance and simple repair; use of available low-cost, low-skill labor; manufacture independent from local utilities; and the ability to use local raw materials and resources in the equipment.[38]

Linguistic and Cultural Considerations

Although previously mentioned within a much broader context, it is appropriate that these factors be reexamined as endogeneous factors. They have a direct effect upon managers and the process of management. They create certain special problems that impact on international technological development.

An example of these types of problems was identified by *Industrial Management* magazine in discussing Britain's potential language problems upon entering the Common Market. It was noted that the days were gone when the Englishman abroad could expect to be spoken to in English. It is at best a disadvantage and at worst a businessman could lose an order, depending on the sensitivity of his potential customer, if he is not able to converse in the particular country's language. It is possible to bridge the language barrier by the use of interpreters, but this is not the ideal solution. The interpreter only goes through the mechanics of changing one language into another. He or she is not an expert in the particular technical field involved and cannot convey all of the subtleties that can be so significant in a business or technical discussion. Furthermore, the use of interpreters is an expensive and cumbersome mechanism.[39]

Recognizing the potential for lost sales and adverse customer reaction, British firms have established programs to provide foreign language training for their executives. It is recognized that there is less incentive for English executives to learn a second language than it is for their European counterparts. This is because English is the key language to the world's expanding markets, with the possible exception of South America. Nevertheless, there are certain situations where it is essential that the executive be bilingual. The speaking of another person's native language is a nice courtesy which often opens up a conducive atmosphere for successful business and technical discussions.[40]

The major language schools in London, Berlitz and Inluinga, have worked extensively with some of the major British firms, such as IPC, Shell, Esso, ICI and Unilever to establish in-company language training programs for the employees. Some companies, such as Cable and Wireless, the telecommunications company, have taken the business of learning languages very seriously and offers courses at all levels from technicians up to top management.[41]

But simply learning foreign languages is not the total answer to successful dealings with foreign technical people. There are great differences in culture which must be understood. In dealing with the Japanese, for example, it is essential to get to know them socially before any business can be transacted. They are very sensitive to the observance of certain courtesies and formalities.

Over the past few years West Germany has become the Soviet Union's largest capitalist trading partner while Soviet trade with the United States has declined. The reasons apparently involve technical, economic, geographic, and historical factors. However, one of the significant factors appears to be the way of doing business. The German formality, their tendency toward long, ceremonial toasts before business lunches, and their deliberate approach to business appear to be more consistent with the Russian mentality than is the American approach.[42]

Differences in cultures have been cited as being major factors in America's superiority in technical innovations over foreign countries. The key people in an American firm, i.e., engineering, marketing, production, etc., work closely together to ensure that a proposed new product properly meets a specific need. In other countries this is not always the case. It is noted that, "the British engineer generally won't talk to a marketing executive in his own company because engineering has a much higher status in the United Kingdom than does marketing." The preoccupation with status, which affects German and Japanese as well as British managers, is cited as a chief reason why Rolls-Royce had such difficulty making a success of some of their most advanced airplane engines. Rolls-Royce was always ahead of or behind the market. This was because the company has been traditionally run by engineers who consider it beneath their dignity to consult with marketing personnel. They put a great deal of research and investment into advanced engines such as the RB211 without determining whether a sufficient market existed. Such a problem is less likely to occur in the United States where particular professional specialities do not automatically confer status which comes only from success. The American manager has a propensity to talk to anyone in the company who can help him or her do the job.[43]

It appears that communications may be a consideration at three levels within the transnational:

Between organization headquarters and a national office.

Within the national organization's management.

Between management of the national organization and the workforce.

The multiplicity of languages and the parallel diversity of cultures in the world economy have a constraining influence on the operation of an international business.

Production workers in a firm generally have the least education and smallest language diversity. It is usually impossible to require these workers to learn the language of the foreign owners and managers. This then dictates that all communication between management and the workers must be in the worker's "tongue." Often it is accomplished by hiring national intermediaries who speak both the national language and the language of the foreign owners.

The situation may become even more complicated when the workers speak more than one language. In an African nation where workers from several tribes may be employed in the same factory, the problem can be acute. It may be necessary to use a "lingua franca" to ease the problem. The lingua franca is a literal language bridge—a vehicle language. The workers will not understand as well in the lingua franca as in their mother tongue. In some instances, it is necessary to use all applicable languages, such as in Belgium where there is great hostility between the French- and Flemish-speaking segments of the population.

In West Germany, sometimes there are workers in a single plant from four different nations. This often necessitates separation of the workforce along linguistic lines. Some bilingual production workers are paid extra to be the interpreter between the German foreman and their national colleagues, e.g., a German-speaking Turk. Even then, many signs in a plant are in several languages. At the Ford Motor Company plant in Cologne, almost half of the work force is non-German. The codetermination meetings with workers required by German law are held in three languages—German, Turkish, and Spanish. At the same plant, meetings with top management are held in English, especially if an American vice-president is present.[44]

Today's technology allows corporate headquarters to keep in constant touch with all world markets. The headquarters' control process involves continuing communication, both oral and written, with all of its foreign operations. Most of these will be in countries with languages different from that of the headquarters' country, but all communications with headquarters will be in the "company language"—usually the language of the home country.

A unique approach to communications problems was taken by Caterpiller Tractor Company. They had to come to grips with the worldwide reality of numerous salesmen, technicians, and repair personnel handling their products. They were instrumental in the development of a unique system of printed communication called Caterpiller Fundamental English (CFE).

CFE is a printed one-way communication which does not require pronunciation or writing of any of the words. It is a condensed, simplified, and specialized form of English designed to speed instruction. Without CFE, service manuals would require translation into numerous languages. Through a 30-lesson course, students acquire a visual understanding of the 800-word vocabulary, although they may not be able to say the words. In this stripped-down, single-purpose language, there are 70 verbs, 450 nouns, 100 prepositions, and 180 adjectives, adverbs, and pronouns. The student's instructional manual includes photographs and drawings of Caterpiller parts and techniques. Also included in the kit is a Pocket Reference in which the student writes a native-language translation of CFE words. Instructors must know English and the student's language.[45]

Values and Attitudes

In evaluating the potential of a piece of machinery or equipment, it is usually sufficient to refer to objective and measurable specifications. Thus, an engineer who knows the horsepower, revolutions per minute, capacity, tolerances, and similar specifications can generally be quite certain of an evaluation. This may not be the case when an analyst attempts to forecast the market potential or economic output of a nation. Evidence points to a nation's inner motivations and values as being the determinants of economic performance and level of development. "A community's attitude toward work can be a more decisive determinant for raising productivity...than material resources, or for that matter even technology."[46]

While there are numerous attitudes and values that can enter into the work environment, only a few deserve attention: attitudes toward time, achievement and quality of work, wealth and material gain, and change.

Modern attitudes toward time are a relatively recent historical development. They are found in industrialized societies and are generally the converse of traditional attitudes toward time. In the modern view, time is perceived as a straight line rather than as a circle. Yesterday is gone forever, today is here only briefly, and tomorrow is almost upon us. Time is measured less by recurring natural events than by the artificial but precise movements of the clock. The hours, minutes, and seconds themselves become important measures of human activities.[47]

Ben Franklin said "Time is money"; therefore, it must be handled with some kind of stewardship. The Russians shared this attitude when in 1923 they distributed leaflets saying:

> Measure your time, control it! Do everything on time! Exactly on the minute! Save time, make time count, work fast! Divide your time correctly, for work and for leisure![48]

Time itself is neutral, and the same time is available to all nations. However, each society or culture has somewhat differing attitudes toward time, and these differences have important economic consequences. In general, the traditional attitudes toward time are found in the less-developed countries, while the modern attitudes are prevalent in industrialized nations. Significantly, Japan alone among the Asian countries has a linear (modern) rather than a cyclical view of time. There is an implied relationship between the attitudes and the economy.

International variations in attitudes toward achievement and work do not fall into a dichotomy as do attitudes toward time. Instead they range along a spectrum according to the degree to which achievement and work are considered necessary, important, and desirable. Of course, in essentially all societies people believe it is necessary to work in order to eat. However, beyond that basic view of work as necessary to survival, attitudes may range toward a much stronger achievement orientation where work is considered desirable—and even a religious or patriotic virtue. Generally, the more positive the attitudes to work, the more productive the society.[49]

To a large degree, international differences in attitudes toward achievement are religiously based. The Protestants—especially the Calvinists—developed the work ethic to a high degree of achievement orientation. McClelland cites a number of studies showing that the need for achievement is still higher among Protestants generally than among traditional Catholics. The most striking example was that of a Mexican village which converted to Protestantism. After ten years, tests were given that showed the Protestant children of the village had a distinctly higher need for achievement than the children in a neighboring Catholic village.[50]

If one accepts the importance of the achievement drive in the economy, there remain very practical and difficult problems. A society that is short on financial capital or the necessities for industrialization can borrow or import them. Even managerial skills can be imported. If, however, the society has a low achievement drive, the remedy is much more complex and long range.[51] The quality, as distinct from the quantity, of a population is critical in leading to a high national standard of living.

Attitudes toward wealth and material gain are obviously crucial in an analysis of a nation's potential as a marketplace or producer of goods. There are several ways to view this consideration. One aspect is simply the degree to which money and material possessions are considered in a favorable light. Another aspect relates to the nature and source of income and wealth.

There are societies that have a less affirmative attitude toward wealth and material gain than we do in the West. For example, to the extent that the Hindu or Buddhist is seeking nirvana the entanglements and preoccupations of material things are avoided. The greater good is in the opposite direction—the absence of desire.

Another basis for limited material aspirations may be the widespread experience of poverty- and subsistence-level living. Long experience of poverty and the improbability of transcending economic and social strategy may severely limit a person's expectations. Corporate planners in the developing countries invariably assume strong desire for high levels of living among the populus—this is not usually the case.[52]

There are differing attitudes toward the appropriate form of wealth among the nations. These have significant impact on how people direct their economic activities. They also affect the supply of funds for savings and investment. Raising capital for industrial expansion is difficult in those areas where cattle, gold, land, or other tangible property is the accepted form of wealth.[53]

Societies also differ in their attitudes toward the appropriate sources of income. Frequently, business and commercial activities rate rather low as a way of earning a living. This affects the caliber of people entering business and the kind of necessary reward system.[54]

For the transnational firm, attitudes toward wealth and material gain have various repercussions. Most directly they affect the recruitment, compensation, and motivation of employees. Employee motivation will vary from country to country, as will the kinds of incentives required. The organization's philosophy, products, machinery, and marketing program must be tailored to suit local attitudes and aspiration levels. For both the firm and the economy, the capability to raise capital for investment and expansion will largely depend on local attitudes, on appropriate sources, and uses of capital.[55]

Attitudes towards change are another basic variable in the formation of an infrastructure. Change may refer to both goods and processes. Change may mean the adoption of new or different goods. It may also mean adoption of a new method of doing things, with or without attendant tools or implements. Societies differ widely in the degree to which change is perceived in a favorable light. At one extreme, in traditional societies, new products or processes may be considered as an undesirable disruption or perhaps as being evil. Attitudes range from a reluctance or resistance to change to a positive welcoming of change, and a feeling that new is better and old is outdated.

Religion helps to explain differences in attitudes toward change. Among those with negative attitudes toward change are the Moslem nations. Islam is not only a faith, it is also a religion organized as a political unity, with integration, rather than separation of church and religion.[56]

Willingness to accept change depends further on the amount of risk the potential adopter perceives in the change. This is an assessment of both personal and social risk and is in addition to the normal risk of innovation, i.e., that the innovation might be unsuccessful. Conservation is often justified. Too often innovations developed elsewhere, however well-intended, have not succeeded in the local context because the laboratory development and testing did not properly consider local environment and cultural peculiarities.

For those agents of change wishing to innovate on an evolutionary basis, several guidelines are appropriate. First, one should determine the deterrents to the change. Second, cultural obstacles that can be modified or adapted should be identified. Third, the innovation must be tested and evaluated in terms of the host culture. Fourth, attempt to demonstrate the innovation locally to hasten its acceptance. Fifth, technical change will be accepted quicker and easier than social or political change. And, sixth, seek within the existing culture those attitudes and values that might be used to support the proposed innovation.[57]

Labor Unions

Labor unions have historically played a crucial role in many nation's politics and industrialization and in the development of the overall economy. It is absolutely necessary that a firm wishing to establish a foreign subsidiary consider the framework of labor unionism within the area of intended operations. While there is often little direct unionism within the laboratory or among engineers and technologists, it is obvious that unionism is a factor once the innovation is moved into the production phase.

Modern European labor unions were formed with the aim of a total social transformation. They still function, in fact, in a much broader sphere than is suggested by the term "interest group." In Europe, their functions embrace many aspects of the life of the working person, to include education and recreation, and they historically have sought (and achieved) major political goals such as rejection of feudalism and the right to vote. European unions are frequently closely identified with political parties and ideologies, particularly socialist ones. Seemingly, the European union members tend to have a much greater sense of worker solidarity than do those of the United States, perhaps because suffrage and other rights were not won by European workers until they took collective action to gain them.[58] Also, European workers are probably stratified in their work environment whereas many American workers are intrinsic about moving into higher economic levels as entrepreneurship or management.

Compared with the labor organizations of the developed nations, the unions of the developing countries represent an economically weaker but politically more explosive force. In general, unionism in developing countries is a house divided against itself. Rudimentary education and lack of experience in industrial labor–management problems diffuse the efforts of the workers to express their protests and to realize hopes. In spite of the rapid growth of unions, effective unionism is rare. The greatest obstacle is the apathy of workers. Unemployment, underemployment, and an irregular labor supply often make the collection of union dues impossible and seriously undermine the union's economic position.

A multitude of small, independent unions usually view the business world from a feudalistic perspective. They form many rival federations, based upon political affiliation, social ideology, or religious beliefs, which resist amalgamation into strong integrated labor movements. Union leaders are usually outsiders—middle-class intellectuals with doctrinaire philosophies, usually nationalist or communistic—who lay greater stress on political issues than on the practical problems of wages, working conditions, and productivity. As a result, most of the remains are tied to some political party and its interests put first. Another form of union leadership comes from the opportunist who capitalizes on the workers' predicament and discontent by extorting employers and seeking political office for personal gain.

Collective bargaining is in its earliest stages in most developing countries. Workers do not understand it, and union leaders tend to prefer to practice politics. Although most developing nations encourage union growth, nearly all restrict collective bargaining by limiting the right to strike, enacting comprehensive labor codes, and providing for compulsory arbitration or labor courts.[59]

Development of Human Resources

Harbison and Myers, in a review of international manpower, reveal that although important progress is being made in the organized, purposeful development of industrial manpower in a number of developing countries, it is often too restricted both in coverage and quality. Training in high-level industrial skills is still a rarity.[60]

For the most part, formal in-service training programs are rare. All too often the supervisors who are to do the training are so busy with their own tasks that they do not have the time for it. The Asians in East Africa and the Syrians and Lebanese in West Africa have effective on-the-job training for their own people both in the wholesale and in the retail trades, but they avoid training any of the African natives.

The study by Harbison and Myers indicates that some Latin American countries are stressing employer-financed programs for vocational training in industrial plants. In Columbia, for example, international firms have sponsored a program of apprenticeship training, night courses for adult workers already employed, and training of plant personnel to organize and operate their own skill-development programs within factories. In some of the more advanced nations more attention is being paid to upgrading the qualifications and improving the performance of people already employed in strategic occupations. On-the-job training has, in general, spread more widely among institutions in the more advanced nations, and often the armed forces are used as a training ground.[61]

The technical and vocational school is seen as a viable alternative for worker training in some nations. In Argentina, Brazil, and Chile the governments have taken steps to establish schools to train people for jobs in industry. Most of the developing nations, however, still rely upon the transnational firm that employs the people to give them training, and that training is seldom done in a formal manner.

Clearly, the quality and efficiency of virtually any organization depends largely upon the overall quality of the persons in the organization. Hence, the nature and quality of the educational process within a country are critical factors in determining the level of ability and expertise of the work force. The most direct connection between education and the transnational firm would be in the training of workers worldwide. Less obvious is the connection between education and the goals and motivations that individual managers bring to their tasks, and the need to develop managerial control systems that have the best chance of yielding goal congruence.

International Science and Technology

Communications

> Anyone who has ever tried to work through an interpreter doesn't have to be told about cultural and language obstacles to an effective transfer of information and thought. It's hard enough to gain real communications within the homogeneous background of one's own family. As backgrounds become more divergent, the difficulties in communication increase in a corresponding manner.[62]

As Peters has noted above, communications is a definite problem in international operations. On the surface one would presume that scientists speak but a single language. While this may be partially true, there are the subsurface realities of aspirations, motives, cultural differences, religion, and hundreds of other "noises" which interfere with the communication linkage between scientists and thus frustrate management of their activities on a global basis. In this section, a number of aspects of personnel-related issues will be highlighted in an attempt to alert the student as well as the practionaire to the scope of the problem and its insidious nature.

Overseas Operations

A variety of reasons may be advanced to explain the existence of separate overseas R&D facilities. According to a National Science Foundation study, the most prevalent reason for maintaining an R&D facility in another country was to adopt products to local market conditions.[63] There are, as has been discussed, obvious differences in markets served by the transnational firm. These differences exist from place to place within a given domestic market and often are even greater among countries. For example, chemical companies develop different mixtures of fertilizers to serve various geographic areas within the United States. Sharper climates, soils and related differences in markets served in other countries require additional modification.

In the NSF study representatives from the 18 companies interviewed stated that Western Europe, Canada, and Japan were the principal locations of their overseas R&D efforts.[64] High-technology industries, such as electronics and electrical equipment, tend to concentrate their R&D efforts in Europe and Japan where there is an ample supply of qualified scientific and technical personnel available. Other factors which affect the placement of foreign R&D laboratories are availability of personnel speaking the "company language," proximity to manufacturing plants, and promotion of goodwill between the company and a particular government. In the NSF study, company officials were noted as favoring, whenever possible, all staffing to come from local foreign nationals.

Availability of Foreign R&D Personnel

According to the National Science Board, a comparative measure of a country's R&D effort, along with its R&D/GNP ratio, is the relationship between the number of scientists and engineers and the size of the population.[65] Table 12-2

Table 12-2. Scientists and Engineers Engaged in R&D per 10,000 Population, by Country

	1965	1975	Change
United Kingdom	10.1	18.8 (1972)	137%
Canada	7.7	10.0 (est.)	130%
France	8.8	11.0 (est.)	125%
West Germany	9.7	16.7	172%
Japan	11.9	22.0 (est.)	185%
United States	25.4	24.8	98%
U.S.S.R.	21.6	43.8	203%

compares such relationships for several major industrialized countries for the years 1965 and 1975.[66] The most striking feature of these statistics is the proportional decline of R&D personnel in the United States when compared with the large increase registered by other countries. It should be pointed out that pure statistics can be misleading. Absolute numbers do not reflect productivity and quality of R&D effort. In some instances the increase in R&D personnel does reflect more aggressively the effort and accomplishment which has competitively compromised the impact of the U.S. technology in world markets. The international R&D manager would probably be concerned with the "absolute" availability of technical personnel from which he could readily staff an organization. These figures, also compared for 1965 and 1975, are depicted in Table 12-3.[67] Again, the United States makes a relatively poor showing when compared to other "R&D intensive" nations. These data might serve to encourage an organization to establish foreign R&D operations in some of these countries.

Factors Affecting the Availability of R&D Personnel

Just as technology is not a static phenomena, so too, the availability of R&D personnel changes with time. Therefore, the R&D manager should become acquainted with some of the factors which influence the number of personnel available to pursue R&D. One of those factors is the support for R&D that is

Table 12-3. Scientists and Engineers Engaged in R&D, by Country (in Thousands)

	1965	1975	Change
United Kingdom	54.6	77.1 (1972)	141%
Canada	15.1	25.0 (est.)	166%
France	42.8	60.0 (est.)	140%
West Germany	57.0	103.0	181%
Japan	118.0	250.0 (est.)	212%
United States	494.1	530.5	107%
U.S.S.R.	499.4	1115.0	223%

given by the government. As an example, let us study the effect that funding changes have had on research and development personnel in the United States. Figure 12-1 depicts the funding trends for R&D in the United States from 1953 to 1977 in constant 1972 dollars.[68] These data illustrate two important factors. First, federal funding for R&D has always constituted at least half of the available money. Secondly, the total R&D funding has suffered from a "rollercoaster" effect caused primarily because of yearly fluctuations in the federal funding. (The nonfederal funding, on the other hand, has shown steady growth since the early 1950s.) Note the rapid rise in federal funding from 1960 through about 1964–1965, followed by a leveling off and eventual decline in federally supplied R&D dollars. This funding curve was in direct response to America's $25 billion space race that started in the early 1960s. Now observe the effects this money availability had in the demand and supply for R&D manpower.

Figure 12-2 shows the demand and supply for new engineers in the United States from 1964 to 1976.[69] During the period that federal R&D money was increasing, there was a corresponding increase in the demand for new engineers, with a peak of over 80,000 new job openings in 1966. However, the subsequent decline in federal support was marked by a similar decline in demand for new engineers which reached its lowest point in 1971. When total R&D funding again increased in 1970, the result was increased demand for

Figure 12-1. R&D funding trends 1953–1977.

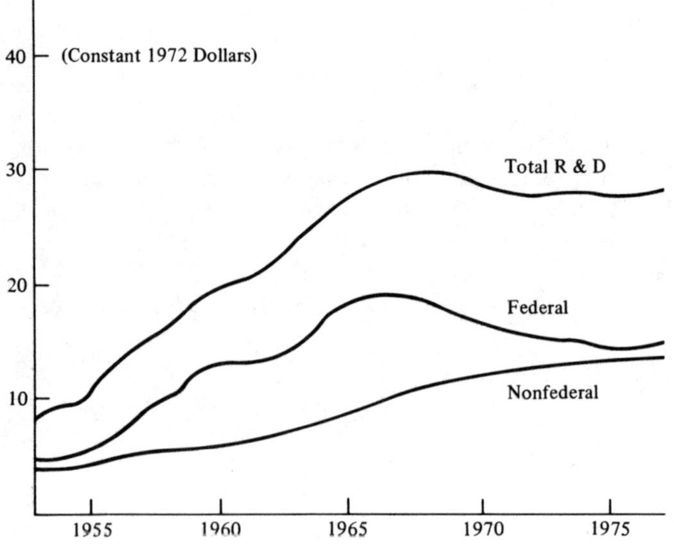

engineers starting about the same time period. The analysis highlights the apparently strong relationship between the government support for R&D (expressed quantitatively in terms of dollars or R&D/GNP) and the availability of trained personnel. Such situations may also exist in other countries, especially if they tend to follow a nonuniform policy concerning support for technology. This is certainly a factor that should be weighed by any organization contemplating an R&D effort overseas.

There is yet another factor illustrated by the supply curve for new engineers in Figure 12-2. The variation in the supply is obviously directly related to changes in demand, but the important point is that there is a long lag-time between increased demand and the corresponding increased supply.

In times of increased demand for a commodity, producers normally will temporarily increase output from existing facilities. However, this is not the case with the production of trained manpower simply because there is a four to six year time lag inherent in the system due to the time required for students to complete a technical degree program. Today's increased demand for technical talent will be satisfied a minimum of four years from now.

This, too, is an important consideration for an international R&D manager. Local technical educational facilities should be investigated for quality and applicability of education and reliability of supply. Regardless of the demand for technical talent, one must analyze the availability of R&D personnel and the accompanying factors that influence that availability since these may

Figure 12-2. Supply and demand for new engineers 1964–1976 (United States).

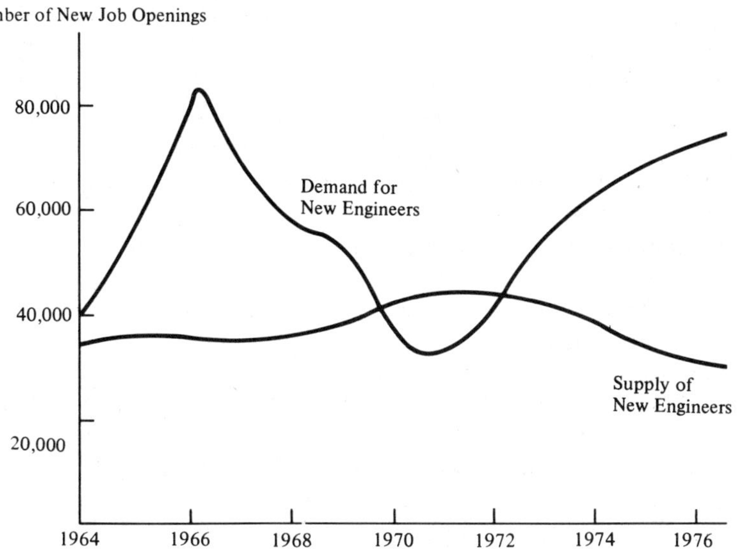

become some of the most important factors influencing the eventual selection and operation of an overseas facility.

Finding Local Talent

Assuming that an organization has considered the factors associated with the availability of technical personnel overseas, the next problem with which it must deal is finding and retaining local talent. If a company is not well-known in the host country, experience has shown that using a personal contact is by far the most productive method for locating personnel with specific training.[70] This local contact, who is essentially an agent of the transnational, can better establish rapport with prospective workers and show them the advantages of working for a transnational organization. Using an agent as an intermediary overcomes the initial language and cultural differences that may make a negative impression on workers.

Local colleges or universities in the host countries are another source of technical talent, both for new graduates or for experienced faculty members. However, the R&D manager should be aware that it may not be easy to entice a researcher away from the academic environment. In many foreign countries, scientists associated with colleges or universities are accorded an unusually high social position which would seriously be degraded by working for a foreign company.[71] Nevertheless, the academic community may be a valuable resource for providing information as to local talent or even as a part-time adjunct work force.

The transnational manager should also be aware that the college graduate, even from some highly rated foreign schools, may not have the same academic credentials or motivation that are characteristic of graduates of home country schools. As Roland Omnes, Professor of Physics at both the Faculty of Sciences at Orsay and the Elite Ecole Polytechnique stated, "A big difference between American and French society is that in the U.S. a man is appreciated for what he does, while in France he is appreciated before he does anything." This translates into saying that anyone who graduates from one of France's "grande ecoles" (highly specialized schools) is set for life no matter what the person subsequently accomplishes.[72]

National employment agencies may also provide services which can be used to locate local talent. However, the successful use of such agencies is highly dependent on the individual countries concerned, the characteristics of their labor markets, and the extent to which the government actively supports a labor/manpower policy. For further information in this area, the reader is referred to Chapter 1 of R.A. Jenness' work *Manpower and Employment: Problems and Prospects* published by OECD.[73]

A new overseas organization can also attempt to hire talent away from local firms or other foreign based industries. This approach is not always possible because of limited worker mobility in many areas of the world.

One final method which can be used to locate talent overseas is a technique called "citation analysis." Suppose a French company wishes to establish a foreign research center whose primary focus will be the development of new technology in abrasives. The French company can identify the major technical publications in the field of interest and subsequently determine those foreign authors (on a country-by-country basis, if desired) that have been referenced (cited) in these works.[74] The results will yield those foreign researchers and their organizations with similar interests and capabilities which could form the nucleus of a new overseas operation.

Some Potential Problems

The transnational firm may face several types of problems when attempting to recruit foreign talent and sustain their foreign operation. One of the most prevalent problems is that of perspective. All too often the transnational manager or scientist views himself as the expert and the indigenous scientist or engineer as a person of lesser talent, skill, and potential. Americans are often thought of as exploiting foreign resources (either material or human), a factor which can make workers reluctant to work for a U.S.-based firm. But, the best way to overcome this problem is to ensure that the U.S. organization will establish an indigenous R&D capability in the host country, not just a capability that will fold if and when American support is withdrawn.[75]

Another situation that the transnational manager may find overseas is, as mentioned, that the lack of worker mobility may prevent the hiring of the people necessary to staff the organization. This is especially troublesome for American managers. In the United States, technical personnel move about freely from job to job as their interests, motivations, and job availability change. This is not true in many foreign countries where history and culture dictate long, perhaps lifetime, employment patterns. Consider, for example, the situation of a young Japanese engineer upon graduation from college. He will most likely seek employment with a firm in or near his hometown. He will live in a company dormitory for an average of three to five years with other junior company employees. He will quite likely marry a woman employed by the company, and they will move to an apartment house provided or owned by the company. The engineer is assured of lifetime employment in trade for total loyalty to the company.[76]

Or consider the situation in Mexico and Central and South America. In these areas, work and employment center around the family. Businesses are passed from generation to generation, and the tradition of a family working for a certain firm is quite strong.[77] Obviously, it would be quite difficult for a U.S.-based firm to break into these types of manpower markets.

A final consideration for the R&D manager is what has come to be called the international nature of science. On the surface this would seem like an asset since "science knows no political or economic boundaries." However, there are increasing instances where national and international scientific organizations have taken political stands and used science as a bargaining tool.

Recently, the Federation of American Scientists has asked the U.S.S.R. to halt a planned sale of a 400 megawatt nuclear reactor to Libya because of the fear that Libya is trying to develop or acquire nuclear weapons technology.[78] In a similar instance, the American Mathematical Society has protested attacks on Jewish mathematicians by the Soviet Union. The protest has escalated to the point that more than 2,400 American scientists have signed personal pledges to end or restrict their cooperation with their Soviet counterparts until political dissidents are released from prison.[79] The use of science to further political or "human rights" issues may become more prevalent in the future and could have an impact on some U.S. operations overseas. Consider the impact on a U.S. company with a subsidiary in China should Chinese political activities become the target of some U.S. or international scientific organization. Although there is nothing that the R&D manager could do in such a situation, he or she should be aware that science is not totally apolitical, a fact that could have an impact on him or her directly at some future time.

The problems associated with assessing the availability of foreign R&D personnel and of R&D personnel and of obtaining services are many and varied. Once these problems are overcome, the transnational manager may face the single biggest challenge: actually managing an overseas workforce.

Managing Foreign R&D Personnel

In a large-scale study of transnational management, Sirota and Greenwood surveyed workers employed in 25 countries by a large manufacturer of electrical equipment.[80] One aspect of the study concentrated on ascertaining the fourteen most important work goals of three different occupational sectors: sales, technical, and service. The nations involved are indicated at Table 12-4, and represent at least 40 employees in all three categories. United States nationals and indigenous workers were surveyed in each nation.

Table 12-4. Countries in the Sirota/Greenwood Study with at Least 40 Individuals in Sales, Technical, and Service Occupational Sectors

Argentina	Israel
Australia	Japan
Austria	Mexico
Belgium	New Zealand
Brazil	Norway
Canada	Peru
Chile	South Africa
Columbia	Sweden
Denmark	Switzerland
Finland	United Kingdom
Germany	United States
India	Venezuela

Results revealed that the top priority goal of technical personnel was training (to improve skills or learn new skills). This goal is not all that apparent to management, who very likely would assume that technicians would be seeking "challenge" or "autonomy" *vis à vis* additional training. Further, other results indicated that:

"Training" and "challenge" were the number one or two goals for all occupational sectors.

"Training" and "challenge" were the top goals for 92% of all countries surveyed.

"Successful company" and "physical conditions" were consistently listed as least important for all countries and occupational sectors.

Although Sirota and Greenwood found a great similarity between the individual and national goals of all respondents, they noted that there were several "country clusters" in which goals were almost identical. Table 12-5 depicts those country clusters and their distinguishing characteristics. A detailed knowledge of these characteristics would obviously aid the R&D manager in appealing to and satisfying these goals for their workers.

Sirota and Greenwood believe that the results of their study have two important applications. First, they can help to overcome our stereotyped view of foreign workers. The study shows that people from other countries tend to place emphasis on many of the same goals as do Americans, and our misconceptions about them may be due to a combination of prejudice and the self-fulfilling prophecy. For example, if employees from a certain country are

Table 12-5. Countries Whose Goals Are Almost Identical (Country Clusters)

Cluster	Characteristics
1. Anglo Australia, Austria, Canada, India, New Zealand, South Africa, Switzerland, United Kingdom, United States	High achievement; Low security.
2. French Belgium, France	Similar to Anglo but more emphasis on security and less on challenging work.
3. Northern Europe Denmark, Finland, Norway	High job accomplishment; Low advancement and recognition.
4. Latin America Argentina, Chile, Columbia, Mexico, Peru	High security and fringe benefits.
5. Independents Brazil, Germany, Israel, Japan, Sweden, Venezuela	Country-dependent. Example Japan: High earnings and challenge; low advancement, autonomy. Example Germany: High security and fringe benefits; high advancement, earnings.

believed to lack management potential, they will be denied management training. If their training and challenge goals are not met, they won't advance in the company, and their performance will suffer. This only serves to substantiate the initial feeling about their limited abilities and makes the prophecy completely self-fulfilling. But if we understand the personal and national goals of other peoples, then we can adapt our behavior accordingly, resulting in increased productivity from all concerned.

Secondly, the results of the study tend to support current models of human motivation developed by American researchers. This is extremely important, because it suggests that Americans can successfully apply the same management techniques in foreign situations that they would use in a domestic company. Some findings, however, indicate that modifications to management theory should be made in selected areas. Most notably, certain goals, such as job security and job autonomy, vary widely with what Sirota and Greenwood interpret as environmental factors.

Foy and Gadon have made a detailed study of worker participation in Sweden, Great Britain, and the United States.[81] In Sweden, the level of worker participation is very high, due primarily to a very low unemployment level (a seller's labor market) and a long history of cooperation deeply rooted in a country's history and culture. But in England emphasis is placed on individual freedom and independence. Adversary relationships between workers, unions, management and government are expected. The result is few incidences of participatory management. In the United States managers have been free to experiment with many forms of participatory management. In short, levels of worker participation or "self-management" is very country dependent. The data collected by Sirota and Greenwood along with those collected by Foy and Gadon indicated that foreign workers tend to have the same goals and, therefore, tend to be motivated by the same things that American workers are motivated by. However, there are major differences (e.g., degree of worker participation) that must be considered on a country-by-country basis.

The Japanese have realized that a complete understanding of the wants of a foreign people is important to the success of a product line. Prior to introducing a new product, they immerse marketing, sales, and advertising personnel in the foreign culture so that the product can be tailored to the idiosyncrasies of buyers.[82] The dramatic success of Japanese products in world markets speaks well of this technique. The American R&D manager should obviously take similar actions to become totally familiar with the people whom he or she will be managing.[83]

Loyalty and Creativity

An understanding of the people involved in R&D in high-technology activities is fundamental to the success of any manager, especially so for managers of international R&D operations. The manager must rely on the loyalty, devotion, knowledge, and most importantly the creativity of his or her workers. The manager can develop an environment where innovation is nurtured, encouraged, and rewarded. Consider, for example, what the American manager has in common with American workers: They are loyal to the same country and, quite likely, to the project on which they are working; they share a common system of values in which success, for the vast majority of workers, is measured by status, monetary rewards, and the acquisition of goods; they tend to be motivated by the work itself and the opinions of their peers. Finally, they share a common language which allows them to communicate with some degree of efficiency.

But these common bonds are often lacking in international organizations. The manager and the workers are loyal to their respective native countries. The workers may tend to feel exploited by the American manager, whom they regard as a businessman rather than as a fellow scientist or engineer. The American manager may question whether his or her management technique, so firmly entrenched in American management theory, is culturally biased and inappropriate in a foreign environment. Effective communication may be blocked because of the lack of a common language. Yet, in spite of all these problems, the manager in an international R&D organization MUST produce—the company's existence depends on it. A very possible solution to the problem lies in the better education of the transnational manager. Just as they learn that technical competence alone is not sufficient to assure success as a manager in a domestic organization, managers also must learn that foreign workers have special wants and needs that must be understood if the human assets are to be utilized effectively.

Summary

As indicated in this chapter, the R&D manager of transnational firms has many subjects to consider when doing business abroad. One of the most important considerations is the people with whom he or she will be doing business. Supervising people and interpersonal relations coupled with understanding of their specific wants and needs may constitute the major element in the success or failure of the international venture. The manager must also be cognizant of the availability of appropriate personnel and understand this factor to intelligently decide on the location, type, and level of effort accorded a project. A knowledge of management and country unique characteristics which require the modification of domestic management techniques is also fundamental to a successful working relationship with the foreign workers.

As change agents, transnational enterprises should recognize their responsibility for the consequences of innovations introduced. Further, they must also recognize the ethical questions of planned change and the desire for participation in the planning process. Projects and programs should be planned and executed in a manner that ensures the cultural stability and possible economic consequences of the recipients being affected by the technological innovation.

This will require that the transnational organization develop an empathetic understanding of the conditions and characteristics of the receiving society. These guidelines call for an increase in the level of sophistication of transnational corporate environmental evaluation. In the final analysis, the future of the transnational corporation in the role of a cross-cultural technological change agent may well hinge on its ability to match transfer and innovation strategy with the goals, interests, and cultural needs of host nations.

Endnotes Chapter Twelve

1. E.J. Kolde, *International Business Enterprise*, Englewood Cliffs, NJ: Prentice-Hall, Inc., 1968, p. 291.
2. "Foreign Ventures—More Firms are Hiring Own Political Analysts to Limit Risks Abroad," *The Wall Street Journal*, March 30, 1981, p. 1.
3. R.D. Hayes, C.M. Korth, and M. Roudiani, *International Business: An Introduction to the World of the Multinational Firm*, Englewood Cliffs, NJ: Prentice-Hall, Inc., 1972, pp. 103–104.
4. C.J. Hayes in *The Dynamics of Nationalism*, ed. Louis L. Snyder, Princeton, NJ: D. Van Nostrand Co., Inc., 1964, p. 2.
5. V. Terpstra, *The Cultural Environment of International Business*, Dallas, TX: South-Western Publishing Co., 1978, pp. 236–239.
6. *Ibid.*, pp. 178–181.
7. D.P. Mukerji, "Mahatma Gandhi's Views on Machines and Technology," *International Social Science Bulletin*, Vol. 6, No. 3, 1954, pp. 441–442.
8. J.J. Servan-Schreiber, *The American Challenge*, New York: Atheneum Publishers, 1968, an English translation.
9. Sanford Rose, "The Secret of Japan's Export Prowess," *Fortune*, January 30, 1978, p. 56.
10. Herbert E. Meyer, "This Communist International Has a Capitalist Accent," *Fortune*, February 1977, p. 137.
11. Kevin Klose, "Science Township in Siberia Spurs Soviet Industrial Drive," *The Washington Post*, February 19, 1978, p. A25.
12. Kevin Klose, "Taming Siberia with Metal Tracks," *The Washington Post*, March 2, 1978, p. A1.
13. Ralph King, "Transplanting Technology to Transform Tropical Africa," *Process Engineering*, December 1976, p. 74.
14. V. Salera, *Multinational Business*, New York: Houghton Mifflin Co., 1969, pp. 394–395.
15. *Ibid.*, p. 395.
16. Edward E. David, Jr., "U.S. Innovation and World Leadership-Facts and Fallacies," *Research Management*, November 1977, p. 7.
17. Edwin Mansfield, "Economic Impact of International Technology Transfer," *Research Management*, January 1974, p. 10.
18. Deborah Shapley, "Technology and the Trade Crisis: Salvation Through a New Policy," *Science*, March 2, 1973, p. 881.
19. Janice R. Long, "Seminar Airs Technology Trade Problems," *Chemical and Engineering News*, May 12, 1975.
20. "Barriers to Technology Transfer Studied," *Aviation Week & Space Technology*, August 21, 1972, p. 13.

21. David, *op. cit.* p. 8.
22. Mansfield, *op. cit.* p. 8.
23. Robert Gilpin, "Technological Strategies and National Purpose," *Science*, July 21, 1970, p. 442.
24. *Ibid.*, p. 442.
25. Ron Amann, Julian Cooper, Bob Davies, "No Change on the Eastern Front," *New Scientist*, November 24, 1977, p. 477.
26. *Ibid.*, p. 478.
27. Christine King, "China—A New Role for Science," *New Scientist*, October 6, 1977, p. 33.
28. "Selling Auto Plants as Well as Autos," *Business Week*, April 5, 1976, p. 40.
29. Masaaki Aoki, "Why Japan Trades in Technology," *Hydrocarbon Processing*, March 1977, p. 90.
30. "Metalworking Will Share in Growing China Trade," *Iron Age*, June 7, 1976, p. 50.
31. "Israel, Seeking Advanced Equipment, Looks for Reliability, Sophistication," *Commerce Today*, March 3, 1975, p. 27.
32. Meyer, *op. cit.* p. 146.
33. Lowell W. Steele, "Barriers to International Technology Transfer," *Research Management*, January 1974, p. 19.
34. Philip H. Abelson and Irene Tinker, "Technology Transfer," *Science*, January 28, 1977, p. 869.
35. Richard N. Cooper, "The International Economic Situation," *Department of State Bulletin*, April 18, 1977, p. 379.
36. R. King, *op. cit.* p. 75.
37. R. King, "Processing Problems in Transplanting Technologies into Africa," *Process Engineering*, January 1977, p. 70.
38. George P. Sutton, "Technology for Underdeveloped Countries—The Problem," *Astronautics & Aeronautics*, December 1972, p. 14.
39. "Small Firms Stall at the Common Market Language Barrier," *Industrial Management*, October, 1972, p. 8.
40. "English Is Not Enough," *Industrial Management*, November 1973, p. 28.
41. *Ibid.*, p. 28.
42. Craig R. Whitney, "German–Russia Trade Holds, America's Slips," *The Washington Star*, February 25, 1978.
43. Sanford Rose, "Why the Multinational Tide Is Ebbing," *Fortune*, August 1977, p. 116.
44. Terpstra, *op. cit.* p. 15.
45. *Business International*, April 6, 1973, p. 107.
46. K. Nair, "Blossoms in the Dust," *The Human Factor in Indian Development*, New York: F.A. Praeger, 1962, p. 190.
47. L. Mumford, *Technics and Civilization*, New York: Harcourt, Brace & Co., 1934, pp. 12–18.
48. R.A. Webber, *Culture and Management: Text and Readings in Comparative Management*, Homewood IL: Richard D. Irwin, 1969, p. 14.
49. Adopted from Terpstra, *op. cit.*, pp. 74–75.
50. D. McClelland, *The Achieving Society*, New York: Irvington Publications, 1961, p. 411.
51. Adopted from Terpstra, *op. cit.*, pp. 79, 80.
52. Nair, *op. cit.*, pp. 192–193.
53. Webber, *op. cit.* p. 189.
54. Vance Packard, *The Status Seekers*, New York: Pocket Books, 1961, pp. 218–219.

55. Adopted from Terpstra, *op. cit.*, pp. 84–85.
56. V.M. Dean, *The Nature of the Non-Western World*, New York: Mentor Books, 1956, pp. 59–60.
57. Terpstra, *op. cit.*, pp. 90–91.
58. For a comprehensive analysis of international unionism see D.H. Blake, "Trade Unions and the Challenge of the Multinational Corporation," *The Annals*, Vol. 403, September, 1972, pp. 35–45.
59. Kolde, *op. cit.*, p. 577.
60. Frederick Harbison and Charles A. Myers, *Manpower and Education*, New York: McGraw-Hill Book Co., 1965.
61. Kolde, *op. cit.*, p. 582.
62. E. Bruce Peters, "Cultural and Language Obstacles to Information Transfer in the Scientific and Technical Field," *Management International Review*, Vol. 15, No. 1, 1975, 75–88.
63. "Reviews of Data on Science Resources," National Science Foundation, NSF 79-304, No. 33, April 1979, p. 1.
64. Western European nations favored were the United Kingdom and Switzerland, in large part because of the high degree of technical expertise available. Non-European locations cited were Brazil, Australia, the Philippines, and South Africa, for the same basic reasons.
65. *Science Indicators 1976*, National Science Board, NSB 77-1, Washington, DC: U.S. Government Printing Office, 1977, p. 2.
66. *Ibid.*, p. 186.
67. *Ibid.*
68. *National Patterns of R&D Resources: Funds and Manpower in the United States 1953–1977*, National Science Foundation NSF 77-310, Washington, DC: U.S. Government Printing Office, 1977, p. 1.
69. Howard E. Wakeland, "Engineering Guidance and Counseling," *Engineering Education*, April 1974, p. 480.
70. J.D. Peno, Jr., "Multinational Corporate Behavior in Host Country High Level Manpower Market: The Implications for Technology Transfer and Foreign Investment Control in the Less Developed Host Countries," *Transfer of Technology by Multinational Corporations*, Washington, DC: U.S. Department of Commerce, March 1972, pp. 45–62.
71. *Educational Review*, January–February 1973, p. 14.
72. Grace Marmor Spruch, "The Trouble with French Science is Frenchmen," *Technology Review*, October–November 1976, p. 13.
73. R.A. Jenness. *Manpower and Employment: Problems and Prospects*, Paris: OECD, 1978.
74. "Citation Analysis: A New Tool for Science Administrators," *Science* April 16, 1975, p. 430.
75. José Lopes, "Developing Countries and Dependent Science," *Impact of Science on Society*, July–September 1977, p. 262.
76. Donald Christiansen, "Japan Today: Assets, Liabilities, and the Future," *IEEE Spectrum*, September 1977, p. 33.
77. Stanley M. David, "U.S. Versus Latin America: Business and Culture," *Harvard Business Review*, November–December 1969, p. 90.
78. "Reactor Sale to Libya Challenged," *Science*, December 22, 1978, p. 1264.
79. Thomas O'Toole, "Jewish Mathematicians Mistreated by Soviets," *The Washington Post*, March 10, 1979, p. A11.
80. David Sirota and J. Michael Greenwood, "Understanding Your Overseas Work Force," *Harvard Business Review*, January–February 1971, pp. 53–60.

81. Nancy Foy and Herman Gadon, "Worker Participation: Contrasts in Three Countries," *Harvard Business Review*, May–June 1976, pp. 71–83.
82. Christiansen, *op. cit.*, p. 33.
83. This parallels the teachings of Professors Richard N. Farmer and Barry M. Richman. They have been at the forefront of a movement in comparative management which espouses the cognizance of native cultures, societies, legal systems, and economic systems prior to management transfers. For more details see, R.N. Farmer and B.M. Richman, *Comparative Management and Economic Progress*, Homewood, IL: Richard D. Irwin, 1965.

CHAPTER THIRTEEN

International Technological Proprietary Rights

Protection and Incentive for Technological Development

Protection for Incentive

The pioneer families on the western frontiers of yesterday ventured forth and conquered the wilderness. They cleared the land, made it produce, and created a homestead. As a reward for their labors, the government granted them title to the new land.

The modern pioneers on the frontiers of science and technology likewise venture into the unknown. They push forward man's knowledge of science and the useful arts, and turn the new knowledge to productive use. As a stimulus to this pioneer, the government grants title to the new idea created. This title is one of a group of industrial proprietary rights which evidence ownership. These rights enable the inventor or innovator to reap a reward and, in doing so, contribute to the overall wealth of the other citizens and the wealth of the particular nation.

In this chapter, we will examine the various technological proprietary rights—patents, copyrights, and trademarks; explaining their nature, legal status, monetary aspects, and international ramifications.

Proprietary Rights Protection — International

Exporters, investors, licensors and virtually anyone doing business abroad have a vital stake in protecting their technological proprietary rights. In most countries it is possible to protect these rights, but it is necessary to acquire protection for each country individually throughout most of the world. There is as yet no overall international patent and trademark "system." With relatively unimportant exceptions, no country recognizes internally the patents or trademarks issued by other nations. There is, however, general agreement among nations on basic rights of patent and trademark owners. These rights are embodied in the *International Convention for the Protection of Industrial Property*. It is commonly referred to as the "Paris Union." The Convention applies to industrial property in its widest sense and covers patents for inventions, utility models, industrial designs, trademarks, trade names, indications of origin, and the prevention of unfair competition. The provisions of the International Convention will be discussed in more detail later in the chapter.

The ultimate goal of the Paris Convention and that of other national and international industrial property right treaties, accords, and conventions is to stimulate innovation, international trade, and worldwide technology transfer by recognizing the inherient rights of the inventor and innovator. It is apparent that technology transfer is more likely to occur under conditions when proprietary rights are protected.

Problems in Protecting Proprietary Rights

There naturally are many difficulties associated with the protection of these rights. Many problems boil down to honest differences of opinion as to the terminology involved in describing the property right. Other difficulties encountered relate to the timing of the application for protection; the laws and degree of enforcement by the individual nations involved, and the relative degree of development of the nations involved in the specific dispute.

Companies spend thousands of dollars establishing brand names as trademarks for their products symbolizing quality and emphasizing certain features designed to entice customers to buy their brands. Much effort and money goes into research to develop industrial properties such as products, processes, designs, and formulas, in order to provide a company with an advantage over competition. Such industrial properties are among the more valuable assets a company may possess. Names like "Sony," "Sharp," "Nixdorf", and "Coca-Cola," or rights to processes like Xerography, cellophane, and the production of computer "chips" are invaluable. These products have international recognition and acceptance.

The failure to protect industrial property rights abroad adequately can lead to the loss of these rights in potentially profitable markets. Because patents, processes, trademarks, and copyrights are valuable in all countries, some transnationals have found that their assets have been appropriated and profitably exploited in foreign countries without license and/or reimbursement. Even more devastating, they often learn that not only is another firm producing and selling their product, or using their trademark, but that the pirating company is the rightful owner in the country where they are operating. Companies must keep vigil for attempts at piracy of their products. Levi Strauss and Company and Bluebell, Inc. were successful in stopping a flow of counterfeit blue jeans into West Germany. Apparently, over $1 million worth of counterfeit jeans were sold before the illegal operations were halted.

It is not uncommon to find situations where manufacturers have licensed local companies (discussed in Chapter Fourteen) to produce their products in return for a royalty which is paid for a while then terminated by the licensee. When inquiries about the stopped royalty payments are made, the licensor is told that the particular process is no longer being used. Further inquiry has often revealed that the process has been changed minimally and the licensee continues to produce the product sans royalty payment. There have been cases where companies have lost the rights to trademarks and have had to buy back these rights or pay royalties for their use. Other culprits have had success in pirating processes and demanding substantial payments from the original owners to stop usage or to deregister their false claim.

The resolution of problems is exacerbated by distances between adversaries, language barriers, legal definitions, and legal jurisdictions. This situation, then, means that the transnational firm must take specific legal steps to assure themselves of protection and then be on guard to enforce this right. Some assurance of legal protection is especially critical where the transnational firm has expended resources, taken a risk position, and promoted a market where there has been technological development.

Legal Environment

The legal systems of the world stem from one of two common heritages—the "common law," derived from English law and found in Great Britain, Canada, the United States, and most other nations that have been under English influence at some point in their history, and "civil" or "code" law, which is derived from Roman law and found in the majority of the countries in the world. The differences between these legal systems are significant and can have a heavy impact upon businesses engaged in international commerce.

Common law has its gensis in tradition, past practices, and legal precedents set by the courts through interpretations of statutes, legal legislations, and past rulings. Common law seeks "interpretation through the past decision of higher courts which interpret the same statutes or apply established and customary principles of law to a similar set of facts."[1]

Code law is based upon an all-inclusive system of written rules (codes) of law. Here, the legal system is generally divided into three separate codes: commercial, criminal, and civil. While common law is recognized as not being pandemic, code law is considered complete as a result of the broad, sweeping provisions included in most code law systems. For example, under the commercial code in a code law country, the law governing contracts is made inclusive with the statement that "a person performing a contract shall do so in conformity with good faith as determined by custom and good morals."[2] Although code law is considered inclusive, it is apparent from the foregoing statement that there might well be some broad interpretation necessary in order to include everything under the existing code.

There usually is a variance in the meaning of commercial law between common law and code law countries. Under common law, commercial disputes are subject to laws which may be applied to either civil or commercial disputes since there is no specific recognition of commercial problems as such. For code law countries, however, there exists a separate code specifically designed for businesses. The commercial code has precedent over other codes when matters of business are under jurisdiction. This provision results from historical recognition that legal problems of merchants are often unique and thus should have special status under the law.

Steps have been taken in common law countries to codify commercial law, even though the primary basis of commercial law is found in precedents set by court decision. Recognizing the need for modernization of commercial practices in the United States, several legal bodies formulated a new uniform code, entitled the Uniform Commercial Code (UCC), which was published in 1952. It was revised in 1958 and 1962. The UCC has been adopted by all the states except Louisiana. It has effectively eliminated a host of differences that existed previously among the laws of the states and has also provided provisions to fill many of the gaps between the prior laws.[3] Great Britain is taking steps to codify their commercial practices.

Those laws that govern industrial property rights offer the most striking differences between common and code law systems. Under common law, ownership is established by use; whereas under code law, ownership is determined by registration. In some code law countries, certain agreements may not be enforceable unless properly notarized and registered; whereas in a common law country, the same agreement may be binding so long as proof of the agreement can be established. While virtually every country has elements of both common and code law, there are sufficient differences between common and code law systems with regard to contracts, sales agreements, and other legal problems that it is necessary for transnational firms to pay particular attention to even the most basic and simplistic legal questions.[4] Legal form and agreement, as indicated, is important where there is a standard product; where there is no product or service precedent and where the state of the art may be affected in an international transaction involving high technology, awareness of possible legal implications is even more important than in prosaic purchases.

Patents

Definition

A patent, as defined by United States' law, is a "grant from the government that conveys and secures to an inventor the exclusive right to make, use and sell an invention for seventeen years."[5] At the expiration of the period of patent protection the patented item reverts to the public domain. The patented item can be, in effect, protected beyond the expiration date by adding subsequent improvements which are also patentable. In such instances where the patent rights have expired only the rights to an obsolete item are available. By employing improvements a more marketable product has probably emerged as a consequence of patentable evolutionary developments.

Patents are typically granted for new articles, but design patents are given for manufactured articles that have been changed in a way that will enhance their sale. Plant patents are granted to individuals who invent, discover, or reproduce a new variety of plant, and are applicable to the new field of genetic engineering. Patent law has also been evolving with respect to computer programs. Initially, computer programs could not be patented, but the commercial necessity of protecting them has led to a revised perception.

Patent laws do vary from nation to nation. This is ostensively due to the differences in application and enforcement between code and common law countries.

Usefulness and Implications

The word patent is derived from the phrase "letters patent," which in earlier times designated the document by which a sovereign ruler conferred a privilege or right to someone. The name was a reference to the fact that the document, addressed to the public-at-large, was sealed in such a way that the document could be unfolded and read without breaking the seal. The person granted a patent has a monopoly over the specific subject matter of the grant for a specific period. In all countries patents are valid for a limited term only; this limit ordinarily secures the profit position of the inventor for a reasonable period, yet does not permanently deprive the public of the free use of the invention. In the United States, after the patent has expired anyone can make, use, or sell the invention without the permission of the patentee but as indicated in the preceding section patent protection can be extended by patentable improvements. In the United States the basic term of 17 years may not be extended except by a special act of Congress.

The American law (similar to those in other common-law countries) was designed to encourage the maximum inventiveness. The system of granting U.S. patents for inventions has evolved with a complex set of objectives including rewarding the inventor and thereby stimulating inventive activity.

Under present American law it is appropriate to distinguish between the grant of a positive right to produce the item and the granting of the right to exclude others from producing the object. In earlier periods probably both were intended, since restrictions existed on the freedom of anyone to engage in particular occupations. Modern development, however, has been toward the concept that only the right to exclude others is granted by the patent, since it is the patentee's own privilege to make and deal with the subject matter.

By having the exclusive right, the patentee is encouraged to manufacturer and put the invention into use since the patentee is free of competition for a time, and the investment in such activities is stimulated. The right to exclude, granted by the patent is stated in different countries. In the United States the "right" is specifically expressed as "the right to exclude others from making, using or selling the invention." In the United States any process or device may be patented if it is novel and useful, and if plans and a working model are supplied.

In the past there have been many significant technical patentable accomplishments by independent inventors in the United States. However, as technology has become more complex many technological developments have been the product of several contributions by different people. With high developmental costs, great risk, required management expertise, and marketing outlets as important factors, the trend has been to large corporations as the ultimate owners and exporters of major patents.

Injurious practices, such as holding back beneficial patents that may make obsolete some widely used product or process, have developed. Other practices, such as acquiring all patents in a given field and granting manufacturing licenses only to those firms that promise to refrain from effective competition, have been repeatedly attacked by the federal government, under the antitrust laws.

Secret and Foreign Patents

So-called secret patents may be issued for inventions that are to be kept secret for purposes of national security; usually in such cases the patent is withheld and the invention is simply not disclosed. Some countries provide for what are called confirmation, revalidation, or importation patents, where a person has obtained a patent in a foreign country. Such patents may more easily be obtained than a local patent. The main advantage is that all the procedural efforts toward issuing a patent have already occurred, the second country can merely enter a record of the first patent. A different system exists in the U.S.S.R. and other socialist countries, where there are provisions not only for patents of the usual kind but also what are referred to as authors' or inventors' certificates. The authors' certificate does not confer any exclusive rights to the invention but records the inventor's contribution, recognizes authorship, and entitles the inventor to receive compensation for the use of the invention (if used).

In such dual-system countries, the inventor generally has the right to choose between applying for an inventor's certificate or patent. Local inventors in Eastern Europe generally apply for inventors' certificates; foreigners apply for patent rights because of certain impracticalities in acquiring inventors' certificates. Citizens of socialist countries obtain very few or no patents. The right conferred by a patent, though it may be expressed in terms of exclusive rights, does not really have the same effect as in nonsocialist countries because of the absence of private enterprise.

Patentability and Procedure

The physical object for which patents may be obtained normally relates to something invented. This includes almost every type of invention of an industrial nature. Different statutes express the subject matter in various ways—in the United States it is defined as "any new and useful process, machine manufacture, composition of matter or improvement thereof." Various items such as scandalous or immoral matter, matter contrary to law, scientific principles, and so on, usually cannot be patented; processes involving only mental steps may not be patented.

To qualify for a patent, an invention must be new, and novel; novelty is usually defined by statute. In most countries, if the invention has become known to the public before the application for a patent is made, it is no longer considered novel and a valid patent cannot be obtained. Usually, any prior use outside the country concerned, without printed publicity, is not considered as defeating novelty. In addition to the requirement for novelty, there has developed, primarily in the more industrialized countries, a further requirement of a subtle character concerning the "inventiveness" or "unobviousness" of the subject matter. In other words, the new subject matter must sufficiently advance the state of the art for a patent to be warranted. The prevalent idea coming into use in European countries is that an invention, to be patentable, must be new and "involve an inventive step," with the further definition that an inventive step is involved if the subject matter is "not obvious, having regard to the state of the art." The intention of these provisions, of course, is to exclude slight or trivial changes from the protection of patents. However, the determination of adequate inventiveness has been one of the most difficult aspects of patent law and has involved the greatest number of conflicts of opinion.

There are several important phases in any patent-granting system—application date, novelty examination, opposition period, and patent grant. Firms that are concerned with patents or anticipate transactions involving patents should also ascertain appropriate policies as to compulsory working requirements, patent validity periods, and publication policies.

In most countries the inventor or person deriving the right from the inventor may apply; in the United States, only the inventor may apply, although the patent may be granted to the assignee. The application for a patent must comply with the formal requirements of the country, including specified forms, documents, procedures, and fees. The application must contain a description of the invention, presented such that it can be accomplished by following the directions, and it must contain one or more statements that define the invention succinctly and serve to limit the scope of the rights requested. An application for a patent must be directed to one invention, but several related inventions, linked by a single inventive concept or otherwise closely related and interdependent, may be permitted in the same application. If the application violates the rules or practices relating to unity of invention, the applicant will be required to "divide" or "restrict" the application to but one invention.

The filing date of the application is important since in general, it marks the point in time at which the novelty of the item must exist and also determines who obtains the valid patent in cases where two or more different persons make application for the same invention. Although the filing date is controlling in most countries, a few countries permit recourse to the date of invention. In general, applications for patents are maintained in confidence by the patent office until after the patent is granted, or at certain stages in the proceedings, or after a certain time interval from the filing date of the application, as may be specified in the statute. The applicant has provisional patent rights in the publication of the application, which become ineffective if a patent is not ultimately obtained.

Administrative Procedures

Broadly, two main types of administrative procedures govern the granting of patents. Under the first system, called the registration system, if the application's papers are deemed to be formally in order, the patent is granted in due course. Whether the patent complies with substantive provisions of the law is determined later by a court if the question arises, as in a suit on the patent. In some countries there may be a refusal of a patent on the face of the papers or an objection based on a charge of "lack of unity." The French law of 1744 was the prototype of this system. The United States subsequently adopted the French system, but a new patent law in 1836 introduced what is usually referred to as the examination or preexamination system. Under this system, an attempt is made in advance to determine whether or not the application complies with the substantive requirements for patents. An examiner searches through relevant prior patents, possibly including those of other countries and publications available to determine whether or not the degree of novelty is sufficient to support a patent. The examination cannot be exhaustive and matters such as the existence of prior use are not investigated before the granting. The examiner, after making the search of the prior art, writes to the applicant and relates the results and indicates whatever action is considered appropriate at that time. If the decision is adverse in any respect, the applicant may present an argument and amendments seeking to overcome the examiner's position. The application is then reexamined.

Most countries employing the examination system carry out only limited examinations, searching primarily through their own prior patents. Few countries have arrangements for obtaining the results of searches made in other countries. The chief reason for this is the formidable expenditure of time and effort involved in such full searches. Because of the heavy workload and increasing backlog of applications, various schemes have been developed to alleviate or expedite the process of examination. In the Netherlands, examinations are reserved only for those applications that appear to have enduring importance and interest, thus saving considerable work on the part of the patent office.

The use of mechanical or computer search has been increasingly used. This shows promise in reducing time, cost, and effort to determine if similar concepts have already been patented or if granting a patent will in some way be an infringement on patent rights already granted.

About two dozen countries that grant patents publish the specifications in printed form, either some time during or before examination or at the time the patent is granted or shortly thereafter. Many countries exchange copies of their printed specifications, which enables them conveniently to build up their files. Most countries publish an official journal in which notices and other information relating to patents and related subjects appear.

A fee is required when an application is filed and, in general, at some later date also. The large majority of countries (United States and Canada excepted) require the payment of periodical fees to maintain the patent in force. One result of the renewal fee system is that patents in which the owner is no longer interested drop out of consideration as subsisting monopolies. If a renewal fee is not paid, the patent lapses, usually a grace period for late payment of a fee is provided. This procedure may make useful concepts available in situations where the many patents have been issued and the patentable item for various reasons has never been exploited.

In the 19th century, in most countries the patentee was required to "work" his invention fairly continuously within a specified period; if he did not, the patent became void or was revoked. Later there developed a compromise procedure. The patent is not revoked for nonworking, but rather, after a specified period, becomes subject to the granting of what are called "compulsory" licenses. If an invention has not been worked, a qualified applicant may seek permission to work the patent (a license) from the patent office or a court. The applicant must pay the patentee whatever royalties may be determined and is prohibited from transferring his or her license to another.

Compulsory licenses serve a number of purposes. They may be extended to advance the public good, by making certain that an invention that is deemed useful is in fact used. Several countries specifically provide that medicines or inventions useful in preparing medicines be subject to compulsory licenses. Although the United States has no general law relating to working or compulsory licenses, the courts have used the device of compulsory licenses in deciding antitrust suits. A company judged monopolistic can be forced, as part of the remedy, to grant licenses to others. Finally, compulsory licenses are also issued to those who have dependent patents. A compulsory license is granted for the main patent so that the dependent one can be properly worked. Licensing is discussed in considerable detail in Chapter Fourteen.[6]

Conventions and Arrangements

The International Convention for the Protection of Industrial Property

The first attempt to provide for international protection was the International Convention for the Protection of Industrial Property (the so-called Paris Union) signed in 1883, with the United States ratifying the agreement in 1887.

The convention has demonstrated remarkable durability as evidenced both by its survival power and its attraction for the newer countries which have come into existence since the convention was created. Membership is divided about equally between developed and developing countries and includes five Soviet satellites, as well as the Soviet Union.

Basic provisions of the International Convention are of two kinds—the rule of national treatment and the establishment of certain principles and rights. National treatment means that all the member countries have agreed to grant the same patent and trademark treatment to nationals of other member countries as they grant to their own nationals. This tends to eliminate discrimination against foreigners.

Each country is free to determine the scope of its own proprietary laws. However, the degree of protection varies from country to country. This principle does not call for reciprocal treatment. This may result in a situation in which nationals of a given country receive less favorable treatment in other countries than is afforded foreign nationals in their own country, or vice versa. The second basic provision of the International Convention was that granting a "right of priority" to foreigners. This specifies that a certain patent owner (e.g., a U.S. patent holder) who files an application in another member country has a 12-month priority over any other applicant filing for the same invention in any other country belonging to the International Convention. The priority for trademarks is six months. The six- or 12-month priority period runs from the date of filing in the country of origin and not from the date the patent or trademark was granted.[7]

The Patent Cooperation Treaty and European Patent Convention

Two recent treaties have enabled transnational businesses to obtain foreign patent protection under more simplified procedures than in the past. The Patent Cooperation Treaty (PCT) entered into force on January 24, 1978 and the European Patent Convention (EPC) did so on October 7, 1977.

The Patent Cooperation Treaty enables a party to file a single application for patent searches among all participating nations. While not a patent system per se, the PCT is an application system which became operational in 1978. It is designed to streamline applications and preliminary examinations in signatory nations. Its greatest use is likely to be outside Europe.[8] The PCT makes it easier to obtain patents by filing one application for all the designated countries. Nevertheless, the inventor will still have to obtain an individual patent in each nation in which patent protection is sought. This is an application-processing system, not an approval system.

The European Patent Convention (EPC) is a patent approval system providing for single application for a single patent, thereby having the effort of national patents in contracting nations. The EPC became operational in 1977 and covers 16 European-area countries.[9] The EPC permits selected coverage in Europe.

Other Conventions

A number of conventions are oriented toward geographical, regional or trade zone. The Inter-American Convention includes most of the Latin American nations and the United States. It provides protection similar to that afforded by the "Paris Union." The Community Patent Convention (CPC) is designed to provide single application for single Common Market patents, subject to the laws of the European Economic Community (EEC). The CPC will provide coverage among the member nations of the EEC. It supplements the EPC; thus, an inventor does not need EPC, only CPC, if coverage is desired only within the Common Market.[10]

Some Guiding Arrangements and Alternatives

Once a patent, trademark or some other industrial property right is registered, most countries require that these rights be worked and properly policed. The United States is one of the few countries where a patent can be held by an individual throughout the duration of the protection period without being manufactured and sold. Other nations feel that in exchange for the monopoly provided by a patent, the holder must share the product with the citizens of the country. Hence, if patents are not produced within a specified period, usually from one to five years, the patent reverts to public domain.

There are numerous drawbacks to the existing international patent system. Perhaps the most serious drawback among them is the protection of these patent rights from infringement. The typical situation is one in which a manufacturer finds that a product of foreign manufacture which imitates his own has appeared and is being marketed as competition. The complainant believes the foreign product, mark, label, packaging or advertising to be a copy of his own and therefore to be an infringement. The difficulty in analyzing and subsequently resolving this issue lies in the absence of any impartial international judicial bodies to hear commercial disputes. Remedies when available are usually initiated through diplomatic channels.

In addition to the abuses of the system, there are other matters which exacerbate the present patent process, especially as it pertains to the United States. The first of these is the limitation placed upon the rate of diffusion of new inventions due to the restricted use of inventions that patents permit their owners. The range of application of new inventions is more narrow than it would be without such restrictions. This also limits the overall quality of research, as it must be based upon knowledge that existed prior to that incorporated into existing relevant patents. Efforts to incorporate and build upon knowledge contained in existent patents (other than that patented by the inventor) entail possible patent infringement. As a consequence the diffusion of existing knowledge and techniques is limited, and the ability to extend the boundaries of knowledge is also obstructed and retarded.

The first disadvantage of the patent system leads to a second disadvantage resulting from the realities of competitive pressures. The primary motive behind industrial research effort is the desire to preserve and/or enlarge, if possible, the company's share and control of the market. When a firm discovers a new or improved product or process which gives it economic advantage, its competition is bound to follow the lead. Often when the originator has obtained a patent, the competitors are forced to invent around this patent in order to remain competitive. In essence, this is a subterfuge requiring the utilization of scarce resources to duplicate an existing technology without offering something substantially different. It might be questioned whether these resources could be more productively employed since only occasionally does this duplication result in anything better. Society usually suffers a loss in the long run.

Are there alternatives to the present systems? Several proposals have been considered over the years. An extreme concept is that the patent system be abolished altogether in order to maximize the range of applications of all inventions. Under such a situation, all knowledge would become a "free good." Another proposal has held that the present system be replaced by a system of awards for inventions from the public sector. By making new scientific and technological knowledge free thereafter, a system of government awards would stimulate inventors, whether private individuals or corporate-backed. Another possibility might be to allow the invention into the public domain but in order to provide incentive, reward the inventor with royalty income from any use of the invention.

It is obvious that the suggested proposals for alternatives do not provide a panacea. This is a complicated problem and it is doubtful that easy agreement could be reached upon a more liberalized concept. Attempts should be made to simplify registration, distribute information, allow the use of technology without restrictive and monopolistic controls, and still provide incentive for innovation by protecting the processes and products that result in unique contribution.[11] To iterate, diffusion and use are critical along with the recognition of the need to maintain incentive and reward for risk and effort.

Copyrights[12]

Definition and Purpose

A copyright is the exclusive right inherent in the generation of creative works. In the context of technology, copyrighted material normally includes advertising and promotional literature, shop manuals and other technical documents.

A copyright is designed to provide "protection" to the creator (the inventor) of original literature or artistic productions. With a copyright, the owner is vested for a limited time period with the sole and exclusive privilege of reproducing copies of the work for publication and sale.

In common law, any author or compiler of data who prevented others from using the work without permission by keeping it secret had a common law copyright. Such a copyright ended when the work was published. Publication originally meant any communication to others, not necessarily in written or printed form. Presently, however, most nations have passed laws protecting the rights of the author/creator for a specified period of time.

On January 1, 1978, a new United States copyright law became effective, completely replacing Title 17 of the United States Code, which had been used since 1909. The new law is divided into eight different chapters, beginning with a discussion of the subject matter and scope of copyright. It includes chapters relating to the copyright duration notice, deposit and registration requirements, infringement, manufacturing requirements, and administration. The copyright law has four essential purposes:

To maximize the availability of creative works to the public.

To give creators of copyrighted works a fair return and to provide users of copyrighted works with a fair income.

To balance the interest of copyrighted users and owners.

To minimize any negative impact on industries regulated by change in the copyright law.

The 1978 law created new effective periods for copyrights. Works created after January 1, 1978 are given statutory copyright protection for the life of the author plus 50 years. Pseudonymous and anonymous publications, as well as those done "for hire" (ghosted) have a copyright term of 75 years from publication or one hundred years from creation, whichever is shorter. For those works already under copyright protection before the new law took effect, their present term of 28 years from date of first publication will remain. If a renewal is applied for, the second term will be increased to 47 years.

Use

The copyright holder is entitled to the exclusive use of all those materials that are copyrighted, subject to a number of exceptions—such as fair use and library reproduction.

Some copying is allowed without payment of fees or permission of the copyright holder under the doctrine of "fair use." Fair use allows reproduction of copyrighted material without permission if the use of the material is reasonable and not harmful to the rights of the copyright owner. Section 107 of the copyright law refers to permissable purposes such as criticism, comment, news reporting, teaching (including multiple copies for classroom use), scholarship, or research. Four criteria are used in considering whether a particular use is reasonable:

The purpose and character of the use, including whether it is of a nonprofit, educational nature or of a commercial nature.

The amount and importance of the material used in relation to the work as a whole.

The nature of the copyrighted work.

The effect of the use on the potential market or value of the copyrighted work.

Libraries and archives can reproduce single copies of certain copyrighted items for noncommercial purposes without violating the copyright law. Notice of copyright on the library or archive reproduction is necessary, however. Wholesale copying of periodicals is not permitted.

Major issues in applying copyright laws relate to computer software, computer databases, and econometric modeling. There are expected to be major court tests in settling these issues over the next few years.[13]

In citing copyright material or the use of such material in research the rules as to copyright infringement or plagiarism are not always explicit. If a substantial portion of the copyrighted material is used, some distinctive idea copied, or an original chart or graph reproduced, the safest approach legally and ethically is to get the copyright holder's permission and pay a royalty if required. There may be a question of what constitutes substantial use and this can ultimately hinge on interpretation. As mentioned, the safest and most ethical approach is to get permission. Citing the reference source may be adequate if a relatively insignificant portion of the copyrighted material is being used.

Trademarks

Identification and Legal Processes

A trademark is a distinctive mark, model, device, or emblem that manufacturers stamp, print, or otherwise affix to the goods that they produce so that the goods can be identified in the marketplace and their origin, goodwill, and quality standards can be vouched for. A trademark can be registered by its owner or user. Exclusive use of the trademark can be perpetual in the United States, although many other nations have limited the period of protection.

In countries with laws patterned on the British system, the period of protection is usually seven years, renewable for seven to 14 years thereafter. In most other countries, it is ten to 20 years. Protection usually depends upon adoption and use; if the owner continues to use it, no one can infringe upon the trademark.

A trademark must be distinctive in order to be registered. It is not enough to merely describe an article or to name a city. For example, it would be unacceptable to register the trademark "Georgia Peaches." There naturally are exceptions to this, however. When particular words have been used for such a long time that the public identifies them with a particular product and its origin, then those words can be registered as a trademark. The same holds for geographic terms that have acquired a meaning other than their location.

Trademarks can grow so common that they become generic names. For example, "Thermos" was originally a brand name for a thermal food-storage container. Now the term has become synonymous with such containers and can no longer be used solely as one company's trademark.

Prompt registration of trademarks is advantageous. In most countries, trademark applicants are not required to present evidence of use of a mark prior to registration. This is different from the U.S. system where a mark must be used in order to acquire legally recognized ownership.

In many countries, the first person to apply for and acquire registration of a mark is recognized as its rightful owner. In the British Commonwealth countries and certain others, the applicant must either show use or specify intended use, in which case the mark must be used within a certain period after registration.

Generally, in code law countries, such as France, the first applicant is entitled to registration and protection of a mark regardless of whether it may have been previously used by another party. In these countries which have no prior use requirements, registrations of marks owned in the United States are sometimes acquired by persons without the authority of the American owner. Such persons then use these registrations to prevent the true American owners of the product (the U.S. trademark holders) from trading their goods in that nation, or compel them to license the marks to the indigenous registrant or to employ the latter as local distributors in order to do business in their country.

Treaties for Trademark Protection

Unlike the present situation in the patent field, it is possible for firms to obtain centralized protection of their trademarks. The Paris Union was the first apparent attempt at internationally institutionalizing the trademark registration process. This treaty is adhered to by approximately 80 nations.

Other important treaties include the General International Convention for Trademark and Commercial Protection of 1929, to which the United States and nine other Western Hemisphere countries are parties. There were predecessor conventions to the 1929 Convention, namely those of 1910 and 1923, which either were allowed to lapse or were superseded by later agreements.

There are several international agreements in effect under which trademark applications can be filed with a central source for protection in a number of countries. Regionally, such agreements currently in effect are the African and Malagasy Industrial Property Agreement (Union) and the Benelux Trademark Convention. Parenthetically, the United States does not recognize either agreement.

The "Madrid Agreement Concerning the International Registration of Trademarks" (the Madrid Convention), which is organized on an international as distinct from a regional basis, is adhered to by 23 countries. Under its provision, a trademark first registered nationally in a member country can be applied for by the owner in the other 22 nations through a single filing with the World Intellectual Property Organization (WIPO) Central Bureau in Geneva, Switzerland. The Bureau, upon receipt of the application, distributes it to the other member countries for processing and, if qualified, registration by each in accordance with its own laws. Countries have the right to refuse protection within one year from the date of publication of the international mark. Under the original agreement text, such registrations were always dependent on the prior home registration; if the latter was ever cancelled, those in the other countries became invalid.

Under a text adopted at Nice, France in 1957, dependence of subsequent registrations on the prior home registration is limited to a period of five years. After that time, such marks may no longer be terminated by a single action directed against the prior home registered mark. This agreement is called the "Arrangement of Nice Concerning The International Classification of Goods and Services to Which Trademarks Apply." It is the most widely used trademark classification system and consists of 34 product and eight service classes. The system is used by the United States and about 60 other countries.

In the early 1970s a new Trademark Registration Treaty (TRT) was drafted. The TRT provides for simplified central filing procedures but differs from the Madrid Agreement in several basic procedural areas: the TRT provides that for a single fee, a trademark application can be filed with the WIPO Central Bureau in Geneva. Unlike filings under the Madrid Agreement, the applicant will not need a prior home registration. The filing of a TRT application will have the effect of a filing in each country designated by the applicant. The mark, after filing, will then be published and circulated by WIPO to member countries whereupon each nation designated by the applicant has 15 months within which to refuse registration under its national law. If no timely refusal is indicated by a designated member country, the mark is deemed registered there. No member country will be able to refuse a mark on grounds of nonuse or cancel it on such grounds for at least three years after its registration. In some instances, nations will have to amend national trademark laws in order to adhere to the TRT; the United States will have to make several adjustments to existing statutes.

Trade Secret

Not Protected by Patent

Intellectual property can normally be protected in only one of two ways—it can either be patented or practiced as a trade secret. A restatement of Torts number 757 indicates that a trade secret "may consist of any formula, pattern, device or compilation of information which is used in one's business, and which gives an opportunity to obtain an advantage over competitors who do not know or use it." Therefore, a trade secret is a resulting discovery/invention which is deliberately produced/used without the benefit of patent protection.

The major difference between trade secrets and patents is that the trade secret possession of technology gives no right to prevent development and use by others, whereas a valid patent is exclusive (denying the unauthorized use of the technology by others). The trade secret owner and user may only prevent wrongful disclosure and improper use by persons with whom a fiduciary or confidential relationship has been established. This then sets the tone for technology disclosure. An aura of confidentiality should be established before trade secret information is passed outside the developing firm. Once this relationship has been established, however, unauthorized disclosure by the second party may result in a lawsuit being filed by the first party for damages at common law and perhaps result in the first party obtaining an injunction from the court restraining the use of the item/information. Since there are no specific statutory laws for the protection of trade secrets, the protection of them under the present legal system in the United States and throughout the rest of the world is tenuous.

Several important trade secrets have rendered huge profits for their developers. A few examples are the secret formulas for Coca-Cola, the formulas for Chartreuse liquor guarded by Carthusian monks for more than 400 years, and the metrallurgical secret for making cymbals protected by the Zildjian family since 1623.[14]

Favorable Situations for Trade Secrets[15]

There are a number of factors that should be considered in making a choice between trade secret and patent protection:

Legal considerations.

Costs.

The economic strength of the company.

Potential benefits.

Political ramifications.

The rate or speed of technological development affecting the invention or process, i.e., state of the art.

Security constraints.

Time and urgency of need.[16]

The filing and prosecution of a U.S. patent tends to cost between $3,000 to $5,000. When foreign protection is desired, the costs are increased proportionally by the number of countries in which protection is sought. Therefore, if protection is deemed necessary in ten countries, costs have risen to at least $33,000 ($3,000 for the basic U.S. patent, plus $3,000 in each of the ten additional nations). Furthermore, generally in foreign countries, as the patent matures, maintenance fees rise sharply. Estimates of the cost of protecting a trade secret are certainly more difficult to ascertain. At best, one can look to the opportunity costs associated with such protection

An invention may not be patented but is practiced as a trade secret. If the trade secret becomes known and is copied and subsequently patented by others, then a monopolistic competitive advantage is lost and profits that would have otherwise accrued during the life of the item are also lost.

Often taking a position of trade secret versus a patent position entails a calculated risk. A consideration is where the technology is developing so rapidly that the time, cost, and effort to obtain a patent are impractical. In such instances by the time the patent is granted technological advances have obsoleted and neutralized the patent. A good case is the early development of transistors.

Another situation where trade secrets might abrogate the need for patent protection is where there are unique skills or uncopiable techniques to process or produce the product. This is exemplified by the inability of the U.S.S.R., in many instances, to produce quality consumer products even though they have access to the basic information.

There are also instances where an invention could have been practiced as a trade secret yet was patented, with an inherent loss of business advantage when the patent expired and became available to competition. There have been cases where the issuance of the patent merely alerted competitors to the existence of the technology. In such instances where legal or technical protection of the patent might be difficult, infringement by competitors is possible because legal redress is no deterrent. Frequently, legal processes are slow and cumbersome. Large organizations may be in a position to exploit patents owned by smaller or less affluent organizations for competitive advantage where the weaker organization is unable to spend the time or cost to show patent infringement.

There are risks and benefits associated with both patents and trade secrets. A general rule as to which option to select is difficult to formulate. Each case should be considered individually, with a detailed and comprehensive analysis of the comparative advantages and disadvantages of each position.

Favorable Situations for Patents

An important step in the patent process is the search of the prior art. These are normally conducted by patent attorneys. Thorough searches are difficult, time consuming, and costly, and may not be conclusive. Patenting is indicated when the claims associated with technology will be sufficiently strong and broad to protect the product and its subsequent modifications adequately and the potential benefits outweigh the costs.

Patents should be considered when it will be difficult to keep a development secret because of its vulnerability to breaches in security or because the invention is susceptible to "reversed engineering." Additionally, patenting is viable when the invention meets the marketing needs of a company, gives it a significant competitive advantage, and requires a large R&D and marketing investment, and if there is a good possibility that others will independently make or disclose the same inventable concept.

A patent may facilitate licensing and cross-licensing agreements. This process may be important to a firm requiring cash, as a patent is, within itself a precise, tangible claim to an invention.

The major commercial benefit arising from a patent stems from the right it gives to the owner to exclude others from practicing the invention. It follows that this right allows the owner to develop the market for the invention, free from direct competition for a limited period of time. This period of exclusivity might be sufficient to enable the company to obtain a major advantage over its competitors and maintain a major share of the market, despite the expiration of patent protection. In many instances, a patented product demands a higher price. This is particularly true in the pharmaceutical field, where surveys have shown prices of drugs to be substantially higher where product patents were held. By keeping the competition at bay, the patent holder could set a higher price and achieve high profits.[17]

Public use of patentable trade secrets for more than one year renders them unpatentable. This factor forces the developer to make the patent decision within a definite time frame. A considerable cost of the patent system arises from uncertainty. It is difficult for even the most experienced patent attorney to predict whether a multimillion dollar investment will be afforded protection by the patent law.

Uncertainty is also present in the area of trade secrets. The secret may be compromised by any number of factors including personnel moving to competitive firms and "reverse engineering." It is apparent that the choice between patenting a process or practicing it as a trade secret is a difficult one.

Know-How

Knowledge—The Use of Technology

Know-how or "technical information" is often more important than a secret process. This may involve knowledge of how to set up a plant or machinery, how to run the plant, or how to make a product in the best way. Know-how then may be a varied assortment of rights, trade secrets, plans, photographs, blueprints, specifications, manuals, and technical assistance. Know-how or the use of technology includes many improved ways of performing operations which are procedural innovations and are not patentable.

Edwin Mansfield has said that:

> Technology is society's pool of knowledge regarding the principles of physical and social phenomena (such as the properties of fluids and the laws of motion), knowledge regarding the application of these principles to production (such as the application of genetic theory to breeding of new plants), and knowledge regarding the day-to-day operations of production (such as the rules of thumb of the craftsman).[18]

Clearly, know-how is an integral part of the technological process. It is often the actual object of a licensing agreement.

As a general proposition, legal protection is afforded know how and stems from the fact that such know-how is "factually exclusive" and worthy of proprietary protection.[19]

This in essence, means that another party may acquire the secret and the rights conferred by the secret only from the originator. The original possessor of the know-how typically is able to obtain redress only if another party has acquired it by unconscionable means. Implied here is the fact that a license agreement provides contractual restrictions on the right to use the know-how and implicitly requires the second party to protect and maintain the secrecy of the know-how.

Originators apparently do not seek patents for know-how because of implicit expense, administrative involvement, or fear of disclosure and subsequent loss of "technological edge."

Arbitration

Quick Impartial Decision Process in Disputes

Unless settled voluntarily, trade differences may have to be settled ultimately through court action. As a rule this means an expensive and time-consuming operation, particularly if litigation takes place in a foreign country. Inconveniences and hazards multiply, exacerbated by language barriers, distances between litigants, dependence upon foreign legal councels, and a relative unfamilarity with foreign laws. To avoid these problems businesspersons throughout the world tend to resort, whenever possible, to voluntary commercial arbitration for the settlement of their disputes. Arbitration affords, in the usual case, a less expensive, private, and faster procedure. Voluntary commercial arbitration is a mutually agreed upon quasijudicial process where the two parties to a dispute submit their differences to an impartial (usually a recognized expert in the area of dispute) third party who renders a decision which is binding on the disputants.

These experts, who usually are appointed by the parties or by an organization designated by the parties, impartially hear and examine the case and weigh and appraise the evidence. They limit their inquiry to the matters and issues agreed to in the arbitration agreement, and decide the dispute in accordance with universal mercantile standards and established business practices. While not foolproof, this system provides the parties with prompt, relatively inexpensive, private, and allegedly impartial settlement of the dispute under principles known and understood by the litigants.[20]

To make it possible for a dispute to be submitted to arbitration, the parties must have agreed to do so either in advance or after the dispute has arisen. If thereafter either of the parties refuses to take part, where there has been prior agreement to arbitrate, the arbitration will proceed nevertheless since the rules to which the parties have agreed contain provision for procedure by default.

The range of cases submitted to arbitration can cover a wide spectrum of disputable issues, but roughly 20% involve licenses for patents, manufacturing processes, know-how, and trademarks.[21]

It has not always been easy or possible to obtain recognition and enforcement in countries foreign to where the arbitration award was granted. As a result, the 1958 United Nations Convention on Recognition and Enforcement of Foreign Arbitral Awards was conceptualized and ratified by 45 nations. In the United States, commercial arbitration awards are legally enforceable.

U.N. Convention

The 1958 Convention supersedes the Geneva Protocol on Arbitration clauses of 1923, and the Geneva Convention for the Execution of Foreign Arbitral Awards of 1927. The United States did not belong to the 1923 and 1927 Geneva agreements, but did have friendship, commerce, and navigation treaties including arbitration provisions with a number of countries. The 1958 Convention enjoys a number of advantages over its predecessors. The principal benefit is the reduced and simplified requirement for recognition and enforcement of awards. The convention clearly stipulates the affirmative actions that must be taken by a party seeking enforcement of a foreign arbitral award. Also, the convention provides for improved freedom of the parties in choosing the authority to arbitrate as well as the arbitration procedure.

In the absence of agreement by treaty, domestic legislation usually does not provide specifically for recognition and enforcement of foreign arbitral awards. The winning party, to enforce a foreign award, had to initiate a judicial proceeding in such country. The 1958 convention established uniform provisions under which the signatory nations agreed to recognize and enforce, within their respective jurisdictions, arbitral awards issued in other member nations. Furthermore, the convention specifies the grounds on which recognition and enforcement may be refused.

The term "arbitral award" refers to awards made by arbitrators deciding differences between legally competent parties, and includes awards made by arbitrators appointed for individual cases and those made by certain permanent arbitral bodies to which the parties have submitted, e.g., an arbitral award by a chamber of commerce.

Under the convention each contracting state refrains from taking jurisdiction of a matter which the parties have agreed to submit to arbitration. As a rule, each member nation recognizes as binding and enforceable the arbitral awards in its jurisdiction. However, recognition and enforcement are not automatically extended to all agreements and foreign arbitral awards. There are certain circumstances under which member states may deny recognition and enforcement of agreements or awards. These include incapacity of the parties or invalidity of the arbitration agreement, failure to provide adequate or proper notice to the parties, the award falling outside the preview of the agreement, and the subject matter being not arbitrable under its national laws.[22]

Antitrust and Technological Proprietary Rights

U.S. Constitutional Provisions

Protection of both patents and copyrights in the United States is based upon a constitutional provision. Article I of the Constitution states, in part, that Congress shall have power "to promote the Progress of Science and useful Arts, by securing for limited Times to Authors and Inventors the exclusive Right to their respective Writings and Discoveries." A U.S. patent for a term of 17 years gives the inventor not the right to use, since this is inherent, but the additional right to exclude all others from the manufacture, sale, and use of the invention.[23]

An inventor must make a full disclosure of the invention in the patent application, and the patent claims define the precise limits of the patent.

The U.S. patent statute provides that a patent shall have the attributes of personal property and that patents, applications therefor, or any interest therein may be further assigned (by licenses—discussed in the next chapter).[24]

A patentee (the owner) or the assignee (the licensee) may file a civil law suit for infringement upon the limits and rights of the patent. This right extends naturally only within the United States. An international agreement such as the Paris Union allows for recognition of infringement at the international level.

From an antitrust standpoint, patents are classified as process patents, product patents, or combination patents. Often a patent may cover a new product and also the process for making it. Product patents covering an entire product are now rare. Combination patents may cover an assembly of various parts, none of which itself is patented and some of which are patented.[25]

Antitrust Aspects of Patents

Patents constitute an exception to the basic rule of competition embodied in the Sherman Act, since, within the scope of the patent claims, the owner has a recognized legal monopoly. The monopoly right is granted as a reward for the benefit to be derived by the public from the invention. The civil courts' concern, however, is whether the owner's (patentee) activities are within the proper scope of the patent monopoly. If they are outside this scope, they are to be tested by the antitrust laws. The courts have also shown a distinct tendency to treat activities relating to patents with more strictness under the antitrust laws than activities relating to other property.

Antitrust problems do not generally arise in the United States in the acquisition of patents, either by grant or by purchase. A company may acquire as many patents as it desires, just as it acquires other property. Antitrust violation may result, however, from the enforcement of a patent obtained by intentional fraud on the Patent Office.[26]

The courts have held that companies can monopolize patents and use them to further monopolize an industry. An example occurred in the parking meter industry where a company acquired and used all important patents.[27]

Patents were highlighted in a number of legal disputes relating to international cartel arrangements in the 1940s and 1950s.[28] In most of these activities however, there were activities far beyond any reasonable use of patents, and the use was to accomplish a forbidden result. Patents in antitrust foreign trade situations usually have involved either the problem of whether a patentee's activities are protected by a legal monopoly, or the problem of whether the use of the patents themselves—acquisition, licensing, etc.—violates the antitrust laws. This is also true of copyrights and, to some extent, of trademarks and know-how.

In the past the antitrust suits brought by the Department of Justice involving patents have only rarely attacked patent validity. In the main, in these cases, the government has attacked certain restrictive practices alleged to violate the antitrust laws which were defended as being within the patent grant or ancillary to the patent grant.

Section 337 of the United States Tariff Act of 1930, as amended, declares to be unlawful unfair methods of competition and unfair acts in the importation of products into the United States or their sale, the effect or tendency of which is to destroy or injure an efficiently operating American industry or to prevent its establishment or to restrain or monopolize trade and commerce within the United States. The President, upon discovering unfair acts, may direct that articles be barred from entry.

This statute gives an American patent owner governmental protection in addition to the normal recourse of patent infringement suits.

Trademarks and Antitrust

Trademarks carry no monopoly rights and accordingly cannot be used to justify monopolization or illegal restrictive practices. Trademarks, however, may become valuable property rights.

The courts have also evolved an antitrust nuisance doctrine applicable to trademarks similar to that applicable to patents. Both antitrust defenses stem from the very cold equity doctrine that "he who comes into a court of equity, must come with clean hands." In order for the defense to be good in trademark cases, however, it has been held that the use of the trademark itself must have been an integral part of the antitrust violation. A case where the doctrine was applied was *Phi Delta Theta Fraternity v. J.A. Buchroeder & Co.*, involving the use of trademarks (fraternity insignia) to implement an alleged conspiracy whereby all college fraternities and sororities would be bound under exclusive jeweler contracts.[29]

Antitrust Laws of European Nations

In describing European antitrust laws, a distinction is usually drawn between those adopting the "prohibition" principle and those adopting the "control of abuse" principle. The general notion of the prohibition principle is that restrictive practices are prohibited, and, in addition, the acquisition of dominant or monopoly power is forbidden. United States laws generally fall into this category. The "control of abuse" principle is that restrictive business practices or a dominant market position may be to some extent permitted, but there will be sufficient regulation to prevent any abuses arising from such practices or dominance. The Common Market laws draw from both principles.

In the Parke, Davis case, the EC Court of Justice held that a patent could be used to violate the antitrust laws; however, the fact that patent rights in one

EC country gave special protection to the patentee did not itself violate EC laws.[30] Thus, an owner in the Netherlands of a patent covering antibiotics could assert the patent to keep out imports of similar products from Italy, which has no patents covering drugs. The Sirena case concerning trademarks also held that the mere fact that a trademark owner could keep others from using the mark did not constitute a dominant position under the laws.[31] The owner must also have power to prevent effective competition in a substantial part of the market. The facts in the case were that a U.S. owner of a trademark for medicated cosmetic cream assigned all rights of the trademark in Italy to an Italian firm which produced and manufactured a cream to which the mark, registered in Italy, was affixed. The Italian firm had sued to prohibit the importation of a similar cream with the same trademark from Germany. The German producer had affixed the mark under an assignment of the German rights by the same U.S. firm. The Italian Court had asked an opinion from the Court of Justice on community law.

The European Common Market antitrust laws are only a part of the European antitrust structure. Four of the original members have their own antitrust laws as do all the new members.

The German law is perhaps the closest of the European laws to that in the United States, undoubtedly influenced by the anticartel laws of the Occupation Forces after World War II. All agreements are declared invalid which, by restraining competition, are likely to affect the production of, or market conditions with respect to, goods or commercial services. Resale price maintenance requirements are illegal with exception, as in U.S. law, for branded products, and books and publications. There are broad exemptions provided for particular types of cartels, such as rationalization cartels organized to take advantage of technical improvements in an industry. A Cartel Authority enforces the statute. Exempted agreements must be filed with the Authority which may object to the registration of the cartel. The Authority may enjoin abuses of their market positions by market-dominating enterprises, and it must be notified of every merger resulting in a market share of 20% or more.

The French law also renders illegal, null, and void all concerted actions, agreements, and combinations that have the purpose or effect of interfering with the full exercise of competitive pricing. Refusals to sell, discriminatory conditions of sale, tying agreements, and resale price maintenance are prohibited. Exemptions may be made by ministerial order as to agreements which have the effect of improving or extending product markets or assuring economic progress by rationalization or specialization.

In 1972 the French government in an anti-inflation measure, tied in competition and restrictions against cartel agreements with price control. Under this order, price control is selectively lifted for industrial products. To illustrate, where there is considerable international competition there will be no price regulation provided the rules relating to competition are strictly observed, that price reports are not circulated in the industry, and that the enterprises will refrain from participating in concerted practices concerning prices.

The Dutch law is a "control of abuse" law. All "regulations of competition" or cartel agreements must be filed with the Minister of Economic Affairs unless such a requirement has been waived. If such an agreement is entered into by a majority of those in an industry and is found by the Joint Ministers to be in the public interest, it may be made binding on all enterprises in the field. If the Ministers find the agreement contrary to the public interest, they may declare it, or a part of it, not binding. If the Joint Ministers find a position of economic power to exist which adversely affects the public interest, they may, after a hearing, regulate the dominant enterprise or enterprises.

The Belgian antitrust law, enacted in 1960, is strictly an abuse law. If an abuse of economic power is found to exist, the Minister of Economic Affairs may obtain relief by royal decree if necessary. Abuse consists of practices that "distort or restrict the normal course of competition" or that "hinder either the conomic liberty of producers, distributors, or consumers, or the development of production of trade."

The Irish Law provides a Fair Trade Commission. The Fair Trade Commission is appointed by the Minister for Industry and Commerce and is empowered to issue rules, after affording an opportunity for representations by interested parties, for fair trading conditions concerning the supply and distribution of any kind of goods or related services. The Commission may also make inquiries into the supply and distribution of goods and present proposed orders to the Minister for Industry and Commerce, who then put them into force subject to confirmation by Act of the Oierachtas (Parliament).

The Danish antitrust law, like those of other Scandinavian countries, depends, as noted, a great deal on publicity resulting from the publication of cartel agreements on a cartel register. A Monopoly Control Authority (M.C.A.) may issue orders to remedy the effects of restrictive business practices if negotiation with the parties concerned is ineffective. An appeal to the courts is provided as to M.C.A. decisions. If the M.C.A.'s orders are not sufficient in a particular case, it must submit a report to the Minister of Commerce who may present the matter to Parliament.

The Monopolies and Restrictive Practices (Inquiry Control) Act of 1948 and the Monopolies and Mergers Act, 1965, provide the machinery for control of monopoly and merger in the United Kingdom. The Department of Trade and Industry (formerly the Board of Trade) may refer to the Monopolies Commission for investigation and for a report if monopoly conditions or restrictions (not covered by agreements required to be registered with the Registrar of Restrictive Trading Agreements) prevail as to the supply of goods or services in the United Kingdom. It may also refer to the Commission for investigating the export of goods from the United Kingdom. The legislation specifies that monopoly conditions exist if one company supplies or purchases at least one-third of goods or services, or if two or more companies acting together supply or purchase one-third of goods or services, in a manner to prevent or restrict competition. Provision for referral of mergers to the Monopolies Commission was made in the 1965 Act under two conditions: (1) where the merger would lead to or strengthen a monopoly or (2) where the gross value of the acquired assets amounts to over five million.

The Monopolies Commission with a membership of up to 25 members is composed of industrialists, lawyers, and economists chosen for their ability and experience. Additional members may be appointed, and the Commission may work in groups to handle several matters at one time. All but the Chairman serve on a part-time basis. The Commission makes reports and recommendations (these are published) to the Department of Trade and Industry, which may or may not act on them. If the Department accepts the recommendations and makes an order, it requires Parliamentary approval. While the Commission's recommendations have been accepted in a number of cases, actual orders were required in only four of them—one prohibiting the merger of the Rank Organization with the De La Rue Company.

Acting on monopoly and restrictive practices references, the Commission may have to make only a factual report, or (what is more usual) a statement on whether monopoly conditions exist in the supply of goods or services, and whether the activities of the parties in question operate against the public interest. Factors relating to the public interest include: efficiency in production and distribution; encouragement of new enterprise; the fullest use of manpower, materials, and productive capacity; the development of technical improvements; and the expansion of markets. The reference may require a "general" report on practices which prevent, restrict, or distort competition in the supply of goods or services or exports.

As to mergers, the Commission reports on whether the merger can be expected to operate in the public interest, and it makes recommendations to remedy undesirable consequences of the merger. The Department, after obtaining a Commission report, may by order prevent the merger or, if the merger is consummated, may order dissolution or take some less stringent action.

The Restrictive Trade Practices Act 1956 and that of 1968 are the laws that concern restrictive business practices. Restrictive agreements between two or more persons carrying on business within the United Kingdom in specified categories, not including services or labor, must be registered with a Registrar of Restrictive Trading Agreements, who must present the agreements to the Restrictive Practices Court. The restrictions specified are those between suppliers or processors of goods as to prices, terms of sale, quantities of goods to be produced, application of processes to goods, persons to be supplied, or areas of supply.

The Restrictive Practices Court reviews the agreements brought before it in terms of the public interest. Agreements containing such restrictions are presumed to be contrary to the public interest unless they fall within seven "gateways" specifying advantages or benefits to the public, and such benefits outweigh the adverse effects of the restrictions. The gateways include: that the restriction protects the public against injury from the goods or their installation, that removal of the restrictions would bring benefits to consumers, that the restriction is necessary to counteract measures taken by others, that it is necessary for negotiation with others controlling a preponderant part of the goods or their market, that employment would suffer, that exports would be reduced, or that the restriction is necessary to protect other restrictions upheld by the Court.

Canadian Antitrust Laws

The present antitrust law in Canada is entirely criminal in nature. The original act, passed in 1889, preceded the Sherman Act. The Combines Investigation Act now contains both the administrative provision for investigation and the former criminal code provisions concerning monopoly and restrictive practices. Because of the disadvantages of the present system of criminal law and in order to strengthen the antitrust law, the Minister for Consumer and Corporate Affairs introduced a bill in 1971 to completely revise the Canadian antitrust law. This bill has been widely discussed and debated and has been reintroduced in Parliament in a revised form. Its revision followed an extensive investigation and report by the Economic Council of Canada.

The present law makes it a crime to conspire or combine to unduly prevent or lessen competition in the production, manufacture, purchase, or sale, or the transportation or supply of any article or the price of insurance; to unduly limit facilities for production, etc. or "to restrain or injure trade in commerce in relation to any article." The act also covers monopolies and mergers which operate "to the detriment or against the interest of the public," advertising that is misleading, and a variety of other restrictive practices.

Enforcement of the act is vested in a Director of Investigation and Research, a Restrictive Trade Practices Commission, and the courts. The Director, with a staff of about 100, conducts inquiries into restrictive practices, monopolies, and mergers forbidden by the act. The three-member Commission hears evidence presented by the Director and by parties under investigation, and makes reports to the Minister of Consumer and Corporate Affairs. The Attorney-General can institute proceedings in the courts against the parties at any stage. The act provides for injunctive and dissolution remedies in addition to, and supplementary to, criminal proceedings. Important reports by the Restrictive Trade Practices Commission in recent years have included Shipping Conference Arrangements (1965), Trade Practices in the Phosphorous Products and Sodium Chlorate Industries (1966), and Electric Large Lamps (1971). The courts have quite generally condemned arrangements for price-fixing, boycotts, and the like—conspiracies that would come under the Sherman Act in the United States. While there have not been many monopoly cases, a number have been brought in recent years. Thus far the courts have required a high degree of concentration with a consequent lessening of competition to hold a merger unlawful.

The new legislation in Canada would also include three enforcement agencies. A Commission having wide investigatory powers would be similar to the present Director of Investigation and Research, and a special tribunal would be set up which, unlike the present Restrictive Trade Practices Commission, would be a court of record to deal with antitrust cases brought before it. The criminal courts would continue to handle antitrust criminal cases, and the civil courts would handle damage actions brought by private parties who are given rights under the new act.

The law makes certain offenses illegal per se and subject to criminal penalties. These include agreements among competitors for price-fixing, bid-rigging, allocation of markets, limitation of production or distribution, preventing new entries into a market or causing withdrawals from it, and group boycotts. Willful monopolization is also a criminal offense. Fines under the law can be as high as $1 million for a first offense and $2 million for the second offense. Other antitrust offenses, such as mergers and noncriminal aspects of monopoly and restrictive agreements generally, would be dealt with by the new tribunal. The new law also contains special provisions for foreign takeovers of Canadian companies.

The present Canadian antitrust laws has been strongly enforced for many years. The exclusively criminal nature of the law has been a drawback, but the addition of injunctive relief in connection with criminal prosecutions has served to remedy this defect somewhat.

It should also be noted that the U.S. antitrust laws have had a significant effect in Canada. Whether this is good or bad depends upon the viewpoint. There has been some resentment in Canada against the operation of U.S. antitrust laws extraterritorially in Canada. It may well be argued, however, that on the whole the U.S. antitrust laws have had favorable effects in Canada as well as in the United States.

Japanese Antitrust Laws

The original antimonopoly law in Japan was enacted under the aegis of the occupying powers which had earlier obtained dissolution of the Zaibatsu combines. These giant commercial enterprises prior to World War II had virtual monopolies in finance, trading, and industry. The law was amended in 1949 and again in 1953 after the Treaty of Peace came into force.

The present law, which still has many similarities to the U.S. Sherman, Clayton, and Federal Trade Commission Acts, states its purpose, inter alia, to be to prevent "the excessive concentration of economic power" and "to promote free and fair competition." The law prohibits private monopolization, unreasonable restraint of trade, and unfair business practices.

"Private monopolization" denotes business activities by which an entrepreneur, individually or by combination, "excludes or controls the business activities of other entrepreneurs thereby causing, contrary to the public interest, a substantial restraint of competition in any particular field of trade." "Unreasonable restraint of trade" includes business activities, whether agreements or concerted action, which fix prices or limit production, technology, products, facilities or customers, causing a substantial restraint of competition as above. "Unfair business practices" include discriminatory treatment, dealing at too high prices, coercing customers, and like practices, which tend to impede fair competition as designated by the Fair Trade Commission in specific industries. Mergers that involve a substantial restraint of competition or in the course of which unfair business practices have been employed are prohibited, and also stockholdings whose effect "may be substantially to restrain competition." Resale price maintenance is banned with some exceptions. The law contains a provision aimed at preventing the resurgence of the Zaibatsu; that establishment of a holding company is prohibited.

The law itself contains various exemptions, e.g., as to depression and rationalization cartels, industrial property rights, designated cooperatives, regulated industries, "natural monopolies," and legitimate acts under legislation for particular industries. At present there are a large number of additional exemptions, including export trade, land transportation, shipping conferences, and insurance, and in particular industries such as coal, machinery, fertilizers, nonferrous metals, and textiles; there are special provisions, e.g., for rationalization cartels.

The Fair Trade Commission is the agency established by the antimonopoly law to enforce its provisions. The Commission is an independent agency attached to the Prime Minister's Office, composed of a Chairman and four other members appointed by the Prime Minister with the consent of both Houses of the Diet. The staff, composed of a General Counsel, Hearing Examiners, a Secretariat, Investigation, Economic and Trade Practice Divisions, and local offices, numbers over 350 persons. The Tokyo High Court has exclusive jurisdiction over Fair Trade Commission cases. Private penalties following a decision of violation are provided for, but this provision has been little used.

There has been a general merger trend in Japan, despite the antimerger provisions, involving primarily small companies but also some very large companies, e.g., the three Mitsubishi heavy industries which had been a single firm prior to World War II. The largest merger was the acquisition by Yawata Iron and Steel Co., Ltd., the largest crude steel producer with 18.5% of the market, of Fuji Iron and Steel Co., Ltd., the second largest steel company with 16.9% of crude steel. After public hearings the Fair Trade Commission recommended against the merger, and brought action to stop it in the Tokyo High Court, alleging that it would restrain competition in railway rails, tin plate for food cans, foundry pig iron, and sheet piles. (Crude steel itself did not come within the interpretation of the law to include only markets in end-use manufactured products.) A consent judgment ordered divestiture of assets in the first three categories above, and that the merged company give technical assistance to other companies as to sheet piles.

The Japanese antimonopoly law, modeled after the U.S. law, has many exceptions; however, as noted, some area which are exempted from the provisions on restriction of competition and monopolization are still subject to the unfair practices provisions. These have been very effective. The Fair Trade Commission has acted vigorously in the face of considerable odds. Concepts of competition and antitrust were distinctly foreign to the Japanese economy. Japan has made great strides in the last two decades in changing over from an economy dominated by large government-supported enterprises with practically monopoly power to an essentially competitive economy. Many Japanese industries are still very much concentrated, but of course this is also true in the United States and in other industrial countries. The largest 100 companies account for 33% of the total capital employed in all companies in Japan. Eight companies account for 79% of the iron and steel industry, 13 companies account for 69% of transportation equipment, and 12 companies account for $91\frac{1}{2}$% of the electricity and gas industries, although the latter two are subject to governmental regulation.[32] Approved export cartels are exempted from the antimonopoly law and, contrary to experience in the United States, Japanese export cartels with governmental approval appear to flourish.

Competition policy overall is now a fundamental principle in Japan with general public and especially consumer backing. The "New Economic and Social Development Plan of 1970" states,

> The Japanese economy is a free economy operating mainly according to the market mechanism...it is desirable that the principle of competition be respected in the private sector and that government intervention be limited to the minimum....[33]

Summary

International firms face a multitude of problems in their efforts to develop successful trade relationships. One of the major tasks is product differentiation. To assist in this identity effort, various patent, trademark, and copyright laws have been developed.

These laws, at both the national and international levels are conceptualized with the primary focus being protection of the rights of the inventor/owner in the marketing of these items. The legal systems of the Free World are divided between the common law and code law adherents.

Laws relating to patents, copyrights, trademarks, and know-how differ throughout the world. Under common law, the first user has legal ownership; under code law, the first to legally register becomes the owner. International conventions have been negotiated to attempt some reconciliation of these differences.

Antitrust laws in the United States are applied to technological proprietary rights. Versions of these laws are now found not only in the United States but in many developed nations as well. The objective is to ensure fair trade and to prohibit abuse of the rights inherent in the issuance of proprietary rights.

Endnotes Chapter Thirteen

1. Leslie L. Lewis, ed., *The Dartnell International Trade Handbook*, 1st edition, Chicago: The Dartnell Corp., 1963, p. 513.
2. *Ibid.*, p. 513.
3. Larmar Lee and Donald W. Dobler, *Purchasing and Materials Management: Text and Cases*, 3rd edition, New York: McGraw-Hill Book Company, 1977, pp. 490–491.
4. For an excellent discussion of the legal complexities facing the international trading company, see Phillip R. Cateora and John M. Hess, *International Marketing*, 4th edition, Homewood, IL: Richard D. Irwin, 1979, Chapter 7.
5. K.W. Clarkson, R.L. Miller, B. Blaire, *West's Business Law: Text & Cases*, St. Paul: West Publishing Co., 1980, p. 258.
6. For a discussion on the history and nature of patents, see George E. Folk, *Patents and Industrial Progress*, New York: Harper and Brothers Publishers, 1942, Part III and Part IV.
7. Vincent Travaglini, "Protection of Industrial Property Rights Abroad," *Foreign Business Practices*, U.S. Department of Commerce, November 1975, pp. 25–26.
8. Nations include United States, Great Britain, West Germany, Switzerland, Cameroon, Central African Empire, Chad, Congo, Gaban, Tago, Madagascar, Malarru, and Senegal.
9. Signatory nations include Austria, Belgium, Denmark, France, Germany, Greece, Iceland, Italy, Liechtenstein, Luxemburg, Monaco, the Netherlands, Norway, Sweden, Switzerland, and the United Kingdom.
10. Sources for the discussion of patent conventions are Haseltine, Lake, and Waters: "New Patent Systems: What They Offer, How They Differ," *Business International*, April 9, 1976, pp. 116–117; "Looking to Europatent," *Business Europe*, September 30, 1977, pp. 305–306; "Foreign Patent Protection Gets Easier," *The Wall Street Journal*, November 21, 1977, p. 6.
11. For an interesting examination of the effects and restrictions upon technology and innovation see Daniel Hamberg, *R&D: Essays on The Economics of Research and Development*, New York: Random House, 1966.
12. See *West's Business Law*, *op. cit.*, pp. 258–260, for a discussion relating to copyrights.
13. "The New Territory Copyrights Will Cover," *Business Week*, November 22, 1976, pp. 86–90.
14. Thomas M. Noone, "Trade Secret vs. Patent Protection," *Research Management*, May 1978, p. 21.
15. *Ibid.*
16. Philip Sperber, *Intellectual Property Management*, London: Clark Boardman & Co., Ltd, 1974.
17. C.T. Taylor and Z.A. Silberston, *The Economic Impact of The Patent System*, Cambridge: Cambridge University Press, 1973.
18. Edwin Mansfield, *Technological Change*, New York: W.W. Norton & Company, 1971, p. 9.
19. D.B. Zenoff, *International Business Management*, New York: Macmillan Co., 1971, p. 91.
20. Ovidio M. Giberga, "Eupreement of Foreign Arbitral Awards Under the U.N. Convention," *Foreign Business Practices*, U.S. Department of Commerce, November 1975, pp. 15–16.
21. V. Travaglini, "Protection of Industrial Property Rights Abroad" *Foreign Business Practices*, U.S. Department of Commerce, November 1975, p. 29.
22. Giberga, *op. cit.*, p. 16. See also summary of commercial arbitration laws of many developed and developing nations at pp. 17–24.
23. Special Equipment Co. v. Coe, 324 U.S. 370, 65 Sup. Ct. 741, 89L Ed. 1006 (1945); United States v. American Bell Telephone Co., 167 U.S. 224, 239, 17 Sup. Ct. 809, 810, 42L, Ed. 144, 154 (1897).

24. 25 U.S.C. Section 262 (1970).
25. W.L. Fugate, *Foreign Commerce and the Antitrust Laws*, 2nd edition, Boston: Little, Brown and Co., 1973, pp. 257–259.
26. Corning Glass Works v. Anchor Hocking Glass Corp., 253F. Supp. 461 (D. Del. 1966), aff'd on this point, 374F. 2d 473 (3d Cir. 1967).
27. United States v. Vehicular Parking Ltd., 54F. Suppl. 828D.Del. 1944, Mod., 61F. Supp. 656 (D.Del. 1945).
28. See, e.g., United States v. National Lead Co., 332 U.S. 319, 67 Sup. Ct. 1634, 91L. Ed. 2077 (1947); United States v. Imperial Chemical Industries, Ltd., 100F. Suppl. 504 (S.D. N.Y. 1951).
29. 251F. Suppl. 968 (W.D. Mo. 1966). See also Clairol, Inc. v. The Gillette Co., 270F. Suppl. 371 (E.D. N.Y. 1967).
30. Parke, Davis & Co. v. Probel, Reece Beintema-Interpharm and Centrapharm Companies, Case No. 24/67, Feb. 29, 1968.
31. Sirena, S.R. v. Eda Garbtt Case No. 40/70, Feb. 18, 1971.
32. See OECD, Annual Reports on Competition Policy and Restrictive Business Practices Legislation and Its Application, Japan, April 1979, p. 48.
33. *Ibid*., p. 56.

CHAPTER FOURTEEN

International Cooperative Arrangements

Technology—A National Resource

Incentives for Cooperation

Technology is by now generally recognized throughout the world as one of the functions that provides for growth and vitality in a nation. It is considered as one of the primary forces of national growth and is increasingly being recognized as an indispensible instrument of national policy. It is also regarded as a national resource. Nations are therefore jealous in their attitudes toward technology. Those nations that are lacking seek it; those that have it are reluctant to lose their "technological edge." Nations on both sides of the "technological fence" are hedging their positions. A natural outgrowth of this dilemma then has been the growing number of instances of international cooperative agreements. Cooperative agreements can provide access to technology which is otherwise not available or economically feasible by reducing risk, making capital available, and pooling knowledge.

In this chapter, the focus will be on the nature and characteristics of some of the more important of the technological cooperative arrangements that assist in the worldwide diffusion of technology.

Licensing

Licensing Considerations

Ostensibly, exporting manufacturers may enter into foreign-base production in one of three ways: (1) licensing, (2) long-term contractual arrangements with local producers (there are many variations of these arrangements as will be seen in this chapter), or (3) direct investment in manufacturing facilities. There are a number of factors that influence the decision to license and the method chosen; these include degree of risk, time horizon of venture, capital availability, quick returns, added income to underwrite R&D to maintain a technologically advantageous position, and political/government pressures. In addition, licensing can be a useful means to test foreign markets, to protect patents and trademarks against cancellation for nonuse, and to establish operations in countries that are sensitive to foreign ownership.[1]

Foreign Technology Licensed in the United States

Some examples of foreign technology that have been licensed in the United States include:

Wankel Engine. The German Wankel rotary combustion engine is licensed to the Curtiss-Wright Corporation, which has the rights to sublicense to North American automotive manufacturers and makers of other types of equipment. The engine is now in a "feasibility study stage."

Plateglass. Over half of the plateglass produced in the United States is made under licenses for the Pilkington "float glass" process developed and owned in the United Kingdom.

Ball-Point Pen. The modern form of the ball point pen was developed by two Hungarians in the early 1940s. Several U.S. companies, including Eversharp and Eberhard Faber Company, licensed the rights for production in the United States.

Cellophane. Of French origin, cellophane was first produced in the United States in 1924 by DuPont, which was assigned the U.S. patent, process, and know-how rights by the French developer.

DDT. Although originally prepared in 1874, DDT's insecticidal qualities were not realized until discovered by J.R. Geigy, a Swiss firm, in 1939.

Helicopters. The first practical design was produced in Germany in 1937. United Aircraft Corporation produced the first successful U.S. design in 1941.

Insulin. Eli Lilly Company, an American firm cooperated with a group of experts associated with the University of Toronto to develop techniques for the factory production of this Canadian invention.

Jet Engine. The jet engine was the result of simultaneous development efforts in England and Germany during the late 1930s and early 1940s.

Magnetic Recording. A Danish invention, it was first produced in the United States in 1903.

Penicillin. Penicillin was discovered in England in 1928.

Polyethylene. The low-temperature process for manufacturing polyethylene was originally developed in Germany in the mid-1950s and has since been licensed to United States firms.

Self-Winding Watch. Primarily a Swiss invention, its development dates back to the 1920s.

The above is far from an all-inclusive list of licensed products but does afford a representative sample. Relatively few Americans appreciate the impact of foreign technology which has been integrated into products and processes that affect our standard of living. By the same token, considerable American technology has been employed in various degrees in foreign countries with substantial impact in those countries.

Granting a License

It is generally accepted worldwide commercial practice that a holder of a tangible or intangible property right may assign (1) the entire interest in the right, (2) an undivided share of the exclusive right, or (3) an exclusive right for use in a specified part of the world. Any conveyance of a less than full interest is a license.[2] A holder may grant a license for a term to any part of the rights. The rights granted can be either an exclusive license to one licensee or a nonexclusive license to one or more licensees.

Since the 1970s there has been a trend toward selective licensing between Western and Eastern European entities. This has apparently come about as a consequence of Soviet recognition that technological parity can be reached in some technologies quicker and cheaper by licensing than by attempting local development.

In developing countries the granting of a license can foster the development of new industries where a major investment could not be justified because of capital limitations or the level of technology does not exist. In addition, licensing often provides for technical assistance in an expanding market as well as a means for integrating improved technology. In some instances, without licensing arrangements the technology could actually be excluded by direct import restrictions or tariff barriers.

Licensing Problems

There are a number of factors that distract from the values of licensing. The potential licensor and licensee should be aware of the following:

Every licensee is a potential competitor.

The licensor uses the licensee's manufacturing and marketing operations and these may not be completely satisfactory. This could result in quality problems and marketing practices that could affect the licensor's reputation.

Allied to the aforementioned is limited control or possible loss of direct control.

Licensing is probably the least profitable way of exploiting a foreign market. It is often a compromise position dictated by factors that preclude direct operation and control.

Licensing Feasibility

Table 14-1 indicates the procedural activities relating to the acquisition of technology via licensing. For the most part, these activities are sequential. The decision not to license may be made at any phase in the sequence. There may be tradeoffs wherein considerations of potential benefits and liabilities require extensive information, as indicated in the various steps, before the decision can be reached.

Prefeasibility studies examine all pertinent internal and external factors associated with financing, producing, and marketing the product. This is the initial overt act and serves to determine those alternatives that deserve further study. The second step in the feasibility stage is the in-house practicability study, which is much more comprehensive. This step should look not only at the economic and technical implications of the technology but also at such implications as they affect the organization's objectives and resources.

Positive recommendations from the initial stages lead to further indepth explorations in the organizational phase. At this point it is necessary to seek inputs from top management and legal and financial entities, as well as from other functions that might be involved. This is the time that a separate new venture group may be established. In any event, top management should now appoint a project (product) manager. The manager would be vested with guidelines, policy enunciations, authority, and objectives and be expected to guide the venture along its future path.

The legal experts should make detailed investigations of patent antitrust implications, legal restrictions, and governmental regulations, both foreign and domestic. Legal obstacles may spell the demise of a venture. Financial experts should become actively involved and continuously apprised of developments so as to maintain a cost perspective of the venture. They should also estimate the tax implications of the proposed transaction. It is necessary in this phase to brief and update top management on new developments on a continuing basis.

The decision phase involves top management and the project leader. If the venture proves to be too expensive, too difficult, or otherwise untenable, management probably will decide to scrap the idea. In Table 14-2 are a

Table 14-1. Organizing Steps for Successful Technology Licensing

Feasibility Phase
Prefeasibility study (marketing and technical evaluations)
In-house practicality study
Organizing Phase
Organizing for exploitation
Top management considerations
Financial considerations
Legal considerations
Decision Phase

number of important Dos and Don'ts that serve to summarize the three phases of this process.[3]

Licensing Sources

A company interested in purchasing the right to practice someone else's invention has a number of sources from which to choose. These sources of patents, trademarks, and technological know-how are divided into the following six categories:

Independent, unincorporated inventors.

Small, incorporated laboratories.

Nonprofit research institutes.

Universities.

Governmental agencies.

Industrial concerns.[4]

Table 14-2. Dos and Don'ts of Technology Licensing

Dos
Study internal technical, marketing and financial needs
Study external markets
Analyze competition
Determine ultimate consumer opinion
Develop interdisciplinary team
Adopt strategic plan
Select project leader
Establish new venture group
Provide balanced organization
Develop realistic capital needs
Study patent/antitrust implications
Determine legal restrictions
Analyze government regulatory requirements
Acquire know-how plus patents
Use techniques followed by successful companies
Require strong support of management
Analyze facts and terminate if necessary
Don'ts
Believe in-house market surveys without objective outside market studies
Back new technology too far from existing product lines
Spread organization too thinly
Expect quick positive results
Allow existing production and marketing to kill project with negative inputs
Allow not-invented-here attitude to prevail
Allow in-house research to suffer from licensing-in or purchase of technology
Use licensing-in for defensive or market control purposes only
Allow creative scientist or engineer to dominate
Allow negative financial department input to overweigh other positive factors
Allow legal counsel to be exclusive negotiators

There are numerous examples of where lone, independent, unincorporated inventors have made significant discoveries. Often these people have lacked the entreprenual incentive, economic wherewithal, or intuitive insight to pursue their invention to economic fruition. These people logically become a natural source for licensing agreements.

The small laboratory is another possible source because such laboratories are developing products and processes for commercial exploitation. They have been known to both sell and buy licensing agreements. Small laboratories frequently suffer from insufficient capital, inadequate market outlets, and inexperienced management. Some partnership arrangement by licensing may provide the prospect for returns which are not probable if there is a sole or independent approach to product or process exploration.

Nonprofit research institutes are prolific sources of ideas, patents, patent applications, and prototypes. They have well-established procedures for negotiating licensing agreements.[5] Universities can also be invaluable sources of ideas. Universities are the birthplaces of vitamin D, streptomycin, bacitracin, the cyclamates, and metal hydrates. The major difficulty in tapping this source is to identify the technology. There are few, if any, listings available.

The government is another excellent source of technology in most Western countries. In the United States, for example, the federal government owns approximately 25,000 patents and currently generates about 2000 per annum. The inventions come mainly from government laboratories. Government-owned inventions also evolve from contractor inventions to which the government has title. Part of 101-4 of Title 41 of Code of Federal Regulations, obtainable from the U.S. Government Printing Office, provides guidelines for licensing of government-owned inventions. The National Technical Information Service (NTIS) established by the U.S. Department of Commerce provides, on a fee basis, technology searches. This is the central source for the public sale of U.S. and foreign government-sponsored research, development, and engineering reports.

Licensing from an industrial firm may be the easiest source of technology. Often the technology sought may have been one that has already been exploited commercially. Adapting a proven and successful technology minimizes trial and error and risk. This often leads to a simple turn-key agreement.

Reciprocal Benefits and Marketing

In some situations, the licensor is only willing to enter into the licensing agreement because of reciprocal license grants. In these instances, the reciprocal license serves as partial compensation. Where a foreign licensee has no reciprocal rights or know-how to offer the licensor at the time a licensing agreement is concluded, a grant-back or feedback commitment with respect to the rights and know-how supplied is often included in the licensing contract. This is termed "cross-licensing."

Cross-licensing is more common than the one-way license. Normally the licensor will want the advantage of whatever improvements the license develops; therefore, even the one-way license is likely to have a reciprocal twist by way of grant-backs. Often foreign licensing has much to offer. There may be incentive if the license arrangement joins two large firms where each have desirable technology which can be exchanged. Furthermore, pooling of patents and reciprocal cross-licensing may be necessary to unfreeze the technology of both parties when they hold complimentary patents which are technically or commercially indispensable to each other.[6]

The overall profitability of licensing transactions tends to increase the revenues attributed to R&D. This source of income may be used to fund additional R&D work.[7] Marketing of technology via the licensing process can also provide a profitable return on spinoff technology developed from major projects that would otherwise lie idle. Often these spinoffs are valuable but not directly useable by the developing company. Marketing technology even to competitors in certain cases can actually enhance its commercial use. Certain industries demand at least two sources for a product before it will be adopted for widespread use.[8]

Some licensees avoid cross-licenses and would rather negotiate a separate agreement covering any reciprocal license grants. The avoidance may be for antitrust reasons. Feedback rights and know-how are commonly made available to the licensor on an exclusive and royalty-free basis. However, if new patents or products are covered by the return grant, the contract may stipulate that licenses will be granted royalties mutually agreeable to the parties.

Income and Tax Regulations

Income from licensing patents, trademarks, copyrights, and know-how is, like most income of a corporation, taxable in the majority of nations. It is usually termed "royalty income." Income from licensing is not limited to *royalties* but includes such items as the following:

Technical assistance fees.

Sale of components or materials to license.

Lump-sum payments.

Technology feedback.

Royalty-free reciprocal license rights.

Fees for engineering services.

Sales of machinery or equipment to licensee.

Management fees.

According to U.S. tax law income from a direct license is taxed at ordinary tax rates, with a credit against the U.S. tax bill for the foreign income tax that is withheld on payments by the licensee. Capital gains treatment may be obtained for licensing income under certain circumstances. If all substantial rights in a patent are transferred, the transaction may qualify as a sale or exchange. This necessitates either transfer of legal title to the patent with registration of the transferee as patent owner, or granting an exclusive license within a particular area for the life of the patent. Sales of trademarks and know-how may also be made by assignment of title or granting an exclusive license in a limited geographic area. The sale of know-how is fraught with problems due to its "intangible" state. It must be clearly established as "property" and the licensee should receive the right to prevent its unauthorized disclosure.[9]

The exchange of patents, trademarks, and know-how for shares in a foreign company constitutes a taxable exchange of a capital asset. This type of transfer has been increasingly used, particularly when the transferee country taxes dividends at a lower rate than royalties. In the United States, the exchange of patents, trademarks, and know-how for shares in a foreign corporation may be tax-free for the licensor if an advance ruling can be obtained from the Internal Revenue Service that the proposed transfer is not for the principal purpose of avoiding taxes.

Export Controls

In the United States, as in most other countries, there are federal regulations which inhibit the outflow of technical data. The Export Administration Act of 1969 authorizes the President to prohibit or curtail exports of commodities and technical data from the United States. Under this authority, the U.S. Department of Commerce administers a control system based on national security, foreign policy, and short supply needs in the United States. Most exports to other destinations require either a validated license for which the exporter must submit a signed application, or a general export license. A general export license is a broad authorization which requires neither an application by the exporter nor the issuance of an export license document.

There are two general export licenses for foreign transfer of technical data. The general export license, "GTDA" (General Technical Data Available to All Destinations), authorizes American exporters to transmit to any destination unclassified technical data of a scientific or educational nature. The other general export license, "GTDR" (General Technical Data Under Restriction), authorizes exports of a broad range of unpublished technical data to free world countries. Such exports are, however, subject to assurances from the foreign importer against the unauthorized use of both the data and its direct product.

Aside from data relating to a few highly strategic commodities, most technical data can be exported to free world countries under these general export licenses. Generally available published data and scientific and educational data may also be exported to Eastern European countries under general license. On the other hand, export of unclassified, unpublished technical data requires a validated license to Eastern Europe, Asian communist areas, and Cuba.[10] Most developed nations have laws which are similar to those of the United States as pertains to licensing exports.

The control of exports can be controversial. A case in point is the export restriction of computer hardware from the Control Data Corporation to the Soviet Union. The computer was to be sold with the understanding that it would be used in the Soviet Union to monitor weather. The sale was held up by export restrictions on the basis that the computer could be adapted to military purposes. Export restriction hinged on possible use, other than alleged purchase use, and the fact that the computer was far more advanced and sophisticated than any computers then available within the Soviet Union. The Control Data Corporation fought the restriction on the grounds that the computer actually did not reflect the current state of the art and that more advanced versions were then available in the United States. Also, it was contended that if we did not consummate the transaction, the Soviet Union could procure similar equipment from foreign competitors.

Antitrust Limitations

Whatever the actual subject matter, or the form, if the license agreement tries to limit the competitive freedom of either party, American antitrust laws may be relevant to the transaction. It should be recalled from Chapter Nine, that many foreign nations have, in recent years, enacted laws which are similar to American antitrust legislation. There are a number of factors that govern whether the transaction is in violation of antitrust laws; these include:

The market.

The territorial restrictions.

Type and combination of restraints.

There are many reasons as to why a licensor and a licensee may not wish to compete. Apart from the licensing transaction, both parties may want the advantages of territorial market division and the division of world markets between themselves. To both, the primary motivation may be the elimination of competition, and the procurement of the license may be of secondary importance.

Given different interests and motivations, several devices may be used to achieve the desired restraint. The strongest limitation is the explicit negative covenant which restricts markets, products, prices, or other terms of sale of either the licensor or licensee. A slightly milder limitation is the stepup in royalty rates if specified territories, output quotas, or terms of sale are transgressed. Where patents are being licensed, an effective territorial restraint may be achieved without explicit contractual provision by dividing the foreign patent rights among the various licensees. Thus, the commercial interests of the parties may assure competitive forbearance and the observance of mutually respected ground rules without need for explicit contractual limitations. Such tactic cooperation may be fortified when the licensor has equity participation in the licensee's company. In instances where licensing leads to restrictive competition the licensing agreement can be subject to legal constraints even though the products manufactured under the license are not themselves restrained or do not flow in domestic markets.

"Covenants not to compete" attached to a transfer of unpatented information are critical antitrust problems posed where there is international know-how licensing. These covenants may take the form of agreements not to sell within certain countries, to sell only to certain customers, to manufacture only specified goods with the licensed know-how, or to apply the know-how in plants in certain countries. The covenants may also restrict quantities to be sold or set prices at which the goods may be sold.

A cross-license in itself is not illegal; an exchange of patents and technological know-how is usually beneficial to all concerned—companies and countries alike. Such an exchange may, however, be for the purpose of restraining trade, which is in direct conflict with antitrust laws. The cross-license, like the one-way license, will almost always be projected into the future, especially if it joins firms separated by distance, law, and language. The exchange will frequently speak of all present and future patents related to a product line rather than to specific existing patents. This may be for the purpose of restraining competition.

Trademarks may also be the matter of international grant, assignment, or license. There may be considerable pressure on the owner to transfer the trademark to a foreign licensee in order to maintain the company's trade name in the foreign markets to which they cannot export because of cost or protectionist barriers. To the extent that trademark registration confers a lawful power to exclude others from use of the trademark in a country's markets, a territorial allocation of trademark goodwill may be accomplished without contractual restraint.

Although there may not be explicit agreement to do so, mutual interest in competitive immunity may lead each competitor to confine production to the licensed mark even though it has no great intrinsic commercial value. The problem is analogous to the use of "paper" or spurious patents to achieve an otherwise unlawful agreement. However, the trademark is even more easily adapted to such purpose, since there is no analogue to the requirement of patentability. And, unlike the patent situation, no license is necessary in order to open the product or process itself to competing producers; only the label is at stake in the case of a trademark. No matter how restrictive a particular foreign licensing agreement may be, a nation's antitrust laws will normally only be concerned if its particular foreign or domestic commerce is affected. Unless licensing is itself commerce within the meaning of the Sherman Act, United States foreign or domestic commerce will be affected by a license arrangement only when the terms of the license either restrict imports by foreigners into the United States or interfere with American export freedom. Accordingly, a restriction imposed on a French license against making sales in Italy would not involve the American antitrust laws even though the licensor was an American.[11]

Licensing as an Operational Strategy

Licensing is a favorite strategy for small- and medium-sized companies as well as large companies. Foreign operations may extend beyond licensing arrangements, which are generally viewed as a supplement to exporting or manufacturing rather than as the only means for entry into foreign markets. Licensing as an operational strategy may be employed when capital is scarce, when import restrictions forbid any other means of entry, when a country is sensitive to foreign ownership, or when it is necessary to protect patents and trademarks against cancellation.

Agency Agreements

Legal Aspects of Agency

By using locally based agents, a transnational firm can conduct multiple business operations simultaneously in various foreign locations. Agents operate "in the name of" the transnational firm. Agency is a common practice in international business activity. It is feasible where the maintenance of a sales force is not economic.

By U.S. law, in agency agreements, one party, called the "agent," agrees to represent or act for the other, called the "principal," subject to the principal's right to control the agent's conduct in matters entrusted to the agent.[12]

An agency relationship can be created for any legal purpose. The respective relationship created by agency law establishes certain rights and duties, which are similar to those that arise from the law of torts and contracts.

Agents must act with reasonable care and exercise skill and knowledge typical to the place where they perform. In addition, they must exercise any particular skills that they possess. Failure to meet these standards allows a principal to bring an action against the agent. Generally, agents must act exclusively for the benefit of their principals in all matters within the scope of the agency agreement. This duty obliges agents not to use unfairly any information or property that they have acquired by virtue of the agency.

The principal must pay the agent the agreed compensation for the services that have been performed. The principal may also provide a suitable place for the agent to work and must use reasonable care to prevent injury to the agent. In a principal–agent relationship, the parties have agreed that the agent will act on "behalf of and instead of" the principal in negotiating and transacting business with third persons.[13] This relationship will affect the principal's rights, duties, and obligations. An agent is empowered to perform legal acts that are binding on the principal. For example, an agent can bind a principal in a contract with a third person. An agent has "derivative authority" to use a degree of independent discretion in carrying out the principal's business.[14] Foreign laws do not necessarily parallel U.S. laws pertaining to agency contracts and agreements.

Classification of Agents

Agents do not purchase goods; they place or take orders; the title to such merchandise (or technology) does not pass to the agent. Agents may be classified in many differing ways. Classed according to selling rights, they may be exclusive, semiexclusive, general, or lessee.[15] An exclusive agent is one who has the sole right in all sales of goods in the territory covered by the agreement. In such a legal agreement the agent is assured of commissions on all sales in the territory.

In some instances agents do not have exclusive rights on all sales of goods in their territories. The semiexclusive agent's rights are modified in various respects. For example, it is frequently found that sales to governments are reserved to the exporter, and the agent has no claim and receives no commission on such sales.

The general agent is an exclusive agent of a peculiar type. Normally where an exclusive agent is appointed, the importer/exporter agrees to appoint no other agents or subagents to that territory without the consent of the exclusive agent. This is not the case of a general agent. Here the principal may appoint as many other agents in that territory as required or desired. It is also possible that a general agent represents more than one client; representation is normally not in lines that are directly competitive.

A lessee is an agent who receives a product (or technology) from the principal and, in turn, leases it to customers. The title is never transferred, as there was no sale.[16]

Selection of Agents and the Contract

Proper selection of agents is an important process. Much of the burden of overseas operations rests on their ability. The main factors to be considered in sifting a list of candidate agents are their character, competence, financial status, reputation, prestige, product lines, sales policies, location, trade group affiliation, nationality, and political influence. All these considerations must be analyzed not only from the present perspective, but with a view toward future transactions as well.

The terms of the agency as finally agreed upon constitute the agency contract. It is customary to reduce the terms of the contract to writing. The terms of the contract should specify the rights, duties, and liabilities of the principal (the exporter/importer) and the agent. Matters that are normally included in this contract are the following:

Principal's concessions and obligations.

Agent's concessions and obligations.

Mutual concessions and obligations.

Jurisdiction clauses.

Termination clauses.[17]

Agency Contract Terminations

There are numerous reasons as to why an agency agreement would be prematurely terminated; among these are poor agent performance, changes in the product, policy changes, and economic fluctuations. Regardless of the actual reason, precipitately terminated agreements usually causes legal problems in international circles.

To deal with the issues created from the agent's point of view, some foreign governments have enacted protective legislation establishing special requirements and procedures to compensate the agent for injury. In those countries with protective legislation, the thrust of the laws is to go beyond the written agreement to the underlying basis of principal–agent relationship. These laws recognize that the agent has a proprietory interest in the goodwill and local market as created for the principal's sake. Accordingly, an economic value is assigned to this interest, and the foreign law entitles the agent to share a part of this value as compensation for the loss of future revenue.[18]

Transnational firms with agents in countries where laws provide for agent protection should have cognizance of the appropriate provisions and should seek to conduct agency arrangements to avoid possible legal liability. Special care should be taken that all contractual provisions are valid under the laws of each country in which the supplier and the agent will conduct their business, and that the agreement fulfills the requirement of local law.

Franchise

Franchise Provisions

Another form of international cooperative arrangement is the franchise. This is a hybrid form of licensing in which the franchiser usually provides market knowledge, in some instances capital support, management training, and expertise, purchasing arrangements, advertising and product identification.

The U.S. Federal Trade Commission has defined franchise as "an arrangement in which the owner of a trademark, a trade name, or a copyright licenses others, under specified conditions or limitations, to use the trademark, trade name, or copyright in purveying goods or services." The franchise system has also been described as an organization composed of distributive units established and administered by a supplier as a medium for expanding and controlling the market for its products.[19] Each franchise dealer is a legally independent but economically dependent unit of an integrated business system.

The growth in franchise operations has outdistanced the law of franchising. There has yet to develop a solid body of national or international laws relating to franchises. In the United States, the courts tend to apply general common law principles and the federal or state statutory provisions where they are applicable.

Types of Franchises

There are three types of franchises: distributorships, chain-style businesses, and manufacturing or processing plants. A distributorship occurs where a manufacturing concern (franchisor) licenses a dealer (franchisee) to sell its product. Often, a distributorship covers an exclusive territory.

A chain-style business operation occurs when a franchise operates under a franchisor's trade-name and is identified as a member of a select group of dealers who engage in the franchisor's business. The franchisee is generally required to follow standardized or prescribed methods of operations. Often, the franchisor requires that minimum prices and standards of operation be maintained. Frequently the franchisee is obligated to deal exclusively with the franchisor to obtain materials and supplies.

A manufacturing or processing plant arrangement is one in which the franchisor transmits to the franchisee the essential ingredients or formula to make a particular product. The franchisee then markets it either at wholesale or at retail, in accordance with the franchisor's standards. A good example of this type of franchise is bottling plants to make soft drinks.

Advantages and Disadvantages

Franchising provides a highly effective means to gain rapid market expansion and exposure with a minimum of capital outlay by the franchisor. Because franchisees make their own investments in order to undertake business operations, they have a strong incentive to make a profit. The franchisee gets the benefit of all of the franchisor's trade names and trademarks. In addition, the franchise carries with it goodwill, product recognition, and customer acceptance as well as the benefits of the franchisor's national and international advertising.

Because there is a dearth of international franchising laws, the tendency thus far has been to favor the franchisor in court cases. Other disadvantages include the reality that the franchisor selects the locations for the franchise, dictates operating procedures, often stipulates capital requirements, may not afford territorial protection, usually reserves the rights to terminate the franchise agreement, and draws a percentage from sales not profits.

Franchises in Practice

Over the past several years, a number of franchisors have initiated foreign operations. For example, there are Kentucky Fried Chicken outlets in Japan, Great Britain, and Germany. There is a McDonald's restaurant on the *Champs-Elysees* in Paris. Volkswagan's automobile franchises are found throughout the world. American motel (hotel) franchisors such as Ramada Inn and Holiday Inn are found in Belgium, France, Italy, Spain, The Netherlands, and Denmark. These are recent entrants. Such companies as Coca-Cola, Pepsi-Cola, Hertz, and various oil companies have franchised internationally for years.

Coproduction

Cooperative Venture

Coproduction, a relatively new international cooperative arrangement, is apparently increasing in use.[20] It is a technique whereby a domestic firm and a foreign firm will enter into agreement to produce a end-item using certain domestic componentry and technology plus certain additional componentry and technology produced in the foreign country. The final assembly of the end-item is accomplished in the foreign country by the foreign firm.[21] In the past, most of the coproduction ventures were in the field of military technology. However, the implications and potential for commercial usage should not be minimized.

As used by the U.S. Department of Defense the term "coproduction" is defined as follows:

> Any program wherein the U.S. government, under the aegis of an international diplomatic level or Ministry of Defense-to-Department of Defense agreement, either directly, or indirectly through specific licensing arrangements by designated commercial firms, enables an eligible foreign government, international organization or designated commercial producer to acquire the "know-how" to manufacture or assemble, repair, maintain and operate, in whole or in part of specific weapon, communication or support system, or an individual military item. The "know-how" furnished may include research, development, production data and manufacturing machinery or tools, raw or finished material, components or major sub-assemblies, managerial skills, procurement assistance or quality-control procedures.[22]

It is important to note that this detailed definition includes the notion that coproduction inherently bears the "blessings" and approval of governmental agencies. It is this aspect which makes coproduction such a valuable consideration for the transnational firm.

Coproduction has often been compared to "cooperative development." The two arrangements are not synonymous. Cooperative development (codevelopment) is a joint venture between nations in the design, research, and development of a specific end-item of equipment to be jointly used. The key objective then, of codevelopment is the *development* of an end-item *vis à vis* the *production* associated with coproduction.[23]

Benefits of Coproduction

Figure 14-1 portrays the interrelationship between the nations and firms involved. The technology was developed by Firm A, which has been actively producing the item. Subsequently, a demand for the product has developed in

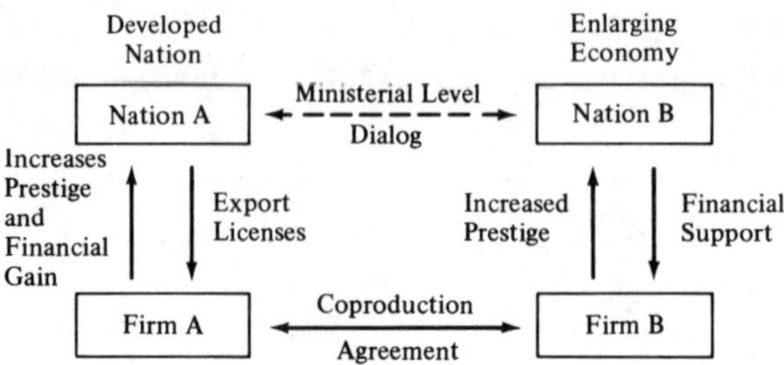

Figure 14-1. Coproduction agreement.

Nation B. For any number of reasons the product is not available in that nation. Negotiations are initiated by one of the four entities identified in Figure 14-1; e.g., either of the firms or either of the national governments. After negotiations, as illustrated in the figure, a bilateral agreement is concluded, with approval of the firms and national governments. The agreement enables Firm B to build the product utilizing some components built in Nation A and some additional components produced in Nation B. The actual technology is provided by Nation A, with the final assembly accomplished in Nation B by Firm B.

An example of a coproduction arrangement is the "Lockheed TRISTAR" aircraft, which is a jointly produced airplane by a British company and the McDonald aircraft company of the United States.

The fuselage and wings are built by McDonald, while the Rolls-Royce engine is built in Great Britain.

Other coproduction arrangements which led to development of weapon systems are the F-16 fighter aircraft, the "Improved Hawk" antiaircraft missile, and the German–French "Roland" missile.

The most ambitious project is the British–German–Italian MRCA (multi-role combat aircraft), both in terms of financial involvement and end-item procurement. Several other ventures include a 155 mm howitzer, being produced by Britain, Italy and Germany, the German–Dutch Flakpanzer anti-aircraft gun, and the British–French "Jaguar" aircraft.

There are a number of practical similarities found in coproduction and licensing agreements. These include the ability to gain entry into new markets with modest investment, relative ease of technology transfer, and increased financial gain. However, there are a number of factors involved in coproduction that are worth noting. These include, from the viewpoint of Nation B:

Providing a new industry which can be translated into other products.

Adapting the pace of industrialization to the capabilities of the receiving country and firm, a variation of appropriate technology.

Providing technology, know-how, and training on an "as needed" basis.

Providing vital managerial guidance and expertise.

Creating a balance between transferred and indigenous domestic input factors.

Enabling the use of a product which under normal conditions might be excluded due to import quotas, currency problems, or balance of payment considerations.

Forming the basis for additional long-term projects and additional commercial dialog.

Coproduction arrangements usually occur when the supplier cannot satisfactorily complete the sale in a foreign market alone. This may be because it lacks sufficient capital to produce directly in the country, because the government of the host country does not sanction foreign firms, or because the customer will not purchase foreign-manufactured items. Often the product coproduced has had a successful marketing life. Coproduction can extend the product life and prove profitable to the product originator by providing a partial market which probably would not exist without a coproduction agreement. The receiving nation benefits from the technology, can develop its own capabilities, and has access to the product cheaper than would be possible by direct purchase.

Coproduction and Developing Nations

Coproduction offers an unusually attractive opportunity to gain entry into the markets of developing nations. It may be used in those instances, as indicated, where there are currency restrictions or balance of payment problems or when there is a possibility of "expropriation." Expropriation is an overt act whereby the foreign host government seizes the property of the outside firm. Because of the "partnership" arrangement and the "umbrella effect" of the comprehensive coproduction arrangement, expropriation risks are greatly reduced.

The significant advantage for the supplier is an extension of the production life of the product which naturally extends the inherent profitability. This effect is seen in Figure 14-2. The figure represents the life cycle of a typical product, passing through stages of research, development, production, market

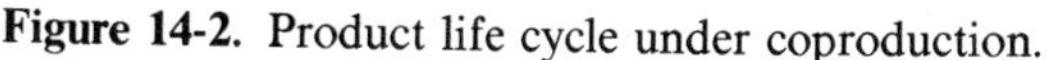

Figure 14-2. Product life cycle under coproduction.

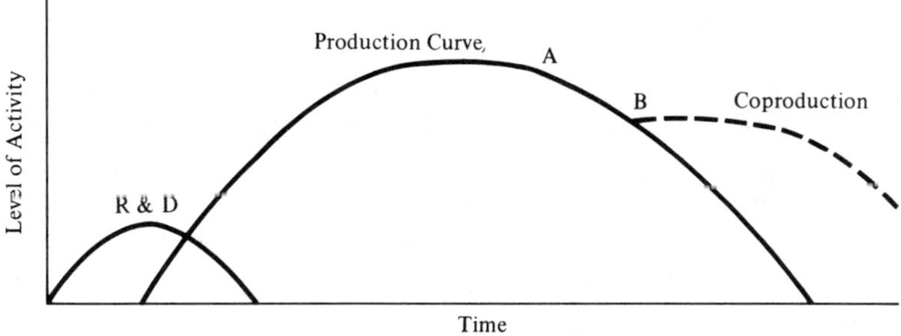

introduction, market saturation, and decline in demand (path A). Note that the coproduction agreement actually extends the life of the product to a significant degree. Very likely this "extra life" (path B) occurs at that point of market saturation in Nation A. Since some of the more technically advanced components are produced in Nation A, under the coproduction agreement there is a continuation of jobs and increased profits for Firm A. This labor effect would not have occurred in pure licensing agreements.

A number of "attendant advantages" of coproduction exist, such as economies of scale, cost reductions, induced demand for parts replacements, the requirement for technical liaison and services, and production continuity. Even though the supplier does not have the entire pie, the remaining piece is large enough to be very attractive. Without coproduction, there, in most cases, would not even be a piece of the pie.[24]

Other intrinsic value offered by the coproduction arrangements in developing nations includes the infusion of money into the project by Nation B, further reducing the risks of the supplier. Risk is also minimized since only proven products are usually coproduced. The extension of the product's life cycle also serves as the spur to generate additional R&D in Firm A for the "new and improved" version because of an increase in market size and incremental profits.

East–West Coproduction

Coproduction has been used by Western nations in trading with the communist countries of Eastern Europe. In those instances, the Eastern partner normally contributes the labor, the raw materials, and the plant, and some of the components. The Western partner usually supplies advanced equipment, production know-how, product design, engineering specifications, managerial expertise, and often international marketing channels.

The concept is an ideal one for dealing with the COMECON nations. It provides for Western investment without becoming overbearing. It also provides needed consumer goods for the communist nations and capital returns due to sales in world markets. The capital return, of course, assists in balancing the international accounts of the Eastern nations.

Examples of East–West coproduction are numerous. The West German firm of Rheinstahl entered into an agreement with the Hungarian Ministry of Machine Building for the construction in Hungary of quarrying equipment, machine tools, and other steel products utilizing Hungarian, as well as German semifinished components. The Austrian firm of Simmering-Graz-Pauker has a coproduction arrangement with the Hungarian group called Komplex to build power plants in India. The project is financed through Hungarian–Indian bilateral clearing arrangements. IKEA, a Swedish furniture company, supplies machinery and designs for the semimanufacture of furniture in Poland under its own technical control. The semimanufactured goods are shipped to Sweden for finishing steps and marketing.

The inducements for these arrangements parallel those previously discussed. The Eastern partner is enabled to produce the sort of items for which there already exists a large demand in local or Western markets. Full capacity economies in Germany, Switzerland, Sweden, and several other European countries have on occasion generated manpower shortages. These shortages have in the past, been relieved by expensive importation and on-the-job training of foreign workers, with considerable social dislocation and expensive new requirements for housing, schools, etc. The Eastern European countries, on the other hand, still have considerable labor surpluses. The Western partners benefit by the opening of markets by the use of the components, parts, and services supplied by the Western partner.

A subjective benefit of coproduction arrangements is that they require a great deal of communication and mutual understanding on a variety of matters. Such ventures tend to push ideological differences into the background and allow for mutual concentration on the task at hand.

This message is being received by the poorer nations of Asia, Africa, and Latin America. Coproduction may well prove the appropriate vehicle by which the developed nations can be induced to assist in raising the living standards and economic levels of the "have-not nations" of the world.

Joint Ventures

Restrictions

Joint ventures have much in common with licensing agreements and often arise from them; as when a licensor accepts equity in return for patent as know-how rights. They are also directly and indirectly encouraged by the refusal of some countries to permit operations by wholly owned foreign subsidiaries. Developing nations, in particular, have been less understanding of and are more reluctant to host large multinational corporations. This has been especially evident since the 1974 United Nations' report on multinational corporations. This report, which was prompted by International Telephone and Telegraph's attempt to interfere with the 1972 Chilean election, found that host nations were beginning to push for a significant measure of local control over foreign investment in their nations. Most apparently favored majority domestic ownership or national regulation and control. However, as a less-favored alternative, the joint venture has been identified as a reasonable arrangement.[25]

Incentives for Joint Ventures

When two or more persons (firms) combine their interests in a particular business enterprise and agree to share in losses or profits jointly or in proportion to their contribution, they are engaging in a joint venture.[26] Cateora and Hess have said that a joint venture is primarily a merger or partnership of two or more participating companies which have combined resources for marketing, financial, and/or managerial reasons.[27] The joint venture is normally created in contemplation of a limited activity or a single transaction, but it can also be used where there is a continuing relationship between the parties to the joint venture.

The joint venture, as a means of engaging in international commerce, has become increasingly prevalent during the past decade. Many countries have adopted favorable postures toward joint business ventures, recognizing the inherent benefits of transferred technology.

Commensurate with this spirit, countries have begun to encourage joint ventures by providing special legal benefits. The resulting laws usually cover such matters as provisions relating to entry and approval procedures, assurances against expropriation, rights to transfer profits and capital, exemptions from taxes, and remission of certain import duties. However, there may be requirements that prior governmental approval be obtained for the project, either as a condition for starting up or in order to assure the parties that their foreign exchange needs will be satisfied. Restrictions on the local partner are apt to be examined carefully, especially as pertains to restraints on exports. Some governments interfere in the setting of royalty rates, while others are sensitive to possible adverse effects on domestic competitors.[28]

One of the strongest motivations for a transnational firm to enter into a joint venture is the significant reduction in political and economic risk as a result of the local partner's contribution to the venture. There are a number of additional reasons that a joint venture would be attractive to the transnational firm:

It enables a company to utilize the specialized skills of a local partner.

It allows the transnational firm access to a partner's local distribution system.

It enables transnational firm to enter markets forbidden to foreigners.

It enables expansion when otherwise constrained by personnel and financial limitations.

Fundamentally, the foreign investor is looking for a return on the investment that commercially justifies investing in one foreign country as opposed to another. Further, the investor usually expects a legal guarantee of the security of the investment: i.e., assurance against nationalization, expropriation, etc. And finally, the foreign investor is concerned with receiving favored licensing and taxation privileges to include earnings and repatriation.

The host country, on the other hand, has its own objectives which must be achieved if a joint venture is to be considered. First and foremost is that the joint venture should be linked to a national economic development plan. In this sense, the venture should enhance through employment, production, and balance of trade, the stature of the host country. Consistent with this objective, of course, is the laying of foundations for a permanent export industry. In line with these objectives there should be a concurrent management and technical skills training program for indigenous personnel as a means to upgrade national personnel capabilities and for the replacement of foreign nationals. Finally, the objectives of the host nation would normally include linking foreign investment to social development, such as construction of infrastructure facilities (railroads, highways, etc.) and educational facilities.[29] There are numerous examples of application of these objectives. Cases in point are a comparison of IBM ventures in India *vis à vis* Aramco ventures in Saudi Arabia.

IBM maintained complete control over its subsidiary and allowed India to be only a market and assembly station, but not a technology development site. This resulted in IBM being nationalized with no recourse but to take minimum compensation. Aramco, on the other hand, helped Saudi Arabia to train its people in the functioning of the oil exploration company and developed the Saudi infrastructure to include a university. This appreciation of host country psychology and involvement in the country's objectives maintained Aramco's viability even after nationalization, earned Aramco favored construction contracts, and allowed Aramco to continue to own an oil refining plant in Saudi Arabia.[30]

Joint Ventures Forms

There are two basic forms of international joint ventures: the equity joint venture and the contractual joint venture. In the equity venture the foreign enterprise or state gains ownership rights to natural resources, plants, equipment, manufactured goods, and the like. In contractual joint ventures the foreign enterprise does not get direct ownership rights to these items. Contractual joint ventures have found great favor with the international banking community.[31]

Joint ventures can also take other forms. A "regional coalition" is a joint venture of regional enterprises. An example is the Triad Holding Corporation, an Arab-owned and managed conglomerate involving Egypt, Iran, Lebanon, Saudi Arabia, and Sudan. "Fade-out" arrangements are joint ventures with a foreign government or corporation, with programmed takeover by the foreign partner at some future time. These arrangements usually include some sort of licensing agreement. A high-technology enterprise is established using foreign capital. The corporation supplying the high technology trains the foreign partner for the eventual takeover.[32]

According to Perlmutter, a new form of organization is forming, which he calls "industrial systems constellations." These are conglomerates with multiple national identities. Nationally oriented companies form joint ventures to achieve a worldwide competitive advantage without sacrificing their national identities. Examples are General Electrical and Hitachi, which formed General Television of America; Dunlop and Pirelli, in numerous ventures producing automobile tires; and American Motors Corporation and Renault.[33]

National reactions to joint ventures vary widely. India specifies maximum foreign participation at 40% in many industries. Nigeria has a long list of business enterprises which are reserved exclusively for Nigerian ownership, plus a second list in which foreign equity is limited to 40%. Japan still severely limits foreign ownership, but in an increasing number of cases, foreign firms are permitted to own a majority of Japanese firms according to a 1976 *Business Asia* study.[34]

The patterns of joint ventures tend to vary from country to country. American companies prefer complete ownership when possible and tend to avoid joint ventures with governments. European companies are more likely to go into joint ventures with smaller ownership and to participate in government- or union-owned joint ventures. Some interesting patterns emerge; only slightly more than one-third of U.S. businesses abroad are joint ventures, whereas over 60% of European foreign businesses are joint ventures. Some 15–18% of European joint ventures are with foreign governments, whereas only about 1% of U.S. joint ventures involve government participation.[35]

Companies have found that they do not necessarily need majority interest to control joint ventures. The list at Table 14-3 is a set of guidelines developed by Business International Corporation for controlling international joint ventures.

Organization and Tax Considerations

Generally speaking, any of the available business forms may be suitable as a vehicle for a joint venture. However, the civil law corporation or English law "public company" is the most widely used form for productive enterprises organized as joint ventures. Its flexibility and adaptability to effective centralized management generally makes it the most advantageous form of organization for large-scale joint ventures.

Table 14-3. Guidelines for Controlling Foreign Joint Ventures

1. Issue two kinds of stock—voting and nonvoting—that will divide the profits evenly but give a majority vote to the U.S. side.
2. Arrange the deal 49–49 with 2% in the hands of a third party friendly to the U.S. side.
3. Provide in the by-laws that the U.S. side will have a majority of directors.
4. Have the by-laws stipulate that the U.S. directors (even though equal in number with the partner's directors) will appoint the management.
5. Have the by-laws provide that in the case of a tie vote, the position of the U.S. side will prevail.
6. Arrange a 50–50 deal, but with a management contract awarded to the U.S. investor.
7. Arrange a contract for the entire output of the jointly owned producing facility to be sold to a U.S.-controlled marketing company. The marketing company should get what it wants from the producing company.
8. A modification of number 7: give 51% of the producing company to the local partner in exchange for 51% of the selling company.
9. Satisfy the pressure for 50% local ownership by putting the local 50% in the hands of a local insurance company that has no interest in management.
10. Better yet, spread the local 50% over a multitude of shareholders. Union Carbide in India and Kaiser in Brazil have thousands of local shareholders.

Another factor that may influence the use of the local law equivalent of the corporation is that the laws relating to matters such as minority stockholders, preemptive rights, and rights and duties of directors are more apt to be established. Also, if there is to be public equity participation, the corporation is the only practicable alternative because it is usually the only company form in which the shares are readily transferable. If equity participations are to be closely held, the "limited liability company," a business form peculiar to the civil law systems, may be suitable for joint ventures of modest size. Like the corporation, this form of enterprise affords limited liability and continuity of existence. Unlike the corporation, the members' shares can be transferred to a nonmember only after consent and after other members have declined to exercise a prior option to purchase. It is usually subject to less regulation than the corporation and may bear a lower tax burden.

Participants may wish to organize the enterprise under the law of a noninterested nation, and operate the joint venture as a branch. Reasons for doing so include a desire to minimize taxes or to withdraw profits to a second country where they may be accumulated free of danger of currency depreciation, political instability, or exchange restrictions.

The place where the joint venture is incorporated is often critical for tax purposes. Corporations created in the United States are taxed here on their worldwide income. Corporations created in a foreign land are generally taxed here on income from sources inside the United States. Organizing as a branch of a U.S. company would subject the joint venture to U.S. tax. If the venture is to operate in Latin America, there is a 14-percentage-point income tax advantage in forming a Western Hemisphere Trade Corporation (WHTC). WHTCs are used by many manufacturers to carry on their operations in Canada and South America.

Foreign corporations have often been used in lieu of WHTCs with the result that no U.S. tax is payable.

U.S. tax on foreign source income earned by foreign corporations is deferred or postponed until the foreign corporation pays dividends to U.S. shareholders. The foreign corporation in most cases will pay some foreign income tax. This payment may be credited against U.S. income tax. If the foreign tax is lower than the U.S. rate, a tax is paid to the United States on foreign source income at a rate equal to the excess of the U.S. over the foreign rate. When the foreign rate equals or exceeds the U.S. rate, the credit cancels U.S. tax on foreign source income.

Antitrust Rulings

While there are very few decisions on the antitrust consequences of international joint ventures, it is clear that the Sherman Act applies. The provisions of this act have been applied to joint ventures between American and foreign firms. For example, the arrangement between the DuPont Company (U.S.) and the Imperial Chemical Industries Company (U.K.) to form a jointly owned Canadian subsidiary for the purpose of selling in Canada, was held by a U.S. court to be an attempt to divide the Canadian market. The decision was that one of the two companies must divest itself of its holding in the joint Canadian company.

In the case *U.S. v. Trinken*, 341 U.S. 593 (1951), it was ruled against an American company and its two foreign partners. Here an agreement not to compete among the companies, interlocked by stock ownership, was held illegal and not a legitimate "joint venture."

Joint ventures which include marketing in their activities are probably the most vulnerable to antitrust actions. Fugate states, "the cases seem to teach that joint marketing ventures between actual or even potential competitors will almost surely run into antitrust trouble."[36]

Foreign joint ventures pass under the applicable foreign antitrust laws. Until recently, challenges on antitrust grounds to American acquisitions or mergers with foreign companies were nonexistent. This situation has changed quickly and European nations, in particular, are moving to pass antitrust laws similar to those in the United States. The first signs came in 1969 when the Commission of the European Committee (Common Market) challenged Continental Can Company's acquisition of various European packaging manufacturers.

Some Additional Factors Affecting Joint Ventures

The ownership pattern of a transnational corporation tends to be related to its organizational structure. Mixed area and matrixed-structured transnational firms tend to avoid joint ventures. They will accept joint venture arrangements if competition requires cost-cutting measures or marketing communication across international boundaries. "Mother–daughter organizations" lean toward wholly owned subsidiaries. Transnationals with international divisions or worldwide product divisions tend to form joint ventures with local enterprises.

Joint ventures are normally encouraged in this country as long as they do not conflict with antitrust considerations. The U.S. government provides guarantees against some of the political risks and, in certain cases, a portion of the business risks, relating to new investment in about 80 of the less-developed nations. The political risks covered are currency inconvertibility, loss due to expropriation, and damage attributable to war, revolution, or insurrection.

American companies fall under the statures of the Foreign Corrupt Practices Act of 1977. Under this law, substantial corporate and individual fines and prison sentences may be levied for making improper payments (bribes) to foreigners to ruin business or influence foreign legislation. Additionally, the Export Administration Act of 1977 and the Trade Act of 1974 prohibit the boycotting of one nation in order to do business with another, and limit most-favored-nations trade status to those countries not deemed to be human rights violators.

At Appendix B is a checklist designed to assist transnational firms in their negotiations with foreign business persons. The list is appropriate for use when considering joint ventures, direct investment, and licensing agreements.

Technological Consortiums

Large Complex Projects

Technological consortiums are ventures between two or more nations and/or between two or more companies where extensive resources are required to accomplish a technological objective. The consortium can involve partnerships between nations, firms, or nations and private enterprise.[37]

The consortium approach to foreign investment can offer a number of advantages: (1) it may reduce the risk of investment by any one entity; (2) it may permit the participating organizations to secure better terms of investment than if each organization negotiated separately; (3) it may reduce the time spent on negotiations with the host government; and (4) it may permit the pooling of resources. Difficulties include the following: (1) those associated with organizing the consortium; (2) reaching agreement on initial investment terms; (3) reaching agreement on day-to-day operations such as division of work; and (4) operational cooperation to transcend the tendency to view participation nationalistically.

Organizational Incentives

As mentioned, technological consortiums have been formed because of perceived need, economic constraints, and technological limitations. In some instances there have been political overtones in addition to the more immediate economic and technological purposes. In the case of the Concorde, Great Britain has not always been such a willing and happy partner. British participation was assured by the French in return for French support of Great Britain's application for European Common Market membership. Technological objectives have been achieved, but the costs escalated far above initial expectations and the direct economic returns have been disappointing.

Many desirable projects are of such size and complexity as to be prohibitive undertaking for a company or a nation. The technological consortium has evolved as an operational form to fill a void and enable the execution of projects which might otherwise not be feasible. The consortium arrangement also encourages internationalism through active participation and commitment.

There are generally three types of innovations which encourage the formation of a consortium: (1) a complex product (e.g., a weapons system), (2) a product designed for multiple customers (e.g., Concorde), and (3) a complex system of organizations and hardware to accomplish an end or deliver a service (e.g., the Washington, DC Metro system).

There are normally four levels of involvement in the consortium process:

Ministerial.

Planning and policy making.

Operational control.

Consortia.

The ministerial level is at the top of the political structure and bears the approval/disapproval authority for consortium programs and organizations. Included are alliance/treaty councils, defense ministers/secretaries, or their direct representatives. The planning and policy making level is usually comprised of representatives of each nation and firm involved in the project. These representatives are empowered to carry out and sanction at the operational level.

The operational level (or executive level) usually consists of an agency or body, with governmental and industrial representatives of each nation and major industry involved. It is responsible for executing the program and for carrying out policies and plans received from higher levels. The consortia levels are divisions created beneath the executive agencies for research, development, and production management. Special divisions may be created for particular purposes such as language, liaison and centers for technical documentation control. Additional industrial subconsortiums sometimes result for development and production of major components.[38]

Some Representative Examples of Consortiums

In 1965, the National Iranian Oil Company (NIOC) established an agreement with a technical consortium consisting of Assienda Generale Italiena Petroli (AGIP of Italy), Phillips Petroleum Company (United States), and Oil and Natural Gas Commission of India (ONGC). Iranian policy stipulated that Iran must be an equal partner in any venture in terms of financial contribution and representation on the Board of Directors. The profits were to be split 75–25% in favor of the host country. The consortium was instrumental in generating tremendous levels of petroleum outputs that were unlikely without the outside technical assistance and initial funding.

In 1971, the World Bank organized a consortium, called the Consultitative Group for International Agricultural Research (CGIAR), to establish and operate a number of agricultural research centers. Eleven centers were established in developing nations. CGIAR now consists of 20 governmental agencies, private institutions, and the World Bank. The efforts of these research centers are concentrated on improving the yield of grains through genetics and disease control, systems of crop rotation, and systems of livestock production. Related objectives involve the adequate domestic production of fertilizer, the adequate distribution of new hybrid seeds, and making fertizilier available to the small farmer. Funding rose from $15 million in 1972 to $42 million in 1975.

Some examples of other consortiums organized to undertake specific technological investigations include the following:

1. *European Atomic Energy Community (EURATOM)*. EURATOM was founded in 1958 to coordinate the progress of R&D of atomic centers in Italy, Belgium, the Netherlands, and West Germany, and has built three reactors. The value of EURATOM has become doubtful to many of the participants. Its main usefulness now is found in its dissemination of information.
2. *European Council for Nuclear Research (CERN)*. CERN was founded in the 1950s to study high-energy nuclear physics. Its budget has included the construction of a large high-energy accelerator in Geneva.
3. *European Satellite Association (ESA)*. ESA was established in the 1960s to design satellites for launch in U.S. rockets. Several rockets have been launched and ESA is currently assisting in the Ariadne and Space Shuttle programs.
4. *Concorde*. This supersonic transport was the joint product of the British BAL Corporation and the French Aerospatiale Corporation.
5. *ATLANTIC Project*. A NATO consortium program to develop a long-range maritime patrol aircraft.
6. *The Alaskan Slopes and North Seas Oil Exploration Projects.*

Tax Obligations and Antitrust Provisions

The tax considerations of the consortium are tied to the nature of the consortium, the percentage of participation and ownership, the organizational form of the arrangement—corporation, partnership, etc.—and the countries involved for tax purposes. The U.S. taxes would likely accrue in accordance with the guidelines as outlined for joint ventures.

To date, consortiums apparently have not run afoul of U.S. or foreign antitrust laws. The probable reason is that because of their scope and magnitude, they have inherently included various governmental participation from the outset. It is doubtful that a consortium could establish a base that would interfere with trade without engendering fierce and swift governmental reactions.

Consortiums — An Overview

Need has been the prime motivator for the establishment of most technological consortiums. While need has been a strong incentive and enabled accomplishment that might otherwise have not been possible, it should be pointed out that there have been some significant problems associated with this operational form. National pride and jealousies inevitably impede progress and cooperation. Differences in operational philosophies, often reflecting cultural differences, have been in some projects disruptive, affecting mutual trust and professional respect.[39] Even though there has been the potential for positive achievement and technological success, consortiums have often fallen prey to petty problems which have sapped their effectiveness and contribution.

Despite problems it appears that technological consortiums will increase in number and impact. Motivational factors and other considerations affecting consortiums include the following:

All participants must be highly motivated and cooperative.

They must have a sense of urgency to develop/produce the item.

Firm requirements and specifications must be agreed to in advance.

High risk, high need, and advanced technology requires a consolidation of resources.

There must be a minimum of government involvement in management and details.

Where possible, there should be a proportionate sharing of risk and resources.

Financial arrangements must be agreed on early.

There has to be a willingness to relinquish some degree of nationalistic interests to achieve other technical, performance, design, or economic goals in the project.

Participants should be interdependent for components.

Summary

There are numerous ways to transfer technology, including international cooperative arrangements. These arrangements have as their aim an internationally generated profit. The two major types of cooperative arrangements are the *licensing agreement* and the *joint venture*. There are several off-shoots of these arrangements to include coproduction, codevelopment, and technological consortiums. Additionally, there are forms of arrangements which allow for special tax considerations—Domestic International Sales Corporations, Western Hemisphere Trade Corporations and Webb-Pomerene Export Associations are examples (discussed in Chapter Fifteen).

The National Industrial Conference Board (NICB) in a study of licensing by 240 American companies has identified the following reasons for licensing:

To obtain extra income from technical know-how and services.

To spread the costs of company R&D programs.

To maximize returns from research findings and accumulated know-how.

To retain established markets that have been closed or threatened by trade restrictions.

To reach new markets not accessible by export from existing facilities.

To enter or expand foreign markets quickly with minimum effort or risk.

To gain cost or other advantages of local manufacture without committing capital abroad.

To augment limited domestic capacity and management resources for serving foreign markets.

To provide overseas sources of supply and services for important domestic customers.

To accommodate military needs of U.S. or foreign governments.

To develop market outlets for raw materials or components made by the domestic company.

To build good-will and acceptance for other company products or services.

To develop sources of raw materials or components for other company operations.

To conserve dollar exchange.

To discourage possible infringement, impairment, or loss of company patents or trademarks.

To bolster a minority-ownership role.

To diversify sources and types of company income.

To pave the way for future investment.

To acquire reciprocal benefits from foreign know-how, research, and technical services.

To further the economic development of a foreign country.[40]

There are, naturally, some drawbacks in the use of licensing agreements; these are as follows:

Creation of potential competitors (licensee).

Potential marketing to undesirables (third countries or specific groups).

Weak control over manufacturing.

Weak control over marketing.

Inability to collect royalties.

Potential for payment reduction through currency devaluations.

The specific rights and privileges in a contract vary with respect to the conditions necessary in order to make the licensing agreement worthwhile for both the licensor and licensee. They are governed by such factors as the bargaining positions of the two parties, and their long-range regional or global production and marketing plans. Patent, trademark, and antitrust regulations of the countries involved also influence the provisions of a licensing contract.

The following specific questions should be considered by a company before drafting a license contract:

How may patents, processes, or trademarks be used?

How will technical assistance be rendered?

Which products are included in the agreement, and to what extent?

What territory is to be covered by the license?

How should the licensor be compensated?

What happens if compensation cannot be paid by the licensee?

If sublicensing is permitted, how should it be carried out?

What are the provisions as to duration and cancellation?

What are the assignment possibilities?

What rights does the licensor have in developments by licensee?

What visitation and inspection privileges are held by the licensor, and on what terms and conditions are they to be exercised?

Can the parent company inspect accounts?

What provisions are there for satisfactory promotional and sales performance and for adequate quality control?

What governmental approvals are required?

What tax factors are involved?[41]

International joint ventures can take many forms depending upon the needs and circumstances of the partners and the conditions under which the collaboration agreement is consummated. Differences between international joint ventures can be traced to factors such as the percentage of the total equity of the joint venture held by each of the partners, the number of partners involved in the joint venture, and their characteristics.

A transnational's ownership of a joint venture may vary from a majority to an equal or minority participation in the equity capital of the joint venture. Joint ventures offer several advantageous features especially when coupled to local partners:

Market access to closed economies.

Market awareness by indigenous partners.

Additional managerial talent.

Additional capital.

Increased morale of indigenous workers.

Market opportunities with local governments.

Access to local raw materials.

Local production.

Special R&D skills.

Joint ventures can also have some unique disadvantages. Hence, transnational firms should carefully weigh the advantages against the possible disadvantages. Some of the prominent disadvantages include the following:

Equity disputes.

Staffing disagreement.

Managerial disputes.

Profit distribution.

Third country distribution disputes.

Production factor prices and availability.

Tax distribution conflicts.

Arrangements such as coproduction, codevelopment, and technological consortiums are hybrids of the licensing arrangement and the joint venture. For the manager, each of the hybrids offers unique strengths and weaknesses. Therefore, in selecting the form of arrangement, where licensing, joint venture or hybrid, consideration should be given to the following factors:

Tax implications.

Equity contributions.

Risk.

Market.

Management and control.

Planning.

Legal considerations.

Governmental and political interest.

Termination provisions.

Endnotes Chapter Fourteen

1. See *Foreign Business Practices*, U.S. Department of Commerce, November 1975, for several informative articles pertaining to industrial property rights in the international environment.
2. W.L. Fugate, *Foreign Commerce and the Antitrust Laws*, Boston: Little, Brown and Co., 1973, p. 267. For a comprehensive approach to foreign licensing see Robert Goldscheider, *1979 Technology Management Handbook*, New York: Clark Boardman Co., 1979.
3. See Willard Marcy "Acquiring and Selling Technology—Licensing Do's and Don'ts," *Research Management* 22 May 1979, pp. 18–21 for an excellent discussion of this process.
4. Murray Senkus, "Acquiring and Selling Technology—Licensing Sources and Resources," *Research Management* 22, May 1979, p. 22.
5. See H. Orlans, *The Non-Profit Research Institute*, New York: McGraw-Hill Book Co., 1972, for a comprehensive listing of these nonprofit institutes in the United States.
6. K. Brewster, Jr., *Antitrust and American Business Abroad*, New York: Arno Press, 1976, pp. 154–155.
7. B.A. Anderson, "Acquiring and Selling Technology—Marketing Techniques," *Research Management* 22, May 1979, p. 26.
8. *Ibid.*
9. *Foreign Business Practice*, *op. cit.*, p. 76.

10. *Ibid*., p. 77.
11. For a complete and detailed discussion of licensing and antitrust laws see W.L. Fugate, *Foreign Commerce and the Antitrust Laws*, Boston: Little, Brown and Co., 1973; K. Brewster, *op. cit*., and, G.E. Folk, *Patents and Industrial Progress*, New York: Harper & Brothers Publishers, 1942.
12. K.W. Clarkson, R.L. Miller, and B. Blair, *West's Business Law: Text and Cases*, St. Paul: West Publishing Co., 1980, p. 544.
13. *Ibid*., p. 545.
14. South-West Law Book.
15. R.L. Kramer, *International Marketing*, Dallas: South-Western Publishing Co., 1970, p. 450.
16. *Ibid*., pp. 451–452.
17. *Ibid*., pp. 453–463.
18. *Foreign Business Practice*, *op. cit*., pp. 1–2.
19. Clarkson et al., *West's Business Law*, *op. cit*., p. 730.
20. Daniel D. Roman, *Science, Technology, and Innovation: A Systems Approach*, Columbus, OH: Grid Publishing, 1980, p. 192.
21. For an in-depth, excellent discussion of military coproduction, see Howard Ivan Lukens, *Coproduction Within the U.S. Helicopter Industry*, unpublished doctoral dissertation, The George Washington University, February 1975.
22. Department of Defense Directive 2000.9. "International Coproduction Projects and Agreements Between the United States and Other Countries or International Organizations," March 26, 1968.
23. *Coproduction Within the U.S. Helicopter Industry*, *op. cit*., pp. 33–34.
24. Roman, *op. cit*., pp. 192–193.
25. Irwin Miller, "Multinational Corporations: The U.N. Report," *Business Horizons*, December 1974, p. 21, and *Multinational Corporations in World Development*, United Nations Department of Economic and Social Affairs, New York: Praeger Publishers, 1974.
26. *West's Business Law*, *op. cit*., p. 591.
27. P.R. Cateora and J.M. Hess, *International Marketing*, Homewood, IL: Richard D. Irwin, 1979, p. 541.
28. *Foreign Business Practice*, *op. cit*., p. 70.
29. W.C. Friedmann and Leau-Pierre Begwin; *Joint International Ventures and Developing Countries*, New York: Columbia University Press, 1971, p. 2.
30. "Tavoulareas: A Wily Negotiator on Aramco," *Business Week*, January 20, 1975, p. 69.
31. J.D. Aronson, "Politics and the International Consortium Banks," *Stanford Journal of International Studies*, XI, Spring 1976, p. 43.
32. David H. Heenan and Warren J. Keegan, "The Rise of Third World Multinationals," *Harvard Business Review*, January–February 1979, p. 108, and, *Multinational Corporations in World Development*, p. 43.
33. "The Rise of Third World Multinationals," *op. cit*., p. 107.
34. "How Companies Resolve Common Problems in Japanese Joint Ventures," *Business Asia*, September 19, 1976, p. 289.
35. Cateora and Hess, *International Marketing*, *op. cit*., p. 542.
36. *Foreign Commerce and the Antitrust Laws*, p. 366.
37. Roman, *op. cit*., p. 193.
38. A.H. Cornell, *An Analysis of International Collaboration in the Organization and Management of Weapons Coproduction*, Ph.D. dissertation. Washington DC: American University, 1969, pp. 180–182, 205.

39. Roman, *op. cit.*, p. 195.
40. E.B. Lovell, *Foreign Licensing Arrangements: Evaluation and Planning*, Studies in Business Policy, No. 86, New York: National Industrial Conference Board, Inc., 1958, p. 15.
41. C.H. Lee, "How to Reach the Overseas Market by Licensing," *Harvard Business Review*, Vol. 36, No. 1. (January–February), 1958, p. 81.

CHAPTER FIFTEEN

International Institutional Arrangements

Early Cooperative Agreements

Objectives

As early as 1910, South American statesmen realized the desirability of an intercontinental alliance to solve economic and technological matters, to provide mutual military assistance in times of aggression from outside the continent, and to preserve peace within the continent.[1]

The alliance failed, largely because of the strong nationalistic (and selfish) tendencies among the signatories. Other early international agencies whose charters included coordinating pure international technological activities were the International Telegraphic Union, founded in 1865, and the Universal Postal Union, founded in 1875.

The first worldwide efforts at international cooperation and organization occurred as a result of World War I. One of the more significant results of the Paris Peace Conference of 1919 was the creation of the League of Nations. The purpose of the league was to maintain peace, arbitrate international arguments, and promote international cooperation. Despite the ardent support of President Woodrow Wilson, the resulting Treaty of Versailles was not ratified by the United States Senate. This omission by the United States no doubt hurt the chances of the League's efforts and no doubt contributed to its demise. The League was, however, successful in resolving many conflicts among smaller states and in providing financial assistance to troubled and developing nations such as Austria, Hungary, and the Balkan states. Unfortunately, the reluctance of the world's great powers to either exercise or respect the provisions of the League Covenant resulted in its virtual dissolution in the Munich Pact of 1938.[2]

With the advent of World War II, the warring nations saw the obvious need for an international organization with more power and clout than the old League of Nations. Thus, the United Nations was born in San Francisco in 1945. Among its purposes were international peace and security, the development of friendly international relations, and the achievement of "international cooperation in solving international problems of an economic, social, cultural, or humanitarian character."[3] In addition, Article 52 of the United Nations Charter permits the establishment of regional agencies "for dealing with such matters as are appropriate for regional action." Article 57 permits the creation of specialized agencies with "wide international responsibilities in economic, social, cultural, educational, health and related fields."

There are multinational bodies and international cooperative arrangements that focus on science, technology and innovation on a regional and a worldwide basis. This chapter examines the role of nonprofit institutions in stimulating business on an international basis, the nature of some of the international institutional arrangements, some of the institutional projects, possible technological implications, and a projection of the future role and importance of these nonprofit institutions.

Role of Nonprofit Institutions in Stimulating Business

United Nations

In addition to the operations of private and national governmental organizations, world trade is promoted through the activities of the United Nations, the Organization of American States, and various other international organizations.

While individual countries promote their own trade and investments, the United Nations is interested in the development of trade of all nations. A primary instrument for worldwide programs is the Economic and Social Council. The Council has observed that long-term development of trade, particularly for the less-developed countries, depends on their ability to export and upon policies affecting basic commodities such as manufactured goods.[4]

The Commission on International Commodity Trade is concerned with the stability of trade in primary products. UNCTAD, or the United Nations Conference on Trade and Development, deals largely with the problems of the lesser-developed countries. The United Nations International Trade Center helps these lesser-developed countries find markets for their exports by providing information on export markets and marketing development and by exporting promotion services and the training of personnel.

The United Nations publishes a wealth of information for and about world markets, such as the *United Nations Yearbook,* the *UN Statistical Yearbook,* and the *Directory of International Trade* and a host of special studies from its specialized agencies on innovation, production, agriculture, and health and technical assistance.

Kurt Waldheim noted the immense contributions made by science and technology toward resolving the problems of mankind. He seemed dismayed, however, that despite the tremendous forward strides of technology there still remained a "gulf between the advanced and the developing countries," and that rather than being reduced, the gap seemed to be widening.[5] Waldheim pursued the theme that developing countries must help themselves, primarily utilizing such conduits as common international institutions franchised to encourage growth and their own organizations for development. He went on to note that "no nation is too small to have within its frontiers the technical and intellectual capacity to recognize what are its needs and to determine what is relevant to those needs."[6]

Waldheim noted, however, that the developed nations and the United Nations can and must give important assistance and advice. He felt that the developed nations must undertake a commitment to assist the developing countries in undertaking research and building up the essential technological infrastructure to make them viable entities and devote a percentage of their own R&D efforts to the developing nations. There is a strong inference that technological assistance for developing nations has both political and economic overtones. Developed nations can technologically assist developing nations by means of aid programs; often the actual vehicle for implementation of technological assistance programs are the transnational organizations.

Regional Organizations

In addition to the efforts of the United Nations, there are numerous regional organizations that exist to promote and facilitate the trade of their members. Some of them carry out extensive publication programs that can provide data and insight regarding marketing conditions and methods within the member's territories. The Organization for Economic Cooperation and Development (OECD) is made up of 19 European countries, plus the United States and several other nations. OECD will be discussed in more detail later in this chapter.

The North Atlantic Treaty Organization, consisting of European nations, plus Canada and the United States, has also been a stimulus to technological innovation through the ambitious support of R&D efforts for new weapon systems. This organization, which was formed by the Allied Powers that prosecuted World War II against the Axis Powers, provides for the national defense of the various members through a combined program of weapons development and troop deployment. The weapons development, production, and distribution is made through the aegis of private industry of the NATO nations.

In the Western hemisphere, cooperation is achieved, at least in part, through the efforts of the Organization of American States. Information helpful to businesses is distributed through its Secretariat, the Pan American Union.

Institutional Arrangements

International Organizations and Technological Promotion

This section examines the role of several international organizations in the discovery, development, and transfer of technology. These include the United Nations Family of Organizations, one regional organization—the Organization of American States (OAS), one independent organization—the Organization for Economic Cooperation and Development (OECD), and one military organization—the North Atlantic Treaty Organization (NATO).

The United Nations Family[7]

The technology development activities of the UN are spread throughout a number of its specialized agencies. These include inter alia: the UN Development Programme (UNDP), the UN Educational Scientific and Cultural Organization (UNESCO), the UN Industrial Development Organization (UNIDO), the World Bank Group, the International Labor Organization, the International Telecommunication Union, and the Universal Postal Union. A large amount of the UN technological activities is controlled by the UNDP, however the other agencies are semiautonomous and carry out programs of their own as well as acting as executing agencies for UNDP projects. The following paragraphs discuss UNDP, UNESCO, UNIDO, and the World Bank Group.

The *UN Development Programme* is the world's largest multilateral technical assistance program. It was created in 1966 by combining the governing bodies of the Special Fund and the Expanded Program of Technical Assistance. The funding and programming of these activities were kept separate until 1971 when they were administratively combined.

The UNDP is not an action agency but does provide funds to other special agencies of the UN who act as executing agencies. The UNDP maintains field representatives in about 94 less-developed countries who work closely with the host government to identify needs for assistance and help in obtaining it, assist in smoothing the path to project implementation, and help to assure smooth follow-ups. The field representative is a key element in the UN program since he or she is responsible for all UN activities within a LDC.

The UNDP has four functions: (1) it carries out surveys and feasibility preinvestment studies to determine economic potential of a country and plan the use of natural resources; (2) it establishes and strengthens educational institutions; (3) it creates and expands research centers; and (4) it supplies technical training and advisory services. As in all UN assistance activities, technical assistance under the UNDP is supplied only on request. In 1972 UNDP supplied funds of about $308 million in programs worth a total of over $500 million (a portion of the cost is borne by the recipient of the aid) in about 135 countries.

UNESCO was established in 1945. The Organization's assistance activities are either permanent activities (such as the exchange of information and documentation, assistance in international nongovernmental organizations, and preparation for international conferences) or short-term special assistance projects. UNESCO activities are within the following categories:

1. Educational projects aimed at eradicating illiteracy, educational planning, improving the status of teacher, and building schools.
2. Natural science projects aimed at developing the structure of science, fostering international scientific cooperation, and applying science and technology to development (specifically hydrology, seismology, and marine science).
3. Social science projects aimed at problems affecting the evolutionary societies.
4. Cultural dissemination.
5. Mass communications projects to free the flow of information and stimulate its distribution.
6. International exchanges of scientists.
7. Technical assistance projects aimed at the extension and modification of all levels of educational facilities, teacher training, teaching of scientists and engineers, assistance to scientific research and technical documentation services, and the development of social science and mass communications teaching facilities.

The UNESCO activities are funded both through its sources of funds and through UNDP.

UNIDO was established in 1966 to promote and accelerate industrialization in less-developed countries. Its functions include:

1. Helping governments prepare requests for technical assistance;
2. Helping governments strengthen national institutions;
3. Coordinating Industrial Development activities of the UN; and
4. Providing research results useful to developing countries.

It maintains 20 some field advisors with regional responsibility for UNIDO activities and sponsors a large number of meetings, seminars, and training courses to assist developing countries to industrialize. UNIDO also uses its own funds and the funds of the UNDP for which UNIDO is an executing agent.

The World Bank Group[8]

The World Bank Group consists of three legally independent financial institutions with interlocking staffs: the International Bank for Reconstruction and Development (commonly called the World Bank), the International Development Association (IDA), and the International Finance Corporation (IFC).

The World Bank, founded as a result of the Bretton Woods Conference in 1944, has as its purpose the loaning of money either to governments or to organizations under guarantees from their government. "The Bank's Articles of Agreement require that loans made or guaranteed by the Bank shall, except in special circumstances, be for the purpose of specific projects of reconstruction or development."[9] The main differences among the organizations are that the World Bank loans long-term money at close to conventional international rates, the IDA loans very long-term money at no interest charging only a nominal service charge, while the IFC loans directly to businesses without government guarantees and may purchase equity offerings. In 1975 the World Bank committed about $4.32 billion in loans, IDA committed about $1.58 billion in credits, while IFC committed about $216 million in investments.

Many of the countries and organizations borrowing from the World Bank Group need technical assistance to help identify good programs, prepare the project proposals, and set up suitable administrative mechanisms. The World Bank has supplied this assistance largely as a part of its normal financial activities. These have included advice on how to prepare projects and on the selection of outside consultants (whose fees can be financed as part of project funds) to assist in preparing and managing a project. In addition, the World Bank has provided technical assistance in areas outside the strict banking relationship. This assistance is limited to areas in which the Bank may be expected to have special competence and where assistance would be particularly useful in obtaining financial assistance for high-priority projects.

The World Bank initially found that most of its borrowers lacked personnel capable of preparing a detailed plan for development. After trying survey missions which attempted to identify development possibilities and to make recommendations leading to a detailed program, and the use of resident advisors, the World Bank now maintains a Planning Advisory Division, which provides "...technical assistance to member countries regarding the appropriate machinery for the formulation and execution of development plans and programs."[10] This assistance includes all forms of management consulting in the establishment of planning agencies and may include resident advisors if desired.

The World Bank also performs several types of studies which provide technical assistance by identifying potential projects for the country. The first of these is the "sector study" which analyzes one economic sector (e.g., communications) within a country or a region in order to derive a coordinated investment plan and identify projects for the sector. The second type is the "feasibility" study which analyzes projects already identified for economic and technical feasibility. These studies are financed either by grants from the UN Development Programme (UNDP), by grants from the World Bank if less than $200,000 is required, or by a project preparation credit from IDA. Within its normal financial activities the World Bank provided about $160 million in technical assistance in fiscal 1975 (June 1974–June 1975). The Bank also acted as Executing Agency for about $5.4 million of UNDP-financed studies.[11]

Organization for Economic Cooperation and Development (OECD)[12]

The Organization for Economic Cooperation and Development (OECD) was founded in 1960 as a successor to the Organization for European Economic Cooperation which had been formed under the Marshall Plan after World War II.[13] OECD policies are designed to obtain maximum economic growth and stability in its member countries, help member and nonmember less-developed countries to expand, and help the expansion of world trade.[14] OECD members include 18 Western European countries, the United States, Canada, Japan, Australia, New Zealand, and Yugoslavia (which has special status). Although primarily concerned with economic cooperation, the OECD members have agreed to cooperate in the scientific and technological areas. In contrast to UN organizations, the OECD efforts include both developed and less-developed countries. The transfer efforts aimed primarily at nonmember developing countries have been concentrated under the Development Assistance Committee, and OECD Development Center, while those concerning member countries have been concentrated under an interdisciplinary secretariat, the Directorate for Scientific Affairs which serves the Committee for Scientific and Technical Personnel, the Committee for Research Cooperation, and the Committee for Scientific Policy.

The Development Assistance Committee (DAC) was established by the major capital exporting countries (in 1969, 95% of the world economic aid originated in DAC member countries) to assist in the development of less-developed countries by increasing the flow of resources through coordination of efforts. In addition to coordinating the assistance efforts of its members, the DAC has a modest program to provide assistance to the less-developed European members in the establishment of policies, plans, and programs for development and in the training of personnel. The Technical Cooperation Working Party guides the technical assistance programs within the nonmember less-developed countries. The Working Party efforts have been limited to attempts at gathering more accurate data and advising members on how to provide assistance.

The OECD Development Center was established in 1963 to create a link between OECD members and nonmembers.

> The purpose of the Center is to bring together the knowledge and experience available in member countries of both economic development and the formulation and execution of general policies of economic aid; to adapt such knowledge and experience to the vital needs of countries or regions in the process of development and to put the results at the disposal of countries by appropriate means.[15]

The Center conducts research on the most important less-developed countries' economic problems, such as industrialization, the role of industrial entrepreneurs in development and in agriculture, employment and investment. Its efforts to transfer technology to less-developed countries have included seminars in developing countries concerning technology transfer among personnel from developed and less-developed countries, the publication of documents concerning these problems, and the Development Enquiry Service to help answer questions raised by the lesser-developed nations.

The Committee for Scientific and Technical Personnel is concerned with the development and utilization of these types of personnel within the OECD member countries. Among its programs are the Center of Educational Research and Innovation founded in 1968. The Center's efforts include development of programs for the socially disadvantaged, curriculum updating, and the development of new methods of teaching.

The Committee for Research Cooperation encourages the exchange of information of scientific and technical research among member countries. Advisory groups within the committee have been established to consult on broadly based R&D management, scientific information, and several specific categories such as transportation. The funds required are minimal since the committee only launches projects through the generation of cooperative research, studies, and demonstration projects.

The Committee for Science Policy encourages the exchange of ideas on scientific policy on the national and international levels. It studies the measurement of scientific activities, the relationship between science and economic growth, the policies of member countries, science and lesser-developed nations, and basic research. One of its more important outputs has been a study on technological gaps within the OECD which indicated that as a result of the diffusion of technology across national borders there were no particular technological gap trade problems among OECD members.

The OECD has been criticized for concerning itself too much with activities outside its objectives,[16] occasionally taking too narrow a view in its deliberations, encouraging too much governmental control over transfers, and not taking any operational responsibilities.[17] However, it was intended to be a deliberative body where member nations can discuss problems in international assistance and encourage and critique each others efforts. As such it has been very useful.

The Organization of American States[18]

The charter of the Organization of American States (OAS) was signed in 1948 at Bogota and became effective in 1951 upon ratification of two-thirds of the members. Its purpose is, inter alia, "To promote, by cooperative action, their (member states) economic, social and cultural development."[19] Compared with the international organizations discussed earlier in this paper, the OAS is unique in that with the exception of the United States all member countries are less-developed countries. The technical transfer activities of the OAS are concentrated in the Inter-American Economic and Social Council (CIES) and its Inter-American Council on the Alliance for Progress (CIAP), the Inter-American Council for Education, Science and Culture (CIECC), and Department of Technical Cooperation of the General Secretariat.

The CIES is one of the action organs of the OAS and is responsible directly to the General Assembly. Its purpose is

> to promote cooperation among American countries with a view to attaining accelerated economic and social development; in accordance with the standards set forth in Chapters VII and VIII of the Charter of the OAS.[20]

In 1963 the CIAP was formed to give impetus to the Alliance for Progress. It is a permanent standing committee of the CIES and is essentially its executive committee. CIAP is authorized to study problems and recommend suitable solutions in the technical assistance area, establish financial requirements of projects and strive for ways of meeting them, review development plans for coordinated economic integration, coordinate CIES committee activities and convene necessary meetings, and review the Pan American Union budget.

The CIECC is another action organ of the OAS. Its purpose is to "promote friendly relations and multilateral understanding between peoples of the Americas through education, science and cultural cooperation; and exchange between member states... ."[21]

The Department of Technical Cooperation of the General Secretariat is responsible for the following:

1. The Program for Technical Cooperation established in 1950 by CIES to provide technical training at high levels at centers in universities within the Western hemisphere.
2. The Fellowship Program.
3. Program of Direct Technical Assistance, which provides experts to help members of the Pan American Union.
4. The Technical Assistance Program of the Special Development Assistance Fund.
5. Special Training Program, which provides short intensive courses outside the OAS area.
6. The University Development Program.
7. Program of Integrated Technical Projects.

The function of the Department is "to contribute to technical development of the American countries by acting as a coordination center for reciprocal cooperative endeavors undertaken by the countries composing the organization."[22]

All these departments and committees administer a broadly based technical assistance program which is designed to develop National Technical Cooperative Programs within its members. In 1972 OAS assistance efforts amounted to almost $17 million of which $4.3 million was for technical assistance and $5.7 million was for training. OAS provides short-term aid in the form of direct technical assistance (advisors) and assistance for the specific needs of educational institutions, and long-term aid in the form of the Regular Training

Program for graduate education, the Special Training Program (see above), Inter-American Centers for training and exchange of know-how, Regional Educational Scientific and Technological Development Programs which provide fellowships to complement national efforts, and Integrated Technical Cooperation Projects which provide Latin American professionals fellowships for use outside the OAS.

One of the more interesting activities within the OAS was the Specialized Conference on the Application of Science and Technology to Latin America (CACTAL) in 1972. CACTAL was convoked by the OAS General Assembly upon the urging of both CIES and CIECC to study ways to transfer technology to Latin America more efficiently. CACTAL's 200 experts analyzed problems on the creation and development of technology as well as the OAS efforts in that area, studied facets of technological innovation and transfer, and studied proposals for cooperation between two or more Latin American countries. CACTAL concluded that each country must establish its own development strategy; the development policy should strive for full employment and freedom; the science and technology policies must be aligned with the economic and social policies; the scientific and technological development strategy should use the systems approach to ensure the cooperation of the whole country; the strategy should eliminate the technological dependence on developed countries; applied, experimental, and basic research should be increased; financing should be domestic; and international aid should only fill in the gaps.[23]

North Atlantic Treaty Organization

The Mutual Security Act of 1953 established a Mutual Weapons Development Program. The purpose of the program was to increase the defense posture of friendly foreign nations by speeding up the R&D of advanced military weapons and equipment. With the reestablishment of a technical base in Europe, the program was subsequently phased out. An added economic benefit of the program is that it assisted Europe in the development of products that were competitive with American items.[24]

In December 1957, at a Paris meeting of NATO Heads of Government, Secretary of State John Foster Dulles proposed the initiation of a "coordinated program of research, development and production of a selected group of modern weapons systems... ." In his address, he stated:

> We envisage the prompt initiation of such a program through a temporary NATO *ad hoc* group, consisting of highly qualified scientists, engineers and production experts who, in conjunction with NATO military authorities, would be responsible to the North Atlantic Council. ...In this endeavor, appropriate pooling of talent, combining of resources, and sharing of research and development information should be selectively arranged. ...In order to assure adequate studies and planning in the field of weapons systems and to relate the program closely to our scientific endeavor in the military field, the United States supports the establishment of an appropriate permanent NATO mechanism for this purpose... .[25]

Recognizing the mutual defense interests and interdependence of participating nations, NATO has made a concerted effort to achieve military, economic, and technological collaboration among its allied nations in the research, development, and production of defense weapons systems. Although member nations agree in principle on the need for such collaboration, they were frequently not in agreement as to how to collaborate and what to collaborate on. In general, arrangements provided for Military Departments of Cooperating nations to make agreements on projects, funding, contractor selections, and information access. However, participation by member nations in effect has been selective and vacillating because of varying attitudes by the nations and their industries.[26]

To achieve, where possible, common programs, investigations by nations of requirements and technology must begin at an early stage. To encourage this cooperation, the Conference of National Armament Directors (CNAD) established six major groups which report to it. These are:

NATO Naval Armaments Group.

NATO Air Force Armaments Group.

NATO Army Armaments Group.

Defense Research Group.

Tri-Service Group on Air Defense.

NATO Industrial Advisory Group.

Each of these agencies exchange technological information in areas of prospective future equipment development. The armaments groups, in particular, work to produce multinational NATO cooperative programs for the development of major equipments and weapon systems. In those cases where cooperative developments do not appear possible, these groups work to achieve demonstrated interoperability as a minimum acceptable alternative.

Competition in the commercial world of the Alliance is important throughout the life of any product, not just at its inception. This too is true in the world of military procurement. For example, in the United States the existence of the F-15 aircraft as an available product ensures that the producer of the F-16 continue to strive for efficiency rather than resort to the comparative inefficiency of no available competition. Once in production, the F-16 can serve as a damper to keep the costs of the F-15 from rising abnormally.

Within NATO, there are naturally problems associated with research, development, production and distribution of weapons systems. For years most of the weapons systems were conceived and produced in the United States. While Europe was encouraged to develop its defense industry through mechanisms such as Euro-Group ,[27] the reality is that since World War II, the other NATO nations have had little chance to compete on a real basis with the United States within the military weapons systems arena. Thus, the present movement towards Rationalization, Standardization and Interoperability (RSI) for NATO arms and ammunition is still for the most part the one-way street of the past—United States selling weaponry to Europe. RSI means *Rationalization* of such things as military tactics and doctrine, *Standardization*, and *Interoperability* of equipment and systems. Whatever the policy of the United States toward developing a viable European arms industry, the reality translates to the basic issues of jobs at home and the pure economics of competition—more arms produced in Europe, less Americans employed, less dollars for the American industry, which leads to less viability for the United States arms industry.

Despite the pure realities, there are some signs of increased cooperation. The U.S. government has encouraged a "family of weapons concept." Here the United States would develop and take the lead in producing some types of weapons for all NATO forces, while the European nations would do the same for other types.[28]

Special Cooperative Arrangements

Webb–Pomerene Export Association

An Act passed in 1918 offers unusual international trade opportunities to American trading firms—the Webb–Pomerene (Export Trade) Act, subtitled "An Act to Promote Export Trade." Basically, the Act provides qualified exemptions for export trade associations from the prohibitions of the Sherman Antitrust Act of 1890 and the Federal Trade Commission and Clayton Acts of 1914. This limited exemption from the antitrust laws is conditioned by safeguards to domestic business competition, and there must be no restraint of the exports of any domestic competitor.

One of the important purposes of the Act was to facilitate exporting by smaller companies. In general, a Webb–Pomerene Export Association (WPEA) may act as the export sales agent of the members, arrange transportation for the goods of the members, agree upon prices and terms of trade for sale of the members' merchandise abroad, and arrange for distribution of the products in foreign markets.

There is a wide diversity in firm size among the members of the associations. Some have corporate members relatively large in size, others are comprised of small business units, and still others are a combination of both large and small producers. A review of available data indicates that the successful export associations generally restrict themselves to a single commodity or group of related commodities. [29]

Operations are most apt to succeed if the industry is one in which a limited number of producers account for the major proportion of production, and these leading producers are association members. Associations formed to handle a diversified line of noncompeting products soon decide that joint export operations are not suitable for exploitation or unrelated goods.[30]

Legal formalities for establishing a Webb–Pomerene Association are relatively simple. The Act requires only that the association file with the Federal Trade Commission (FTC) within 30 days after its organization:

A verified written statement identifying office locations or places of business.

Names and addresses of all officers, stockholders, and members.

If incorporated, a copy of certificate or article of incorporation and by-laws; or, if unincorporated, a copy of the articles or contract of association.[31]

The act also requires associations to file on the first of January every year a statement incorporating any changes in the above information which may have occurred during the calendar year. WPEAs cannot participate in cartels or other international agreements which would reduce competition in the United States, but do offer four major initial benefits: (1) reduced export costs, (2) expanded promotion, (3) trade barrier reductions, and (4) improved trade terms.[32] Other advantages include stabilized export prices; standardization of grades, contract terms, and sales conditions; adjustment of claims; and combating commercial combinations that may have played one exporter against another.[33]

The major disadvantage lies in the fundamental inability of members to cooperate. Some associations suffer from poor management. Other associations have encountered keen foreign competition.

Western Hemisphere Trade Corporations[34]

The Revenue Act of 1942 initially enabled the qualifications of firms for special legal and tax considerations as Western Hemisphere Trade Corporations (WHTC). To claim the status of a WHTC, under the 1954 Internal Revenue Code a domestic corporation must meet the following qualifications:

Entire business activities must be conducted within the geographical limits of North, Central, or South America and the West Indies.

Its gross income for the 3-year period immediately preceding is derived from (a) sources outside the United States (95% or more) and (b) the active conduct of a trade or business.

A corporation that meets these qualifications is allowed an additional tax deduction of $\frac{14}{48}$ of its taxable income. The practical consequence is to tax a qualifying corporation on only about 70% of its profits.

All WHTCs must be domestic corporations created or organized in the United States under the laws of any state or the District of Columbia. An exception is made for corporations formed in Canada or Mexico solely to comply with the laws of those countries. Such a corporation is treated as a domestic U.S. corporation for purposes of qualifying for the preferential tax rate. To so qualify, the Mexican or Canadian corporation must be included in a consolidated return. The WHTC may be called upon to pay income taxes in the countries with which it transacts business.

Domestic International Sales Corporations

The Internal Revenue Code of 1971 permitted U.S. firms to establish Domestic International Sales Corporations (DISC) which are entitled to a tax break on export income. This benefit is designed to permit manufacturers and nonmanufacturers to generate a pool of tax-deferred earnings, which can be utilized to expand and modernize export production facilities, intensify or initiate export promotion efforts, or provide more favorable credit terms to export customers.

In order to qualify as a DISC, a corporation is required to confine its activities almost entirely to export selling and certain related activities. As long as the DISC remains qualified, one-half of its export income is deferred from taxation. However, this deferral only applies to that portion of its earnings which it retains and uses for export development purposes. Once a distribution to shareholders is made (and the law requires 50% of export income be deemed distributed), it is taxed to the shareholders at their normal rates. A corporation, to qualify for the DISC benefit, must

Be a domestic corporation.

Have at least 95% of its receipts from qualified export sales.

Have at least 95% of its assets used in export.

Have but one class of stock.

Have a minimum capitalization of $2,500.

Make an election to be treated as a DISC.

Have a separate bank account.

Keep separate books of account.[35]

Enactment of the DISC represents recognition by the United States Government of the economic importance of exporting to the well-being of the nation. It effectively endorses the joint and cooperative effort between business and government to enable a viable United States international commerce position.

Standardization Programs

Informational Requirements

Scientific and industrial progress has transcended national boundaries and it is imperative that every nation keep itself informed of advances in other countries. One of the objects of standardization is to know what problems have already been solved, which work is proceeding, or which research still needs to be done. This will help to eliminate or minimize more contributive duplication of effort and the waste of scientific manpower, which no country can afford. International standardization has played a major role in this process of cross-fertilization by its unification of scientific and technical language.[36]

ISO (International Organization for Standardization)

The International Organization for Standardization (ISO) is the specialized international agency for standardization, comprising in 1975 the national standards bodies of 81 countries. The work of ISO is aimed at worldwide agreement on International Standards with a view to the expansion of trade, the improvement of quality, the increase of productivity and the lowering of costs. ISO work covers virtually every area of technology, with the exception of electrotechnical questions, which are the responsibility of the International Electrotechnical Commission (IEC). ISO brings together the interests of producers, users, governments, and the scientific community in the preparation of "international standards." ISO work is carried out through some 1,630 technical bodies. More than 100,000 experts from all parts of the world are engaged in this work which, by 1978, had resulted in the publication of more than 2,800 ISO Standards, representing some 30,000 pages of concise reference data.[37]

There are some serious problems, however, with the ISO Standards. There is essentially a tug-of-war underway between one group, which includes the United States, Australia, Japan, and Canada, and another group, which includes those nations aligned with the European Economic Community (EEC). The problem is that the highly industrialized nations oppose ISO recommendations that fall far short of sophistication levels already attained. On the other hand, European nations and some developing nations oppose standards stricter than those they are comfortable working with. The balance of power appears to rest with the EEC group because they hold most of the competitive secretariats and can thus control much of the committee actions. Also, all nations have the same voice, one vote. This means that a tiny country can effectively cancel the vote of the United States, Japan, or Canada.[38]

ECE (United Nations Economic Commission for Europe)

The United Nations Economic Commission for Europe was established in 1947. Its membership includes the European membership of the United Nations, including the Soviet Union and the United States. Nonmembers participate from time to time when matters of particular concern are being considered; for instance, Japan participates in meetings concerning motor vehicles. The ECE's work on standards is conducted through subsidiary functional committees and through the meetings of the Government Officials Responsible for Standardization Policies (GORSP).[39] The four main objectives that have been set by GORSP are (1) the safeguard of public health and safety, (2) the improvement of the environment, (3) the promotion of scientific and technological cooperation, and (4) the removal of technical barriers to international trade resulting from disparate standards and technical regulations and their application.[40]

Metrication

The United States has compromised its world trading position to some extent by its reluctance to adopt the metric system of weights and measures. In a world that is estimated to be more than 90% metric, the United States was the last industrialized country in the world to take some official action toward conversion. That action was the Metric Conversion Act of 1975 which was signed into law by President Ford. The Act provides for "voluntary conversion."[41]

The slowness of the United States to convert to the metric system has stemmed mainly from lack of public acceptance. However, just recently the American Society of Mechanical Engineers (ASME) softened its policy regarding the publication of codes and standards in metric units. The original policy mandated the use of metric units in all of ASME's new standards. The revised policy states that codes and standards shall be published in metric units at the appropriate time as determined by industry, government, public, and society needs.[42]

The large transnational firms have spearheaded the metric conversion in the United States. Most of them have adopted special programs to phase in the new units over a period of time. They have also established training programs to orient their employees to the new system.[43]

International Cooperative Arrangements, Technology, and Management

The Range of Cooperative Arrangements

International Cooperative Arrangements enable a company to penetrate foreign markets by exporting its products from the home country; by licensing its patents, trademarks, processes, technology, or know-how to foreign producers; or by manufacturing its products in the foreign market itself. The foreign manufacturing facility could be a wholly owned subsidiary of the transnational company or set up as a joint venture, with the transnational firm and one or more local partners sharing ownership in the subsidiary. The form the cooperative arrangement ultimately takes would be dictated by the type of technology, political controls, economic factors, and management philosophy.

Decisional Impacts

The decisions that management takes regarding the company's worldwide policies on technological development and the subsequent exploitation of the technology by diffusion methods such as licensing and ownership of its foreign subsidiaries are strategic decisions. These decisions have long-range consequences in terms of overall organizational structure and the scope of worldwide operations. The decision to export some or all of its products does not have the same type of major impact on the firm as a decision to license a product to a foreign producer. The firm may decide unilaterally to stop exporting to a certain country without much problem but a decision to curtail licensing operations in a foreign country cannot be easily implemented when a foreign license is involved under a licensing agreement. Similarly, a decision to curtail production in a joint venture in one country, in favor of increased levels of production in another country to serve third markets, would not be easy to implement because of the objections of the local partners.

Dependence on purchased technology also has limitations. Where the technology is purchased, the purchasing organization is not the original entrant into the market. Competition may be severe, profits may be affected, and control can restrict operational latitude. Another aspect is that the firm which has no technology to sell may find it difficult to buy; in some industrial fields cross-licensing and know-how exchange agreements provide incentives for doing business.

If the technology is in a dynamic area, i.e., electronics, communication, or genetic engineering, to cite a few examples, there is the need for constant invention, innovation, and diffusion. Many organizations, which have enjoyed market entry and initial success resulting from innovations, have subsequently seen their position erode as technological competition has caught up or passed them.

In technologically volatile areas organizational survival is predicated on innovation and markets where there are rewarding economic returns. Organizations operating internationally or affected by internationally operating organizations must not be oblivious of technological developments and the range of direct or cooperative arrangements that are possible for economic market exploitation.

Labor Objections to Cooperative Arrangements

Opposition to the transnational enterprise has surfaced in many developed nations. One American labor leader stated the problem in these words:

> There seems to be a kind of speedup on the part of multinational firms to transfer plants, production, products, and technology—and jobs—outside the borders of the United States. Entire industries, growth industries, in fact, badly needed here, and many thousands of urgently needed jobs are exported. To many of us in the labor movement it portends a mass exodus.[44]

This feeling is common as regards joint ventures, coproduction, technological consortiums, and codevelopment activities and, to a lesser extent, licensing. Labor sees these arrangements as a move on the part of management to circumvent the higher wages in the developed nations.

In the United States, for example, labor views technology transfer as an "exporting" of jobs. Labor sees the transfer as making possible the rapid duplication in foreign countries of sophisticated manufactures based on U.S. technology, much of which was developed at the expense of U.S. taxpayers in government-sponsored research projects. The contention is that if the transnational firm did not license technology to foreign producers or to their own foreign affiliates, it would take much longer for foreign countries to manufacture competitive products which might either displace U.S. exports or displace homemade products in the U.S. market. Labor also feels that the transnational firm often can deliberately circumvent national policies to the detriment of labor. The labor movement views the transnational as moving "beyond the laws" of a particular nation.[45]

In-depth empirical studies of the employment effects of transnational activities contradict these views of labor. In a study of nine industries, the net employment effects of technology transfer are positive in six and zero in the other three.[46] A study conducted by the U.S. Tariff Commission, using several difficult scenarios concluded that the activities of the U.S. firms operating overseas had virtually no effect upon U.S. employment.[47]

Hawkins, using rank correlation statistical techniques, concluded that foreign activities rarely displaced U.S. workers in absolute terms.[48] However, while jobs are not necessarily at stake in transnational operations, there is little doubt but what the labor movement does in fact lose is power. The transnationals can move production, while labor cannot shift workers to follow.

Arrangements with State-Owned Companies

American managers, according to some theorists, are often reluctant to establish cooperative ties with public agencies. Apparently this reaction is based in part on the high antipathy that U.S. managers hold toward governments, their own or any other.[49]

Europeans react differently. They have lived at close quarters with their governments for many years. In Europe the public sector is itself a major actor in industry, both at home and abroad. In many instances, these companies have already had considerable experience in carrying out joint venture arrangements with governmental agencies. For some Europeans, cooperative arrangements with government-owned industries or agencies are judged desirable and advantageous. They are more inclined to assume that these relationships provide political protection, as well as the probability of governmental assistance in the event that they fall into serious difficulty. This has particularly been true in West Germany, France, and Great Britain. A large measure of Japan's economic success can be attributed to compatible working relationships between the government and industry.

Transnational firms face many problems, but none so potentially threatening as that posed by state-owned companies. Although foreign state-owned companies have not as yet mustered a serious competitive challenge to the transnational corporation, the spread of state ownership during the latter 1970s has rapidly changed the nature of international competition. Serious potential competition is seen in the chemical and airline industries. William Sneath, Chairman of Union Carbide, predicts that by the mid-1980s companies owned or controlled by governments will account for nearly 50% of the competition in the chemical business.[50] Most foreign flag airlines are government owned and virtually all are government financed or otherwise aided. The state has an ownership stake in 19 of Europe's 50 largest industrial companies.[51] Investment in government-owned enterprises accounts for more than 25% of all investment in Sweden, 50% in Austria, and 35% in Italy. The basic industries of coal, steel, and petroleum are partly or wholly nationalized in most European nations.

With the increasing power of state-owned companies, transnationals will often find that they must deal either through these nationalized firms or as a partner with them in order to do business in a particular nation. A reality, however, is that cooperative arrangements with national firms lessen the likelihood of expropriation or takeover.

The Need for an Effective International Technology Brokerage

Much of the worldwide wealth of technological information continually generated in university laboratories, governmental agencies, research institutes, and industrial laboratories, representing huge investments, has not been adequately defined, evaluated, cataloged, or exposed beyond the originating organizations. In this era of information explosion and rapid technological change, the problems of finding needed information, disseminating technical information of value, and then actually utilizing the information in the production process have become acute.

Clearly, there is a need for more effective technology transfer process than currently exists. Nationally and internationally there is a need to effectively move technology to firms or countries where there is slack capacity and market potential. Most middlemen dealing in technology transfer and utilization are limited in the scope of their activities and are relatively ineffective.

There exists a unique possibility for imaginative, perceptive individuals and agencies to step into this void. The problem is illustrated in Figure 15-1. Many organizations have idle resources, others have technology which is under-

Figure 15-1. Role of technology brokerage agency.

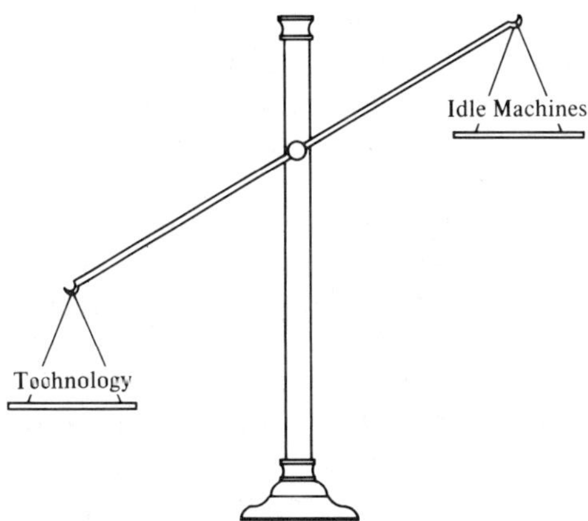

utilized or is not directly compatible with their immediate operational objectives.

International Technology Brokerage Agency (TBA) could act as the balance, transferring the technology from the source to the user, on a worldwide basis. TBA would go far beyond the current role of the middleman. As envisioned, it would have a diverse technical staff for information gathering and evaluation. Existing middleman processes rarely have the resources for a comprehensive approach.

The objectives of the Technology Brokerage Agency are

1. To seek, identify, and catalog technology.
2. To seek, identify, and list industries with idle capacity.
3. To act as a linking pin between sources and users of technology.
4. To facilitate horizontal transfers of technology.

The Technology Brokerage Agency would, therefore, match appropriate sources of innovation, scientific information, and technology with firms having identified needs. The brokerage, acting as a transnational enterprise, would seek technology and innovation on a worldwide basis, negotiate with both parties, and effect the best possible cooperative arrangement—whether licensing agreement, joint venture, coproduction agreement, or direct sale.

It is recognized that the diffusion step of the transfer process poses many problems. Past efforts at large-volume technology transfer have been stymied and frustrated by the bureaucratic structures of the various nations, by the lack of information between "haves" and "have nots," and by the lack of resources and incentives.

The TBA could be organized along the lines of a classic brokerage house. A number of affiliated agents who could operate as "listers of technology", and "listers of capacity" (business contracts). The TBA would maintain a computerized data base operating much like the system illustrated in Figure 15-2. Note that the data base enables a match between available technology and a particular business contact.

The enterprise could operate much like a real estate brokerage—matching sellers with buyers on a commission basis. In this same sense, agents would put together contracts between those selling technology and those buying. The agents would often rely upon the computerized data base. Agents would be paid on a commission basis—just as are real estate agents.

Another possibility is that transnational firms could participate in such an activity on an annual subscription basis. Information generated by such an organization would undoubtedly transcend the economically feasible capabilities of any single organization.

There are many permutations possible for a Technology Brokerage Agency. A TBA would go far beyond the present approaches. Current methods for matching technology and need are primarily based on organizational search and match capabilities or the use of various types of international middlemen. In both instances, capabilities are limited by information and ability to identify

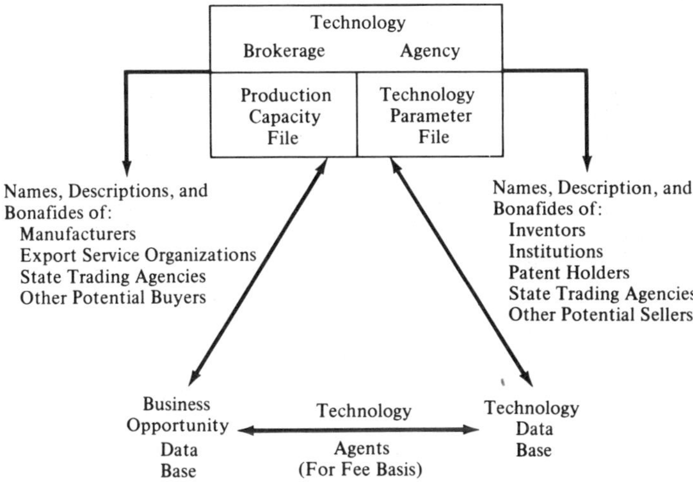

Figure 15-2. International technology brokerage agency.

and evaluate technical possibilities. A TBA could employ many specialized people in many different nations who could coordinate efforts to identify needs, match relevant technologies, and provide a bridge over which technology could effectively be transferred.

Summary

This section has sketched the technical assistance programs of the major international nonprofit organizations.

The United Nations Family is, of course, the largest and concentrates on aid to less-developed countries. OECD member countries have provided the majority of the technical assistance aid in the free world. OECD itself has been concerned mainly with coordination and has been involved in transfers between developed and developing countries. The OAS has been organized mainly by less-developed nations and has been concerned with transfers to and among less-developed nations. NATO is charged with the mutual, balanced defense of all its member nations; thus, technology is mainly diverted to weapon systems and other defense-related objectives.

The various standardization programs are attempting to optimize the world's scientific and technological efforts. The ISO's contribution has already significantly minimized scientific duplication.

Specialized associations such as WPEA, WHTC, and DISC are furthering the placement and transfer of technology by the transnational firm.

However, despite all the efforts of the various agencies, there is a growing need for a worldwide technological brokerage effort. Such an effort, very likely, through the operation of free enterprise initiatives, will provide the key to maximum technology transfer.

Endnotes Chapter Fifteen

1. Ann Van Wyner Thomas and A.J. Thomas, Jr., *The Organization of American States*, Darcas: Southern University Press, 1978, pp. 3–11.
2. W.E. Caldwell and E.H. Merril, *The New Popular History of the World*, New York: Gregstone Press, 1950, pp. 603–605 and 666.
3. D.C. Coyle, *The United Nations and How It Works*, New York: Columbia University Press, 1969, p. 214.
4. *United Nations Yearbook* (Various editions).
5. Kurt Waldheim, "Technology for World Peace," *Technology Review*, June 1973, p. 73.
6. *Ibid.*, p. 74.
7. The discussion in the paragraphs concerning the United Nations, the United Nations Development Programme, the United Nations Educational, Scientific and Cultural Organization and the United Nations Industrial Development Organization has been synthesized from the following:

   a. Jack E. Vincent, *Handbook of the United Nations*, New York: Barron's Educational Series, 1969.
   b. United Nations, *Everyman's United Nations*, 8th ed., New York: United Nations, 1968.
   c. *U.S. Participation in the United Nations*, report by the President to the Congress for the year 1970, Department of State Publication 8600, International Organization and Conference Series 96, Washington, DC: The U.S. Government Printing Office, 1971.
   d. *Yearbook of the United Nations 1972,* Volume 26, Office of Public Information, New York: United Nations, 1975.
   e. Coyle, *op. cit.*
8. The discussion of the World Bank Group is based on the following:
   a. *Policies and Operations—The World Bank, IDA and IFC*, Washington, DC: The World Bank, 1971.
   b. *World Bank Annual Report 1975,* Washington, DC: The World Bank, 1975.
9. *Policies and Operations, op. cit.*, p. 31.
10. *Ibid.*, p. 48.
11. *World Bank Annual Report*, p. 67.
12. The OECD discussion is based on the following:

    a. *The OECD at Work*, Paris: Organization for Economic Cooperation and Development, 1964.

    b. *The OECD at Work for Development*, Paris: Organization for Economic Cooperation and Development, 1971.

    c. Henry G. Aubrey, *Atlantic Economic Cooperation*, The Case of the OECD, Published for the Council on Foreign Relations, New York: Frederick A. Praeger.
13. Aubrey, *op. cit.,* p. 4.
14. OECD, *Choice and Adaptation of Technology* p. 2.
15. *Ibid.*
16. Aubrey, *op. cit.*, p. 115.
17. U.S. Department of Commerce, *Factors Affecting the International Transfer of Technology Among Developed Countries*, Report of the Panel on International Transfer of Technology, Washington, DC: U.S. Government Printing Office, 1970, pp. 45–46.
18. The OAS discussion is based on the following:
    a. OAS, *Annual Report of the Secretary General to the General Assembly*, OAS Official Records, OEA/Ser. D/III. 22, Washington, DC: General Secretariat of the OAS, 1972.
    b. *Report of the Secretary General July 1969–December 1970,* Washington, DC: Secretariat of the OAS, 1970.

c. M. Margaret Ball, *The OAS in Transition*, Durham, NC: Duke University Press, 1969.

d. Thomas and Thomas, *op. cit.*

19. Thomas and Thomas, *op. cit.*, p. 414.
20. OAS, *Report of the Secretary General, op. cit.*, p. 34.
21. *Ibid.*, p. 41.
22. Ball, *op. cit.*, p. 285.
23. *U.S. International Firms and R, D & E in Developing Countries*, Office of the Foreign Secretary, Washington, DC: National Academy of Sciences, 1973, pp. 51–60.
24. LTC Eugene J. Vittetta, USA, "The Quandry of Cooperative Weapons Development with European Allies," Thesis, Industrial College of the Armed Forces, 1972, pp. 36–38.
25. U.S. Department of State Publications 6606, *NATO Meeting of Heads of Government, Paris, December 1975*, Texts of Statements, Washington, DC: U.S. Government Printing Office, March 1958, pp. 67–68.
26. Cpt. A.H. Cornell, USN, "An Analysis of International Collaboration in the Organization and Management of Weapons Coproduction," Ph.D. dissertation, The American University, 1969, pp. 180–182, 205.
27. Euro-Group consists of all European NATO nations; e.g., excludes Iceland, Portugal, Canada, and the United States.
28. "Splitting up NATO's Arms Trade," *Business Week*, October 23, 1978, p. 111.
29. *Foreign Business Practices*, Washington, DC: U.S. Department of Commerce, November 1975.
30. R.L. Kramer, *International Marketing*, Dallas: South-Western Publishing Co., 1970, pp. 528–534.
31. *Foreign Business Practices, op. cit.*, p. 57.
32. P.R. Cateora and J.M. Hess, *International Marketing*, Homewood, IL: Richard D. Irwin, 1979, p. 560.
33. Kramer, *op. cit.* pp. 534–535.
34. See A.P. David, "The Western Hemisphere Trade Corporation: The Bountiful Tax Accident," *Harvard International Law Journal*, Vol. X, Winter 1969, pp. 101–149; and Paul Seghers, "Advantages of Operating as a Western Hemisphere Trade Corporation," *Practical Problems in Taxation of Foreign Operations*, New York: Journal of Taxation, Inc., 1965.
35. *Foreign Business Practices, op. cit.*, pp. 93–94.
36. *World Standards for World Progress*, Geneva: International Organization for Standardization, pp. 1–2.
37. ISO Memento, Geneva: International Organization for Standardization, 1978, p. 2.
38. Brian Wakefield, "Will ISO Standards Bring U.S. to Its Knees?" *Iron Age*, April 7, 1975, p. 43.
39. Vincent D. Travaglini, "ECE Recommendations on Standardization Policies," *ASTM Standardization News*, December, 1977, p. 19.
40. *Recommendations on Standardization Policies*, Geneva: United Nations Economic Commission for Europe, 1977, p. 3.
41. John Obrzut, "Metric Movement Grows—Are We Ready For It," *Iron Age*, October 10, 1977, p. 45.
42. *Ibid.*, p. 46.
43. *Ibid.*, p. 46.
44. Statement of Paul Jennings, President, International Union of Electrical, Radio and Machine Workers in U.S., Congress Joint Economic Committee, Subcommittee on Foreign Economic Policy, *A Foreign Economic Policy for the 1970's*, 91st Congress, 2nd session, 1970, part 4, p. 814.

45. *A Trade Policy for America: An AFL-CIO Program*, Washington, DC: AFL–CIO, undated, p. 9.
46. See R.B. Stobaugh et al., *Nine Investments Abroad and Their Impact at Home: Case Studies on Multinational Enterprises and the U.S. Economy*, Boston: Harvard Business School, Harvard University, 1976.
47. U.S. Tariff Commission, *Implications of Multinational Firms for World Trade and Investment and for U.S. Trade and Labor, Report to Committee on Finance*, U.S. State Department, Washington, DC: U.S. Government Printing Office, 1978, pp. 641–672.
48. R.G. Hawkins, U.S. Multinational Investment in Manufacturing and Domestic Economic Performance, Washington, DC: Center for Multinational Studies, 1972, p. 22.
49. Jasish La Palombara and Stephen Blank, *Multinational Corporations in Comparative Perspective*, New York: The Conference Board, Inc., 1977, p. 41.
50. Bureau of National Affairs, *International Trade Reporter's U.S. Export Weekly*, March 7, 1978, pp. 1–2.
51. *The Economist*, December 30, 1978, p. 51.

CHAPTER SIXTEEN

Technology, World Trade, and the Transnational Firm

The Operational Environment

Unionism

It has been noted that managing worldwide corporate systems requires the wisdom of Solomon and the patience of Job.[1] It is no trivial nor easy feat to appreciate the differences in culture, language, and national law, to say nothing of problems with technological facilities, personnel availability, and attitudes toward labor.

Europeans have difficulty understanding that American companies willingly build plants in low-labor-cost areas such as Ireland, Korea, and Southeast Asia. The European priority is different: Keep the employment up at home.

European trade unions are much tougher than American unions, and it is not necessarily a matter of corporate democracy. The real difference is that the European trade unions become deeply involved in the actual operations of the company. They control work hours, manning levels, hiring rates, the employment impact of new projects, and the current evolution of corporate social conscience. American unions are by no means so deeply involved or influential. They are interested more in keeping full membership roles and ensuring acceptable pay and benefit increases. White-collar unions are relatively rare in the United States, and industrywide unions exist only in steel, rubber, glass, and wet milling.[2] In the United Kingdom or the Scandinavian countries, a single trade union may go on strike and paralyze an entire nation. The military in several northern European nations have been unionized.

Strikes and walkouts (often termed "industrial action") are frequent challenges for the managers in Italy, the United Kingdom, and Belgium. In

Scandinavia, industrial disputes are usually settled by negotiation. In other countries, the police may become involved very rapidly. Japanese unions have been known to snake-dance through major cities as contract-renewal time approaches.

Local Employment Practices

Local employment rules differ from country to country. In most of Europe, employee incompetence is not a justification for termination. A Swede might say that an employee's inability to cope is the company's fault because the person was not properly trained. It is virtually impossible to fire an employee in Sweden. In Belgium and West Germany, the penalties for wrongful dismissal are severe. An employee who has been working for little more than six months may be entitled to as much as three years' salary if terminated.

Work habits vary widely as well. An American executive will often spend only two weeks with the family in the summer and perhaps another week during the Christmas holidays. For the rest of the year, the person may work far in excess of 40 hours a week, often including weekend work. The executive will likely initially suffer from "cultural shock" when put into an international managerial role. Work habits often significantly vary from country to country. The Frenchman goes to the seashore for four weeks every year. The Swede takes six weeks vacation every year and enjoys long weekends sailing. Most Danes, in addition to the summer holiday, take a two-week midwinter vacation when the weather becomes oppressive. The Norwegian engineer will normally leave work at 3 p.m. during the winter months so as to enjoy some cross-country skiing.

American companies frequently modify organizational structure to reflect changes in operational objectives. Reorganization is a common practice to achieve improved efficiencies. A shift in operational emphasis and individual assignments is almost a normal activity. Unless such shifts reflect drastic action necessitated to cope with operational failures they do not have any negative individual connotation.

Europeans are more conservative and are apt to be much more individually sensitive to organizational changes. In essence, organizational structure is normally more rigid in Europe than in the United States. A change in assignment, unless clearly promotional, is prone to be interpreted negatively. Also, strata may at least in part be determined by cultural constraints, and this adds restriction to altering organization structure.

Technology and World Trade

The Transnational and Developing Countries

Industrialization is a key factor in the economic development of most countries. It offers prospects of a growing availability of manufactured goods, increased employment, improved balance of payments, greater efficiency, a technologically more sophisticated work force, and modernization throughout an economy. The transnational is especially well-suited to expanding the export market of a developing country and can introduce industry that has a comparative advantage on the world market. Further, through its diverse international operations it can absorb products that are manufactured in excess of domestic market demands. The surplus can be used to generate capital which can be employed to develop additional resources.[3] Based on the aforementioned, a transnational has the potential to assist a developing nation overcome the lack of industrialization and to provide for growth in domestic skills in labor, management, and entrepreneurship.

The decade of the 1980s may be the greatest trade era in world history as the developing countries accelerate their economic growth, and their tremendous resources become more accessible. Their increasing capacity will create markets so huge as to defy description; in terms of potential opportunity for the transnational corporation, the possibilities of the international marketplace will be virtually limitless. Consider the market profile alone. The approximately 100 nations which make up the developing world contain more than two-thirds of the earth's entire population, and by the year 2,000 their numbers will reach a projected five billion.[4]

International Investment and Multinational Enterprise

The Organization for Economic Cooperation and Development (OECD) has developed guidelines for the transnational firm as part of a broader understanding on various investment issues. The OECD Ministers have signed a "Declaration on International Investment and Multinational Enterprises," which includes several interrelated elements:[5]

A reaffirmation by OECD members that a liberal international investment climate is in the common interest of the industrial nations.

An agreement that they should give equal treatment to foreign-controlled and national enterprises.

A decision to cooperate to avoid "beggar-thy-neighbor" actions, pulling or pushing particular investments in or out of their jurisdictions.

A set of voluntary guidelines, defining standards for good business conduct which the Ministers collectively recommended to transnational corporations operating in their territories.

A consultative process under each of the above elements of the investment agreement.

Some Pros and Cons of the Transnational Enterprise

John Diebold has identified a number of positive and negative statements and attitudes relating to the transnational enterprise. Table 16-1[6] represents some of the issues raised by Diebold. Technology, the transnational enterprise, nationalism, and world trade are obvious pieces of the same pie. In order to

Table 16-1. Issues of the Transnational Enterprise

The Transnational Enterprise (TE)	
Its Proponents Say	**Its Critics Say:**
1. By focusing on economic rationality, the TE represents the interests of all against the parochial interests of separate nations. It is the most effective available counter to rampant nationalism. Its only political weapon is that it can remove its benefits from developing countries that are politically unreliable or confiscatorily antibusiness: and this is an incentive toward responsibility that is in poor countries' own interests.	1. The TE removes a significant part of the national economy from responsible political control. It is an invasion of sovereignty and frustrates national economic policies.
2. The TE is the best available mechanism for training people.	2. TEs do not train people in entrepreneurial skills needed in developing nations.
3. The TE is effective in diffusing technology.	3. The transfer of technology is often minimized because (a) R&D is generally carried out by the parent company; (b) the training of nationals of the host country for R&D posts is often neglected; (c) the technology itself is often closely held.
4. The TE is the most promising instrument for the transfer of capital to the developing world.	4. The cost of the capital brought by the TE is far higher than the host government would be charged as a direct borrower in capital markets. The profits of the TE are exorbitantly high, and too low a proportion of them are reinvested.
5. TEs have been proven to be the only effective instrument for economic development.	5. The rationalization of production is sometimes a tax dodge.
6. The TE enhances competition and breaks local monopolies.	6. Its sheer size and scope represents unfair competition to local enterprises.
7. Management of the TE is becoming increasingly flexible, sensitive to local customs, and genuinely international in fact and in spirit.	7. The interest of the parent company must remain dominant and the TE cannot ever become genuinely international.
8. The TE is an agent of change which will ultimately reduce barriers to communications between peoples and establish the basis for a stable world order.	8. Far from breaking down barriers between peoples, the TE aggravates tensions and stimulates nationalism.

capitalize on the potential world markets, the transnational must successfully integrate local resources, appropriate technology, and nationalistic considerations.

Technology and Economic Growth

When published in 1972, *The Limits to Growth*[7] delivered a grim and controversial warning: The world must halt industrial and population growth or risk collapse within 100 years. To environmentalists, it was a profound and sober message, and the book became a keystone to their worldwide movement.

But to some economists, it was considered an intellectual farce, a computerized update of the questionable theories of Malthus.

The impact of the Malthusian conception is difficult to exaggerate. It focused upon the implications of limited resources for the prospects for economic growth, and it specifically linked the problem to the rate of population growth. It has long been accepted that to forestall the realities of Malthusian "doom" society has to turn to technology. As Simon Kuznets has said:

> Any emphasis on relative scarcity or irreproductible resources, as a factor in determining low levels of economic performance extending over a long period, must be countered with the question why no successful effort has been made by the victims of such scarcity to overcome it by changes in technology. To be retained, the hypothesis must, therefore, be rephrased: the have-not societies are poor because they have not succeeded in overcoming scarcity of natural resources by appropriate changes in technology, not because the scarcity of resources is an inexorable factor for which there is no remedy; and obviously human societies with low levels of economic performance are least able to overcome any scarcities of irreproducible resources by changes in technology; but this is a matter of social organization and not of bountifulness or niggardliness of nature.[8]

Although the antigrowth economists,[9] have had an impact upon world opinion, economic growth remains a goal of practically all governments of the world. The transnational enterprises seem determined to help satisfy this goal.

If modern economic growth is strongly related to the productivity-raising effects of technological innovation, and if societies involved recognize this connection and desire these same results, they will then devote resources to induce further technologican innovation. Societies will consider the value of enhancing the stock of basic knowledge and thus the broader the technological base from which inventions and improvements can be made. They will judge the value of increasing the supply and strengthening the motivation of inventors and innovators. The use of resources and national energies stimulating the flow of technological innovation could materially improve economic growth.[10]

Trade enables a nation to take advantage of international specializations. A country is inclined to export products with low opportunity costs with an expectation of importing goods and techniques with high opportunity costs. A more favorable theoretical allocation of the factors of production occurs when factors such as technology and other technical skills are transferred to a second country where they are scarce. There these factors will be combined with relatively abundant factors of labor and natural resources in order to produce goods and services. This theoretical natural flow and allocation of factors is indeed occurring within the world and is contributing to an actual reallocation of factors and a rise in efficiency of the world economy.[11] An important agent of transfer is the transnational enterprise. Much in the same fashion that national corporations helped establish and build national economies, so have the transnational firms helped integrate national economies into a world economy.

Root has described the transnational firm as "first and foremost an innovator."[12] Through its wide-ranging organizational structure, the transnational spreads new concepts, new products, new production processes, innovations, and new approaches to management and innovation on a global scale. A note of caution is necessary, however; the positive contribution of the transnational to the world economy does not imply a positive and universal economic contribution to each and every country, although there is an implication that all nations can share in the benefits of a more efficient and more dynamic world economy if they are willing to make the effort and commitment of resources.[13]

Underlying Economic Implications

Viewed in historical perspective, the transnational corporation has demonstrated surprising vitality and flexibility in adjusting to economic and political changes. It has, indeed, demonstrated the ability to survive and expand, even when governments were attempting to surpress its growth.

Until the 1930s, most countries paid little attention to the capacity of transnational corporations for moving across international boundaries. Except for purposes of trade, no reasons existed for imposing restrictions at their boundaries. By the mid-1930s, however, Lord Maynard Keynes, the economist, had demonstrated that it was possible to pursue maximum income and full employment objectives within national boundaries. As nations began to articulate national goals and priorities, they were confronted by entities that could move across boundaries, institute policies, and undertake activities which could frustrate these efforts. Governments discovered that international corporations by their activities abroad have demonstrated the porosity of such boundaries.

This apparent conflict between the transnational corporation with its supranational point of view and the nation state with its national economic concerns and special interest groups has given rise to a host of economic and political problems. Both adherents and opponents acknowledge that transnationals are here to stay and probably will continue to grow and expand in the future. At issue, at this point, is the degree of freedom that should be allowed or the extent and nature of regulation that should be imposed upon present operations and future growth.

There is a general uneasiness about the transnational corporation and its impact. There is no denying that their operations within nations frequently result in outward flows of monies—often contributing to deficits in national balance of payments. This outward flow of capital can strengthen competitors and contribute to a decline in export growth—thus, weakening a particular domestic economy. One national reaction is to impose mandatory foreign investment controls.

There is a similar ambivalence toward the transnational corporation as viewed by the capital-receiving country. There is fear that giant corporations will devour native industries and impose alien controls over their economy. On the other hand, those countries do not dispute the fact that the international corporations have contributed substantially to their welfare and technology, and there is understandably a reluctance on their part to do anything to disrupt the benefits already attained by the presence of these companies. Yet in a world of rising economic nationalism, there is a kind of inchoate uneasiness that economic policy formulation is slipping into foreign hands and that something needs to be done to retrieve the levers of economic control and to reassert political sovereignty.

Some Proposed Guidelines

In 1972, the International Chamber of Commerce (ICC) issued its "Guidelines for International Investment," which address the needs of both home and host countries. The major concern of the ICC was that any code contribute to a positive climate for increasing international investment and growing world trade. The ICC intends that any subsequent code will neither distract the competitive position of transnational firms *vis-à-vis* national companies, nor discriminate between privately-owned, state-owned, and mixed enterprises. Also in 1972, the International Organization of Employers and the International Labor Organization (ILO) worked in collaboration on a code which resulted in the "ILO Tripartite Declaration of Principles Concerning Multinational Enterprises and Social Policy."

Regional groups, such as the Andean Pact countries and the Organization of American States have attempted to establish uniform transnational investment rules. The EEC is also interested in a new investment guarantee formula, but its efforts are directed more toward governments than toward transnational firms. The EEC is attempting to include investment guarantees in a number of individual country agreements that could eventually add up to a universal code.

The greatest potential for a truly universal and comprehensive code of conduct for international business is found within the U.N. Since 1972, various U.N. bodies have been simultaneously drafting at least six codes.[14] One proposed code concerns illicit payments which, however, has been running afoul of governments. Some national bodies are extremely sensitive to surveillance of how contracts are issued. A second code concerns restrictive business practices, and a third is aimed at revision of the Paris convention covering patent laws and property rights.

A fourth U.N. draft code was directed at developing a "Code on International Accounting and Reporting." Those groups in favor of this code claim full disclosure of key financial and nonfinancial data is essential to understanding transnational performance and likely impact. Western delegates, however, displeased with proposals, apparently felt that U.N. interest in disclosure was more motivated by antibusiness sentiment. The most controversial disclosure requirements concern employment and production data, transfer pricing policies, environmental impact information, and capital investment programs. Western delegates suggest such proposals are unrealistic until uniform accounting standards are adopted, and inequitable unless national firms (which compete with transnational enterprises and some of which are state-owned) are subject to the same requirements.

The two most crucial and comprehensive U.N. efforts focus on the general "Code of Conduct for Transnational Corporations" and the "Code of Technology Transfer" (the Code on Technology Transfer was discussed in Chapter Three as it relates to the Third World egalitarianism movement). The Group of 77 (Third World nations) supported mandatory, legally binding codes directed toward transnational firms only. Eastern bloc nations proposed mandatory codes for privately owned transnational corporations. The Western group insisted on a voluntary code addressed to both governments and transnational firms (including state-owned, mixed companies, and privately owned). There have been proposals by the United States that the behavior of national corporations also be considered. The U.N. Center on Transnational Corporations has been tasked with reconciling these conflicts and developing a draft acceptable to all interest groups.

Major issues have been the determination of jurisdiction for settlement of disputes and the nature of enforcement mechanisms. There has been encouragement as most nations do agree that the objectives of the codes should be to facilitate technology transfer, stimulate foreign investment, and assist in stimulating economies of developing nations.

As far as the "Code of Conduct for the Transfer of Technology" is concerned, there has been some definite progress. Rival drafts have been prepared by the developed nations and the Group of 77 countries. There are areas of agreement. The main points still at issue are the following:

1. Which precise "restrictive business practices" are to be prohibited.
2. Whether the code is to be voluntary or legally binding.
3. Whether the code should incorporate the principle of special preferences for less-developed countries.
4. Whether legal problems in technology contracts should be subject to international arbitration or settled nationally.
5. Whether the code should include guarantees offered by suppliers to purchasers.
6. Whether the code should include general prohibitions and restrictions as to terms of "technology contracts."[15]

Whatever the final forms of agreements, meetings and discussions such as those discussed lead to conciliatory national and bloc attitudes and positions. Even voluntary codes would create standards and guidelines against which to judge transnational behavior and strategies.[16]

In response to another but related issue, American business executives believe that they are losing business to foreign competitors, because U.S.

companies must abide by the Foreign Corrupt Practices Act of 1977. The act, unique among the industrialized countries of the world, prohibits U.S. companies (to include those acting as transnational corporations) from engaging in "questionable payments" to foreign officials, agents, or political party leaders. Penalties for violation of the law range from $1 million for each corporate offense to $10,000 per offender with jail terms of up to five years for individual offenders. Businesses are concerned that they may be victims of vagueness as it is difficult to differentiate between bribes and "facilitating payments" (tips paid to low-level officials to speed up service). Some companies, such as Lockheed and Northrop, insist that the law has not hurt their overseas business; others have not been similarly fortunate. Dow Chemical Company apparently lost the opportunity to develop a petrochemical complex in Indonesia because the company was unable to pay a "promotion fee" to prominent Indonesians.[17] Until some international body is able to draft an universally acceptable "conduct of business" accord, it is not likely that the world's businesspersons will refrain from freely engaging in questionable practices. There is little doubt but that bribes and under-the-table payoffs occur in worldwide business transactions. What may be an unfair practice to one society is acceptable within another.[18]

Technology and Management Organization

Management and the Operational Environment

Within the transnational enterprise there will likely be a large number of different management styles represented and, of course, differing methods of organization reflecting the operational environments of the nations served. These factors add an uncalculable factor to an assessment of a degree of difficulty of international management. Organizations must be sensitive to the operational environment as it might affect operational objectives. Good operational practice should relate human resources and personnel contribution to organizational objectives, accommodate indigeneous cultural idiocrasies, encourage coordination and cooperation, and recognize the contribution of functional components. In practice, the operation usually emphasizes functions rather than objectives, discourages espirit de corps, breeds functional disequilibrium, and fails to convey perspective.

Organizational Forms and Life Cycles

Transnational organizations should be structured to integrate people, functions, operations and objectives. The organizational structure and fiber can become the vehicle for communicating objectives and directing operational flow. There is often confusion between organizational forms and the mechanics of implementation. There are several possible organizational forms, and differing variations are likely and exist simultaneously within the transnational firm.

Organizations can be departmentalized (organized) along functional lines, by geographic location, by product mix, by purpose of service or process, as a project, as a hybrid or matrix, or free form. Some or all of these forms may be used within a single transnational corporation.[19]

Organizations grow and develop personalities. Most organizations also experience a life cycle with operational characteristics unique to each phase.[20] Each of the first three phases of the organizational life cycle (infancy, adolescence, and maturity) have desirable characteristics. Management should assess the organizational operational phase and make the necessary transitional adjustments. Ideally, a transnational organization should have the enthusiasm, free flowing information, and flexibility of infancy; the focus of objectives, goals, and confidence of adolescence; and the experience, reputation, growth, reasonable stability, and market position of the mature organization. It follows that the stagnation associated with the fourth possible phase, senility, should be avoided.

Organization and R&D

The human resource is especially a critical factor in achieving successful R&D objectives. Complex projects usually require diverse and high-level professional skills. There are both advantages and disadvantages in transnational organization for R&D. The advantages pertain to the blending of skills from different cultural and educational environments. The products resulting from such R&D have to have international appeal and application. A composite international approach not only provides for the blending of the requisite skills but it also mitigates against provincial bias. The potential negative aspects of an international approach stem from possible divergent operational philosophies, a strong or biased orientation predicated on educational processes and limitations, and nationalistic tendencies which can circumvent the real need for an international approach.

As an example, there are close cultural ties between the Americans and British. A common language facilitates communication. However, there are distinct differences in operational philosophy. While there are exceptions, as a generalization, it can be said that American R&D is managed. On the other hand, R&D activities in Great Britain are considerably less organized and structured than in the United States. A frequent complaint expressed to one of the authors during consulting assignments in Great Britain is the frustration generated by different operational philosophies where joint technological projects have been undertaken. British scientists and engineers operate in a relatively laissez-faire environment, whereas their American counterparts are much more aware of and sensitive to managerial constraints.[21]

Attitudes

The international transfer of entrepreneurial skill is a distinctive and unique function of the transnational system. There are a number of attitudes of the international manager which deserve mention. A recent study was conducted on a sample of 211 managers—101 West Germans and 110 Americans. The sample was derived from German and American expatriate managers who were assigned to the regional headquarters of their respective multinational organizations in Latin America and Western Europe. The subjects were middle managers in automotive manufacturing, pharmaceutical production, and worldwide banking organizations. The study organized data on a nationality, regional, organizational, and hierarchial basis. Several findings were noteworthy:

Regardless of nationality or regional location, expatriate managers considered subordinates to possess lesser amounts of managerial ability than the respondents.

Respondents judged superiors to have greater managerial ability than peers of respondents.

Expatriate managers tended to be more critical of their subordinates than they were of their superiors.

American managers in Western Europe tended to have less overall confidence in their subordinates than did German managers.

Both German and American managers were critical of Latin American subordinates as to perspective and initiative.[22]

Trade Strategies of Transnational Firms

Strategic Management

The characteristics of the target market, the organization's goals and objectives, and the nature of the work force all intensify the challenge facing the international manager. Strategic management is essential. Strategic management is largely an interface of three mechanisms:

A planning framework that cuts across organizational boundaries and facilitates decision making.

A planning process that stimulates entrepreneurial thinking.

A corporate value system that reinforces managers' commitment to the corporation's strategy.

Many organizations attempt to make strategic decisions at only two strategic levels—decisions that affect the shape and direction of the enterprise as a whole, and those that affect only a subsidiary. This is restrictive planning. The successful transnational firm is likely to encompass a planning framework spanning five levels:

Product / market planning, accomplished at the unit where product, price, sales, and service are planned and competitors identified.

Business-unit planning, produced by organizational entities sufficiently large and homogeneous to exercise control over most significant factors; thus, controlling market position and cost structure.

Shared resource planning, discharged by those units that share corporate resources; effect here is to avoid suboptimization.

Shared concern planning, performed by agencies who in combination are seeking to devise strategies that meet unique customer needs in terms of geography or technology.

Transnational corporate level planning, consummated by corporated headquarters to identify worldwide technical and market trends, set corporate objectives, and marshal financial and human resources to implement those plans from the subordinate levels.

Without a detailed, yet flexible process, strategic planning would degenerate into a bureaucratic exercise. Because it is difficult to produce creative, comprehensive strategic plans consistently and reliably, the successful transnational enterprises challenge and stimulate their manager's thinking and creativity by

Stressing competitiveness, ensuring an awareness of the competitor's strategy, likely policies, and goals.

Focusing on a theme reinvigorating the planning process by directing all plans toward a specified theme such as expansion, new technology, or alternate distribution channels.

Negotiating objectives, allowing subordinate elements to participate in the allocation of resources commensurate with overall transnational objectives.

Demanding strategic insights, avoiding competition by reformulation of perception, identifying pertinent strengths and weaknesses at all levels.

The value system of the transnational firm provides the third, albeit less visible linkage between planning and action. Four common traits tend to be shared in successful strategically managed firms:

An awareness of the value of teamwork.

High entrepreneurial drive.

Apparent open lines of communication.

An open belief in the organization and its objectives.

Thus, as corporations become even larger in the future there will be increasing demands upon managers at all levels. The tenets of strategic management as outlined may prove to be the key to success.

General Strategies

Strategic advantage analysis and diagnosis is the process by which the strategists examine the transnational organization's financial accounting, marketing/distribution, production/operations, personnel/labor relations, and corporate resources to determine the specific strengths and weaknesses. With this knowledge, management can effectively exploit opportunities and meet threats. Once managers have analyzed each function of the business from the perspective of strategic management, they can begin to select and settle upon specific strategies.

The primary strategies and their associated substrategies in outline form are the following:

- I. Stable growth strategies
  - A. Incremental growth strategy
  - B. Profit (harvesting) strategies
  - C. Stable growth strategy
  - D. Sustainable growth strategy
- II. Growth strategies
  - A. Internal growth strategies
  - B. External growth strategies
    1. Merger
    2. Joint venture
    3. Vertical integration
    4. Grow-to-sell
- III. Turnaround strategies
- IV. Retrenchment strategies
  - A. Divestment
  - B. Liquidation
  - C. Captive company
- V. Combination strategy

Stable growth strategies are those pursued when a firm continues to seek the same or similar objectives, increasing the level of achievement by the same annual percentage, continuing to offer the same products/services as in the past. The transnational's main strategic decisions focus on incremental improvement of functional importance. The firm plans growth at approximate historical levels and rates.

Incremental growth, as a substrategy, calls for the firm to set as its objectives the relative achievement levels accomplished in the past, adjusted for inflation. Profit (harvesting) strategies are those whose main objective is to generate cash for the corporation or stockholders. Market share may be sacrificed in order to generate the cash. A stable growth substrategy is characterized by the firm's reducing objectives from growth level to incremental growth level in order to focus upon improved efficiency and greater effectiveness. A sustainable growth strategy is an incremental growth strategy chosen by top management because of unfavorable external conditions, such as an adverse political restructuring in a particular nation.

Growth strategies, as a category, are characterized by an individual firm's increasing the overall level of objectives. The company is seeking returns at a much higher level and rate than in the past.

As a substrategy, an internal growth strategy focuses on raising the level of objectives achievement higher than past levels by increasing sales and profits from existing product/service line. Diversification may well fall into this subcategory, and is characterized by a firm's adding products and services, improving technology, increasing production, or adding to the number of customers. Another substrategy is that of external growth. In this instance, a firm raises its objectives to a level of achievement higher than that which an extrapolation of its past level suggests and does so by increasing sales and profits through mergers, joint ventures, vertical integration, or grow-to-sell strategies.

A merger occurs when two or more businesses combine. One company may acquire the assets and liabilities of the other in exchange for stock or cash, or both companies may be dissolved so that assets and liabilities can be combined and new stock can be issued. A joint venture involves an equity arrangement between two or more independent enterprises which creates a new organizational entity.

Vertical integration is characterized by the extension of the firm's business definition in two possible directions: A backward integration strategy has the firm entering the business of supplying some of the firm's present inputs; a forward integration strategy moves the firm into the business of distributing its output by entering channels closer to the ultimate customer.

Turnaround strategies are pursued by the firm whose level of achievement is below its past level. Management is seeking to raise the level of achievement. In this situation the organization will normally attempt to improve its relative level of efficiency. Technology may play a key role in this strategy.

Retrenchment strategies are also appropriate for the firm whose level of achievement is below past marks. If the firm wishes to continue to serve its public in the same sector or product/service line, it may have to reduce its product or service line. Strategic decisions tend to focus on functional improvement and reduction of organizational units with negative cash flows.

Divestment substrategy entails the selling off or liquidation of organizational divisions or subsidiaries. The liquidation substrategy calls for the selling off or shutting down of subsidiaries or even a major portion of the parent. A captive company substrategy is one in which a firm reduces its major functional activities and sells 75% or more of its products or services to a single customer.

Combination strategies are distinguished by firms whose main strategic decisions focus on the conscious use of several primary strategies (i.e., stable growth, retrenchment, etc.) at the same time in several subordinate organizations or among subsidiaries. Another type of combination strategy involves the use of several primary strategies at different future times.

Once a reasonable number of strategic alternatives are considered, the top managers choose a strategy. This decision should be within the context of strategic management and consideration of the following four factors:

Perception of external dependence.

Attitudes toward risk.

Awareness of past strategies.

Power relationships and organizational structure.[23]

Strategies of R&D

While the preceding discussion centered on strategic strategy, there are a number of accepted strategies that relate directly to the R&D arena. In most instances, a successful research and development strategy is the result of careful evaluation and critical analysis of the various interrelationships that link together corporate strategy (as discussed above), assessed capability, corporate resources, environmental analysis, and individual R&D projects. The primary R&D strategies are as follows: offensive, defensive, gap, maverick, and acquisition.[24]

An *offensive strategy* is one in which a transnational firm identifies new markets, develops products to fill those needs, and arranges the necessary product distribution system to support this penetration. This is a high-risk, high-potential-payoff strategy. The emphasis is upon the market and the development of the suitable product.

A *defensive strategy* is characterized by a low-risk, low-payoff situation. In this instance, most of the technical effort is developmental in an attempt to minimize risk factors.

Licensing has already been discussed in previous chapters. As a pure strategy, however, it provides a relatively low-risk, moderate-payoff situation. In this case the risk of research has been absorbed by the patent holder, and usually most of the developmental work has also been accomplished prior to the agreement. Remaining risk lies in the area of market research and market development.

Gap strategy allows for the late-arriving transnational firm to exploit gaps and "soft spots" existing in present, in-place produce lines and markets. The new firm, rather than meeting competition head-on, seeks to identify virgin fields not yet plowed by competition. Oftentimes there are actual gaps existing in competitors' product lines which may prove lucrative.

Maverick strategy or "entrepreneural strategy" is one pursued in an extremely high-risk, moderately high-payoff situation. In some instances the characteristics and attributes of new technology may severely reduce the market for a given product or product line. The market leader is vulnerable to the new technology and may perceive negative consequences if the new technology is introduced by the leading producer. This provides a space for an entrepreneural spirit who is willing to lose and has the necessary expertise to take the chance. This strategy is often used in the high-technology electronics and computer fields. The strategy enables the application of a new technology in which a company has expertise to new products in someone else's market where innovation reduces the size of the total market.

Acquisition strategy is essentially of two sorts—people acquisition and company acquisition. In the former, an alternative to buying a competitor's technology through licensing is to acquire their key staff as perhaps a complete project team. While more risky than licensing, this alternative offers the opportunity for future, more long-run benefits.

Acquiring divisions or subsidiaries of competitors is often adopted as a policy where R&D budgets are constrained or nonexistent. Such a move greatly reduces the start-up cost of a R&D effect and also minimizes the initial risks of research as they were absorbed before the acquisition.

Ownership Patterns and Organizational Control

Diversity of organizational form prevails in the world of international business and the dynamics of organizational development continue to produce changing patterns of ownership and operation. Essentially all transnational firms differ in the extent to which they wish foreign interest to participate as owners in their foreign subsidiaries. Some companies avoid any foreign equity participation in their ventures. Others actively seek to conduct activities as joint ventures on the basis of either a majority or minority ownership interest. Still others want only a contractual management relationship with foreign business firms and no (or only a nominal) equity interest of their own.

For those firms insisting on 100% ownership, a concern for the effectiveness of management appears to be one of the most important reasons. Some parent companies are apprehensive about management interference. They fear a loss in efficiency and effectiveness should they have to share management with minority interests. A related reason for preferring full control has to do with intracompany pricing of components. Companies in some industries show sizeable shipments of unfinished goods within the company. When the goods have independent market values, the form of ownership is unimportant. But when the components do not carry prices quoted in independent markets, cross-shipments within the transnational organization can give rise to serious conflicts of interest between owners and the minority partners.

There are a number of other factors that act powerfully to favor full ownership. In some cases the parent company may lack confidence in the ability of the foreign businessperson expressing an interest in participating. Sometimes, the wholly owned firm reflects unsatisfactory past experience with shared ownership. An inability to agree on key policies may block a joint operation. Different philosophies or the lack of experience in dealing with foreigners may well dictate the use of 100% ownership. Also, as indicated, conflicts can develop when components rather than a complete product is the objective of the operation.

Many transnational corporations are willing to participate with some minority factions providing they retain a majority controlling interest. In most cases, local ownership participation benefits all partners by providing expertise on indigenous matters. It is often good from the public relations standpoint to have local equity participation. The parent company does not lose control over the firm's operations. The majority interest assures the parent a loud voice in such matters as rate of return, rate of growth, and overall strategy.

There have been occasions when a transnational firm will actually aggressively seek a minority interest in overseas operations. This situation can occur when the transnational needs additional capital or if it is desirable for political reasons to have locals as participating owners. In other cases, transnational firms prefer a minority interest because they (1) do not wish to be responsible for financing most or all of the venture, (2) have enough to do on the basis of a long-term management contract, or (3) are confident of being able to carry on in an influential way by virtue of their strength in the R&D of new products.

Effective firms adjust their organizational structure to fit their changing strategy. Once a strategy is chosen, it must be implemented by changes in people, changes in policy, and most often changes in organizational structure. Transnational firms utilize different management structures in order to control their business activities across international boundaries. The major structures used are the following:

Mother–daughter.

International division.

Worldwide product.

Area.

Functional.

Mixed.

Matrix.[25]

In the *mother–daughter* management structure a loose relationship is maintained between the parent company and its subsidiary. In this structure the foreign subsidiary president reports to the president of the parent company. The heads of functional departments also report directly to the parent company president. The management relationships tend to be advisory rather than controlling. This structure is popular among many Continental European Transnationals. It has not been used by U.S. transnational firms since 1967. Figure 16-1 displays the basic features of the mother–daughter structure. Positions included within dashed lines are often included on formalized boards of management in the Netherlands, West Germany, and Switzerland.

The *international division* form of transnational organization has been very popular with United States corporation. In this form, one officer exercises control over most international operations of the firm, see Figure 16-2. This officer usually has direct access to the chief executive officer, thus ensuring concentrated attention to business opportunities at the highest executive levels.

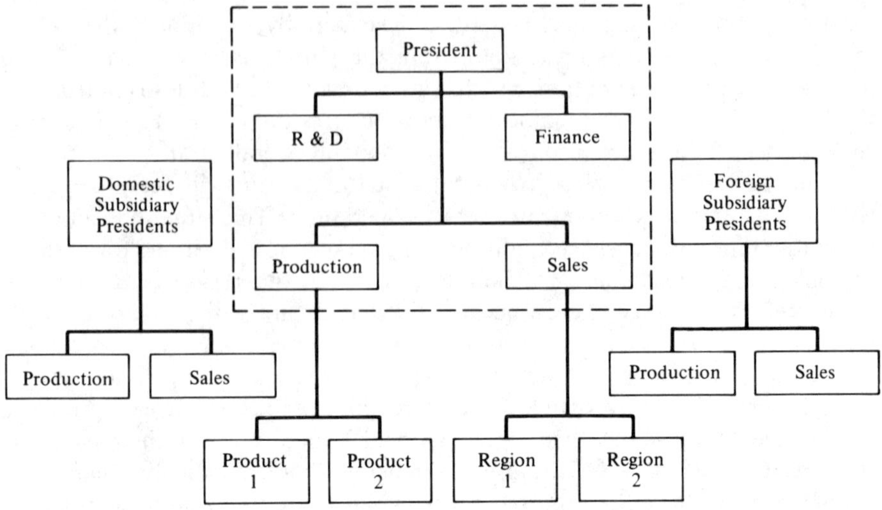

Figure 16-1. Mother–daughter organization structure.

Such a line of command requires that the activities of the international division and the domestic divisions be coordinated so that resources can be intelligently apportioned between the two. This coordination is especially important when the geographic distance between the international division's officer and corporate headquarters is large. The international division structure is most effective with corporations whose overseas markets are small compared with their home markets.

For firms with widely diversified operations, the *worldwide product* provides for international product coordination that international and regional organizations lack. In this form each major product head has line authority over all national and international operations dealing with his product, as in Figure 16-3. This form has the advantage of allowing the profit center (product) to develop the international market expertise around the needs of the specific product. A major disadvantage of this form of organization is the relative ease with which the domestic product manager can lose sight of his international markets.

The *regional, or area organizational* structure allows for economies of scale in manufacturing and marketing, especially in firms with little product diversification and wide-scale geographic dispersion. In the regional structure, line authority for most operations is divided among regional managers, For example, Dow Chemical Company is organized among worldwide regional lines. Regional managers for the United States, Latin America, Europe, the Pacific, and Canada all report to a world headquarters group. This group, as does the president in the international division structure, can continually review the

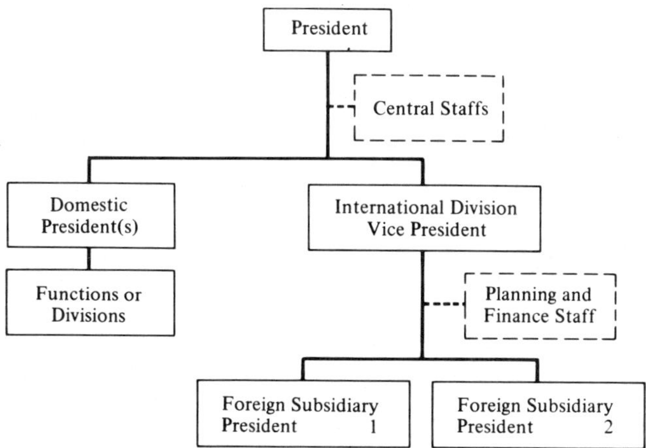

Figure 16-2. International division structure.

total operations of the firm. The disadvantages of the regional structure are that product continuity on a worldwide scale is difficult. Coordination between geographic areas in R&D or product planning is especially difficult. This problem can be partially eased by combining world headquarters and corporate headquarters and by centralizing all R&D. As an example, Xerox corporation flatly prohibits local units to carry on R&D work. Eastman Kodak company maintains a centralized group which is tasked with dealing out R&D tasks to overseas units and coordinating their efforts. Figure 16-4 illustrates this organization.

Figure 16-3. Product organizational structure.

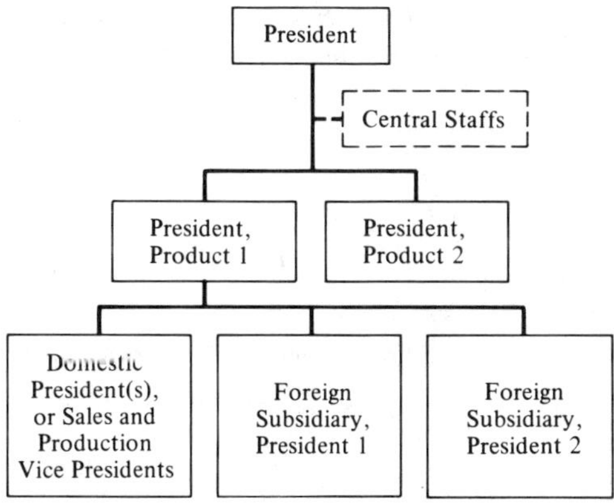

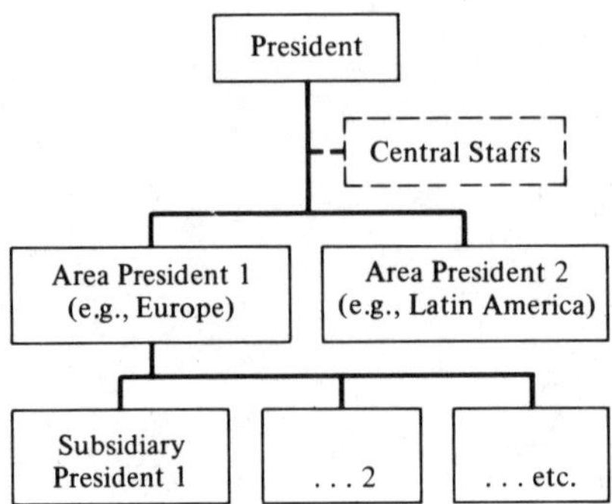

Figure 16-4. Area or region structure.

In the *world functional structure*, control is organized through the functional division chiefs who control both domestic and foreign operations. This structure is not effective in controlling international operations unless the firm deals in a highly technological and homogeneous product line. In this case, the functional heads are able to exercise effective control over their areas of interest, coordinating the product line and, at the same time, keeping up with technological changes within the industry. Figure 16-5 is an example of the functional organization.

The independent local unit structure is effective in small corporations where unit self-sufficiency can be encouraged. In this structure the corporate headquarters try not to influence the operations of their foreign subsidiaries. An example of this structure has been practiced successfully by Anderson, Clayton Company, a diversified corporation with subsidiaries in Mexico and Brazil. Although the corporate headquarters is in Houston, the subsidiaries are expected to operate autonomously.

As multinational corporations grow in size and complexity their control has become more complex. For firms with the problem of managing a large geographic dispersion and a large product diversity simultaneously, no one organizational structure mentioned above can be completely appropriate.

Figure 16-5. Functional organization structure.

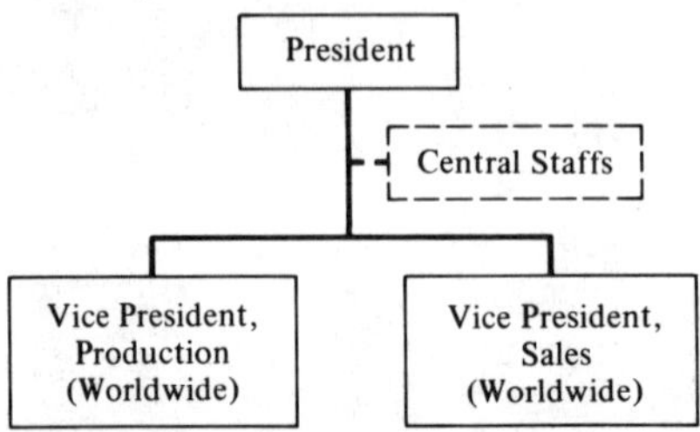

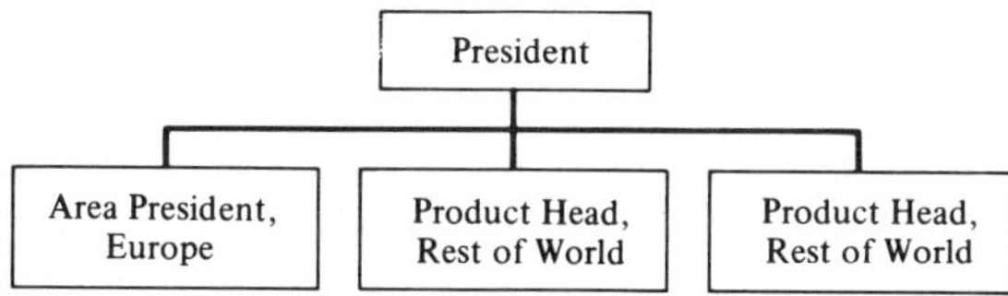

Figure 16-6. Mixed organization structure.

Mixed and matrix structures can be used for the coordination of both product and area knowledge, or the area and functional knowledge, etc.

The lines of authority can be mixed in many ways. Textron Corporation, for example, maintains a mixed structure. In this mixed structure single lines of authority exist throughout the organization (see Figure 16-6); a world product structure is used for all functions except financial and legal which use a worldwide functional organization. Ciba-Geigy Ltd., on the other hand, has adapted an area-product matrix structure that gives its product divisions responsibility for product management and profit. Technology, personnel, and long-range planning and finance are managed in an area structure at corporate headquarters. Where product and area R&D lines cross, the product division has dual lines of authority; see Figure 16-7.

The mixed and matrix structures have the advantage of centralized control of important functions such as R&D, thus reducing expensive duplication effort. At the same time they allow the individual product managers to exercise control over the profit centers. The dual lines of authority in the matrix structure allows flexibility and centralization of effort. In the rapidly changing business environment this is especially important. The matrix structure allows for rapid organizational response to change. If a firm needs to emphasize its product line worldwide, the product lines of authority can be stressed. If, however, the market conditions in one geographic area necessitate an area or marketing emphasis, the worldwide area or functional structures can be stressed.

Figure 16-7. Matrix organization structure.

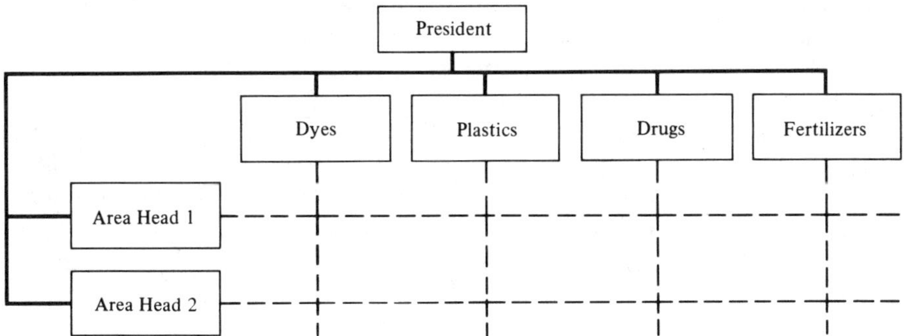

Most large multinational corporations have grown through the evolution of mother–daughter, to international division structures, onto mixed or matrix organizations.

Centralized vs Decentralized Management

Organizational and control considerations of a transnational corporation are tied not only to ownership patterns but also to the relationship between parents and subsidiaries.[26] This relationship has significance because it attempts to resolve the special problems of coordinating and guiding the many members of a transnational's corporate family.

In many instances, decision making is centralized in the parent organization. The subsidiary is furnished detailed operating plans and in turn submits comprehensive reports to world headquarters at frequent intervals. Such direct supervision will likely affect the subsidiary in terms of initiative, flexibility of response, reaction to local problems, exploiting local opportunities, and the handling of local operating problems. The transnational headquarters will usually have difficulty in maintaining this degree of rigidity. It is doubtful that corporations practicing rigid, centralized management procedures could grow to the size of most transnational corporations. The basic problem of information flow and feedback would be stifling and likely self-defeating.

The opposite pole is decentralization, which constitutes almost complete delegation of decision-making authority to the subsidiary. However, the parent normally sets the key goals to be attained by the subsidiary. A necessary condition for such a decentralized parent–subsidiary relationship seemingly is long experience in transnational operations.[27] This situation provides for maximum flexibility and freedom of action for subsidiary managers. However, virtual subsidiary autonomy tends to induce subgoals and suboptimization. Complete decentralization of effort denies to the subsidiary the breadth of resources and experiences of parent managers; it may also limit the flow of information and productive exchange between different subsidiaries, which may become intraorganizationally competitive rather than cooperative.

Either complete centralization and complete decentralization represent undesirable extremes. A middle ground approach is much more usual and innately more effective. While studies have been made seeking to identify a universal formula, thus far none has been discovered. There appears to be far too many factors to allow for a generalized approach in solving this important dilemma.

The type of organizational structure adopted by the transnational enterprise should be conducive to good management but also should be appropriate to the society in which it is located. A decentralized organizational setup is consistent with a participatory management style but may not be appropriate in some cultural environments. A more centralized bureaucratic structure would be better oriented to a traditional society where rules and regulations provide a formalized framework for working relationships. Such a bureaucratic structure would not normally be appropriate for an R&D division where it is important to encourage innovation, free-thinking, and creativity. If the society were characterized by social stratification, this would tend to suggest a vertical organization, which again is more centralized and traditional. In Britain it has been the custom of many companies to place on the board of directors only those of the higher social classes. The social status may also indicate in some countries what work schedule you adhere to (i.e., the higher the status the later you arrive at and leave work).[28] These types of customs must be respected if the nationals are to fit into the company organization. Another indication of the significance of making structure compatible with custom is evident in Japan. In Japan too much individuality is viewed as immature. Thus, the traditional "Ringi System" is consistent with a group decision-making process whereby a proposal is circulated to all affected units for review or approval and after many group meetings may receive the final go ahead.[29] This would not be a country in which to establish a centralized organization. Related to this is the nature of the population. In Japan there is a homogeneous population, whereas in the United States the population is heterogeneous, reflecting many different cultures.

The majority of U.S. firms with subsidiary operations overseas still tend to centralize their R&D efforts within the continental United States. The reasons for this decision include the ability of a centralized R&D staff to integrate requirements worldwide,[30] the access to the highly trained technical personnel needed to run such an effort, the cost of moving and maintaining sophisticated equipment for R&D labs in remote locations, the risk of political instability and the potential loss of state-of-the-art technical equipment and data, and the problem of duplication of effort from decentralized R&D efforts. However, there are some firms which believe all these disadvantages are more than counterbalanced by benefits. One executive who believes in decentralized R&D stated that what duplication does result appears to pay off through the development of better products. Furthermore, some firms feel that international executives need more influence in product development since they have the first-hand knowledge of the cultural and consumer needs and potential world markets.[31] ITT employs a worldwide R&D effort. Currently, more than 25,000 scientists and engineers work in ITT labs throughout the world. The microwave-radio relay system carrying 1,800 speech channels in a single radio beam was developed by a European company. Honeywell also believes that each overseas market should be able to provide the controls, technology, and service demanded by local conditions.[32] It is felt that cross-fertilization through the multinational firm can be productive in the research process as well as the results. To cite another example, RCA's policy is that decentralized research facilities can provide technical assistance to European and Asian licensees while also providing a means of monitoring European and Asian electronic developments and keeping the company's domestic laboratories posted.[33]

The incentives for decentralized research facilities appear to be growing. As Europe and Japan, particularly with respect to the chemical, drug, and electronics industries, become more competitive with American firms, the need to decentralize becomes more attractive. The trained technical personnel are available and new ideas/concepts are viable.

The R&D situation in developing countries however, is a different story. The technological gap between these countries and the developed countries does not appear to be closing, despite the fact that as much as 1% of their GNP may be allocated to R&D. This is somewhat of a false sense of accomplishment for a developing country because there still may not be an adequate base of science/technology and trained personnel. The concept of quality versus quantity of R&D in a developing country appears to be problematic. There is normally state sponsorship of the R&D effort which proceeds through three stages. The first is characterized by abundant financial support, where there is a lot of pomp, ceremony, and excitement about the "new" effort. The second stage is five to eight years later, the "operational stage," when funds are more difficult to obtain and generally support personnel are lacking. The final stage would be the diffusion of knowledge into society, but by this time support has faded and nothing of consequence has been accomplished.[34] The fact that the R&D effort throughout all stages is essentially state-owned and traditionally managed accounts for the emphasis on the "number" of scientists working rather than the "quality" and experience of an individual scientist. This in itself may be self-defeating to an R&D effort. In addition, a political crisis during any of these stages may disrupt the R&D organization to the point where it may not be able to regain its position once the turmoil is over. Another important factor is that R&D funding or scientific placement in many developing countries is related to political acceptance rather than professional credentials.

Environmental Analysis

Corporate managers are coming to recognize that successful overseas operations, perhaps even survival, depend on the quality of observation and analysis of host-country environments. Factors militating the assessment include mounting criticisms of the transnational firm's motives and objectives, revelations of corporate misconduct, national and international campaigns to devise codes of conduct, and the political volatility of many places where foreign investment exists or may wish to expand.

Forces within the societies of the world are insisting upon a voice in what a transnational enterprise may or may not do. These forces are attempting to inhibit the undesirable consequences accruing from business activity; they are interested in seeing industry share more of the social costs of operations and business activity. We have seen the results of their concerted interest and concern—the proposed United Nations' codes of ethics relating to the transnational firm.

While these vibes are recognized there is a difference of opinion among transnational managers as to the best approach. A certain amount of analysis is accomplished by all successful transnational firms. At the highest level of generality, they are seeking to ascertain the degree of political stability, the attitudes and policies toward foreign investment, the reliability of the government regarding commitments made to the foreign investor, and the best way for the transnational to present itself to the public and government of the host country. Also, the foreign investor should attempt to become familiar with the laws of the host-country which may affect its operation.

There are a number of other dimensions that deserve the attention of top management of the transnational enterprise. While subject to change, the answers to the following points will be invaluable in shaping the trade strategies:

1. Primary development goals of the host government, degree of internal consistency, amount of domestic controversy that they engender, identification of groups favoring sets of priorities.
2. Relationship between central, regional, and local governments; assessments of relative power and influence of each level.
3. Local or regional pressures for devolved political and/or administrative authority.
4. Degree of professionalism, technical capability, basic attitudes, and values of all levels of public bureaucracies.
5. Nature and quality of planning ability and machinery of all governmental levels.
6. Assessment of governmental ability to turn plans into legislation and legislation into practice.
7. Identification of sectors where the aspirations of indigenous governments and the activities of the transnational affiliate might be made attractively complementary and those areas where conflict may be expected.
8. Basic attitudes and demands of action groups, both real and potential.
9. Proposed policies and regulations affecting foreign investors, both existing and potential.
10. Identification of likely points of misunderstanding and assessments as to how to avoid mistakes and conflict.[35]

Trade Problems of Transnational Firms

Some Significant Problem Areas

The rapid growth in recent years of the transnational enterprise has not occurred without significant problems. There are many significant problems, both facing and created by the transnational, which deserve mention—some have previously been discussed, while others are complex and beyond the scope of this text. This section will identify and assess several remaining matters which are deemed worthy of further discussion: negotiations, political and economic risk, problems with state-owned companies, transfer pricing, taxes, and information flow.

Negotiations

Increasingly, negotiations are used as a means of deciding the boundaries within which a transnational enterprise may initiate, function, and terminate operations within a specific country. It is therefore useful to have cognizance of the most prevalent provisions, the basis for strength for the parties involved, and the essential behavioral factors which are brought into play.

As nations tend to "belong" to special interest groups (OPEC, COMECON, EEC, Group of 77, etc.) so do they recognize and learn from recent events. Thus, the foreign negotiation will likely rely partly on other recent negotiations to serve as models. What has recently transpired between other transnational firms and the government, or between similar types of corporations, or between the same firm in similar countries will serve as a common reference and will set the precedent.

Kapoor has identified the dimensions of the negotiation procedure—Figure 16-8.[36] It should be pointed out that this model is dynamic and changes with time and situation.

Negotiations tend to transpire without the context of *common interests*, *conflicting interests*, *compromise*, and *criteria* or *objectives*. The process of negotiation is one of molding these interests into a common plan or agreement,

Figure 16-8. Dimensions of negotiation (*Source*: Adapted from A. Kapoor, Planning for International Business Negotiation, Cambridge: Ballinger Publishing Co., 1975, p. 2.)

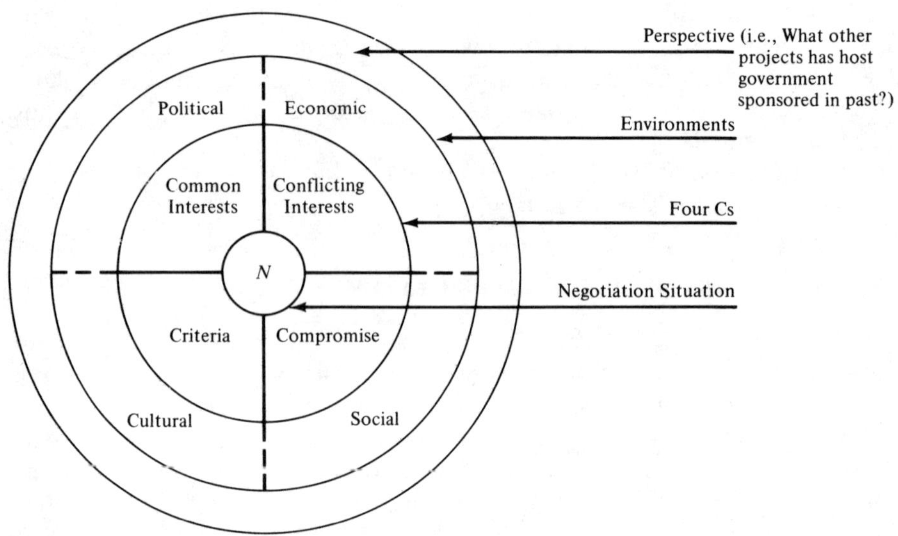

of seeking to combine "something to negotiate for" with "something to negotiate about," giving and taking on various points in an attempt to determine an acceptable objective and its criteria for achievement.

The environment of the negotiations is of importance. The "mind set," attitudes, and strategies of the negotiators are influenced by the political, cultural, social, and economic settings of both parties. The factors and their relative importance will vary from country to country, from firm to firm, and from time to time.

There are some key mistakes often made in negotiations, which can be grouped under four major headings: cultural, governmental, decision making, and organizing. The first of these, cultural, relates to comparative management concepts wherein the negotiator lacks knowledge as to the foreign nation's customs, history, environment, and ways of thinking. The failure that results is that negotiators do not understand why counterparts adopt particular stances and are unable to place themselves in the other person's shoes. One of the most obvious problems that can develop is that there is insufficient attention to "saving face" for the opponent. This can lead to a breakdown of the negotiations and a loss for both sides.

The second series of mistakes focuses on the participatory role that a foreign government plays in the negotiating, planning, regulating, and managing of industrial ventures.[37] A lack of recognition as to the nature and role of foreign governments in this context can undermine a sound negotiating position.

In comprehending the relevance of decision-making characteristics to negotiations, it is imperative that the negotiating team study the business structure, personalities, skill-level, organizational objectives, and goals of their opposing team. All these aspects influence the decision-making process during the negotiations. Quite often there is a failure to recognize that approval within one level of an organization does not necessarily guarantee implementation at another level. The negotiating team must represent an organizational level capable of implementing the agreements, or the negotiations may be fruitless. Furthermore, and perhaps most significantly, there should be sufficient time allocated for the negotiations. It takes more time to complete the negotiation process in some instances than others. Americans are for the most part conditioned to change and rapid decision making, whereas foreigners are usually oriented to a more lengthy and involved decision-making process. The Orientals, especially, are careful negotiators—not hurrying, ensuring the atmosphere is one conducive to negotiation, and then conducting the negotiation over a period of time which is often considered excessive to the Western mind. If the negotiations are approached with tight time constraints, there may not be sufficient time for any time commitments. Worse yet, the foreign concerns may interpret the short timeframe as indicative of the lack of seriousness to do business with them and the little value placed on a lasting association.

Finally, it is necessary to examine the mistakes made in organizing for the negotiations. The most serious of these relate to planning considerations including the lack of planning for changing negotiating strength, insufficient planning for communications between decision makers and negotiators, and inadequate attention to the training of executives in the art of negotiation. Inattention to these factors may result in frequent interferences by higher officials from both sides and the inability for either side to accommodate and react to changing and conflicting interests.[38]

Negotiations are serious business situations, and for several years, business professors at several universities have conducted simulated, role-playing negotiations based upon past case histories.[39] This technique is proving to be a valuable device; by practicing roles and researching culture and history, business negotiators are in a better posture for negotiations.

Risk Management

There are a number of special risk elements that are confronted in international business activities—political, financial, regulatory, and tax. They arise from causes such as the existence of different currencies, monetary standards, and national goals, but they are all measurable through their effect on profitability and ownership.[40] We will examine the elements of political risk now, reserving discussions of tax risk as part of the analysis of tax impact upon the transnational firm later in this chapter. Economic risk was analyzed in Chapter Three. Various facets of regulatory risk have already been discussed throughout the text.[41]

The transnational corporation faces a number of different political risk exposures through the cycle of business involvement. These political sanctions, each involving a differing degree of political risk are

Confiscation.

Expropriation.

Nationalization.

Domestication

Confiscation occurs when a foreign investment is taken over by a government without any reimbursement. *Expropriation* occurs when a foreign investment is taken over by a government but some form of reimbursement was made; the original owners did not willingly sell. While confiscation and expropriation deal with the taking of property, *nationalization* refers to ownership by the government. As an example, a transnational's property may be confiscated expropriated and then operated by the government and/or subsequently turned over to the private sector. *Domestication* is that process whereby a government, by various means, forces a foreign-held corporation to relinquish control, including actual ownership, to nationals.

Of the sanctions, confiscation and expropriation are apparently the most frequently used and most critical politically induced risks of international business.[42] Of the modern takeovers, the more noteworthy include Guatemala's takeover of foreign-owned banana plantations in 1953, Brazil's takeover of U.S.-owned electrical power plants, the expropriation of Anaconda's and Kennecott's holdings in Chile, and the expropriation and nationalization of Cerro's holdings by Peru.[43] In the four years between 1970 and 1974, 34 Latin American, African, and Asian nations expropriated $1.2 billion worth of U.S. and overseas investments.[44]

Why does a nation feel that it must seize foreign investment? Many reasons are given in an attempt to rationalize the move. Most, however, boil down to the belief that the country's goals and self-interest can best be served by government or national ownership rather than by foreign control of a particular industry.

Domestication is fast becoming a favorite tool of host countries in bringing the transnational enterprises' activities in line with national interests.[45] Rather than outright moves (confiscation or expropriation), concern over foreign investment is translated in a series of subtle restrictions on the firm's freedom of operation—an attempt to domesticate the foreign investor. Governments can declare that ownership must be passed to nationals, or they can suggest that greater local ownership will avoid unprofitable changes in import quotas and exchange rates. The government may suggest that more supplies and component parts be purchased locally. Other tactics include a requirement to promote locals to high management positions, greater decision-making powers vested in local personnel, and a requirement for more products to be produced locally.[46]

Some industries are more susceptible to sanctions than others. Public utilities are a frequent target for expropriation since it is universally held that they are critical to growth and defense. High-technology firms are tailor-made for the confiscation tactic as a nation can rapidly transfer wealth, property, and technology from foreign to local hands with a minimum of problems. Domestication will likely be used against the full range of mid-to-high-technology corporations.

It should be noted that government takeover does not always mean total loss for the foreign investor. In many cases the government will reimburse the transnational firm for the perceived value of the losses. The reimbursement is seldom felt to be "equitable" by the foreign owner, but there is less stigma attached to governmental intervention when such payment is made.

When assessing the advisability of entering into or continuing an international investment, there are six demanding questions related to the nation:

1. How stable is the political system?
2. How strong is the government's commitment to encouraging and supporting foreign ownership?
3. What is the expected tenure of the present government?
4. What changes would be enacted by successors to the present regime?
5. What would be the likely efforts of these changes?
6. What actions and decisions must transpire now?[47]

Answering these questions is seldom easy. However, once answered, they help form the basis for defensive action. Very basically, there are five risk exposure strategies that are open to the transnational manager to varying degrees:

Avoidance.

Equity sharing.

Hedging.

Insurance.

Retention.[48]

Avoidance is an attempt to shy-away from the high-risk situation. At times the risk can be shifted to a third party. The company may find it necessary to forsake a particular venture because the risk as assessed is higher than allowed by company policy or is not prudent at that time. *Equity sharing* is an attempt to spread the risk. This becomes more difficult as the risk factor becomes more apparent. *Hedging* is an attempt to avoid loss by a forward sale—perhaps in terms of currency or commodities. Hedging may incur high interest penalties as well as constraints on local borrowing. *Insurance* is normally available for international operations through a variety of international agencies. For example, The Overseas Private Investment Corporation (OPIC) is a federal agency insuring U.S. companies against seizure of overseas properties by foreign governments, from property damage from war, and from their inability to repatriate profits. The Agency for International Development (AID) has a credit insurance feature. However, the bulk of the insured international business undertaken by U.S. firms is covered by FCIA, a group of over 75 American marine, casualty and property insurance companies which cooperate with the Export–Import Bank in providing protection for both commercial and political risks.

Retention is often forced upon the international manager. Not so much a strategy within itself, retention is more a result of the infeasibility of other strategies. There are times when the transnational corporation must absorb substantial risks, since the managers will be unable to shift, hedge, or transfer all political risks in all instances.

It is important to recognize that political risk is manageable once known. There can be little doubt that political risk management requires reliable information, early warning systems and signals, and strategies to reduce risk exposure and to maintain bargaining leverage with host governments. These inputs and outputs to the transnational's operational and planning system must be timely and constantly revised in light of new political situations.

State-Owned Businesses

Transnational firms face many forms of international competition, but a growing competitive threat comes from state-owned companies abroad. For the most part, these companies are heavily subsidized by their governments and are not required to earn profits comparable to those of their privately owned competitors.

State ownership of businesses is becoming a familiar aspect of the European economic scene. The national government has an active ownership investment in 40% of Europe's 50 largest industrial concerns.[49] The largest industrial company in their respective nations is owned by the governments of France, Italy, Great Britian, Austria, Mexico, Brazil, and India.[50]

Internal growth and diversification provide convenient means for the state-owned company to meet its commitment to expansion. The ability to grow, succeed, and thrive even without earning profits places the state-owned company in an enviable position. Today few industries are immune to competition from these state enterprises. State-owned and -operated industries may not be profitable, but they may be subsidized by governments because these industries support political goals. Governments may also support nonprofitable industries to foster selected technological development or minimized dependency on foreign industries. A good example is extensive foreign subsidization of commercial aviation.

Private enterprise operates under the shadow of potential economic failure. The state enterprise has no such specter. State ownership confers apparent immortality on an enterprise. It would not be politically feasible for a government to allow their company to go bankrupt, no matter how large their deficit.

The state-owned company has a series of built-in, guaranteed markets such as garnering all governmental defense and other governmental-related business activities. This ploy also allows the government to acquire more power to influence and control purchasing decisions of large segments of the economy.

State financing provides the state enterprise with a unique advantage for expansion. Because there is no requirement to pay dividends, all profits, if any, may be poured back into expansion projects. Most nations deploying state-owned firms also provide them indirect assistance in the form of tariffs, restrictions, or quotas. These subsidiaries are frequently hidden and difficult to trace, and they provide lucrative "props" for the enterprise.

In another strategy, governments will often use state-owned companies to assist domestic corporations by selling and purchasing goods or services at prices above or below market value. Banks provide special, low interest rates to exporting firms; purchases will be made to foster work and thus avoid layoffs; and other equally insidious methods may be used to stifle competition from the transnational companies.

Actions by state-owned companies will probably become increasingly bothersome in future years. Transnational corporations will have to do constant economic battle with them. It is likely that the transnational will lose frequently. The transnational can be saved in the long run by measurable, visible, and tangible increases in technology and productivity. The very nature of the state-owned enterprise militates against dramatic advances in technology and innovation—their "Achilles' Heel."

The Transnational Firm and Personnel Management

Considering the numerous problems involved, the selection, promotion, and remuneration of managerial personnel for overseas operations becomes a matter of importance. Circumstances usually compel transnational managers to operate more autonomously than their domestic counterparts. It should be recognized that the overseas manager occupies several roles: representative of the transnational firm, manager of the local firm, resident of the local community, citizen of the host state or of another, and member of a profession. Likely sources for the transnational manager include home country nationals, host country nationals, and third country nationals.

Robinson has identified three primary problems involved in the selection of transnational managers:

Nationality.

Choice of prerequisites.

Validation of prerequisites.[51]

While there are several sources for managers, there is an apparent trend for the transnational firm to hire more local national personnel in management positions. By doing so, the firm enjoys lower aggregrate costs and receives from the employee an innate knowledge of the culture, environment, and political setting. However, this action is not without problems; indigenous personnel often resist transfer and may well be of a lesser quality than potential managers from other nations.

Regardless of the source, there are a number of factors that must be recognized when selecting managers for overseas positions:

Technical capabilities.

Skills as a manager.

Personal motives.

Empathy and emotional stability.

Family status.

The candidate should be evaluated in terms of his or her technical knowledge and capability to do the job. Candidates should know and have practiced the fundamental principles of management. It is well that the transnational ascertain and understand the motivating forces behind candidates' applications. There should be definite, positive reasons for seeking and accepting posts with transnational corporations. Candidates should be sensitive to cultural differences and similarities between their own and those of the host nation (if different). They must be willing to accept value differences in other people and be tolerant toward foreign cultural patterns. They must be emotionally stable in order to survive the mental ordeal of transnational assignments. Candidates should recognize that a transnational manager has to be a corporate diplomat. Finally, the family of the candidate (especially those transferred within the corporate structure) must be resilient and capable of adjusting to change.

Promotion and remuneration are important considerations within the transnational firm. A company has to decide whether to limit management careers to national operations, whether to move managers into the worldwide stream (transnational), or whether to move the individual from his or her native country to corporate headquarters and return (binational). Each strategy has natural advantages and disadvantages; each successful transnational firm has definite personnel management policies. The choices of remuneration are more limited. Here there are only two basic strategies—dual scale or international scale.[52] The dual scale is a situation where, for example, American personnel are on an American salary scale, and all others are on the local scale. The international scale is less discriminatory; all employees are on an international scale plus they receive a variety of extras. Commonly included as extras are a cost-of-living differential, an expatriate bonus to compensate for being away from home, and personal adjustment payments such as language training, moving allowances, children's education, home leave, entertainment, and special health and accident insurance. Pay also varies widely between companies.

Seldom are the subsidiaries of transnational companies composed only of white-collar personnel. Technical and semiskilled personnel can comprise the bulk of the staff. Most transnational managers, therefore, must deal with a local labor force. One of the most apparent international differences in labor–management relations is how each group views its relationship with the other. When there is little interface between the two groups, there can be problems in reaching corporate objectives. This separation will often be enhanced by "class differences" between management and labor.

In many nations, labor groups vote largely in bloc. This results in labor demands being met primarily through national legislative means rather than through collective bargaining means. Companies in a given country may deal with several different unions. The pattern will likely vary, but normally multiple unions tend to weaken management's position since any one may be in a position of holding up production, particularly if there is conflict among unions.[53]

In the United States there have been strong criticisms of the transnational process by the labor unions. The claim is made that direct foreign investment takes jobs away from American laborers. Studies by the U.S. Department of Commerce have refuted this claim.[54] Indeed, foreign operations apparently provide jobs for American workers in three ways:

1. Manufacture of capital equipment to be used in the new plants overseas.
2. Production of components to be processed further at foreign plants.
3. Manufacture of U.S. goods that would not be sold abroad unless the company were established there.[55]

Management tends to argue that in the long run, direct foreign investment is good for a nation and is also necessary to the growth and survival of commercial enterprise. They feel that a threat of job displacement should not be used as an excuse to limit foreign trade or investment. Without the freedom to expand internationally, national firms would soon lose their competitive edge, thus damaging the nation's balance of payments and prosperity. This latter factor would then erode the earning power of the firm, destroy its capital base and effectively impair the R&D capability from which new products spring.[56]

Taxing the Transnational Firm

The area of tax planning is crucial for any business, whether domestic or transnational, since it has a profound effect on profitability and cash flow. Taxation has a strong impact on the choice of (1) location in the initial investment decision, (2) legal form of the enterprise, (3) method of finance, and (4) method of arranging prices between related entities.[57]

Tax practices throughout the world differ significantly from those found in the United States. This can often cause problems for the transnational firm. Lack of familiarity with laws and customs can and does create serious problems. In many nations, tax laws are rather loosely enforced which causes great variance between the effective and statutory tax rates. In some nations, such as Spain and Italy, taxes are generally negotiated between the tax collector and the taxpayer. A variance among countries in generally accepted accounting principles can cause differences in determination of taxable income and thus affect cash flow. Different countries treat the taxation on earnings of the foreign subsidiaries nonuniformly.

Value-added taxes (VAT) has been used as the tax basis for most Western European countries since 1967; it is also referred to as TVA or tax on value added. VAT has been instrumental in facilitating intra-European trade based upon a uniform tax system. A VAT is computed by applying a percentage rate on total sales less any purchases from other business entities. Each independent company is taxed only on the value added at each stage in the productive process. Thus, if one company was fully integrated vertically, the tax rate would apply to its net sales because it owned everything from raw materials to finished product.

In many countries there are tax incentives for foreign investors. Generally, when nations are desirous of foreign investment, such as some of the developing countries, they will exclude certain types of investments from taxation. Others, such as Puerto Rico, excuse investors from paying taxes for a certain period of time. Brazil has allowed firms operating in certain regions of that country to utilize their earnings for expansion without taxing them. These tax-holiday policies are designed to influence the flow of investment funds.

U.S. tax law for the transnational firm is extremely complicated. An entire chapter could be devoted to this subject alone and would barely scratch the surface. In the interest of brevity the following principles serve to summarize the effects of U.S. tax laws:

1. *Equity on a National Basis*. If one firm is taxed on its earnings, then all firms should be taxed on their earnings, irrespective of source (foreign or domestic).
2. *Neutrality*. Foreign subsidiaries should be taxed similarly as U.S. subsidiaries to prevent follow-on discrimination against U.S. investments.
3. *Place of Incorporation*. Profits generated by foreign corporations are not subject to U.S. tax until repatriated to the United States.
4. *Avoidance of Double Taxation Through Tax Credits*.
5. *Form Versus Substance*. The substance of a transaction should determine taxability, not just the form.
6. *Substantial Business Purpose*. Any action that effectively reduces taxes should have a substantial business purpose and not be done simply for tax minimization purposes.
7. *Exceptions and Incentives Based on Public Policy*. This allows the federal government to accomplish certain national objectives through tax policies.[58]

Tax pressures are being applied to the transnational enterprise from three directions: (1) the individual nations in which it operates, (2) the United Nations, and (3) its home nation. Many of the developing nations are beginning to extract greater tax revenues from foreign investors, often subtly threatening some sort of nationalism or expropriation move. The U.N. has published studies expressing deep concern over the problem of taxation. Differences in tax rates, according to one such study, "in the definitions of taxable income, in the principles that govern taxing jurisdiction and in practices in making allowances for foreign taxation" have led to greater sophistication on the part of the transnational in minimizing tax liabilities.[59]

The United Nations is apparently concerned, as are individual nations, over the allocation of profits to the benefit of the transnational firm and to the detriment of the countries that rely on tax revenues to finance developmental projects. The U.N. is attempting to postulate an international charter whereby nations can join together in allocating transnational enterprise profits so that each country can collect tax revenues based on its contribution to the transnational's production and sale and not based upon some arbitrary intracompany pricing scheme.[60]

It is apparent that the transnational corporation needs to consider profits and cash flow when making investment and operational decisions. Tied to the initial investment decision is the financing decision. Both debt and equity financing have tax consideration. If the transnational corporation is trying to maximize its worldwide cash flow, it should try to concentrate profits in tax havens or in low-tax countries. Proper planning and timing of dividend remittances can allow a transnational the advantage of some tax relief.

The transnational operational manager as well as the financial executives must be cognizant of the complexity of worldwide tax laws. The following is a partial checklist designed to assist transnational managers with their tax planning:

1. Identify opportunities to reduce paper profit (depreciation, inventory, etc.).
2. Analyze tax havens.
3. Consider organizing special subsidiaries to minimize taxes (DISC, WHTC, etc.).
4. Have cognizance of major changes to local tax laws.
5. Weigh tax costs against profit benefits when making expansion decisions.
6. Verify that unjustified tax assessments are disputed.
7. Develop operational strategies that parallel tax avoidance strategies.
8. Analyze appropriate accounting principles for possible loopholes.

Another consideration that has an impact upon taxation is transfer pricing. A transfer price is the price on inventory sold between related organizational entities. For example, a low transfer price from parent to subsidiary would reduce cash in the parent, and thus reduce relative income due to the low value placed on intracompany sales. If, however, the corporate tax rate to the subsidiary is considerably lower than that of the parent, it would be advantageous to price transferred goods at high levels. Major considerations in setting transfer prices include:

1. Concentration of cash.
2. Minimization of taxes.
3. Reduction of risks due to inflation and exchange rate changes.
4. Competition.
5. National economic and tax restrictions.
6. Needs of foreign interests.
7. Public relations.
8. Fair profits for subsidiaries.[61]

As the transnational firm crosses national boundaries it will likely encounter accounting systems that differ from those of the parent country. These systems dictate the nature and content of reports presented for creditors, local investors, prospective investors, and the government, all the while adhering to the accounting principles of the parent country.

There are several major differences in accounting principles worldwide. Most European nations are much more conservative than the United States in their presentations of financial statements. Consolidated statements, for example, are not required in many countries such as West Germany and Japan. The transnational firm must take into consideration the accounting function and its inherent complexities when making investment and tax-reduction decisions.

In several countries, notably the developed nations, R&D costs can be used to help reduce the tax bill. In 1974, in the United States, the Statement of Financial Accounting Standards No. 2 was issued by the Financial Accounting Board. The major features of these "generally accepted accounting principles" as related to R&D costs are as follows:

1. Costs to be identified with R&D activities include the direct costs of materials, labor, and the equipment, facilities and intangibles acquired or constructed for a particular project which has no alternative future use; depreciation or amortization of equipment, facilities and intangibles used with a particular project that do have alternative future uses; and a reasonable allocation of indirect costs.
2. General and administrative costs not clearly related to R&D activities and any capital costs including interest are to be excluded from R&D costs.
3. All R&D costs are to be charged to expense when incurred; only items historically deferred by government regulated enterprises may not be expensed.
4. R&D activities as defined by the National Science Foundation (NSF) are those recognized for finance and accounting purposes, although some social science R&D is allowed on an exception basis.
5. Disclosures made in financial statements are to be limited to total R&D costs charged to expense.[62]

MIS and Transnational Corporations[63]

A well-run transnational organization devotes a great deal of energy and attention to the proper management of its resources. Cash management, physical asset management, inventory management, and human resource management are familiar areas, but a very critical corporate resource has been virtually ignored—information. Information is not only that which is required to manage the far-reaching edges of the transnational's horizons, but also includes technical information as well. The concept of information as a resource leads directly to focusing attention on available information of an enterprise.

For the transnational firm, the problem of developing a conduit for information flow is a particularly critical item. Assessment of subsidiary performance and the organizational control system that it facilitates depends partly on the flow of information between the transnational parent and subsidiary. Although international communication is no longer the difficult matter it once was, it is still a matter of concern. The transnational must place a premium on an effective information system mainly because of distance, diversity, and instability in foreign environments. If speed and comprehension is paramount, then the costs of information gathering and processing increase exponentially.

The types of information required by a transnational enterprise in order to exercise its control and operation functions vary depending upon the firm's strategies and goals. Data required for comprehensive transnational management of subsidiaries usually fall into three categories:

Environmental information.

Competitive position.

Internal subsidiary operations.[64]

Many transnational firms are now facing data crises in a number of different areas—marketing, human resources, and financial are the most noteworthy. The problem simply stated is one of knowing what data to collect and how much. Reliable information is needed from all geographical areas of interest on competitive pressures, the financial environment, consumer tastes and life-styles, market characteristics, and industry conditions. And, while the information is available, it becomes a challenge to the local manager to collect it in a timely and comprehensive fashion. It is also extremely important that the information be accurate and that it is properly integrated and acted upon. Data collection is exacerbated by items such as cultural differences, language differences, and political differences. Without adequate preparation, an entire product introduction campaign can be foiled by avoidable mistakes. For example, in Malaysia, the color "green" denotes the dangers of the jungle and conveys a completely negative image—green should be avoided when marketing goods in that area.

It is necessary for the transnational organization's data collector to understand the definition of the data and its frequency of collection. Standard demographic data such as average age, income statistics, occupational items, and size of households may not be available within certain countries. National income data, foreign trade figures, and consumer expenditures are usually difficult to locate and obtain in developing countries. There seldom will be uniformity of terms in published reports issued by the governmental agencies in developing nations. The term "family income" represents different things depending upon the indigenous agency collecting the data. "Family" in many countries includes grandparents, uncles, and cousins.

Standard definitions may not exist for either industry or product categories. Overall country data could obscure regional differences. Gross national product figures are often collected at different times by governmental agencies so that information cannot be easily compared. The data collector must use a satisfactory measure so that there is understanding as to what is collected and its relative accuracy. Data must be separated from what really are not data. Secondary data must be checked carefully for bias and timeliness. Good data collection requires good research (remember the saying "garbage in—garbage out").

As data are received, the effective transnational will use management information systems (MIS) to transform it into meaningful and useful information. An MIS is a system, manual or automated, which gathers data, and in terms defined by management, translates this data into meaningful information to be used in managing the organization. As defined, there are two primary hurdles to be overcome in order to develop an effective MIS—management must know what information they require in order to effectively manage and data must be collected to meet these needs.

It is beyond the scope of this text to completely analyze the informational requirements of transnational managers. However, there are several points that should be noted. Far too often in the past, MIS were developed to satisfy only the needs of the functional managers—marketing, finance, personnel, etc. This led, within the average transnational corporation, to a flow of data upward through the organization within functional areas only. While assisting these functional managers at the various levels, seldom was the information synthesized in a form that was usable by managers in other functional areas, at similar organizational levels. As a result, either too much or too little data was collected. There was excessive redundancy in data collection and analysis, causing notable deficiencies in timeliness of managerial response, accuracy, or perception of degree of accuracy of information, and lack of coordination between agencies within the organization.

It is our opinion that new computer software technology, notably data base management and structural programming techniques, now enables a transnational organization to develop management information systems which effectively pass data both vertically and horizontally within an organization in a timely manner. Additionally, data communications technology is sufficiently advanced that worldwide data collection can become virtually "real time," making use of high-grade telephone/telegraph circuits and communications satellites.

The onus is upon transnational managers to conceptualize their information needs, express a requirement to management information systems developers, and to insist upon involvement in the systems development process. Speed, accuracy, and effectiveness are the noteworthy capabilities of MIS, but are only possible if managers work closely with systems developers and constantly restate their requirements and express their interests.

Disinvestment, Trends, and Beneficial Technology

Causes of Disinvestment

As has been stated, all is not "wine and roses" for the transnational corporation. The worldwide involvement demands constant attention to changes in governments, moods and attitudes of people, changes in tastes, and naturally, cognizance of technological changes affecting their products and those of their competitors. There have been several recent instances of "foreign disinvestment: by some of the transnationals. This move usually is caused by: (1) poor investment decisions, (2) loss of competitive advantage or shifts in market demand, or (3) nationalization or expropriation.[65]

Trends

No consensus has been reached regarding future disinvestment trends. Many knowledgeable business observers believe that the rash of disinvestments represent a sorting out of ill-conceived investments in the 1960s and 1970s. Product life cycle in international relationships is perhaps the most adequate general theory explaining this problem. Transnational corporations, according to the theory, need accept the concept that foreign investments are born, grow, mature, and become senile. This acceptance will lead to less surprises, and more well-planned approaches to investment and disinvestment decisions.[66]

Beneficial Technology

Despite contrary arguments, transnationals return beneficial technology to their home nations. In some instances, acquiring foreign technology is the goal of an overseas investment. The Minnesota Mining and Manufacturing Corporation, for example, purchased Ferrania, an Italian firm, in order to improve its own film products. TRW Corporation acquired the Pleuger Company of West Germany because Pleuger had developed a superior submergible pump.[67]

All too often, domestic restrictions of one kind or another can force a transnational to go overseas for development work. Union restrictions in developed countries often contribute to this move to overseas development. Otis Elevator Company, required by unions to construct elevators and escalators on the construction site, used their West German subsidiary Flohr-Otis G.m.b.H. to develop a line of compact, simplified, prefabricated elevators, and escalators currently being sold throughout Europe.[68]

Sometimes technology reflows result from the efforts of transnational firms to meet competition in foreign markets. Other times when a new product fails to find a market in a country, a transnational can transfer production to a more receptive country, redefine the product through experience, and then reintroduce to the original country. In the former case, Englebert, Uniroyal's French subsidiary, was forced to develop a steel-belted radial tire to compete with Michelin. Englebert developed a competitive tire and it was subsequently introduced by Uniroyal to American consumers. As an example of the latter instance above, Bendix, licensed to produce disc brakes, shifted production to a French subsidiary because of noninterest in the United States; eventually, Bendix reintroduced disc brakes, which were used by Ford Motor Company in the Pinto automobile in 1969.[69]

Third World Transnationals

The world of the established transnational is also being further complicated by multinational firms chartered in developing countries. Third World multinational corporations may be categorized as those from (1) resource-rich developing countries, (2) labor-rich, rapidly industrializing countries, and (3) market-rich, rapidly industrializing countries.[70] With the increasing propensity for developing nations to band together, the Third World multinational will loom as an ever-increasing threat to the established transnational corporation. There should be little doubt that these new corporations are threats. They have important resources backing their entrance into the international market places. They have the capability for making major contributions. They will probably be competitive and effective.

As analyzed in this chapter, there are numerous factors that have an impact upon technology and the transnational organization. Transnational managers must be properly selected, strategy carefully conceived, plans comprehensively developed, and operations cohesively conducted. There are many natural enemies of the transnational firm, but perhaps its worst enemy is itself.

Endnotes Chapter Sixteen

1. "Going Global," *Datamation*, Vol. 26, No. 9, September 1980, p. 131.
2. Louis E. Boone and David L. Kurtz, *Contemporary Business*, 2nd edition, Hinsdale, IL: The Dryden Press, 1979, pp. 173–175.
3. C. P. Kindleberger, *Economic Development*, New York: McGraw-Hill Book Co., 1958, p. 91.
4. These figures are based upon OECD 1980 projections.
5. Signed on June 21, 1976.
6. Adopted from John Diebold "Multinational Corporations: Why Be Scared of Them?", Foreign Policy #12, National Affairs, Inc., in association with Carnegie Endowment for International Peace, New York, Fall 1973, pp. 79–93.
7. Dennis Meadows et al., *The Limits to Growth*, New York: The Club of Rome, 1972. The message of this book was discussed in Chapter 3.
8. S. Kuznets, *Economic Change*, New York: W.W. Norton & Co., 1953, p. 230.
9. The antigrowth movement is exemplified by G.J. Mischan, who wrote *The Costs of Economic Growth*, New York: Praeger, 1967, and *Technology and Growth*, New York: Praeger, 1970.
10. Argument adopted from S. Kuznets "Technological Innovations and Economic Growth," *Technological Innovation: A Critical Review of Current Knowledge*, P. Kelly and M. Kranzberg, ed., Advanced Technology and Science Study Group, Georgia Institute of Technology, January 1975, pp. 510–513.
11. F.R. Root, *International Trade and Investment*, Cincinnati: South-Western Publishing Co., 1973, pp. 567–568.
12. *Ibid.*, p. 568.
13. *Ibid.*, p. 568.
14. None have been approved at this writing.
15. *Mobilizing Technology For World Development*, J. Ramesh and C. Weiss, editors, New York: Praeger Publishing Co., 1979, pp. 89–90.
16. Sec "UN Technology Meeting Lacked Clear Direction," *Science*, Vol. 205, September 21, 1979, pp. 1236–1238, Working Paper No. 10, Commission on Transnational Corporations, Eighth Session, United Nations Economic and Social Council, January 7–18, 1980; "Report of the Intergovernmental Working Group on a Code of Conduct on its Fifth, Sixth, and Seventh Sessions," Commission on Transnational Corporations, United Nations Economic and Social Council, April 11, 1979; "Transnational Corporations: Certain Modalities For Implementation of a Code of Conduct in Relation to its Possible Legal Nature," Commission on Transnational Corporations, Sixth Session, United Nations Economic and Social Council, December 22, 1978; and "Transnational Corporations: Code of Conduct; Formulations By The Chairman," Commission on Transnational Corporations, United Nations Economic and Social Council, December 13, 1978.
17. "Business Without Bribes," *Newsweek* February 19, 1979, pp. 63–64.

18. Dan Morgan, "Executives Say Bribe Law Costs U.S. Companies Business," *The Washington Post*, March 10, 1979, p. A20.
19. For a comprehensive discussion of organization form see W.F. Glueck, *Management*, 2nd edition Hinsdale, IL: The Dryden Press, 1980, Chapter 11; and, for those organizations especially suited for use in R&D organizations see D.D. Roman, *Science, Technology and Innovation: A Systems Approach,* Columbus, OH: Grid Publishing Co., 1980, Chapter Eleven.
20. See Chapter Eleven.
21. See Roman, *op. cit.*, pp. 346–353 for discussion of these factors within the science and technology setting.
22. For an analysis of the study see "Leadership Attitudes of American and German Expatriate Managers in Europe and Latin America", by E. Miller, B. Batt, R. Hill, and J. Cattaneo as reported in *The Proceedings 1980 Academy of Management*, Detroit, MI, August 1980, pp. 53–57.
23. W. Glueck, *op. cit.*, p. 264.
24. B. Twiss, *Managing Technological Innovation*, London: Longman, 1974, pp. 56–61.
25. For more detailed information on transnational organizational structures, see J.N. Behrman, J.J. Boddewyn, and Ashok Kapour, *International Business — Government Communications*, Lexington, MA: D.C. Heath & Co., 1975; L.G. Franco, *The European Multinationals*, Stamford, CT: Greylock Publishers, 1976; and, R.D. Hays, C.M. Korth, and M. Roudianai, *International Business: An Introduction to the World of the Multinational Firm*, Englewood Cliffs, NJ: Prentice-Hall, 1972.
26. M.Y. Yoshino, "Toward a Concept of Managerial Control for a World Enterprise," *Michigan Business Review*, Vol. 18, No. 2, March 1966, pp. 25–31.
27. V. Salera, *Multinational Business*, Boston: Houghton Mifflin Co., 1969, p. 383.
28. M.Z. Brooke and H.L. Remmers, editors, *The Multinational Company in Europe: Some Key Problems*, Ann Arbor: The University of Michigan Press, 1972, p. 120.
29. W.M. Fox, "Japanese Management: Tradition Under Strain," *Business Horizons*, August 1977, p. 79.
30. M.G. Duerr and J.M. Roach, *Organization and Control of International Operations*, New York: The Conference Board, 1973, p. 24.
31. *Ibid.*
32. H. Martyn, *Multinational Business Management*, Lexington: D.C. Heath and Co., 1970, p. 150.
33. *Ibid.*, p. 154.
34. J.A. Sabata, "Quantity vs. Quality in Scientific Research: The Special Case of Developing Countries," *Impact of Science on Society*, XX, 1970, pp. 185–186.
35. J. LaPalombara and S. Blank, *Multinational Corporations in Comparative Perspective*, New York: The Conference Board, 1977, pp. 60–61.
36. Ashok Kapoor, *Planning for International Business Negotiation*, Cambridge: Ballinger Publishing Co., 1975, p. 1.
37. *Ibid.*, p. 7.
38. *Ibid.*, pp. 10–11.
39. J. Fayerweather and A. Kapoor, "Simulated International Business Negotiations," *Journal of International Business Studies*, Spring 1972, pp. 19–32.
40. Hayes et al., *International Business*, p. 23.
41. For a comprehensive discussion of regulatory risk see *Antitrust, Uncertainty, and Technological Innovation*, Committee on Technology and International Economic and Trade Issues of the Assembly of Engineering, National Research Council and Office of the Foreign Secretary,

National Academy of Engineering, National Academy of Sciences, Washington, DC, 1980, p. 1.

42. For a comprehensive review see James K. Weekly, "Expropriation of U.S. Multinational Investments," *MSU Business Topics*, Winter 1977, pp. 27–36.
43. "Cerro Takes Loss of $45.6 million in Peru Seizure," *The Wall Street Journal*, March 12, 1974, p. 26.
44. P. Nehemkis, "Expropriation has a Silver Lining," *California Management Review*, Fall 1974, p. 15.
45. P.R. Cateora, "The Multinational Enterprise and Nationalism," *MSU Business Topics*, Vol. 19, No. 2, p. 21.
46. P.R. Cateora and T.M. Hess, *International Marketing*, Homewood, IL: Richard D. Irwin, 1979, pp. 160–164.
47. F.R. Root, "Assessing and Managing Political Risk," *The Wall Street Journal*, October 3, 1980, p. 15.
48. *Ibid.*
49. *The Economist*, December 30, 1978, p. 51.
50. "State-Owned Business Abroad: New Competitive Threat," *Harvard Business Review*, March–April 1979, p. 162.
51. R.D. Robinson, *International Management*, New York: Holt, Rinehart, and Winston, 1967, p. 72.
52. *Ibid.*, p. 82.
53. J.D. Daniels, E.W. Ogram, and L.H. Radebaugh, *International Business: Environments and Operations*, Reading, MA: Addison-Wesley Publishing Co., 1976, pp. 458–460.
54. "U.S. Multinational Enterprises and the U.S. Economy," in *The Multinational Corporation: Studies on U.S. Foreign Investment, Part I*, U.S. Department of Commerce, March 1972, pp. 18–24.
55. R.B. Stobaugh, "How Investment Abroad Creates Jobs at Home," *Harvard Business Review*, September–October 1972, p. 119.
56. *Ibid.*, p. 126.
57. A.J. Raedler, "Taxation Policy in Multinational Companies," in *The Multinational Enterprise in Transition*, ed. A. Kapoor and P.D. Grub, Princeton: The Darwin Press, 1972, p. 30.
58. P.F. Brantner, "Taxation and the Multinational Firm," *Management Accounting*, October 1973, pp. 11–13.
59. *Multinational Corporations in World Development*, United Nations, 1973, p. 66.
60. Daniels et al., *op. cit.*, pp. 177–178.
61. See Lars Nieckels, *Transfer Pricing in Multinational Firms*, New York: John Wiley & Sons, 1976; and J.S. Arpan, "International Intracorporate Pricing," *Journal of International Business Studies*, Spring 1972, pp. 1–18.
62. "R&D Expenditures and Corporate Planning," *Research Management*, January 1980, XXIII, pp. 23–26.
63. MIS for the transnational enterprise is a topic which deserves extensive treatment. Dr. Puett has been involved in international MIS development over the past 15 years and is convinced that transnational enterprises have spent far too little time, money, and thought in this area.
64. Salera, *op. cit.*, p. 386.
65. G.G. Gattis, "U.S. Foreign Disinvestment," *The American University Business Review*, Washington, DC, Vol. 2, No. 1, Fall 1979, p. 35.
66. *Ibid.*, p. 41.

67. "A Return Flow of Technology From Abroad," *Fortune*, August 1973, p. 63.
68. *Ibid.*
69. *Ibid.*
70. D.A. Heegan and W.J. Keegan, "The Rise of Third World Multinationals," *Harvard Business Review*, January–February 1979, pp. 102–103.

SECTION VI:

Epilog

CHAPTER SEVENTEEN

Present and Possible Future Impacts

Some Technological Considerations

Technology and the World Environment

As a generalization, people want a better life. A better life can usually be transcribed as freedom from want, access to and possession of at least some of the nonessentials or luxuries, good health, a reasonable life expectancy, the absence of emotional stress engendered by a politically and economically unstable environment, and satisfying human relations resulting from gratifying work experience, intellectual stimulation, and personally rewarding leisure activity.

Prior to the 20th century it was possible in many societies to live a lifetime little influenced by technological change. Societal change, resulting from technology, has rapidly accelerated in this century. Change and technological development have not come in comparable degree to all societies. There have always been societal differences based on technological development. Technological development has often been the product of environment such as culture, climate, terrain, natural resources, and geographic location. What has been significant in the 20th century is the increasing disparity in technological development between different societies.

Technology is a product of human endeavor. To halt or eliminate technology would be to eradicate the human race. As long as there are people there will be inquisitive and intellectually aggressive individuals who will probe and experiment. Unfortunately, while technology has contributed to a better life in some instances and for some societies, it has also led to unforeseen negative affects in other instances. It most certainly has been a wedge driving greater world societal inequality.

Will technological expansion continue at a rapid pace? Plateau? Or actually diminish? If the recent past is any indicator of the future, technological expansion will continue at a rapid pace. However, not all people feel technological change is beneficial. Some people feel the problems resulting from technological change have outweighed the benefits. There are many advocates for a simpler lifestyle. Is it possible to retreat technologically or maintain the status quo? Is this desirable? To what extent will technological change have an impact on future society? Technological development cannot be isolated, and it must be recognized that there are international impacts.

If the thesis advanced in a preceding paragraph is accepted, that the human spirit is naturally inquisitive and technological development is inevitable, it then becomes imperative that technology be understood and managed.

Perspective

It is only during the latter half of this century that the implications of technological change have come into focus. The initial phase, awareness, has dawned. The next phase, coping with and managing technology, is evolving.

The recognition of a need for the management of science, technology, and innovation is, as has been indicated, a relatively recent phenomena. It is maintained that recognition and understanding are preliminary to solution. The balance of this chapter attempts to identify some of the problem areas associated with national and international technological development and some technological development prospects which are imminently nonexistent or are on the horizon.

Problems

Technology — Cure or Cause

Technology has been a factor in solving some problems and has been a factor in creating other problems. The world has figuratively grown smaller; internationalism has increased because of greater individual mobility, quicker and more sophisticated means of communication, and intensified interdependence between people and nations, which circumvents artificial political boundaries.

The world is becoming increasingly complex. Human survival is contingent on adaptability and solving the problems generated by complexity. Problems resulting from technology are often amenable to solutions by technology. Not all solutions are easy or, if possible, palatable to all societies. Most of the more intense problems are of relatively recent origin and are technology related. Candidate problems begging technological solutions are impressive. Just a few of these areas are touched upon in the following paragraphs. Technological problems are classified for discussion as environmental, productive, and cultural. Actually, there is much overlapping, and problems are not exclusively contained within any one classification.

Environmental Problems

Environmental problems can be segregated as being the by-product of technology and as problems created by natural circumstances where technology can neutralize or eliminate undesirable natural characteristics.

Technology has often resulted in an insatiable demand for natural resources. Often resources expended are not regenerating. Many natural resources, once considered plentiful, are rapidly diminishing. Moreover, some natural resources which are critical components in modern technology are unevenly distributed or nonexistent in some parts of the world.[1] No better example can be given than oil. The problem is compounded in many nations by high dependence and consumption of products made from natural resources that are alien to those societies.

Transnational organizations have often been the vehicle to discover, develop, and exploit natural resources. Technologically critical natural resources have frequently been native to developing countries. Inadequate technology and capital limitations in such countries have been factors leading to their development by foreign organizations. The transnational has often initially been welcome in these situations. In many instances after the first sense of euphoria of the host country has dissipated, there have been feelings of resentment. Host country hostility usually reflects the impression that natural resources are being used outside the country for the betterment of other societies and a benefit analysis is unfavorable to the host country.

Developed nations are invariably industrial nations. Industrial nations are high energy consumers. Few industrial nations are energy self-sufficient. There are diminishing supplies of traditional energy sources. Unless cheap and bountiful alternative energy sources are developed the existing world economic structure is in extreme jeopardy. Technology must be used to solve energy requirement problems. Alternatives as to energy sources or more effective use of energy represent tremendous developmental opportunities.

Energy developed from internal resources is only one important area where shortages are evolving. Developed nations, in particular, have been extravagant users of natural resources. Often products have been designed for early obsolence and wastefully discarded. Technology can fruitfully be employed to utilize natural resources better, to find substitutes for nonrenewable resources, to help devise better systems for waste management and disposal, and to develop economic processes for recycling.[2] Each of the aforementioned areas affords incentives for commercial development. No doubt with increasing pressures resulting from some of the problems cited, transnational organizations will move into these evolving opportunity areas.

Another environment problem associated with technology is pollution. The environment has become contaminated. The natural habitat has been affected. Also, technology-generated contamination has led to many industrial diseases affecting humans.[3] Pollution problems are usually not local or political.

Pollution originating in one geographic location and in one political domain can spread to infect other areas. Pollution is a very serious threat to the quality of life. Pollution, in its many forms is a international problem which requires an international cooperative effort for effective solution. If quality of life standards are to be maintained or improved it is imperative that technological effort be directed to the elimination of harmful pollution.

Most of this section has related to environmental problems resulting from technology. Technology can also be employed to improve natural conditions. A good part of the world is unhabitable or marginally habitable because of climate, terrain, or location. Technology can be a factor to harvest more effectively ocean and space resources, to improve agricultural yields, to convert salt water to usable fresh water economically, to reclaim wasteland, to neutralize debilitating climatic conditions, and to minimize the consequences of periodic natural disturbances.

Productive Problems

There are many problems associated with productive technological development. An attempt is made to touch on some of the more relevant difficulties.

Technologically directed production essentially, involves technical and productive feasibility and market or economic prospects. Most so-called new products are not really new products. Rather, they are evolutionary developments and are improvements from existing products.* The development of a really new product is a high-risk endeavor. In new product development in a complicated technology the technical and marketing risks are considerable and the resource requirements are generally extensive.

In the United States there has been an organizational trend toward financially dominated management. Financial people, by reason of their conservative functional orientation, are conditioned to expect short-run predictable results. This attitude is incompatible with the long-term high risks and unpredictability of technological development. In short, a risk-avoidance posture is not conductive to technological development.

Immediately after World War II the United States was the unquestioned technological leader in the world. The U. S. position has since eroded along several technological frontiers. Major competition in high-technology products has come from Japan and West Germany, in particular, as well as several other developed countries. Almost invariably in each situation where technological competition has taken place there has been a willingness to forego short-run profit, venture capital has been made available, and in many instances government has provided varying degrees of support for industry.

Direct head-to-head competition may not be technically or economically feasible in the future. The technological complexity, the extensive resource requirements, and the need to develop world products with a broad market

*Genetic engineering offers great promise for new plant and animal strains.

base will act as motivations for technological cooperation. Cooperation on complex technological projects is increasingly being manifested in technological consortiums.

The expansion of knowledge in electronics, medicine, genetic engineering, space, and the remote sensing of the earth's resources, as a few examples, are making it possible to create products that were heretofore undreamed of. Such prospects are, of course, exciting; such prospects are also frightening and fraught with potential problems.

New products often obsolete existing products. Capital investment may be negated by superseding developments. Are there enough riches in the world to discard equipment, facilities, and products that are obsoleted by newer developments? Attendant to product obsolescence is human obsolescence. What impacts will new technological developments have on the present labor force and existing skills? Rapid technological change requires a constant and orderly transition. The human factor is critical and cannot be overlooked. In the final analysis the true wealth of any nation or society is its people. Human obsolescence resulting from technology is a very real threat.

New products are often operationally unpredictable. Even if new products are exposed to exhaustive premarket tests and evaluation, unforeseen problems frequently occur in actual use. The more drastic the technology changes, the higher is the probability that, at least initially, there will be the need for product redesign and modification.

Associated with defective products are such problems as organizational reputation and image as well as potential legal liability. There has been a growing consumer movement in the United States. There have been several individual and class action suits brought against companies for injuries resulting from defective products. Quality control and maintenance of quality standards is extremely important. As indicated, when products are really new they are apt to have "bugs" so that quality standards and control are usually very difficult in the early product life stage. This is a problem and is a factor creating pressure for evolutionary and predictable product development vis à vis a revolutionary development where there may be product unknowns.

There is still another problem associated with product development. There are no international product quality control standards, and governmental regulations vary extensively between nations. A cardinal example is food and drug regulations and quality control in the United States versus controls employed in other nations. Many pharmaceutical products unacceptable in the United States by our standards, are available within other countries.

A few of the more relevant production problems resulting from technology have been mentioned in the preceding paragraphs. One more very important problem should be addressed and that is the ability to overproduce relative to the effective market demand. Automation, robotization, and computerization are a few technological developments that have materially changed the production processes. It is becoming increasingly possible to produce more and more goods with fewer and fewer people. No societal segment is immune from such technological encroachment.

It is often maintained that technological displacement is a temporary phenomena and that in the long run technology will be instrumental in creating more jobs than it eliminates. There may be validity to such arguments. No attempt is made to support such contentions positively or negatively. However, it is contended that a very real short-run transitional problem does exist. Traditional supply and demand economic theory appears to have broken down. Overproduction, resulting from sophisticated technological developments appears to be a more normal trend than the exception. How can surplus labor be accommodated in industrial societies? The problem is even more traumatic in developing nations where huge surpluses of unskilled labor exist. The difference between present low-skill levels and a shift of requirements for new high-skill levels intensifies the labor disparity between developed and developing countries.

The shifting production and skill requirements presents one of the greatest technological challenges in the world. Technology has magnified rather than minimized such problems; technology is required to solve this world problem of unemployment or underemployment. There are apparently, as yet unanswerable questions: What technology or technologies can be developed to solve these problems and where does the initiative lie for such technological development? With government? With industry? Or, a partnership between government and industry?

Cultural Problems

Cultural patterns can have a strong influence on technological development. Culture can be reflected in potential institutions, religious beliefs, and societal mores. In most countries of the world there is a separation between the state and religion. However, the degree of separation varies; the religious influence on political doctrine in some nations is considerable.

Often where religious and political systems are intertwined there is definite cultural bias against technology that might affect tradition. Usually, such societies are not technologically progressive. Many examples can be cited where there is a religious and subsequently politically subservient population. More often than not the educational level and general intellectual attainment in such an environment is not conducive to a dynamic technology.

The political situation can also provide motivation for or retard technological development. Political instability is a deterrent to technological investment. Significant technological change usually involves a long-term commitment. There is understandable reluctance to make such a commitment with the attendant risk and capital requirements where there is an uncertain political future. As has been mentioned several times in this book, governmental policy can also be extremely influential in encouraging technological development.

Interface with many different nationals, from developed as well as developing countries, has indicated a very positive concern with the need for innovation, improved productivity, and problems of motivation. It would appear that problems relating to innovation, productivity, and motivation are universal. Without lengthy discourse it is also maintained that cultural influences are extremely important motivational factors to encourage or discourage innovation and subsequent productivity.

Another very serious problem in technological development is the question of proprietary right. Most new technology is developed in industrially advanced nations. In many instances such technologies are eventually modified and transferred to less technologically advanced societies. Developing nations, often the recipients of transferred technology, are frequently resentful because of technological dependence and a feeling of exploitation. There have been several instances where advanced technology was originally welcomed and eventually expropriated.

Developed nations are becoming wary of transferring technology where there is considerable risk and investment. Reluctance to develop and transfer stems from the possibility, as mentioned, of expropriation and also the fact that the transferee may eventually become a competitor. Competitive advantage is possible at a result of less-expensive labor and operations as well as not having to contend with technological developmental costs.

There is no easy answer to the issues raised. It does appear that there is a growing schism between the developed and the developing nations on the legal and moral rights to technology. There is no satisfactory international law covering rights and use of technology. Nations zealously guard their sovereignty and any legal redress attempted within a nation's sovereign domain is apt to have a very unsympathetic reception.

The sociological setting reflects cultural patterns. Some societies are more materialistic than others. In some societies, materialism is equated with "the better life." In such societies, there normally is a pronounced work ethic. In other societies, materialism has negative connotations. Still in other societies, there are economic conditions that discourage work because material acquisition of any consequence is beyond the expectations of the average worker.

Many factors have been mentioned that affect the quality of life. At the beginning of this chapter an attempt was made to describe the elements of a better life. All societies do not provide equal opportunity for achieving the better life. Human rights differ in various political jurisdictions. Value systems also are subject to a wide variation due to religious, political, and cultural influences. Considering the existing range of societal variations, it would appear that, in most instances, the development of universal technologies is not feasible.

Some Possible and Some Probable Technological Changes in the Future with International Impact

Growing Internationalism

Persuasive arguments can be advanced that technology is facilitating internationalism. Many technological developments, possible and probable, are motivational for internationalism and are instrumental in the lowering of national barriers. Isolationism, as a political philosophy, is not feasible in the light of growing international technological interdependence. It has become apparent that no nation has a monopoly on knowledge or brain power, let alone the material resources required for many essential products. In short, increasing technological and related economic interrelationships are intensifying international interactions and forcing technologically cooperative arrangements which in the past would have been virtually impossible because of political constraints.

"Futurism" is demanding increasing attention and respect. Many scenarios on short-, intermediate-, and long-run future international developments are possible. An entire volume could be directed to such conjecture. Needless to say an extensive, in-depth treatment is beyond the scope of this book. In the following paragraphs of this section some of the more likely developments which have technological and international impacts will be mentioned. It is unrealistic to assume that all the changes suggested will be universally adapted or that changes which are generally probable will occur at the same intensity or within the same time frame for all nations.

Cultural Changes

Many societies are in some phase of cultural change. The extent and rate of change are apt to be greater in technologically advanced societies than in societies strongly rooted in tradition. In the United States, the term "generation gap" has been widely used to denote the difference which has taken place in a very short span of years. The difference in value systems and lifestyles between parents and children in the latter half of the 20th century has become very pronounced.

Several factors have contributed to the change in the cultural system. Education, once regarded as a privilege or luxury is now considered a right. The level of education of the general population has increased with a subsequent change in life expections, human or people awareness, and societal concern. Women have moved into occupations previously considered male bastions. Additionally, women are assuming greater managerial responsibilities in organizations. Traditional or stereotyped male/female roles are being modified.

With better education and career prospects and less economic dependence on males, many women are delaying marriage and the raising of families. Inflation, the desire for career identification, and increased materialism have been pressures encouraging two wage earners in the family. The long-run prospects are for demographic changes such as fewer children per family, eventual population stabilization, and a shift in the age composition in the population to a much larger percent being older. People are living longer and retaining their physical and mental vigor longer. Early retirement represents a loss to society by taking these productively capable people out of the system. Retirement costs of older workers may, at least in part, be born by younger workers. This puts additional strain on the system and lowers the overall system productivity. A solution to this problem is certainly indicated. Perhaps some technological development will provide an answer?

Cultural changes are taking place at the most rapid rate in the history of humanity. In many societies changes are not only rapid but are revolutionary relative to past cultural practices. It can be questioned as to what now is a tradition in such societies, or in fact does a tradition indeed exist. In most developed nations there is a trend toward a better educated population. Education is no longer for the classes, it is now for the masses. A better educated population will probably be more discerning and apt to reject inflexible cultural traditions. Young people will be more inclined than their ancestors, or their parents for that matter, to explore socially and question rigid institutionalism.

Political and Economic Changes

Political disruption has been relatively common in the world. Political disruption has at times been gradual or transitional and at other times has been revolutionary and possibly violent. Some societies have been more vulnerable to drastic political change than other societies. Political stability or peaceful transitional change can provide incentive for national technological development. Some degree of predictability and continuity is environmentally essential for capital accumulation and technological investment.

Many nations, particularly the Soviet bloc countries, have adopted five-year plans which frequently incorporate many technological objectives. At times national planning has been less than satisfactory. The United States, with notable exceptions such as the space program, has not generally made a formal long-term technological planning commitment. Often desired technological direction can be inferred from political support of projects. More often however, the government management of technology has been crises stimulated rather than on the basis of calculated planning.

Technology should have increasing international impact. Forward-looking political and economic organizations will have to evaluate their role and participation in future technological development. Organizational role and participation will be to some extent influenced by diminishing nationalism predicated by increasing international interdependence. It may be far into the future, but there is a reasonable probability that there will be diminishing quality of life disparities between nations. In line with increasing international social awareness more science, technology, and innovation activity will be directed to socially oriented projects. Firms doing business internationally could be well advised to look into commercial prospects of socially directed effort.

Quality of Life Changes

There should be significant changes affecting the quality of life; many of these changes are the result of technology. In the future more production will be possible with less human effort. Work will be less tedious and dangerous. There will be more individual interpretive latitude. Hopefully work will be more pleasant and aesthetically rewarding.

In many of the developed nations there appears to be a trend toward shorter work weeks, flex time, and longer vacations. It follows that people will have more leisure time. Perhaps it will become generally feasible to schedule work so that periodic sabbaticals will become a norm. Sabbaticals can provide new experiences, intellectual stimulation, and a change of pace to avoid or minimize human obsolescence.

There is the possibility that in the future there may be some career stratification based on demographics. Modular career patterns could be at least a partial answer to boredom and early retirement.[4]

Undoubtedly the quality of life will be affected by medical technology. Barring any catastrophic natural or human induced event there is good future probability for better health and increased lifespan. The entire health care field has great promise for technological development. Technology will assist in eliminating or controlling many diseases, retard aging, eliminate or minimize birth defects, and by artificial processes enable the replacement of diseased or injured organs.

Communication

International communication is still not simple, but there is progress. Communication difficulties arise from language, cultural, and space differences. In many places language differences are no longer insurmountable barriers since internationally educated people can usually communicate in a second language such as English, French, Spanish, or German. Cultural problems also can be surmounted by a little research and a willingness to adapt to local customs. Proximity has helped to minimize previous problems resulting from physical separation and culture.

Many technologically related factors have contributed to improved communication. Satellite communication systems have made information transmission cheaper and more accessible. International television has been a most effective communication device to transmit quickly news and pictures of events of worldwide interest.[5] People are more mobile. Exposure to different people and different cultures is enlightening and helpful in developing an international understanding and dialogue.

Computer technology has perhaps been the most revolutionary development in communication. Computers in their various applications have had a profound impact throughout the world. Technology has moved so rapidly in the computer area that failure to anticipate and expand the technology is tantamount to inviting operational and market failure.

Cooperative Effort

A recurring theme throughout this text is the growing international nature of business and technological innovation. It would seem possible to do business on an international scale with no direct technological innovation. However, upon reflection, the basis for trade or exchange is usually some product or service that is unique or not economically or technically feasible for one of the parties to the transaction. The product or service invariably is representive of some phase of technology.

It appears that some form of cooperative effort between nations and between businesses is becoming a relatively common practice.[6] Cooperative effort is dictated to minimize risk, pool knowledge,[7] have access to and effectively use natural resources, establish a market base, and eliminate or neutralize technologically induced ecological problems which have international repercussions.

In the past cooperative effort has been restricted by a strong sense of nationalism and the desire to achieve a competitive advantage. Changing world conditions have led to a reassessment and frequently subsequent modification of national policy. What appears to be evolving is the increasing need for mutual ventures where the ultimate benefits circumvent provincial interests. In essence, technological cooperation is being forced by the recognition that technological development is imperative for political and economic survival.

Industry Prospects

Technological awareness and relevant and economically feasible innovation are critical factors, especially so for the business organization operating in the international marketplace. A significant part of awareness is information. Information must be germane and intelligently interpreted to identify diminishing prospects and emerging opportunity.

Many new skills, career patterns, technologies, and products are evolving. Some fields or products appear to be on a downward trend, being superseded or obsoleted by technological developments. A total comprehensive list of fields that offer promise for technological opportunity probably is not possible. Following are some fields or technologies where future prospects seem to be encouraging:

Microelectronics.

Communications.

Computers.

Food processing.

Energy.

Health—genetic engineering.

Ocean resources.

Leisure.

Education.

Transportation.

Environment.

Space.

Chemistry (development of synthetics).

Remote sensing of earth's resources.

Waste management—recycling.

Some Concluding Observations

Capital Requirements

Many emerging or prospective technologies require tremendous capital expenditures for R&D activity. Cost escalations for such activities have been so considerable as to price major technological explorations out of the realm of any one political or business organization. As previously indicated, the emerging nature and sophistication of many technologies have encouraged cooperative effort. Cooperative effort has for the most part been among the industrialized developed nations. Developing nations have initially been excluded or have had relatively little impact in many of the more recent and relevant technological developments.

A possible solution to encourage more uniform world technological development and greater participation would be the establishment of a new world technology monetary fund. The fund could be directed toward internationally relevant technological development and could provide the necessary capital required for such development. All nations could contribute and participate in the technological benefits resulting from the investment capital.

The suggestion is an oversimplification of a complex task but the potential international benefits of such a plan could warrant a studied look at the feasibility of this recommendation. A few immediate advantages suggested are the availability of capital for high-risk but potentially internationally beneficial technology, participation and contribution of many nations encouraging a "one world" approach helping to dissipate inherent international animosities, the creation of a broader market base, and closing the technological gap between the developed and developing nations.

Better Management

Managing science, technology, and innovation as a viable concept is a relatively new phenomena. The study of international business as an academic discipline is also of recent origin. We think that the recognition of the interrelationship between international business and technological innovation represents an additional step forward.

There are many problems in the world stemming from political or economic sources. Considering the magnitude of problems in the world a cursory look could leave the impression that many of the difficulties are insolvable. Many technology-related problems are so extensive that the resources or jurisdiction of any one organization or political entity would be severely strained at best or probably inadequate to reach a satisfactory solution.

It has been said that what is past is prologue. Present and potential future events seem to dictate a new and more enlightened managerial approach to cope with the evolving world environment. Future successful managers will require a much broader perspective. Problems will be far more complex and international in scope. Managers will have to divorce themselves from provincialism.

Technological development in the future will probably proceed along more orderly, better planned, and managed approaches than has been the case in the past. Information gathering and interpretation will be fundamental to technological forecasting and assessing both the potential positive and negative aspects of a developing technology. Additionally, more concern in the future will be necessary to evaluate the appropriativeness of a technology before any significant commitment is made to that technology.

Better management can be instrumental in resolving many of the present and potential future problems. Better management in the future will be dependent on responsiveness to the international environment and the changes taking place in that setting.

The Transnational Business Organization

Prior to World War II transnational business organizations generally operated unobtrusively. Since World War II it can hardly be said that the transnational has become flamboyant, but the nature and extension of their operations has given them considerably more visibility.

The transnational organization may be a unique vehicle to accomplish internationally by more subtle means that which is often not overtly feasible. The transnational, by entrepreneural advantage in different political jurisdictions, can transcend national barriers. The factors of production are land, labor, capital, and entrepreneurship. The entrepreneural activities of transnationals can be used to effectively blend the factors of production from different countries into a viable economic product. It may be that the transnational is one of the best vehicles for technology transfer. It may also be that due to locational advantages and available resources that the transnational firm is and will continue to be a prime developer and promoter of technological innovation.

Endnotes Chapter Seventeen

1. "Getting Serious About Strategic Materials," *Science*, Vol. 212, No. 17, April 1981, p. 305.
2. *Ibid.*
3. See "Medical Sleuths—Fear of Toxic Materials Creates More Demand For Epidemiologist," *The Wall Street Journal*, April 14, 1981, p. 1.
4. "An Aging Work Force Strains Japan's Traditions." *Business Week*, April 20, 1981, pp. 72–85.

5. It has been reported that a British invention of a TV with a three-inch screen will be marketed some time in 1982. *Industrial Research*, April 1981, p. 44.
6. To list just a few examples: The European Common Market, The Soviet Union Bloc, Andes Nations, OPEC, The Concord, the Airbus, etc.
7. A good example is the employment of Israel's trained human resources by U.S. Companies. "Israel—A Bargain for the U.S. in High-Tech Engineers," *Business Week*, April 20, 1981, p. 44.

Appendix A

Technology Source Identification

General

Listed are various sources that will assist in locating and transferring technology worldwide. Most of the directories may be found in World Trade Center (WTC) libraries, located in major U.S. and foreign cities. Consult local telephone directory for specific street address and telephone number of WTC library.

Directories on International Companies

American Register of Exporters and Importers (90 W. Broadway, New York, NY 10017). Provides information on Steamship Lines, Freight Fowarders, American Chamber of Commerce in Foreign Countries, Foreign Chamber of Commerce, Embassies, Foreign Trade Associations.

Bottin Europe (annual) (Societe Didot—Bottin, 1 rue Sebastien Bottin, Paris 7^{e}, France). Provides information for Importers/Exporters, Producers and Manufacturers, General information by country and city including government offices, trade offices, and Chamber of Commerces.

Directory of International Engineering and Construction Services (National Constructors Association, 1012 Fourteenth Street, Washington, DC 20005). International engineering and construction firms.

Who Owns Who: Australasia and Far East: A Directory of Parent, Associates and Subsidiary Companies (O.W. Roskill & Co., Ltd. 14 Great College Street London S.W. 1P-3 R.V. England). Parent associates and subsidiary companies in Australia and Far East.

Who's Who in Finance & Industry (previously named Business & Industry) (A.M. Marquis Co.). Includes selected principal businesses.

Who's Who in Foreign Trade—Roster and Directory (Foreign Trade Association of Southern California, Los Angeles, CA 90017). Classified—company and individuals in trade in Southern California.

Meier's Adressbuch der Exporteure und Importeure (International directory published in German translated as Directory of Export and Import) (Rudolf Dudy K.-G. Hamburg 1, Banksstr. 20-26, Germany). Geographically by country and city. Some trademarks.

Jane's Major Companies of Europe—1975 Edition (annual) (The Charterhouse Group, 1 Paternoster Row, St. Pauls, London EC 4P 4HP England). Western European companies' financial structure, operating result, and business activities.

Directory of Swiss Manufacturers and Producers (Swiss Office for the Development of Trade, Dreikonigstrasse 8 CH-8022, Zurich, Switzerland). Swiss companies' line of business, cross-indexed by product.

Dun and Bradstreet Principal International Business: The World Marketing Directory—1975 Edition (annual) (Dun and Bradstreet Inc., 99 Church Street, New York, NY 10007). By country, import and exchange regulations, shipping and transportation ports and services, weights and measures communications, radio, cable, mail, laws, insurance, export terms and practices.

World Wide Chamber of Commerce Directory (Johnson Publishing Company, Inc., Box 455, Loveland, CO 80537). Chambers of Commerce in U.S. American Chambers of Commerce abroad, Canadian Chambers of Commerce, foreign Chambers of Commerce in principal cities throughout the world, foreign embassies and consulates located in the United States and U.S. consulates and embassies throughout the world.

Europ Production (ABC Edition) (Europ Export Edition GMBH, D-61 Darmstadt, Germany, Berliner Allee, Postfach 4034). The universal register of European exports, by products and suppliers.

Kelly's Manufacturers and Merchants Directory, (Neville House, Eden Street, Kinston-upon Thames, Surrey, KTI IBY, England). By country and product, international companies' addresses.

Local Phone Book (Yellow Pages) of Foreign Countries (Available from local telephone company). By city and product, companies' addresses and phone numbers.

International Yellow Pages (R.H. Donnelly Corporation). By country, city, and product, companies' addresses and phone numbers.

Newspapers and Magazines

All leading U.S. and foreign newspaper and magazines.

F&S Index International (Monthly) (Predicasts Inc., 11001 Cedar Avenue, Cleveland, Ohio 44106). Cross-referenced index on world magazines.

Trade Association Publications

Committee for a National Trade Policy, Inc.

National Council of American Importers, Inc.

Trade Relations Council of the United States, Inc.

International Executives Association of New York.

International Trade Club of Chicago.

American Society of International Executives.

U.S. Department of Commerce Publications and Services

Agent/Distributor Services (ADS). The ADS is used to locate foreign import agents and/or distributors. The essence of the service is the determination of a firm's interest in a specific export proposal and willingness to correspond with the U.S. register. Information is supplied on one to six qualified representatives.

Trade Opportunities Program (TOP). This service provides information about foreign firms that could act as agents or distributors for products. Through TOP's Notice service, the U.S. company, as a subscriber to TOP, specifies the products and the countries for which it would like to receive notices of overseas representation opportunities. This information is automatically matched by computer against representation opportunities identified by foreign Service Officers (worldwide). The U.S. subscriber is notified of matches.

Foreign Traders Index (FTI). A collection of information about foreign firms maintained in a master computer file. The file contains information on more than 150,000 importing firms, agents, representatives, distributors, manufacturers, service organizations, retailers, and potential end-users of U.S. products or services in 130 countries. This information is made available through the Export Mailing List Service, the FTI Data Tape Service, the FTI Data Tape Service, and Trade Lists, discussed below.

Export Mailing List Service (EMLS). The EMLS consists of special targeted retrievals for individual requesters wishing to obtain lists of foreign firms in selected countries by commodity classification. Retrievals provide data as to name and address of firm, name and title of chief executive, year established, relative size, number, cable address, and product or service codes by SIC number.

Foreign Traders Index (FTI) Data Tape Service. Through this service, information on all firms included is The FTI for all countries (or in selected countries) is available to subscribers are magnetic tape. Users can retrieve various segments of the data through their own computer facilities.

Trade Lists. The Department of Commerce maintains up-to-date lists of foreign buyers, distributors, and agents for various products in many countries. These trade lists give names and addresses of foreign companies dealing in specific products in more than 100 countries. They also identify importers and dealers, giving names and addresses, the size of each firm, the size of its sales force, the territory covered and other pertinent information such as the acceptable language of correspondence.

World Trade Directory Reports. These reports provide detailed commercial information of individual overseas firms whose names you might, for example, have obtained from the trade lists. They describe the size of the firms, products handled, sales territories, and names of owners and officers. They also cover the type of organization method of operation, capital, sales volume, general reputation in trade and financial circles, and names of any U.S. firms represented by the overseas firm.

Agent Distributor Search Service. This service consists of a survey performed on-the-spot by a U.S. Commercial Officer. He looks for qualified firms that are willing to handle your product in a specific country or area. Each survey costs $25.00 and takes an average of 60 days to complete.

Overseas Business Reports. These reports provide detailed economic and market analysis on approximately 100 specific countries.

Global Market Surveys. These reports provide detailed economic and market analyses by product in the world markets and detailed market analyses on selected countries.

Checklist—U.S. Department of Commerce (Field Offices). A list of several hundred international business publications.

Foreign Commerce Handbook. U.S. Chamber of Commerce, Foreign Commerce Department. A general guide to import and export services and information. Lists all principal information sources, including regulations, texts periodicals, government and commercial sources.

An Introduction to Doing Import and Export Business. U.S. Chamber of Commerce, Foreign Policy Department. A handbook introducing the principles, problems, practices and techniques involved in foreign trade operations.

Other Information Sources

Exporters Encyclopedia (Thomas Ashwell and Co.). Details the documents and method of handling shipments to every country in the world. Reference tables and summaries of government requirements, shipping, communications, packing, marking and invoicing requirements. (Generally similar to a Dun and Bradstreet publication of the same title.)

Export and Import Procedures (Morgan Guaranty Trust Co. of New York). A summary of the methods of financing and payment of international transactions and the handling of financial instrument in importing and exporting.

Exporting to the United States (U.S. Treasury Department, Bureau of Customs). A general guide designed to inform foreign suppliers as to regulations and procedures for preparing and documenting shipments to the United States.

Handbook of International Purchasing by Paul H. Combs (Cahners Books, 221 Columbus Avenue, Boston, Massachusetts 02116). Guide to foreign buying, terms of payments, and other aspects of purchasing abroad.

Revised American Foreign Trade Definitions (National Foreign Trade Council).

Trade Terms (*Terms Commerciaux*) (International Chamber of Commerce).

Uniform Customs and Practice for Documentary Credits (1962 Revision—Brochure No. 222) (International Chamber of Commerce).

Financing of U.S. Exports (The First National Bank of Chicago, 1975).

Export and Import Financing Procedures (The First National Bank of Chicago).

Understanding Futures in Foreign Exchange (International Monetary Market).

Exchange Rates, Monthly Foreign (Federal Reserve System Division of Administrative Services).

Pick's Currency Yearbook (Pick Publishing Corporation).

Customs House Guide (Import Publications).

Tariff Schedule of the United States (Annotated) (1963, including supplements) (U.S. Tariff Commission).

Special and Administrative Provision of the Tariff Act of 1930 (1960 Edition) (including Supplement 1, 1965) (U.S. Tariff Commission).

American Import and Export Bulletin (monthly) (Import Publications).

Customs Regulations of the United States (U.S. Treasury Department).

Customs Information for Exporters to the United States (U.S. Treasury Department).

Treasury Decisions (U.S. Treasury Department).

Comprehensive Guide to U.S. Government Import/Export Forms (Customs Consultants).

Import Manual (Trilling Publications).

Export Form Guide Book (Unz and Company).

Export/Import Traffic Management and Forwarding (Alfred Murr Shipping Digest).

Air Shippers Manual (Import Publication).

Exporter's Guide to Cargo Insurance (American Institute of Marine Underwriters).

Marine Insurance (Insurance Company of North America).

Arbitration in Foreign Trade (American Arbitration Association).

Sources of Credit Information on Foreign Firms (U.S. Department of Commerce, Bureau of International Business Operations).

Foreign Trade Service — Foreign Import and Exchange Regulations (Chase Manhattan Bank of New York).

Doing Business in (*Specify Country*) (American Management Association Bulletin).

International Commerce (Quarterly) (Foundation for the Advancement of International Business Administration).

Air Transportation Magazine (Monthly) (Budd Publications).

International Management (Monthly) (Dun and Bradstreet).

National Foreign Trade Council, Inc. (10 Rockefeller Plaza, New York, NY 20020.

Foreign Trade Association of Southern California (3921 Wilshire Boulevard, Los Angeles, California).

National Council of American Importers (New York, New York).

Local Consulates of Foreign Countries (Local Telephone Book).

International Divisions of All Major Banks (Local Telephone Book).

International Chamber of Commerce (38 Cours Albert Ier, Paris VIII, France).

Local Trade Commissions of Foreign Countries (Local Telephone Book).

International Executives Association (432 Park Avenue, New York, NY).

World Trade Council (United States Chamber of Commerce, Washington, DC).

Council for International Progress in Management (845 Third Ave., New York, NY).

Organizations and Institutions Involved in International Technology Transfer

International Organizations

Financial

World Bank

International Bank for Reconstruction and Development

Institutes

International Maize and Wheat Improvement Center (DIMMYT) Mexico

International Rice Research Institute (IRRI) Philippines

International Institute for Applied Systems Analysis (IIASA)

International Scientific Organizations by Discipline, e.g., Physics, Chemistry etc.

Aviation/Astronautics

International Civil Aviation Organization (INCAO)

International Astronautical Federation (IAF)

International Council of thc Acronautical Sciences (ICAS)

Multinational Organizations

The United Nations

Economic Commission for Europe

Food and Agricultural Organization

World Health Organization

International Atomic Energy Agency

Regional Economic Commissions for Asia, Far East, Latin America, and Africa

United Nations Educational, Scientific and Cultural Organization (UNESCO)—Science Policy Division

United Nations Industrial Development Organization (UNIDO)

International Labor Organization (ILO)

Advisory Committee on the Application of Science and Technology to Development (Subsidiary of Economic and Social Council)

General Agreement on Tariffs and Trade (GATT)

Organization for Economic Cooperation and Development (OECD)

Scientific Affairs Directorate

Committee for Scientific and Technical Personnel

Committee for Science Policy

European Nuclear Energy Agency (ENEA)

Development Assistance Committee (DAC)

European Organizations

European Space Research Organization (ESRO)

European Launch Development Organizations (ELDO)

EURATOM

European Coal and Steel Community (ESC)

International Institute for Management of Technology (IIMT) Milan, Italy

European Civil Aviation Electrical Organization (EUROCAE)

North Atlantic Treaty Organization (NATO)

NATO Armament Groups

Military Agency for Standardization

Anti-Submarine Warfare Research Center—Italy

Advisory Group for Aerospace Research and Development (AGARD)

SHAPE Technological Center

Information Exchange Groups (IEG)

Standing Committees on Technology Exchange

Mutual Weapons Data Exchange Agreements

NATO Industrial Advisory Group (NIAG)

Asia

Asian Center for Technology Transfer & Investment (ACTTI)

Organization of American States

Organization of American States—Dept. of Scientific Affairs

Standards Organizations

- Organization for International Standardization (ISO)
- International Electrotechnical Commission (IEC)
- American National Standards Institute (ANSI)
- British Standards Institute
- ABC Standards Group—American, British, Canadian

Transnational Corporations

- R&D laboratories abroad
- Manufacturing, marketing, and service organizations
- Training and education of foreign nationals—workers, technicians, managers
- Investment in local production and use of local suppliers
- Programs of technological upgrading of indigenous industries and suppliers
- Introduction of advanced management practices and technological influence

U.S. Government Agencies

- DOE Cooperative Agreement, Technology Exchange Programs
- DOD
  - Cooperative R&D programs
  - Bilateral coproduction agreements
  - Consortia production programs with NATO/allied countries
  - Military sales
  - Defense Security Assistance Agency
  - Exchange Scientist Program
  - NATO Navy Advisory Groups
  - Information exchange groups
  - Mutual weapons data exchange agreements
  - Military attaches
  - ONR London
- NASA
  - Office of International Affairs
  - Cooperative R&D Programs
  - Technical data and publications services
  - Exchange agreements
- Department of Commerce
  - Patent Office, ESSA, Bureau of Census
  - Clearinghouse for Foreign Scientific and Technical Information
- Department of State
  - Science and technology offices
  - Embassies, missions, consolates, etc.
- Agency for International Development
- National Science Foundation
- National Academy of Sciences

Industrial Trade Associations

AIAA—American Institute of Aeronautics and Astronautics
AIA—Aerospace Industries Association
NSAI—National Security Industrial Association
EIA—Electronics Industries Association

Appendix B

Foreign Investment and Licensing Checklist*

This checklist of factors to consider prior to negotiation of a foreign direct investment or licensing agreement is designed to assist businessmen in development of their own checklists when exploring investment and licensing opportunities abroad. It does not purport to be complete but does cover problems associated both with developing countries and the developed nations.

Foreign investment and licensing agreements are often closely linked, licensing sometimes being an integral part of the direct investment. Occasional references to licensing will therefore be found in the section on foreign investment. Businessmen contemplating only licensing abroad should, in addition to studying the section on licensing, carefully check the factors listed under the headings of "Government Laws and Regulations" and "Financial Factors" in the foreign investment section.

Section I

Foreign Investment Checklist

A. General

1. Expansion of opportunities for overall growth and long-term profitability.
2. Current and long-term advantages and disadvantages.
3. Careful selection of areas on which to concentrate.
4. Competitive capability.

*Source is Office of International Investment, U.S. Department of Commerce, Washington, DC 20230

5. Experience of others, United States, foreign, and domestic.
6. Desire and capacity of local foreign enterprise to participate.
7. Adequacy of local foreign market or need for export to third countries (What do the prospective customers need and want; what can or will they buy; and how many consumers will there be?).

B. *Market Prospects*

1. Estimated size, trends, and potential of market in the country (by quantity or value, broken down, if possible, by city or region), purchasing power, and population distribution.
2. Export markets and estimated size.
3. Nature, source and extent of competition:
   a. Domestic (quality, value).
   b. Imports (quantity, quality, value, and source).
4. Sources of market information:
   a. Government statistics and special reports.
   b. Chambers of Commerce, banks, and trade, industry, agriculture associations.
   c. Private marketing research agencies.
   d. Market surveys available.
5. System of distribution of goods and merchandising and sales practices or techniques (domestic, and export or import):
   a. Wholesaling, retailing, manufacturers representatives, exporters, forwarders, etc.
   b. Peculiarities with respect to specified commodities or product lines.

C. *Government Laws and Regulations*

1. General political/economic future; attitude of the government of the country toward U.S. or other foreign private investment; and types and forms of investment preferred. Is U.S. private foreign investment welcomed in general or in particular lines? Is there a specific policy statement relating thereto and to industrial investment? Is the policy followed in practice? Is equity sufficient to assure required profits and control of assets and technology, yet low enough to minimize exposure to hazards of nationalism?
2. International agreements:
   a. Treaty of Friendship, Commerce and Navigation with the U.S.;
   b. Membership in GATT, International Monetary Fund, World Bank, etc.;
   c. Convention with the U.S. on the Avoidance of Double Taxation;
   d. Investment Guarantee Agreement with the U.S. (If a developing country);
   e. Most-favored-nation treatment with third countries;
   f. Trade arrangements with third countries;
   g. Customs Union, Common Market, etc.
3. Governmental assurances as to remission of profits, royalties, technical service fees, and repatriation of capital.

4. Specific laws affecting the following:
   a. Foreign investment, including licensing;
   b. Specific industries; e.g., manufacturing, petroleum, mining, etc.;
   c. Registration or incorporation of wholly or partly-owned enterprises, permits and time required, etc.;
   d. Provincial, municipal or other local laws;
   e. Percentage and form of foreign ownership;
   f. Monopolies and restraints to trade;
   g. Insurance.
5. Regulatory or administrative practices affecting the prospective foreign investor. Is national treatment or most-favored-nation treatment accorded in respect of the following:
   a. Foreign operations (types of investment excluded);
   b. Tariffs, including any preferential treatment accorded third countries;
   c. Import or export quotas or permits;
   d. Treatment in respect of licensing;
   e. Customs procedures, method of evaluation of duties, and time required in clearing goods;
   f. Free ports (sea or air);
   g. Price maintenance or discrimination;
   h. Taxation;
   i. Profits, and use of funds generated in third countries;
   j. Legal and judicial protection;
   k. Availability of patent, copyright, trademark and other protection;
   l. Treatment of local branch of foreign entity and of U.S. personnel, including residence requirements and limitations of stay, if any;
   m. Leasing or acquisition of land or other real property.
6. Tax rates affecting the proposed enterprise with respect to (1) initial plant and equipment and spare parts therefore, and (2) raw materials and components for manufacture in the country, and (3) end products and sales, and the following:
   a. Import duties;
   b. Exchange taxes;
   c. Property/real estate taxes;
   d. Corporate taxes, income and dividends;
   e. Personal income taxes, national and foreign;
   f. Municipal/local taxes;
   g. Other taxes or charges (also ascertain the effect of U.S. taxes on the investment).
7. Tax concessions:
   a. Types of exemptions or deferrals;
   b. Duration of exemptions or deferrals.
8. Other governmental, regional or municipal incentives or inducements to private foreign investment.

D. *Financial Factors*

1. Convertibility or possibility of effective utilization of resources (availability of foreign exchange); financial stability or security.
2. Local capital interested in joint ventures:
   a. Identity;
   b. Financial capacity;
   c. Extent and nature of possible financial commitment;
   d. Other possible participation.
3. Banking facilities available and nature of credit facilities offered, short, medium and long-term (conditions, terms, interest rates, etc.):
   a. Domestic;
   b. Foreign;
   c. Governmental or other lending institutions and facilities.
4. Availability of loans from U.S. sources, governmental and private.
5. Availability of funds or other resources from third-country operations.
6. Availability of local legal and accounting services.
7. Currency, exchange rates, and controls.
8. Capital repatriation and remittance of profits, licensing flat fees, royalties and other payments.
9. Third country transfers.
10. Availability of U.S. Government insurance covering nonbusiness risks, such as, expropriation, convertibility, war risk, civil strife, insurrection and rebellion, in developing countries.

E. *Materials*

1. Availability of domestic materials (quantity, quality, continuity, and price) and identity of suppliers (firms, location, and general capacity).
2. Availability and prices of imported materials on local market, and availability and price by direct import.
3. Availability of continuing supplies of spare parts for machinery and equipment, of perishable tools, and of steel for maintenance use.
4. Availability of local machine shops, tool and die shops, pattern shops, plant maintenance services, forging capacity, and foundry capacity.
5. Subcontracting possibilities.

F. *Communications and Transport*

1. Telegraph, radio-cable and telephone facilities.
2. Sea and river.
3. Rail.
4. Truck and road.
5. Air.
6. Time and costs in moving goods between major cities and from raw material areas to production and to consumption areas.
7. Particular packaging and handling problems.

G. *Labor and Management*

1. Labor supply (skilled, semiskilled, unskilled); availability for 1, 2, and 3 shift operations; availability of clerical, supervisory and executive personnel (quality and supply).

2. Labor organization and labor-management relations:
   a. Unions, federations, etc.;
   b. Leadership and membership;
   c. Ratio and importance of organized and nonorganized labor;
   d. Cultural differences and customs.
3. Wage rates (male and female):
   a. Minimum rates (skilled and unskilled);
   b. Estimated average rates (skilled and unskilled);
   c. Fringe benefits and traditional bonus payments (if any).
4. Labor laws and regulations:
   a. Policies of government and labor;
   b. Wages, hours, retirement, and termination;
   c. Nationality requirements and hiring practices;
   d. Health or workmen's compensation insurance;
   e. Sick leave;
   f. Vacations (whether or not paid), holidays;
   g. Other allowances;
   h. Severance pay.
5. Labor stability.
6. Practices and availability of labor housing:
   a. Costs;
   b. Other social overhead.
7. Mobility of labor and availability of worker transportation.
8. Labor efficiency and trainability: Available measures of output of labor (quantity or weight of product output per unit of time) or informed estimates of comparative labor working conditions and efficiency to levels in other countries (skilled and unskilled) in specific fields. Availability and quality of vocational, technical and administrative schools.

H. Plant and Physical Facilities

1. Land:
   a. Urban and suburban costs (per square foot or square meter);
   b. Availability of plant sites adjacent to urban areas with good sources of supply of water, electric power and transport.
2. Buildings: Local costs (per square foot or square meter). and time factor for normal or specific types of construction, and special problems:
   a. Single story;
   b. Multistory.
3. Water supply:
   a. Adequacy, quality, pressure; method of distribution;
   b. Waste disposal.
4. Power supply:
   a. Availability, reliability, and costs from local public utilities;
   b. Comparative costs of local private factory power generation for use of individual plants;
   c. Availability and local costs of oil, coal, or other fuels.

I. Other Important Factors

1. Languages and customs, formalities and protocol.
2. Cost of living.
3. Accounting, reporting, and auditing requirements.
4. Special local considerations, such as housing, food, health problems and medical facilities, advertising media and methods.
5. Status of required U.S. personnel, method of payment, allowances, taxation, etc.
6. Views of other U.S. investors in noncompetitive lines in the area under consideration.
7. Specific elements relating to the particular investment under study.
   a. Effect of foreign venture on U.S. operations or on overall growth:
      1. Assignment of direct responsibility for project to senior officer of parent firm;
      2. Capability of financing and staffing, and backstopping effectively.

J. Concluding Considerations

1. Best form of investment for specific case (license; joint participation, and nature of association; branch; subsidiary; etc). Consider pros and cons of joint venture with foreign government or agency of that government.
2. Method of operation or administration *vis-à-vis* U.S. organization and projected foreign facility.
3. Selection of best form of financing.
4. Final evaluation of long-term advantages and disadvantages of a specific foreign operation in a specific area and field; and effect on parent domestic organization.
5. Include an arbitration clause for settlement of disputes in a joint venture agreement with foreign private or governmental partner.
6. If it is decided that an enterprise is to be established, the clearest possible advance understandings should be developed with the foreign host government and with the foreign private participants or associates.

K. Sources of Assistance and Information

1. U.S. Department of Commerce. In addition to the services of its 42 field offices located throughout the United States and in Puerto Rico, specialized information for potential investors and licensors is available from the Department's Office of International Investment, Office of International Commercial Relations and Bureau of Domestic Commerce. A wide range of current and periodically updated information is provided by the Department's publications, including the biweekly *Commerce Today*, Overseas Business Reports, Trade Lists, and World Trade Directory Reports.
2. Overseas Private Investment Corporation.
3. Foreign Embassies, Consulates General, Consulates and Trade Offices in the United States.

4. U.S. Embassies, Consulates General and Consulates during exploratory visits in countries of investment or licensing interest.
5. Chambers of Commerce, trade associations and industry organizations.
6. Foreign Departments of private banking institutions.
7. Private foreign investment counseling entities; international marketing research and advertising agencies.
8. Other U.S. investors or licensors in the foreign area of interest.
9. Books and articles on foreign investment and licensing as available in many public and private libraries.

Section II

Licensing Abroad Checklist

A. Field of agreement. Must be very explicitly defined and leave no shadowy borderlines.
B. Territory within which license is operative and as to which licensee is permitted effective operation. Manufacture vs. sale of lease rights.
C. Exclusivity of license. Circumstances in particular country will dictate extent of this. In any case provide the following:
   1. Reservation of licensor to convert from exclusive to nonexclusive (or contra).
   2. Option of licensee to convert (pro or con) under conditions of specific performance.
D. Payments by licensee to or on behalf of licensor.
   1. Royalty
   2. Advance payment over and above royalty for the following:
      a. Goods and services;
      b. Plans and engineering;
      c. Promotional and sales program;
      d. "Good faith" guarantee;
      e. Option re future improvements.
   3. Future (after specified period) assistance in respect of manufacturing technique.
   4. Taxes imposed by national or local authorities (other than income tax). E.g., stamp taxes, registration taxes, payroll taxes, property taxes, insurance, and the like.
   5. Cost of obtaining and maintaining patents, trademarks, and copyrights.
   6. Designate royalty currency and consider effect of inflation exchange rates, convertibility, government restrictions, etc.
   7. Vest right in licensor to buy into licensee on anticipated bases. Sometimes desirable to have option for conversion of royalty obligations to equity interest.

E. Rights and privileges (or restrictions of licensee regarding use of licensor's trademarks. Consider nature and origin of trademarks to be used, manner of use and conditions under which misuse may be penalized. In no event assign trademarks to licensee or even to licensor's foreign licensing subsidiary or foreign base company.

F. When patents are involved, follow these procedures:
   1. Provide for "patent marking" as may be required under law of country in question.
   2. Protection of licensee against infringement by competitors. Unwise to undertake ligation unnecessarily—*always retain* full *control* of such litigation *by licensor*.
   3. Include specific statement that licensor undertakes or assumes no obligation or warranty that licensed operation is free of liability for potential infringement of third-party patent rights.
   4. Limit "future" re licensor patent rights initially available to licensee within field of agreement.
   5. Under appropriate circumstances, give licensee conditional option to obtain future patent rights.

G. When license is not based upon patent rights, and hence is a "know-how" and technical assistance agreement, follow these procedures:
   1. Limit licensee's initial rights to "know-how" and technical information then in being.
   2. If "futures" are required at outset, limit to improvements *developed on a commercial basis* within not more than one year advance of the effective license date.
   3. Establish best possible bases for continuing assistance to licensee as means of retaining him as an effective operating representative.
   4. Provide for available, but always optional, marketing and promotional assistance by licensor to licensee.
   5. Provide for control of timing and extent of "know-how" transfer and of general information that may be required by licensee.

H. Commercial operations under license (whether or not based upon patent rights):
   1. If more than one product is to be manufactured, schedule order of production to guard against licensee overextending initial operations.
   2. If processes are involved, spell out areas of application and use by licensee; and establish control and periodic review by licensor.
   3. Reserve to licensor's right to require discontinuance of a particular product or process under designated conditions of economy or ineffective license operation.
   4. Provide for conditions under which licensee may or may not manufacture competing or noncompeting products. Reserve the right to screen licensee's operations periodically in this respect.

5. Establish standards of achievement to be met by licensee under penalty of termination or modification of the license.
6. Establish right of licensor to institute and enforce standards of quality with particular relation to use of licensor's trademarks where permitted.
7. Establish right of licensor to inspect licensee's operations, to receive and evaluate samples of product, to audit books and to survey licensee sales and advertising effort at periodic intervals. Such rights must be exercised at stated intervals by licensor. Occasional waivers may result in loss of these rights.
8. Include provision as to licensor's right to export for parallel competition with licensee under certain circumstances.
9. Provide for control of changes in models or products produced under the license.

I. General
1. Training of licensee personnel in advance of and during licensed operations: Where–when–how many at a time–for how long? Establish basis for payment of costs of same and distinguish from royalty obligations.
2. Provide for special research and engineering by licensor on behalf of licensee. Define clearly and limit as to scope, time and timing. Assess costs against licensee on a cost-plus-percentage basis.
3. Provide for confidential treatment by licensee of licensor's proprietary information. Consider available means of enforcing this.
4. Include, when appropriate and possible, provision for reverse flow of "know-how" and patent rights. Consider "mutual assistance" concept in light of antitrust considerations.
5. Provide for handling of future disputes between licensor and licensee. Arbitration normally is not too satisfactory a recourse and some countries bar this procedure.
6. Spell out licensee's rights as to sublicensing and as to assignment of original license. Limit such rights and always require approval of licensor.
7. Establish circumstances and conditions generally under which agreement may be terminated in advance of natural life. Consider difference between termination and cancellation. Consider, also, laws of the country in which the licensee is situated.
8. Include advance disclaimer by licensor as to responsibility for licensee's operations under the agreement as they may affect third parties or any foreign government. Also disclaim any responsibility for licensee's representations of warranty to third parties. Additionally, licensor should be free of responsibility for damages or other liability resulting from faulty design or workmanship on part of licensee.
9. Consider effect of future changes in ownership or key personnel of licensee. Reserve right to modify or terminate if changes unsatisfactory to licensor occur.

10. Verify source and quality of raw materials, components, repair parts, and the like.
11. Designate jurisdictional law that is to govern interpretation of the agreement. Also designate place of execution and be sure that actual execution is effected at such location.
12. When license is exclusive for manufacturing and selling in a certain territory, consider optional extension of rights to adjoining territory for nonexclusive selling.
13. Assure compliance with government regulations and restrictions—both United States and foreign.
14. Define rights and obligations of both parties after termination. Effects of waivers.

Selected Bibliography

Ackoff, R., *Redesigning the Future*, John Wiley and Sons, New York, 1974.

Ammer, Dean S., *Materials Management and Purchasing*, Richard D. Irwin, Homewood, IL, 1980.

Ansolf, H. Igor, *Corporate Strategy*, McGraw-Hill Book Co., New York, 1965.

Archibald, R.D., *Managing High-Technology Programs and Projects*, Wiley (Interscience), New York, 1976.

Barnard, Chester, *The Functions of the Executive*, Harvard University Press, Cambridge, MA, 1938.

Basiuk, Victor, *Technology, World Politics, and American Policy*, Columbia University Press, New York, 1977.

Behrman, J.N., Boddewyn, J.J., Kapour, A., *International Business–Government Communications*, D.C. Heath and Co., Lexington, MA, 1975.

Bereano, Philip, *Technology as a Social and Political Phenomenon*, John Wiley and Sons, New York, 1976.

Bergstem, C.R., and Krause, L.A., ed., *World Politics and International Economics*, The Brooking Institution, Washington, DC, 1975.

Bhalla, A.S., ed., *Towards Global Action for Appropriate Technology*, Pergammon Press, New York, 1979.

Blake, S.P., *Managing for Responsive Research and Development*, W.H. Freeman and Co., San Francisco, 1978.

Boorstin, D.J., *The Republic of Technology: Reflections on Our Future Community*, Harper and Row, New York, 1978.

Brewster, K. Jr., *Antitrust and American Business Abroad*, Arno Press, New York, 1976.

Bright, James, *Research, Development, and Technological Innovation*, Richard D. Irwin, Homewood, IL, 1964.

Bright, J.R., ed., *Technology Forecasting for Industry and Government*, Prentice-Hall, Englewood Cliffs, NJ, 1968.

Bronowski, J., *The Origins of Knowledge and Imagination*, Yale University Press, 1978.

Brooke, M.Z., and Remmers, H.L., ed., *The Multinational Company in Europe: Some Key Problems*, The University of Michigan Press, Ann Arbor, 1972.

Cateora, P.R., and Hess, J.M., *International Marketing*, Richard D. Irwin, Homewood, IL, 1979.

Caves, Richard E., and Jones, Ronald W., *World Trade and Payments: An Introduction*, Little, Brown and Co., Boston, 1973.

Cetron, M.J., *Technological Forecasting*, Gordon and Breach, New York, 1969.

Cetron, Marvin J., and Ralph, Christine A., *Industrial Applications of Technological Forecasting*, John Wiley and Sons, New York, 1971.

Chacholiades, M., *International Trade Theory and Policy*, McGraw-Hill Book Co., New York, 1978.

Chandler, Lester V., *The Economics of Money and Banking*, 5th edition, Harper and Row, New York, 1969.

Chase, R.B., and Aquilano, N.J., *Production and Operations Management: A Life Cycle Approach*, Richard D. Irwin, Homewood, IL, 1981.

Clarkson, K.W., Miller, R.L., and Blaire, B., *West's Business Law: Text and Cases*, West Publishing Co., St. Paul, MN., 1980.

Combs, P.H., *Handbook of International Purchasing*, Cahners Books, Boston, 1971.

Coninx, R.G.F., *Foreign Exchange Today*, John Wiley and Sons, 1978.

Corbin, Arnold, *Changing Marketing Strategies in a New Economy*, Bobbs-Merrill Education Publishers, Indianapolis, 1977.

Coyle, D.C., *The United Nations and How It Works*, Columbia University Press, New York, 1969.

Daniels, J.D., Ogram, E.W., and Radebaugh, L.H., *International Business: Environments and Operations*, Addison-Wesley Publishing Co., Reading, MA, 1976.

Dean, V.M., *The Nature of the Non-Western World*, Mentor Books, New York, 1956.

Dean, Genevieve C., *Science and Technology in the Development of China*, An annotated bibliography, Mansell Information Publishing, London, 1974.

Duerr, M.G., and Roach, J.M., *Organization and Control of International Operations*, The Conference Board, New York, 1973.

Eckaus, Richard, *Appropriate Technologies for Developing Countries*, National Academy of Science Printing Office, Washington, DC, 1977.

Ellsworth, P.T., and Leith, J.C., *The International Economy*, Macmillan Publishing Co., New York, 1975.

Evans, T.G., *The Currency Carousel*, Dow Jones Books, Princeton, NJ, 1977.

Folk, George E., *Patents and Industrial Progress*, Harper and Brothers Publishers, New York, 1942.

Franco, L.G., *The European Multinationals*, Greylock Publishers, Stamford, CT, 1976.

Freeman, A.M., *International Trade: An Introduction to Method and Theory*, Harper and Row Publishers, New York, 1971.

Friedmann, W.C., and Begwin, Leau-Pierre, *Joint International Ventures and Developing Countries*, Columbia University Press, New York, 1971.

Fugate, W.L., *Foreign Commerce and the Antitrust Laws*, Little, Brown and Co., Boston, 1973.

Gee, E.A., and Tyler, C., *Managing Innovation*, John Wiley and Sons, New York, 1976.

Gerstenfeld, A., *Innovation*, University Press of America, Washington, DC, 1976.

Gerstenfeld, A., ed., *Technological Innovation: Government/Industry* Cooperation, John Wiley and Sons, New York, 1979.

Glueck, W.F., *Management*, The Dryden Press, Hinsdale, IL, 1980.

Goldscheider, Robert, *1979 Technology Management Handbook*, Clark Boardman Co., New York, 1979.

Gyorgy, A., and Kuhlman, L.A., ed., *Innovation in the Communist Systems*, Westview Special Studies on the Soviet Union and Eastern Europe, London, 1978.

Haas, E.B., Williams, M.P., and Babai, D., *The Uses of Technical Knowledge in International Organizations*, University of California Press, Berkeley, 1978.

Haberler, G., *The Theory of International Trade*, William Hodge and Co., London, 1936.

Hamberg, Daniel, *R&D: Essays on the Economics of Research and Development*, Random House, New York, 1966.

Harbison, Frederick, and Myers, Charles A., *Manpower and Education*, McGraw-Hill Book Co., New York, 1965.

Hayden, Eric W., *Technology Transfer to Europe*, Praeger, New York, 1976.

Hayes, R.D., Korth, C.M., and Roudiani, M., *International Business: An Introduction to the World of the Multinational Firm*, Prentice-Hall, Englewood Cliffs, NJ, 1972.

Jewkes, J., Sawers, D., and Stitterman, R., *The Sources of Invention*, Macmillan Publishing Co., New York, 1969.

Johnson, R., and Gummett, P., *Directing Technology: Policies for Promotion and Control*, Croom Helm, London, 1979.

Jones, H., and Twiss, B., *Forecasting Technology for Planning Decisions*, Macmillan Press, London, 1978.

Kahler, R., and Kramer, R.L., *International Marketing*, South-Western Publishing co., Cincinnati, 1977.

Kapoor, A., *Planning for International Business Negotiation*, Ballinger Publishing Co., Cambridge, 1975.

Kapoor, A., and Grub, P.D., ed., *The Multinational Enterprise in Transition*, The Darwin Press, Princeton, 1972.

Katz, J.E., *Presidential Politics and Science Policy*, Praeger, New York, 1978.

Kelly, P., and Kranzberg, M., ed., *Technological Innovation: A Critical Review of Current Knowledge*, Advanced Technology and Science Study Group, Georgia Institute of Technology, Atlanta, 1975.

Kindleberger, C.P., *American Business Abroad: Six Lectures on Direct Investment*, Yale University Press, New Haven, 1969.

Kindleberger, C.P., *Economic Development*, McGraw-Hill Book Co., New York, 1958.

Kindleberger, Charles P., *International Economics*, 5th edition, Richard D. Irwin, Homewood, IL, 1973.

Kistiakowsky, George, *A Scientist at the White House*, Harvard University Press, 1976.

Knight, Thomas J., *Technology's Future: The Hague Congress on Technological Assessment*, International Society for Technological Assessment, Washington, DC, 1976.

Kolde, E.J., *International Business Enterprise*, Prentice-Hall, Englewood Cliffs, NJ, 1968.

Kramer, R.L., *International Marketing*, South-Western Publishing Co., Dallas, 1970.

Kuznets, S., *Economic Change*, W.W. Norton and Co., New York, 1953.

Lall, Sanjaya, and Streeten, Paul, *Foreign Investment, Transnationals and Developing Countries*, Westview Press, Boulder, CO, 1977.

LaPalombara, J., and Blank, S., *Multinational Corporations in Comparative Perspective*, The Conference Board, New York, 1977.

Lawless, E.W., *Technology and Social Shock*, Rutgers University Press, New Brunswick, NJ, 1977.

Lee, Lamar, Jr., and Dobler, D.W., *Purchasing and Materials Management: Text and Cases*, McGraw-Hill Book Co., New York, 1977.

Lewis, Leslie L., ed., *The Dartnell International Trade Handbook*, The Dartnell Corp., Chicago, 1963.

Long, T. Dixon, and Wright, L., *Science Policies of Industrial Nations*, Praeger Publishers, New York, 1975.

Mansfield, Edwin, *The Economics of Technological Changes*, W.W. Norton and Co., New York, 1968.

Mansfield, *Technological Change*, W.W. Norton and Co., New York, 1971.

Martyn, H., *Multinational Business Management*, D.C. Heath and Co., Lexington, 1970.

McClelland, D., *The Achieving Society*, Irvington Publications, New York, 1961.

Meadows, Dennis, et al., *The Limits to Growth*, The Club of Rome, New York, 1972.

Medreder, Z.A., *Soviet Science*, W.W. Norton and Co., New York, 1978.

Meyers, S., and Marquis, Donald G., *Successful Industrial Innovations*, National Science Foundation, Washington, DC, 1969.

Mischan, G.J., *Technology and Growth*, Praeger Publishers, New York, 1970.

Mischan, G.J., *The Costs of Economic Growth*, Praeger Publishers, New York, 1967.

Mumford, L., *Technics and Civilization*, Harcourt, Brace and Co., New York, 1934.

Nau, Henry R., *Technology Transfer and U.S. Foreign Policy*, Praeger Publishers, New York, 1976.

Nehrt, L.C., *International Finance for Multinational Business*, Intext Educational Publishers, Scranton, PA, 1972.

Nieckels, Lars, *Transfer Pricing in Multinational Firms*, John Wiley and Sons, New York, 1976.

Noble, D.F., *Science, Technology, and the Rise of Corporate Capitalism*, Alfred A. Knopf, New York, 1978.

Okolie, C.C., *Legal Aspects of the International Transfer of Technology to Developing Countries*, Praeger Publishers, New York, 1975.

Orlans, H., *The Non-Profit Research Institute*, McGraw-Hill Book Co., New York, 1972.

Packard, Vance, *The Status Seekers*, Pocket Books, New York, 1961.

Phatak, A.V., *Managing Multinational Corporations*, Praeger Publishers, New York, 1974.

Poats, Rutherford, M., *Technology for Developing Nations*, The Brookings Institute, Washington, DC, 1972.

Ramesh, J., and Weiss, C., ed., *Mobilizing Technology for World Development*, Praeger Publishers, New York, 1979.

Ricardo, David, *The Principles of Political Economy and Taxation*, Penguin Books, New York, 1971.

Roback, S.H., Simmonds, K., and Zunick, J., *International Business and Multinational Enterprises*, Richard D. Irwin, Homewood, IL, 1977.

Robinson, Austin, *Appropriate Technologies for Third World Development*, Macmillan Press, London, 1979.

Robinson, R.D., *International Management*, Holt, Rinehart, and Winston, New York, 1967.

Rodgers, Joseph L. Jr., *Environmental Impact Assessment, Growth, Management's and the Comprehensive Plan*, Ballinger Publishing Co., Cambridge, MA, 1976.

Roman, Daniel D., *Science, Technology and Innovation: A Systems Approach*, Grid Publishing Co., Columbus, OH, 1980.

Root, F.R., *International Trade and Investment*, 4th edition, South-Western Publishing Co., Cincinnati, 1978.

Rostow, W.W., *The Stages of Economic Growth: A Non-Communist Manifesto*, Cambridge University Press, Cambridge, MA, 1960.

Salera, V., *Multinational Business*, Hougton Mifflin, Co., New York, 1969.

Samuelson, Paul A., *Economics*, 10th edition, McGraw-Hill Book Co., New York, 1976.

Schumacher, E.F., *Small is Beautiful*, Harper and Row, New York, 1975.

Servan-Schreiber, J.J., *The American Challenge*, Atheneum Publishers, New York, 1968.

Schor, Donald A., *Technology and Change*, Delacorte Press, New York, 1967.

Snyder, Louis L., ed., *The Dynamics of Nationalism*, D. Van Nostrand Co., Inc., Princeton, NJ, 1964.

Sperber, Philip, *Intellectual Property Management*, Clark Boardman and Co., London, 1974.

Speigel-Rosing, Ina, and deSolla Price, Derek, ed., *Science, Technology and Society*, Sage Publications, London, 1977.

Strasser, G., and Simons, E.M., ed., *Science and Technology Policies*, Ballinger Publishing Co., Cambridge, MA, 1973.

Taylor, C.T., and Silberston, Z.A., *The Economic Impact of the Patent System*, Cambridge University Press, Cambridge, MA, 1973.

Teich, Albert H., ed., *Technology and Man's Future*, St. Martins Press, New York, 1972.

Terpstra, V., *The Cultural Environment of International Business*, South-Western Publishing Co., Dallas, 1978.

Thomas, Ann Van Wyner, and Thomas, A.J. Jr., *The Organization of American States*, Southern University Press, Darcas, 1978.

Twiss, Brian, *Managing Technological Innovation*, Longman Group, London, 1974.

Webber, R.A., *Culture and Management: Text and Readings in Comparative Management*, Richard D. Irwin, Homewood, IL, 1969.

Wells, L.T., Jr., ed., *The Product Life Cycle and International Trade*, Graduate School of Business Administration, Harvard University, 1972.

Zenoff, D.B., *International Business Management*, Macmillan Co., New York, 1971.

Government Publications and Miscellaneous Reports

Department of Commerce, *The Multinational Corporation*, Washington, DC, 1972.

Department of Commerce, *Technological Innovation: Its Environment and Management*, Washington, DC, 1967.

Department of Commerce, *The Small Business Market in the World*, Washington, DC, 1979.

Department of Commerce, *Overview of the Export Administration Program*, Washington, DC, October, 1979.

Department of Commerce, *Foreign Business Practices*, Washington, DC, 1975.

International Monetary Fund, *Balance of Payments Concepts and Definitions*, Washington, DC, Pamphlet Series No. 10, 1968.

National Aeronautics and Space Administration, *Spinoff 1980—An Annual Report*, Washington, DC, 1980.

National Science Foundation, *National Patterns of R&D Resources: Funds and Manpower in the United States 1953–977*, NSF 77-310, Washington, DC, 1977.

National Science Foundation, *Science Indicators—1976*, Washington, DC, 1977.

National Science Foundation, *Federal Laboratories and Technology Transfer: Institutions, Linkages, and Processes*, NSF-RA-R-74-018, Washington, DC, March 1974.

UNESCO, *An Introduction to Policy Analysis in Science and Technology*, No. 46, Paris, 1979.

UNESCO, *Science Policy and the European States*, #25, Paris, 1971.

United Nations, *Guidelines for the Study of the Transfer of Technology to Developing Countries*, TD/B/AC, 11/9, New York, 1972.

United Nations, *Recommendations on Standardization Policies*, UN Economic Commission for Europe, Geneva, 1977.

United Nations, *Multinational Corporations in World Development*, New York, 1973.

World Bank, *Policies and Operations—The World Bank, IDA and IFC*, Washington, DC, 1971.

World Bank, *Appropriate Technology in World Bank Activities*, Washington, DC, 1976.

Index